Judicial Deceit

Tyranny & Unnecessary Secrecy at the Michigan Supreme Court

Peninsula Press

Judicial Deceit

Tyranny & Unnecessary Secrecy at the Michigan Supreme Court

Chief Justice Elizabeth A. **Weaver** *(retired)*

David B. **Schock**, *Ph.D.*

Published by Peninsula Press
Glen Arbor, MI 49636

ISBN 978-0-9894101-3-7

Edited by Amee Schmidt. Cover design by Amanda Mary. Book designed and typeset by Amee Schmidt with titles and text in Californian FB.

Contents

Prologue

This book is filled with examples of judicial deceit, tyranny, and unnecessary secrecy at the Michigan Supreme Court. These examples represent just a little more of what I have called the tip of the iceberg—a most dangerous iceberg of misuse and abuse of government power.

And why am I bothering to tell it now? Because I believe there needs to be a record of what judicial deceit, tyranny, and unnecessary secrecy did to individuals and to the law, what it did to a third of the government—the judicial branch, and what it did to the whole government. It's not unique to the Michigan Supreme Court. It applies to some other courts, and no doubt it applies and runs through the other two branches of government. It's a tragedy. The Michigan Supreme Court was politicized, became at times disorderly, unjust, unprofessional, and like the other branches, created its own expensive spin machine. The need is for reform at, in, and of the Supreme Court. (See Appendix A for my Seven-Point Plan for Reform.)

I witnessed what has happened. And so I'm telling what I experienced. I view it as a very serious issue: our culture is in danger—our country, our civilization. Part of that danger—in too many places—is the lack of an open, independent, and unbiased judiciary. I follow as true Mary Baker Eddy's Bible-based admonition: "Designate those as unfaithful stewards who have seen the danger and yet have given no warning."[1] So I am giving the warning. To me it's a Noah event: "People, build your boats!" In this case that means, "People, demand reform and get it!"

As a steward, I stayed on the Supreme Court for almost 16 years, and the last 10 or 12, I was really striving to try to get it fixed from within. It didn't happen, because there weren't four justices on the court to even see the danger totally, nor who were independent enough that they would stand up and lead, nor who would want to do something about it.

And it isn't for me to solve alone; it's for people to wake up and realize, that when you give government power to intelligent people and allow them to act in unnecessary secrecy, it can encourage them in the worst human propensities: deceit, hatred, revenge, and lust—lust for power. Then, later or sooner, even good people will do bad things. We each have a responsibility to be vigilant and to address those propensities when we encounter them in ourselves and others.

My responsibility now is to let people know. I care about the individuals in this state, especially the children. I care about all our citizens, and they all have the right to fair, just treatment in the courts,

---

1 Mary Baker Eddy, *Science and Health with Key to the Scriptures*, Published by the Trustees under the Will of Mary Baker G. Eddy, (Boston, Mass.), 1875, copyright renewed 1934, Chapter XVI—The Apocalypse, 571:13-14.

and to be able to have confidence and trust that those who have the power to settle disputes in a peaceful way will do so; that they have judges and justices who are not deceitful, tyrannical, and will not be unnecessarily secretive.

It's important. I did everything I could from "within," and now I'm on the "without;" I voluntarily got out August 2010. And this is my last duty from my Supreme Court judicial experience. I was entrusted with the opportunity to serve the people, and it's for them that we offer this book.

Michigan Supreme Court Chief Justice Elizabeth A. Weaver, retired

Note to Readers

This book is laid out as a history, and history happens in order, sometimes. But just because we start at the beginning and—with a very few exceptions—stick to chronology, that does not mean that the reader is obligated to read it that way. Let us encourage you to dip in any place you like. If you find them needless, after reading the Introduction, skip the first two chapters of how Elizabeth Weaver came to the Michigan Supreme Court, maybe parts of Chapter 3 concerning the work of a justice. You might want to skip five or so pages of Chapter 4 that lay out the farm-team system of a powerful Governor for bringing malleable judges along.

Perhaps you want to go to:

Chapter 8 to learn about Justice Markman's unconscionable treatment of subordinates, or his need to bring a gun to work.

Chapter 11 to understand the arbitrary treatment of support staff at the court.

Chapter 15 to learn how the Michigan Supreme Court created law (which is not its job) in child adoption.

Chapters 15, 16, 21, or 24 to learn how long-serving and diligent local judges were threatened and punished by various justices of the Supreme Court, aided and abetted by either or both the State Court Administrator or the Judicial Tenure Commission (JTC), the court's own investigatory branch intended to objectively examine judicial conduct.

Conversely, consult chapters 13, 23 and 28 to learn of instances when local judges were nearly allowed to get away with smoking pot, were allowed to retire with honors after pleading guilty to a petty theft, or who had allowed perjured testimony and were not held up for public scrutiny, all again courtesy of the JTC.

Or go to Chapter 20 to learn how the Supreme Court rewrote the common law in its *Trentadue* decision, thereby restricting reasonable discovery...and Chapter 23 for the ways the Supreme Court whittled down the environmental rights of individuals in the state to go to court and to have standing before the law.

And there's more, much more. But to get there, we needed to include much of what transpired along the way. And that takes time and pages; don't be constrained by the way we approach the subject.

There is plenty of deceit, tyranny, and secret dealings for almost anyone who is interested in justice to find something herein that is remarkable. ...And not just those in the state of Michigan: if it's happening here, it can be happening in any of the other 49.

But know that this is our best effort to tell the story in detail.

Introduction

If you live in an area with good judges and good courts, you are fortunate. You recognize that in any court case, there is going to be a winner and a loser. And sometimes the loser is not convinced the court has acted correctly. That can lead to an appeal. And if the appeal is disappointing, the two-time loser might see the need for yet another appeal. In effect this could be a verdict in, say, a circuit court, an appeal to the Court of Appeals, and appeal from that court to the Supreme Court. If the Supreme Court is corrupt, it really doesn't matter what happens at the two lower courts; even if they were correct, there is no reasonable expectation that justice will ultimately prevail.

Because the Supreme Court can take up whichever of the cases on appeal and any administrative issues it wishes, it can—in short order and with much secrecy—change the law and the climate of law in the state. When that happens, the court has become corrupt.

Whenever and wherever the course of justice is diverted by ideology, or political or personal gain, the process has become corrupt.

The lust for control, prestige, dominance...what the philosopher Eric Voegelin called *libido dominandi*, the desire to dominate. And, with the *libido dominandi* there result the drive for unnecessary secrecy and eagerness for—and apparent delight in—tyranny and deceit, more forms of corruption. And when you toss in additional general nastiness, sloppiness, and creepiness, it's enough to make almost anyone wonder what in the world has really been going on.

We offer this chronicle of corruption at Michigan's high court, an especially sad chapter in this state's history. We recognize this is, after all, the public's business done on the public's dime. And at stake is the public trust and the trust of the public, both seriously compromised.

This book is the work of a public servant (a retired chief justice of the Michigan Supreme Court) and a private individual (a former professor), both of whom believe their Master when he said (Luke 8:17) "For nothing is secret, that shall not be made manifest; neither anything hid, that shall not be known and come abroad."

The authors assert that it is time.

So, how likely is it that a retired chief justice and a former college professor would join forces to lift the hem of the judicial robe to reveal the soft underbelly of that corrupt high court? First, readers need to know something of the authors.

The Retired Chief Justice

The reader will learn much in this book about Elizabeth "Betty" Ann Weaver. Most of it will come in the form of her own words as a co-author of this book. In late 2011, she began a series of discussions with co-author David Schock about her time on the bench. Throughout, her conversational voice from those discussions is in *italics* (her previously published comments—quoted in the media or in opinions and memos, for example—are treated as any other quoted material).

Before you judge the content of her ideas and assertions, you need to know something about Elizabeth Weaver. Beside the brief biographical information on the back book cover, the first two chapters detail her rise to the Supreme Court. Her progress might seem unlikely, against all odds. That's part of what makes it remarkable. In writing this book, she reveals much (but not the entirety) of what transpired in her nearly 16 years (including two years as chief justice) at the Michigan Supreme Court. While she served on the bench, she did her best to share with the public what had been going on. Sometimes she was heard. At other times, her voice was stifled. Her sense of a duty to the citizens of Michigan did not diminish once she left the court in 2010.

In the Prologue, she says:

I witnessed what's happened.[2] And so I'm telling what I experienced. I view it as a very serious issue: our culture is in danger—our country, our civilization. Part of that danger—in too many places—is the lack of an open, independent, and unbiased judiciary. I follow as true Mary Baker Eddy's Bible-based admonition "...designate those as unfaithful stewards who have seen the danger and yet have given no warning."[3]

Eddy's words are drawn from I Corinthians 14:8:

> But if the watchman see the sword come, and blow not the trumpet, and the people be not warned; if the sword come, and take any person from among them, he is taken away in his iniquity; but his blood will I require at the watchman's hand.

> This book is an obligation that's been placed on Elizabeth Weaver. It's part of doing right and fearing not.

2 Elizabeth Ann Weaver interview by co-author Schock, video recording, Glen Arbor, Mich. Schock interviewed Justice Weaver in a series of conversations that began 31 October 2011, and that are continuing. Weaver's voice throughout are in italics.
3 Mary Baker Eddy, *Science and Health with Key to the Scriptures*, Published by the Trustees under the Will of Mary Baker G. Eddy, (Boston, Mass.), 1875, copyright renewed 1934, Chapter XVI—The Apocalypse, 571:13-14.

"Do Right and Fear Not."

Weaver displays the motto prominently about her home and office.[4] She shares it frequently with audiences at her speeches.

"Do right and fear not" relates especially to Weaver's work at the Michigan Supreme Court. She had helped some members of the majority to get there, mentored them, encouraged them.

It took a long time for me to realize that they had deceived me. And having realized that I helped create this opportunity for wrongdoing, this problem, I had some responsibility to try to fix it.

Never once did she rage against them or condemn them as individuals. She would, however, hold their actions up to scrutiny. But as individuals, she didn't—and doesn't—hate them.

I would have been destroyed if I hated. I know that hate destroys you eventually. I don't hate anybody, but I was hugely disappointed in them. And I have been appalled and repulsed by their wrongdoing.

The desire, always, is identify and redress wrongs, reform behavior, and then go on.

I feel every justice has a duty to let the public know something if it is serious. And having taught first grade, I know the difference between tattle-tale-ing and serious matters. And the business of the Supreme Court is serious. And I don't expect anybody to be perfect, so it wasn't a matter of people's human idiosyncrasies or failings in any given moment. But we're dealing about justice and fairness and properly doing the people's judicial business—with citizens, employees, authorities and other judges, and the whole public sense of justice.

When Weaver has said that her fellow justices were wrong and misguided, that their actions were not worthy of them, she actually was holding them in high regard; they were fully capable of making different and better choices. Further, she didn't want them punished, didn't want to get even; she just wanted them to stop their bad behavior and start acting like the rational and reasonable adults she knew they were called to be.

These were people that I liked and had helped, and then I was finding that it wasn't as it should be. So it occurred to me that being on the Supreme Court was like dealing on a daily basis with hatred, lust—particularly lust for power—revenge, and deceit. Those are the human propensities, negative propensities, and human failings that we must not entertain. And we should get rid of them in ourselves, and see that they don't have to be a part of our lives.

---

4 That aphorism is cross-stitched and hangs in a frame on a wall in one of the houses where Mary Baker Eddy lived, 23 Paradise Road, Swampscott, New Hampshire, now a museum. Justice Weaver is a sincere student of Christian Science. She begins and ends her day with prayer and Bible study; she teaches Sunday school at her local church in Glen Arbor. She eschews alcohol, tobacco, caffeine, any other drugs, stimulants or depressants. She doesn't doctor in the conventional sense; she didn't take the state health insurance during all her time on the bench. Well, that's not completely accurate, she said: she took the dental insurance but never used it.

And what I have learned is this: to deal with hatred, you have to handle it with kindness; to deal with lust, you need chastity, purity; to deal with revenge, you need a sense of charity, and forgiveness in trying to get it straight; and to deal with deceit—which seems to be the most insidious of all because it fools you—you need honesty, truth-telling.

She admits she felt the slings and arrows that were directed her way. It was wearing. There were times when the words and actions of her former colleagues drove her to tears, she says. But she knew that those words and actions harmed her detractors even more than they harmed her. She made every effort to stand up to the onslaught, and never stood down from telling the truth, even if in the near term it brought down more scorn. And it had to be the whole truth, not shaded or compromised. She knew her struggle was for larger purposes.

At times, she admits, it was a challenge.

But it was MY challenge. And I don't have any animosity with respect to these people.

And you'll find that while this book deals with serious subjects, there is room for friendship and humor. Elizabeth Weaver laughs much and easily, and loves a good party. She delights in meeting political candidates whom she respects, likes being in a crowded room at events, and always manages to strike up a conversation. She loves good food and cooks up a legendary red beans and rice. She loves to play golf and tennis and follows sports, especially those of her adopted State of Michigan teams. She loves going to the Final Four and the Rose or Sugar Bowl.

She has never been married, never had children. But that allows her to call ALL children her grandchildren. She taught first grade, high-school French, and college-level introductory law. She enjoys young people. At close hand, she's watched many of them grow to their majorities. Most of her life has been devoted to their wellbeing, and she will do whatever is necessary to protect them, especially the youngest and most vulnerable of them.

The Former Professor

I (Weaver's co-author, David Schock) met Weaver in the fall of 2006 in my work as a documentary filmmaker.[5] That came about because some creative people with the 20th Circuit Court (Ottawa County) wanted help to educate the community.

Why? Most people don't know what the various courts do. District? Circuit? Probate? How to convey the differences among the courts to an audience?

Videographer Phil Blauw and I took to the sidewalks to informally survey people about their perceptions. The results were interesting and often hilarious.[6] The most

5 For much of the book, I remain "co-author Schock," a practice I drop when I become a participant in events, late in this book.
6 David B. Schock, *You and the Courts*, Ottawa County, 2007, http://www.miottawa.org/.

notable supposition was that a probate court was the place that set the terms of your probation. The most knowledgeable subject was a former state prisoner. He'd been through it all.

The idea was that we'd intercut the erroneous answers with commentary by a judge. My first thought was that I'd like to use the chief justice of the Michigan Supreme Court. At the time that was Cliff Taylor. No, said an advisor to the film...whoever else, not Justice Taylor. Instead, he suggested I work with Justice Weaver.

Well, okay, but I voted for Justice Taylor. Come to think of it, I voted for Justice Weaver, too. In fact, I pretty much automatically voted for the incumbent. They all were just doing a great job.

Uh-huh. So, feeling a little bit like I was settling for second best, we set up the early evening session with Justice Weaver at the newish Hall of Justice in Lansing.

When I arrived, my first thought was that in any other country, it would have been named the Palace of Justice. ...A sweeping vista allowing the towering hall its pride of place. This edifice is built at a grand scale of enduring materials.[7] We ascended to the top floor, looked out over a darkling Lansing, and went about setting up our equipment in a book-lined room. Shortly thereafter, a rather short woman with blond hair came into the room and introduced herself: Betty Weaver. She was pleasant, asked about our time frame, and then went to don her robe for the shoot.

In the film, Justice Weaver delivered the overview of the courts:

The great majority of people never HAVE to go to court, and so most of them spend their lives without ever going INTO a courtroom. They do know that there are courts...they know there are judges in their city and county and at the Supreme Court...and that's about it. But they don't really know what happens at the courts or how the courts CAN and DO affect their lives.[8]

Her answers went a little long—not a surprise to anyone who knows her; she is voluble—but I knew I'd be able to shave them down in editing; we were getting what

CourtsLE/20thcircuit/courtvids.htm.
7 The court website describes the Hall of Justice this way:

The Michigan Hall of Justice was designed and built to house the Michigan Judicial Branch of government. It's a space where the Supreme Court, Court of Appeals and their respective support organizations have been brought together under one roof to serve the people of Michigan.

The Michigan Hall of Justice is a six-story building characterized by a dome in the center and gently sweeping curves that face on axis with the State Capitol. A building whose colonnades were designed as arms to reach out and invite citizens to approach the Hall of Justice. A building whose glass dome lets light into the judiciary. A building of limestone, granite and marble that symbolize the permanent things on which our constitutional republic is founded - Justice, Freedom and Self-government under the rule of law. [The Michigan Hall of Justice, Michigan Supreme Court, http://courts.michigan.gov/Courts/MichiganSupremeCourt/PublicInfoOffice/Documents/The%20Michigan%20Hall%20of%20Justice.4.pdf.]
8 For a good grounding in the courts and their functions see Michigan Judicial Branch, State Court Administrator's Office, Michigan Supreme Court, http://courts.michigan.gov/Administration/SCAO/Resources/Documents/other/OrgChart.pdf.

we needed. It didn't take all that long, and when we were wrapping up, I asked if she might like to join us for dinner. She would, and so would her intern. (She was almost always accompanied by an intern, an advanced-level law student of real promise who would also serve as her driver and general factotum. These interns always had a front-row seat for what transpired.) We adjourned to Emil's for some good Italian and conversation.

I didn't know it at the time, but just then she was being beleaguered by other members of her court. They were suppressing her dissent in a case because she was saying things they didn't want known, embarrassing things about how they'd made decisions. Shortly thereafter they would launch Administrative Order 2006-08, the infamous "gag order" that they hoped would keep her from talking.[9]

So we talked of the job of being a justice and the work of the court. She observed:

You'd think that the Supreme Court would be the fairest in the land, the most objective, professional, orderly, fair, filled with the best and brightest minds, dedicated to achieving justice for all the state's citizens.

We agreed.

Well, you'd be wrong.

And she lifted the curtain just a little to reveal incidents of the smothering of dissenting voices, backstabbing, character assassination, and intrigue. Much of it was motivated by the desire for gain—political gain—and for power.

I observed that it wasn't right for justices at the state's highest court to behave that way. To myself I added "...That is, if it's really so." It seemed unlikely and improbable, and I reasoned Justice Weaver's account might be an exaggeration. Wouldn't I otherwise have read about all this in the newspapers?

Nevertheless, before we went our separate ways, I volunteered: "Well, let me know if you need help with that." I certainly hoped she'd like the final production of *You and the Courts*, but I pretty much thought that would be the end of our association. Justice Weaver did indeed enjoy the finished film, in fact, so much so that she wanted extra copies to send out.

And some time later came the phone call that I really hadn't considered likely: Yes, she COULD use some help getting the story out about what had been happening at the Supreme Court. I had to scurry, researching the issues, reading opinions, trying to make sense of a wide range of events, all related to her assertions. And everywhere I turned, I found she was correct; there was no exaggeration or hyperbole.

---

9 We'll see this again subsequently. It flies in the face of both the Michigan Constitution and the Code of Judicial Conduct (the courts own rules for ethical behavior). You can read the "gag order" here: http://www.icle.org/contentfiles/milawnews/Rules/Ao/AO-2006-8.pdf.

February 2007 saw us[10] in Traverse City at her regional branch of the Supreme Court. The view from her office across the street to Grand Traverse Bay was stunning, a far different kind of elegance than the Hall of Justice presented. The result of that sit-down interview was *Conflict at the Court*, an hour-long piece.[11] She dropped the dime on the bad behavior at the court. The completed film went lots of places...the League of Women Voters, various media outlets (with no appreciable response), to legal scholars, other judges and—via them—to the others at the Supreme Court.

By releasing the film in the spring of 2007, we were staying away from the political tricks both parties play during election season. We wanted the film to stand on its own and not be used primarily for campaign fodder; this was way too important. My only hesitation in the whole project was the thought that I should have interviewed several other justices. It took me a long time to work through that. Had I done so, I'm convinced there would have been no film. The concern that other voices were needed was offset by the realization that they were heard on a nearly daily basis in their actions at the court. These voices were not only in the majority; they were intent on dominating any conversation, no matter what.

All I had to do was read the ways they interacted with Justice Weaver. She may have been raising issues, but others were quick to characterize her as a disappointed crank. She stayed with the issues; they sank to *ad hominem* attacks.

Some of the rhetoric directed her way by the chief justice indicated she was "behaving like a petulant 'only child' [...]"

> Justice Weaver is more or less 'Holding her breath' until she gets her way. . [...] She hopes, as a child engaging in a tantrum, that one of the adults will given [sic] in and allow her to dictate [...]. . [...] (In fact ever the concilia-tor, I even suggested Justice Weaver use a hunger strike as a vehicle as it seemed to have the potential for everyone to be a winner) we cannot give Justice Weaver this power to bludgeon her colleagues by threats of outra-geous statements needlessly embarrassing to third parties.
>
> It is a sad situation that Justice Weaver has made here [...].[12]

That was simply because she dissented from the court's choice of chief judge for Kent County's Probate Court. But that dissent raised a stink because it revealed a court at work making law, not interpreting it.

She's also been called a bag lady, mentally ill, terminally ill, and—perhaps most eloquent of it all—"implacably evil."

---

10 This time the videographer was Dennis Hart.
11 David B. Schock, *Conflict at the Court*, 2007, penULTIMATE, Ltd. (Grand Haven, MI). You can see it here: http://www.mymicourt.com/?page_id=23
12 Clifford W. Taylor, "Memorandum," 17 July 2006, unpublished.

I looked up "implacable" for its exact meaning. It means "irredeemably". Rippy (Chief Justice Robert P. Young, Jr.) is a very smart man. I have my faults but...

She is not implacably evil. *I don't believe anyone is implacably evil.*

All these comments were made by her colleagues, people with whom at one point or another she had been friends. That's the tragedy of it. She has reason to believe that they have spread untrue rumors about her; she knows that others have been warned not to stand too close to her in public and not to converse with her if they valued their careers. It was a little like fourth-grade bullying, but it was nearly ceaseless.

By that point in early 2007, the court had become a war zone.

And I waded into it with hesitation. She understood. She'd have trouble believing it herself, she acknowledged, if she hadn't been through it. And, document-by-document, she laid it out, explaining what had gone on. A pattern of behavior at the court emerged. First, the majority would do something beyond the bounds...make up laws and policies on the fly. Then Justice Weaver would object and chronicle what had happened. Next, few would note her objection, or they might reply with disdain. And something would explode and the majority would look bad. Finally, they would blame her for all of it.

And it took time to peel back the layers of obfuscation. But once I did, there—at the center—would be the wrongdoing, malignant and odious. She would repeatedly remark that her revelations were just "the tip of the iceberg."

But who was taking the time to verify her allegations? Not the media.[13] They were following the squabbling; that was the news, not the substance of the disagreements. They were observing the tip that was above water, not diving below to see the submerged portion of the issues.[14]

So, we made the film, and I started watching and reading, paying close attention. I received a very special education, something that would amount to an extra post baccalaureate degree in civics and law. I learned to trust her: Weaver didn't lie or shade the truth, even when it might have been convenient or very helpful for her reputation to have done so. That didn't mean she might not be wrong about an assertion, but when she learned she had erred, she would acknowledge her mistake and set the record straight. So, if she was telling the truth, that meant that somebody else was lying; there was no way for both sides to be correct on these matters. I started recognizing the lies. And I quickly understood one lie would lead to discovering another; they were connected. But much of that lay ahead.

---

13 As a result of what I perceived as media indifference—and taking advantage of new technologies—I started writing about the Supreme Court after the film was released. I would post at the site I used to chronicle unsolved homicides, http://www.delayedjustice.com. The content grew so fast that I needed to spin off another website, the same one that now displays *Conflict at the Court*, http://www.mymicourt.com.
14 Changes in the practice of news gathering, and the economy also worked against allowing serious and able journalists the time required to follow complex and ongoing issues.

With the film out, the court had to take a back seat to what was next on my plate.

There was unfinished business, the fruit of earlier labors. From 1994 to 2006, I had taught at Hope College, a small, liberal-arts college. I taught both as an adjunct (part time) associate professor in the English Department and then, in the fall of 2000, full time in the Communication Department. My doctorate was in English (creative writing and literary criticism), but my life's work was writing, producing, and making documentary films.

In the fall of 2003, I taught a documentary class, and I invited students to walk with me through the process as I made a film. The subject of my proposed film was Janet Chandler, a Hope College student who had been murdered 24 years before. The result was a lengthy film, *Who Killed Janet Chandler?* In addition to a local theatrical release, the film also showed on a local Public Broadcasting station 25 years to the hour of the discovery of her body along an expressway.

The film generated enough buzz that the Michigan State Police and the Holland Police Department in the late spring of 2004 fielded a four- (and later, five-) member cold case team, whose only business it was to work the case full time.

In the process of their 18-month investigation, all kinds of things happened. I finished a film about the Ku Klux Klan in Michigan. Also, I had completed one more murder-related film—*Jack in the Box*—and was in the middle of a third—*Finding Diane*.

By the time of the first arrest in the Chandler case, February 8, 2006, I had conveyed my intention to discontinue teaching at Hope. Subsequently, five other suspects would be arrested and arraigned.

The arrests were big news, and more than once, I had to talk down overeager network show producers who wanted to feature the college professor who solved the crime. "He didn't," I'd tell them. "The police solved it." All the college professor and his videographer and associate producer Phil Blauw did was tell the story.

That wasn't quite complete, but it served to keep me off the morning news shows.[15] The more complete explanation was that Phil and I had made a special cut of the film that the cold case team used in its interrogations. We also fed all the tips that came to us (and there were many) directly and immediately to the cold-case team members. I was busy working with the team even after I left the college in the spring of 2006; that involvement would continue for the next several years.

The fall of 2007 saw the trial of four of six of Janet Chandler's killers (two had pled earlier). NBC had licensed my film to use in an episode of *Dateline*.[16] The network also hired me to make their recording of the trial in addition to my own.

---

15 One assistant producer for either NBC or CBS asked "But don't you want to be famous?" I didn't, and I explained why: my dog already loved me.

16 Jack Cloherty, producer, "Conspiracy of Silence" NBC *Dateline*, 23 May 2008, http://www.msnbc.msn. com/id/24792743/ns/dateline_nbc-crime_reports/t/conspiracy-silence/#.Ty2Bw80bFQQ.

The four were convicted Nov. 1, 2007, after nearly three weeks of *voir dire* (selecting the jury), instruction, testimony, arguments, and deliberations... everything that makes up a trial. They would spend life in prison without the possibility of parole. And it was likely that one who pled would live out his days there, too, with a 20-40 year sentence. The woman who pled received the shortest sentence, 10-20 years. The five men were employed by Wackenhut, a private security company.[17] Those five had been part of a large number of guards that been sent to Holland to "police" a strike at a paint company.

The head of the strike detail for Wackenhut (also the corporation's agent in charge) was the primary actor in the premeditated murder of Janet Chandler. And it was possible that some of her attackers (the Attorney General's office puts it at between 10-12 men who raped her, but there may have been more) were on the Wackenhut clock while they were assaulting her.

It took some time, but when things had calmed down a little, the Chandlers found an attorney who was well qualified to explore the possibility of suing Wackenhut, the company that had hired, trained, and fielded the guards. Although the company didn't know what was going on in its name while the attack and murder were in progress, it was possible that after the fact, Wackenhut may have tried to cover up the involvement of the guards. Wackenhut may have played a role in delaying the solving of the crime. But that would remain to be proved in court.

There were plenty of attorneys who wanted the case and were willing to promise the moon. The attorney who did get the case, Rob Gaecke, couldn't promise anything except a lot of work against formidable odds. In the first place, the suit couldn't be launched in a state court.

Why? The crime occurred in Michigan. Why couldn't the case be filed in a local circuit court?

"Well, it's like this," said Gaecke, "In Michigan you have only three years from the commission of the crime until the clock runs out on filing a lawsuit."

Three years? The case wasn't solved for a full 27 years. That would have meant that the Chandlers would have had to have filed their suit in 1982. Who were they supposed to sue? How was this fair? How was it even possible? Were there other states like this? Why and when did Michigan adopt this standard?

The answer was this: The Michigan Supreme Court established the new law in the July 27, 2007, *Trentadue v Buckler Automatic Lawn Sprinkler Co.* decision.[18]

---

17 Wackenhut is now part of G4S: http://www.g4s.us/en-us/.
18 *Trentadue v Buckler Automatic Lawn Sprinkler Co.*, No. 128579, Michigan Supreme Court, 25 July 2007, http://publicdocs.courts.mi.gov:81/OPINIONS/FINAL/SCT/20070725_S128579_81_trentadue4dec06-op.pdf.

That opinion handed down by the court in a split decision meant that while the prosecution, the police, and the family were readying for this most unusual trial in a most unusual case in the murder of Janet Chandler, the Michigan Supreme Court was overturning its own precedent that long had served as the law of the land. Before and historically under common law—the code we inherited from centuries of practice—the law had held that the clock started ticking when the evildoer was revealed.

I discovered that Justice Weaver had filed a vigorous dissent in the case.[19] And that fixed her more firmly in my mind as a voice of reason and common sense. What were the rest of these folks thinking? *Qui bono?* Who benefits, indeed? In the case before the Supreme Court, the beneficiaries were the insurance companies that otherwise would have had to pay a whole lot.

"We have this big black cloud over Michigan," said Gaecke of the *Trentadue* decision.[20] Of course, Gaecke is a plaintiff's trial lawyer, the kind of lawyer a lot of people profess not to like until they need one.

With Gaecke's revelation, I was transfixed in the matter of justice for Janet Chandler and my assessment of the court. This intersection of the Michigan Supreme Court opinion and the verdict in the Chandler case left no doubt in my mind that something was desperately wrong at Michigan's highest court. And this had become personal.[21]

I was about to learn a whole lot more after I received a message from my favorite justice.

Justice Weaver, though she had a secretary and four law clerks, from time to time needed some editing help. Could I go over some administrative documents, the work of her crew? That was help I could offer.

There were others who needed assistance, in particular Probate Judge Pamela O'Sullivan in Macomb County. The State Court Administrator (and chief of staff), Carl Gromek—another Supreme Court appointee—had savaged her. She wanted to let people know what was going on. So, I lent a hand there, too.[22]

And could I listen?

Sometimes Justice Weaver needed to hear herself talk through the problems confronting her. She had about her what she called her "kitchen cabinet," a term dating to the

---

19 She was joined by Justice Michael Cavanagh. You can read that dissent here: http://www.justiceweaver.com/pdfs/128579-Opinion.pdf. We'll also be taking a deeper look at the case in Chapter 20.
20 Rob Gaecke, telephone interview with author, 4 February 2012.
21 Gaecke, representing Janet's parents, ultimately filed suit in a U.S. District Court, alleging that Wackenhut engaged in fraudulent concealment of facts that had bearing on the case. The suit was initially dismissed and Gaecke appealed. In early December of 2011, I travelled to Cincinnati with the Chandlers to witness that appeal. The appeal was denied in a split decision (2-to-1) as was a request for reconsideration. Gaecke appealed to the U.S. Supreme Court, but that court declined to take up the case because of the Michigan Supreme Court's ruling that became law. [John Tunison, "Victim's parents can't sue killers' employer," *Grand Rapids Press*, 2 October 2012, A3.]
22 You can read her letter to then-Chief Justice Clifford Taylor in Chapter 21.

presidency of Andrew Jackson and used (by his critics) to denote an informal group of advisors. She would turn to the cabinet both to sound out her concerns about the operations of the court and her ideas to correct them. She'd also listen to the responses. I don't want to make it sound like I was doing a lot; I wasn't. But I was more and more alarmed by what was happening at the court. This was serious. The other justices at the time were Cliff Taylor, Maura Corrigan, Marilyn Kelly, Michael Cavanagh, Robert P. Young, Jr., and Stephen Markman. And they were acting in ways they shouldn't.

A Treasure Trove

The story in this book is told through court documents, internal communications, and detailed conversations. The book also compiles media accounts and other interviews that put the history in context. But much of the substantiation comes from Weaver's copious files.

Weaver is by her own reckoning an inveterate saver. ...Memos, scraps of paper, newspaper articles. She has them all, and she pretty well knows how to find them. She also had a habit of dictating summaries of conversations as soon as possible after they occurred. This was how she kept track of all the work of the court.

These boxes and boxes of materials, hours of cassette recordings, video recordings...all will be going to the Clarke Historical Library at Central Michigan University. That's the same place that holds the papers from her predecessor, Senator/Justice Robert P. Griffin. Oh, the archivists there will have a job ahead of them, but perhaps nowhere else is there such a career documented in just such a way. Scholars may find a veritable trove.

Finding Justice

If we raise issues that resonate, we hope you will do something about it: become a court watcher, study the issues and the judges and justices, write, call, ask to see your legislators, the Governor, join a citizens group that works for change. You'll find at the end of this book one plan—a Seven-Point Plan—for reform of the Michigan Supreme Court that Justice Weaver has been working on for years. It maintains elected justices and refines the appointment process to fill vacancies, checking and balancing some of the authority the Governor has under the state Constitution. It's a plan. Doesn't have to be your plan, but it's a place to start. The goal is to give you a fair shot of achieving and receiving justice.

And while it's a plan for Michigan, that doesn't preclude its use in any other state. Michigan may be at the bottom of some surveys in terms of the autonomy and authority of its Supreme Court, but other states have their own problems. If the excesses we lay out here happened in Michigan, they can happen almost anyplace else, too.

Critics will rightly note I am not an attorney. But some of my best friends are. They are students of order, respecters of custom, convention, and continuity, and much more that I value. I really like most attorneys. As my closest lawyer friend told me "I paid a lot of money to learn to think this way." Jon Muth, one of the people we interviewed for this book, said it might be a good thing I'm not one of their number. In the first place, I can't be sent to the dread Attorney Grievance Commission (that's an agency of the Supreme Court that deals with attorneys who are accused of having done wrong). Were I an attorney, I might find myself disbarred.

And what about Elizabeth Weaver? They've already tried to get her...sending her to the Judicial Tenure Commission and the Attorney Grievance Commission...all to no avail. A majority of the Supreme Court also botched an attempt to censure her. Who knows what the new majority will try next?

Richard Weaver (no relation) wrote a little book, *Ideas Have Consequences*.[23] They do. This present book really is the idea that the Michigan Supreme Court can be better, in fact, can be the best court in the land...if people demand it.

At the outset, neither Justice Weaver nor I wanted to write this book. But it's here. And we hope it will be of service to the cause of justice and lead to real reforms. We trust there will be consequences, and we have faith that those consequences can be good.

And in reference to the question asked early in this chapter...how likely it was that a former college professor and a retired chief justice of the Michigan Supreme Court would collaborate on such a work?

Under the circumstances, it was inevitable.

23 Richard Weaver, *Ideas Have Consequences*, University of Chicago Press, (Chicago, Ill.) 1984.

Chapter 1

From the State of Tulane to the Bench

How do you hijack a state supreme court? In Michigan, it took a confluence of factors at the turn of the century (the 20th to the 21st), including the unchecked appointment powers of a Governor who was determined to control the courts (as he did the executive and legislative branches) and justices beholden to him who were willing to ignore the common law, the state Constitution, and common sense. In the process, they would act deceitfully and in unnecessary secrecy.

That took some doing. After all, the justices usually arrived at the high court by the process of election. But in Michigan, when a justice resigns, the Governor steps in to appoint whomever he or she chooses. That happened three times—well, three and a half—in the span of two years in the last half of the 1990s. The result was a stacked court.[24] And a stacked court whose appointees were less than qualified—through lack of experience or judicial temperament—for their new jobs. Oh, they were plenty smart, but that wasn't enough.

It's probably happened before in this state, certainly it has in others[25], but we might not know about individual stories that make up this larger narrative unless there was someone on the inside who was keeping track.

There was: Justice Elizabeth "Betty" Ann Weaver (chief justice 1999-2001).

She didn't start off as someone who set out to chronicle the excesses of her fellow justices. She was set on effecting reforms at the court and the rest of the state's judicial system. As a lower court judge, she certainly had seen the need.

She had arrived at the Supreme Court January 1, 1995, via the elective process. She had been elevated from the Michigan Court of Appeals, where she had served a full six-year term and then two years of a second term. Before that, she had served for 12

---

24 A stacked court is the result of appointments by an executive officer (in this case a governor) of judges who are more likely to deliver favorable verdicts. Those judges (or justices) take newly vacated seats. In contrast, a packed court is the appointment of supernumerary judges to offset other votes on the court. Franklin Delano Roosevelt developed a plan to pack the U.S. Supreme Court with more justices to achieve his ends in New Deal legislation.
25 The Louisiana Supreme Court under the late Governor Huey Long comes to mind.

years in Leelanau County as a trial judge in the Probate and Juvenile Court. In all of her seven elections, she was never defeated. And she was never appointed to her seat on the bench; she always won her seat on the bench as an electoral decision of the people.

This daughter of the South had grown up in New Orleans and is quick to call you "Darlin'." Her father, Louis Edgar Weaver, was a sign painter who had come to New Orleans from the Illinois and Indiana farmlands where his Irish, English, Scots, and German forebears settled. He had finished 8th grade, moved west and worked as a cowboy, and then went off to fight with the Marines in the First World War. During the war, he was twice wounded and was subsequently reported killed in action.[26] When he married, he was 15 years older than his young and spirited bride, Mary Alva Groff Weaver. Elizabeth was the youngest of their three children. *And my Daddy loved his daughter.*[27] That didn't stop him, though, from playing cutthroat Hearts games with her, offering no concession because of her youth or sex. *Oh, no. That was serious business, and I learned how to be strong.*

Elizabeth also learned plenty from her mother, a real Southerner but a descendent of Dutch Canadians on her father's side and German immigrants on her mother's side. The family had money at some point, but it had dissipated. Her mother had finished high school, but early—at age 16—and for that reason was not awarded her diploma; that was the policy in that school district at that time.

This hand-me-down tricycle was Elizabeth "Betty" Ann Weaver's first vehicle. And it was her very own. She treasured it and the independence it gave her. She's on the sidewalk in front of her family's New Orleans' home.

Both parents had high aspirations for their children.

And my mother was the most devoted supporter in my life until she passed in 1977.[28] *She provided* <u>*unselfish, unfailing*</u> *love, discipline, opportunity, and example of Christian character and leadership.*

26 Weaver wrote about that event in one of her high school essays. Imagine the family's reaction to the soldier showing up at the front door after all had thought him dead.
27 As a reminder, Weaver's voice throughout is in italics.
28 Her father had passed a year earlier.

Before my arrival, she was healed of a diagnosed cancer in one visit to a Christian Science practitioner, and she saw I was exposed to Christian Science by attending Sunday school and her example.

Mary Alva Groff and Louis Edgar Weaver at about the time of their marriage. Elizabeth's mother had graduated from high school as a 16 year old. For some administrative reason that meant she could not be awarded her diploma. Elizabeth's father, 15 years older than her mother, had left school after eighth grade, gone west to work as a cowboy, fought in World War I as a Marine (where he had been twice wounded and then mistakenly listed as killed in action) and then came south to New Orleans where he found work as a sign painter.

Even as a child, Elizabeth felt the pull of justice. She had two older brothers, Robert (Bob) and Richard (Dick), and one of her earliest recollections involved both them and her innate sense of justice. It transpired as the story of *The State Of Tulane*:

There's a difference of about five years between each of us, so I learned about justice early. In fact, real early. My Dad had wanted to be a lawyer so—my older brother, Bob, was going to be a lawyer,[29] and he had gone to what they call Pelican Boys State, sponsored by the American Legion, and he learned a lot about government—or more about government. He came home, and he organized our family, at least us kids, into a state, and it was called the State of Tulane. (It was Tulane because my brother intended to go to Tulane University.) And we were each parishes. I was Beauregard Parish, named after the school I was going to. And we had voting, but it was keyed to our ages: as I recall there were 14 votes for Bob, ten for Dick, and five for me. So my older brother had to get one or the other of us to win, but my second brother and I had to be together or we were going to lose. And we had laws, and we had rules, and we had courts, and we had government.

Elizabeth with brothers Dick (left) and Bob. Their father held the law in high regard as a profession, one he'd said he wished he could have pursued. Bob had given thought to becoming a lawyer but was disabused of the idea when he went to college: His professors told him he was too smart to go into law. Both brothers became instead Ph.D. chemical engineers. Elizabeth studied languages in her undergraduate career (majoring in French) but had worked in a law office since she was 15. She was drawn, she said, to the ideal of justice and fairness under law.

---

29 Both brothers wound up as Ph.D. chemical engineers.

One time I violated one of the laws, and I went on trial. My older brother was the prosecutor, but he was also the judge. And I made an offense, apparently, with Dick, my second brother. I had done it, but I had a good reason, because, probably, he had done something to me first.

I was on the witness stand, and my older brother was cross-examining me, and said, "Did you do it?" Well, I wanted to say, "Yes, but..." and give the reasons. And he said, "You can only answer 'Yes' or 'No.'" Still, I wanted to answer more than "yes" or "no." And he said, "You can only answer 'Yes' or 'No.'" It was badgering—bullying—and I didn't like it. And it didn't seem like justice to me if you can't explain. So I went to what I considered the supreme court; I left the room, crying, and I went and found my mother. She came in and found out what was going on and adjudicated the matter, and she disbanded the state. The whole State of Tulane was abandoned, and it was never to be talked about again. It wasn't.

Now, I don't talk about this in any way to disparage my brothers because they both were very good to me. But I did learn to defend what I thought, what I stood for, even at probably age five at the time of the State of Tulane. So I got that initial dealing with a lack of separation of power, rotation in office, and the need for just general fairness and justice, which was intuitive to me.

By the time she was 15, she was learning on the job in a law office:

My Sunday school teacher Jimmy Coleman was a lawyer, and pretty much turned out to be a second Dad to me in many ways, and eventually I had some summer jobs at the law firm. I got to put pocket parts in the books and do different things.

In what is likely a scene from a high school drama club production, Elizabeth Weaver stands at the ready, pencil in hand. The thespian in front remains unidentified, but the young woman in the plaid skirt is Gnann Williams Cather. *She's my best friend from junior high and high school and Newcomb. She and I not only were champion debate partners but we also did minor parts in the school plays. I was a bridesmaid for her. She lost her home to 10 feet of water from Katrina and she and her family had to live in Baton Rouge for four or five months. When I went down after she returned to New Orleans she wanted me to go with her to her devastated home. It was only her second time to go there since the flood...a very difficult experience. I had stayed there on a number of visits to New Orleans. We are still in touch of course. She came from New Orleans for my surprise retirement party.*

She had planned to study math or science (although she didn't much like the lab work) at Newcomb College[30] there, but instead studied languages...German, Russian, Spanish, and majored in French. She graduated in 1962 on the Dean's List, as a member of Mortar Board and Phi Beta Kappa, as a member of Who's Who in American Colleges and Universities, and she won the French Government Excellence in French Award.

Elizabeth Weaver (right) with two friends at their 1962 graduation from H. Sophie Newcomb Memorial College, the women's coordinate of Tulane University, New Orleans. *We graduated from Newcomb first and then Tulane, a fun and busy day. On the left is Marilyn Reilly Cohen. I always called her "Reil." She majored in English. She married her junior high boy friend— Stephen Cohen (also a friend of mine) who became a doctor. Marilyn became an English teacher. They had two children. Years later, Marilyn decided to go to law school and is a successful lawyer in the New Orleans area.* In the middle is Rona Simonin O'Reagan. *I called her "Ro." She majored in education and became a teacher and actually taught overseas in the American School for children of armed service personnel in northern Africa, perhaps Libya. Ro married Richard O'Reagan and lives in Jackson, Mississippi. Ro's dad was in the oil business. I think and was older like my dad. Her parents were true Cajuns and her mother had a marvelous Cajun accent and spoke Cajun French as well as English. She was a great cook. At the time the photo was taken, the trio had been friends for much of their lives. We all went to Beauregard Junior High together, then to different high schools, and then Newcomb together. I believe Reil, Ro and I were all Phi Beta Kappas. I am still in touch with them. They both came to my induction into the Newcomb Hall of Fame.*

So it was very clear that I should do something after college. ... I met up with somebody, a gal at an LSU football game, who was going to law school, and it just was as obvious to me as anything that that's what I should do. I talked to my parents, remembering my dad had wanted to be a lawyer — although, this was odd for a girl to be a lawyer. I didn't know any women that were lawyers.

She talked with her brothers about the idea as well.

And no one thought, "Well, that's the craziest thing ever." They didn't try to discourage me. So, I went to law school. I had a very naïve idea that I would learn it all there and be a lawyer. I studied with people, and I did well in law school.[31]

One of those study partners was Anita Connick, one of four women in her law class at Tulane (of 104 in her class and from a total of 400 students in the school). Anita and her husband, Harry, Sr. ran a local music and record store, while both of them attended law school. Harry was a year or so ahead of his wife and Weaver.

---

30 H. Sophie Newcomb Memorial College, or Newcomb College, was the coordinate women's college within Tulane University. She was selected the 2005 Alumna of the Year for the college.

31 According to two sources: both the 2005 and the 2009 *Michigan Manual*, she was inducted into The Order of the Coif, an honorary legal scholastic society, served as an editor of the *Tulane Law Review*, and clerked for Judge Oliver P. Carriere of the Louisiana Civil District Court. [http://www.legislature.mi.gov/documents/publications/manual/2005-2006/2005-MM-0519-0531-Supreme.pdf; http://www.legislature.mi.gov/documents/publications/MichiganManual/2009-2010MichiganManual/09-10_MM_V_pp_09_Weaver.pdf.] She also was an honor graduate, and among the top ten students of her class.

They were considerably older than I was—but they put themselves through college and law school with their music store. And we all finished. And so Anita practiced out of her home because she had two little kids, and I was with the law firm ... the Sunday school teacher's law firm. But I was doing some other cases in family [law] and other things. And I would go out to the Connick's—and little Harry, Jr. was just a little kid, you know, four or so—and Anita would say, "Well, Little Harry, play for Betty," and he'd knock out the "Saints" and all that. And I'd say, "That's good, little Harry. Keep that up."

He did.[32]

And Anita went on to be a judge, and I went on to be a judge, and we were always in touch. And I have albums of Harry Connick's, signed.

Shortly after her graduation in 1965, Weaver went to work as a title specialist for Chevron Oil.

I had a good beginning job, but there was definitely a glass ceiling there, and I didn't intend to be there a long time. I had this interest in young people and juvenile matters and, particularly, the law in relation to that. And I felt that I needed to broaden my horizons to other than New Orleans, but only temporarily.

She had been offered the job of Dean of Girls at the University of Georgia. The work would deal with young people, but it wasn't a job that appealed. And there was another offer in Nashville.

You notice still in the South.

But she was destined to travel much farther from home. That journey began by providence or chance at her brother Bob's wedding. One of the members of the wedding party was a man who led the private and exclusive Leelanau School[33] in northern Michigan's Glen Arbor. Glen Arbor is in the southern part of Leelanau County, an area that stretched up to Northport at the tip of the Leelanau Peninsula.

He kept trying to convince me to come up here, and I was looking more at high school. And in this totally different place—how much more different could it be than New Orleans with the snow and everything? So I decided I would do it.

The first year she worked as a counselor and taught French. By the second year, she served as Dean of Girls in addition to her teaching.

---

32 Harry Connick, Jr. is a jazz pianist, vocalist, conductor, and actor of international renown. His home is still New Orleans.

33 The Leelanau School had been founded by Cora and Skipper Beals as a summer camp for boys in 1923. The camp expanded to serve as a nine-month school in 1929 and went coeducational in the early 1940s. (http://www.leelanau.org/index.php?option=com_content&view=article&id=56&Itemid=10).

What a change! From hot and steamy New Orleans with its crush of people and myriad cultures to the old-growth hard- and piney-woods of cool northern Michigan. From salt water to fresh. From a population densely packed into cantonments, or quarters, to a rural county northwest of Traverse City, with fewer than 11,000 people.[34] That first winter of 1966-67, she stayed in a house directly on the shore of Lake Michigan near the mouth of her beloved Crystal River. Snow found its way through every crack and crevice, piling in small drifts on the inside of the windows. And, because this broadening of her horizons was to be temporary, she had not completely severed her ties with her New Orleans' employer.

I was still involved with the law firm in New Orleans, and I was on a wrong cycle. I was in New Orleans in the summer and here in the winter. If anything, it should be the opposite.

As an independent young woman, she liked being on her own. She liked teaching, and stayed with the job at the Leelanau School for two years. Then she waited tables and, starting in 1969, taught as a substitute in the area public schools. The teaching appealed.

And so I was connected. And there would be a job, but I needed to have a teaching certificate.

So, she determined to get it, and her emphasis would be elementary education. One reason for her choice was that drugs were showing up even in northern Michigan. She said she recognized them as a threat and felt that she needed to reach children at a younger age...as young as possible in order to prepare them for the choices they would face.

And so I called Central Michigan University. The head of the Education Department kindly talked to me, and he let me in, like, the next day. And in two more days, I was down there to start the semester. In 14 weeks, I took 20 hours in education courses. That's all I needed—I had a law degree, and I had other degrees, and I did my practice teaching right there in Mt. Pleasant with Mrs. Minnie Epple at Fancher School, and then I got my certificate.

She remembers the weekly drives through snowstorms to get back and forth to Mt. Pleasant, indicating her study consumed a winter semester.[35]

Dr. Alan F. Quick was the man who made all of that possible at CMU, in those days known as "The Friendly School." He both administered her program and served as one of her teachers. He remembers her as a most able student:

> She wanted to be certified, so I helped her. I got to know her and enjoy her as a student. And she was an excellent student. I had a History of Education class she took from me, and I can remember the paper she wrote; it was

---

34 There were still fewer than 22,000 residents at a population density of 62.5 persons per square mile in 2010, according to the U.S. Census Bureau (http://quickfacts.census.gov/qfd/states/26/26089.html).
35 During the week, she stayed in Mt. Pleasant.

very good. She was ambitious, and she had little trouble ... just zoomed right through. I can remember looking back at Betty as a student; I could see she was going to be an asset to our whole society. You want to help everybody as much as you can, but there are those students who make it a real pleasure.[36]

There was the Southern accent, too, said Quick, and her reciprocated kindness, kindness that would run through her life: "I have a letter I received from her when I retired. It was a nice letter."

And then I was able to teach first grade.

After earning her teaching certificate from Central Michigan University, Elizabeth Weaver taught first grade beginning in 1972 at the Glen Lake Community School in nearby Maple City.

She did, beginning in 1972 at the Glen Lake Community School in nearby Maple City. Mary Frixen, herself a teacher, had met Weaver in the late 1960s, shortly after both of them had moved into the community.

> She taught my son in first grade. She was an excellent teacher. [....] Betty doesn't go into anything unless she can be outstanding at it. She accepts nothing but top quality from herself.

> I have been an elementary principal and before that a middle school teacher. As a principal, I DO believe that when kindergarten and first grade teachers die, they go straight to heaven.

> And she did an outstanding job. She was compassionate without babying them. She was supportive, encouraging of them, perceptive—seeing what each child needed and meeting those needs. She was innovative for her time;

---

36 Dr. Alan F. Quick, telephone interview with co-author Schock, 26 November 2011.

she pushed the curriculum. I was very happy with her as my son's first grade teacher.[37]

Weaver also reflected on her growing desire to stay in Michigan and to find ways to use <u>all</u> her talents and training. She was determined not to allow her legal career to slide.

Because there's no reciprocity between Louisiana and any other place, I had to take the Michigan Bar, which I did. I was able to study for the Michigan Bar while I was teaching. And I became a lawyer here.

She took and passed the exam in the spring of 1973. Bar number P22059. She opened her own practice, running it out of her home. A teacher/lawyer, or lawyer/teacher?

Newly sworn as a Michigan attorney, Weaver stands by the sign on her road advertising her services. Her law practice and full-time teaching kept her busy.

The teaching had given her a solid introduction to the community. She knew the families and pretty much the way things worked in this rural, off-the-beaten-path part of Michigan that constituted one of the lesser-discovered summer resort havens; it was almost too far away from any place else to be an easy commute.[38] At the time she arrived, she said, lakefront footage was going to $50 a foot. It wouldn't stay that way long, though.

But then, neither would she remain a teacher very long; she had seen a path for herself that would combine her love for young people and her love for law: administering juvenile justice in the form of a probate and juvenile judge.[39]

There was a wonderful probate judge here, Myles C. Kimmerly, and he was going to retire in '76, and so that would be time enough for me to do what I needed to do, because I was already nine years a lawyer. And so that all worked out, and I passed the Bar. But then the judge passed on.

37 Mary Frixen, telephone interview with co-author Schock, 30 December 2011.
38 That's changed. In the summer of 2011, ABC's *Good Morning, America*, reported the Sleeping Bear Dunes National Lakeshore (including Glen Arbor) was voted its "Most Beautiful Place in America" and "one of the nation's best-kept secrets." (http://abcnews.go.com/Travel/best_places_USA/sleeping-bear-dunes-michigan-voted-good-morning-americas/story?id=14319616#.TtETb8lfoco.)
39 Much of the work with juveniles is now handled in the state's circuit courts, a result of the reorganization of Michigan's court system.

Kimmerly's death in 1973 meant Governor William Milliken would make an appointment of a judge who would serve until the 1974 general election.

And I was considered, but I was not political; I was non-partisan, and I didn't belong to any party. So I didn't get appointed.[40]

The appointment instead went to Marion Yoder, a former prosecuting attorney and the favored nominee of the established Republican Party. Would Weaver challenge him in the upcoming general election? First she talked it over with her parents. They were supportive. Then she spoke with her close Michigan friends, first among them Joy Taylor. "I thought she should go for it," said Taylor. "It made sense to me."[41]

Taylor, busy raising young children and teaching, gave her support in doing some driving. Weaver says that her best help was assessing people's strengths and trustworthiness.[42]

Weaver also consulted a close friend who was both a Christian Science practitioner and teacher.

These people don't give you advice, but if requested, they will pray specifically for you, including knowing that you will listen for, accept, and act upon the thoughts God is ever sending to you. She believed that I would be good for it and I should do it. She urged me to discover and develop all my talents.

And she spoke with others whose opinions mattered to her, especially the mother of one of her former students, Mary Frixen, who recounts a discussion:

> She and I had become friends, and we discussed the possibility to her going into the probate court. It seemed a perfect fit. But she was vacillating... should she tackle this? She was not an incumbent and she'd have to defeat (Yoder).
>
> She has always been very concerned for young people. That's really her driving concern. Teaching was another arrow in her quiver of skills she'd use later in life. It just added to her knowledge base.
>
> There was only one criticism I ever heard and that was she had no children of her own. But she did. And every teacher I know of says the same thing...

---

40 Growing up in the South, she observed that if you wanted to vote, it had to be as a Democrat. What other party was there? With her move to Michigan she fostered a reflective, conservative outlook and identified herself, ultimately, as "an independent common-sense Republican." Whenever she has claimed party affiliation, it has been as a Republican. Whenever she has been nominated by a party, it was the Republicans. She has sometimes in latter years been accused of being a RINO—Republican In Name Only. She says that's not the case, and if anyone has moved away from the base it's been the Republican Party.
41 Joy Taylor, telephone interview with co-author Schock, 3 January 2012.
42 Those abilities also would come into play in subsequent elections in a much larger way. Joy Taylor is probably her closest friend and, since 1981, her neighbor along the Crystal River.

they talk about "My kids." Every child who was in her classroom was her child.

I always felt she had more to offer as a judge of children than as a teacher—not that she wasn't excellent at it [teaching]—but that her road had further to take her. She's always been about service...how to serve. She could offer Leelanau something nobody else in the county could. [43]

So, anyway, I decided, "Well, I'm qualified," and there was an election for the remainder of the term. And so—I did have a lot of friends because I was active in the community and all that, and a respected teacher. It was a political base, as it turned out, but I didn't plan it that way. So, in '74 I ran. And I went door-to-door, and I just ran on a very positive "I'm-qualified" campaign.

FIRM and FAIR
Uniquely Qualified

B E T T Y   W E A V E R
for
PROBATE JUDGE
Vote November 5th
Leelanau County

Weaver had planned to run for probate judge in Leelanau County in 1976 when the incumbent, Myles C. Kimmerly, was scheduled to retire. He died in 1973, and while she put her name forward for consideration, Governor Milliken picked former prosecutor Marion Yoder, a Republican favorite. Undeterred, Weaver ran against a heavily-supported Yoder and won by 400 votes.

While she was an independent, she came toward the Republican Party as a result of the suggestion in 1974 from another local woman. Connie Binsfeld, from nearby Maple City in the Leelanau Peninsula, was running as a Republican for the House of Representatives at the same time Weaver was running for her probate judgeship.

I was interested in being a judge, and to me it was non-partisan. Along the way, however, I came to know Connie Binsfeld.

The Republicans hadn't been particularly welcoming to Binsfeld in a way that was familiar to Weaver.

When she beat them in the primary, the Republican establishment supported the Democrat candidate openly.

A lesser woman might have thought the party system didn't have much to offer her; after all, the established powers were trying to keep both Binsfeld and Weaver out. But Binsfeld saw and shared with Weaver that there was something of value there.

43Mary Frixen.

I basically agree with accountability for actions, and opportunity. So I found that I agreed with Republican principles. (Of course many Democrats I know also have those principles.)

And she felt that it would be good for me to be involved in the parties. And so there were opportunities to meet people, and I came to realize that there are a lot of very good grassroots people in these parties. I had a lot of support from people across the line. I would go to any party or thing that I was invited to.

And she went, not only to parties, but any place she could meet people throughout the county. Friend Mary Frixen volunteered to help as much as she could...given her commitments to her young family, teaching, and operating a resort: "I was glad to help and I wound up as campaign treasurer. I drove her around some, but my contribution was mostly taking money and writing a letter to every donor. She had others doing the driving."

Sometimes they'd take her or she'd drive herself, going door to door over the county's nearly 350 square miles. Imagine a petite young woman pulling up at your front stoop in her white 1964 Olds Cutlass (bought used for $1,800) in the summer or early fall of 1974, drawling out her request for your support for her candidacy as THE probate judge in your northern Michigan refuge. Things had come far for women. But that far?

I got elected by 400 votes. But, of course, in Leelanau County I think there were only 4,000 votes ... a lot of people don't vote for judge anyway. I was a juvenile judge in many senses of the word, and it wasn't well-received necessarily by the establishment—this person from the southern part of the county—I don't know that anybody had ever been elected for county office from down here—not in recent times. ...And this person was a woman, and young. But it was the right timing, and I unseated the incumbent, and that was it.

Connie Binsfeld also was elected and began a political career that took her from the House to the Senate and eventually to the position as Lieutenant Governor from 1991 through 1998 under Governor John Engler. She and Weaver would work together many times on substantive issues, most notably for the benefit of children. But in 1974, both Binsfeld and Weaver were just at the beginning of what would be grand adventures.

Taking her first oath of office, Monday, Dec. 30, 1974, Elizabeth Weaver was sworn in by Circuit Judge William R. Brown. Her term began Jan. 1, 1975, and she would serve as a probate judge for 12 years. The *Traverse City Record-Eagle* reported there were about 60 well-wishers in the audience in the Leelanau County courthouse in Leland. (*Traverse City Record-Eagle*)

Weaver took her oath of office two days before her term began on Jan. 1, 1975. The *Traverse City Record-Eagle* memorialized the event:

> LELAND—"Solomon asked the Lord for wisdom, knowledge and an understanding heart," said Betty Weaver. "This morning I honor that prayer."
>
> An audience of about 60 well-wishers saw Miss Weaver take the oath of office as Leelanau County judge of probate early Monday.
>
> The oath was administered by Circuit Judge William R. Brown to the 33-year-old attorney who unseated veteran Leelanau lawyer Marion Yoder in the November election.
>
> Yoder had served the remainder of the term vacated by the death of former Probate Judge Myles Kimmerly.
>
> Following the brief ceremonies Judge Weaver cited the Hebrew king's prayer and said she shared it. The thought, she said, came to her on the way to the ceremony which installed her as judge of probate.
>
> "I am very happy," she said. "I recognize that the people of Leelanau County have placed their trust in me. I will live up to it."
>
> One who shared Judge Weaver's feelings was Circuit Judge William R. Brown who administered the oath of office.
>
> "I regard it as a privilege to preside at the installation of Judge Weaver," he said following the ceremony. "I wish her the best of everything."[44]

The job of the probate judge in Leelanau County was only part time—usually two days a week, but some of the same hours she had been spending at school. So, she left the classroom, and she took much of what she'd learned there with her to the bench.

I just took my common sense to the court, a sense that everyone needs to be accountable and responsible for what they do; and that every young person deserves an opportunity to discover and develop their talents, but they're responsible to do it. That's what I learned at home, and that was just what I've learned from my faith, too. I mean, it's just a matter of good American values: we're all responsible for discovering and developing our worth, but we should have an opportunity to do it.

For the young people who appeared before her bench, it all started with their realization that she was going to hold them responsible for their actions.

And so I established that, which isn't remarkable, but it seemed to be remarkable in an age of excuses.

---

44 "Betty Weaver sworn in as probate judge for Leelanau County," *Traverse City Record-Eagle*, 31 December 1974, 5.

First would come probation. If that wasn't effective, *we had a safe place to get people's attention.*

Jail.

People don't learn unless you have their attention. So I became famous for holding young people accountable in the Leelanau County Jail, where we could see the child every day. They were safe—much safer than going to some downstate detention facility, where they would be mixed, probably, with armed robbers, murderers, and rapists who were under 17.[45] *We didn't need that. We needed young people to realize that if they were going to break and enter people's homes and then wouldn't abide by their probations, that they could lose their freedom.*

Youthful offenders who ignored her first warning might have found themselves in a cell (without cellmates) for a maximum of 30 days.

Joy Taylor recalls a conversation at a parent/teacher conference with a parent of one of her young students. People knew Taylor lived next to Weaver and the matter of "The Judge" came up. "And this Dad said to me, 'Weaver? She put me in jail.' There was a long pause and then he said 'It was the best thing that ever happened to me.' His wife agreed. Knowing him, it was true."[46]

Her former campaign treasurer, Mary Frixen, remembered one young student who had crossed the line. Before appearing before Weaver's bench, the student asked Frixen what he should do. "I told him to tell the truth; that she would know if he was lying. And to say he was sorry only if he truly was. He needed to know that she was not going to let him off easily and it was up to him."[47]

In the end, the student reported to her that his encounter with Judge Weaver was "like dealing with a dragon with two heads."[48] Frixen reported that the former student/offender is now a police officer.

Her actions received widespread attention. In 1978, almost midway into her first full term of office, she was featured in a two-page spread in *People Magazine*:

---

45 Incarceration of juveniles has changed drastically since then, in large part to Weaver's efforts leading various committees and task forces. According to her biographical entry in the 2005 Michigan Manual:

Justice Weaver was appointed to the Michigan Commission on Criminal Justice by Governor William Milliken; to the Michigan Committee on Juvenile Justice by Governors James Blanchard, John Engler, and Jennifer Granholm. She was also appointed to chair the Governor's Task Force for Children's Justice and the Trial Court Assessment Commission by Governors Engler and Granholm. She has served as chair of the State Bar of Michigan Juvenile Law Committee and as president of the Top of Michigan Probate and Juvenile Judges Association. In addition, Justice Weaver has served on the National Council of Juvenile and Family Judges and as secretary of the Probate and Juvenile Judges Association of Michigan. (http://www.legislature.mi.gov/documents/publications/manual/2005-2006/2005-MM-0519-0531-Supreme.pdf.)

46 Joy Taylor, 5 January 2012.
47 Mary Frixen.
48 Ibid.

In this photo that was shot but not used in the *People Magazine* article, photographer John Collier captured the interaction between Judge Weaver and one of her youthful charges. Collier was a *Detroit Free Press* photographer who also took select freelance assignments. (John M. Collier.)

The young prisoners—under Michigan law they must be at least 15—are locked in plain barred cells with only the barest amenities. They have a toilet, washbasin, table, chair and a mattress on a steel shelf. There is no television, but school lessons are delivered daily, along with any books the inmates request. "It's not easy to put them in jail," says Judge Weaver, 36. "I do it for a purpose—to give them time to think. We counsel them daily and have them write essays on what they've learned."
....

"People have to learn to be responsible for their actions, and the courts just happen to be the system we have for making people accountable. Fear of punishment never made a young person truly honest, but it keeps him honest until he reaches a moral decision on his own. Juvenile offenders do not want to see my court again."[49]

The article's author, Julie Greenwalt, sought out an unnamed dissenting voice who found fault with Weaver's approach: "'You might scare hell out of a kid,' objects another juvenile judge, 'but what does it do to his future? Putting a child in jail is a degrading experience.'"

Judge Weaver made sure no child was degraded.

Embarrassed, maybe. But it gave us a chance to reach the child in a way that he or she would know that we cared very much. And that it was their responsibility to do right. And this was their opportunity.

The *People* piece concludes this way:

She insists on letters of apology to victims of juvenile crime ("I believe that people should learn to say 'I'm sorry'") and reads every essay she assigns young defendants. "Remember," she admonishes them, "I want the paper written properly, neatly, nothing sloppy." The initial results are encouraging. One young inmate improved his reading two grade levels during his 27 days behind bars, and juvenile crime in Leelanau County has dropped 18 percent since Judge Weaver took office. "We have an opportunity to do right by these kids," says Her Honor. "Goodness gracious, what a shame if we didn't make use of it!"[50]

Her fame spread.

I went on Good Morning America *and, also,* To Tell The Truth—*and they actually got me, but it took them quite a while.*

49 Julie Greenwalt, "When a Kid Goes Wrong Judge Betty Ann Weaver Tries Some Unusual Therapy: Jail," *People Magazine*, 16 January 1978, Vol.9. No. 2., 56-57, http://www.people.com/people/archive/article/0,,20069996,00.html.
50 Ibid.

One of her colleagues, a second-generation probate judge, was Eugene "Bud" Moore in Oakland County.[51] He was a little older, had been on the bench a little longer, and her work caught his attention. He says they probably met at a summer meeting of the probate judges.

> I was from a great-big county, over a million people; she was from a little-tiny county in Northern Michigan. However, she was from a county that I loved because we have a cottage on Crystal Lake, which is just south of her county. And I spent a lot of time up on Glen Lake because I have a couple of sisters who have cottages on Glen Lake. So we had a lot in common to talk about.[52]

> They shared committee work, in particular, trying to implement changes brought about by the 1967 U.S. Supreme Court decision *In re Gault*.[53] That decision meant minors had the same rights to due process that adults had... "the right to timely notification of charges, the right to confront witnesses, the right against self-incrimination, and the right to counsel."[54]
>
> And so we were writing the juvenile court rules basically to implement much of the Gault decision. One of the big issues was whether or not kids should be put in jail. And Oakland County has a juvenile detention facility. They've got a couple programs. Leelanau County has nothing except the jail. So if you wanted to make an impact on a youngster's life in Leelanau County, you put them a night or two in jail, and that's what Betty Weaver did. And she and I disagreed about that (laughing). But she pointed out to me the fact that, you know, "I don't have your alternatives up here. I can't put them in a juvenile home. Your juvenile home is probably just as nasty as my jail. And in my jail up here there's somebody who is gonna be watching this kid every minute, and it isn't such a horrible place after all." So that's how we first met.[55]

They would initially share two disagreements: minors in jail and which lake was more beautiful, Glen or Crystal.

But even their disagreements didn't divide them, said Moore: "You become friends with people that you don't always agree with, and I think we both learned a lot from each other."

---

51 Oakland County Probate Court Chief Judge Eugene A. Moore retired in the summer of 2010 after 44 years on the bench. [Tom Kirvan, "Distinguished Servant: Chief Probate Court judge to retire on a 'high note,'" *Detroit Legal News*, 26 July 2010, http://www.legalnews.com/detroit/1001812.]

52 Eugene "Bud" Moore, video interview with co-author Schock, 13 March 2012, Oakland County.

53 "*In re Gault*–387 U.S. 1 (1967)," Justia.com, U.S. Supreme Court Center, http://supreme.justia.com/cases/federal/us/387/1/case.html.

54 "*In re Gault*," Wikipedia, http://en.wikipedia.org/wiki/In_re_Gault.

55 Eugene "Bud" Moore.

In this unpublished photo, Weaver is on the Lake Michigan shore with her beloved longhaired dachshund, Hansie. (John M. Collier.)

Moore says her influence as a probate judge was felt throughout the state.

> I do think she had an influence of compassion and an influence on insisting that cases that came in to the juvenile court were just as important as any other case. And while the probate court is looked upon by some as a lower court than the circuit court, I think she made it well known to her colleagues, and in opinions she wrote, that some of the most important cases that they decided were cases involving kids and families.[56]

---

56 Ibid.

At the same time, there were proposed reforms for juvenile justice within the state, reforms she and several other young probate judges thought would fly in the face of common sense.

And so I, and a judge from Detroit [Wayne County]—Judge Gladys Barsamian (who was a juvenile judge elected the same time I was), and Judge Donald Owens, who was the juvenile judge from Lansing [Ingham County], were the three young judges at the time who stood against what was going to be bad reform.[57] And from that, I became known more throughout the state.

Well enough known that when it came time for elections of judges to the Michigan Court of Appeals in 1986, she contemplated running. Again, she sought input from her small group of trusted friends, among them was Joy Taylor. Taylor put it this way:

> She seeks advice, and she weighs it carefully. She has a group she trusts, and she knows she can get good advice and thinking from them.
>
> Then she steps back, and she literally talks it over with God. I don't know how else to put it. She goes to the source, the only source that will have influence.[58]

Weaver also gives a lot of credit to her supporters.

These are remarkable people and they helped me understand that everyone has a role to play. I was a soldier. Without their support...well.... But I did have their support.

And we realized that there was a need to have on the Court of Appeals someone with probate juvenile experience so we wouldn't get these crazy opinions that we were getting. So I ran for Court of Appeals.

There were two seats coming open in the court's Third District[59]...and eight candidates: Weaver, David Sawyer of Grand Rapids, Gary R. McDonald of Saginaw, Janet Neff of Grand Rapids, Alan Cropsey of DeWitt, Thomas M. Burns, Jr., of Gaylord, Nathaniel Stroup of Petoskey, Randy Tavohnen of Elsie.[60]

We had the Kent County Prosecutor and son of a retired congressman out of Grand Rapids [Sawyer]. And we had an Irish sitting judge [McDonald]. And when they found out I was going to run, a woman was thrown in, who later did become a judge—but not during my elections [Neff]. And one of the spouses of a sitting Court of Appeals judge was running [Stroup], and the son of a judge who was leaving [Burns, Jr.].

---

57 They were soon joined by probate judges Michael J. Anderegg and Randall Hekman.
58 Joy Taylor.
59 Michigan's Court of Appeals is now divided into four districts, but at the time of Weaver's election there were only three. The offices for those courts were in Detroit, Lansing, and Grand Rapids. She served in the Third District, geographically the largest, which stretched up the west side of the state and into the Upper Peninsula, encompassing 66 of the state's 83 counties. The main office then was in Grand Rapids but Weaver maintained a regional office first in Glen Arbor and, later, after a fire in an adjoining office, in Traverse City.
60 Primary Elections guide, *Grand Rapids Press*, 31 July 1986.

The odds were long against her.

Highly unlikely. I was from a county of, now, 14,000.

But she had a little help. Along the way, she came under the consultative guidance of the first woman elected to Michigan's Supreme Court: Justice Mary S. Coleman. Justice Coleman had left the court in 1982, but as chief justice she had appointed Weaver to the Judicial Coordination Council for the Michigan Supreme Court.

Justice Coleman became a mentor to me. She was the first woman to get to the Supreme Court—in '72, and she was the first woman to be a probate juvenile judge on the court. I was the second.[61]

Mary S. Coleman, the first woman to serve as the chief justice of the Michigan Supreme Court, was the honorary chair for Elizabeth Weaver's Court of Appeals campaign in 1986. Of Weaver, Coleman wrote: "As a statewide leader and communicator—an experienced trial judge, attorney, educator and juvenile expert—Betty Weaver has the diverse background and qualifications so needed on our appellate courts. Judge Weaver had the character, courage and commitment needed for the Court of Appeals."

And the then-chief justice of the Michigan Supreme Court, former Governor G. Mennen "Soapy" Williams, also backed her candidacy. He had earlier appointed her to the special *ad hoc* committee regarding part-time probate judges.

So we had one from the Republicans and one from the Democrats, both of whom really cared about the judiciary. Coleman was my honorary campaign chair, and Soapy Williams wrote me a letter of recommendation on his own—well, I got this letter saying he would recommend me, and he said, "Do what you want with it." And, eventually, one of the other candidates—a Democrat—insisted he write them a letter of recommendation.

Weaver had simply told Williams that she was going to run. He reached across the party line and endorsed her candidacy.

...Because I worked with him and because he, as the chief justice, saw the trial judges. He wasn't hierarchical—and he took some heat for that.

And then there was her campaign strategy.

All I needed to do was come in second. There were a lot of favorite sons in that election, and my way of presenting things was that, one, I'm the only one with probate judge experience. And I'm from up here.

61 Justice Coleman was the third woman state Supreme Court justice in the nation. She became the Michigan's first woman chief justice in 1979 [Women and the law, Michigan Supreme Court Historical Society, http://www.micourthistory.org/women_and_law.php?w_id=13]. Weaver became the state's third woman chief justice in 1999.

And then I'd say, "I know that you have a favorite son, but you have two votes, and I only need one to be your adopted daughter." And all they had to do in all the places where there were favorite sons was just give that second vote to me.

There would be two ballots...the August primary to narrow the field to four and the November general election to select the two winners.

And out of the eight, improbably, seemingly, I came in second both times. And I got to be the adopted daughter.

She positioned herself as a second-choice candidate, and it worked. Judge David H. Sawyer came in first. The two would run for reelection at the same time in 1992.

And then the next time I was elected, I received the most votes, more than my colleague [Sawyer]. He joked about it. It was like 60,000 votes more.[62] And we were both unopposed.

Her move to the higher court was a mixed blessing for those who served as her colleagues. Judge "Bud" Moore from Oakland analyzed it this way:

> I hated to lose her as a probate juvenile judge because she was one of the best. She had a very innovative program; she worked with kids. In a small county, and with smaller caseloads, you can be somebody who sees the kid every day, jail or no jail; or see a child in his own home. Betty was working with that youngster and family all the time. So when she left that job and became a Court of Appeals judge, we missed her.[63]

Weaver became the first probate juvenile judge to serve on the Court of Appeals. Moore said she brought valuable experience:

> The Court of Appeals needed to have people who were on that bench, who had been juvenile and probate judges and knew what it meant to be in the trial court, and she reflected that when she took that bench. And oftentimes, Court of Appeals judges either go right from being a lawyer to being on the Court of Appeals, or they get appointed because they're a political pal of the Governor, or they may have been in the criminal court system, the circuit court. But rarely do you see probate. And so we were glad to have her there because she would bring her experience to cases on the Court of Appeals— which involved youngsters and families, neglect and delinquency. It's good to have that kind of a person on the Court of Appeals. So it was a loss in one way but a gain in another.[64]

It was obvious, she said, that the Court of Appeals offered a much broader field on which to take action, especially with respect to her interests:

---

62 According to the *Michigan Manual*, Weaver received 675,339 votes and Sawyer received 614,697. [Michigan Legislative Service Bureau, comp., "Official Canvass of Votes, General Election November 3, 1992," *Michigan Manual 1993-1994* (Lansing, Mich. 1993), 863.]
63 Eugene "Bud" Moore.
64 Ibid.

Juvenile matters and juvenile justice, and abuse and neglect, and the need to have our young people have the opportunity to discover and develop their worth, and to let them know that they are going to be accountable for what they do.

This is the Court of Appeals Weaver had joined with her 1986 election. At that time, she was one of only two women on that court. Front row, from left: Daniel F. Walsh, Michael J. Kelly, Chief Judge Robert J. Danhof, Chief Judge Pro Tem John H. Gillis, Donald E. Holbrook, Jr., Richard Maher. Middle row: Walter P Cynar, Roman S. Gribbs William R. Beasley, Myron H. Wahls, David H. Sawyer, and Gary R. McDonald. Back row: Martin M. Doctoroff, Elizabeth A. Weaver, Harold Hood, Joseph B. Sullivan, Barbara B. MacKenzie, and John H. Shepherd. The Court of Appeals was created in 1963; cases were first heard in 1965, and there were nine judges in all. By the time Weaver arrived, there were 18 judges, a number that grew to 28 by the time she moved on to the Supreme Court. The number of judges was revised downward to 24 in 2012 as a part of court restructuring and is to be achieved through attrition. [About the Court, Michigan Court of Appeals,http://courts.mi.gov/courts/coa/aboutthecourt/pages/about.aspx.]

But there were others substantive issues, too; in fact, all the rest that came before her. She labored away at the Court of Appeals, and she saw a need for reform throughout the state's court system. That reform, she judged, would best come from the state's highest court.

I decided that there was a need on the Supreme Court for the same sense of justice. I wanted to find reforms to see that we served the public better.

Chapter 2

Betty Weaver Slept Here[65]

Reflection: Sword or Shield?

The power of a state supreme court is equal to and arguably more than the other two branches (the executive and the legislative). In Michigan, the seven members of the high court have a corrective function to make sure that whatever the Governor or the members of the House and Senate or the courts get up to squares with the Constitution and the laws. As paragons of the state's court of last resort, they handle the challenges to make sure that what transpires is in accordance with all that's gone before. The concept is called *stare decisis*…Latin for "standing by that which has been decided." The process calls for a deep understanding and respect for the past.

That's not to say that all must be as it was. Our governing charters, state and national constitutions, rules, and laws, are subject to change. And there are times when the high courts change the course of history. Think, perhaps, of *Brown v Board of Education*, an opinion that served to sunder the rules keeping black and white children from attending the same schools and—theoretically—receiving the same educational opportunities.

Simply put, the court is a force that serves as the last word. And it can be either a sword or a shield. Which is best? Are there times when each is appropriate?

Yes, said Weaver, but in the main the court should serve as a shield, and justices must know restraint.

I did not believe that courts should use their vast power—which is, to me, the ultimate power— without restraint. To be able to say what a law or a rule means is more powerful than those who wrote it and those who signed it, i.e., the Legislature and the Governor. If you can just say what it means, regardless of what it might actually say, that's real power—and then, people have to follow it.

---

65 In talking with people about Elizabeth Weaver, this is one of the most common observations: "Oh, she spent the night at our house." It was true: she spent a lot of nights in supporters' guest bedrooms in her quest for a seat on the Michigan Supreme Court in 1994.

So, I think the power to interpret—because the law isn't always clear, or even when it is clear—should be used as a shield to protect people's rights, to see that there is justice and fairness, and not use it as a sword to go forward and promote policies, to promote ideologies, to promote agendas. The role of a judge is not to be an agenda pusher, whether it be of special interests[66] or the individual agendas of the judges, their ambitions to either remain in office, to move into higher office, or ideologies and philosophies. They should not be thinking, "this is the way the world should be, and all I need is four votes, and it doesn't matter what the Legislature, the Governor, or anyone else says because I want to promote these policies." And worst of all, it should not be promoting the agendas of bias and prejudices, either.

So that power should not be used as a sword. It should be used as a protection so that there is justice, and an equal justice under the law.

Historically, courts have sometimes taken a stand that a law that has been passed is wrong—not that it's necessarily unconstitutional, but it's wrong. What should a justice do?

You have every power to say that, and that you don't agree with it, and that the Legislature should look at it, and they should change it, and that the world should know that this is not right. If it is a crime against nature or a serious matter, a really serious matter, then one cannot be like certain judiciaries in totalitarian areas, such as the judiciary in Nazi Germany, which went along with anything. Then you just stand up knowing you may be eliminated as a judge. Every judge needs to be willing to do what needs to be done in accordance with the very highest sense of right and take the consequences. I think honesty is always the best policy, and it is the power. So you would take an honest position.

But you're not going to change the law because you think the speed limit should be 75 and it's only 65. You may not think that law is fair, but it's not for a judge to change it. Whereas, if the law is we're going to kill every other child, you're not going to go along with it and you're not going to enforce it, and you take the consequences.

And there can be consequences. With that in mind, Judge Elizabeth Weaver sought to be Justice Elizabeth Weaver.

A New Campaign

What was behind her thinking...and the thinking of her supporters?

We felt there was a need for justices who were closer to the trial courts, and justices also more interested in reforming the way our courts operated. It seemed my particular experience as the juvenile judge was an asset. The only one who had ever been there before was Justice Mary Coleman, who was my mentor.

---

66 Special interests, said Weaver, are important: *Special interests make the world go 'round. But they never should be in control of the judiciary, and judges and justices shouldn't be in their pockets.*

...And there was my interest in making the whole justice system work better.

One of the ideas was to promote the idea of judges, even judges of differing court distinctions, to fill in for each other. That would mean a circuit judge might go down the hall to sit in for a probate judge, a district judge for a circuit judge.

The public doesn't care what the title of a judge is. A judge is a judge to them. And if they're sitting waiting, waiting, waiting for matters, and someone—another judge—is in the building, but they weren't elected to do that...we needed to serve people better. I thought I would be able to help bring those reforms about, including seeing that there were good judicial services, and particularly with respect to children and families.[67]

One of the supporters of that concept was former (and by the time she was considering running for the Supreme Court, the late[68]) Chief Justice G. Mennen "Soapy" Williams. She also received continuing support from former Chief Justice Mary S. Coleman and also from then-sitting Justice Dorothy Comstock Riley and her husband, Wally.

They were very supportive of my getting there, among many people, but Dorothy was on the court. And as early as 1991 at the Engler Inaugural,[69] the Rileys were encouraging me to run for Supreme Court. I wasn't interested in doing it at that time, but they did encourage me, and continued to encourage me.

Regional diversity also played a part.

We needed people who weren't all from the Detroit area; although at the time I came to the Supreme Court, I took Justice Robert Griffin's place.[70] But Justice Griffin had spent most of his career in the U.S. Congress, and until his coming to the court had not been particularly involved in the Michigan Courts or the Michigan justice system. And Justice James Brickley was living up here, but his career had been downstate, too, in service as Lieutenant Governor and President of Eastern Michigan University.

So to have someone from the small areas—because this is a vast state, and one size doesn't fit all— needed to be understood. ...Not just the people from the Detroit-Lansing beltway.

Yes, but one of her opponents <u>was</u> from the north. Further, he was a legacy contender and a fellow Michigan Court of Appeals judge: Richard Allen Griffin,[71] son of the

67 At the time, the idea was revolutionary. A tiered pay structure and hierarchical organization worked against it. In time, Justice Weaver and others who promoted the idea would succeed.
68 Williams (born Feb. 23, 1911) had died Feb. 2, 1988, the year after leaving the court. He and Weaver shared membership in Phi Beta Kappa and Order of the Coif.
69 Interesting to note that Governor Engler made no mention of the courts in his inaugural address, January 1, 1991. [John M. Engler, "Michigan: Inauguration Speech," 1 January 1991, http://www.michigan.gov/formergovernors/0,1607,7-212-31303_31317-1976--,00.html.]
70 Justice Griffin called Traverse City home. He served in the U.S. House of Representatives from 1957-1966, when he was appointed to the U.S. Senate. He was elected that same year and then re-elected in 1972. He came to the Michigan Supreme Court in 1987 and served through 1994. [Biographies, Robert P. Griffin, Michigan Supreme Court Historiacl Society, http://www.micourthistory.org/bios.php?id=107.]
71 He is now a federal Judge on the U.S. Sixth Circuit Court of Appeals in Cincinnati.

departing Justice Robert Griffin. With that background, it would be understandable that the Republicans would put his name on the ballot. But how did Weaver get there? And was she the only other one who wanted it?

There were two seats coming open: that of Justice Robert Griffin (and because of his age, he was not going to be able to run again[72]) and Justice Conrad Mallett, Jr. Mallett was running for his first full term (he'd been appointed in 1990 and had run for a partial term in 1992).

There was one other who wanted it: Maureen Pulte Reilly. As far as she was concerned, it was a natural. She was a woman with the Reilly name and from Detroit and she had money in her family. She had gotten to the Court of Appeals.[73] But she did not want to work for the Supreme Court nomination, and she was of a mind that they should beg her to do it. Engler didn't like that, I don't think. And Griffin didn't want her.

Perhaps because Pulte Reilly would be too strong a contender.

The only time Rick Griffin ever talked to me about running, he came down the hall to my office at the Court of Appeals to talk with me. He wanted me to run for Supreme Court because he knew I was thinking about it. I thought it was awfully nice of him—we could both run and we could both win. I realized as time went on that probably he wanted me in the race as what he perceived as the weak candidate. ...Push Pulte Reilly out, and he'd win.

Support also came from a couple who were her good friends at the time, Cliff and Lucille Taylor. Mr. Taylor also was then a sitting judge on the Michigan Court of Appeals. Perhaps more important, Mrs. Taylor was Governor John Engler's chief legal counsel. *At the time, they were interested in reform. One afternoon, Lucille and I sat down to draw up a plan of reforms of the appointment system.*

And Governor Engler also helped Weaver to the court in 1994.

He let it be known that I was okay, and I was an acceptable second candidate, sometimes called the "throwaway candidate." You had to have two, and I was satisfactory. He let Brooks Patterson know it was okay to make the nomination for me. I don't think he did any serious money raising for me.

But as far as Griffin went, said Weaver, their one conversation about the matter was the only conversation about it.

I never heard from him again once it was clear I was going to get the nomination. Pulte Reilly eliminated herself and the Taylors viewed me as a good candidate, and that maybe I could win.

Rick Griffin took a stand that he was not going to accept any PAC money...well, his dad probably could have gone out and gotten all the money he needed. But not taking PAC money was his important

---

72 You can't be 70 or older and take office as a justice. [Judicial Branch, Michigan Government, http://www.michigan.gov/som/0,1607,7-192-29701_29703---FI,00.html.]
73 She served from 1989 through 1998 [Past Judges, Michigan Court of Appeals, http://coa.courts.mi.gov/court/judges/pastjudges.htm].

campaign issue. In terms of not taking the money, he was many years ahead of his time, but it was a Pyrrhic effort.

Both Griffin and Weaver were nominated by the Republican Party at its nominating convention in late summer.[74] The Democrats at their convention put forward incumbent Conrad L. Mallett, Jr., (from Detroit) and Donald R. Shelton, who was then serving on the bench in the 23rd Circuit Court (Washtenaw County).[75] Independent George Killeen, of Burton, successfully petitioned to have his name included.

Certainly there was support at home. Neighbor and friend Joy Taylor[76] observed that Weaver would make an excellent justice: "It never dawned on me that she shouldn't go for it or that she wouldn't make it. I just felt it was the next step for her, that whatever she had to bring to it was what was needed."[77]

The other Taylors, Cliff and Lucille, also encouraged her to run and helped her, said Weaver: *And Cliff Taylor said I was a great campaigner.* The late Gary R. McDonald, who had lost to Weaver in her first Court of Appeals race, had noted her abilities. *He warned others: "Never run against her. She will win."* (McDonald later successfully reached the Court of Appeals.) All she had to do was launch a campaign. Part of that process was fashioning her message. She had been warned by Justice Dorothy Comstock Riley and others not to allow the Republican Party to manage it:

So they advised me to not use the party apparatus as far as doing your publicity, your media; that what could happen was that the Supreme Court at that time, for the Republicans, was on the bottom of the list of whose ads got run, even though it might be your "buy" and your money that was raised for you, it could be dropped and replaced with ads for candidates' or issue ads of higher importance from the party's perspective.[78] So they advised me to use a PR group that they had used, who were not in the politics business; they actually were out in the real world, representing Universal Studios and different things, and they just picked a few candidates that they liked. And they had done Justice Levin; they did Judge White ("Judge White, Just Right."); and they did Dorothy Comstock Riley. So, they were just non-partisan about it.

The public relations firm was Marontate & Company, then of Auburn Hills.[79]

---

74 In Michigan, it is possible to have your name included on the ballot for Supreme Court through petition. As well, any incumbent justice may simply declare and have her or his name on the ballot, but the more common practice is through party nomination.

75 Michigan Campaign Finance Reform website: http://www.mcfn.org/pdfs/reports/SCAppendix.pdf.

76 No relation to Cliff and Lucille Taylor.

77 Joy Taylor, telephone interview with co-author Schock, 3 January and 11 January 2012.

78 Weaver's media firm made television buys directed at prime time, most often the evening news. The party would buy large blocks of time—including prime time—and then schedule what it saw as the most important elections (gubernatorial) when most viewers would be watching. As she said, the Supreme Court candidates would slot to less-viewed day parts or no slot at all. *That's what happened to Republican-nominated candidate Judge Hilda Gage in her unsuccessful 1996 campaign for Supreme Court. I tried to help her and urged her to go with Marontate.* (Subsequently discussed.) *After the election, she had money left over that wasn't spent. If she had gotten her ads run she probably would have won.* Hilda Gage, now deceased, was a Michigan Court of Appeals judge and a former Circuit Court judge of Oakland County (two years as chief judge).

79 The firm is now Berline, Inc., of Bloomfield Hills.

They were really great. They were good at placements, and they knew who could do television and who couldn't, and who could speak to the camera directly and who couldn't. For instance, I could, and so they made their ads accordingly.

They were very good, and very independent. And they liked that, I think, about me. I interviewed them, and they decided to do me, and they came up with "Weaver—We Need Her," which was a wonderful, and remains a wonderful, slogan.[80]

And while she had a message and those who could help craft it, she didn't have much money to pay for it. In fact, there were a series of problems that were threatening her candidacy.

The money wasn't coming, and my sister-in-law who had committed to being the campaign manager had to leave right at the crucial part of the campaign.

Joy Taylor recollected that "Betty would call [from the road] and the news was just awful and at a crucial time, the end of August."[81]

And for all her willingness to help, Taylor had to return to her classroom teaching. What would happen to the campaign? Joy consulted a mutual trusted friend. She was positive, said Taylor, this was a right idea and that a right idea carried within it all that was necessary for its attainment. It was the right idea for her to go forward with it. Still, said Taylor,

> we were struggling financially, and Betty was being told she needed "X" dollars for the TV campaign to get her face out there. And Betty was worried about the money, but she was also thinking of the totality of the campaign, everything she had to do, all the travel, meeting all the people, television interviews. It was daunting. We were meeting about what to do, and one of the volunteers said "You're going to have just what you need when you need it." She was so sure of it. So was I. I knew she would have it. I didn't know where it was going to come from or how, but I was sure.
>
> I said "Betty, don't worry. Don't worry. We'll find the right people. The money will come."
>
> I knew the campaign was the right idea, her election was the right idea. And whatever we were going to need would be supplied. And from that moment, the money started pouring in...well, not pouring in, but enough, and it came in steadily and from earnest people.[82]

And the right people came, too. Among other volunteers, Stephen Sonke came from Virginia. He quickly became the *de facto* fundraiser and an occasional driver.

80 The firm would go on to handle Justice Weaver's second campaign in 2002. *And in 1998, I actually encouraged them to take Maura Corrigan. They did, and that's one of the reasons she won.*
81 Joy Taylor.
82 Ibid.

He was steadying calming influence, willing to try to do something very difficult: raise money for a candidate who is not perceived as strong. I was not involved with raising money. But I think Steve talked with Chuck Yob,[83] and he would tell him who to go to. At least I think so.

According to Joy Taylor:

> Everything took a turn. It became a break-even campaign. It was phenomenal, and what was going on was very obvious to me at least.
>
> The more we listened and we trusted it would come, the more things happened. The whole scenario we're talking about is that Betty's life has been based in prayer. She knows how to listen for guidance and ideas and to pursue her highest sense of right.[84]

Weaver demonstrated through her particular way of campaigning: indefatigably. She says she always believed that the right people would come forward at the right time to take on any and all activities necessary. And that she'd have plenty of energy, the right contacts, enough money. It's her theory of supply, and it seems to have worked.

Known as an indefatigable campaigner, Weaver embraces a supporter during her 1994 run for the Supreme Court. Campaigning was demanding and time consuming. But it was a joy and energizing to meet and communicate with people at a grassroots level and to get to know every part of the state better.

There were the right people at the right time. Some of them were generational friends and associated in several ways with earlier times in her life. Two of her drivers—second cousins from New Orleans—were a grandson and grandnephew of her Sunday school teacher and first law mentor, Jimmy Coleman. One of the reasons they came north to volunteer was the great care that Weaver took of them when they were boys. One of them, volunteer Wendell LeGardeur shared their history:

> She's known my family from New Orleans for a long time. And I've always known her because I went to summer camp where she lives. I came to the Leelanau Camp [in Northport] the first time when I was 8 years old. My

(Continued on page 52)

83 A Michiganian from Hesperia, Yob was then a member of the Republican National Committee.
84 Joy Taylor.

Two of Leelanau County's three members of the Michigan Women's Hall of Fame: Elizabeth Weaver (inducted 2005) and Emelia Christine Schaub (inducted 1990). The third member is Weaver's long-time friend and former Representative, Senator, and Lieutenant Governor Connie Binsfeld (inducted 1998).

Running for the Supreme Court in 1994, Elizabeth Weaver met in the front of the Leelanau County Courthouse to discuss her campaign with her old friend Emelia Christine Schaub. Schaub, then 103, had been the state's first practicing woman prosecuting attorney who was first elected in 1936 and was then re-elected five times serving through 1946.

I was the second woman lawyer in the county and she was absolutely welcoming. In fact it was she who in the 1973 ceremony at the Leelanau County Courthouse proudly made the motion for my admission to practice law in Michigan.

Schaub began her working career operating a store and telephone exchange. She then enrolled as a student at MacLachlan's Business University (now Davenport University) in Grand Rapids. She subsequently worked as a secretary in an insurance agency and then as a student again while she earned her law degree at the Detroit College of Law.

The Michigan Women's Historical Hall of Fame has chronicled the highlights of her career:

One of Emelia Schaub's great achievements was the work she did on behalf of the impoverished Ottawa and Chippewa of Leelanau County. In 1943, on behalf of the County Board of Supervisors, Schaub petitioned the state of Michigan for title to lands which the county would hold in trust for the Leelanau Indians. The lands requested were those in the plot of Peshawbestown, which had been lost for non-payment of taxes. Seventy-seven acres were turned over to Leelanau County to serve as a de facto reservation. In tribute to her act, Emelia Schaub was made an honorary member of the Ottawa and Chippewa tribes.

Schaub's work had lasting consequences. In 1978 the Grand Traverse Band of Ottawa and Chippewa Indians applied for Federal recognition. They were granted this primarily because they had an established land base in Peshawbestown and had lived there continually for 128 years.

When in 1926 she successfully defended James Corbett charged with murder, she became the first woman lawyer in Michigan to win a murder case. In 1932 Schaub obtained a Writ of Habeas Corpus for an alien who had been detained in prison for over a year while U.S. Immigration Officials tried to find grounds for deportation. In 1936 she obtained a refund of over $5,000 in tuition paid by 13 Detroit women when the instructor running a sewing school without a license failed to fulfill her agreement with them.

Schaub was an organizer and secretary of the Leelanau Foundation of Northport, Michigan. Later she helped found the Leelanau Historical Society, Inc. and was president, museum director, and member of the board of directors until 1986. She was a charter member of the Traverse City Zonta Club and first secretary of the Leelanau Chamber of Commerce. In addition to her community activities, Schaub was secretary and treasurer of the Women Lawyer's Association.+

Emelia was unselfish, smart, strong, independent, and easy to love. I was blessed to know her and have her help and support.

+ Emelia Christine Schaub, The Michigan Women's Historical Center and Hall of Fame, http://hall.michiganwomen.org/.

parents stuck me on a plane, there were two changes before I arrived. The very first weekend, there was Betty. She came up and took me away.[85]

Her interventions would become regular.

> She would come and rescue me. She would take me for a Saturday and I'd go to her house...play and swim in the Crystal River and have picnics. Those are great memories.[86]

Wendell LeGardeur, left, and Jamie O. Coleman

Judge Elizabeth Weaver stands with Governor John Engler and Lieutenant Governor Connie Binsfeld in the 1994 campaign. With them is Jamie O. Coleman, one of Weaver's campaign volunteers. Binsfeld had been a strong support in Weaver's career of public service, right from the start in her run for probate court. *I am continually grateful for her support. Together we were able to work to ensure common sense in juvenile law even before I went to the Court of Appeals.*

85 Wendell LeGardeur, telephone interview with co-author Schock, 28 December 2011.
86 Ibid.

At the time of Weaver's Supreme Court campaign, LeGardeur had just graduated from Colgate and served a stint as a camp counselor. He followed up on the work of his cousin, Jamie O. Coleman, who'd spent the previous seven weeks on the road.

"Jamie broke the ice on that one," said LeGardeur. "He had such a great experience and it just fit right in for me. I remember it was an amazing experience. I had no idea how wonderful it would be."

Part of it was the transportation, said LeGardeur.

> She had this conversion van that had been donated by a supporter. And it was her Weaver-We-Need-Her-Mobile. And she called me her chief *aide de camp*. I'd do anything she needed. We drove all over the state. I was impressed with her grassroots-style of support. She was always eager to meet anyone to share her message.[87]

Essential to her campaign was the Weavermobile, an older but updated Ford conversion van. We put 40,000 miles on it. It was wonderful and we could get tons of campaign literature and our signs inside, even our big signs. *We'd load it up with all the heavy stuff—we didn't want to ship it—so that we could take it all to the volunteers. We covered a lot of territory in the Weavermobile, and I was so grateful we had it.* The season for a Supreme Court candidacy begins unofficially in the spring; the official season begins when the parties make nominations in August. That meant 40,000 miles in about five months all the while doing the work of the COA.

Ever thrifty and with limited funds, he said Weaver had the idea to avoid unnecessary expense.

> We would have friends in every city in Michigan, and we never stayed in a motel. Somebody always would open their house and there was always a separate room for each of us. It was very efficient. And it makes so much sense: you don't pay for rooms and you get a supporter.

> Some people need some time for just themselves, but Betty didn't need that. I guess she was able to get that time when she slept. She was a great planner, had it all organized in advance.[88]

LeGardeur drove her from the Upper Peninsula to Detroit and all points between.

87 Ibid.
88 Ibid.

And she would go anywhere. We went to churches...all different kinds of churches, but I remember especially a Baptist Church in Detroit. She would start with her situation and give her spiel, and everybody would listen.[89]

It changed the somewhat shy young man.

It took me a day of watching her work the crowd to get it. If I was going to do this, I would have to go "all in." It taught me how important it is to get to all people. Everybody is an opportunity to explain your side to and to get them to listen. And you didn't have to bore everybody to death. She would start her talks with "Like Henry the Eighth told each of his wives...'I won't keep you long.'"[90] She could get across her message and keep it simple.[91]

Weaver says she watched him transition from someone with the windows rolled up and a little scared of Detroit and its reputation to a windows-down-handing-out-campaign-flyers-at-stoplights kind of guy. "It definitely changed my life," he said. "I learned how to be more outgoing."

And there was plenty of fun, too, LeGardeur explained.

I can remember one time when we met a Korean group and we did some kind of commercial. And she wanted to learn hello and goodbye in their language. It became part of the commercial.[92]

"*Kamsahamnida* (Thank you)," said Weaver in Korean when she was reminded of the incident. After 17 years, she remembered. But, then, she HAD been a language major.

And then there were the food stops. One in particular still has his mouth watering. Heading out of town, they would vector through Birmingham to Le Petit Prince, a bakery at the intersection of 14 Mile and Pierce for Les Grenouilles[93] ...frogs...specialty pastries in the shape of the amphibian. But there also were baguettes, croissant, and other French delicacies to bring back to Glen Arbor.

Joy Taylor concurs that the meeting and greeting was essential:

She went county by county throughout the entire state and met the people of Michigan. I think they got to know her sincerity and that she was caring. There wasn't a county she missed. She went to every courthouse in every county.[94]

---

89 Ibid.
90 She still uses the line and it still evokes an appreciative laugh.
91 Wendell LeGardeur.
92 Ibid.
93 Always risky for a non-French speaker. According to the owner, the feminine singular is *la grenouille*. The bakery, there since 1978, has been turning them out all this time.
94 Joy Taylor.

Elizabeth Weaver and neighbor and best friend Joy Taylor stand on the floor of the 1994 Republican Party nominating convention where Weaver's name was put on the ballot.

The contest against an incumbent (Justice Mallett) and a highly favored local son (Judge Griffin) gave Weaver little pause, at least as far as LeGardeur could tell:

> I hadn't done a lot in politics, but she had so many wonderfully eager volunteers to support her. I never felt we were an underdog and in an uphill battle. She was very confident. Everywhere we went, we were greeted with many supporters. The connection she made with the local people...they would remember her like it was yesterday. It was a real achievement.[95]

In the end, it really was "a real achievement." She came in second in the race for two open seats, and she spent less than any of the other major-party candidates.

Eugene "Bud" Moore was still on the bench then as a probate judge and he watched her run with a certain sense that it was inevitable:

> Knowing Betty, I wasn't surprised. I mean, I think she decided that this is where she could have the most impact. I wasn't sure if she was going to get elected, but she—you know, there's nobody that worked harder than she did to get to that—to any job. She just is a dynamo, and she made it.[96]

Here's how the totals broke out:

Conrad Mallett, Jr., spent $374,101 and garnered 1,090,830 votes. Weaver spent $196,995 and received 984,925 votes. Richard Griffin spent $198,178 and received 961,902 votes. Donald Shelton spent $519,901 and tallied 595,115 votes. Independent George Kileen spent $63,940 and received 449,788 votes.[97]

95 Wendell LeGardeur.
96 Eugene "Bud"Moore, video interview with with co-author Schock, 13 March 2012, Oakland County.
97 Michigan Campaign Finance Reform website: http://www.mcfn.org/pdfs/reports/SCAppendix.pdf.

There were some other outside expenditures, notes Rich Robinson of Michigan Campaign Finance Reform:

> The Michigan Democrat Party made independent expenditures of $34,000 supporting Mallett and $16,000 supporting Shelton. By the '96 election, the parties made independent expenditures totaling $1 million and the overall cost doubled from '94. The '94 election was the last of an old era.[98]

...The end of an era that was perhaps the perfect time for an independent Republican to come to the court.

Of the entire campaign, Weaver reflected: *It was a very pleasant campaign, very cordial.*

Governor John Engler beams in the glow of his re-election and Elizabeth Weaver, in the background, celebrates for him at the festivities at the Lansing Center. At that point, however, Weaver was unsure whether she had prevailed. *I had not yet won even though Engler's win was decided. It would be through the night and to about 7 or 8 a.m. the next morning when Griffin called and congratulated me that I had won. That made for a very long day and night: traveling from Glen Arbor to Lansing, having fun visiting with friends at the gala celebration and waiting for the result through the long night and morning with Candice Miller for Secretary of State and Andrea Fischer for the U. of M. board. Their victories like mine were not determined until the wee hours of the morning.*

---

98 Rich Robinson, e-mail to co-author Schock, 27 December 2011.

On the High Court

January 1, 1995, Weaver was invested with her office.

And what a gathering in the Capitol Rotunda that proved. James H. Brickley administered the oath. He would shortly assume the duties as chief justice from then-Chief Justice Michael Cavanagh.[99]

In the ceremony, Brickley welcomed all and introduced the first speaker, Ingham County Probate Judge Donald Owens, someone who had served with Weaver when she was a probate judge, and someone who later would rise, with Weaver's help, to the Court of Appeals. Owens introduced notable guests, many of whom already had played—or would later play—instrumental roles in Weaver's time at the court.

Brickley then read into the record a letter from Michigan's first woman Justice (and first woman Chief Justice) Mary S. Coleman (retired). She was in Florida and unable to attend, but she brought home the importance of Weaver's experience as a trial judge.

> Dear Betty,
>
> It is with deepest regret that I cannot be with you as you take the oath of office as a justice of the Michigan Supreme Court.
>
> It will be a turning point in your life unlike your other judicial experience. Your own background will bring a new perspective to the membership, as has each justice. Your personal work with neglected, abused and delinquent children will be especially valuable. There is no substitute for every-day challenges of a broad spectrum of decisions which must be made concerning some of life's most basic problems. I think the nation has belatedly realized that early intervention is the key solution of crime as we know it.
>
> I know that you will be an asset to the court in many ways. You have demonstrated intelligence and commitment to excellence in all phases of your life. I recall that you were valedictorian in high school, then on to Phi Beta Kappa, and then *Tulane Law Review* editor and Order of the Coif.
>
> Your judicial experience on the probate and juvenile court and on the Court of Appeals was outstanding. Your leadership abilities as chair or president of important facets of our state life has been impressive. There is sound reasoning for my full confidence in you as a justice.
>
> Few people realize the broad extent of responsibilities which the Michigan Constitution places upon the third branch of government. The "One Court of Justice" mandate has not yet been fully realized. The obligation of "super-

---

99 *Chief Justice Cavanagh wasn't there that day. He was, I think, going to Canada or something for New Year's Day.*

intending control" over all Michigan courts, and to a large extent, over the legal profession as a whole remains an awesome challenge.

However, I know that you will meet your challenges with intelligence, plus common sense. Also I feel confident that you will look into the future as you and the court submit decisions of precedent. I expect the Supreme Court will become a part of you so long as you live, as it has with me. It is the keystone of justice in Michigan.

Best wishes,

Mary S. Coleman, Chief Justice, Michigan Supreme Court (Retired).[100]

The main body of remarks came from the next speaker, Court of Appeals Judge Maura D. Corrigan, someone Weaver thought of as part protégé and all friend.[101]

May it please the court, Justices Brickley and Levin, family and friends of Betty Weaver, public officials who have gathered here today, on this happiest of New Years in 1995, I have the signal honor of moving that the oath of office be administered to Elizabeth Ann Weaver, as the people of Michigan have willed by their votes this past November.

Then-Court of Appeal Judge Maura D. Corrigan delivers her paean to Elizabeth Weaver during the Jan 1., 1995 investiture. Corrigan described Weaver as a person of integrity, probity, truthfulness and directness who would bring her "Do-right-and-fear-not" belief to the high court. Corrigan would later find that attitude inconvenient when her own intrigues repeatedly were brought into the light.

It falls to me to tell you something about my friend, Betty Weaver, who takes this oath of office today. In case you all wondered, I wanted to let you know that there really is only one Betty Weaver. I heard repeatedly on the campaign trail from people around the state—because on occasion I called myself surrogate Betty Weaver—I heard that there must be more than one Betty Weaver because that woman was everywhere, and indeed she was. I know you will permit me a story from the campaign trail.

100 "Special Sessions: The Honorable Elizabeth A. Weaver Investiture Ceremony," Michigan Supreme Court Historical Society, 1 January 1995, http://www.micourthistory.org/special_sessions.php?get_id=85.
101 Neither the mentoring relationship nor the friendship would last beyond 2002. Viewed in that light, the comments are poignant.

My husband and I attended a reception, and we arrived in the parking lot the same time that the Governor arrived and the then Judge Weaver's van arrived in the parking lot. I want to let you know that the Governor made a beeline for the reception, but Judge Weaver went after the hapless and un-witting voters that happened to be parking their cars in the parking lot as well. So she cornered every eligible voter in every part of the state. That tells you a little about Betty Weaver, the campaigner. There is only one Betty Weaver and she is a singular woman.

Of course, you all know that Betty has 20 years experience as a probate and appellate judge. She will be the fourth of the sitting justices of the Michigan Supreme Court who have served as Court of Appeals judges. But she will only be the sixth of the 55 judges who have ever served on the Court of Appeals to join the Michigan Supreme Court. Betty became a citizen of Michigan by choice, not by birth. As a student in Louisiana, as Justice Coleman already told you in her letter, that she distinguished herself very early as Phi Beta Kappa, Order of the Coif, and editor of the *Tulane Law Review*, I think, evidences her quick legal mind, her incisive mind, and her great capacity for mental effort. Betty fell in love with Michigan and moved here. She taught school in Leelanau, and became a probate court judge after a stint in private practice in small and large firms.

But these historical facts about Betty Weaver don't really tell you anything at all about her character.

In preparing for today, I reviewed the recent publication of the Michigan Supreme Court Historical Society, and that publication indexes all of these sorts of ceremonies that have been held here through the years. I read those for a while, ceremonies of investitures and memorials and portrait unveil-ings involving some of the great leaders of the court. I read about Justice Cooley and Justices Marston and Potter and Williams and Mary Coleman, herself, and I think it's fair to say that in all of those events, people describe the justices who have served on the Michigan Supreme Court as people of honesty, integrity, and energy. Betty Weaver shares these hallmarks of the great justices of our state.

Honesty, she is breathtakingly direct. One of her favorite expressions, which all of you justices will soon know is: Let's cut the comedy. I expect you will hear that soon. She is not a person who minces words. She is not a person who wastes words. She loves words, and she loves what is true.

In terms of the other hallmark I spoke of, integrity, Betty is a woman of pro-bity. She is a whole person. She knows who she is. She speaks with common sense and simple wisdom and energy. I already told you, I think I am pretty sure that she never sleeps. Her energy is boundless.

The more that you give Betty Weaver to do, the better she likes it, and the knottier the problem, the better she likes it. But beyond this, I want you to know she is no procrastinator. She knows her job is to decide cases and to decide them now. She will decide cases, she will be forceful in argument and her opinions will display her strong convictions. That said, I want you to know that Betty Weaver does not suffer from judgitis. She has no divinity complex that I can detect. She is totally without pretense and without pretension. She will become your true friend. When you meet Betty it is true to say, she makes you want to help her out, and she will help you.

The best part of Betty Weaver, though, I save for last, and that is, that Betty Weaver will make you laugh. She has a wonderful sense of humor. You will experience a range of laughter with Weaver, from the simple giggle to the cackle to the shrieks of laughter, to the side-splitting belly laugh, because Betty loves life. She loves a good story, and she will have you in stitches from time to time.

For me, making this motion today is really bittersweet, because Betty is my friend and I will miss her as my friend and colleague on the Michigan Court of Appeals. But you on the Supreme Court are lucky to be having this justice join you today.

Ever since I was a young lawyer, I remember that various chief justices of the Supreme Court, Justices Brennan, Williams, Coleman, Riley, and Cavanagh, spoke of the need for the Michigan Supreme Court to become a collegial court. Betty Weaver will dedicate herself to the principle that when the Michigan Supreme Court works together, it best serves the public good. Justice Weaver, I thank you for the opportunity of moving for the administration of this oath. It is, as someone wrote, a covenant with the People of Michigan and with God.

Chief Justice Brickley, I now move that you administer the oath of office to Justice Weaver.[102]

---

[102] "Special Sessions: The Honorable Elizabeth A. Weaver Investiture Ceremony."

Elizabeth Weaver takes the oath of office as a justice of the Michigan Supreme Court from Justice James Brickley, Jan. 1, 1995. Holding the bible is Richard M. Taylor, her neighbor Joy's nephew. *I have known him since his childhood. He volunteered in the campaign. He is a member of the State Bar of Michigan and a research attorney.* The oath itself was a simple statement that she took seriously: *I, Elizabeth Weaver, do solemnly swear that I will support the Constitution of the United States and the Constitution of the State of Michigan. And that I will faithfully discharge the duties of the office of justice of the Michigan Supreme Court according to the best of my ability, so help me God.*

The oath administered, there were additional comments. Those from her fellow probate judge Gladys Barsamian (retired) were especially apt. They had known each other a long, long time.

> Betty and I met over 20 years ago when we were both fortunate to be chosen to serve our respective communities as probate judges, Betty in Leelanau County and I in Wayne County. We met in judge's school.[103]

> What I soon discovered was that we had two things in common: our desire to be the best probate judges we could be, and our profound concern for the families and children of the state of Michigan. And I believe those two things we had in common caused us to develop a close personal and professional relationship that I cherish.[104]

103 Newly elected or appointed judges often need help to get up to speed. What is called judges school, or baby judge school, is really a series of programs offered through the Michigan Judicial Institute, developed and implemented in 1977 by the Michigan Supreme Court. [http://courts.michigan.gov/education/mji/Pages/default.aspx].
104 Unlike the relationship with Justice Corrigan, the friendship between Judge Barsamian and Justice Weaver remains warmly supportive.

We both became active in the Michigan Probate Judges Association to improve our skills and to work with our colleagues for the improvement of the juvenile justice system. That was another thing that we had in common. We believed that our responsibilities extended beyond sitting on the bench.

Betty became involved with numerous commissions and committees. She served on the Commission of Criminal Justice, the Committee on Juvenile Justice, the Michigan Council of the Michigan Supreme Court, a special committee to study and report on the role of part-time probate judges, a committee to develop a case docket tracking system for probate court, just to name a few.

As a probate judge, she achieved national recognition for juvenile programs, being featured on *Good Morning America* and in *People Magazine*.

Soon Betty became aware of the need for probate court expertise on the appellate courts of our state and decided to seek election to the Michigan Court of Appeals, Third District.

She was successful. And in keeping with her objective, she has educated her appellate court colleagues in probate matters and has been responsible for important decisions impacting families and children, prominent among them are *Sands v Sands* and *In re Sterling*.

Despite her position with the Court of Appeals, Betty has remained loyal to her roots and continues to maintain an interest in probate and juvenile court matters and is currently serving as Chair of the Governor's Task Force on Children's Justice Concerning Abuse and Neglect.

Under her leadership, the committee has issued a comprehensive report advocating many changes and improvements in the system where children are the victims. Betty and her committee are about the business of implementing their recommendations.

As you know, it didn't take long for Betty to recognize the need for expertise on the highest court of our state, and apparently the people of the state of Michigan agreed with her. Again, the families and children of Michigan will be better off by her being there. Recently a study was completed on one hundred persons who were considered to be very successful in their personal and professional lives. All available information on these people was examined, in an effort to find out what they might have in common.

Finally a universal quality was discovered: Every single one of these highly successful people was a good-finder. Good-finders, by definition, are people who look for and find what is good in themselves and others in all situations in life. Good-finders are actively aware that God has done uniquely beautiful things in themselves. Good-finders look only for what is good in others and vocally affirm them explicitly and gratefully, appreciating the goodness and giftedness of others.

Good-finders look for what is good in all the situations of life. Good-finders know that the best blessings almost always come into our lives disguised as problems. Good-finders know that there is a promise in every problem, a rainbow in every storm, warmth in every winter; our Betty Weaver is a good-finder.[105]

Among others, Steve Sonke had a chance to say a few words, but he limited himself to comments about serving as one of Weaver's drivers and his interactions with the public:

One time I was out there, I came across a man operating some heavy machinery, so I walked up to him and asked him who he was going to vote for the Supreme Court and if he knew Betty Weaver. He says: "Yeah, I know Betty Weaver. She threw me in jail."

Well, I didn't expect this conversation to go very far, and I was trying to think of a way out. He quickly followed up with: "But I would vote for her, because she helped me out. She straightened me out, and the sentence was just." A second person I ran into, who was actually a person I talked to fairly often in the course of the campaign, was following all of the campaign workers, not only for the Supreme Court but for all of the other offices. In one of those conversations, she said: "Well, Betty certainly deserves to win, because she is the hardest working of all the candidates."[106]

Finally, Justice Weaver had a chance to offer remarks. Her mother and father figured large in her formative influences. And she ended with this.

Now, as I formally am vested with the office of Justice of the Michigan Supreme Court, I am humbled by the trust that you and the people of Michigan have invested in me.

I am keenly aware of the responsibility assumed, the challenges to be faced and met, and the opportunity to make a positive difference for the individual, the judiciary, and the state.

My promise is, as my parents said, to do my very best. To continue to work, to help the judiciary to fulfill its important role of aiding in seeing that every individual understands, he (or she) is accountable and responsible for his actions. That every individual has the opportunity to discover and develop a conscious sense of his own worth.

---

105 "Special Sessions: The Honorable Elizabeth A. Weaver Investiture Ceremony."
106 Ibid.

As I assume this important office, my prayer today is that of the Psalmist, "Give me understanding and I shall keep thy law; yea, I shall observe it with my whole heart."

Thank you all so very much for coming. We have a reception, and I understand that I now get to exercise the prerogative of a justice of the court by using this gavel and closing this session of court, and the reception is now on.[107]

And the party was on.

---

107 Ibid.

Chapter 3

The Court of Last Resort

A state supreme court IS the last resort within a state's judicial system. The only place to go beyond it is the federal system of courts, with the U.S. Supreme Court as the last resort of last resorts.

As specified in Michigan's 1963 Constitution, this ultimate court, the Michigan Supreme Court, has general supervisory control over all courts—all of the state's trial courts and the other appellate court—the Michigan Court of Appeals. To aid in the administration of all the courts, the Supreme Court appoints a State Court Administrator (SCA) and his/her office, the State Court Administrative Office (SCAO), and other assistants of the court as may be necessary.[108]

The Supreme Court also sets court rules and policies, investigates and disciplines errant judges through its Judicial Tenure Commission (JTC) and wayward attorneys through its Attorney Grievance Commission (AGC), educates new judges and updates sitting judges—and other court personnel—through its Michigan Judicial Institute, and tests individuals educated and trained in the law who seek authority to practice in Michigan through its Board of Law Examiners. In addition, there is an office of Dispute Resolution, a Learning Center, Child Welfare Services, a Court Reporter and a Recorder Certification Program, an office of Finance, a Foreign Language Interpreter Certification Program, a Foster Care Review Board Program, a Friend of the Court Bureau, an office of Judicial Information Systems, a Reporter of Decisions, an office of Trial Court Services, an office of Supreme Court General Counsel, an office of Human Resources, a Clerk's Office, and an office of the Court Crier.[109]

There are hundreds of people who work for the state to make the courts work. And over all of them are seven justices who hold the responsibility to make sure everything goes according to the rules and who—one would hope—will have the wisdom and experience to decide what is just in the matters that come before them.

---

108 Constitution of Michigan of 1963 Articles VI, Sections 3 and 4, http://www.legislature.mi.gov/ (S(3d5m5k45blxvr4450rnxhcyy))/mileg.aspx?page=getObject&objectName=mcl-Constitution-VI. And for a directory of Supreme Court offices and programs, see http://courts.michigan.gov/supremecourt/Directory. html.

109 The Court Crier opens, closes, and records sessions of the court. In addition, s/he deals with building-related issues, supplies, and in-house copying.

But there is a tendency for justices to see themselves in a way that is fundamentally different from trial judges. Eugene "Bud" Moore, now a retired probate court judge, explains:

> The judicial system is different than most other systems. Trial judges, for instance, certainly get their cases appealed, and they get reversed from time to time on appeal. But, basically, when you're a trial judge, you're in your own domain, and you don't have to convince your colleagues of anything because you make the decision. And if you're a smart trial judge, you'll recognize that what makes most trial courts work are certainly the lawyers who participate, but also the people who work within the court system. Juvenile courts never could survive if they didn't have outstanding people who are dedicated in helping kids. And any judge who thinks "I am the one who makes my juvenile court successful" is crazy. What makes that successful may be some leadership, but most of all it's the day-to-day, in-the-pits grind of men and women who love kids and families and work with them. And I think Betty knows that, and Betty experienced that. And when she left that type of domain, where people around her were very, very important, and went into a domain in which the most important person is the justice—which, I think, is the way many, many appellate and Supreme Court judges think—that's a different world, and I think it was harder for her.[110]

Not because she'd come to think that justices were inherently superior but because she would be surrounded more and more by other justices who did.

As the newest of the seven, Elizabeth Weaver was sworn in Jan. 1, 1995 as Michigan's 98th Supreme Court justice and was ready to go.

Well, there wasn't any particular orientation; you just showed up. And there weren't any particular written rules, but you're the new kid on the block, so you just listen and pick it up. There was a general desire to get along, I think; and even though I wasn't the chosen candidate of some, everyone was pleasant enough. I just tried to learn and see what was going on. And Justice Riley was very helpful and friendly to me. I figured out how to do the job and pretty much learned the dynamics of the court.

On the court at the time were Chief Justice James H. Brickley and Justices Dorothy Comstock Riley, Michael F. Cavanagh, Patricia J. Boyle, Charles L. Levin, and Conrad L. Mallett, Jr. With Weaver's arrival, the political balance on the court was much the same as before. Both she and retired Justice Robert Griffin were considered conservative Republicans.

My coming didn't philosophically change too much, but Griffin wasn't known to be particularly interested in court reform and other related matters. But we both were pretty straightforward, calling-them-as-we-see-them types.

---

110 Eugene "Bud" Moore, video interview with with co-author Schock, 13 March 2012, Oakland County.

The 1995 Michigan Supreme Court, from left: Justice Elizabeth A. Weaver, Justice Charles L. Levin, Justice Michael F. Cavanagh, Chief Justice James H. Brickley, Justice Conrad L. Mallett, Jr., Justice Dorothy Comstock Riley, and Justice Patricia J. Boyle.

Justice Levin had been there longest of all, beginning Jan. 1, 1973. He had served on the Court of Appeals (where he had first been elected in 1966 and subsequently won reelection). In 1972, he ran for the Supreme Court as an independent, forming his own party,[111] and prevailed against a field of seven others. He was elected at the same time as Weaver's mentor, Justice Mary Coleman.[112]

And Justice Levin was pretty well known to be quite liberal, from an active Democrat family background. But you never were quite sure what he was going to do. He was quite independent and pleasant. And he listened.

Next in length of tenure was Dorothy Comstock Riley. But measuring her time on the court requires an explanation. An unsuccessful candidate (against Michael Cavanagh) for the Supreme Court just the month before, she had been appointed by Governor William G. Milliken on Dec. 9, 1982, to fill the seat of Justice Blair Moody, Jr. Moody had

111 Elisha Fink, "Michigan Lawyers in History—Justice Charles Levin: A Scholarly Independent." *Michigan Bar Journal*, September 2000, Volume 79, No. 9.
http://www.michbar.org/journal/article.cfm?articleID=126&volumeID=11.
112 "On and Off the Court," Michigan Suprme Court Historical Society, http://www.micourthistory.org/on_and_off_the_court.php.

died Thanksgiving evening of that year, but that was after running for and winning his seat in a reelection, defeating among others, Riley. Justice Riley had been the Wayne County Assistant Friend of the Court, a Wayne County Circuit judge, and had served on the Michigan Court of Appeals.[113]

In what remains one of the most convoluted series of events, Justice Riley was removed from the position by her fellow justices on the Supreme Court. According to former Chief Justice Thomas E. Brennan's[114] recounting, Riley's ouster was engineered by sitting Justice G. Mennen "Soapy" Williams and Attorney General Frank J. Kelley. Williams was counting votes to be chief justice. Kelley argued that Riley's appointment was valid only as long as Moody's current term, which expired Jan. 1, 1983. Then it would have been up to the incoming Governor, James J. Blanchard, to make another appointment to fill the spot until the next possible election.[115]

The matter of timing is critical for the Michigan Supreme Court. Each justice on the court sits for an eight-year term. At least one seat on the Supreme Court comes up for election or re-election every two years; most often—three out of four times—it's two seats. Each seat is tied to an election year in the eight-year cycle. The goal is for an orderly transition to allow for overlapping experience; it wouldn't do to have all justices up at the same time.

And in the event of a vacancy on the court through death or retirement, the Governor selects a justice—and it is only the Governor who can make the appointment under the state Constitution. But the appointment lasts only until the swearing in after the next general election. If the appointee is successful at that election, s/he will need to stand for election again at the end of the inherited term if it's less than eight years.

And that's what would have happened if Justice Riley's appointment had been considered valid. Justice Riley would have served until the election of 1984. If elected then, she would have served out the remaining six years of Moody's, term.

But that's not what happened, according to then-retired Justice Thomas E. Brennan:

> Chief Justice Williams went around the table, asking each member of the court to express an opinion about the case of *Attorney General v Riley*.
>
> The split was predictable.
>
> The "K" Kavanagh and the "C" Cavanagh both felt the Attorney General was right. So did the chief justice. Brickley and [James L.] Ryan were inclined to

---

113 Ibid.
114 Ibid. On the court from 1967 through 1973.
115 For a compelling account of the story, consult Thomas E. Brennan's first-hand account at his website, oldjudgesays [http://oldjudge.blogspot.com/2011/01/partisan-judges.html]. Brennan, the youngest chief justice in Michigan's history, was by that time off the court but jumped into the fray, filing an amicus brief and offering his help to Riley's defense team. (And, yes, it did come down to Riley being the defendant.)

go the other way. Which, again predictably, left the matter up to Charles L. Levin.

Chuck Levin, the only surviving member of the court on which I served, is a very intelligent man. I remember him as a man who spoke and wrote in very long sentences. No combination of words or ideas was too complex or convoluted to overload his brain or his pen.

He was, and remains, a scrupulously gentle and caring human being who shows up at the most inauspicious funerals and sends thoughtful, if not timely, notes of condolence, appreciation or congratulation. That gentility spills over into his decision making.

He never jumps to a conclusion. Indeed, the very notion of a conclusion is nearly anathema to him. He is never happier than when a fork in the road has a multitude of prongs.

When it came time for Chuck to express his initial impression of the Riley case, he deferred. It was his usual way. He wanted to hear what the others would say. He wanted to weigh all the factors.

And so the discussion continued. But nobody changed their mind. It came back to Levin. As he often did, he began by summarizing the arguments on both sides, noting the strengths and weaknesses of each. Finally, he admitted what he so frequently had to admit.

He couldn't make up his mind.

That said, he reluctantly deferred to the ancient, logical, and common sense rule of judicial decision making. The plaintiff always has the burden of proof and the burden of persuasion. If you make a claim, you have to prove your claim. If you want the court to do something, you have to prove your entitlement. The Attorney General hadn't convinced him that Justice Riley should be ousted.

And so he said, "I guess I'm with Dorothy."[116]

So it was three to three, and she would stay.

But Levin was "with Dorothy" only for a short time.

One time he stopped appearing to be independent is when he voted against throwing Riley off the court, and then he changed two days later and voted for her to be thrown off the court. And it was

116 Thomas E. Brennan, "In the dugout (Number 11)," oldjudgesays, http://oldjudge.blogspot.com/2011/03/in-dugout-number-11.html.

Levin's vote that tipped the thing. First, the headlines read, "She stays." Two days later the headlines were "Levin switched" because it appeared he got huge pressures from the Democrats.

In a bit of legerdemain, the court reconsidered the matter and the new vote stood four to two. "...it is ordered that the said defendant, Dorothy Comstock Riley is hereby ousted and excluded from the office of justice of the Supreme Court."[117] The court, argued Brennan, didn't have the authority to do that. But who was to gainsay them? ...Perhaps if she appealed the matter to a federal court? But no, she wasn't going to do that, said Brennan; it would be too distracting to the business of the Michigan Supreme Court.[118]

In the end, she was booted off the court, leaving Feb. 16, 1983. But she was returned by the public in the 1984 general election (nominated by the Republicans), defeating sitting Justice Thomas G. "Thomas the Good" Kavanagh (a two-term justice nominated by the Democrats and first elected in 1968), and independent Robert Roddis.[119] It's understandable that there may have been some wounded feelings. Nevertheless, by 1987, Riley was elected chief justice (and reelected in 1989), and ran for and won another eight-year term against then-Court of Appeals Judge Marilyn Kelly in 1992. And she was there to welcome Justice Elizabeth Weaver.

I knew that Justice Riley was glad that I was there. She and I became close, talked, and enjoyed collegiality and friendship.

Justice Brickley came to the court by yet another Milliken appointment and at nearly the same time as Justice Riley. He was named to the court Dec. 27, 1982, to replace retiring Justice Coleman. There was a little more than two years left on her term. Brickley ran successfully in 1984 (the next general election), 1988 (to fill the end of Justice Coleman's cycle), and again in 1992, nominated each time by the Republicans.

117 Thomas E. Brennan, "Completely alone (Number 15)," oldjudgesays, http://oldjudge.blogspot.com/2011/03/completely-alone-number-15.html.
118 In referring to a similar kind of appointment (Hugh B. Clarke, Jr., 54-A District Court in Lansing), this one made by departing Governor Jennifer Granholm and opposed by incoming Attorney General Bill Schuette, the May 24, 2011, *Grand Rapids Press* opined this way:

The Michigan Constitution says a judicial vacancy "shall be filled by the governor." The constitution further specifies, "The person appointed by the governor shall hold office until 12 noon of the first day of January next succeeding the first general election held after the vacancy occurs."

Those are plain and straightforward words and they affirm the Michigan governor's power to make the appointment. All seven justices—hailing from the Republican and Democratic Party—agreed with that assessment. Mr. Clarke will serve on the District Court bench until Jan. 1, 2013.

The mystery is how a plurality (sic: actuality it was a majority—4 to 2) of the Supreme Court in 1982 could have come to a contrary conclusion. The ruling was patently political, seeking to curb one of the constitutional powers of the governor's office for partisan gain. This ruling should set to rest this question about the judicial appointment powers of the governor. [Editorial, "How the Michigan Supreme Court got it right on judicial appointments," 24 May 2011, http://www.mlive.com/opinion/grand-rapids/index.ssf/2011/05/editorial_why_the_michigan_sup.html.]
119 "On and Off the Court," Michigan Suprme Court Historical Society, http://www.micourthistory.org/on_and_off_the_court.php.

Justice Brickley was a very decent man.

Justice Michael Cavanagh, nominated by the Democrats, was elected in November of 1982 and took office Jan 1, 1983. (He had defeated Riley in that election by a quarter of one percent of the vote.[120] Before that, though, they had been colleagues and friends on the Court of Appeals for seven years, often sitting together on the three-judge panels. Further, Justice Brennan notes, "As a young lawyer, Cavanagh had been an investigator for the Wayne County Friend of the Court's office. His supervisor was Dorothy Comstock Riley."[121]) He was brand new to the court when the Riley matter exploded. He is now the longest serving justice on the court. He won reelection in 1990, 1998, and 2006. He will be forced to leave the court Jan. 1, 2015 because of his age.

Justice Cavanagh, like everyone, was pleasant. He was known as quite liberal on all matters. I was known as a conservative, truly independent woman coming to the court. So it appeared we had little to agree upon. But gradually over the years, particularly once the Englerites took over, I think we both realized we agreed on more than we had thought, particularly our desire for a fair and just process for all.

Justice Riley's replacement (appointed by incoming Governor James J. Blanchard) was Patricia J. Boyle, a Democrat. She had been an Assistant United States Attorney, Director of Research, Training, and Appeals in the Wayne County Prosecutor's Office, and a judge in the Detroit Recorders' Court. She stepped down from a federal judgeship, a lifetime appointment (made by President Jimmy Carter) as a U.S. District Court Judge for Eastern Michigan, to take the seat on the Michigan Supreme Court.[122] It was an unusual move.

Justice Boyle was friendly to the new justice.

The day after I was elected in 1994, I drove to Detroit from Lansing and visited with Justice Boyle. She was very gracious and welcoming. I was surprised when she told me how much she disliked elections as I remarked on how much I had enjoyed the learning and the people. Years later in reflecting on those remarks, I realized it was the difference between being elected without political appointment, without the incumbency designation, and without special-interest financial support— which was my case—or feeling one needed those things to be elected or re-elected. Just consider that $18 million was spent in the 2012 Supreme Court election.

Justice Boyle was collegial, intelligent, hardworking with a good sense of humor. We shared a mutual enjoyment of the farcical English sit-com Keeping Up Appearances.

Also on the court was Conrad L. Mallett, Jr. Mallett had been a last-minute appointment, Dec. 21, 1990, made by outgoing Governor Blanchard. Mallett, only 37, had replaced

120 Thomas E. Brennan, "Picking the chief (Number 3)," oldjudgesays, http://oldjudge.blogspot.com/2011/01/picking-chief-number-3.html.
121 Thomas E. Brennan, "A time to write (Number 12)," oldjudgesays, http://oldjudge.blogspot.com/2011/03/time-to-write-number-12.html
122 "On and Off the Court," Michigan Suprme Court Historical Society, http://www.micourthistory.org/on_and_off_the_court.php.

Dennis Archer.[123] Justice Archer was himself another Blanchard appointee who served from January 2, 1986, to December 18, 1990. He would go on to serve as Detroit's mayor from 1994 to 2001.[124]

Mallett had been a second-generation Detroit political activist. He'd served as legal advisor and director of legislative affairs to Blanchard from 1983 to 1984, then as Executive Political Director and Senior Executive Assistant to Mayor Coleman Young of Detroit, 1985-86, and as a partner in the law firm of Jaffe, Rait, Heuer & Weiss, Detroit, from 1987 through 1990. His appointment came as a real surprise to most, including the incoming Governor:

> Republican Governor-elect John Engler said the Mallett selection was "clearly not one he would make," said a spokesman.
>
> Engler doesn't question Mallett's ability as an attorney, spokesman John Truscott said, but said he is too closely identified as a political person.[125]

Reporter Eric Freedman agreed that politics did and would play into the appointment:

> Conrad L. Mallett, Jr., brings political rather than courtroom skills to the Michigan Supreme Court.
>
> Mallett's selection to replace Dennis W. Archer is a political reward by his former boss, lame duck Democratic Governor James J. Blanchard.
>
> Like Archer, who he will replace, Dec. 28, Mallett comes to the court without previous judicial experience. But unlike Archer, he is not a well-known trial lawyer and is more familiar with legislative corridors and conference rooms than with the inside of courtrooms.
>
> [...]
>
> He has never argued a case in the state Court of Appeals or the Supreme Court, according to Supreme Court computer records.[126]

Blanchard defended his choice, putting him at the top of a list of ten other candidates, and noted:

> Mallett "Was at the very top of the list from the very beginning."

---

123 Ibid. In all, Blanchard made three appointments to the high court, but only two of them ever served at the same time.

124 Keith Bradsher, "Detroit Mayor will not seek another term," *New York Times*, 18 April 2001, http://www.nytimes.com/2001/04/18/us/detroit-mayor-will-not-seek-another-term.html?ref=denniswarcher.

125 Gregory Huskisson, "Mallett gets partisan reaction; Blanchard says high court choice shows 'a strong sense of fair play,'" *Detroit News* and *Free Press*, 22 December 1990, 1A.

126 Eric Freedman, "Mallett lacking judicial expertise," *Detroit News*, 23 December 1990, 1C.

"Conrad Mallett will bring youth, energy and a strong sense of justice to the Supreme Court," [Blanchard] said. "All things being equal, I would consider a minority because I feel the courts should reflect the diversity of the state."

In choosing Mallett, Blanchard passed over a number of prominent blacks with judicial experience. They include Appeals judges Harold Hood and Myron Wahls, Wayne County Circuit judges Cynthia Stevens and Claudia Morcom, Genesee County Circuit Judge Valdemar Washington and former Detroit Recorder's Chief Judge Samuel Gardner.

"There were certainly some superb candidates and it was a surprise," said Henry Baskin of the State Bar's Judicial Qualifications Committee.[127]

Engler would have a chance to lead the effort to unseat Mallett in the election of 1992. As Governor and head of the GOP in Michigan, Engler hand-picked Wayne County Circuit Court Judge Michael Talbot to square off against Mallett in what would be an unseemly contest:

[T]he Talbot-Mallett race is far from gentlemanly.

Not when Talbot paints Mallett as "Blanchard's revenge." Not when Mallett accuses Talbot of "intemperate conduct and not being qualified."

The gloves came off last week when they squared off on public television's *Off the Record*:

• Talbot on Mallett: "I don't think he knows criminal law. What did he bring to (to the Supreme Court) other then as a political advisor to the mayor of Detroit and to the then-Governor (Blanchard)? Period."

• Mallett on Talbot: "He has an unusually high rate of 'being chastened by the Court of Appeals,'" referring to several criminal convictions overturned because of Talbot's courtroom conduct.[128]

Mallett prevailed in the election.[129]

Mallett had been on the court four years by the time Weaver got there. But he was the first of the justices to call her and welcome her to the court. Theirs would prove an effective relationship.

Justice Mallett was really interested in trying to enact reforms—he was young on the court. He was very grateful to Justice Riley for supporting him when he got there, and helping him. And he and I got along fine. What I found during the course of the first year was Mallett would not try to write excuses.

---

127 Ibid 6C.

128 Eric Freedman, "Talbot, Mallett swap barbs in bitter court race," *Detroit News*, 28 September 1992, 1B.

129 Talbot would subsequently rise to the Court of Appeals as a result of an Engler appointment (covered in Chapter 4).

If he was making a decision that he felt he had to make—maybe it was on Workman's Comp., or this, that, or the other thing—he generally didn't particularly justify it; he just said that's the way he was doing it, and that was it.

The court as a whole, she found, was a smoothly functioning group.

Because of the way Justice Riley had been removed and the very bad publicity that had ensued, and then Justice Riley being elected overwhelmingly—there was a real desire not to have friction, at least a desire to have it appear that everything was all as it should be. And I was there as an independent justice—but perceived differently as a big Republican. It was a learning experience, but people were pleasant enough.

Pleasant enough...an assessment shared by Grand Rapids' attorney Jon Muth. Muth served as president of the Michigan Bar in 1994 and 1995.

> I thought the court functioned reasonably well. [...] The State Bar officers had a meeting on a regular basis with the chief justice where we would talk about issues that were germane to the court and germane to the bar. And I started to attend those meetings probably in about 1993. I was meeting with the chief justice [Michael Cavanagh] on a fairly regular basis during that period of time. And I didn't really have the sense there was significant dysfunction at the court. There were differing views, certainly, but it was not apparent to me that there were significant internal divisions and very harsh political antagonisms.[130]

In any case, things went along—there was a pleasantness about it. There were disagreements sometimes over the way cases went. In my perception, there were some agendas with respect to Workmen's Comp. and to labor unions, particularly American Federation of State, County, and Municipal Employees, AFSCME. There were differences about whether to pursue trial court reforms such as the pilot projects, but the pilots proceeded relatively harmoniously.[131]

When Weaver arrived, she changed the sex balance on the Court: for the first time in its history there were three women.[132]

It had been, really, a male institution until the coming of Mary Coleman. She had told me how difficult it was when she first arrived. She took her concerns home. I guess I don't want to say exactly what she told me; she did her crying at home—the way she was treated. She was an outsider. She was the first interloper into the club, you know, a male club. This was a very male institution. But I will say that was in '72 that she was elected. By '78, they chose her as their chief justice.

---

130 Jon Muth, interview with co-author Schock, video recording, Grand Rapids, Mich., 17 January 2012. Muth would go on to serve as Weaver's attorney in 2006 during a court-related matter. He would also face the Attorney Grievance Commission for a conversation he had with her in 2010. You'll be able to read more about both of those events in subsequent chapters.

131 We'll hear more about those pilot projects. They were intended to reform the courts for increased efficiency. They resulted in the resignation of one of the justices.

132 Editorial, "How the Michigan Supreme Court got it right on judicial appointments," *Grand Rapids Press*, 24 May 2011, http://www.mlive.com/opinion/grand-rapids/index.ssf/2011/05/editorial_why_the_michigan_sup.html.

When I got there, it wasn't male dominated. A lot of that had passed. In other words, Justice Coleman had been chief justice, Justice Riley had been chief justice, and Justice Boyle was there. We all kind of settled around so we did things in a refined, businesslike way.

Part of that business early on was electing Justice Brickley as chief justice, taking over from Justice Cavanagh.

And so my vote did go to Brickley, and it would be Brickley, Riley, and myself who would be—in general—the moderately conservative independent justices who were Republicans on the court.

The position of chief justice was not merely ceremonial; there was a lot of extra work attached, as well as extra staff. The job—with its attendant prestige—was bestowed for two years at a time. Cavanagh had just served a total of four years.

Neither Justice Levin nor Justice Boyle had ever served as chief justice...with the exception of the one hour that Justice Levin spent as chief justice.[133] Everyone liked Brickley. Cavanagh visited Brickley up north, and so he had influence with him about things.

We had a lot of cases,[134] but we did not have mean-spirited memos, and we didn't have memo traffic constantly to everything. And we didn't have the technology to have unwisely considered e-mails too often throwing stuff back and forth, which is just a lot of unnecessary work. We did our work, and we really sent work out that was significant; and then at the conference—it was on Thursdays then—we discussed things and then we moved from one item on to the next.

And there was not a power block of four on all issues and, particularly, there was a respect for the institution—the workers, the staff. And the workers were not there to protect and promote the agendas of justices.

I was interested in minutes because I think records are important. We didn't have a real orderly way about the minutes. And so, we did get minutes every few months. And I was assigned—it fell to me because I did look at them—to be the person who really would bring it up if there were some inaccuracies or, to me, if they weren't complete. But there were never any arguments in those years as to what actually did happen.

At the time of her election (and until 2002), the Michigan Supreme Court claimed as its home the second floor of the G. Mennen Williams Law Building, a "temporary" home until something better could be built.[135]

I never officed in Lansing. When the Michigan Hall of Justice was built, it wasn't built to put the justices there but to bring the various offices into the same building in Lansing. The State Court Administrator, Michigan Judicial Institute, the Bar Examiners, and the Court of Appeals all were in different buildings. The idea was to get the offices and agencies of the Supreme Court into one

---

133 The agreement was made among the justices as Levin was retiring from the court in 1996.
134 *I think with Mallett [as chief justice] we did 118 opinions one year. That was the highest that we did. That's a lot of opinions, maybe too many.*
135 "Homes of the Michigan Supreme Court," Michigan Supreme Court Historical Society, http://www.micourthistory.org/court_homes.php.

building. I believe it was also the idea of some to get all the justices into one office only in Lansing. It did not happen, and it SHOULD not happen. It is a bad idea to have all the justices clustered in Lansing.

Oh, and there actually WAS a room assigned to her in Lansing, but it was the size, she said, of a small bedroom.

...A little cubbyhole. And the offices were cramped, worn, and dated, really from the Milliken administration. But we functioned.

Like others on the court, Weaver maintained a regional office.

Justices Boyle, Levin, and Mallett had offices in Detroit. Chief Justice Brickley was up here [in Traverse City]. I always was willing to be in the state office building in Traverse City, but there was no room. So my offices went into Grandview Plaza. It was a very nice office with 3,000 square feet.

Into that space, she put the five employees of her office of the court, their offices, a reception area, her office overlooking Grand Traverse Bay (just across the street), and storage, lots and lots of free storage. At the time of her investiture, she had two administrative secretaries and three law clerks. As time went on, the balance shifted to one secretary and four law clerks, a result of computerization.

There wasn't as much need for someone to type, but there were always plenty of administrative matters to deal with. In fact, administrative work is so important, it's as important as case work. So that fourth law clerk would deal with a lot of that.

It was more the functional needs of the office rather than any monetary concerns.

A beginning law clerk was paid less than an experienced secretary. But they caught up. And there was always plenty of work. Everybody did everything that needed to be done.

Nor did Weaver cycle lots of law clerks through her office, a practice sometimes undertaken to give as many young lawyers as possible a chance to see a supreme court up close.

I did not and do not believe in turning over law clerks every two years in order to give more young lawyers the experience or get fresh-out-of-law-school ideas. To be turning over clerks and training new ones every two years is very inefficient and a waste of time. Unpaid law student interns supply all the fresh up-to-the-minute input needed.

Weaver lived about 25 miles west and north of Traverse City. She usually drove that commute, unless she was heading to Lansing as she did pretty much once every week. And then it would fall to an intern—a law school student or recent graduate—to drive the 400 or so miles round trip.

They did a lot of schlepping. I had interns since I was a probate judge. They were never paid. I think I spent more time with interns than anyone else.

On that three-and-a-half or four-hour drive between Lansing and Traverse City, she worked, slept, or talked with the interns.

And there were always other long trips...to Detroit or where have you. They've told me they cherished the times we drove.

Weaver would learn of their lives, hopes, and interests. She is still close to many of them, tracking their careers and families, even officiating their marriages, celebrating their accomplishments, but also consoling them when life dealt them hard knocks. For their parts, they responded to her friendship and interest. And they were in a unique position to see what was really happening. They were, after all, privy to whatever might occur.

And I took them wherever I went—I didn't have a spouse—so if I met the presidential candidates or Governor and got a picture with them, or went to the Final Four, they were there. And there was always the business of the court. If you let them have a real learning experience, they were going to understand a lot about what really was going on, the way business was done and the way you did business. Of course, everything they saw and heard was totally confidential, but they were learning. They got to see what it was to be a law clerk.

And they didn't have to do it on an empty stomach: *I always fed them.*

And if they were really good, the interns would sometimes go on to become law clerks in her office on those rare occasions when a spot opened. And those interns and law clerks—while they worked long and hard—often had a front row for history. Retired Probate Judge Eugene "Bud" Moore made note of their presence.

> Rarely did I ever see her in a setting where we were at a judicial meeting, or the Governor's Task Force meeting, or something that was official, that she didn't have a law clerk or intern with her. And one of the first things she did was introduce that person. She made that intern or law clerk feel at home in the room and not a "somebody" that the justice had dragged in there. And I think that's true of everywhere she went.[136]

When she was working in Lansing, she would often need to stay overnight. Her lodging of choice was the Michigan State University Kellogg Center.[137]

There would be times, of course, when the weather made travel impossible, and other times when her physical presence was not required. She would link up by telephone

---

136Eugene "Bud" Moore.
137 *In 2011, they had calculated since 2002 I had been at the Kellogg Center 700-plus times.* The number is probably more than doubled for her court career, especially because two of those years she served as chief justice (1999-2001) and was downstate four or five days a week.

from her Traverse City office. Toward the end of her tenure on the court, she could have linked via videoconference, but she chose not to. It would have been difficult and distracting to set up and use. She discovered that by recording the telephone feed, she could go back over matters to make sure she understood what people were saying.[138]

The Work of a Justice

The workload of a justice is unrelenting. This is from the court's 1999 annual report:

> The Supreme Court receives annually approximately 2,200 to 3,000 applications for leave to appeal from litigants seeking review of decisions by the Michigan Court of Appeals. Each of the Supreme Court's justices is responsible for reviewing each case at a rate of 200 to 300 a month to determine which should be granted leave. Justices analyze each case up to three times before a decision to grant leave to appeal is made. The court issues a decision in all cases filed with the clerk's office. Cases that are not accepted for oral argument may be decided by an order with or without an opinion. These orders may affirm or reverse the Michigan Court of Appeals, may remand a case to the trial court, or may adopt a correct Court of Appeals opinion. In these instances, the court deems further briefing and oral argument unnecessary. This system saves litigants and the public the considerable time and expense of full-scale briefing and argument where none is needed.

> In addition to this extensive review of cases, the typical workload of a justice includes:

> - reviewing 35 to 50 cases for conference several times a month;
> - preparing 12 to 18 cases each month for oral argument;
> - writing and reviewing majority opinions, concurrences, and dissents;
> - preparing for administrative meetings concerning court rules, discipline issues, board appointments, and the like several times a month;
> - attending to educational and communication responsibilities; and,
> - performing a variety of civic obligations, including speeches, classroom visits, and conferences.[139]

In 1994, the court received 3,188 applications for review, an all-time high number of cases.[140] By 2010, the number, which had been steadily dropping, was at 1,960.[141] Whichever the number, the court grants leave to hear only a small percentage of the cases that are appealed to it.

---

138 This practice led to an interesting series of events in the campaign of 2010.
139 *Michigan Courts: Striving for Excellence*; Michigan's One Court of Justice, 2000 Annual Report, Michigan Supreme Court, http://courts.michigan.gov/Administration/SCAO/Resources/Documents/Publications/Statistics/1999/1999%20Michigan%20Supreme%20Court%20Annual%20Report.pdf .
140 Ibid.
141 Michigan Supreme Court Annual Report 2010, Michigan Supreme Court, http://courts.michigan.gov/Administration/SCAO/Resources/Documents/Publications/Statistics/2010/2010%20Michigan%20Supreme%20Court%20Annual%20Report.pdf.

The Supreme Court's authority to hear cases is discretionary. [...] [T]he Court grants leave to those cases of greatest complexity and public import where additional briefing and oral argument are essential to reaching a just outcome.[142]

That means that there are a lot of people working to winnow down the numbers of cases to the most important.

We had a central staff in Lansing responsible for reviewing every application as timely as possible. And so the feeling was that the people who worked there were not in fear of their jobs all the time; that their opinions were welcome even if we didn't like them. I felt we had staff that would generally be willing to say, "Well, maybe you better look at this." It was nice if people did it in a nice way, but even if they didn't, it was better to hear from our staff.

We had about 18 lawyers that were commissioners. They were experienced. I knew that their opinions might even be correct as opposed to ours, and it was better to hear it from them. My approach, always, is to have people tell me what they really think. I don't need people around me that are telling me what they think I want to hear. And I would rather hear it then than later because I didn't feel I was always right, but I always stuck with what I believed was right. So, I would like to know if I'm off the track. After considering all points of view, I then decided what I believed was right.

Their job was to make substantial reports—Commissioners Reports. They were known as CRs or Greenies (because of the color of paper).

In the Greenies, the commissioners would analyze the legal issues in each case and include a complete history, usually in ten to twenty pages.[143]

And our job was to review the reports. We would get anywhere from 200 to 400 of those on a monthly basis. Different justices can do it different ways. Some have interns and clerks review them. I—following Justices Coleman and Riley—did that work myself. I felt that it was very important decisional work. Clerks and interns are good, but they don't necessarily have decisional judgment. It made for a heavy caseload; you had to do some every night.

Upon their study, the justices would decide which cases they'd discuss during their weekly conferences. They might circulate memoranda expressing their views on the matters before them. They might ask commissioners for more information. Usually only a quarter to a third of the cases filed would come up as subjects for discussion. And at each conference, the justices might consider 25 to 40 cases. And the discussions about cases might spill over into conversations outside the conference.[144]

---

142 *Michigan Courts: Striving for Excellence*; Michigan's One Court of Justice, 2000 Annual Report.
143 For an in-depth understanding of the work of the commissioners, see Shari M. Oberg and Daniel C. Brubaker, "Supreme Review: Insights on the Michigan Supreme Court's Consideration of Applications for Leave to Appeal," *Michigan Bar Journal*, February 2008, 31-33, http://www.michbar.org/journal/pdf/pdf4article1327.pdf.
144 Ibid.

The Supreme Court usually gives a very brief reason when it denies an appeal. Most often the language relates that the justices "are not persuaded that the question(s) presented should be reviewed by this court."[145] Sometimes the justices will decide that until further proceedings at lower courts, the case is "not ripe" for consideration. If leave is granted, the court schedules a hearing for oral arguments, public hearings that are held usually in the first week of the month in the court sessions that run from October through May. All parties granted leave come to present their sides in timed arguments. For their part, the justices ask questions and offer comments. They are not supposed to indicate which way they might be leaning, but court watchers sometimes can tell.

After the oral argument, the justices meet to talk over the case and reach a preliminary conclusion. They may not all agree, in which case a justice or justices may file a dissenting opinion that will be published with the majority opinion. One of the majority, usually in rotating order, will take on the work of writing the opinion with his or her clerks. Sometimes in the process of discussion, research, and writing, the justices change their minds and come down on a different side of the argument. When the first draft is written, the opinions are circulated for revisions and clarifications. The final opinion is signed and entered. The court must enter its decisions by July 31 of each year, or the case must—if requested by a party—go back to be heard again.[146]

It's not just the cases. I learned that a great part of the work was also administrative. A huge part of the court is in its making the rules; it doesn't matter what the Legislature says if the court makes the rules. And that's a real issue in deciding who has standing, who doesn't, how long you have to file your complaints. And we had all kinds of rules as well as having two administrative bodies that are supposed to be the arms of the court: the Judicial Tenure Commission (JTC) and the Attorney Grievance Commission (AGC).

The court, through its website, agrees that there is a lot more work than just hearing cases.

> The Michigan Constitution places on the Supreme Court the responsibility to supervise the entire state court system. As a result, the Supreme Court must consider a wide variety of matters relating to court rules, rules of evidence, disciplinary rules, administrative orders, appointments to various boards, budgetary matters, and a host of related concerns.
>
> These administrative matters are handled by the court during regular conferences [...] at public hearings during the year. Where there is a proposal to change a court rule or take other action, the court will often publish the proposal for comment, and then decide what to do only after reviewing the comments of all those who respond.[147]

---

145 "How a case is decided," Michigan Supreme Court, http://courts.michigan.gov/Courts/ MichiganSupremeCourt/Clerks/Pages/How-a-Case-is-Decided.aspx.
146 Ibid.
147 Ibid.

Making suggestions and recommendations for any changes having to do with the court system is a serious undertaking. But that's how reforms are made, and Weaver was intent on making things better throughout the state's courts. And because she had the reputation as a conservative justice and had openly expressed her desire to work on reforms, sitting Republican Governor John Engler, also known for his conservative inclinations, appointed her as chair of the Michigan Trial Court Assessment Commission August 16, 1996. The commission had been established by the legislature under Public Act 374 of 1996[148] and Weaver was one of the 23 appointees made by the Governor.[149]

But by then, Engler controlled the legislature, and the commission wouldn't exist if he didn't sign the bill to approve it.

We were trying to gather data to assess needs...whether we had too many, enough or not enough judges. We were looking for ways to better meet the needs and to serve public. Margaret Chiara was the executive director.

At the time—1997—Chiara had already been a two-term county prosecutor, and she was the first woman president of the Michigan Prosecuting Attorney's Association of Michigan.[150]

It was in Weaver's work with the Commission that she first really talked with Jon Muth, a former Michigan Bar Association president. He remembers:

> And we worked closely together there; we had some similarities in the views and the approaches, and we sort of had a natural bonding.

> I went into service on the Trial Court Assessment Commission with only one goal, and that was to see what recommendations that we could make that would make the Michigan judicial system more fair, more accessible, and more efficient. My sole goal was to advance the rights and the opportunities of Michigan citizens to get a fair shake in the courts. ...A totally apolitical agenda. I didn't care what judges went, I didn't care what judges stayed, I didn't care what courts got expanded and which were shrunk. And I think Betty had somewhat the same approach: looking at the public interest. Although, she was a great deal more politically astute than was I.[151]

148 Robert Bowerman, bill analysis, Public Act 298 of 1998, Senate Fiscal Agency, 23 March 1999, http://www.legislature.mi.gov/documents/1997-1998/billanalysis/Senate/htm/1997-SFA-0808-E.htm.
149 Pat Masserant, "Governor appoints Trial Court Assessment Commission," State of Michigan press release, 16 August 1996, http://www.state.mi.us/migov/gov/PressReleases/199608/trialcou.html.
150 The Michigan Women's Historical Center and Hall of Fame, "Margaret M. Chiara," http://hall.michiganwomen.org/honoree.php?C=0&A=207-208-209-210-211-212-217-213-214-216. Chiara and Weaver would continue to serve together. In 1999, Chiara became the policy and planning director for the Office of the Chief Justice of the Michigan Supreme Court. Weaver was the chief justice at the time. The two would work together frequently thereafter. Weaver says she considers Chiara a close friend and holds her in high regard. Chiara would go on to serve as Michigan's first woman U.S. Attorney (Western District of Michigan) until March of 2007. That is a whole other story that appears in Chapter 11.
151 Jon Muth.

Astute or otherwise, she says she was being deceived at that point by the Governor. He was someone who should have been a natural ally.

Both were willing to take on entrenched and powerful figures. Neither one thought waiting for an opportunity until others would accord them their turn was the right course. Both had a sense of vision of what might be. Both were realists, espousing the belief of Otto Eduard Leopold, Prince von Bismarck's assessment that "Politics is the art of the possible." And both were willing to work as hard as needed to make what they wanted to happen a reality.

Like Weaver, Engler never lost an election for public office. And both were Republicans. But they had differing views on the concept of public service and the desirability of transparency in governance.

In retrospect, Engler saw the commission as a way of getting rid of judges in certain areas, adding them in others, and getting control of the courts. He saw it as an opportunity ultimately for achieving his ends.

The work of Trial Court Assessment Commission would last only two years and halt quickly, even though there was an ongoing need.

It didn't quite go the way Engler wanted it. That's why it ended suddenly.[152] But Muth and I were independent in our assessment, and we worked seriously at it.

She wouldn't discover the Governor's deception behind the creation and dissolution of the Trial Court Assessment Commission until several years later, but there were intimations along the way.

---

152 It ended with the passage of Public Act 298 of 1998. [Robert Bowerman, bill analysis, Public Act 298 of 1998, Senate Fiscal Agency, 23 March 1999, http://www.legislature.mi.gov/documents/1997-1998/ billanalysis/Senate/htm/1997-SFA-0808-E.htm.]

Chapter 4

Governor John Engler: Managing the Farm Team

To understand what happened during Justice Weaver's tenure at the Supreme Court, it's essential for the reader to know who else was in the mix...political figures, state officials and staffers, judges, justices. Their names will come up again and again in the flow of the book. It's also helpful to know how these people came to their positions and power. One of the questions always is this: to whom <u>might</u> they be beholden?

For judges or justices, there are only two ways they get to the bench: election or appointment. So it's good to know the answers to these kinds of questions: If they come through election, were they heavily promoted by a political party and with the blessings of political leaders? If they were appointed, by whom, how, and why?

The Constitution specifies that for judges and justices, the appointer-in-chief is the Governor. And that Governor when Weaver came to the court was John Engler. He was crucial to all that happened thereafter. His politics, his dealings, and especially his appointments set the course for the future of justice in Michigan.

Circumstances were aligning so that before he left office on Jan. 1, 2003, Engler would appoint many judges. ...Three to the Supreme Court and 16 to the Court of Appeals.[153] The Associated Press put the total number of his judicial appointments to the appellate and trial courts at 188,[154] but Engler himself, speaking before the National Press Club in 2005, put the number at more than 200, and he boasted of the impact he had on the Michigan courts.[155] There are about 520 judgeships in the state. That means he appointed just under 40 percent of the judges in Michigan.

And that doesn't count all the other judges he helped to their benches through his support in the elective process.

---

153 That's by our count reviewing the relevant *Michigan Manuals*. The AP puts the number of judges appointed to the Court of Appeals at 17 [Associated Press, "Engler loses top justice," *Traverse City Record-Eagle*, 8 November 2008, http://record-eagle.com/2008election/x75063246/Engler-court-loses-top-justice/print.].
154 Associated Press, "Engler loses top justice."
155 C-Span, "Judge John Roberts Supreme Court Nomination" at the National Press Club, 10 August 2005, http://www.unz.org/Pub/CSpanTV-2005-00270?View=FullVideoDetails.

As for the appointments and assistance to election, there was a tautology involved. Your friends are your friends because they share your values. And your values are motivated by the highest ideals. The same goes for your friends' motives. They are the people best suited to help you achieve your goals, goals that are themselves motivated by your ideals and right beliefs. It makes sense and is only wise to appoint them whenever possible to positions of trust and authority.

So, when does it turn from idealism into cronyism? When does it cross the line from independence into sycophancy?

And how did Engler get in a position to wield such authority?

When John Engler[156] took office as Michigan's 46th Governor on Jan. 1, 1991, he brought his considerable political experience to bear on the state's problems. His was a big journey from Beal City to Lansing, a lot further than the 80 or so miles to the south; he would rise from the feedlots to national prominence.

He grew up on a cattle farm, devoting his energies to work at home, school, 4-H, and Future Farmers of America activities. He was a young man with promise and a plan.[157]

Engler got his start as career politician in 1968 after watching and helping his father, Matt, in a primary election as the senior Engler challenged incumbent Russell H. Strange of Mt. Pleasant for his seat in the Michigan House of Representatives. Matt Engler lost, but his son John kept thinking about how somebody might capture that seat from the seven-term incumbent. At the time of his father's defeat, the young Engler was a rising junior at Michigan State University, studying agricultural economics. In his senior year, he and fellow student Thomas Plachta drafted a plan as a class assignment to challenge Strange once again. (The paper received an A-minus.) Initially, the blueprint was for somebody else to serve as the candidate...but it didn't work out that way. John Engler mounted a campaign to successfully run in the primary, defeating Strange by 159 votes, and then went on to a win in the general election, claiming nearly 60 percent of the votes. The first opportunity for the 22-year-old to cast a ballot coincided with his victorious candidacy. As such, he was the state's youngest legislator of all time.[158]

Of Engler, the fledgling legislator, Lucille Taylor (subsequently his chief legal counsel when he was governor) observed:

156 Co-author Schock knows John Engler, but not well. He knew John's father, Matt, better, and as a newspaper reporter and editor interviewed him when he was head of the Michigan Beef Industry Commission. He also knew John Engler's first wife, Colleen House Engler, but he never met his second wife, Michelle DeMunbrun Engler. In the interest of full disclosure, Schock voted for Engler every chance he had. And he had also received an inquiry from one of John Engler's staffers shortly before Engler left office about whether he might be interested in a seat on a state commission. The co-author declined.
157 Gleaves Whitney, *John Engler: The Man, the Leader and the Legacy*, (Chelsea, Mich., Sleeping Bear Press, 2002). Whitney has been the director the Hauenstein Center for Presidential Studies at Grand Valley State University since 2003. Co-author Schock has known Whitney since the mid 1980s. For more about Whitney, see http://hauensteincenter.org/staff/ or http://www.gleaveswhitney.com/. In his book, Whitney gives a generally positive review of the Governor's career; they were, after all, colleagues and friends. The book is not, however, a whitewash. There are plenty of comments from Engler's detractors as well as his supporters.
158 Ibid., 42-55.

My first impressions of him were that, though he was young, he was not willing to wait his turn. He was always thinking about how to make Republicans the majority in the House. He wanted to change the agenda. It seemed he had amendments on every bill. Often he did not clear those amendments with the party leadership; so, many times, he wouldn't even get the votes of his own caucus. But he never gave up.[159]

Some in the legislature, she said, found him annoying. Others found him useful and effective. He was unabashedly supportive of his party and apparently would sometimes sacrifice his own interests for the good of the Republicans. Those on the other side were flummoxed. The deputy chairman of the Democratic State Central Committee wrote Engler's hometown paper, Mt. Pleasant's *Daily Times News*:

We are extremely concerned, and we hope that you will send to Lansing in '73, a new state Representative. We have nothing against youth; we have nothing against males, but the young male you sent to Lansing is voting a hard-line Republican vote. He is extremely partisan and unwilling to listen to the other side.

If you call yourself anything other than "quite conservative," John Engler is not representing you. Although he is young and makes a nice image, we urge you to take a good long look at his philosophy and the way he conducts himself....[160]

There wasn't much middle ground on Engler. People either seemed to warm to him or they didn't, trusted him or not. His conservative credentials were well in order, and although he described himself as a fiscal conservative, he took liberal stands in some other areas: lowering the voting age, environmental legislation, and drug law reform.[161] Still, he read serious books, believed in limited government, tax cuts, and trimming the size of state government, including its staff. The residents of his district liked him very much, returning him to the House in 1972, 1974, and 1976.

The first time I met him, Engler was a power in the House. He was already in the power structure. I was working with [Rep.] Connie Binsfeld on juvenile reform that was being proposed—and it was not going to be good reform. People in the Milliken Administration and Democrat leaders—Lynn Jondahl, Perry Bullard, and Mark Clodfelter[162]—were proposing a whole new juvenile code.

159 Ibid., 59.
160 Robert Mitchell, 62. And in more disclosure, co-author Schock was later editor for a time of that same newspaper, by then renamed *The Morning Sun*.
161 Ibid., 64.
162 H. Lynn Jondahl, a Democrat, was a member of the Michigan House of Representatives for 22 year—1973-1994—from the 59th District (1973-92) and the 70th District (1993-94). In 1994, he ran unsuccessfully in the primary for governor. [Joice to Jonelle, Political Graveyard.com, http://politicalgraveyard.com/bio/jolley-jondahl.html.] He is from Okemos and is on the board of directors and immediate past chairman of the Michigan League for Public Policy (formerly the Michigan League for Human Services). [Board of Directors, Michigan League for Public Policy, http://www.milhs.org/about-us/board-of-directors] Winston Perry Bullard, a Democrat, served in the Michigan House of Representatives from 1973-92 and represented the 53rd District. He was from Ann Arbor. Bullard also was active in the ACLU and Common Cause. [Buffum to Bulloch, Political Graveyard.com, http://politicalgraveyard.com/bio/buffum-bulloch.html.] Mark A. Clodfelter, a Democrat, was a member of the House of Representatives from 1975-1980. He was from Flint (81st

The government was going to be less accountable...and in the name of the children. The other members of the Young Turks—that's what they called us—probate judges Don Owens, Gladys Barsamian, Randy Hekman, Michael Anderegg, and I—became very concerned. I enlightened Connie that we were likely going to have reforms that would make things worse. Connie agreed and understood. It's through her I came to know John Engler. We had a working relationship, and he seemed to listen. It was important to get him to understand the point of view of judges.

Binsfeld also served as a go-between with Weaver and then-Governor William Milliken.

Because of that, Milliken appointed me to a commission on juvenile court reform.[163]

But of his own career, Engler had determined that the Republican leadership under Governor Milliken was too moderate. According to friend Colleen Pero, "John had [...] been thinking about how to take over the Republican Party from Milliken's people— and not just thinking about it, but doing it when the time was right."[164]

Never shy, Engler found friends who shared his sentiments, people he would rely on, and he launched his own reform movement, beginning with his attempt to change the party's leadership at the Michigan Republican Convention in 1977[165] and then his drive in 1978 to unseat state Senator Jack Toepp (R-Cadillac) in the primary. Engler won with 54 percent of the vote. His margin of victory in the general election was even higher: two-to-one.[166]

He unseated Senator Toepp and that was quite a big deal. He then became the state Senator for here [Leelanau County]. I really didn't have dealings with him as a Senator for Leelanau County...I had

---

District). [Clippert to Clynick, Political Graveyard.com, http://politicalgraveyard.com/bio/clippert-clynick. html#249.39.41.]

163 Ultimately, the resistance to the reforms doomed their enactment, but it took time: *The issue came up in 1975 and subsided in 1981.*

164 Whitney, 68. Colleen Pero is an attorney who started working at the Capitol in 1974. Not only is she one of Engler's close friends, but also she is married to Dan Pero, Engler's former chief of staff and campaign manager. And she would effect the introduction between Engler and his second wife, Michelle DeMunbrun. After his time as Governor, Engler would go on to head the National Association of Manufacturers and continue to work closely with Dan Pero, who is president of American Justice Partnership and compiles a blog at http://americancourthouse.com/about. Dan Pero was campaign chairman for the unsuccessful gubernatorial runs of Richard "Dick" Posthumus in 2002 and Michael Cox in 2010. Colleen Pero is former co-director of the Michigan Political Leadership Program at MSU, and was Justice Cliff Taylor's campaign manager in 2008. In October of 2011, she was appointed by the Michigan Supreme Court as commissioner-at-large to a three-year term with the State Bar of Michigan. [Marcia McBrien, "Colleen Pero of Laingsburg appointed to State Bar of Michigan Board of Commissioners by Michigan Supreme Court, 6 October 2011, http://courts.michigan.gov/News-Events/press_releases/Documents/PR10-06-11SBMappt.pdf.] In July of 2012, Governor Rick Snyder appointed her to the Board of State Canvassers to fill the remainder of a term that was to run through Jan. 31, 2013. ["Snyder makes appointment to Board of State Canvassers," 27 July 2012, http://www.michigan.gov/snyder/0,4668,7-277-57577_57657-281404--RSS,00.html.] She was reappointed for a full four-year term ending in 2017. [Ed Wesoloski, "Two appointed to Board of State Canvassers," The MiLW Blog, 29 January 2013, http://milawyersweekly.com/milwblog/2013/01/29/two-appointed-to-board-of-state-canvassers/?utm_source=WhatCounts+Publicaster+Edition&utm_medium=email&utm_campaign=MiLW+Daily+Alert%3a+Butzel+Long+asks+for+government+bailout+on+pensions&utm_content=Two+appointed+to+Board+of+State+Canvassers.] She also served as campaign manager for Judge Colleen O'Brien's failed 2012 bid for the Michigan Supreme Court.

165 Ibid., 73.

166 Whitney, 75–76.

*about as much to do with him as when he was the state Representative for Mt. Pleasant. I never
thought of him representing Leelanau County.*

*I thought John Engler was a little bit rough around the edges and he was not a particularly good
speaker. But until he became Governor, I wasn't paying that much attention.*

Like always, as a new state Senator, John Engler had a plan. Gail Torreano joined him
in 1980 to run his Senate office. She described his agenda:

> He said that we would be working on three goals:
>
> To help make the Senate Republicans the majority;
> To help him become Senate majority leader;
> To help him become Governor.
>
> Put these three goals in perspective. In 1980, he was still serving his first
> term in the Senate. He was low man on the totem pole. He was just one of
> 14 Republicans—there were 24 Democrats then—so he was very much in
> the minority. But he didn't hesitate. He planned far in advance, and he was
> certain of himself.[167]

And that's pretty much the way it worked out. ...With a little help from the influence
of a new President, Ronald Reagan. (Engler did not favor Reagan's candidacy for
President, supporting instead Senator Howard Baker. Still, he benefitted from the shift
in public sentiment.[168])

And things were looking up when Governor Milliken announced he would not seek
reelection in 1982. The Milliken old guard wanted Lt. Governor James Brickley, but
Engler supported Dick Headlee, a leader of the 1970's tax revolt and the author of a
popular property tax measure, the Headlee Amendment. Brickley wound up on the
Supreme Court, Headlee ran unsuccessfully against James Blanchard. Engler, however,
won his own re-election battle handily, with more than 60 percent of the vote.[169] And
the balance of power in the Senate was still in the hands of the Democrats, but less
firmly so: it was 20-18; the Republicans had picked up four seats. Further, just after the
election, Engler was picked by his own party to serve as the minority leader beginning
in 1983, in effect becoming the voice of the Republican Party under a Democratic
Governor.[170]

Engler's shift from the minority leader to the majority leader came thanks to Governor
Blanchard's imposition of a 38 percent boost in the state's income tax. Angry voters
recalled first-term Democrats David Serotkin (Mt. Clemens) and Philip O. Mastin
(Pontiac). That left the balance at 18 all. Democrat Senator Lana Pollack related a

---

167 Gail Torreano, 80.
168 Ibid., 81.
169 Ibid., 85.
170 Ibid., 86.

conversation she'd had with ousted David Serotkin: "[H]e was sure that while Allen Cropsey was the foot soldier behind the recall campaigns, John Engler was the general, the brains behind this bold assault on Democratic Senate leadership."[171]

The result was the election of two Republicans in a special election January 31, 1984. The 20-18 balance was then in the Republicans' favor.[172] Engler had no votes to spare; if one of his caucus defected and the Democrats held as a party block, the balloting would be tied. So, he knew he had to work with the minority insofar as possible.

During that time, he had some communication with Weaver.

I continued to have contact with him on juvenile issues. I managed to be appointed by Governor Blanchard because I was a dissenting voice to committees. If nothing else, I was some kind of voice of reasonable opposition. I remember how some of this became beyond Connie, and she suggested I talk with Lucille Taylor.

It's likely that was the first time Weaver talked with her. That meeting would be important.

The 1986 election saw William Lucas, the Republican candidate, challenge incumbent Jim Blanchard. John Engler's then-wife, Colleen House Engler, was Lucas' running mate for Lieutenant Governor. But she wasn't the next in line for such a position, at least by seniority.

Connie was in contention for the spot on the ticket with Lucas. She wasn't happy about being passed over, but in the end, it was the best thing that could have happened to her.

That was the same election that saw Weaver reach the Court of Appeals.

It's during that election that I got to know a lot about the elective process. There were a lot of occasions to meet Colleen House Engler. I liked both Bill Lucas and Colleen. I always thought she was a far better communicator than her husband.

Lucas went down to the incumbent, 32 to 68 percent.

That was a Titanic candidacy. If they had won, John and Colleen might have continued as a couple, but it was unlikely that Lucas was going to win. She didn't run for her House seat, and she was out of a job. And she was out of her marriage.

They would divorce later that year.

In his own race, Engler prevailed over his opponent with almost 60 percent of the vote. He told friends it would be his last run for the state Senate: he was either going to be Governor or run for the U.S. Senate.[173]

171 Ibid., 92.
172 Ibid., 93.
173 Ibid., 100.

He opted for the Governor's chair in 1990. And he worked hard for it, uphill all the way. As might be expected, the *Detroit Free Press* endorsed Blanchard, *the Detroit News*, Engler. Former President Ronald Reagan came to speak for Engler, but the survey news wasn't good. Two days before the election, the pollsters put Blanchard ahead by 14 points.[174]

In the end, analysts determined that Blanchard and his team didn't work as hard, didn't have a message to sell, and couldn't motivate Detroit voters to get to the polls. Engler won by less than one percent of the vote.[175] But those 17,000 votes were enough to avoid a recount, said Lucille Taylor "but not enough to be a mandate. We all came into this office with the general public thinking: We are an accident; John Engler is the accidental governor; this is the accidental administration."[176]

Accidental or not, Engler went on to win both condemnation and acclaim for slashing $200 million from the state's budget to avoid insolvency; the Blanchard administration had not balanced its books and had left a fiscal mess. The state's welfare program was top on the cutting order. Then came reductions in staff to reduce the size of the state government.[177]

Much of Governor Engler's first term was filled with necessary actions: meeting the deficit and enacting Proposition A, the tax proposal to restructure funding for schools throughout the state. He and his staff had their hands full.

But one of the necessary obligations of a Michigan governor is to appoint judges and justices in the event of a vacancy that cannot be filled by an election. Those appointments range from the lower trial courts—probate, district, and circuit—to the Court of Appeals and even to the Supreme Court.

Appointments to the Court of Appeals

There is a pattern to the Court of Appeals appointments in Michigan reminiscent of baseball.

It IS like the farm system. Lucille Taylor talked to me about it one time. They didn't think much of the probate and district courts, so if you were young or very inexperienced, or they didn't particularly like you or didn't trust you, that's where you would go. The circuit court appointments went to people they were grooming, people who might go on to bigger and better things. Now, they didn't always judge people correctly, and there were some disappointments. And if they prove to be too independent that would be as far as they would go. But if they thought they could control you....

Just like the big leagues, promising young players were brought into the system and moved up when there was an opening. All they'd have to do was be willing to play ball to the coaches' and general managers' liking.

---

174 Ibid., 138-139.
175 Ibid., 150-151.
176 Ibid., 180.
177 Ibid., 193.

When Weaver took her oath of office for her first eight-year term on the Supreme Court, Engler was taking the oath of office for his second four-year stint as Governor. In that time, he had made only four appointments to the Court of Appeals: Michael J. Connor in 1991; Clifford W. Taylor and Maura Corrigan, both in March of 1992; and Henry William Saad in December of 1994.

Connor earned both his B.A. and J.D. at the University of Notre Dame. He began his legal career as a bailiff and law clerk in the U.S. District Court. He moved into criminal trial practice in the Detroit Recorder's Court.

> [...] both as an assistant prosecutor and as a defense attorney with the Legal Aid and Defender's Office. In 1970 he was appointed Chief of the Recorder's Court Division of the Wayne County Prosecuting Attorney's Office and he served in that capacity until his appointment to the Recorder's Court Bench in 1973.[178]

He was re-elected to the post until he was appointed in 1981 to the Third Circuit Court (Wayne County), by Governor Milliken. He was serving there when John Engler appointed him to the Court of Appeals in 1991.[179] Connor left the bench in 1995.[180]

Taylor was the husband of Engler's chief legal counsel, Lucille Taylor. He had earned his undergraduate degree from the University of Michigan in 1964 and his J.D. in 1967 from George Washington University. He served as a line officer in the U.S. Navy from 1967 to 1971. Taylor had never served as a trial court judge, but he had worked from 1971 into 1972 as an assistant prosecuting attorney for Ingham County. He left that job for private practice with Denfield, Timmer & Seelye (later Denfield, Timmer and Taylor) where he worked for 20 years.[181]

And there are those, who would argue that you don't have to have judicial experience to be a justice.[182] And I don't argue you have to. Justice Griffin didn't, and he did a fine job. You're going to start at the beginning. Now, whether you should go to the Court of Appeals? Bob [Robert J.] Danhof did. I think he was in George Romney's administration and was an Attorney General candidate. He turned out to be a very good judge.

But Cliff didn't have any particular outstanding qualifications for the job. If he weren't friends with John Engler, he wouldn't have gotten appointed. But that's—oftentimes—what is wrong with an appointive system without checks and balances on it. The appointing governor shouldn't fill the place with partisans and political friends lacking the highest noteworthy experience and qualifications.

178 *Michigan Manual 1991-1992* (Lansing, Mich. 1993), 597.
179 Ibid.
180 Past Judges, Michigan Court of Appeals, http://courts.mi.gov/Courts/COA/judges/Pages/Past.aspx.
181 John Truscott, "Governor Engler Appoints Court of Appeals Judge Clifford W. Taylor to the Michigan Supreme Court," 21 August 1997, http://www.state.mi.us/migov/gov/PressReleases/199708/taylorto.html. See also Clifford Taylor, Judgepedia, http://judgepedia.org/index.php/Clifford_Taylor and Biographies, "Clifford Taylor," Michigan Supreme Court Historical Society, http://www.micourthistory.org/bios.php?id=111.
182 Robert Griffin had been a U.S. Senator, but he'd never served as a judge before he was elected to serve for his one term (1987–95) on Michigan's Supreme Court.

Weaver had met Taylor first when he was the Republican candidate against Attorney General Frank Kelley.

I remember the first time I encountered Cliff was when he was running for A.G., I think, in probably '90, up at Garfield Township. And he was running against the Eternal General, Frank Kelley, and so it was a sacrificial candidacy. He and I got on fairly well.

Well enough so that over time they would play a little tennis and golf together, share events with each other's family and friends, even stay in each other's houses.

He even referred to me as like a sister.

Corrigan graduated *magna cum laude* with her B.A. in 1969 from Marygrove College, and from the University of Detroit with her J.D. in 1973, also *magna cum laude*. She first served as a law clerk at the Michigan Court of Appeals to the Honorable John Gillis.[183]

> She then moved on to become an assistant prosecuting attorney in Wayne County from 1974 to 1979; in 1979 she was appointed Chief of Appeals in the U.S. Attorney's Office for the Eastern District of Michigan. In 1986, she was promoted to Chief Assistant U.S. Attorney, becoming the first woman to hold that position. In 1989, Corrigan became a partner in the law firm of Plunkett and Cooney, specializing in litigation and appeals.[184]

I had certainly supported Maura to be appointed to the Court of Appeals. And I had tried to mentor her to some degree. She and I became friends. I moved on to the Supreme Court; she was on the Court of Appeals. She spoke at my investiture. I supported and helped her become Chief Judge of the Court of Appeals—I opened the door for her to attend some particularly educative seminars around the country.

Sometimes they traveled to the same meetings together.

When we went to some event at the University of Kansas, we had good times looking for the Oregon Trail where it starts out; and she likes blue glass, and we were looking for that; and I was looking for a certain kind of Franciscan china, no longer made.

Saad was a *magna cum laude* graduate of Wayne State University Law School. He had also earned his undergraduate degree in business at the university.

> Prior to joining the bench, Judge Saad was a partner at Dickinson, Wright, Moon, Van Dusen and Freeman, where he practiced law for 20 years. He was also an arbitrator for the Michigan Employment Relations Commission and a hearing referee for the Michigan Department of Civil Rights.[185]

183 Biographies, "Maura Corrigan," Michigan Supreme Court Historical Society, http://www.micourthistory.org/bios.php?id=113.
184 Ibid.
185 Second District Judges, Michigan Court of Appeals, http://www.courts.michigan.gov/courts/coa/judges/

But he also had never before served as a trial court judge.

In his next term—1995-1999—Governor Engler would add an additional six appointees at the Court of Appeals: Robert P. Young, Jr., and Stephen J. Markman in 1995; William C. Whitbeck and Hilda Gage in 1997; Michael J. Talbot and Kurtis T. Wilder in 1998.

Young graduated from both Harvard College and Harvard Law School.

> In 1978, he joined the law firm of Dickinson, Wright, Moon, Van Dusen and Freeman, becoming a partner in the firm in 1982. Beginning in 1992, [...] Young served as vice president, corporate secretary, and general counsel of AAA Michigan.[186]

Again, no experience as a trial court judge.

Markman earned his undergraduate degree at Duke University and his law degree at University of Cincinnati College of Law.[187] He had experience at the federal level.

> From 1989–93, Justice Markman served as United States Attorney, or federal prosecutor, in Michigan, after having been nominated by President George H. W. Bush and confirmed by the United States Senate. From 1985–1989, he served as Assistant Attorney General of the United States, after having been nominated by President Ronald Reagan and confirmed by the United States Senate. In that position, he headed the Department of Justice's Office of Legal Policy, which served as the principal policy development office within the Department, and which coordinated the federal judicial selection process. Prior to this, he served for seven years as Chief Counsel of the United States Senate Subcommittee on the Constitution, and as Deputy Chief Counsel of the United States Senate Judiciary Committee.[188]

When he came to the Court of Appeals, he had most recently been working at Miller, Canfield, Paddock and Stone in Detroit.

Whitbeck earned his bachelor's degree from Northwestern University and his law degree from the University of Michigan.[189]

> In private practice for over 20 years, Judge Whitbeck was a partner in the law firms of Honigman Miller, Dykema Gossett, and McLellan, Schlaybaugh & Whitbeck.

pages/biosd2.aspx.
186 Chief Justice Robert P. Young, Jr., Michigan Supreme Court, http://courts.michigan.gov/courts/michigansupremecourt/justices/pages/chief-justice-robert-p-young-jr.aspx.
187 Stephen J. Markman, NNDB website, http://www.nndb.com/people/124/000167620/
188 Justice Stephen J. Markman, Michigan Supreme Court, http://courts.michigan.gov/courts/michigansupremecourt/justices/pages/justice-stephen-j.-markman.aspx.
189 Fourth District Judges, Michigan Court of Appeals, http://www.courts.michigan.gov/courts/coa/judges/pages/biosd4.aspx.

Judge Whitbeck also served in the administrations of three Michigan Governors: George Romney, William Milliken, and John Engler. He served on the transition teams of President Ronald Reagan and Governor Engler. Judge Whitbeck served in the U.S. Army Reserves for six years and was honorably discharged in 1972.

Judge Whitbeck was an assistant to Governor Romney, special assistant to Secretary Romney at the U.S. Department of Housing and Urban Development, and area director of the Detroit Office of H.U.D. in the Milliken administration, he served as Director of Policy in the Michigan Public Service Commission. He served as counsel to Governor Engler for Executive Organization and director of the Office of State Employer.[190]

While Whitbeck had significant relevant experience, he had never served as a lower court judge before his appointment to the Court of Appeals.

Gage earned her undergraduate and master's degrees with distinction at University of Michigan and her law degree at Wayne State University Law School, graduating *magna cum laude*.[191] She was elected in 1978 to the Oakland County Circuit Court where she also served as chief judge.

Gage was appointed to the Court of Appeals in 1997, after serving as a judge and chief judge of the Oakland County Circuit Court, to which she was first elected in 1978. Appointed to both the Michigan Civil Rights Commission and the Michigan Sentencing Guidelines Commission, Gage was the first woman to serve as chairperson of the National Conference of State Trial Judges of the American Bar Association. She was also the first woman president of the Michigan Judges Association and the first woman to chair the Michigan Judicial Tenure Commission.[192]

Talbot was another two-time Engler appointee. Talbot, who earned his undergraduate degree from Georgetown University and his law degree from the University of Detroit, began in private practice. He was first appointed as a judge of Detroit Common Pleas in 1978 and then Detroit Recorder's Court in 1980 by Governor Milliken, and to the Third Circuit Court (Wayne County) bench in 1991 by Governor Engler. Engler also appointed him to the Court of Appeals in 1998.[193]

Wilder was still another two-time Engler appointee. He earned both his undergraduate and law degrees from the University of Michigan. He began his career in Detroit with

190 Fourth District, Michigan Court of Appeals, http://www.courts.michigan.gov/courts/coa/judges/pages/biosd4.aspx.
191 "Judge Hilda Gage Elected to National Center for State Courts Board of Directors" Michigan Supreme Court Office of Public Information, 30 August 2002.
192 "Hon. Hilda Gage Mourned by Michigan Supreme Court, Court of Appeals; Gage Remembered as Trailblazer," Michigan Supreme Court Office of Public Information, 14 September 2010.
193 First District, Michigan Court of Appeals, http://www.courts.michigan.gov/courts/coa/judges/pages/biosd1.aspx and Michael Talbot, Judgepedia.org, http://judgepedia.org/index.php/Michael_J._Talbot.

Butzel Long, P.C., and then with the Lansing law firm Foster, Swift, Collins and Smith, P.C. John Engler appointed him in 1992 to the 22nd Judicial Circuit Court (Washtenaw County). He served part of his tenure there as chief judge.[194]

In his last term, Engler would appoint others to the Court of Appeals: Jeffrey Collins, Brian K. Zahra, Donald S. Owens, and Patrick Meter in 1999, and Christopher M. Murray and Pat M. Donofrio in 2002.

Collins was <u>another two-time Engler appointee</u>. He earned his bachelor's from Northwestern University and his law degree, *cum laude*, from Howard University School of Law.[195] He began his career with Bell and Hudson, in Detroit, started his own practice, and was appointed John Engler as a judge of Detroit Recorder's Court in 1994. When that court was abolished in 1997, Collins moved into the Third Circuit Court (Wayne County). With Engler's encouragement and the Republicans' nomination, he ran for the Michigan Supreme Court in 1998 but lost. Engler appointed him to the Court of Appeals in late 1998 and he took office in 1999.[196]

Zahra was <u>another two-time Engler appointee</u>. He earned his bachelor's degree from Wayne State University and his law degree (with honors) from the University of Detroit Law School. He began his legal career clerking for Judge Lawrence P. Zatkoff of the U.S. District Court for the Eastern District of Michigan. He left for private practice with the Detroit law firm Dickinson, Wright, Moon, Van Dusen & Freeman, and was later a partner there. In 1994, Engler appointed him to Third Circuit Court (Wayne County) where he served until December of 1998, when the Governor tapped him for the Court of Appeals (he took office in 1999). Governor Rick Snyder appointed him a justice of the Michigan Supreme Court in 2011.[197]

Meter was <u>also a two-time Engler appointee</u>. He earned his bachelor's and law degrees from the University of Notre Dame, where he also taught undergraduate Spanish and worked as a juvenile probation officer. He began his legal career in 1973 as a prosecuting attorney and then chief assistant prosecuting attorney for Saginaw County. He served until 1984 when he entered private practice with Braun, Kendrick, Finkbeiner, Schafer and Murphy. In late 1991 Engler appointed him as a judge on the 10th Circuit Court (Saginaw County) and then appointed him to the Michigan Court of Appeals in 1999.[198]

Owens, a long-standing probate judge from Ingham County, was one of the Young Turks described earlier, the group comprised of Owens, Weaver, Gladys Barsamian, Randal Heckman, and Michael Anderegg. The account of his appointment to the Court

---

194 John Truscott, "Governor Engler Appoints Wilder to Court of Appeals" 31 December 1998, http://www.state.mi.us/migov/gov/PressReleases/199812/Wilder.html.

195 About Us: Jeffrey Collins, Collins and Collins, P.C., http://www.collinslegal.net/aboutus.html

196 David Ashenfelter, "New Wayne County deputy Jeffrey Collins is low-key but highly regarded," *Detroit Free Press*, 4 November 2011, http://www.freep.com/article/20111104/NEWS06/111040437/New-Wayne-County-deputy-Jeffrey-Collins-low-key-highly-regarded.

197 Justice Brian K. Zahra, Michigan Supreme Court, http://courts.michigan.gov/courts/michigansupremecourt/justices/pages/justice-brian-k.-zahra.aspx.

198 *Michigan Manual 2001-2002* (Lansing, Mich. 2003), 599.

of Appeals is filled with political intrigue and is fully described in Chapter 7. Owens earned his bachelor's, master's and law degrees from the University of Michigan. He served as an Ingham County probate judge from 1974 to 1999, when Engler appointed him to his seat on the Court of Appeals.[199]

Murray was yet another two-time Engler appointee. He graduated from Hillsdale College and the University of Detroit School of Law.[200]

> He practiced law with Keller, Thoma, P.C., in Detroit from 1990 until 1995, while from 1995 to 1997, he served as deputy legal counsel to Governor John Engler. In 1997, he returned to Keller, Thoma, and remained there until his appointment to the Wayne Circuit Court on January 10, 2000.[201]

Engler appointed Murray to that Third Circuit post and then, in 2002, raised him to the Michigan Court of Appeals.

Donofrio received both his undergraduate and law degrees from Wayne State University. He began his legal career as a founding partner of the law firm of Romain, Donofrio, Kuck and Egerer, P.C. Donofrio was yet another two-time Engler appointee, first to the 16th Circuit Court (Macomb County) in 1997, and then to the Court of Appeals in 2002.[202]

The Deal That Engler Wouldn't Make

Engler, early in his political career, had said that he was working against the old, entrenched party machine:

> I feel the major problem in Lansing today is that there exists a special and unhealthy relationship between many elected officials and varied powerful interest groups. At some point these politicians cease to represent the total public interest, and choose instead to represent the private special interests.[203]

How easy is it to drift into becoming your own powerful interest group when you are one of the most successful political figures the state has ever seen? And these appointments...should they be considered good government? ...Or political favors? Personal favors? Rewards? And how much of it remains hidden, unnoted?

---

199 Fourth District Judges, Michigan Court of Appeals, http://www.courts.michigan.gov/courts/coa/judges/pages/biosd4.aspx.
200 First District Judges, Michigan Court of Appeals, http://www.courts.michigan.gov/courts/coa/judges/pages/biosd1.aspx.
201 Hon. Christopher M. Murray, Institute of Continuing Legal Education, http://www.icle.org/modules/directories/contributors/bio.aspx?PNumber=P43849.
202 Second District Judges, Michigan Court of Appeals, http://www.courts.michigan.gov/courts/coa/judges/pages/biosd2.aspx.
203 Gleaves Whitney, *John Engler: The Man, the Leader and the Legacy*, (Chelsea, Mich., Sleeping Bear Press, 2002) 68.

With the Governor, there had been at least one very public *quid pro quo* and it dealt with the 1998 election. That year Frank Kelley let it be known that he was stepping aside. With the right candidate, the Republicans could pick up the office.

John Smietanka was intent on running for Attorney General.[204]

This would be Smietanka's second run for the Attorney General's office. The first effort was in 1994—another sacrificial run against Kelley and one Engler supported. That was at the same time Weaver was campaigning for the Supreme Court and Governor Engler was running for his second term. Weaver, Smietanka, and Engler often appeared at a number of the same events, and Weaver had a chance to listen to their talks. Weaver observed that Engler was not a compelling speaker.

He had tons of confidence and knew how to influence people, but not as a dynamic speaker.

But Smietanka was less engaging.

Smietanka was mind-numbing on the campaign trail. His speeches were long and boring. He'd start out by asking the audience to remember a series of numbers and he went from there. It was complex and the audience was lost.

In the 1998 election, the Governor wanted someone other than Smietanka. He wanted to nominate Scott Romney—someone he thought would fare better with voters—but the issue was out of Engler's direct control and headed for the floor of the party convention. That wasn't how Engler liked things.

Andrea Fischer Newman was the finance chair for all three of Engler's gubernatorial campaigns. She is also a very close friend. This is her recall of the event:

> For John Engler, the 1998 convention in Grand Rapids should have been a moment of triumph. It was probably one of the low points in his career.
>
> Engler just didn't want Smietanka to run in the convention against Scott Romney. Engler didn't think Smietanka would be as strong a candidate as Romney when he faced a Democrat in the general election. So Engler offered Smietanka the sun and the moon and the stars—a judgeship, the Court of Appeals, anything to keep him from running. Smietanka wouldn't budge. And [Chuck] Yob said he would remain loyal to Smietanka, despite the Governor's view that Romney would be a superior candidate in the general election.

204 Smietanka had been in private practice, served 12 years in the Berrien County Prosecuting Attorney's office (eight years as the prosecutor), 12 years as a U.S. Attorney for the Western District of Michigan. While there, he served as Principal Associate Deputy Attorney General in 1990-91 at the U.S. Justice Department. He was nominated by President George Walker Bush in 1992 to serve as a judge in the Sixth U.S. Circuit Court of Appeals. The appointment languished and expired in the U.S. Senate Judiciary Committee. He has returned to private practice as a partner with Smietanka, Buckleitner, Steffes and Gezon. [http://www.smietankalaw.com/sbsg_john.htm.] He also serves as a radio talk-show host for WRHC, Three Oaks, Mich. [http://www.radioharborcountry.org/index.cfm?View=Host&hostID=18.]

Yob also made it an issue of who controlled the GOP: John Engler or the grassroots? Yob kept saying that the Governor should not be in control of the party. The grassroots should be. Furthermore, Yob said, there were grassroots Republicans who couldn't stand Engler. Clearly Yob was using Smietanka as a rallying point for his own vision of the party.

Yob's actions made Engler angry. At the convention the Governor probably would have exploded if he had confronted Yob face to face.

The vote was very close. Smietanka won; Romney lost. The vote was a referendum not just on Romney, but on John Engler. And John Engler lost. He was bitterly disappointed. Michelle was so upset after the vote she was in the bathroom crying.

One of the reasons the Governor lost was that the state party was different now under Betsy DeVos. Before 1998, when Spence Abraham and then Dave Doyle chaired the party, the Governor could have counted on their direct help. But Betsy didn't think it was appropriate for the state party chair to intervene in a fight on the convention floor. Because Engler couldn't count on Betsy's help, he didn't have the organization in place to deal with Smietanka's candidacy. So Engler was down on the floor, doing everything on his own.[205]

"The sun, the moon, the stars—a judgeship, the Court of Appeals, anything...," Andrea Fischer Newman had said.

Perhaps the ultimate "party" favor? Or perhaps there was still something not offered.

Smietanka wanted the Supreme Court. Engler would not give that; it was too important for him to try to get control of the court, and Smietanka was too independent. If Engler had gone to the floor of the convention and simply said that "You have to make up your minds, but here's why I don't want Smietanka: he lost in '94 and is unlikely to win this time," I think he'd have been much better off. And I think he was right about that; if Romney had won the nomination, he'd have had plenty of money and the name recognition. Instead John Engler wanted keep the control and failed to make his case. The convention showed Engler.

Smietanka narrowly defeated Romney in the convention vote and failed in the general election 48 to 52 percent against his Democratic opponent, Jennifer Granholm.[206]

In the end, Engler created Granholm.

This fracture of the Republicans may have done much to drive the Governor to wrest whatever control he could wherever he could...the enemies weren't just the

---

205Andrea Fischer Newman, quoted in Whitney, 316.
206Ballotpedia, "Jennifer Granholm" http://ballotpedia.org/wiki/index.php/Jennifer_Granholm.

Democrats...they were other Republicans who didn't agree with him. The effect would be polarizing, especially at the Supreme Court.

By that fall of 1998, Engler had already made his first appointment to the Michigan Supreme Court. By that time, too, there had already been a change of personnel as a result of age limits and election. We've been so intent on the farm teams that we need to go back and chronicle the big league.

Election and Appointment at the Supreme Court

In the fall of 1996, there were two seats coming open on the Supreme Court. One belonged to James H. Brickely. The other seat was that of Charles Levin, who was too old to run for another term. The Republicans had nominated Brickley, again, and Sixth Circuit (Oakland) Court Judge Hilda R. Gage. The Democrats nominated Marilyn J. Kelly and William B. Murphy, both then serving on the Court of Appeals. Jessica Cooper, also of the Sixth Circuit Court—but of no political affiliation—gathered enough petition signatures to make it on the ballot. Libertarians put forward Jerry J. Kaufman and David H. Raaflaub.[207]

Brickley won handily with 1,340,993 votes. He had raised $228,977 and had independent expenditures (IE) by the Michigan Republican State Central Committee of $223,697.

Kelly came in second with 1,124,618 votes. She had raised $553,274 and had IEs of $97,885 from the Michigan Democratic State Central Committee. Interestingly, there were IEs of $25,764 invested to defeat her by an organization called Justice for Michigan Citizens.

Gage, who placed third, had 971,519 votes. She had raised more than any other candidate: $723,570, and she had an additional $327,576 from the Michigan Republican State Central Committee and $150,386 from the Michigan State Victory Committee (funded by the National Republican Senatorial Committee).

Fourth place finisher Murphy received 899,545 votes and outraised his fellow Democrat, Kelly, with $699,354. The Michigan Democratic State Central Committee plunked down three times as much as it did for Kelly: $289,900. Justice for Michigan Citizens also upped the ante against him with IEs of $78,024.

Independent Cooper received 483,412 votes and raised $148, 931. She had no IEs.

Kaufman came in with 316,943 votes, and Raaflaub garnered 86,069. Neither raised a dime.[208]

207Barbara Moorhouse and Richard Robinson with David Hogg, *Special Interests v Public Values - Funding Michigan Supreme Court Campaigns - 1994-2000* "1996 Supreme Court Election" (Michigan Campaign Finance Network, Lansing, Mich.), 25, http://www.mcfn.org/pdfs/reports/SCAppendix.pdf.
208 Ibid.

Weaver assessed the spoiler in the race was having TWO sitting Sixth Circuit Court judges:

Those were Hilda Gage and Jessica Cooper[209]: two strong, powerful trial judges from Oakland County. And Marilyn was a third judge from Oakland who had been on the Board of Education and had the Kelly name. And Gage and Cooper both were strong—but they negated each other.

Then, too, there was the matter of Gage keeping control of her campaign message.

Hilda went with the party and let them run her media. I had tried to get her not to do that. And it was a mistake, because in the end, she had lots of money left that didn't get spent. So she had money but no ads, and it could have made a difference.
And then Marilyn slipped in. That's how she got there.

Like Weaver, Kelly had prepared for a life of language. She earned her B.A. from Eastern Michigan University, studied at the LaSorbonne, University of Paris, earned her master's at Middlebury College, and taught French language and literature in Grosse Pointe Public Schools, at Albion College, and EMU. She attended and graduated with honors from the Law School at Wayne State University. She practiced courtroom law for 17 years before she ran for and was elected to the Court of Appeals in 1988. She was re-elected in 1994. Her election to the Supreme Court in 1996 didn't change the political balance on the court, but things were a little different, according to Weaver.

So Marilyn came. She was known as a liberal Democrat and was in the majority with Cavanagh; it was Cavanagh and Mallett and Marilyn and Boyle.

And even though the Democrats held the majority, the court only sometimes locked up on political lines.

There was a power block on workman's compensation and union issues, but there wasn't a power block on crime, and there wasn't a power block on some of these other things. So it wasn't as firm a power block as it would be later.

Coincident with Justice Kelly's swearing in at the court was the election of a new Chief Justice. Brickley had served his two years and didn't seek another term.

Brickley didn't want to be the chief justice again.

The office fell to Conrad Mallett, Jr.

When I got to the court, my goal was to reform the judicial services for the people of Michigan. And Justice Brickley started leading in that, and after his term, Justice Mallett led in it. There was a need to reform how we should select justices. But the highest priority was to get better judicial services for the people through all the trial courts, and that's why we had our pilot projects.

---

209 Gage has since died. Jessica Cooper is the first woman prosecuting attorney for Oakland County. For more information, see Jessica R. Cooper, Oakland County Prosecutor, Oakland County, http://www3.oakgov.com/prosatty/Pages/elected_off_bio.aspx.

The pilot project involved five courts around the state.

And there was resistance on the court to doing that, but there was enough leadership from Brickley, and then from Mallett and myself, to move it forward, and we had our pilot projects.

The pilot projects—and legislative lack of support—would later change the face of the court. But that was a little later and there was an immediate change in the offing.

After six years in office, Governor Engler would have his first opportunity to make an appointment to the Supreme Court when Justice Riley stepped down effective Sept. 1, 1997.[210] She had been struggling physically.

Justice Riley began not to be well, and it turned out to be Parkinson's. Justice Riley had goals that she made clear to me.

The most important was her idea to create a new home for the court, the Hall of Justice.

And that was coming along. So, I think that really kept her alive for as long as it did, and she got to see it dedicated; she got to be in it; and her husband was so good to her in taking her everywhere. And Justice Boyle described Justice Riley as like fine bone china, seemingly fragile but very strong; and I think that was true.

When it came to the rumors of who would serve as Justice Riley's replacement, Weaver had lots to consider. Cliff Taylor was a friend. But so were some of the others including Maura Corrigan, Lucille Taylor, and Hilda Gage. In her opinion, they all were qualified.

And so, that day that Justice Riley called the Governor, she called me; she called the Taylors, and that night the Taylors had me for spaghetti dinner at their house—I had many dinners at their house in East Lansing. Remember, it's Justice Riley leaving; the Republicans are under a lot of attack, Engler and his group. I didn't always think it was fair, but I didn't realize people weren't telling the truth all the time.

That night Cliff was ecstatic because he was going to the Supreme Court. Interestingly enough, I perceived, and Lucille perceived—she was the Governor's legal counsel—that Cliff might not be the right appointment at that time, because it could be better to have a woman.

Taking Justice Riley's seat would mean that Cliff would have to run in 1998, and then he would have to run again in 2000 for the full term. And it was going to be very contentious, so it might be wiser to appoint a woman, such as Lucille Taylor, as a matter of fact, or Maura Corrigan, or Hilda Gage. It might be better for Cliff.

Cliff was just, you know, like if there was champagne, he was breaking it out. And Lucille was very low-keyed about it, as was I, because, yes, it would be great, and because I was going to be fine with having Cliff on the court.

210 Biographies, "Dorothy Riley," Michigan Supreme Court Historical Society, http://www.micourthistory. org/bios.php?id=102.

But it was the Governor's decision; it wasn't made. It was already in the paper, all these names of these possible justices. I mean, there were a lot of possibilities as well as him. But for Cliff, it was a done deal.

Now, the next morning, I got a call from Lucille, and she said, "I have had the worst night of my life, because Cliff thinks that I am more loyal to John Engler than him, and that you and I do not want him as the next justice. You have got to call him and tell him that, of course you would support him."

And she said, "I have told the Governor to take my name off the list."

So I did call Cliff and said, "Cliff, of course I'm interested in you being here, and I support you, but it's the Governor's decision."

Later in the summer, Weaver spoke with the Governor about the possible appointment of Cliff Taylor to the court.

I met with Engler at the Governor's Breakfast here in Traverse City for the Cherry Festival parade, and he asked me what I thought. And I said, "Well, I know that you are friends with Cliff, as I am, and Cliff would be a wonderful justice," as I thought he would be. "I support him while I understand, too, that the person has to get elected, and that a woman would be good. It is your decision. And whatever you decide to do, I will support." And I left it at that.

The Governor opted to go with Cliff Taylor. And what Taylor imagined as Weaver's coolness at his appointment would come back to dog her increasingly from the time after Taylor, Markman, and Young won the 2000 election through Taylor's later serving as chief justice (from 2005–2009).

For some reason, he didn't understand that I wholeheartedly supported his appointment and his subsequent election.

Taylor's appointment seemed a conflict of interest to some at the time, and it came up in the 2000 election when Taylor was running for his first full term:

> Some in the Michigan political realm are criticizing the marriage between a Michigan Supreme Court justice and Gov. John Engler's chief attorney, calling it a conflict of interest.
>
> Republican appointee Clifford R. Taylor and wife, Lucille, link the top levels of the judicial and executive branches. The state Constitution keeps the two branches separate as part of the system of checks and balances on state policy.
>
> Critics said the Taylor's union upsets the balance. The Taylors said Supreme Court debates aren't part of their dinner conversations and that they've avoided potential conflicts. [...]

"People talk about it all the time," said former Democratic Michigan Gov. James Blanchard. "There's no way I would have tolerated my counsel being married to a justice on the court."

Lucille Taylor said she's taken steps to avoid conflicts, not just since the Governor named her husband to the Supreme Court in 1997, but since her husband first joined the bench as a Court of Appeals judge in 1992. [...]

Clifford Taylor said he disqualifies himself whenever this wife's legal advice is at issue in a case. That's happened up to four times since he joined the Supreme Court, he said. [...]

"When you have the Governor promoting a particular legal agenda, large chunks of which are being ruled on by the state Supreme Court, that does produce a strong possibility of conflict," said David Moran, a law professor at Wayne State University Law School in Detroit. "I don't see how you get around it."[211]

And it came up again when his opponent in the 2008 election, Diane Hathaway, who defeated him, put it this way: "Cliff Taylor is a walking conflict of interest, and he has got to go."[212]

The arrangement, said Jon Muth, would have required that there be no pillow talk about matters before the court.

It looks like Cliff would have had to have made an extraordinary effort to avoid the influence of the Governor's office. Maybe he did it; I don't know. But it would have had to have been an extraordinary circumstance. And, you know, there are stories that are told going back to Soapy Williams on the court. He was the chief justice, and there were certainly issues in certain cases before the court where it's rumored that he heard from Solidarity House. So it's not brand-new that these things are talked about.

Certainly, there were a lot of rumors about communication between the Engler Administration and Justice Taylor. Again, there's no proof of that, and never any proof that came out that Soapy Williams was marching to the tune of the UAW. But if that sort of thing was happening, that's blockbuster.[213]

211 AP report, "Marriage of Supreme Court justice and Governor's chief attorney disputed" *The Argus Press* (Owosso, Mich.), 6 September 2000, 9, http://news.google.com/newspapers?nid=1988&dat=20000903&id=7T4iAAAAIBAJ&sjid=sqwFAAAAIBAJ&pg=1551,403646.
212 "Hathaway set to unseat the leader of the Republican majority of activist judges known as the 'Gang of Four'" The Conservative Media, 7 September 2008, http://liberalmedianot.blogspot.com/2008/09/hathaway-set-to-unseat-leader-of.html.
213 Jon R. Muth, video interview with co-author Schock, 17 January 2012, Grand Rapids.

Nobody was there to overhear them if they were talking shop, but as far as Cliff Taylor—either as the walking conflict of interest or the spouse of restraint and circumspection—observers chalked up ONE for the Governor.

There would be others. And soon.

Their coming would usher in a fundamental change of the thought at the court.

Judge Eugene "Bud" Moore watched it happen and had discussed it with Weaver:

> Well, I think that she recognized—she may have thought that long before she became a justice—that a system of electing and appointing appellate judges and Supreme Court justices is not what it should be; and that the trial bench is basically an elected bench. Now, certainly, from time to time there's a vacancy and the Governor will appoint somebody. But if you want to be a trial judge, basically you're going to go out and circulate petitions, and you're gonna have to campaign, and you're gonna get on the ballot and campaign again, and you'll get elected or not elected. It's totally different than when you have been appointed by a Governor—you bring, I think, to the bench a different picture when this happens.
>
> I personally believe that as long as we continue to have a system where highest-level judges are not beholden to the people but are beholden to how they got there, we will continue to have problems. I don't know what she thought before she got on the Supreme Court, but I'm sure it didn't take her very long when she got there to find out that these appointed justices—both Republican and Democrat—didn't get there the way she got there. That fact made a difference in their attitude toward the court.[214]

214 Eugene "Bud" Moore, video interview with with co-author Schock, 13 March 2012, Oakland County.

The 1998 Michigan Supreme Court, from left: Justice Marilyn J. Kelly, Justice Michael F. Cavanagh, Justice Patricia J. Boyle, Chief Justice Conrad L. Mallett, Jr., Justice Elizabeth A. Weaver, Justice Clifford W. Taylor, and Justice James H. Brickley. At this point, the court is predominantly Democrat by a 4-3 margin.

Chapter 5

The First Million-dollar Baby; Goodbye Conrad, Hello Robert.

Cliff Taylor was the newbie on the court and was facing an immediate re-election, and it was time for Patricia Boyle to go. In fact, there would be three seats in the wind. Here's a summary by the Michigan Campaign Finance Network of where things stood:

> Before the 1998 election, there were four Democrats and three Republicans on the court. Two seats with eight-year terms were up for election, one of them open. Justice Patricia Boyle (D) decided not to run for re-election. Justice Michael Cavanagh was up for re-election, having first been elected in 1982. In addition, there was a seat with two years remaining in its term on the ballot. Justice Dorothy Comstock Riley (R) had retired in 1997 and Governor John Engler appointed Court of Appeals Judge Clifford Taylor to fill the vacancy.
>
> For the two-year term, the Republicans nominated Justice Taylor, and for the eight-year terms, they nominated Court of Appeals Judge Maura Corrigan and Judge Jeffrey Collins, who was serving on the Detroit Recorder's Court. The Democrats nominated Justice Cavanagh and Judge Susan Borman, who was serving on the 3rd Circuit Court (Wayne County), for the eight-year terms. For the two-year term, the Democrats nominated Judge Carole Youngblood, also serving on the 3rd Circuit Court. The Libertarians again nominated Jerry Kaufman and David Raaflaub for the eight-year terms, but no one for the two-year term. The Reform Party nominated Matthew Abel for the eight-year term.[215]

Boyle's serving out was simple, said Weaver: *She just didn't want to run again.*

She had early on told Weaver just how distasteful she found the elective process. And even though she was both the incumbent and had Big Labor money behind her, it

---

215 Barbara Moorhouse and Richard Robinson with David Hogg, *Special Interests v Public Values—Funding Michigan Supreme Court Campaigns—1994-2000*, "1998 Supreme Court Election," (Michigan Campaign Finance Network, Lansing, Mich.), 2002, 31, http://www.mcfn.org/pdfs/reports/SCAppendix.pdf.

wasn't enough to entice her to stay. She had, after all, run twice—in 1984 and 1990—after her 1983 appointment by Governor Blanchard.

Because Boyle was a Democrat-nominated and aligned justice, her leaving would create an advantage for the Republicans. Cavanaugh was likely to be rock strong; his seat was not in serious danger. But neither of the other two replacement candidates from the Democrats would be as strong as Boyle had been, especially given the political climate. A strong sitting Republican Governor could provide substantial help to his party's nominees, and those nominees might have the further distinction of already having been helped by that same Governor; there might be entangled alliances. Heck, there were entangled alliances. Taylor was already on the high court after the appointment by Engler. And both he and Corrigan had been appointed to the Court of Appeals. Engler had also appointed Collins to the Detroit Recorder's Court in 1994 (and would then bring him to the Court of Appeals in 1999 after his loss in this Supreme Court race).

All during the political season leading up to the election, the court had been doing its business, part of which included reform efforts dear to Weaver's heart.

Mallett was the chief justice, and he was interested in reform as was I. And we were pushing the courts to make changes that would better serve the public; better judicial services for the public. That meant pushing some of the old ideas of hierarchical trial courts where the circuit judges were king of the mountain. And one of the changes that happened was that the pay scales were evened up pretty much. District court judges still get a thousand-dollars less, but it's not the dramatic difference it had been. And the salaries of probate and the circuit judges became the same.

The reforms started through a series of pilot projects.

And we had five of them going, and they were operating in counties that ranged from big to small: one in Washtenaw County, one in Barry County, one up in Lake County, one in Berrien County, and one in the 46th Circuit Court in Otsego, Crawford, and Kalkaska Counties where Judge [Alton Thomas] Davis was.

The idea behind the project was that a judge is a judge is a judge.

And by assignment, they could help each other out. So if the district judge wasn't busy, he could go help someone else, and if the circuit judge wasn't busy, she could help out in another court. They could help out each other rather than having people stacked up in the halls of the district court. Anyone could probably take pleas and those kinds of things; give people their rights. There are so many things that if you're a judge and you've been qualified to be a judge, you ought to be able to do. And that's a lot of the work.

That wouldn't mean that the judges would spend an inordinate amount of time out of their own courtrooms, just enough to keep traffic moving in the halls of justice.

You'd keep them, though, in their specialties with respect to children and families, and the civil matters.

These pilot projects were important, and they didn't come easy, but we found judges who were willing to do it in various places, and they were overall successful. It didn't cost more money, and we served people that much better.

It's now the way business is done in most courts in the state.

It started with Brickley when I got to the court. And then when Mallett became the chief justice, there was more. Brickley was open to it and Riley was, but there were various resistances along the way from the trial courts as well as within the Supreme Court, as you might imagine. Cavanagh was not particularly interested in it. But Mallett and I were, and he was the chief justice. We were a team. It was a great combination. He's there from Democratic Detroit—big city point of view; and I'm from the North, from the out-state and Republican point of view, and both were taking the proper stands, and we were getting people to go along with it. The bottom line was that we made progress.

It was going to take legislation to implement the pilot project across the state. Mallett and Weaver split up to speak with the leaders in both the Senate and the House.

And I got the Senate, which was controlled by [the late William] Van Regenmorter, a Republican, and I worked on getting it done in the Senate.

Mallett drew the House and went to consult with Kwame Kilpatrick, the minority floor leader for the Democratic Party.

Kilpatrick made promises to Mallett to get it done in the House. Certain things got passed in the Senate, but Kilpatrick didn't produce. Kilpatrick, as I remember it, did not fulfill his commitments to Chief Justice Mallett, and Mallett was very disappointed about that. And my understanding at the time—I don't know what Mallett would say now—but Kilpatrick betrayed him, and I think he was very displeased about it. I think Justice Mallett had expressed his dismay at, and somewhat perhaps embarrassment of, not being able to succeed with the Democratic House.[216]

Mallett was actually disgusted with the Democrats, said Weaver. But it's an ill wind that blows no good...to somebody.

In the meantime, Engler and his disciples, cohorts, and his protégés were viewing Mallett....

...With an eye to getting him off the court.

Anyway, Mallett had guaranteed me that he wouldn't leave. I remember being with him at the Traverse City Airport in approximately October of that fall—this would be before the election—

---

216 One of the reasons may have been the dissolution of the Detroit Recorder's Courts, and their replacement with Circuit Courts. It made it far more likely that inner city black Detroiters would be judged by whites from elsewhere in the county. The move had political ramifications.

and he said that he would stay and continue leading. I really wanted him to stay because we were accomplishing reform. Not easily. And he told me he would.

Mallett was in his second year of a two-year stint as chief justice. That's how it worked...the chief justice was elected by fellow justices for two years at a time. Weaver was planning that Mallett would continue.

I would have voted for Mallett to continue as the chief justice. Why not let him? It was a great combination.

Weaver and Brickley had the controlling votes. Assuming Cavanagh would be returned and that a single Republican would come new to the court, Weaver and/or Brickley could make it so. Democrats Cavanaugh and Kelly would vote for Mallett—as would Mallett himself—and then, so would Weaver and, likely, Brickley. A majority plus one. There existed the very real possibility of the Democrat chief justice leading a Republican dominated court whose majority was composed of Brickley, Weaver, Taylor (who had replaced Riley and would be retained in the election) and a newly elected Republican.

Meanwhile, back on the campaign trail, there was a whole lot of spending going on. And while Weaver certainly was hoping that her friend Maura Corrigan would make the cut, it began to look like it might not happen; she was behind in the polls.

And Governor Engler had been very active in her campaign and in raising money. For her ads, Justice Corrigan used the firm that I had used [Marontate and Co.] and that Justice Riley had used. And I recommended that she do that and not let the party control her campaign advertising. Corrigan did go with Marontate.

But there really wasn't enough money to run the ads, no matter who was controlling them. And then in the crunch, the party—or at least the Governor—stepped up their support for her candidacy. Here's how Nancy Perry Graham summarized it in a 2001 issue of *George* magazine when she was reporting on Ohio and Michigan courts:

> Michigan business executives say they learned about raising money for Supreme Court races from the trial lawyers and unions who consistently outspent them until 1998, when the business community helped raise more than $2 million to elect Republican Justices Taylor and Maura Corrigan. With Corrigan behind close to Election Day, Governor Engler stepped in and, with the assistance of his friends at the Michigan Manufacturing Association, helped her raise $300,000 for a TV blitz in the last 11 days of her campaign. She won by four percentage points.[217]

That $300,000 from Engler at the end could very well have changed the outcome of this election. It was a near thing.

---

217 Nancy Perry Graham, "The Best Judges Money Can Buy," *George*, December/January 2001, 90.

When the election was done, Justice Cavanagh was safely and solidly returned. Cliff Taylor was in for the two-year short ride, and new at the court was Maura D. Corrigan, Governor Engler's other chosen one.

Here's how it broke down for the two eight years seats:

Michael F. Cavanagh led the field with 1,443,218 votes, total money raised of $255,073, and with independent expenditures (IEs) of $6,890 from the Michigan Democratic State Central Committee.[218]

Maura D. Corrigan came in second with 1,085,725 votes, total money raised of $1,033,339 (almost a buck a vote), and IEs of $30,780 from the Michigan Republican State Central Committee.

I heard that Justice Maura Corrigan was the first person to have a million dollars. She was the first million-dollar baby. This was a new thing.

Third-place finisher Susan D. Borman tallied 904,947 votes, raised $663,183, and had IEs of $19,256.

Fourth-place went to Jeffrey G. Collins with 464,457 votes, $202,163 raised and IEs of $6,572 from the Michigan Republican State Committee.

Libertarian Jerry Kaufman came in fifth, receiving 221,414 votes. He raised nothing and there were no IEs.

Reform candidate Matthew Able came in sixth and captured 139,273 votes, raised no money and had no IEs.

Libertarian David Raaflaub came in last with 63,202 votes. He also raised zip and had no IEs.

For the two-year seat, Clifford W. Taylor received 1,221,306 votes (out-tallying Corrigan) and raised $986,566. *Almost a million dollars.*

His opponent, Carole F. Youngblood, gathered 1,037,868 votes, almost as many as Corrigan and more than fellow Democrat Susan Borman. She raised $592,297.

Taylor had IEs of $6,572 (the same as Collins but far less than Corrigan) and Youngblood had $6,890 (the same as Cavanaugh but far less than Borman).[219]

---

218 Barbara Moorhouse and Richard Robinson with David Hogg, 31-37.
219 Almost half of Corrigan's war chest came from political action committees—PACS. In addition to that $500,497, another $340,511 came from large individual donors. Chief among all of them were the Michigan Republican State Central Committee $64,144; Associated Builders and Contractors of MI/ABC PAC $34K; Michigan Bankers Association/MI BANK PAC $34K; Michigan Chamber of Commerce PAK $34K; Michigan Restaurant Association PAC $34K; Posthumus Leadership Fund $34K; Michigan State Medical Society/MI Doctors PC $33, 943; Blue Cross and Blue Shield of Michigan/BCBSM PAC $33K; Michigan Health and Hospital Association/Health PAC $32,500; and Detroit Regional Chamber PAC $30,500.

All this money has not gone unnoticed, nor—depending on your viewpoint—unlamented or unlauded. Writing in the *New York Times* in 2000, William Glaberson reported of the 1998 Supreme Court election:

> The politicking is becoming increasingly explicit. As the battle over liability laws has moved into the courts in the last few years, business groups and their trial lawyer adversaries have been increasingly open in describing the battle to win judgeships in bold political terms.
>
> In a newsletter last fall, for example, the Michigan Manufacturers Association[220] told its members about the importance of this year's state Supreme Court election. The newsletter flatly outlined the group's political goal. In the last election, it boasted, contributions from the manufacturers' political action committee "swayed the Supreme Court election to a conservative viewpoint, ensuring a pro-manufacturing agenda."[221]

Immediately after the election, there was a party for the victors. Weaver attended the state Republican "do" in Lansing. They were celebrating—among others—the victories of Corrigan and Engler. And it was there she received "the look."

At that time, I was just glad that Maura was elected because that wouldn't change anything; Mallett would still be there, right? So we just got one more person that's supposedly interested in reform. That's what I was interested in.

[Barbara Moorhouse and Richard Robinson with David Hogg, 33.]

Far and away most of her money came from manufacturing and other business interests, perhaps those affiliated with the Michigan Manufacturing Association. That was followed by finance, insurance, and real estate concerns.

Fully 65 percent of Cliff Taylor's funding came from large individual donors: $643,913. Small individual donors (making contributions of $200 or less) accounted for $141,318, and PAC funding totaled just $131,936. The bulk of his support came from lawyers and lobbyists, followed by manufacturing and business, and then support from the finance sector. [36]

Taylor's ten top contributors included the Michigan Republican State Central Committee $55K; Posthumus Leadership Fund $34K; Chrysler Corporation $30,950; PVS Chemicals $18,600; Ford Motor Company $16,425; General Motors Corporation $14,950; Amway Corporation $13,750; Michigan Health and Hospital Association/Health PAC $10K; Meijer, Inc. $8,450; and Clifford W. Taylor, himself $8,267.

To be fair, Michael Cavanagh's support came in the main from PACS and large individual donors: $106,146 and $88,280 respectively. His ten largest donors were Michigan Trial Lawyers Association/Justice PAC $34K; the United Auto Workers/UAW MI V PAC $34K; Sommers, Schwartz, Silver, and Schwartz, P.C. $25,449; Michigan Education Association/MEA PAC $10K; Michael F. Cavanagh himself $5K; Citizens for Public Education $5K; Archer's Vision for A Brighter Future $4,766; Sachs, Walman, O'Hare, Helveston, Bogas & McIntosh, P.C. $3,975; Joseph D. Reid $3,400; and Sueann Lyons Walz $3K. Most of his funding came from lawyers, lobbyists, and labor. [35]

220 John Engler would later land as president and CEO of the National Association of Manufacturers. January 2011, Engler was named the president of the Business Roundtable [BRT President, Business Roundtable, http://businessroundtable.org/about-us/brt-president/].
221 William Glaberson, "Fierce Campaigns Signal a New Era for State Court," *New York Times*, 5 June 2000, http://www.nytimes.com/2000/06/05/us/fierce-campaigns-signal-a-new-era-for-state-courts.html?scp=1&sq=William%20Glaberson,%20Fierce%20Campaigns%20Signal%20a%20New%20Era%20for%20State%20COurt,%20June%205,%202000&st=cse&pagewanted=2.

Weaver was circulating and looking around the room when she noticed the Governor studying her.

I just remember so vividly Engler's looking at me at that big party celebration when Maura was elected. And he looked at me with one of those looks that was very NOT happy. And as I'm talking to him, it occurs to me that he might be thinking: "The court will be 4-3 Republican. But Brickley and Weaver are the key votes and they are both independent and not controllable...either could vote for Mallett for chief justice and he'd be chief justice."

Or, perhaps he was having gas pains or indigestion.

I don't think so. I will not soon forget that look.

Whatever the Governor was thinking, the election was significant for several reasons, not least because it marked the first time a Michigan Supreme Court candidate raised more than a million dollars.

Maura got elected. That then meant that come January and the chief justice vote that there would be a shift from 4-3 Democrat to 4-3 Republican with Brickley and me as the key independent Republican votes.

Prior to that, Mallett had the votes from the Democratic side, because Maura's spot was Boyle's.

So, for the first time since 1976, the court was Republican. 4-3. But what Weaver didn't know that November election night and until early December was that the court was being readied to become more so: it was soon to go 5-2.[222]

So yes, somehow or other, Chief Justice Mallett was leaving, stepping down, heading off the bench. In October, he had been telling Weaver that he wasn't leaving.

And that changed from fall—October or so—to December, when he announced that he was going to resign and leave. He didn't tell me ahead of time.

Mallett made his announcement Dec. 5, 1998, and it would be, he said, effective Jan. 2, 1999.[223]

And I believe that he was enticed to go by Governor Engler.

Even Brian Dickerson, a well-known columnist of the *Free Press*, had said there was some kind of deal on the table with the Governor. Although he wrote he thought it was a pledge exacted by Mallett to have him replaced with another Black American from Detroit. The new guy would be the third such succeeding in that chair, lending credence to the concept that it was a legacy seat.[224]

222Judy Putnam with Ed Golder, "'Judicial conservative' named to high court; Robert P. Young, Jr. gives GOP a 5-2 majority next year." *Grand Rapids Press*, 31 December 1998, B4.

223Associated Press report, "Michigan top justice to resign," *Toledo Blade*, 12 December, 1998, 6, http://news.google.com/newspapers?nid=1350&dat=19981212&id=x0BPAAAAIBAJ&sjid=mgMEAAAAIBAJ&pg=5681,4199990.

224Brian Dickerson, "High Court Justices, politics can't stay apart," *Detroit Free Press*, 2 September 2010,

Following the 1998 election and Justice Mallett's resignation, the court moved to a 5-2 Republican balance. Here is the first court of 1999, from left: Justice Marilyn J. Kelly, Justice James H. Brickley, Justice Robert P. Young, Jr., Chief Justice Elizabeth A. Weaver, Justice Michael F. Cavanagh, Justice Clifford W. Taylor, and Justice Maura D. Corrigan.

An Associated Press account of his resignation quoted Mallett: "'This is an exciting, yet sad time for me,' Justice Mallett, 45, said. [...] He said he might run again for public office."[225]

Exciting but sad. Especially sad for Weaver.

I really didn't want him to leave. We were a great team. I was not yearning to be chief justice.

With Mallett's announcement, Weaver reflected on the look that John Engler had given her at the Republican election celebration. Was there even more to it than she had first imagined?

http://www.freep.com/article/20100902/COL04/9020388/High-court-justices-politics-can-t-stay-apart.
225 Ibid.

The "look" was early November. Maybe he knew at that time and had already talked to Mallett. I don't know when it all occurred, but obviously, Mallett and he discussed it between the time at the airport and it being announced publicly that Mallett was leaving.

Or, it might have been something else...a dawning recognition:

By the first week of December, Mallett's announcing that he's resigning, and Engler's saying that he's appointing Young. I do believe that Engler saw getting rid of him as a great way to put Robert Young on the court.

This would be the same Robert Preston Young, Jr. who Engler had put on the Court of Appeals in 1995. He was calling one up from the minor leagues. Here's the press release by John Truscott:

> Governor John Engler today named Court of Appeals Judge Robert P. Young, Jr. to be the 102nd jurist to serve on the Michigan Supreme Court. Young fills the vacancy created by the resignation of Chief Justice Conrad Mallett.
>
> "Today is a great day for justice, for the rule of law and for the people of Michigan," said Governor Engler." A brilliant scholar with a keen legal mind and a solid moral compass, Justice Young will make Michigan proud." Judge Young has served on the Court of Appeals for the 1st District of Michigan (Wayne, Monroe and Lenawee counties) since 1995. In 1996, he received more votes than any other appeals court candidate in the 1st District.
>
> Previously, Young was vice president, corporate secretary and general counsel of AAA Michigan. Prior to taking that position in 1992, he was a partner in the law firm of Dickinson, Wright, Moon, Van Dusen Freeman, where he practiced law for fifteen years. Young also served as a Michigan Civil Service Commissioner and as a member of the Board of Trustees of Central Michigan University.
>
> Young, 47, graduated cum laude with a Bachelor of Arts degree from Harvard College in 1974, and received his Juris Doctorate from the Harvard Law School in 1977. In addition to writing and teaching in his profession, Young has participated in a wide variety of professional and community activities, including the State Board of Law Examiners, various committees of the State and Federal Bar, the State Bar of Michigan, the Detroit Barristers Association, the Wolverine Bar Association, and the National and American Bar Associations.[226]

226 John Truscott, "Governor Engler Appoints Court of Appeals Judge Robert Young, Jr. to the Michigan Supreme Court; Praises Young as 'Brilliant Scholar' with 'Solid Moral Compass,'" 30 December 1998, http://www.state.mi.us/migov/gov/PressReleases/199812/Young.html.

There was more about his civic contributions. But for all that, he had no experience as a justice; this would all be new to him.

So at that point, guess who has to be the chief justice? It was apparent in their eyes that now I would be; I had to be the chief justice. And I knew it, because there would be no one else who was able to do it.

Wait! What?

It was hard enough work. I didn't have any desire to be the chief justice, but who else was available to do it? Maura's just walking in the door; Cliff certainly couldn't do it. He was not popular—he was lucky to get re-elected in 1998. Now he's gonna have to run in 2000. And because Mallett's leaving and Young is taking Mallett's seat, Young's going to have to run in 2000. So they're both up for re-election; they can't possibly be the chief justice. And certainly it wasn't going to be Kelly or Cavanagh; so who would it be?

Cliff told me, "You have to be the chief justice." And I remember thinking, "Yes, I do, but it's not because you're telling me I have to do it." He told me like, "That's your role now," you know? ..."That's what we're saying you have to do." He was probably representing what the Governor felt. For me it wasn't that. I knew I had to. I knew that I would have to be the chief justice because the reforms needed to continue. And I really was not happy that Mallett was leaving.

But he wasn't quite gone yet.

Mallett actually didn't go until after noon on the 1ˢᵗ of 1999. And exactly when he left is a little fuzzy. It's somewhat a little foggy as to when Justice Young's appointment got made. I tried to get records; I don't know that I have them. Young came on either January 2ⁿᵈ or the 3ʳᵈ. The date is not exact.

The Michigan Supreme Court Historical Society website notes it was Dec. 30, 1998, but that was also the date of the announcement by Governor Engler.[227] Was Young immediately sworn in?

It wouldn't matter: you can take the oath of office ahead of time, but it does not become effective until the office is vacant.

And Mallett himself said in the AP story of his resignation that it would be effective Jan. 2. Which was it? Or did Michigan have a supernumerary justice for several days?

An extra judge would be quite unconstitutional.

And why the discrepancy at the Michigan Supreme Court Historical Society website that shows both Mallett and Young on the court at the same time? Simply an error or obfuscation? The Michigan Manual also is imprecise on the matter.

---

227 On and Off the Court, Michigan Supreme Court Historical Society, http://www.micourthistory.org/on_and_off_the_court.php?on_off=1.

Weaver said one of the reasons probably had to do with Justice Mallett and his pension. In order to collect anything other than what he put in plus interest, Weaver explained it <u>might</u> have been that he needed eight complete years—January 1 through December 31—on the bench.[228] If that's the case, he needed to serve into 1999.

Mallett had to have eight years, and without any question, he would have eight years if he served through noon January 1.

So, for a day or a few days, Michigan might have had a delay in the swearing in or seating of its newest justice, or maybe even an unconstitutional supernumerary justice. Whichever way it rolled, it was, perhaps, part of the deal.

And then Mallett was off—and Young was on—the court. And it's possible that Young also needed the full year of 1999 for his future pension. That might explain the overlapping listing. But the reality was that Young came later to the court.

Exactly when, I'm not sure, but certainly after Maura because she always had seniority over him. Justice Corrigan came onto the Court for Justice Boyle one moment after noon of January 1, 1999, and Justice Young took office after her.

Weaver was elected chief justice Jan. 6. By that time, Young was definitely on the court.

And I think I was elected by Brickley's vote, my vote, Young's vote, Corrigan's vote, and also Taylor's vote. What Kelly and Cavanagh did, whether they voted for me or not, I don't remember. It wasn't contentious because it was presumed.

There was a little lapse before the office investiture of the newest justice, Robert P. Young, Jr. He had been summoned to the high court with little time to plan any ceremony.[229] Six weeks later, on Feb. 18, 1999, judges, justices, family, and friends, gathered for the official oath of office and speeches.

As the chief justice, Weaver offered a welcome:

> Isn't this just a magnificent gathering? It is such a happy occasion for us to be able to welcome officially to the Michigan Supreme Court our newest justice, Robert P. Young. I can tell you that he is a hard worker. We already have had a session of oral argument; his questions are prepared, interesting,

---

228 Ibid. In all, according to the Michigan Supreme Court Historical Society, Mallett served eight years and 12 days. Had he wanted to collect the maximum amount under that now-obviated retirement plan, Weaver said he would have needed to stay either 16 years and be 60 years old or stay 18 years and be 55. His eight full calendar years would give him something less than the maximum of 60 percent of his yearly salary (which was $124,770 in 1998) when it came time for him to retire.
229 While the Michigan Supreme Court Historical Society has a record of Young's investiture, it doesn't have one for Justice Corrigan.

and right to the point. With no further ado, I want to welcome our modera-
tor for this afternoon, Ms. Beth DunCombe.[230]

C. Beth DunCombe was president and CEO of Detroit Economic Growth Corp. (and
Detroit Mayor Dennis Archer's sister-in-law).

As introductions went, Weaver's welcome was restrained. Her assessment was based
only on what she'd seen on the bench.

For his part, Young promised to uphold the constitutions of the United States and
the State of Michigan in his oath of office administered by Damon Keith, judge of the
U.S. Sixth Circuit Court of Appeals. After an invocation by Reverend Nicholas Hood,
III, pastor of his home church, Plymouth United Church of Christ, speeches followed
by Oakland County attorney Harriet Rotter, Edsel Ford, Detroit Mayor and former
Supreme Court Justice Dennis Archer, Attorney General Jennifer Granholm, and
Governor John Engler. Finally, his audience heard from the state's newest justice.

Justice Young is erudite. His entire investiture speech is well worth reading. In these
selections, he offers an interesting look into his character.

> I am particularly gratified to be appointed by you, Governor Engler, because
> I know you have actually read my decisions, and you would be surprised at
> how uncharacteristic it is that an appointing Governor has ever read any-
> thing that their appointees have written. [...]

> On a personal note, I joined the judiciary a few years ago at some personal
> financial sacrifice to my family, but I did so because I believe in public ser-
> vice and because of my passion for the law. I come from a family whose fairly
> recent history has not always included the faith that equality under law ap-
> plied to us. Indeed, I share in common with Justice Mallett the fact that for
> all our fancy education and professional attainments, when we remove our
> judicial robes, our status is frequently uncertain. [...] You can't be who I am
> without being willing to take an unpopular course for the sake of a just prin-
> cipal. I am, above all I think, fiercely independent, and I believe that the law
> must be applied equally and justly to all. Thus, as a judge, I have been willing
> to go it alone when I have concluded that the law requires a course different
> than that followed by my fellow judges. [...] For the more than 20 years of my
> practice, I have been a consumer of the decisions of the Supreme Court, and
> for most of that time, the court has seemed to me to be less conscious that
> its decisions had to be applied by we mere mortals, by trial judges, lawyers,
> their clients, and the public at large, so that we could organize and plan our
> lives with a clear understanding of and conformity with the law [....]

230 "Swearing-in ceremony for Justice Robert P. Young, Jr., February 18, 1999," Michigan Supreme Court
Historical Society, http://www.micourthistory.org/special_sessions.php?get_id=45.

We are, my six colleagues and I, literally the custodians of the law. What we do or what we fail to do has far-reaching implications, not only for the individuals whose cases are before us, but for everyone in the state. Our decisions are the final word and largely unreviewable. Unquestionably, we must ensure that the law is applied equally without respect to who a particular person is, but the merit of her cause, and we must similarly ensure that the constitutional liberties we have enshrined in our state and federal constitutions are enforced and vigorously protected. I am concerned that over a period of time, the public has come to regard the judiciary as merely another public arena, an alternate forum in which to make public policy. However, our constitution assigns each of the three branches of government specific responsibilities, and each branch must jealously guard the boundaries that separate them. While the judiciary provides an important check on unconstitutional actions by the other two branches of government, I do not believe that the judiciary is an auxiliary legislature. Nor is the judiciary free to intervene in public policy decisions of the political branches and remake them.

[...] The people of Michigan have chosen to be governed by our state constitution, and I do not believe that the judiciary, no matter how well intentioned, should contravene that expression of the people's will.

Similarly, our statutes represent the will of the people as expressed through our elected representatives. Courts must be careful to avoid nullifying that will unless the legislation at issue is plainly unconstitutional. As a result, my judicial philosophy requires that I first give deference to the political branches of government, that is, the legislative and executive branches, by avoiding policymaking in the guise of deciding cases and by interpreting the constitution and statutes consistent with the plain meaning of their language. Second, that I consider the impact of my decisions beyond the case at hand. Third, that I craft decisions with concern for the ease with which they can be applied. And, fourth, that I decide cases on the narrowest basis possible in order to reduce the incidence of adverse, collateral, and perverse unintended consequences.[231]

It wouldn't necessarily work out that way. In the end, there were perverse—but intended—consequences. But it was clear that Young understood the power of court and intended to use it.

In his speech, Justice Young also gave thanks to Justice Mallett. After all, Mallett was his ticket to the bench.

Unfortunately this ceremony could not have been possible had my friend, the recently retired Chief Justice Mallett, not chosen to re-enter the private sector and rejoin his old firm, Miller Canfield. Justice Mallett ably led this

---

231 Ibid.

court and the judicial branch of government during a very difficult time of change and reorganization. He did so with his accustomed grace, charm, and intelligence. I think we all owe him a debt of gratitude for his many accomplishments and contributions, and it is my great regret that I cannot serve on this court with him.[232]

And while Young may have felt gratitude, the Democrats definitely didn't. They were not pleased.

And, remember, the Democrats weren't asking Mallett to leave. In fact, his name became mud. The Democrats were convinced that he betrayed them. Before that, Mallett had been seen as an up-and-coming young Democrat star. And many, many Democrats concluded with his leaving that Engler had taken over the court.

There was even a cartoon in the *Detroit Free Press* that showed John Engler leading a choir of Supreme Court justices—Taylor, Corrigan, Young, and Weaver—singing the right (and right-wing) song under his direction. The illustration was titled "Johnny Engler and the Supremes."

While she disputed the accuracy of the *Free Press* editorial page cartoon, Weaver thought it clever and well done. Governor Engler is leading his vocal group through its paces. From left are justices Cliff Taylor, Maura Corrigan, Robert P. Young, Jr., and Elizabeth Weaver. (*Detroit Free Press.*)

---

232 Ibid.

It's interesting that Brickley was not in it. He was NOT in the Engler camp by any stretch of the imagination. He was never an Engler fan or follower.

Neither was I, but that was the perception, especially by the Democrats. I didn't like it, but I thought the cartoon was quite amusing. I got and kept a copy of it because I enjoy political satire whether it's right or not. I knew it wasn't true, but people thought I was in the choir because I hadn't yet had to take on Engler.

All this because Conrad Mallett wanted to leave. And make no mistake: Mallett had been a rising young star and was talked of as a possible potential mayor for Detroit or a future Governor. He was only 37 when he was appointed to the Michigan Supreme Court by Governor Jim Blanchard. Weaver says that may not have been the best time for him to come to the court.

He came too early. Where else was there for him to go in the courts? He seemed not inclined and was not likely going to be appointed to a federal district judgeship, the U.S. Sixth Circuit Court of Appeals, or the U.S. Supreme Court.

So, when he left the court, Mallett signed on as a partner with Miller, Canfield, Paddock & Stone. He'd worked there earlier as an associate from 1980 to 1983.[233]

Weaver is grateful for the time they had on the bench, and she values a gift Mallett gave her at his departure from the court.

And in the book on Thurgood Marshall[234] that he gave me in leaving, he inscribed in it that I had been his co-captain for almost two years, and that we had almost won the game; but that we would win, and then he said, "I love you." I was very fond of him, in a perfectly businesslike way. There was a deep appreciation for his being willing to stand up and fight for these principles of reform.

Then so we each went on—my intention was that the court would continue with reform. And, in retrospect, I don't believe that Governor Engler was interested in the reforms I was interested in. I think he was interested in taking over the court.

And she'd find out to what degree in short order.

And as far as Young was concerned, Weaver says his coming to the court brought one of the best minds in decades.

Often he and I would come to the same conclusion...as long as I didn't let him know where I stood before he reached his. There is no doubt to me that he is a gifted legal scholar and a most able thinker. And that's what makes all this that much more tragic.

233 Jeffrey McCracken, "Mallett may exit Miller, Canfield, for DMC," *Crain's Detroit Business,* 5 July 1999, http://www.crainsdetroit.com/article/19990705/SUB/907050882.
234 The book was Juan Williams' *Thurgood Marshall: American Revolutionary*, Times Books, Random House (New York), October 1998.

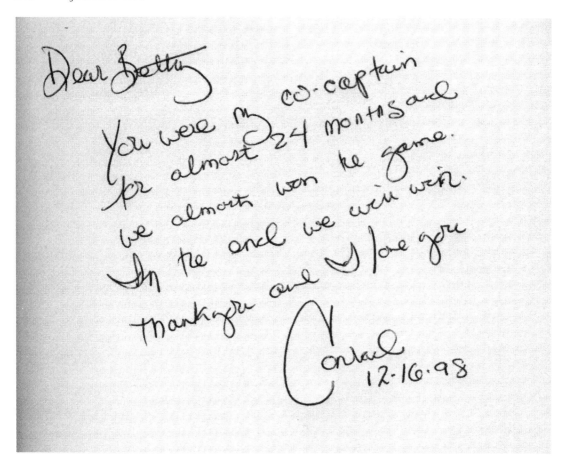

In this inscription of Juan Williams' Thurgood Marshall: American Revolutionary, Mallett wrote to Weaver: "Dear Betty: You were my co-captain for almost 24 months and we almost won the game. In the end we will win. Thank you and I love you. Conrad 12-16-98."

Chapter 6

Does One Dare Speak His Mind?

Justice Young and *Brown v Board*;
Justice Taylor Goes After Ford;
An Unsatisfactory Investigation

In the *fin de siècle* Supreme Court, things were heating up.

Now, by February or March, I met with Taylor and Young because they had already gotten into difficulties. Young had gotten all kinds of people in an uproar about him just after he'd been invested—where Dennis Archer said how outstanding he was. Then, Young talked about Brown v Board *as a wrongly reasoned case.*

Young was quoted as saying to a group of trial lawyers that the case had been "wrongly decided," a phrase he'd later have to explain.[235] Young reportedly had made and repeated his position on several occasions.

His comments could not have been better fodder for his critics. At issue was the 1954 U.S. Supreme Court decision that struck down school segregation. To have a sitting state Supreme Court justice criticize it was anathema to many, and for the justice to be the only African American on his court was beyond the pale.

The immediate reaction against him built until it became an issue in the 2000 election and beyond.

At a dinner for the NAACP that spring, the Michigan Democratic Party passed out flyers critical of Young and his statement. Young reacted.

> According to a press release issued by Marketing Resource Group, Inc., and paid for by Young's campaign committee, Young sent a letter to Democratic

---

235 Nancy Perry Graham, "The Best Judges Money Can Buy," *George*, December/January 2001, 77.

Party Chairman Mark Brewer,[236] insisting on a retraction of "outright lies" in the flyer.

Young asserted that the flyer falsely accused him of being a "[s]taunch believer that *Brown v Board of Education* was wrong" and of "guilt by association" because Young is a member of the Federalist Society, which "believes that *Brown v Board of Education*, outlawing racial segregation in schools, was wrong and seeks to overturn this historic advancement in civil rights."

In his letter demanding a retraction, Young said that he has "always supported *Brown*, publicly and privately" and that the flyer "is nothing more than an attempt to create an ugly, racist campaign to impugn me as Michigan's only sitting African American justice."[237]

According to Mark Behrens and Cary Silverman, writing later in the *Cornell Journal of Law and Public Policy*, the event resulted in Young accusing "the NAACP of race baiting."[238] Behrens and Silverman referenced William Glaberson, writing in the *New York Times*:

In an interview, Justice Young said he had long publicly supported the desegregation ruling. He asserted that he had said he simply shared the views of some critics who say it was based "too much on sociology."

His public response, Justice Young said, was "a moral call to conscience about whether race baiting has any role in the political discourse in a judicial election."

In an interview, Mr. Brewer, the Democratic chairman, said there would be no retraction and that civil rights would continue to be an issue. "It is not a lie," Mr. Brewer said of the flier's description of Justice Young's views. "It is true. He has told a number of people throughout Michigan that *Brown v Board of Education* was 'wrongly decided.' Those were his exact words."[239]

In an editorial, the *Detroit Free Press* weighed in:

The indignant reaction of Justice Robert Young might seem less intemperate if he hadn't invited this kind of attack. Young prides himself on his conservative judicial philosophy and associates with elements of the legal com-

236 Mark Brewer served as the Michigan Democratic Party Chair from 1995 until 2013, when he was replaced by Lon Johnson.
237 Briefly Speaking, "Supreme Court Justice Seeks Retraction," *Michigan Lawyers Weekly*, 15 May 2000, http://milawyersweekly.com/news/2000/05/15/supreme-court-justice-seeks-retraction/.
238 Mark A. Behrens and Cary Silverman, "The case for adopting appointive judicial selection systems for state court judges," *Cornell Journal of Law and Public Policy*, Volume 11, Number 2, Spring 2002, 284, http://www.shb.com/attorneys/SilvermanCary/TheCaseforAdoptingAppointive_2002.pdf.
239 William Glaberson, "Fierce Campaigns Signal a New Era for State Court," *New York Times*, 5 June 2000, http://www.nytimes.com/2000/06/05/us/fierce-campaigns-signal-a-new-era-for-state-courts.html?scp=1&sq=William%20Glaberson,%20Fierce%20Campaigns%20Signal%20a%20New%20Era%20for%20State%20COurt,%20June%205,%202000&st=cse&pagewanted=2.

munity that hold views on civil rights that are antithetical to the NAACP, host of the huge dinner where Democrats distributed the anti-Young pamphlet. His howls of protest also seem a bit excessive, considering that Young was part of the recent Supreme Court majority that overturned a judicial conduct rule for campaigns on the grounds of free speech. The justices said an exchange of ideas and meaningful debate should not be quelled—even if a candidate finds some of the campaign material objectionable.

[...]

Young does not take issue with the results of [the *Brown v Board*] decision, and acknowledges that, as a minority, he has benefited from it. But he has on several occasions questioned the reasoning behind it. The justice told the *Free Press* editorial board that *Brown* was based on "'sociology'—which should be left to sociologists—and not the law."

This is the same rationale other conservatives have used to chip away at *Brown*'s legal foundation.[240]

There are critics aplenty of how the decision was rendered. The Federalist Society, a conservative group that included all of the Republican Justices then on the Michigan Supreme Court (including Weaver), lists in its cannon books that are critical of the judicial reasoning in the case.[241] Many of its members are critical of the opinion "as have [been] a wide range of legal scholars and commentators."[242]

Nancy Perry Graham spoke with Young about the incident that gave rise to the flap. She reported her analysis in *George*:

Sitting in his office, he insisted that he was criticizing the reasoning the court used to support its result, not the result itself. "It's hard to consider that an African-American would want to return to the Jim Crow era," he said.[243]

Maybe unleashing his thoughts at a meeting of trial lawyers wasn't the wisest place to make such a comment.

It was totally unnecessary to talk about; it wasn't an issue anywhere.

Common sense would indicate that was so, but a source in Glaberson's reportage might disagree...there could have been a point to it all, or at least a point to be capitalized upon:

240 Editorial, "Justice Young Protests over Campaign Literature seem injudicious," *Detroit Free Press*, A.6, 12 May 2000.
241 "Conservative and Libertarian Legal Scholarship: Constitutional Law," The Federalist Society, http://www.fed-soc.org/resources/page/conservative-libertarian-legal-scholarship-constitutional-law.
242 "Reducing Injudiciousness in Judicial Elections," Brennan Center for Justice, New York University School of Law, 2 July 2004, http://www.brennancenter.org/content/resource/reducing_injudiciousness_in_judicial_elections/
243 Nancy Perry Graham, "The Best Judges Money Can Buy."

Some of the court's critics say that despite the vitriol over the landmark civil rights case, the real issue is the court's reputation as a harshly conservative panel that regularly sides with business, prosecutors and insurance companies. The critics say Justice Young's reaction may have been partly to distract attention from criticism of the court.

One source of that criticism was an analysis of 57 of the court's rulings last year. The analysis was published in a union newspaper, *Michigan A.F.L.-C.I.O. News*, and then described in a newspaper for Michigan lawyers, *Lawyers Weekly*.

In an interview, the article's author, Mary Ellen Gurewitz, the general counsel of the Michigan A.F.L.-C.I.O. and the State Democratic Party, said the results were "stunningly one-sided" with criminal defendants, for example, losing 15 out of 15 cases decided by the Michigan Supreme Court. People claiming injuries lost 12 out of 13 cases she examined.

Several of the Republican justices have countered that Ms. Gurewitz's analysis was a politically motivated attack on the court and a manipulation of statistics.[244]

Even if Young was seeking only to deflect criticism of the court through the dustup, there was a cost.

And he was in difficulty.

Even so, Young continued and continues to expound on the matter. When the Federalist Society organized a conference in 2004 around the 50th anniversary of the Supreme Court opinion in *Brown v Board*, one of the speakers was Justice Young.[245]

Going After Jim Ford

Young wasn't the only one feeling some heat because of something he said or did. Justice Taylor caught some of his own because of his penchant for what he saw as the need for revenge. In this case, he wanted to punish an attorney who had the temerity to say what he thought about a decision of the high court.

The matter at hand involved the death of motorcyclist Richard Husted, who had been struck and killed by Henry Dobbs. Dobbs was driving his employer's truck, which turned out to be uninsured. And while the truck had been uninsured, Dobbs had his own insurance through Auto Owners Insurance Co. *Michigan Lawyers Weekly* summarized the case:

---

244 William Glaberson, "Fierce Campaigns Signal a New Era for State Court."
245 2004 National Lawyers Convention, "Celebrating Brown v Board of Education's Promise of Equality: How Well Are We Doing Fifty Years Later?," Federalist Society, 11 November 2004, http://www.fed-soc. org/publications/page/2004-national-lawyers-convention-celebrating-brown-v-board-of-educations-promise-of-equality-how-well-are-we-doing-fifty-years-later.

Auto-Owners determined that this [business use] exclusion applied and refused to provide coverage or to defend Dobbs in the wrongful death suit. Consequently, Dobbs did not appear at hearings in the wrongful death action and a default judgment was entered against him for $1.25 million.

Dobbs then sued Auto-Owners in Kalamazoo County Circuit Court. He claimed that Auto-Owners breached its duty to defend him and acted in bad faith by refusing to settle the wrongful death claim. Dobbs moved for summary disposition, arguing that the policy's business-use exclusion was ambiguous and that public policy required Auto-Owners to provide "portable" residual liability coverage when a policyholder has an accident while driving another's uninsured vehicle.

Auto-Owners also moved for summary disposition, arguing that the exclusionary clause was enforceable and not against public policy.

The trial court granted Auto-Owners' motion. The Court of Appeals affirmed in an unpublished opinion. The Supreme Court denied leave to appeal.

Thereafter, plaintiff Marcia Husted, personal representative of the decedent's estate, filed a writ of garnishment against Auto-Owners. Auto-Owners moved for, and was granted, summary disposition. The trial court held that Michigan's no-fault act did not require Auto-Owners to provide residual liability coverage that "travels with" a policyholder.

The Court of Appeals affirmed. The Supreme Court initially denied leave to appeal, but later granted Dobbs' motion for reconsideration. The high court remanded the case to the trial court for additional fact finding. The Supreme Court then granted leave to appeal.[246]

James B. Ford, of Kalamazoo, was the attorney for Marcia Husted. "[I] argued that the Michigan No Fault Statute required Auto Owners to insure Dobbs whenever he drove 'a motor vehicle,' not just his own vehicle."[247]

Justice Taylor wrote the opinion denying Ford's argument. And Taylor's reasoning hinged on the meaning of that "a," said Ford:

Justice Taylor had previously written several opinions holding that "a" means "any," but he refused to apply that reasoning when it would work against an insurance company.[248]

Weaver signed on to Taylor's opinion, as did Corrigan and Young. Kelly wrote the dissent and was joined by Brickley and Cavanaugh, all three calling the decision "unconscionable."

246 Traci R. Gentilozzi, "Ins. Co. Not Obligated To Provide Residual Coverage; 'Business-use' Exclusion Not Against Public Policy," *Michigan Lawyers Weekly*, 10 May 1999, http://milawyersweekly.com/news/1999/05/10/ins-co-not-obligated-to-provide-residual-coverage/.
247 James B. Ford, e-mail to co-author Schock, 29 February 2012.
248 Ibid.

The case[249] was problematic for several reasons, not least because of what was in process: a change in justices. At the time it was argued, Oct. 8, 1998, Justices Boyle and Mallett were still on the court, Justice Corrigan was not yet elected, and Justice Young was still a gleam in Governor Engler's eye.

"This was a $4 million case. And I was told later by a lawyer who claimed to know, that after oral arguments, I won the first vote 5 to 2," said Ford.[250]
The two against would have been Taylor and Weaver.

"Then when Justice Corrigan was elected, the vote went to 4 to 3, and when Young was appointed to replace Justice Mallett in January the plaintiff lost 3 to 4."

And then came *Michigan Lawyers Weekly* looking for Ford's reaction to the ruling. A former Air Force pilot who flew 65 combat missions as a flight commander in Vietnam,[251] Ford did not soft pedal his thoughts:

> [T]he ruling was "completely political" and "makes no sense when compared to the language and history of the no-fault statute." [...]

> "This is almost an absurd decision on its face," Ford commented. "And until widows and orphans can donate as much money as insurance companies [to judicial campaigns], we'll continue to see these types of decisions."

> Ford also emphasized that he argued this case in October 1998, when Conrad Mallett was chief justice of the Supreme Court. Accordingly, Ford noted that the plaintiff likely would have prevailed if the decision would have been rendered before Mallett's resignation from the court in December 1998.[252]

Ford soon found himself looking down the barrel of an Attorney Grievance Commission complaint. A reminder, the AGC is that body that brings to heel straying attorneys. Most often a complaint is kept quiet. The AGC doesn't make public the fact that it is investigating an attorney. Almost no lawyer wants his clients and fellow attorneys to know that he or she is being investigated for possible infringement on the code of conduct. In fact, the only time the AGC would release information about an attorney would be when it found cause for disciplinary measures.

And there was initially a quiet way out, said Ford.

> I was really surprised that a grievance had been filed over it. It was the last thing I had in mind. I was simply speaking from the heart when I was commenting on the case.

249 *Husted v Dobbs*, No. 104447, Michigan Supreme Court, 27, April 1999, http://courts.mi.gov/opinions_orders/case_search/pages/default.aspx?SearchType=1&CaseNumber=104447&CourtType_CaseNumber=1
250 James B. Ford, e-mail to co-author Schock, 29 February 2012.
251 "Ford, James B." FindLaw, http://pview.findlaw.com/view/1411091_1.
252 Traci R. Gentliozzi, "Ins. Co. Not Obligated To Provide Residual Coverage."

They made a number of offers to me. If I would simply apologize everything would be forgiven. Once they grieved me, though, I was willing to see it through to the end. But I had not intended that or wanted it when I started out.[253]

Ford didn't care about quiet. In the first place, the grievance didn't pass the smell test, starting with the complainant, Eric Doster.

> The general counsel of the Michigan Republican Party [...] filed [the] grievance against me, and the [Attorney] Grievance Commission took a very aggressive stance toward the whole situation. They asked me questions about my personal and political beliefs, my opinions, my fees and billing in this case and any intentions I might have to run for political office in the future. They told me that the answers to these questions would be shared with the Republican Party's general counsel.

> All of this [happened] despite clear U.S. Supreme Court opinions that give attorneys the same free-speech rights as anyone else, once a case is over.[254]

And why would the AGC share all the information it gathered with the complainant? The rules, said Richard L. Cunningham,[255] the attorney at the AGC who handled the case. Cunningham, a former Wayne County Prosecutor (1984-1991)[256] and a Detroit Recorder's Court judge,[257] explained it this way: "[T]he rules clearly say that the AGC is supposed to provide the information to the complainant, not to the grieved attorney."[258]

That's an odd way to do business and seems to give a distinct advantage to the complainant. Ford commented about that:

> And the complainant in this case was anything but neutral. He was the general counsel for the Michigan Republican Party, and admitted that he discussed the case with Justice Taylor before he filed the grievance.[259]

Might Taylor have suggested that Doster file the grievance? Other lawyers came to that conclusion, in an article in *Michigan Lawyers Weekly*: "It is widely suspected that

---

253 James B. Ford, telephone interview with co-author Schock, 27 February 2012.
254 C. Jesse Green, "1999 Lawyers of the Year; James B. Ford, Kalamazoo," *Michigan Lawyers Weekly*, 27 December 1999, http://milawyersweekly.com/news/1999/12/27/1999-lawyers-of-the-year-113799/.
255 Cunningham also was a Vietnam veteran, a combat infantryman. Later he served as an instructor at Fort Benning, Georgia. ["Election 2008 Michigan Voter Guide," *Detroit News*, http://apps.detnews.com/apps/election_guide/index.php?requestType-lookup&lookupType-Judges&all_candidates_id-460.]
256 "Fifteen candidates seek Wayne Circuit judgeships," *The Observer*, 7 November 1994, 6A, http://www.cantonpl.org/sites/default/files/observer/1994/11_Nov%201994/11-07-1994.pdf.
257 Patrick Keating, "Richard Cunningham seeks judicial seat," *Michigan Chronicle*, 30 July 2008, B.5.
258 Richard L. Cunningham quoted in C. Jesse Green, "Cunningham Speaks On Handling Of Ford Grievance;
Attorneys, Including State Bar Officials, 'Don't Have A Clue,'" *Michigan Lawyers Weekly*, 21 February 2000, http://milawyersweekly.com/news/2000/02/21/cunningham-speaks-on-handling-of-ford-grievance/.
259 James B. Ford, e-mail to co-author Schock, 29 February 2012.

Eric Doster had been requested, directly or indirectly, by Justice Taylor to file the grievance against attorney Ford."[260]

It was possible, said Weaver:

Somebody likely called Doster...or he called somebody. I know Doster, and it's not like him to have done this unless he discussed it with somebody.

But would that somebody have been Taylor?

He would have been very upset and he must have made remarks about it. But whether it was Taylor, or Lucille Taylor, or somebody else I don't know.... But this is the way they worked. Cliff used to say "Call So-and-So," or he'd tell me that he called somebody to take care of things. Over the years, I listened as they'd call people and have somebody else do it. That's the way they operate.

Doster denied it: "The grievance speaks for itself. Don't try to read anything into it. And don't try to say that anyone asked me to do it because that isn't the case, I assure you."[261]

Cunningham, of the AGC, also later denied the possibility:

> Absolutely not. I don't believe that. I saw nothing to support that. Eric Doster is experienced in disciplinary matters. He serves on hearing panels and he is on the ethics committee at his law firm. I can accept his explanation that he filed this grievance because this was the most outrageous comment he had seen in the press.[262]

Really? "Most outrageous"? Remember, Ford responded to the opinion in *Husted v Auto Owners* and the funding that insurance companies provided for political campaigns. He made no *ad hominem* attacks on Taylor, used no rough language. How does it compare to Governor John Engler's comments when he decided to warm the backside of Ingham County Circuit Court Judge James Giddings?

> James B. Ford's claim that his comments to the media are constitutionally protected is not the first time the argument has been made: Governor John Engler, a member of the Michigan Bar, asserted that same argument when he was investigated for derogatory comments he made about Ingham County Circuit Court Judge James Giddings.

260 C. Jesse Green, "Justice Takes Road Trip; Taylor Talks To Jim Ford's Hometown Paper," 13 December 1999, http://milawyersweekly.com/news/1999/12/13/justice-takes-road-trip/.
261 C. Jesse Green, "Many Fear 'Chill' From Grievance Over Remarks; Lawyers Rally In Support, State Bar Neutral," *Michigan Lawyers Weekly*, 25 October 1999, http://milawyersweekly.com/news/1999/10/25/many-fear-chill-from-grievance-over-remarks/.
262 C. Jesse Green, "Cunningham Speaks On Handling Of Ford Grievance; Attorneys, Including State Bar Officials, 'Don't Have A Clue,'" *Michigan Lawyers Weekly*, 21 February 2000, http://milawyersweekly.com/news/2000/02/21/cunningham-speaks-on-handling-of-ford-grievance/.

The Attorney Grievance Commission investigated Engler—at Giddings' request—after the Governor publicly called the judge a "lunatic" who "got his law degree from a mail-order school" in October 1993. The comments, made after Giddings ruled against the Department of Corrections in a prisoners' rights case, were widely reported by the media.

Engler, a Republican, responded to the AGC investigation in writing, asserting that his remarks were made in his capacity as head of the executive branch and were also protected by the First Amendment.

"[A]n attorney cannot be professionally sanctioned for exercising a constitutional right," the Governor wrote, citing case law to support that proposition.

Engler further said he viewed the complaint to the AGC based on the exercise of his constitutional rights "as intended to chill or curtail those constitutional rights."

Moreover, Engler cautioned the AGC about "being manipulated in this manner" and suggested that the commission "adopt a posture consistent with the [F]irst [A]mendment and summarily reject these complaints."[263]

And for his personal attack, Engler faced no sanctions:

A request for investigation was dismissed after Mr. Engler, through Justice Clifford Taylor's wife, Lucille, warned the Attorney Grievance Commission about being politically manipulated and suggesting that the Attorney Grievance Commission "adopt a posture consistent with the First Amendment and summarily reject these complaints." The Attorney Grievance Commission, in the letter dismissing the complaint, even offered to provide assistance to Engler in the future.[264]

Further, noted Ford, Justice Taylor had used the same kind of language himself:

...I went back through Justice Taylor's previous dissents, and found one, when he was in the minority, where he himself had described a majority opinion as absurd.[265]

And Taylor hadn't been threatened with a trip to the Judicial Tenure Commission, the sister agency of the AGC that's intended for wayward judges (including justices).

---

263 Traci R. Gentilozzi, "Free Speech Claim Already Successful; Governor Cried 'First Amendment,'" *Michigan Lawyers Weekly*, 25 October 1999, http://milawyersweekly.com/news/1999/10/25/freespeech-claim-already-successful/.
264 Michael Alan Schwartz, letter to the editor, "Where Were Bar Members When Fieger Spoke Out?" *Michigan Lawyers Weekly*, 7 February 2000, http://milawyersweekly.com/news/2000/02/07/where-were-bar-members-when-fieger-spoke-out063/.
265 James Ford, *I Lived in Those Times*, Fortitude Publishing (Kalamazoo, Mich.) 2009, 551.

So why even bother with Ford if the issue was already clearly defined? Why would Ford face the AGC for a perceived transgression of much smaller magnitude than the Governor's? From Ford's viewpoint it was simple:

> It was intended as intimidation against lawyers who would criticize the court. They wanted to send a message to the rest of the Bar that you'd better not say anything critical of this court. And for Doster, it was political. He wanted Republicans to retain control and he didn't want anyone to criticize what they did.[266]

Further, said Ford, the AGC indicated to him that it was serious in taking up the matter:

> The AGC has the authority to ignore frivolous grievances, but they did not do so in this case. Instead, when Mr. Cunningham of the AGC contacted me, he informed me they would be playing "hardball" with me on this issue.[267]

Cunningham never denied the "hardball" comment, but he later did deny ever speaking directly with Ford in this matter, saying he worked only through Ford's attorney, Detroit's Ken Mogill.[268]

Mogill had a reputation as a grievance fighter and Ford said he helped out for the good of the cause.

> My out-of-pocket cost was virtually none. Ken Mogill did this for free because he felt so strongly about it. It was quite demanding in terms of time. And, it of course is an aggravation and a great distraction. But at the same time, it was a battle that I was pretty willing to engage in because I felt so strongly about it.[269]

The matter resulted in weekly articles and letters to the editor of the *Michigan Lawyers Weekly*. In one of those missives, a group of Kalamazoo lawyers lionizing Ford, joined in:

> We are not going to stand by idly and watch Ford fight this battle alone. As we understand his statements, we are in complete agreement with him. Not only was the opinion in *Husted v Auto Owners* absurd, it was unconscionable.

> [...]

266 James. B. Ford, telephone interview, 27 February 2012.
267 C. Jesse Green, "1999 Lawyers of the Year; James B. Ford, Kalamazoo," *Michigan Lawyers Weekly*, 27 December 1999, http://milawyersweekly.com/news/1999/12/27/1999-lawyers-of-the-year-113799/.
268 C. Jesse Green, "Cunningham Speaks On Handling Of Ford Grievance; Attorneys, Including State Bar Officials, 'Don't Have A Clue,'" *Michigan Lawyers Weekly*, 21 February 2000, http://milawyersweekly.com/news/2000/02/21/cunningham-speaks-on-handling-of-ford-grievance/.
269 James. B. Ford, telephone interview, 27 February 2012.

The outcome of the case was predictable based upon the political make up of the Supreme Court. It is our guess that nine out of 10 lawyers in this state could have predicted that justices Taylor, Weaver, Corrigan and Young would vote to rule in favor of Auto Owners.

Finally, it is our assumption that the political make up of the Supreme Court will remain the same or become even more predisposed to the agenda of the Engler wing of the Republican Party until adequate financial contributions are made by the opposition.

Benjamin Franklin is said to have made the following statement to the other members of the founding fathers immediately before the signing of the Declaration of Independence: "We must all hang together, or assuredly we shall hang separately."

We are going to hang with Jim Ford. We invite any of our colleagues who has the courage of his or her conviction to join us.[270]

Twenty-seven Kalamazoo-area attorneys signed, inviting their own AGC investigation. It didn't stop there. A full page *Detroit Free Press* ad followed with the signatures of 100 Detroit attorneys.[271]

One of the issues was this: the AGC is a commission of the Michigan Supreme Court. How can you have the appearance of complete objectivity in such a case? Ford raised the issue in a letter to the editor:

[...] I do believe that members of the Bar should be alarmed that the Grievance Commission, operating in secret as an agent of the Supreme Court, can attempt to intimidate and inhibit debate on matters of public policy in which the Supreme Court Justices and members of the Grievance Commission itself have established a personal and financial interest.[272]

In a subsequent interview, Ford drew the noose a little tighter:

It is also worth noting that the members of the AGC serve at the will of the Supreme Court. Perhaps that is the reason why Mr. Cunningham and several members of the commission donated substantial amounts of money to Republican candidates in the 1998 election.[273]

---

270 Letter to the editor, "Attorneys Support Colleague In Grievance Case," *Michigan Lawyers Weekly*, 27 September 1999, http://milawyersweekly.com/news/1999/09/27/attorneys-support-colleague-in-grievance-case/.

271 James Ford, *I Lived in Those Times*, Fortitude Publishing (Kalamazoo, Mich.) 2009, 551.

272 James B. Ford, letter to the editor, "AGC Members 'Secret Agent' Of Supreme Court Of Michigan," *Michigan Lawyers Weekly*, 11 October 1999, http://milawyersweekly.com/news/1999/10/11/agc-members-secret-agents-of-supreme-court-of-michigan/.

273 C. Jesse Green.

The issue kept getting press. In the end, said Ford: "I'm told Engler intervened and said 'They're just beating the hell out of us and you have to drop it.' And they did."[274]

On October 28, 1999, the AGC officially gave it up. But even then, it wasn't a clean "drop" when the AGC dismissed the grievance.

> The AGC's letter also cautioned Ford against "making false statements" criticizing judges.
>
> [...]
>
> Ford took exception to the AGC's warning and its statements regarding insurance companies.
>
> "I might be putting myself back out on a limb," Ford told *Lawyers Weekly*, "but these issues are important and they need to be addressed."
>
> In his response, Ford told the AGC, "There is good reason to believe that insurance companies are violating both the letter and the spirit of MCL 500.2074 which prohibits them from making either direct or indirect political contributions."
>
> Ford also made specific allegations regarding insurance money and judicial elections, referring to "laundered" funds, political action committees (PACs) and individual contributions, which he claimed are connected to the insurance industry.
>
> Mogill also responded in writing to the AGC, supporting the accuracy of Ford's remarks.
>
> But Mogill also questioned the AGC as to why it addressed Ford's comments about insurance companies in the first place.
>
> "[T]he accuracy or inaccuracy of Jim's comments about insurance company contributions is irrelevant to the commission's business," he wrote.
>
> "[T]he accuracy or inaccuracy of a statement about whether an insurance company is making improper campaign contributions is a comment on the company's integrity, *not* that of a judge," Mogill stated in his letter.[275]

In essence, the AGC gave Ford yet another platform to flog Taylor, Doster, the insurance companies, the elective system, and the AGC. It was the gift that kept on giving: "I went to the newspapers with everything," Ford said. "I released their letter."[276]

---

274 James B. Ford, telephone interview, 22 February 2012.
275 C. Jesse Green, "Grievance Over Attorney's Critical Comments Dismissed But Lawyers Say Free-Speech Issue Will Linger, *Michigan Lawyers Weekly*, 8 November 1999, http://milawyersweekly.com/news/1999/11/08/grievance-over-attorneys-critical-comments-dismissed/
276 James B. Ford, telephone interview, 27 February 2012.

And there was more critical coverage in the Dec. 6 edition of *Michigan Lawyers Weekly*:

> The Republican-dominated "new" Michigan Supreme Court has proven to be one of the most controversial in years and some attorneys say that the court's rulings in 1999 lend credence to criticism that it has engaged in "unprecedented" activity, has an "agenda" and has become "too political."

> [...] According to Detroit attorney Kenneth M. Mogill, the Supreme Court itself is responsible for the "bad press" it's getting.

> "What makes this year's Supreme Court decisions so striking is that people's fears have been so thoroughly born out," Mogill said. "We predicted that the court would run roughshod over the rules. Well, we were optimistic."

> Kalamazoo lawyer James B. Ford made similar observations.

> "There is little doubt that something very different is occurring this year, as compared to last year," he said.[277]

Taylor wasn't buying it, and Young chimed, in, too, responding to the issue.

> But Justice Clifford W. Taylor told *Lawyers Weekly* that attacks such as these are political.

> The Michigan Democratic Party "will use anything, will distort and misrepresent anything, to bring the court into disrepute," he observed.
> Justice Robert P. Young, Jr., agreed.

> "I am troubled by the lack of skepticism," he told *Lawyers Weekly*. "The very notion that any court—much less the Supreme Court—ought to be deciding cases on the basis of who won last is absurd."

> Taylor also criticized the State Bar of Michigan in regard to the recent attacks on the high court.

> "The leaders of the State Bar seem to be so timid in dealing with it," he said.

> "The State Bar leaders are timorously lurking on the sidelines, worried about which 'side' to take."[278]

For Ford, it came back to insurance company contributions. In a subsequent interview in *Michigan Lawyers Weekly*, he expanded on the case he had made about their seeming violation of the state's law. In large part, he was able to make his point and people

---

277 C. Jesse Green, "Decisions From The 'New' MSC During 1999; Some Say Bias; Others Say It's 'Just Politics,'" *Michigan Lawyers Weekly*, 6 December 1999, http://milawyersweekly.com/news/1999/12/06/decisions-from-the-new-msc-during-1999/.
278 Ibid.

were eager to hear it because a Supreme Court justice (or, as we'll learn, justices) had singled him out for such special attention.

Ford again noted his belief that the insurance companies were violating MCL 500.2074, which outlaws contributions to political parties or persons. He told *Michigan Lawyers Weekly*:

> [Insurance companies] certainly make political contributions indirectly in a variety of ways, through their PACs [political action committees], their executives, their attorneys, and as I point out in my [response] letter [to the AGC] through the organizations they belong to.
>
> The Michigan Bureau of Elections reported that Justice Taylor, for example, received a direct contribution in the amount of $2,500 from Blue Cross/Blue Shield on Sept. 29, 1998. Whether this was a violation of the law or simply a reporting error, I cannot say. I pointed this out to the AGC.
>
> [...]
>
> I'm relying on the analysis as evidence that my opinion is accurate: that the four Federalist Society members on the Supreme Court have a bias against plaintiffs and in favor of defendants, and that these judges are deciding cases according to their political views of what they think the law should be instead of simply interpreting the language and intent of the Legislature and the Michigan Constitution.
>
> The analysis demonstrates, I think convincingly, that the court will not issue decisions that are fair to plaintiffs until the composition of the court is changed.
>
> In my opinion, the only way plaintiffs will receive more favorable decisions from the Michigan Supreme Court is to change who sits on that court, and the only way to do that under our current system is for people who believe in justice to make greater contributions in both hard and soft money for judicial campaigns. It is shocking to see the sources and amounts of money involved in the 1998 Supreme Court judicial campaigns.
>
> My analysis of decisions shows that, in 1998, when there was a Democratic majority in cases when there was an individual versus an insurance company or corporation there were 45 decisions: 22 for plaintiffs, 23 for defendants.
>
> In 1999 (up until when I did my analysis in August), there were 20 decisions only one for the plaintiff and 19 for defendants. And the one plaintiff decision was a remand. So we have seen a startling turnaround.
>
> Further analysis shows a similar overwhelming bias in reasoning, all in favor of insurance companies. And if you look at who financed the campaigns, in

1998 it was almost exclusively corporate/business/insurance company interests who provided around $1 million apiece for the two Republican can-
didates.[279]

Another whack!

And because the AGC complaint had been dismissed, almost everybody involved
could talk about it in detail. (The exception was Cunningham, who was still bound by
official silence—until it was lifted by the court Feb. 11, 2000. And there was plenty of
indication that he wanted to talk; he'd petitioned the court.)

Among those speaking out was Justice Taylor, but it was as if he hadn't realized yet
that his statements and actions could sometimes create unanticipated consequences.

Ford related what happened Nov. 5, 1999:

> After the grievance against me was dismissed, I got a phone call. There was a
> workers' compensation seminar [at the State Bar] where Taylor was speak-
> ing. After it was over, somebody asked Taylor what he thought about the
> grievance dismissal. He was unhappy and said he didn't think I should be
> able to criticize him. But if that was so and I could, then he also should be
> able to criticize me. And he said he intended to criticize me, and that be-
> cause his position as a sitting justice was more powerful than a trial lawyer,
> he was basically going to destroy my practice.[280]

More press. Ten of his Kalamazoo colleagues were concerned and wrote a letter to the
Michigan Lawyers Weekly.

> The following is part of a published account of what he said during that
> speech: "... Justice Taylor indicated that if lawyers wanted the right to criti-
> cize judges, then judges had the same right to criticize lawyers. However, he
> did not stop there. Justice Taylor went on to indicate that judges have more
> credibility than lawyers, and that judicial attacks on lawyers could have a
> significant negative impact on lawyers' ability to earn income."[281]

That was not the end of Taylor's words and actions, said Ford: "A couple of weeks
later, he came to the *Kalamazoo Gazette*. When he came in, all he wanted to talk about
was what a bad lawyer I was."[282]

The late Charlotte Channing was the editorial writer and political columnist for the
Gazette. This is how she started her piece:

279 C. Jesse Green, "1999 Lawyers of the Year; James B. Ford, Kalamazoo," *Michigan Lawyers Weekly*, 27 December 1999, http://milawyersweekly.com/news/1999/12/27/1999-lawyers-of-the-year-113799/.
280 James B. Ford, telephone interview, 27 February 2012.
281 Letter to the editor, "Attorneys Say Justice's Comment Cause 'Grave Concern,'" *Michigan Lawyers Weekly*,
27 December 1999, http://milawyersweekly.com/news/1999/12/27/attorneys-say-justices-comments-cause-
grave-concern/.
282 James B. Ford, telephone interview, 27 February 2012.

Jim Ford has become quite a burr under the saddle of the Michigan Supreme Court. So much so that Supreme Court Justice Clifford Taylor made a trip to Kalamazoo this week to make his arguments to the *Kalamazoo Gazette* in a case that has become a *cause célèbre* among attorneys and newspapers around the state and has cast that state's high court as political thugs.

It is rare for a Supreme Court justice to descend from the bench to comment on what is being said about the court. Though nominated by political parties and picked by the voters on the nonpartisan section of the ballot, once elected, justices mostly hover unflappably above the unseemly political fray and ignore criticism hurled at them.

But not this time.[283]

C. Jesse Green picked up the story for *Michigan Lawyers Weekly* expanding on the incident:

Gazette reporter Charlotte Channing, who wrote the article, told *Lawyers Weekly* that Taylor's trip to Kalamazoo was "peculiar" and "unprecedented."

"Justice Taylor just called us and asked for a meeting. He initiated the interview," she said. "It was my assumption that he was going to come and be proactive and talk about all the good things the court has done in this term. We had no idea what on earth he was driving at. He didn't say 'I want to come down and defend myself against Jim Ford' or 'I want to come here and suggest that Jim Ford is a dupe.'"

In the *Gazette* article, Taylor referred to Ford as an "unwitting pawn for these people" and said Ford was in "a den of long knives and does not know how they are using him."

Ford confirmed that he interpreted Taylor's original remarks at the workers' compensation session as a threat. "I have no idea what else they could mean," he said.

But Taylor denied that his original remarks at the seminar were intended as a threat. "I was merely pointing out the consequences of taking the lawyers free speech issue too far," Taylor said. [...]

Meanwhile, Ford acknowledged that Taylor's trip to Kalamazoo and comments were unprecedented. "I would not want to try to figure out why Justice Taylor would do this," he said.

[...] "Other attorneys have contacted me and suggested that a grievance should be filed against Justice Taylor with the Judicial Tenure Commission."

---

283 Charlotte Channing, "State Supreme Court doesn't favor big guys, jurist says," *Kalamazoo Gazette*, 2 December 1999, C1.

Ford concluded, "I firmly support [Taylor's] right to free speech, as well as my own. And I think that right probably protects even foolish or vindictive statements."[284]

The Kalamazoo lawyers who supported Ford saw the incursion as a further warning sign:

> Justice Taylor told the *Kalamazoo Gazette* that the reason for the controversy is greed. He accused Jim Ford of griping because he lost a large fee. Justice Taylor accused Ford of being an "unwitting pawn" of the "long knives" of the opposition political party.
>
> Members of the highest judicial body in this state should not personally attack individual attorneys in the hope of causing a "significant negative impact" on that attorney's ability to earn income. In a free society, it is important that all citizens, including attorneys, have an opportunity to comment on the actions of elected officials.
>
> The threats made by Justice Taylor on Nov. 5, 1999, and his visit to Kalamazoo should cause grave concern to all of us, lawyer and nonlawyer, Republican, Democrat and Independent.[285]

What Has Happened Here?

As this was playing out, Chief Justice Weaver wanted to know what was really going on.

I was concerned. So was Al Butzbaugh, then president of the State Bar. Both of us apparently questioned how it had been handled. The AGC didn't seem to have any rules about how things got done and when they got done. There was no end to these things. It needed to be carefully looked into. And my job as chief justice was to see that the Supreme Court performed properly and that so did all those acting under its authority. And if it meant that Justice Taylor had done something he should not have done, it needed to be exposed. I believed that by doing so, I was helping him. The accusations were flying that he had caused this to happen. If he HAD—and I knew enough to know it was possible he had—we needed get to the bottom of it. If he set this in motion, he had to apologize for it and clean it up. And if he hadn't, we needed to know that. It had to be cleaned up.

Her first step was a letter on Dec. 9, 1999, to Brian D. Vincent, then the chairperson of the Attorney Grievance Commission:

---

284 C. Jesse Green, "Justice Takes Road Trip; Taylor Talks To Jim Ford's Hometown Paper," 13 December 1999, http://milawyersweekly.com/news/1999/12/13/justice-takes-road-trip/.
285 Letter to the editor, "Attorneys Say Justice's Comment Cause 'Grave Concern,'" *Michigan Lawyers Weekly*, 27 December 1999, http://milawyersweekly.com/news/1999/12/27/attorneys-say-justices-comments-cause-grave-concern/.

Dear Mr. Vincent:

On December 1, the president and executive director of the State Bar provided the Supreme Court with copies of documents concerning the investigation of Kalamazoo attorney James Ford, the respondent in a recently dismissed case, who had made the documents public. On December 3, I was able to review the documents in depth, and then provided the justices with copies for their own review.

Because the Attorney Grievance Commission is "the prosecution arm of the Supreme Court for the discharge of the Court's constitutional responsibility to supervise and discipline Michigan attorneys," (MCR 9.108(A)), the Supreme Court must be assured that the commission's procedures meet the highest possible standards of integrity and fairness. It is our conclusion that the documents that have been made public in the matter reveal a record of investigatory tactics so flawed that the court is compelled to address them directly and immediately.

The documents we have reviewed include:

• A letter dated September 9, 1999, from the commission's investigator to the respondent's attorney. This letter details the process that the investigator intended to use, which the investigator himself described as "an extremely unusual procedure." The process included steps by which the complainant in the case would be allowed to view factual information and legal arguments provided by the respondent, but the respondent would not necessarily be able to view similar materials provided by the complainant. The process outlined raises questions about the impartiality of the commission's investigatory procedure in this case.

• Interrogatories served on respondent during the investigation. The interrogatories include questions that could not be relevant under any conceivable theory of misconduct related to the grievance. The most egregious of these questions concern the respondent's membership in professional and civic associations. We can think of no legitimate rationale for investigative interrogatories to pose such questions and no legitimate excuse for permitting their use. Such lines of investigative inquiry are never appropriate, and must not be repeated.

The staff actions as evidenced by the documents discussed above cast doubt on the credibility and integrity of the investigatory phase of the attorney grievance process in this case. The court expects that the commission will immediately begin to take all steps necessary and appropriate to correct the errors that have occurred in order to restore the confidence in the grievance process that had been undermined by the "extremely unusual procedure" and questioning employed in this case. The public must be assured that lawyers who violate the high standards of the profession are subject to appropriate discipline. At the same time, lawyers must be assured that the scope of investigation into possible misconduct is appropriate and that the investigation is conducted fairly, without bias of any kind.

To this end, we direct you to advise this court within 30 days of the receipt of this letter of the steps that the commission is undertaking to assure that the "extremely unusual procedures" employed in this case will never be repeated.[286] These steps should include, at a minimum, a process of staff training in professional standards of investigation, and a supervisory structure designed to promote consistency and fairness.

Finally, the court has received a copy of a letter from you to the State Bar president, declining to answer his questions concerning the conduct of the investigation in this matter. In your letter to the president you assert that the commission and its staff have acted in an even-handed, fair, impartial, and apolitical fashion. I am certain that we can all agree that nothing short of that standard is acceptable. The lawyers of this state, and the public, must know this to be true. Therefore, I am providing a copy of this letter to the State Bar president, and will keep him fully advised of the corrective steps that the commission undertakes in response to this letter.[287]

I can assure you I didn't just decide to sit down and pen this letter. I would have done this with the knowledge of the whole court, and I had a lot of thought and review on it. Margaret Chiara, Al Lynch (he was head of the commissioners and a really bright guy; he would tell you what he thought if you asked him), Janet Welch (she had worked as a commissioner and then she had been Justice Griffin's law clerk before becoming legal counsel to the court; she is now the State Bar executive director) all would have gone over this. Before this letter went out, everybody would have seen it.

Even Taylor and Young? Wouldn't they have objected?

They didn't say a word.

Then came the matter of an outside investigation. She turned to a retiree from the high court—Justice Theodore Souris—and appointed him as a special master. He had conducted a similar investigation nearly a decade before, so he had experience with the AGC. Beyond that, he was a Democrat and was not likely to cover up anything for the sake of political convenience. Weaver asked him to do two things: determine if there were any reason the file couldn't be opened to public inspection as long as the parties

---

286 Other extremely unusual procedures would find their way into employment more than a decade later when Weaver was sent to the AGC by Maura Corrigan. The process still was messy and disorderly in 2011.
287 Elizabeth A. Weaver to Brian D. Vincent, letter, 9 December 1999. This letter may have been published on the State Bar website and is referenced as "Chief Justice Letter" in *Michigan Lawyers Weekly*, 27 December 1999, 24.

wanted it opened (Ford and Cunningham[288] most certainly did and none of the others objected); and to see if there was any interference from the Supreme Court in all of this.

If there were something to all this, I didn't want the investigation to be seen as a political matter. If there were something to all of it, I wanted to get to the truth of it.

Souris concentrated on any communications from the court to the AGC or public comments by justices during the period of the complaint. In the body of his Feb. 11, 2000 report he turned up little, if anything, that seemed to form a connection.

> There is no factual basis to believe that any member of the Supreme Court acted inappropriately to compromise the AGC's investigation. I have found no evidence of any contact related to the investigation of the complaint against Mr. Ford by any member of the court with any commissioner of the AGC or with any member of its staff from the date of Mr. Ford's criticism of the court as published in the May 10, 1999, issue of the *Michigan Lawyers Weekly* until after Oct. 28 when the AGC dismissed the complaint.

> Moreover, I have found no evidence of any other inappropriate conduct by members of the court such as, for example, public criticism of Mr. Ford or of the AGC's investigation in speeches or media interviews prior to dismissal of the complaint.

> Neither the complainant nor the respondent nor the AGC provided any evidence of any public comment or writing related to this matter by any member of the court during that same period and I have found none. There have been several instances of public comments by Justices Clifford B. Taylor, Maura D. Corrigan and Robert P. Young, Jr., subsequent to the dismissal of the complaint against Mr. Ford. Had they been made before its dismissal, such comments by members of the court properly could have been construed as attempts to influence the investigation. The justices seem to have avoided such public comment scrupulously during the investigation to avoid influencing it.[289]

In the end, Weaver said she was disappointed with Souris' investigation. He didn't get to the heart of the matter to figure out if Taylor did or did not, directly or indirectly, set Doster in motion. There was not much there...at least not in the body of his report.

It was in Attachment 2—notes of Souris' interviews with the participants—wherein the possibility of mischief arose.

---

288 C. Jesse Green, "Former AGC Lawyer Wants To Go Public On Ford Grievance; MSC Investigation Will Determine Whether He Can," *Michigan Lawyers Weekly*, 7 February 2000, http://milawyersweekly.com/news/2000/02/07/former-agc-lawyer-wants-to-go-public-on-ford-grievance/.
289 Theodore Souris, "Report of Theodore Souris to Supreme Court," 11 February 2000, unpublished.

In his interview with Doster, Souris learned of the initial communication between Doster and Taylor:

> [Doster] said he received no encouragement from any justice before he filed his complaint with the AGC. He remembers discussing Ford's comments about the court with Justice Taylor, but he does not remember telling the justice that he intended to file a complaint.[290]

How likely was that?

"Doster was a paid political operative," said *Michigan Lawyers Weekly* reporter C. Jesse Green. "He gets paid to operate on behalf of his client. This was not an impartial bar member sitting somewhere who was suddenly impassioned to act."[291]

Souris' findings indicated that Doster had spoken with Justice Taylor before he filed, but Doster said he didn't do so at Taylor's urging. Further, Doster couldn't even remember whether he'd told Taylor he was going to do so. Finally, all on his own, he filed. And Souris concluded Taylor didn't have a role in it. This leaves Doster's action of filing the AGC complaint against Ford inexplicable.

Only Doster and Taylor know the truth about the who, when, what, and why of any communications between them about Ford and Doster's subsequent filing of the complaint.

Souris also learned from Doster that there was one other justice and a Court of Appeals judge involved:

> Eric B. Doster, the complainant, views the controversy as an entirely political effort by trial lawyers to defeat [...] incumbents who will be candidates for election this November. Justice Taylor and [Court of Appeals] Judge Stephen Markman [...] and, perhaps, Justice Young, mentioned during casual conversations with Doster after he filed his complaint against Ford that the issue, whether a subjective or objective standard should be used in weighing attorney speech, "was an issue that needed to be addressed." He described the nature of these conversations as expressions of regret by friends for the public abuses and grief Doster was absorbing for what they believed was a legal issue.[292]

This report raised the issue of *ex parte* communication.

"And there is evidence here of *ex parte* communication," said reporter C. Jesse Green.[293]

---

290 Theodore Souris.
291 C. Jesse Green, telephone interview, 28 February 2012.
292 Ibid.
293 C. Jesse Green, telephone interview, 28 February 2012.

Judges and justices are not supposed to have conversations with parties of pending or impending matters at the court,[294] and this matter could have come before the Supreme Court if the AGC had reprimanded Ford or recommended that his law license be suspended and then Ford had appealed the ruling. Taylor, Young, and Markman (who would shortly be on the Supreme Court) could have been faced with either disqualification, or if they'd hidden the matter, even a trip to the Judicial Tenure Commission.[295]

"The fact that the Supreme Court might rule on it eventually was all you needed," said Green. "The Supreme Court would have been the ultimate arbiter of the matter."[296]

Then there was the revelation by Cunningham himself that there was very little to the complaint, certainly not enough to jam up Ford.[297] And Cunningham told Souris that he had been looking for a way out:

> He said he had been looking for a basis for dismissal in Ford's "subjective" intent in making his comments about the court, sufficient to conclude that Ford's comments were political and, thus, justified dismissal of the complaint.[298]

That "'subjective' intent" turned out to be a big issue. Cunningham probed to know Ford's state of mind. And he wanted a lot of other questions answered, too, questions that had nothing to do with the incident. Ford described the questions in his subsequent book *I Lived in Those Times*:

> [T]he Attorney Grievance Commission sent me a questionnaire demanding to know every organization I have ever belonged to, my political views on a range of topics, and various other questions with very heavy Joe McCarthy overtones.[299]

---

294 Canon 3(A)(4) of the Code of Judicial Conduct states:
> A judge shall not initiate, permit, or consider *ex parte* communication, or consider other communication made to the judge outside the presence of the parties concerning a pending or impending proceeding [....], [http://coa.courts.mi.gov/rules/documents/8michigancodeofjudicialconduct.pdf.]

295 Of course, if the JTC recommended action against them, the matter would go to the Supreme Court. It would have wound up an awful mess. And we'll see later the renewed possibility of just this kind of mess.

296 Ibid.

297 In Souris' report he noted:
> Mr. Cunningham's memorandum discloses that he concluded for that record that this matter was "not the case to litigate the limits of an attorney's First Amendment protection." Mr. Ford's comments presenting the "low end" of offensiveness, when compared with other cases, Mr. Cunningham wrote. Those other cases, he concluded, likely will provide judicial guidance regarding the "upper limits" of offensiveness and "it is best to await final resolution of some (of the) pending cases involving 'over the top' attorney statements before litigating cases such as this."

[Theodore Souris.] N.B.: Those other cases were referring to Geoffrey Fieger.

298 Theodore Souris.

299 James Ford, *I Lived in Those Times*, Fortitude Publishing (Kalamazoo, Mich.) 2009, 552.

It seemed pretty intrusive and certainly raised the eyebrows of the chief justice. In a *Detroit News* column by George Weeks, Weaver said there was no reason for such prying:

> "There can be no legitimate, excusable reason for such investigative interrogatories—ever," she said in a Monday interview. "We will not have it!"[300]

Cunningham claimed, though, that he had been instructed to do so.

> I actually got slapped around a bit by the Attorney Discipline Board[301] for not doing enough of this sort of investigation and asking enough of these questions in the [prior] *Fieger*[302] case. I approached *Fieger* using an objective standard and the ADB said, "No! Use a subjective standard and inquire into the surrounding circumstances."[303]

So, he was just following orders.

Green closely studied Souris' report:

> The conclusion was fairly innocuous, but if I recall correctly there was plenty of material in the report to act on if the Supreme Court wanted to. The findings in the report were <u>not</u> innocuous.

> Did Doster or Taylor or Young or any of them come out later and say *"mea culpa"*? No, not that I'm aware of. Was there enough evidence they spoke about this at the time and made allusions to it? Yes, all this stuff is there. In any other context there would be more than enough for an investigation. I don't know why it didn't happen. The whole thing stinks. And there was even more.

> The whole thing was messier even than what you've read. How unseemly.[304]

Ford made out okay. But did he think Taylor vengeful in coming after him in his own home town? "Without a doubt," Ford said. "But it didn't hurt my practice as far as I can tell."[305]

300 George Weeks, "Chief justice rebukes discipline panel," *Detroit News*, 28 December 1999, 15.A.
301 The ADB is yet another agency of the court. It defines itself as: "the adjudicative arm of the Michigan Supreme Court for discharge of its exclusive constitutional responsibility to supervise and discipline Michigan attorneys." [http://www.adbmich.org/.]
302 Over the years, there have been several actions against Southfield attorney Geoffrey N. Fieger concerning first amendment rights. He will figure prominently in several later chapters. This instance deals with Fieger's representation of the family of an inmate who was found dead at one of the Ionia correctional facilities. Fieger claimed the prosecutor was covering up a murder. ["Attorney Speech—Public Statement—Remanded For Hearing," *Michigan Lawyers Weekly*, 20 October 1997, http://milawyersweekly.com/news/1997/10/20/attorney-speech-public-statements-remanded-for-hearing/.]
303 C. Jesse Green, "Cunningham Speaks On Handling Of Ford Grievance; Attorneys, Including State Bar Officials, 'Don't Have A Clue,'" *Michigan Lawyers Weekly*, 21 February 2000, http://milawyersweekly.com/news/2000/02/21/cunningham-speaks-on-handling-of-ford-grievance/.
304 Ibid.
305 James B. Ford, telephone interview, 27 February 2012.

Cunningham later said Ford had devised the entire situation as a test case for attorney free speech...and Ford was so much more appealing than bad-boy attorney Geoffrey Fieger, who also was facing a series of grievances at the AGC.[306]

Reporter C. Jesse Green asked Cunningham the question:

> Q. Do you think that might have been a strategic, legal move by Mogill and Ford to set this up as a great test case on the issue of attorney free speech?
>
> A. Absolutely. On these facts, there was no danger of any serious consequences. No one was going to lose a license over this. Since there was no risk, why not use it to get the political hay out of it.[307]

Earlier, Ford had said he had never before seen himself as a poster child for free speech, but he'd wear the mantle if needed:

> Attorneys should not be expected to give up their First Amendment rights when they take the bar. As I've said, the U.S. Supreme Court has already dealt with this issue and found that, once a case is resolved, attorneys have as much freedom to speak as anyone else. I think that issue was pretty clear already.
>
> The standard for attorneys should be the same as that for any other citizen. But every once in a while, we have to remind ourselves of that.
>
> There is also a distinct possibility that the rules [of professional conduct], if strictly enforced, would conflict with attorneys' constitutional rights to free speech.
>
> [...]
>
> If this recent attempt to silence attorneys had been successful, then the public as a whole would have been hurt. They would not have had the information they needed the next time they went to the voting booth to select Supreme Court justices or court of appeals judges. If attorneys cannot comment about the things that go on inside courtrooms, if we cannot be forthright in the media, how will the public ever gain access to this information?
>
> I would hope that this controversy will now lead to some changes in the rules and that other lawyers will not have to undergo a similar experience.

---

306 Michael Alan Schwartz, "Where Were Bar Members When Fieger Spoke Out?" *Michigan Lawyers Weekly*, 7 February 2000, http://milawyersweekly.com/news/2000/02/07/where-were-bar-members-when-fieger-spoke-out063/.
307 C. Jesse Green, "Cunningham Speaks On Handling Of Ford Grievance; Attorneys, Including State Bar Officials, 'Don't Have A Clue,'" *Michigan Lawyers Weekly*, 21 February 2000, http://milawyersweekly.com/news/2000/02/21/cunningham-speaks-on-handling-of-ford-grievance/.

As for judges, those who are criticized can pursue the same remedies in slander as anyone else. If they have not been slandered, if the comments are not illegal, then judges should just accept the criticism.[308]

Michigan Lawyers Weekly voted Ford one of its top ten attorneys of the year. In his comments at the honor, he added:

> Maybe I am a bit naïve, but I suspect that we are not going to see many, if any, duplications of what I went through. I'm sure that people who might think of filing grievances for political purposes are now going to be reluctant to do so. I hope that I won't have to be a model for anyone else.[309]

Alas, he has been a model for others including Justice Weaver.

And Richard L. Cunningham? He resigned. In a Jan. 10 interview, still not able to speak entirely freely about his investigation, he vented his irritation at the State Bar and Weaver for seeking an explanation for his investigative behavior. In fact, he said he found their actions "unjust."

> The State Bar of Michigan has recently issued a press release which severely criticizes me for my conduct in a recent grievance investigation. (See, "State Bar President's Statement," *The State Bar News*, page 24, Dec. 27, 1999.[310]) It also posted a statement, and several documents, concerning the investigation on its web site. Immediately following this action, I tendered my resignation to the Attorney Grievance Commission. I here offer my explanation for doing so.
>
> State Bar officials have lauded themselves for their role in obtaining decisive and immediate action regarding my investigative techniques. However, decisiveness and immediacy are no virtues when done without any semblance of fairness. The State Bar purports a motivation to ensure the integrity of the grievance process. But their actions belie their words. Although there are several procedures available at law to address such concerns, they deliberately chose to ignore them. Instead, they chose a method which precluded me from even defending or explaining my actions.
>
> The materials posted on the web site include a letter written by the chief justice, after her private meeting with the State Bar officials. It was written without even questioning me on the matters, or giving me any opportunity to be heard. It is this total lack of opportunity to even address the issues that I find so unjust. I see a big difference between rejecting my side of the

308 C. Jesse Green, "1999 Lawyers of the Year; James B. Ford, Kalamazoo," *Michigan Lawyers Weekly*, 27 December 1999, http://milawyersweekly.com/news/1999/12/27/1999-lawyers-of-the-year-113799/.
309 Ibid.
310 Co-author Schock has been unable to chase this down. It may refer to a *Michigan Lawyers Weekly* article of that date and page.

story after hearing me out, and simply refusing to consider anything I have to say.[311]

Without the risk of an *ex parte* communication, how was Weaver to have communicated with Cunningham while he was working the case? And after the complaint was dismissed, Weaver wanted to find out what was happening not only in the Ford situation, but in the rest of the operations at the AGC, too. In particular, she wanted to learn if Cunningham's actions were typical and followed approved policy. Cunningham was not the one to answer that question.

In the end, Weaver worked through Souris' actions to both investigate what Cunningham and the AGC had done <u>and</u> to free Cunningham to speak freely, which he subsequently did and at length (but certainly without any sense of gratitude). In a subsequent interview, Cunningham told reporter C. Jesse Green, "Most attorneys don't have a clue what the rules are, or how this system works. And that includes those in charge of the State Bar."[312] And then he went on in an extended question and answer to again blame the Bar and the Supreme Court.

> They still have never done what you are doing now: just ask me questions and give me an opportunity to explain just what happened, and why.
>
> Understand, I am not in any way attacking Chief Justice Weaver's integrity or anyone's integrity for that matter. But I do question her judgment and the judgment of the court. I don't see that as her letter, alone. She specifically said in the letter that she shared it with the court.[313]
>
> To just jump in and to make that sort of a move, those sorts of accusations, without making any attempt to discover what really occurred, that does not reflect a judicial nature. I'd expect more from judicial officers.[314]

He's the one who mishandled the investigation and had asked the egregious questions. Further, he ignored the fact and knew or should have known that neither I nor anyone on the court under the rules could chat privately with him about what he was doing. He could have and should have dismissed the Doster complaint right away in light of what was done with the one against Engler. But he didn't. Why? Afraid for his present and/or future jobs? Or his own philosophical agenda? Who knows?

There may have been a reason. One could argue that he was Engler's man at the AGC. That <u>judgeship</u> on the Detroit Recorder's Court? Ah, he had run for it[315] and lost in

311 Richard L. Cunningham, "Letter to the Editor: AGC Lawyer Resigns In Light Of Bar, MSC Actions," *Michigan Lawyers Weekly*, 10 January 2000, http://milawyersweekly.com/news/2000/01/10/agc-lawyer-resigns-in-light-of-bar-msc-actions/.
312 C. Jesse Green, "Cunningham Speaks On Handling Of Ford Grievance; Attorneys, Including State Bar Officials, 'Don't Have A Clue,'" *Michigan Lawyers Weekly*, 21 February 2000, http://milawyersweekly.com/news/2000/02/21/cunningham-speaks-on-handling-of-ford-grievance/.
313 With his criticism, Cunningham could have been inviting exactly that same kind of attention that Ford faced, but there was no Doster to advance it. And the matter was moot.
314 C. Jesse Green, "Cunningham Speaks On Handling Of Ford Grievance; Attorneys, Including State Bar Officials, 'Don't Have A Clue.'"
315 Press release, "Detroit Bar evaluates judicial candidates," Detroit Bar Association, 6 July 1990.

the fall of 1990, but he'd been appointed to the court Sept. 6, 1991, by John Engler. Interestingly, he took the place at the Recorder's Court of another Engler rising star, Michael Talbot (who was moved by Governor Engler's appointment to the Third Circuit Court [Wayne County] before his eventual Engler appointment to the Court of Appeals). Cunningham lost his bid for election to the Detroit Recorder's Court and ended his career there Dec. 31, 1992. In 1994, he ran for a judgeship in the Third Circuit Court and lost.[316] Subsequently, he went to the AGC.

And Cunningham could have stayed; there was no one forcing him to resign, said Weaver. As far as she knew, no one had asked him to. But he reported that his integrity had been questioned and that was enough reason for him to leave.

He could have stayed, learned from the rebuke, and brought forward any legitimate complaints and ideas to the court after the Doster complaint was dismissed. He obviously was comfortable and satisfied with the way he and the AGC operated.

And the Ford matter wasn't the only very public case he was pursuing at the time: Southfield attorney Albert L. Lopatin had run afoul of the AGC in the early 1990s for misconduct and had been reprimanded. Cunningham wanted in 1999 to further punish him by additionally suspending his license for 45 days. There were plenty who thought enhancing an already delivered punishment was odd, not the least of whom was Lopatin who said, "It's crap."[317]

And Cunningham had put himself out of a job all the while blaming the way the Attorney Discipline Board had told him to go about his business, blaming the State Bar, Weaver, and the rest of the court. And he'd put himself squarely and repeatedly in the middle of the Ford controversy.[318]

After decamping from the commission, Cunningham re-entered private practice (criminal defense). In 2008, he ran again for a judgeship in the Third Circuit (and was endorsed by the *Free Press*[319]). He lost.[320] But in December of 2008, he found another niche in state government: he was appointed an Assistant Attorney General.[321] He

316 "Fifteen candidates seek Wayne Circuit judgeships," *The Observer*, 7 November 1994, 6A, http://www. cantonpl.org/sites/default/files/observer/1994/11_Nov%201994/11-07-1994.pdf.
317 C. Jesse Green, AGC Wants Enhanced Discipline For Semi-Retired Practitioner; 'Retribution' Or Easing 'Perception" Of System, *Michigan Lawyers Weekly*, 27 December 1999, http://milawyersweekly.com/news/1999/12/27/agc-wants-enhanced-discipline-for-semiretired-practitioner/
318 Interestingly, *Michigan Lawyers Weekly* would vote him a 2000 Lawyer of the Year. In an interview with C. Jesse Green on that occasion, Cunningham continued blaming the high court and Weaver in particular. Green reported that he
　　[H]as devoted much of his time throughout this year speaking to lawyers and judges on the balance between attorney free speech and the ethical obligation bar members owe the public and the judiciary. Ironically, on many of these occasions Cunningham has appeared alongside Ford.
[C. Jesse Green, "Lawyers of the Year (60888): Richard L. Cunningham (Detroit)," *Michigan Lawyers Weekly*, 25 December 2000, http://milawyersweekly.com/news/2000/12/25/lawyers-of-the-year-60888/.]
319 "The best choices for Metro area judicial seats," *Detroit Free Press*, 23 October 2008, http://www.freep.com/article/20081023/OPINION01/810230407/The-best-choices-Metro-area-judicial-seats.
320 "Election results in judicial, prosecutor races," *Michigan Lawyers Weekly*, 10 November 2008, http://milawyersweekly.com/wp-content/plugins/tdc-sociable-toolbar/wp-print.php?p=31164.
321 Michael Cox, *Biennial Report of the Attorney General of the State of Michigan for the Biennial Period Ending December*

is now listed as division chief for the Criminal Division in the Michigan Attorney General's office.[322]

As for Taylor, he looked worse and worse the more he tried to settle the score.

And Doster had given the Democrats issues to use against his candidates in the fall of 2000.[323]

Young and Markman were on record as having entered the mess. Before it was over, Justice Maura Corrigan would join the fray, protesting with Taylor and Young that the "new" court was not an activist court, not pro-business, not pro-insurance.[324]

The rest of the Supreme Court and its Attorney Grievance Commission looked really bad, too, and there had been a lot of time invested and a lot of resources; this horsing around didn't come free.

The only one who came out of this looking okay was Ford.

It was a mess, and it was a public mess. And it was all so unnecessary.

And it took the chief justice away from her top priority, as would the further antics of Taylor and Young.

All I wanted to do was continue with the reforms, and Young and Taylor would not do it. They said "Nope. All that's important is being elected." I kept saying, "If you do the right thing, it doesn't matter. And we're here to do the right thing. If you don't get re-elected, you don't get re-elected." I had faced that many times, but these are people who had never been elected other than after they were appointed to the office and then were incumbents, and they had big money behind them.

So, running for re-election or retention was paramount to them. But it didn't stop them from missteps. Taylor had another flap with two northern Michigan judges, both of them circuit court judges: Kurt Hansen of Gladwin and former State Representative Joseph Swallow of Alpena.

And they were accusing the court of not being an independent judiciary and being in the hands of Engler.

Why was Taylor in a tussle with them?

31, 2008, (Edwards Brothers, Inc., Ann Arbor, Mich.) 2009, xxviii, http://www.michigan.gov/documents/ag/2007-2008_Biennial_Report_of_the_Attorney_General_307858_7.pdf.
322 Contact list, Attorney General, State of Michigan, undated, http://www.michigan.gov/documents/Attorney_General_121914_7.pdf.
323 They still prevailed in the Supreme Court races.
324 C. Jesse Green, "Is The 'New' MSC Engaging In 'Unprecedented' Activity? Critics say 'Yes' While Justices Defend Court," *Michigan Lawyers Weekly*, 13 December 1999, http://milawyersweekly.com/news/1999/12/13/is-the-new-msc-engaging-in-unprecedented-activity063/.

Justice Taylor was the least politically astute (with the exception of Steve Markman...but he came later). And Justice Young—for all his intelligence—was often unwise.

They were indiscrete. Adding to their indiscretions, Taylor and Young found in each other a proclivity for sophomoric humor. On more than one occasion, Weaver had to tell them to stop their silliness and their locker-room antics.

I repeatedly had to tell them to "Cut the comedy." I love a good joke, and I love to laugh, but what they were offering up really wasn't funny. Most of the time, it was offensive.

They seemed to feed on each other, she said. And when they really put a foot in it, they'd turn to her to help them out.

I really was more like a big sister they'd ignore until they needed my help.

They needed her help with *Brown v Board* and with Ford. She gave it, but in doing so, she crossed party lines by bringing in Justice Souris. She was investigating one of Engler's own, and she was willing to expose the inner workings of the court. She was asserting her independence as chief justice. Those would be moves not likely to endear her to Governor Engler.

I guess not.

Chapter 7

Dodgy on *Dart*;
So Long, Jim,
And Hello...um...Steve

James Ford's suit of *Husted v Auto Owners* wasn't the only case to have the dis/advantage of the split court...two justices leaving while two new ones came. With more than 3,300 filings and 100 written opinions a year, that would apply to a fair number during that time.

One of the most interesting of that lot was *Dart v Dart*, a divorce loaded with sex and money. Lots and lots of money. At issue was a substantial chunk of the Dart Container Corp.[325] fortune. Also at issue was the possibility of a justice having an unacknowledged business relationship (but not necessarily an improper one) with one of the families.

Those being divorced were Katina Estelle Dart as the plaintiff-appellant (the one seeking redress in the Michigan court) and Robert Charles Dart as the defendant-appellee.

One of the attorneys who worked on the case and will remain unidentified described it as "spectacularly tawdry." Here are the background facts of the case from the Supreme Court opinion:

> Plaintiff [Katina Dart] and defendant [Robert Dart] were married in 1980 and were residents of Okemos, Michigan, until 1993, when they moved to England. The couple owned a large house in Okemos, situated on thirty-nine acres of land, valued at $1,500,000. The parties had two children. The defendant is the son of the founder of Dart Container Corporation, one of the largest family-controlled businesses in the United States. The defendant's earned income for the years 1992, 1993, and 1994, was $313,009, $563,917, and $281,548, respectively. Between 1990 and 1993, the family's annual expenditures ranged from $300,000 to $600,000. The move to England made possible a September 1993 transfer of several hundred million dollars to the defendant from family trusts.

---

325 Dart, http://www.dartcontainer.com/.

In 1974, before the marriage, the defendant's father established a trust for the benefit of defendant and his brothers. For the transfer to occur, defendant had to renounce his United States citizenship and relocate outside the United States. The plaintiff refused to renounce her United States citizenship, and she also refused to renounce the citizenship of the children. She claims that, despite the relocation to London, England, she has always considered herself a resident and domiciliary of Okemos, Michigan.

In 1993, the parties jointly purchased a house near London for £2.75 million, and began renovations that took over a year to complete and cost another £3.5 million. They enrolled the children in the American School of London. Between 1993 and 1995, plaintiff asserts that she and the children made regular trips to Michigan for holidays, medical care, vacations, haircuts and other activities. Also, she maintained her Michigan driver's license and voted regularly in Michigan elections.[326]

Katina Dart did not give up her American citizenship. She came from immigrant Greeks, who much appreciated American citizenship.

There were problems in the marriage, but poverty was not one of them.

In September 1993, defendant received his distribution from the family trust which had a present, net value of £274 million (approximately $500,000,000).

In the fall of 1994, plaintiff announced that she wanted a divorce. She revealed that what she had previously described to the defendant as a "one night stand" in 1989 had actually been a regular, adulterous affair with a man in Greece. The plaintiff asserted that she and defendant agreed to postpone the divorce action until she and the children returned to Michigan after the 1994-95 school year.

Despite the putative agreement, defendant filed for divorce in England on February 3, 1995. Plaintiff was served with process at the parties' home the following day. She contacted her American attorneys, and they filed a similar suit on her behalf in Michigan in the Ingham Circuit Court four days later.[327]

So, Robert was suing Katina for divorce in England and she was suing him for divorce in Ingham County. And her attorney at the time, John Schaeffer, said he filed suit only a day after Robert's service on Katina, not four.[328]

So the allegations were that the divorce laws in England are much more favorable to wealthy men than women, and at some point Charles, The Prince of Wales, and his wife, Princess Diana, were not

---

326 *Dart v Dart*, No. 110361, Michigan Supreme Court, 20 July 1999, Find Law, http://caselaw.findlaw.com/mi-supreme-court/1226304.html.
327 Ibid.
328 John Schaeffer, telephone interview, 2 March 2012.

getting on and were subject to divorce, and that there were some allegations that the English law had been particularly fixed to favor the Prince of Wales in the divorce.

Michigan Lawyers Weekly reported that Katina alleged as much in her suit:

> Plaintiff contends that the English judgment violates public policy because it treats women as "'second-class citizens,'" provides for only limited discovery, fails to consider the wife's contribution to the family and the "fault" issue.[329]

Now, what we're dealing with here is big numbers, so for all of us regular people who are not dealing in billions of dollars, any millions seem like a lot. So, in the case of Princess Diana, I guess she got millions, but apparently not as many millions or billions as she might have.

I don't know about the royalty, but that's only some thought as to why the divorce went there by the husband, and the wife filed here. So it was going to be a jurisdiction, residency, and domicile issue.

First, through attorneys in Michigan, Robert challenged the jurisdictional authority of the Ingham County court. The court, under Chief Circuit Judge William E. Collette, asserted it DID have the jurisdictional authority in relation to the divorce and the children. It reserved consideration of the couple's property for a subsequent decision.

Katina also challenged the English court, and that court asserted its right to rule on the case.

Then Robert claimed in Ingham County ("on the basis of *forum non conveniens*"[330]) that having any matter decided there would pose an undue hardship.[331] The court disagreed and further asserted its jurisdiction in the property part of the divorce.

But the English moved it right along.

What happened next was chronicled in the Supreme Court opinion:

> On October 27, 1995, a "decree absolute" of divorce was entered in the English court. This was followed by a seven-day trial in March 1996 in which plaintiff filed an answer claiming the "full range of financial ancillary relief available to a wife under the Matrimonial Causes Act [of] 1973."
>
> Both sides presented expert witnesses who testified regarding the parties' assets and plaintiff's reasonable needs. On March 21, 1996, the English court issued a lengthy opinion in which it determined defendant's total net worth to be "about £400 million."

329 "Family Law—Foreign Judgment—Upheld," *Michigan Lawyers Weekly*, 23 June 1997, http://milawyersweekly.com/news/1997/06/23/family-law-foreign-judgment-upheld/.
330 The Latin phrase translates to "forum which is not convenient," [Law.Com, http://dictionary.law.com/Default.aspx?selected=779].
331 *Dart v Dart*, No. 110361.

The court ruled that the reasonable needs or requirements of plaintiff, in light of her pre-divorce lifestyle and habits and the available assets, entitled her to £300,000 ($450,000) a year for life. However, the court held that, "In seeking to achieve justice [the court is] not limited to the reasonable annual expenditure of the wife—or to such other matters—described as constituting her 'reasonable requirements.'"

The court awarded the plaintiff a lump sum of £9 million ($13,500,000), the amount it felt necessary to achieve an equitable distribution. The plaintiff was also awarded the house in Okemos, Michigan, and its contents, that the parties agreed were worth approximately $1.5 million. She was awarded four paintings and her jewelry. The court also set child support in the amount of $95,400 a year for both children.

Defendant was awarded four automobiles and the balance of the marital estate. The English court expressly found that plaintiff was not entitled to a substantial share of defendant's family wealth. It was not a product of the marriage and had not been generated by the efforts of either party.[332]

The allegation was that the English court didn't really allow for proper discovery. There was a lot of talk in the opinion of the English judge about fairness, but whether she really got her right to discovery as she would in America was certainly an issue. She claimed she didn't.

So there was a judgment, then, that awarded the wife $14 million, which sounds like a lot of money to most all of us, but I guess if you're living on a billion lifestyle, it's not a lot.

Katina's attorney sought relief from the English judgment at the Ingham County court.

Two phrases kept cropping up in this case: "comity" and "*res judicata*." "Comity" is "[t]he principle that one jurisdiction will recognize the executive, legislative, and judicial acts of another jurisdiction and will give effect to the other's laws."[333] In essence, it means that one court will defer to the jurisdiction of another. And the doctrine of "*res judicata*" means "a legal issue that has been finally decided by a court between the same parties, and it cannot be ruled on again."[334]

The trial judge, Judge Collette, ruled that the English judgment didn't need to be recognized, so that the matter would proceed in Ingham County Circuit Court.

According to *Lawyer's Weekly*:

> The Michigan court denied the motion, finding that the "English system of law was repugnant" to Michigan's public policy and that the English court's

---

332 *Dart v Dart*, No. 110361.

333 "Comity," Legal Information Institute, Cornell University Law School, http://www.law.cornell.edu/wex/comity.

334 "Res judicata," Legal Information Institute, Cornell University Law School, http://www.law.cornell.edu/wex/res_judicata.

decision "violated plaintiff's 'right to have a fair and equitable distribution of property.'"[335]

So, that, needless to say, was appealed by the husband.

And the matter went to the Michigan Court of Appeals where it was reversed. Appeals court judges Richard A. Bandstra, Richard A. Griffin (son of Justice Robert Griffin [and Weaver's former opponent for her Supreme Court seat]) and E. Thomas Fitzgerald upheld the English court authority and "[t]he English judgment is the final order."[336] They would give it comity, and as far as they were concerned the matter was *res judicata*.

Of course, that ruling was not to Katina's liking.

So it came to our court. There seemed to be something that we really needed to look at here. One of the commissioners was recommending that we should take it, and it was a commissioner's report by a very experienced, good commissioner.[337]

Leave was granted Oct. 12, 1998, while justices Boyle and Mallett were still on the job. The court records aren't clear on all those who voted to grant, but Weaver says she recalls that all the rest except Taylor—and possibly including him—voted for it. But Taylor indicated there were issues he wanted to consider that had not been raised in either the trial court or the Court of Appeals.

When we were considering the grant, when we voted to grant, Justice Taylor had indicated that he was going to send a memo on it, and he showed an unusual interest in this case.

At that point, Cliff was running for the remainder of Dorothy's term and would have to run again in 2000. He indicated he thought we should deny.

That would have let the Court of Appeals decision stand in favor of the husband.

He said at several conferences that he was going to send a memo.

But week after week, he didn't.

Now, he was busy with the election, so he didn't bother with the memo. He had higher priorities: to get elected. And he knew enough about the court to understand that we were not going to hear the case until the next year, so that memo didn't get sent until much later.

The case was set for oral argument in April, which is oftentimes the last month the court would hear arguments in order to get their opinions out by the end of July.

---

335 "Family Law—Foreign Judgment—Upheld," *Michigan Lawyers Weekly*, 23 June 1997, http://milawyer-sweekly.com/news/1997/06/23/family-law-foreign-judgment-upheld/.
336 Ibid.
337 Weaver says commissioners would face conditions at an increasingly politicized court that would lead some to hand in their papers: *We later lost many of them.*

But now we had the oral argument in front of a different panel with what I would call the Engler three [Taylor, Corrigan, Young].

At the oral argument, there were enough lawyers to draft a national constitution. Two firms represented Katina Dart: Carson, Fischer, P.L.C.; and Butzel, Long, P.C. They even brought in Harvard Law School professor Arthur R. Miller. Robert Dart was represented by attorneys from Dickinson, Wright, P.L.L.C. That was Justice Young's former firm (1978-1992). ...All that firepower for a combined 30 minutes of argument.

So when we heard oral arguments, I always dictated where I was in the case after the arguments and after the conference discussions. After we heard an oral argument, then we usually took an initial vote on how we felt about the case. I also kept my own vote sheet and the vote sheet the clerk kept and sent to us. And in looking at my notes, I see that I voted to reverse. I thought, as the commissioner had, that there were arguments that maybe it could be affirmed, but I was concerned about these jurisdictional and domicile issues and the allegations and the arguments that the woman hadn't been given her right to have full discovery. And although there's no question that 14-million dollars is a lot of money— certainly it is to me—I guess it's all relative.

The real issue was: had she gotten her rights? The trial judge [Collette] had talked about that we had freed ourselves from English law, you know, at least 200 years before. So that's where it was, and we wanted to make sure she got her due—she was an American citizen—even though her husband had given up his citizenship.

So with that in mind, that's where it went, and the votes, apparently, were Taylor, Young, Corrigan, and Kelly to affirm the Court of Appeals reversal of the trial court. Kelly really surprised me on this. And it was Brickley, Cavanagh and myself that would reverse and remand it, and let the case be decided in America rather than in England.

Oral argument had occurred in April. In May, I at last got this memo from Justice Taylor. You're always interested in what your colleagues have to say. You assume that they have no special interest in the case or that they would tell you.

Even after Taylor reiterated to the entire court that he was sending a memo, it was addressed primarily to one justice.

So, I get this memorandum. "To Chief Justice Weaver only." Then it says: "Copy: Justice Corrigan and Justice Young only." And this is dated May 7, 1999, and in it Justice Taylor writes to me:

> As you may recall, I am of the opinion that the trial court should have dismissed Mrs. Dart's complaint for divorce on account of no jurisdiction, i.e., Mrs. Dart had not resided in Michigan 180 days immediately preceding the filing, nor had she resided in Ingham County for the 10 days immediately preceding the filing of the complaint. I believe Justice Corrigan and Justice Young indicated agreement with this position.[338]

He's alerting me that he has them on his side.

---

338 Clifford W. Taylor, "Memorandum," unpublished, 7 May 1999.

At best, I can remember that you took the position[339] that the English divorce need not be recognized by Michigan because Mr. Dart was not a resident of England and therefore was not entitled to obtain an English divorce.[340]

...He can be a citizen but not necessarily a resident there. And I guess that was one of the issues.

And then Taylor goes on to try to convince me to change my vote, to change my position.

I am writing this memo to bring two reasons to your attention, which may lead you to consider joining my jurisdictional analysis. First, if the Ingham circuit court [sic.] never obtained jurisdiction, the court could not determine whether the English divorce should be ignored on the basis that Mr. Dart was not a resident of England. [...] Said another way, whether or not Mr. Dart was a resident of England can only be reached if the Ingham circuit court [sic.] had jurisdiction over Mrs. Dart's complaint for divorce.

Second, it appears Mr. Dart did in fact meet England's residency requirement for seeking an English divorce.[341]

Taylor was making a case that the trial court had no jurisdiction because Katina was not a resident of the U.S. In Taylor's analysis, she had to be a resident for 180 days in order to qualify for a divorce here. Even though she was a citizen, owned a home in Michigan, and made frequent trips to her home in Okemos.

When Weaver wouldn't sign on immediately to serve as the fourth vote, she said he went lobbying Justice Kelly.

In fact, after the oral argument, Kelly went to their side. He was concerned about me so he worked on Kelly; she was leaning his way.

Kelly had voted so in the conference after the arguments, said Weaver, but Taylor needed to make sure.

In a subsequent 25-page memorandum on June 11, Taylor argued what he thought was a dissenting opinion that he was circulating:

Plaintiff failed to meet either the state or county residency requirements of our divorce statute. In view of my conclusion that the trial court was without jurisdiction, it is unnecessary to decide the issues reached by the Court of Appeals. The judgment of the trial court should be reversed and the Court of Appeals opinion should be vacated.[342]

---

339 Weaver annotated her copy of the memorandum with this: "This is not the position we took at all."
340 Clifford W. Taylor, "Memorandum."
341 Ibid., and Weaver noted "We agree that [he] met residency—our question is domestic."
342 Clifford W. Taylor, "Memorandum," unpublished, 11 June 1999.

The language and reasoning he used, said Weaver, were a departure from anything she'd seen from him before. He was reaching, overloading his arguments. Weaver's copy of the June 11 memorandum is limned and annotated with comments contesting facts and interpretations. In the long run, one of her clerks wrote on the cover:

> Chief:
>
> We already know we're not w/CWT on jurisdictional issue. I'm guessing that MK [Marilyn Kelly] will want to respond to his "dissent." Beginning on page 20 he makes it sound like we've completely ignored the statute, which is hardly the case, in my opinion.[343]

Weaver wrote on the memorandum her observations after reading it:

> CWT needs to settle it or he'll look very foolish here. Get the emotion out. Get the accusations out. Trying to guess what majority think.[344]

I pay attention to what he's saying. This was a case that was relatively close. There's an argument that you should want to give due to the other country's laws—they had the case in front of them, you know. On the other hand, we're dealing with an American citizen.

And then Taylor had asked me for a quick response:

"I would appreciate hearing from you regarding this information as it will, I believe, probably be dispositive of this case."[345]

When I did look into the jurisdictional issue, I did not agree with him at all. He was interpreting that if you wanted to get divorced, the statute says that you have to live in the county 180 days immediately preceding the filing of the divorce. Well, the position in this case was the husband was arguing she had left Ingham County to go somewhere for a few days. That doesn't make sense. For instance, if the case was in Leelanau and it's adjacent to Grand Traverse that would mean you couldn't go into Traverse City for 180 days; what a ridiculous argument that would be. It was a bizarre textualist argument.

I was concerned about Justice Taylor's view, and if Corrigan and Young and Kelly adopted that, it would be outrageous that people were supposed to be frozen in time and not leave their county for 180 days in order to get a divorce.

And Taylor might have had some influence over Corrigan and Young. After all, Taylor was the senior justice among the three; he had helped them get to the court.

But you have to use some good sense. So, in the end, I did reject those arguments, and apparently, so did Young and Corrigan at some point.

343 Ibid.
344 Ibid.
345 Ibid.

But Taylor still wasn't settled on the matter.

He was extremely interested in the case and was doing everything he could to get a result. He tried one crazy idea and when that didn't fly, he tried another until he got a result. I didn't know what was behind his reasoning.

If his thinking wound up in the majority opinion, it might pose problems. So, she changed her stance and announced to her fellow justices she was joining the majority. Why? No matter which side she was on she wasn't going to sway the vote.

I took Justice Taylor at face value—that he had no axes to grind in this case. And this case was close. So, okay, I looked at the legitimate points.

She found enough of them to come his way, but the rest of Taylor's logic represented a threat to established law.[346] She joined the majority to ameliorate the threat; she could have a voice in crafting the opinion, steering the decision away from issues the court didn't need to deal with.

What eventually happened was that we came to an agreement.

In the end, Justice Kelly wound up writing the opinion and much of Taylor's far-flung logic was avoided.

The majority opinion was this:

> We hold that principles of comity and *res judicata* mandate that the Darts' foreign divorce judgment be enforced. The English court decided the property distribution issue on the merits, and no evidence was presented showing that plaintiff Katina Dart was denied due process. We affirm the decision of the Court of Appeals.[347]

Weaver wasn't exactly thrilled with it, but the analysis and conclusions were better than they might have been.

And she didn't have a lot of communication with Brickley and Cavanagh, who in the end wrote to reverse and remand. Cavanaugh concluded his dissent with this:

> Accordingly, while not, in large part, disputing the authorities cited by the majority as a general matter, I am nonetheless convinced that the operation of the English system of marital asset division in cases involving substantial assets reflects considerations very different from our own, and that such considerations cast a shadow on the decision sufficient to preclude Michigan courts, with our well-established criteria for property distribution in

---

346 *In one sense it made new law by our giving England authority in our courts.*
347 *Dart v Dart*, No. 110361.

divorce cases, from recognizing a decision that is not only from another land, but truly foreign to the concepts underlying Michigan law.[348]

It was a short dissent. And Justice Brickley signed on to it. And they didn't really pick up the mantle on it. But Justice Brickley wasn't at all the conferences. This was May. Unbeknownst to us, by August—as soon as the term was over, he would announce that he was retiring for his health, and so he wasn't in on a lot of the discussions, and I don't know that he wrote anything about it other than he would have granted for the wife—reversed the Court of Appeals.

It wouldn't be until much later—years later—that Weaver would learn that Taylor's unusual interest in *Dart* might not have been related to just the legal issues involved.

It's not unreasonable to assume that as a sitting Supreme Court justice, you might have a party in a case come before you who was someone you might have known from your previous legal work as an attorney.

At the time of *Dart v Dart*, there was in place the 1985 Code of Judicial Conduct, MCR 2.003 (an update of the 1955 code). In particular, a justice could have been disqualified from serving on a case by challenge in the form of a motion from one of the parties, or the justice could raise the issue her- or himself. Four of the list of six circumstances leading to consideration for recusal included (but were not limited to):

(1) The judge is personally biased or prejudiced for or against a party or attorney.
[...]
(3) The judge has been consulted or employed as an attorney in the matter in controversy.
(4) The judge was a partner of a party, attorney for a party, or a member of a law firm representing a party within the preceding two years.
 (5) The judge knows that he or she, individually or as a fiduciary, or the judge's spouse, parent or child wherever residing, or any other member of the judge's family residing in the judge's household, has an economic interest in the subject matter in controversy or in a party to the proceeding or has any other more than *de minimis* interest that could be substantially affected by the proceeding. [...][349]

The ultimate authority of the justice's recusal, though, rested with the justice him- or herself.

Michigan Supreme Court Justices followed a tradition that permitted the challenged justice to search his own thoughts and mind to determine whether or not he was capable of performing impartially. The lack of a clear ethical standard concerning judicial recusal allowed the public confidence

---

348 Ibid.
349 Michigan Court Rule 2.003 (amended 1995). http://coa.courts.mi.gov/rules/documents/1Chapter2Civil Procedure.pdf.

in the impartiality of the judiciary to sink even lower. The old recusal laws required Michigan citizens to accept recusal decisions on faith. A justice was not required to explain his or her decision to either participate or not participate in a case. More importantly, even when a party asked a justice to step aside from a pending case, traditional practices allowed the justice to simply deny the request and participate in the decision without any explanation for his or her decision to deny the recusal request.[350]

If a justice didn't want to step off a case, the justice didn't have to step off. And there was no mechanism in place to remove a sitting justice from any particular case.[351]

To her knowledge at the time, none of the seven justices had anything to do with the *Dart v Dart* divorce beforehand, or the Dart family and their enterprises.

And it wasn't until 2007 that Weaver learned that Taylor earlier MAY have had some kind of relationship with the Darts through Dart Oil and Gas Corp. (now a subsidiary of Dart Energy).

That's when Steve Scofes, Katina's brother, contacted Justice Weaver and told her that Justice Taylor had previously done law work for the Dart empire.

Certainly on the website for Miller Canfield—where Taylor now serves "Of Counsel"—he makes much of his petrochemical experience: "Prior to his judicial appointments, Justice Taylor was in private practice, specializing in tort defense, oil and gas land acquisition, and litigation for major oil producers."[352]

Lansing and the Dart Energy headquarters in Mason are some 15 miles apart. The oil and gas community in Michigan is a small and tight fraternity.

But where was the proof that the association was more than proximal? The research to make the connection would prove out over time.

Early research revealed that the Taylors and the Darts (or their enterprises) seemed to keep showing up on the same lists of donors for worthy causes. One is the Michigan Supreme Court Historical Society. Stephen H. Dart contributed someplace between $100 and $249 in 2002. In 1989 Lucille and Clifford Taylor had bestowed more than $5,000. (And, for the record, Elizabeth Weaver gave something between $1,000 and $2,499 since 1989.[353])

---

350 Aaron D. Hanke, "An Extreme Makeover: Why Michigan's Judicial Recusal Standards Needed Reconstruction and Why More Work Remains to Be Done," *University of Detroit Mercy Law Review* [Vol. 88.97, Fall 2010] 97-154, http://www.law.udmercy.edu/udm/images/lawreview/v88/88lHanke.pdf, citations eliminated.
351 The code was changed in 2009, Weaver leading the way, but only after another bitter fight; that dustup will be covered subsequently in Chapter 17.
352 "Clifford W. Taylor," Miller Canfield website, http://www.millercanfield.com/CliffTaylor.
353 "A look back at 2003; Society update Year-in-review," Michigan Supreme Court Historical Society, 6-7, http://www.micourthistory.org/pdfs/newsletters/winter2004.pdf.

The Michigan History Foundation lists Lucille and Cliff Taylor as donors at the $1,000-plus level and the Dart Foundation at $50,000-plus.[354]

The Mackinac Center lists the Dart Foundation as a $20,000 contributor.[355] In May of 2012, that institution named Taylor to its board, and in January of 2013, it elevated him to board chairman.[356]

It was even reasonable to think that Taylor might have done some work in restructuring the Dart corporations after a family dustup.[357]

But the research that remained to be unearthed was between the covers of some old Martindale and Hubbell directories.[358] That yearly listing of law firms and lawyers shows partners, staff, areas of practice and specialty, and, sometimes, representative clients.

And there it was: beginning in 1984 and continuing 1989, Taylor's law firm, Denfield, Timmer and Taylor, listed Dart Oil and Gas Corp. among its representative clients. Certainly Dart followed Auto-Owners Insurance Co., and Mobil Oil Co., and a host of others...but...it...was...there.

REPRESENTATIVE CLIENTS: Auto-Owners Insurance Co.; National Indemnity Insurance Co.; Pennsylvania Insurance Co.; Travelers Insurance Co.; Getty Oil Co.; Mobil Oil Co.; Ohio Farmers Insurance Co.; Bankers Life & Casualty Co.; Western Casualty & Surety Co.; Indiana Insurance Group; Western Surety Co.; United States Aviation Underwriters, Inc.; American Home Assurance Co.; American Underwriters Group; Netherlands Insurance Co.; Guarantee Insurance Co.; Mills Mutual; American Aviation; Lincoln Mutual Co.; Amoco; Maryland Casualty; Dart Oil and Gas Corp.; Pennsylvania Manufacturer's Association Insurance Co.; Federated Insurance Co.; Amoco Production Co.; American Society for Mass Spectrometry; Employers of Wausau; Jersey

Firms pay to be listed in the Martindale-Hubbell Law Directory. Ironic that what suffices for a brag-book resulted in the revelation that Taylor's old firm, Denfield, Timmer and Taylor, had a business affiliation with the Darts.

354 "Donors of Michigan History Foundation," Michigan History Foundation, http://www.michiganhistory.org/donors.
355 "Mackinac Center for Public Policy," Sourcewatch, http://sourcewatch.org/index.php?title=Mackinac_Center_for_Public_Policy.
356 Ted O'Neil, "Taylor Named New Chairman of Mackinac Center Board of Directors; Former Supreme Court Justice Replaces Olson," Mackinac Center for Public Policy, 14 January 2013, http://www.mackinac.org/18166.
357 Elizabeth Lesly, "The Darts: Fear, Loathing, and Foam Cups," Businessweek, 10 July 1995, http://www.businessweek.com/archives/1995/b343279.arc.htm.
358 Martindale-Hubbell Law Directory, Summit, N.J. 1980-95. [Also see http://www.martindale.com/.]

Steve Scofes also had told Weaver that Katina's attorneys in the case approached one of Taylor's law clerks; they urged that Taylor step off. No response.

In contrast, the primary attorney for Katina Dart before the Supreme Court, Robert M. Carson of Carson Fischer, P.L.C., denied any knowledge of such an event.[359]

Taylor certainly hadn't served as an attorney for the family-run corporation within the prior two years, nor had he been affiliated with a firm that had. And he hadn't worked on the divorce case. But what of numbers 1 and 5 of the disqualification criteria? Was he truly objective or was there a lingering bias? Large amounts of money can exert an influence.[360] And was there the potential for gain from the corporation or the family if he ruled for Robert Dart? Could he possibly have more than a *de minimis* interest, perhaps anticipating campaign contributions for his upcoming election battle? No Dart name shows up the in the 1998, 2000, or 2008 campaign contributors.[361] But campaign contributions can be directed in non-obvious ways, all of which are perfectly legal (now even more so than in earlier years, following the *Citizens United* decision at the U.S. Supreme Court). There is no indication of collusion on the part of the Dart family, Dart Container, or Dart Energy, but with the structure of subsequent PAC support, it's hard to tell that the Darts <u>didn't</u> support him.

You can give money without your name being associated with the gift...perhaps you give to a group that is supporting a candidate or an issue. And under the current laws and rules, there's nothing to

---

359 Robert M. Carson, telephone conversation with co-author Schock, 2 March 2012.

360 In 2005, *Forbes* listed Dart Container as number 276 on its list of the top 500 corporations with revenues of $1.39 billion. [http://www.forbes.com/lists/2006/21/biz_06privates_Dart-Container_RLR7.html.] By 2008 that had risen to $1.54 billion but the corporation had dropped to a ranking of 316. [http://www.forbes.com/business/lists/2008/21/privates08_Dart-Container_RLR7.html.]

And while there is no link from this divorce case to anything improper or illegal on the part of the Darts or their corporations, *Forbes* reported the IRS had taken issue with earlier corporate expenses:

> Styrofoam-cup czars Kenneth B. Dart and Robert C. Dart improperly billed $11.6 million of personal security costs to their Dart Container Corp., the Internal Revenue Service says. In a U.S. Tax Court filing, Dart Container argues the money—half of it spent for corporate aircraft—was a valid business expense due to "specific threats and other facts and circumstances." But it admits other family members benefitted. The wealthy brothers both gave up U.S. citizenship and now live in the Cayman Islands. With additional claims the feds seek another $4.4 million in taxes for 1996 and 1997.

[Janet Novack and William P. Barrett, "The Informer: Their cups runneth over?," Forbes.com, 29 October 2001, http://www.forbes.com/forbes/2001/1029/028.html.]

Novak and Barrett kept on the story and filed this one July 21, 2003, under "Gone but definitely not forgotten":

> Back for the umpteenth time in U.S. Tax Court: Dart Container Corp., the Mason, Mich. Styrofoam cup maker owned by brothers Kenneth B. and Robert C. Dart, who gave up citizenship and live abroad. This case: The Internal Revenue Service says Dart owes $19 million more in 1998 and 1999 taxes, primarily for wrongly deducting $45 million in "interest" payments, related to division of the family business in 1986 to settle a lawsuit by feuding sibling Thomas J. Dart. Dart Container says *it's* owed a $10 million refund. Last year Dart entities paid $26 million in taxes—from 1994.

[http://www.forbes.com/forbes/2003/0721/052.html.]

361 Michigan Committee Statement of Organization, Department of State, http://miboecfr.nictusa.com/cgi-bin/cfr/com_det.cgi?com_id=508576.

prohibit it. I suspect Dart was a good contributor. It's possible Dart contributed substantially to Taylor's, Corrigan's, and Engler's campaigns. But this is speculation.

A personal tie to the Darts would go a long way to explain why Taylor's behavior during the divorce case had been uncharacteristically odd, said Weaver.

There were so many changes of opinion. In retrospect, I could see there was a lot of jostling around to get a result. I didn't know that at the time. It didn't seem like it was the world's most unjust case. Had one known that Taylor had such an interest in the Darts that would have enlightened one that he was willing to do anything as long as he got a result.

What he did wasn't illegal, but it certainly wasn't transparent. It may have changed the course of justice for the Darts, especially Katina.

Had I known, I would have taken it into account, and for transparency asked him to reveal then and there his significant business history with the Darts.

And in retrospect, it raised questions about why Taylor kept silent, why he didn't at least mention that he'd done work for and known the Darts.

I still believed that Cliff was making stupid mistakes in matters like the Ford case rather than being intentionally deceptive.

His silence did not serve his chief justice well. It wasn't the act of a friend. And it didn't line up with Weaver's standard of conduct: *When in doubt get out!*

You do what you can. At the time, I felt that I should have done something more, but I didn't know what. I and my clerks worked on the case, and we followed the issues. We did what we could within the constraints of the majority vote.

In retrospect, I should have been more attentive to that little voice that was telling me something wasn't right here. I couldn't pinpoint the reason at the time. What I didn't realize was that I needed to be suspicious of the objectivity of someone I thought of as a trusted colleague.

Instead, I still worked to help him get re-elected.

"I don't need this."

At this point in her judicial career, Weaver found it inconceivable that her fellow justices—especially Taylor, Young, and Corrigan—would try to deceive her. She knew for certain that Brickley would not. She could deal with the fact that Kelly and Cavanagh were actually working against the new justices.

There were two factions: the Englerites and the Kelly and Cavanagh faction. Kelly and Cavanagh had as their goal the defeat of Taylor and Young in the election; they were really a part of trying to tear them down. And the Englerites' goal was to be elected at any costs. And I was in the middle thinking the people who were up for re-election were being unfairly mischaracterized. To some extent, I was right. But they were at each other's throats, and I was trying to keep all of them from destroying themselves and the court. It was a war. And it seemed like I was herding warring cats.

But she was slowly coming to a realization about Taylor and Young.

This was the beginning of the awakening as I call it. I was working with them on their campaigns for their re-election in the fall of 2000, and I considered that they were dealing with me straight; that criticisms of them were a result of things they were not necessarily handling properly.

But I was also very frustrated with Taylor and Young because they didn't want to take the stands on reform, right from day one. It was clear to me they were not going to stand up for our pilot programs.

The demands of serving as chief justice are huge. There are lots of extra hours, the need to supervise a whole other staff (in addition to your own office with your own clerks and administrative assistants) dedicated to the running of the court, and the responsibility of leading the entire state judiciary. Weaver spent more time in Lansing than anyplace else, coming north most—but not all—weekends. The demands of the office took up enough time that in the spring of 1999, she had to miss one of her most anticipated joys, the Final Four.

Now you know what an MSU basketball fan I am (and U of M, too)—so I was passing up going to the Final Four.[362] I was so busy trying to keep the thing from flying apart. And I said to them, "Look, I don't need this. I don't need to be the chief justice. In fact, I don't even need to be here. I'm eligible to retire."

Now, I didn't say it as a threat; I was just saying it because this is what I felt. I didn't want to deal with it. I was really very disappointed in them and very disgusted.

When I said that, that must have scared the willies out of them because I guess they were thinking further than I was about what an effect that would have on the court if I decided to get off or just wouldn't have anything to do with it anymore. Because I always had strong support from a lot of the judiciary and just general public—I was elected by the people to get to the court and, you know, that makes a difference to have that grass-roots support that gives you 25,000 more votes than somebody else.

But if she had left, wouldn't that have given Governor Engler great joy?

Yes. But it only would have been worse; then they would have had three people to re-elect in the fall of 2000. And remember, they were still hoping that Brickley would go because Brickley's health was somewhat in question. And so in that case, they would have had four people to try to re-elect. They didn't need me leaving. I think it went back to Engler, because he would avoid me, but he didn't give

---

362 MSU did win the Midwest regional final and went to the Final Four where it was eliminated in the first national semifinal, going against Duke. [http://en.wikipedia.org/wiki/1999_NCAA_Men's_Division_I_Basketball_Tournament].

me any gaff as I think he's known to have done to others. In retrospect, I think they were concerned about setting me off.

I was just telling them that's what I felt at that moment. I didn't threaten. I just said, "I don't need this."

Brickley Leaves

Unknown to the rest of the justices, at the time the court decided *Dart v Dart*, Justice James Brickley was on his way out.

And they were always hoping that Brickley would go—wishing him off.

The downside of Brickley's leaving was this: there would be three Republican justices up for reelection at the same time, perhaps an easier target for Democrats to retrieve one or two seats.

There were indications earlier on of the change.

Justice Brickley was apparently having health problems. He was coming down less often to Lansing for conferences, participating instead by phone or sending his votes in writing.

And I bumped into him at the hospital in Traverse City; I was visiting somebody there. He was having tests; he told me. But he did not indicate he was going to resign.

In fact, he was looking for replacement staff.

I actually recommended that someone apply who would be very good as a law clerk for Brickley, and if I had known Brickley was leaving I would have said, "Don't bother." And I even asked Brickley if he wanted the application, and he did want it. But I think he was deciding. And I think as things went along, it probably didn't look really good for him; he decided: "Why do I want to do this job any longer?"

Chief Justice Elizabeth Weaver sits with President Gerald Ford at a State Bar event in Grand Rapids, Sept 15, 1999. It was earlier that morning before the event that she learned the Governor was going to appoint Stephen Markman to the Supreme Court.

I don't remember exactly whether he announced he was resigning and finished the term or finished the term and then announced. I believe he finished the term through July, and as far as one knew, he was going to stay. But I think things got worse; and so then he resigned.

I know I was very disappointed because I didn't want him to leave because, you see, his vote and my vote were very important. And Brickley was not an Englerite. So he was not of a mind to warm up to Taylor and Young.

After 16 years, nine months, and four days, The Honorable Justice James H. Brickley stepped down Oct. 1, 1999. At the time of his resignation, he was the longest serving justice on the court.[363] He died two years later, Sept. 28, 2001.[364]

So, there <u>would</u> be three seats up for election. But before that, the Governor would make his next appointment: Stephen Markman.

The selection wasn't her call. And Markman was not Weaver's first choice. Or her second choice. Or, even, her third. She'd had dealings with him before. In fact, he had been appointed by the Governor to the Court of Appeals' seat Weaver had vacated when she moved to the Supreme Court.

I came to know Markman through Cliff Taylor. And Cliff talked about Steve Markman as better than sliced bread. And I thought: "He really must be something," you know? I had never met him, never heard of him. Cliff wanted me to meet him. So, one day—we were in the Kewpee Doll [Weston's Kewpee Sandwich Shoppe] in Lansing, having lunch, and whether Cliff had invited him to come by, or he just was there, he came over. And I was certainly taken aback at this guy who Cliff thought was the most wonderful in every way. My initial thought was this is really an odd-guy.

She was underwhelmed.

That's very unusual for me, but immediately I corrected it in that I thought "Okay, Cliff says he's fine, and it just must be one of those days, and there must be a lot more to him. Can't judge the book by the cover."

Then, I go to a Prosecutors' Association reception, and Markman's there. So he comes up to me, and he's really right there in my face—and he's got to know why we reversed him, and why I voted to reverse him on "X" case. Well, I'm saying, "What are you talking about, Steve?"

At the time, the court might have received 3,300 filings, and under Mallett's leadership, the court delivered more than 100 opinions a year, about twice what the court does now.

363 "On and Off the Court," Michigan Supreme Court Historical Society, http://www.micourthistory.org/on_and_off_the_court.php.

364 "Biographies: James Brickley," Michigan Supreme Court Historical Society, http://www.micourthistory.org/bios.php?id=103.

Two justices—Elizabeth Weaver of the Michigan Supreme Court and Paul Stevens of the United States Supreme Court at the Grand Rapids event.

"What case are you talking about? I haven't any idea what you're talking about." Apparently I believed, "You were wrong and that's it. Get over it." I remember being reversed and sometimes I'd thought, "Okay, but if I was in that chair I'd be right."

But he was wanting to have a deep discussion about why he had been reversed on this particular thing. I thought, this was weird; it was the wrong place and manner. And I said, "You know, if you really want to know, don't pick a reception. Get in touch later saying, 'This is case "X." Would you look at it and can you tell me what's wrong?'" But for Steve it was: "Why were we wrong about his case?"

Those kinds of skills would not warmly commend him to anyone's attention. And initially, it seemed unlikely that it would be Markman on the high court. The understanding was that Brickley's replacement would be a woman.

That was definitely the word. Maura agreed, I agreed, the Rileys agreed—and remember, Taylor had taken Riley's spot—that it should be a woman, because you've got Young and Taylor up for re-election, and they are lightening rods already. And if you had a woman, at least that would probably be an easier person elected. So, it was pretty much a given that's what was going to occur.

Unless the Governor wanted to ensure that Taylor and Young would have a better chance of being elected by including a weaker pick; a woman might well outpoll them.

Whenever Markman's name was mentioned, I was totally negative on him. I let it be known that I would never want him appointed.

I made it very clear to Lucille and Cliff and, at some point, I just said so: I didn't think he was electable.

I conveyed that Markman was not a good candidate; he's odd, to say the least. I just didn't think he needed to be at the Supreme Court. I did know that he was Mr. Conservative: he taught at Hillsdale College, and that Jim Barrett, then president of the Michigan Chamber of Commerce, was a Markman fan.

But Markman wasn't the only contender for the job; in fact, as much as he wasn't Weaver's first choice he also, apparently, wasn't the Governor's, either.

And there were some women that would have made good candidates. And, too, we needed a trial judge.

The only former trial court judges on the Supreme Court were Michael Cavanagh and Weaver. None of the rest of them had served as so much as a magistrate. Adding another without trial bench experience would handicap the court, said Weaver.

Because I am the chief justice, I'm being informed by Lucille, the Governor's legal counsel, who they're considering, and at different times. I've always felt it is the Governor's business; under the constitution he or she gets to make the decision without any checks such as consent from the senate or advice from a citizen committee.

But nonetheless, they are consulting me, because they don't want a lot of problems. So it comes down that Liz Hardy is mentioned. She grew up in Traverse City, and she is a successful lawyer in Birmingham. Lucille knew that whenever her name was raised, I would always say, "I don't think so." A lot of people like her—she's received awards and all that.[365]

But she was not right for the court, in Weaver's opinion.

But I know I was called on the Friday afternoon before the Monday and Tuesday that we were going to be in Grand Rapids with President Ford and with U.S. Supreme Court Justice Paul Stevens for the State Bar Meeting, at the Amway Grand; and they were now close to doing it; and I was told that it was going to be Nanci Grant.

Nanci L. Grant was then serving in her third year as a judge of the Sixth Circuit Court (Oakland County). She is now the chief judge of the circuit,[366] a member of the Judicial Tenure Commission, and a past president of the Michigan Judges Association. She earned her B.A. from the University of Michigan and her law degree from Wayne State University.[367]

Nanci Grant is the daughter of the Probate Judge Barry Grant and was a circuit judge in Oakland County. She would be a very formidable candidate; relatively young; but she had been elected overwhelmingly. She was part of the Jewish community there and had access to money to run, and I knew her dad [Barry Grant] very well, and I knew her some. And she was going to be the person.

Well, Probate Judge Gene Moore is a very close friend of mine and very close with Barry Grant; he knows the Grants very well. Because I didn't know Nanci very well, I wanted to call and see what Judge Moore thought of her.

---

365 Elizabeth Phelps Hardy is a member of Kienbaum, Operwall, Hardy, and Pelton, P.L.C. She has earned repute for defending corporations from lawsuits and has earned honors, including being named as one of *Crain's* "Detroit's Most Influential Women," and "2008 Power Lawyer." It's also of interest that former Justice Patricia J. Boyle has served "of counsel" to the firm since 2002. [http://www.kohp.com/attorneys/hardy. html.]

366 Weaver said that having Nanci Grant named chief judge was difficult: *It was quite a fight to get her appointed the last time when I was on the court.*

367 "Michigan Judicial Tenure Commission," http://jtc.courts.mi.gov/commission.htm#ngrant.

Probate Judge Eugene "Bud" Moore had served since he was first elected in 1966. One of his opponents in that race was Barry Grant. The two have remained life-long friends. Moore described his first hearing that the daughter of his old friend might have been headed for the high court:

> I've known Nanci all her life. And I got a call from Betty Weaver, and she said the Governor is about to make an appointment to the Supreme Court, and I'd like to get your views on somebody. This was at night...typical. Okay! She says, "What do you know about Nanci Grant?" Well, I think if my wife had been in the room, she'd have had to pick me up off the floor. I had no idea that Nanci Grant would ever be appointed to the Supreme Court. Holy Mackerel! I'd known her as a kid; she was a good circuit judge, had been on the bench maybe two years, I liked her very much, but, my God, of all the people in Michigan.... But anyway, I said, "I know Nanci. I think she's probably a moderate. I think she's conscientious, extremely hard working; any job she gets, she will do an excellent job on it. And the most important, she is a hell of a good campaigner. When she gets appointed, there isn't anybody I can think of who will work harder to stay on the bench." Betty knew that I knew her father, so I was telling her what I thought. But I was dumbfounded that the Governor was thinking of appointing her because it never would have occurred to me.[368]

And she was young, very young. Yes, agreed Moore: "Yeah, well if you like somebody you keep them there a lot longer. And if you appoint them when they're young...."

He told me that she would be excellent. And I felt that while it was not my decision at least I wanted to know what kind of reaction there would be. Because she's relatively young—which I don't have any objection to—and she had earned her spot. And Grant isn't a Kelly name or what-have-you, but the name, she, and her dad were well respected in Oakland County. So, fine: it's going to be Nanci Grant; that's what I understood.

That was a Friday afternoon, and Lucille called me. I'm not calling them; I'm not pushing, you know? It's their decision. They knew what I felt about Markman when it had been floated by me. But as far as Nanci, this was it, and I had said, "Fine," and I would let Lucille know if I had any other thought. I had no other thought; it was fine with me.

We arrive in Grand Rapids, and there's going to be a presentation of these things for helping the indigent—those various funds that the Bar is trying to help people. And while that's going on, Lucille tells me—this is in a downstairs part, and there's a press conference with Engler—and some monies that had been raised for this client relief fund—and Lucille tells me she's got to see me.

So we go outside that room. And Lucille tells me that it's not going to be Nanci Grant; that she refused to take it. And I said, "Well, what about [Michigan Court of Appeals Judge Richard]

368 Eugene "Bud" Moore, video interview with co-author Schock, 13 March 2012.

Bandstra?"[369]—because I felt Bandstra was another really good one. And she says, "Well, he refused to take it. So it's going to be Steve Markman."

And I said, "You have got to be kidding?" And I could not believe it. I said, "In my opinion this is a serious mistake. I'd like to talk to the Governor."

So, after the indigent funds presentation is over, the Governor, Lucille, and I went over to the Cornucopia deli at the Amway and we sat there. And I said, "Why didn't Nanci Grant take it?"

"Well, she didn't want it."

"Well, what about Bandstra?"

"Well, you know Bandstra; he always wants a sure thing. And he wouldn't take it because he was afraid he wasn't going to win."

And so I said, "There's got to be somebody else better than Markman." I said, "He's going to be such a difficult person. You've got two problems already; now you're going to have three. And you could have had a woman; but at least if you had Bandstra, he's very well-respected." I said, "Can't you think about it?"

"No. We're going to announce it tomorrow."

So, I think I went and got Maura, because Maura was against having Markman.

Corrigan was her ally at the time in urging against Markman's appointment, but there was a reason that went beyond just his unsuitability for the job; she had a score to settle.

I later learned from Justice Corrigan that her husband, Joe Grano, who was a law professor at Wayne State University, had dealt with Markman.[370] (Grano was a very conservative professor. And Maura had been a student and then eventually married him. And he was older than Maura.) Well, he and Markman had worked together, I believe in D.C. Markman had a reputation there. And I also learned that when Maura had wanted to be appointed by Bush One to the U.S. Attorney's Office for the Eastern District, that she had asked Markman to help her. And what Markman had done was go around her and then go to Spencer Abraham, who was at the time the head of the party, and had told Abraham that he wanted to be appointed. And so, Markman was appointed and not Corrigan; and her husband, Joe, had never gotten over that. But Justice Corrigan didn't tell me that at the time, when she joined me in opposing Justice Markman's appointment. I still didn't know any of those details about all that until later.

---

369 Bandstra is now chief legal counsel to Michigan's Attorney General, Bill Schuette. Before that, he served on the Michigan Court of Appeals for 16 years. Before that, he was a member of the Michigan House of Representatives. ["Breaking: Court of Appeals Judge Richard Bandstra to Retire January 8," State Bar of Michigan (SBM) Blog, 6 December 2010, http://sbmblog.typepad.com/sbm-blog/2010/12/breaking-court-of-appeals-judge-richard-bandstra-to-retire-january-8.html.]

370 Joseph D. Grano was a distinguished professor of law and an expert on the Warren Court's social policies and an outspoken critic of the Miranda Ruling. He also was the author of *Confessions, Truth, and the Law*, [University of Michigan Press, Ann Arbor, Mich., 1994]. Grano died in early 2002.

And Maura tried to talk to Lucille. Well, they didn't give her the same time that they gave me. I was the chief justice.

So Maura's appalled. So what are we going to do? I have dinner with Justice Riley and Wally at the top of the Amway that evening, and everyone is really disturbed and they—the Rileys—are definitely against that. Of course, Justice Riley is retired, but they head the Historical Society—they founded it. So they were going to do what they could. I think, they talked to the Governor on the phone—I wouldn't swear to that. But I know I talked to the Governor with Lucille at the Cornucopia; I <u>would</u> swear to that. So, it was going to be Markman.

Elizabeth Weaver poses with her dear colleague and friend, retired Chief Justice Dorothy Comstock Riley, and her husband, Wallace Riley, at the Grand Rapids Bar event.

That wasn't quite all the story. Weaver would soon learn much of the rest.

I then talked to Judge Moore as to what happened, because I didn't get any satisfactory answer to it. So Judge Moore tells me this: Justice Young called Nanci Grant and invited her down to the Comerica Building—where they were housed at that time—on, I think it was, a Sunday afternoon. And he told her what a terrible job it was, and that she had a young child and she would not be able to do it, et cetera and so-forth, and talked her out of it. And so, she did withdraw. She then called and got out—and said she wouldn't take it.

Judge Moore confirmed the story:

> I found out a week later from her father that she had gotten a call from the Governor asking if she'd take the appointment and she said—and I'm getting this second hand through her dad—she said "I will think about it." She had a young son at the time, who had a problem with his heart and was going for open-heart surgery at University of Michigan Hospital. And somebody suggested to her—I can't remember who it was—suggested that she go down and meet in Detroit with these current justices. And whether they talked her out of it or not, I found out a week later that she turned it down. Her father has regretted it ever since. ...You should ask him; I shouldn't speak for him. But I've regretted it ever since. Probably Nanci hasn't regretted it; I've never asked her, but she likes what she does.[371]

371 Eugene "Bud" Moore.

And was the person who talked her out of the appointment Justice Robert Young, Jr.?

> That's the name I've heard. They were going to move offices to Lansing and no longer have a Detroit office.[372]

> For years and years and years, I was sworn to secrecy and absolutely didn't tell anybody. And I was with her father once when he told somebody, and I almost fell off my chair. And I said "Does that mean this is no longer a secret?" and he said "Well...mmm-mmm-mmmmmm."[373]

It was no longer a secret. But at the time it occurred, the matter was under wraps.

So they could tell me, quote, "the truth": that they'd offered it to her. What they didn't tell me is that they had Justice Young talk to her to talk her out of it; how terrible it was going to be, what a terrible job it was. Now, Justice Young had been there only since January.

In any case, I wanted to know what happened with Bandstra. They had told me "You know Bandstra. He wants a sure thing." I thought that as somewhat off the mark. So I talked to Bandstra, and he said they told him there'd be no money for his re-election, and he couldn't win. Who would take it?

Now, was there money for Markman? Yes. But there'd be no money for Bandstra. Bandstra, who had been a law clerk to [U.S. Supreme Court Justice Antonin] Scalia and who was a fine judge, et cetera; and he was the chief judge of the Court of Appeals, and I strongly supported him for it.

Now, Nanci Grant never told that to anyone at the time, but I understand that she has since made it known. But that's how it happened. And I never told Maura or anyone about what Moore had told me about what came down, but I know it came down, and Moore knew it, too. And that's what happened.

So, I think that ends that story, right?

---

372 This has been a perennial issue, closing branch offices. It comes up most regularly when the prospect of cost cutting is raised. Or it was raised as a political issue. Weaver's Traverse City office was a favorite target of Cliff Taylor when he was running unsuccessfully for re-election in 2008.
373 Eugene "Bud" Moore.

Chapter 8

The Swearing In, A Replacement, The Swearing Out, And One in the Chamber

So, it was Stephen Markman who would be the 103rd justice of the Michigan Supreme Court. First things were first.

Among those close and very interested in the filling of the Brickley vacancy on the court, I think my opposition to a Markman appointment was pretty well known. I'm open about things. I believe that Markman knew of my opposition. But it was the Governor's choice. Now, when Markman did get appointed, then he asked me to swear him in by coming up immediately to Traverse City, to my office, and I was glad to swear him in. And I had a little something there, a small reception at my own expense. And his family came—his wife and both his young sons.

That was October 1, 1999, and the swearing in would get him on the job, but the formal ceremonies took a little time to plan.

He scheduled his investiture downstate at a time that I could not be there; I don't remember why. He then got Justice Kelly to do it.

The official investiture, Nov. 12, 1999, came with all kinds and sorts of laudatory comments. Former coworkers praised his scholarship, his even temper, his collegiality, his quick intelligence. Much was made of his work as a United States Attorney (federal prosecutor) in Detroit and later assistant Attorney General of the U.S.

Governor Engler let it be known that he was so very pleased:

> I am certainly proud to be here today and to welcome to the Michigan Supreme Court a jurist who brings with him unquestioned integrity and intellectual rigor. Justice Markman embodies everything one attributes to a Supreme Court justice: independence, compassion, fairness, respect for the law, and the desire to see the rule of law upheld.

When I announced Steve Markman's appointment in late September, lawyers and judges from across the political spectrum praised Justice Markman. He was praised in the media. *The Detroit News* called Judge Markman, "a choice for excellence." Even my critics at the *Free Press* said, "No better person could have been selected to replace Jim Brickley than Steve Markman." I quote from their editorial. "He brings a strong legal background and an excellent reputation for integrity and judicial scholarship. Judge Markman gives the court an intellectual honesty and a willingness to judge cases on their facts." Now, when the *Free Press* and *News* agree, that's news.

This is [...] the third opportunity that I've had and the third privilege, and I view it as such, to appoint a justice to the Michigan Supreme Court. It is a responsibility that I approach with the utmost gravity and seriousness, knowing that my decision affects the lives of all of us who live in Michigan.

[...]

[Y]ou join the Supreme Court at a critical time in its history. Our founders designed divided government, assigning the duty to the Senate and House of Representatives of writing the laws, the executive of administering the laws, and the judiciary of interpreting the laws. The vesting of legislative, executive, and judicial powers in the Senate and House, Governor, and our one court of justice, headed by the Supreme Court, still leaves the challenge posed in Article 3, Section 2, that no person shall exercise powers properly belonging to another branch.

Obviously, four of seven justices in the branch, having the power to interpret laws, could exercise virtually unlimited power. [Emphasis added.]

Commendably, the Michigan Supreme Court today has chosen to exercise judicial restraint. This restraint represents a welcome return to first principles, and a much needed antidote to judicial activism. Few things have undermined the rule of law more than seizing from our elected legislators the right to debate, compromise, and defeat or enact the issues of the day.[374]

With that, the Engler court was in session. And what a session it was going to be. Todd C. Berg, in *Michigan Lawyers Weekly* observed:

With the election of Justice Maura D. Corrigan and the appointments of Justices Robert P. Young and Stephen J. Markman, all in 1999, a conservative voting bloc emerged that would drastically change Supreme Court jurisprudence.[375]

374 "Special Sessions: Swearing-in Ceremony for Justice Stephen J. Markman," Michigan Supreme Court Historical Society, 12 November 1999, http://www.micourthistory.org/special_sessions.php?get_id=139.
375 Todd C. Berg, "Taylor-made judicial career: Conservative 'textualist' leaves MSC with no regrets after electoral defeat ends his 11-year run," *Michigan Lawyers Weekly*, 29 December 2008, http://milawyersweekly.com/news/2008/12/29/taylormade-judicial-career/.

The second 1999 Michigan Supreme Court, and the court as it would stand (or more appropriately, sit) for the next nine years, from left: Justice Michael F. Cavanagh, Justice Maura D. Corrigan, Justice Stephen J. Markman, Chief Justice Elizabeth A. Weaver, Justice Clifford W. Taylor, Justice Marilyn J. Kelly, and Justice Robert P. Young, Jr. Weaver would serve as chief justice until 2001.

The Governor had flat-out appointed to the Michigan Supreme Court three of the seven justices—Taylor, Young, and Markman—and at least half appointed Maura Corrigan through elevating her to the Court of Appeals and then bankrolling her Supreme Court run.

Had any Governor before or since held such sway over the judiciary?

Probably so. Since the days that Michigan started electing justices there have been other Governors who have more or less engineered the court. Engler's predecessor, Jim Blanchard (1983–1991) also appointed three justices. Bill Milliken (1969–1983) appointed five, as did G. Mennen "Soapy" Williams (1949–1961). Governor Fred Green (1927–1931) appointed four, and Alex Groesbeck (1921–1927) appointed three. Governor Kinsley S. Bingham (1855–1859) holds the record on appointments: six. But they were also doing double-duty as circuit judges.[376]

376 "On and Off the Court," Michigan Supreme Court Historical Society, http://www.micourthistory.org/on_and_off_the_court.php?on_off=1.

Perhaps it says something about the appointment process. Weaver often decries the unchecked appointment powers that a Michigan Governor uses when there is a vacancy on the court. She envisions reforms that would make any gubernatorial appointment contingent upon confirmation. The process also wouldn't begin with the Governor, but, instead, a meeting of stakeholders who were serving on a qualification commission.[377] The problem, she notes, is much larger than just the appointment process, but that's a big part of it.

It's our justice selection process of party nominees and unregulated, untraceable, unaccountable, unidentifiable, deceitful spending, unchecked gubernatorial power to appoint justices for vacancies, lack of rotation in high office, and unnecessary secrecy that's doing us in.

The run or tenure of the Engler-selected court, in itself, was notable: this court would sit *en banc*, so to speak, for the next nine years and three months...until then-Chief Justice Cliff Taylor was replaced after being unelected in the fall of 2008. That term of consistent justices on the high court (once Michigan became a state) was exceeded only by the court that was formed with the election of Justice Thomas Cooley in 1864.[378]

As the new justice on the bench, Markman set out to distinguish himself as a team player. Unfortunately for Weaver, he was playing for the wrong team. Her move for reforms fell on deaf ears. In the first place, she was against the hierarchical structure that bound the judges of the trial courts from filling in for each other.

And Steve Markman, of course, believed that the hierarchy was very good. He truly believed, and would argue to us, against these ideas for reforms. Markman said he felt it was unconstitutional to assign; yet Article VI, Section 23 says you can assign people to specific needs or over periods of time.

Specifically, Article VI, Section 23 of the Michigan Constitution not only makes provision for the Governor to make appointments for vacancies, but it also gives the high court the authority to make adjustments: "The Supreme Court may authorize persons who have been elected and served as judges to perform judicial duties for limited periods or specific assignments."[379]

I mean, come now, how's that unconstitutional? And Markman said he believed by assigning judges we were deceiving the public—because according to him, everyone who goes into the voting booth

---

377 For a reading of her proposal for reforming the Supreme Court and for a recent talk outlining the needs for reform, and see Appendix A in this book. Also, you can read the plan and the talk on her website: http://www.justiceweaver.com/pdfs/Sevenpointplan.pdf, and http://www.justiceweaver.com/pdfs/GRTALK61112.pdf.

378 Cooley would go on to serve a total of 21 years before stepping down after he was defeated in the election of 1885. And it was Justice Isaac Marston who arrived at the court in 1874 to change the composition of the court. He replaced Justice Isaac P. Christiancy. While Cooley had a lengthy service record on the court, he is by no means the record holder. That distinction goes to the 24th Justice, James Campbell, who served 32 years, two months, 26 days. The second-longest sitting justice is Michael Cavanagh, who took office Jan. 1, 1983. There are ten others who served longer than 20 years. ["On and Off the Court," Michigan Supreme Court Historical Society, http://www.micourthistory.org/on_and_off_the_court.php?on_off=1.]

379 Constitution of Michigan of 1963, Article VI, Section 23, http://www.legislature.mi.gov/(S(bbmf4smpbwnpce45frbqik45))/mileg.aspx?page=getObject&objectName=mcl-Article-VI-23.

knows what the difference is between a probate, a district, and a circuit judge. And so he felt the court could not possibly assign someone who's been elected as a probate judge to do circuit court work, or circuit judge to do probate. Well, that just shows you how lacking in common sense and out of touch with reality he was on these issues.

It wasn't just the assignment issue that set him off.

He and Taylor were against the drug courts.[380] We went down to Kalamazoo and had a hearing about them. Taylor told a judge and others they would support the drug courts. They didn't—and this is when I realized they would tell certain people something, and then tell others something else. But they behaved like children, and people talked about it; they were so disdainful.

Replacing Markman

In the nature of orderly succession, Justice Markman had taken Justice Weaver's spot on the Court of Appeals when she came to the Supreme Court. And now that he was at the high court, his old seat was vacant, and the Governor would have one more of his opportunities to fill it. By all reckoning, the seat should have gone to Weaver's long-time friend Donald Owens, one of the "Young Turks"[381] and a probate judge from Ingham County.

Judge Owens was a noted probate juvenile judge from Ingham County, who had been appointed by Governor Milliken in '74. So now we're in '99, he's been repeatedly re-elected, and he's a very experienced trial judge. He had testified many times at the legislature, and had also been considered a leader and described by a professor at the Yale Law School as the best probate judge in the country. He had tremendous expertise in juvenile and probate law, and he was very bright.

Actually, Owens had been slated to take an earlier vacancy, that of Judge Barbara McKenzie.

She was the second woman on the Court of Appeals; I came in after her, the third woman there. And she and I were very good friends. When she retired, Owens was supposed to get that spot—it had been discussed. I had heard both from Lucille Taylor and from the Governor, that Owens would get that appointment.

Well, then I get a call from the Governor himself, telling me that he was not going to appoint Owens because he was going to appoint [10th Circuit Court (Saginaw County) Judge Patrick] Meter. Why?

---

380 The drug courts (really the Drug and DWI Treatment Courts) were a series of highly structured programs intended to work with substance abusers. Those who wanted to go through the drug court in order to avoid jail time (the alternative) were subject to regular and random testing, counseling, and frequent appearances before trial court judges who would monitor their progress. At the end of their programs, the participants were awarded graduation certificates. The program was highly lauded and had been highly effective at keeping substance abusers straight and sober and out of jail. It also saved the state money by avoiding incarceration. ["Drug and DWI Treatment Courts," Michigan Courts, http://courts.michigan.gov/scao/services/DrugCourts/DrugDWI.htm.]

381 The "Young Turks" was a group of young probate judges that included Weaver, Donald Owens, Gladys Barsamian, Randall Hekman, and Michael Anderegg. They led responsible reforms.

Because Meter was from the Saginaw area and close to the northeast part of Michigan, and he would be able to get (circuit court judges) [Joseph] Swallow and [Kurt] Hansen to calm down with their accusations about the court being controlled by Engler and that it had no independence...that the Engler court was an attack on the independence of the judiciary.

Meter was a circuit judge and a qualified person. ...Not as qualified as Owens in my opinion, but qualified. And he turned out to be an independent, very good Court of Appeals judge. But the Court of Appeals needed the experience of a probate juvenile judge on it. And Owens was in every way— intellectually and by common sense and communicative abilities—the best choice. Nevertheless, I said to the Governor that it was his choice, obviously.

I wasn't keen on Meter's appointment but, again, the message was that Owens would get the next appointment.

But that didn't mean it was going to play out that way. And, for a time, it didn't look like it would.

I got a call from a district court judge, Laura Barnard out of Lapeer County, who I knew well. And I had known her father-in-law, who was an excellent probate judge of Oakland County—long deceased. So, she had been very supportive of my election—that would be the '94 election—and she is a very decent person. She had had some difficulties over there politically, and she was still very young, and had not been a judge very long. But nevertheless, she was called by Lucille Taylor, she told me, and asked if she would consider taking the appointment to the Court of Appeals.

This would have been for the very same seat, said Weaver, that the Governor had promised to Don Owens.

And it would involve having to run immediately because this is the fall of '99, and the election is in November of 2000. I was really taken aback by the call because my understanding was Don Owens was going to get that appointment. So I immediately was able to put two and two together, or one and three, and I realized that she was being asked to do this because there had been a need for a woman to have been appointed to the Supreme Court, and Markman had been appointed to the Supreme Court instead of a woman. And, therefore, Owens seemingly was being tossed off the list again, this time by someone I knew and liked—Judge Laura Barnard. And I told her point blank that I would not be supporting her; she was seeing if I would. I told her I would support Judge Owens. I said, "I would think seriously about getting involved because Owens is ready, in my opinion; you're not." So that was rather blunt, but I think we've remained friends anyway.

So the next thing that occurred was that I called Judge Owens and said to him, "Don, have you heard about the appointment to the Court of Appeals?" And he said, "No, I haven't heard anything yet. I'm waiting to hear from them." And I said, "Well, I think you better get on it if you're really interested in it, because I just got a call from a woman judge, who's been asked to consider taking the appointment. And I can tell you it has nothing to do with who belongs on the Court of Appeals, who's best qualified, but it has to do with this idea of now throwing a high appointment to a woman, to deflect the criticism of not appointing a woman to the Brickley position." And I said, "If you're interested, and if I were you, I would call the Governor's office right away and say how interested you are."

I believed he should do that. I was beginning to awaken to the modus operandi of the Englerites that if they did not hear from him, they'd appoint a woman and tell him they didn't think he was still interested in the appointment because they hadn't heard from him. I further said to Owens: "And then get your people who want you to be appointed to let the Governor know." And I think Judge Owens did that, and as a result he was appointed because he had a bandwagon of judges around the state and all kinds of people who were urging that he should be appointed to the Court of Appeals. And so he was.

Owens' investiture was Jan. 7, 2000.

Chief Justice Elizabeth Weaver and Justice Clifford Taylor flank newly invested Court of Appeals Judge Donald Owens, Jan. 7, 2000.

I, as the chief justice, presided, but I also was asked by Judge Owens to speak. Justice Taylor had been a groomsman at Judge Owens' wedding, and so he was asked by Judge Owens to speak as well. There was a big affair of close to 700 people at the Wharton Center—Judge Owens is very popular, very well known in that area—and lots of Court of Appeals judges were there on the stage, everybody in their robes.

The fact of the matter is, when Justice Taylor spoke, he belittled Judge Owens. Furthermore, he went on to say uncomplimentary things about the Court of Appeals, passing off the judges there as not too significant, which, needless to say, did not make the Court of Appeals judges happy. And when the thing was over, there were a few Court of Appeals judges who surrounded him and really gave it to him, because Court of Appeals judges—unless they have ambitions for some higher office —generally were not too afraid.

So as Taylor and I were getting our coats, Cliff said to me, "Do you think I misspoke?" And I said, "Cliff, yes. You have a very clever sense of humor, but sometimes it's not kind, and there's a place for just clever remarks, but it isn't in front of huge numbers of people at a serious event." And I said, "You are up for re-election, and you want to reserve your caustic humor for joking amongst friends, because it doesn't necessarily come across well."

At that moment, we were close enough as friends that he would say that, because that takes a lot of courage to ask somebody if you misspoke. But he had been pretty well besieged by the Court of Appeals judges before we got off the stage.

At the time, I still believed that Cliff was making stupid mistakes rather than setting out on an agenda. And at the time, I was supporting Justice Taylor and Justice Young for re-election.

She would soon see how well they would follow campaign finance rules.

But first there was a more pressing matter that demanded her attention: the behavior by her newest justice when he physically blocked the way of one of the court employees who was trying to leave his office.

Good Help Is Hard to Find

Justice Stephen Markman was having trouble just getting started.

The first thing was that he couldn't get secretaries. He was coming from the Court of Appeals, and his secretary there wasn't coming, apparently. Now, this was an unusual problem, but it fell to me as chief justice: he came to me and said he needed secretaries. Justice Brickley had been up here in Traverse City, so he had his secretaries up here. He had one or two, I think, and then he had other people; his clerks were up here, pretty much; maybe he had a clerk downstate sometimes.

Markman needed two secretaries and three law clerks. So Weaver went to one of Justice Brickley's secretaries, Christine DesBeauchamp, to see if she might help out. And it <u>might</u> have worked out even better than if Markman had brought his secretary from the Court of Appeals.

Just because you were in the Court of Appeals doesn't mean you know how the Supreme Court works, and you need people to process the paper. The more they know the better. And I asked her [Christine] if she would be willing to go down to Lansing, and it would all be paid for—you know, it wouldn't be at her expense—to go down and help Justice Markman get established while he's getting secretaries.

This is unusual not to find secretaries. You know, most people have a lot of people who want the jobs. They're good jobs, and there are usually good people to find.

In any case, she committed to going there for three weeks and then she'd see what would happen, how it would work out. At the end of the three weeks, it came back to me that she wasn't staying...she WOULDN'T stay. So I talked to her because Markman still needed help. He still needed people. So I asked her, you know, if she would consider staying longer. She would not. Period. Not working for him. That was that.

Hmmmm. That was odd.

I conveyed this, I think, to Lucille Taylor and to Cliff Taylor that he needed help. They knew it, too, I think. But a secretary that had been with him at one time at the Court of Appeals would not work for him.

There would be some concern as to what would be done to these people. I mean, even though I opposed him being there, he was there; I accepted that, and I tried to help him. I got the people to come down and did what I could. And it was settled, and I saw that he had secretaries.

The next thing that happened was I got a report that Justice Markman had a problem with his computer—which can very easily happen—and the male technician had gone down to his office. We were all in the old buildings at this time. And the technician was not able to solve the problem as quickly as Justice Markman wanted—or at all. And Justice Markman was really mad and lost it with the technician, so that the technician had left the office, crying—this is a male—and had said he would never go back there.

Now, this is rather unusual. It is very frustrating when you lose your material on the computer, but it isn't anyone's fault except, perhaps, your own. It's certainly not the fault of the technician who has come out to try to help you. They usually can get it solved eventually. ...Maybe not even while you're there and not when you'd like it, but eventually.

This was then rumored through the court, and it came to me—was reported to me—as true. Also I was informed that others heard about it. So when you have an employee that won't go back and help somebody, and he left crying....

I decided to talk to Justice Markman about it; that this is not the way we treat employees, you know; we don't do that. And so I asked him to come down the hall to my Lansing chief justice office; we were on the same floor.

So I sat down with Steve and I said, "Steve, it's been reported that, you know, you had problems with your computer and that the technician—that you really lost it with him, and that the technician went crying from your office and doesn't ever want to come back to your office."

He went off the charts with me. He launched into it that I didn't like him. It wasn't a matter of not liking him. It's true; I had not wanted him to be at the court as a justice; I never denied that; but I certainly had helped him and was trying to help him then because—I said, "You don't realize you don't treat people that way. You are up for re-election, and you don't need this if for no other reason because it won't help you get re-elected. The best reason, though, is that you just need to treat people with respect."

I could hardly get any of that out because he was furious with me, I think cursed me out—and went out of the office in a rage.

Others found him odd and didn't seem to enjoy working with him.

At some point, he had a law clerk simply tell him off and leave. And these things would get around. This was in a building where the staff was closer than the present building, the Hall of Justice. With the people who were there, things were known; the staff was right there.

Weaver decided she needed to involve Cliff Taylor, Markman's advocate.

So I decided to tell Taylor that "you better get Steve under control because this is not good. It's not good for his re-election if nothing else."

Taylor wasn't the only one she talked with at that time.

After the experience with the technician, I was at the Final Four in Indianapolis. That was in 2000. I had missed the one the previous year in Tampa, but I went to this one. And I was in my full New Orleans, Mardi Gras regalia—boas, glitter, green wig. I took a whole bunch of people down to Indianapolis and, of course, we won. But there were many events, and this was really great—a lot of fun. And waiting to get into an event, I was in line with Jim Barrett, then president, now former president but still active, of the Michigan Chamber of Commerce. He had always been supportive of me—the Chamber had wanted a fair court, supposedly, when they didn't have one. Barrett is a decent man—but they wanted control of the court in the end. And I didn't know that for Barrett, Markman was tops and, in fact, probably had pushed Engler to appoint him. Markman is supposed to be the ultimate conservative.

Justice Elizabeth Weaver attended the 2000 Final Four in Indianapolis to support one of her favorite adopted teams: Michigan State University. Here she is pictured with MSU alumnus Governor John Engler. It was at the Final Four that she told the former president of the Michigan Chamber of Commerce that she and he needed to discuss the excesses of newly appointed Justice Stephen Markman. That word circled back to Justice Cliff Taylor who let her know that he was angered by her actions. At that point, she knew she was dealing with a systemic problem.

Anyway, I'm in line with Barrett, waiting to get in to the event, and we're all dressed up, and I say to him, "We need to talk about Justice Markman. This isn't the place, but we need to talk. So let's be in touch, and maybe you would give me a call?" because I had the technician deal. And I'm thinking, somebody better talk to this man and see if he can get his act together.

Instead of him calling me, he calls Taylor. Cliff Taylor comes down the hall to talk to me and to tell me that he was really ticked that I had talked to Jim Barrett about Markman. Well, don't tell me that, you know? But I knew it was pointless to talk to Barrett then because he'd talked to Taylor. My assessment at that point was that these people don't want to know; they probably knew a lot worse than I knew anyway.

Markman's bad behavior wasn't done. And the next thing Weaver knew about it, Markman's secretary was carried out of the building on a stretcher by paramedics and loaded into an ambulance.

His secretary, Gerri, had had what they thought was a heart attack. They'd called an ambulance, and she'd been taken to the emergency. And what was discovered was that it wasn't a heart attack; it was the stress she was under for the job. And she would not be coming back.

The chief justice has as her or his job the wellbeing of the entire staff. Weaver wanted to know what was going on. She found out soon enough when she received a letter from the secretary.

And this thing was copied to myself, Margaret Chiara, the personnel and policy person, and Ron Stadnika. He was the chief financial officer, and that's where the records of the court were kept. We had no human resource person then.

In it, the secretary gave the reasons for her leaving. The missive was addressed to Markman as the primary recipient, but it's obvious it was intended for the chief justice; Markman was throughout referred to in the third person.

MEMORANDUM

TO:Justice Stephen J. Markman
cc: Chief Justice Elizabeth Weaver, Margaret-Mary Chiara and Ronald Stadnika
FROM:Gerri Kozachik
DATE:June 15, 2000
RE:Notice of Resignation

This letter will serve as my resignation from my position at the Michigan Supreme Court as secretary to Justice Stephen J. Markman. For reasons explained herein, I cannot continue to work through a traditional period of notice.

The immediate reason for my resignation stems solely from concern for my health and follows the recommendations of my physician, who attributes my recent attack of chest/heart pain to work-related stress. There is an ever-present level of tension and stress that exists in Justice Markman's office that, quite frankly, has made working for him unbearable.

It was always clear that Justice Markman was a demanding boss, but I first witnessed the full force of his temper after his former secretary left which was two weeks after I started. Justice Markman had a confrontation with a technician from the computer department who was trying to remedy a problem with his computer. Justice Markman yelled at this individual and told him to 'get out of my office' and that he needed 'someone who was competent to get in here and take care of things.' The tone of this tirade was inappropriately severe under the circumstances and it not only caused the technician to flee, but frightened me that I would be subject to similar treatment for minor mistakes or for not being able to please Justice Markman quickly enough. Unfortunately, these fears were realized. The unpredictability of when a normal office occurrence would be followed by an overreaction by Justice Markman left me in a constant state of alert, and dread of misspeaking, mistyping, or not being able to find a file. Finally, two recent episodes have given rise to my current course of action.

On May 10, 2000, there was a confrontation between me and Justice Markman. Janet Welch from the chief's office had stopped in to talk with Justice Markman for a few minutes if he was free. I went in to his office to check with him and he said that was fine. Before I left the office, he asked me a question regarding the computer and a document he was working on. I tried to help him solve the problem, however, was unsuccessful. I could tell he was getting frustrated and I asked him to "please don't get frustrated with me." He pushed his chair back and told me that he was getting very frustrated with me. He left his office to let Janet know that he couldn't talk with her right then and came back into his office and proceeded to tell me that he couldn't believe that his secretary didn't know how the computer program worked. My reply to him was simple. I never get to use the program. Justice Markman and the law clerks do their own typing and correction. I don't have exposure to the programming unless I copy a document over and work with it on my own. This exchange became heated. After the exchange about the computer, he stated that I was "the most unfriendliest person he has ever worked with in his life." What started as a work-related issue turned into a personal attack and for the first time in my life, I experienced an anxiety attack accompanied with hyperventilating. During this confrontation, I became extremely emotional and pleaded to be allowed to go to the restroom, but he told me to stay in his office. Every time I tried to stand, he would say 'just sit down, relax.' I was not allowed to leave. Justice Markman stayed between me and the door and when a scheduled appointment finally compelled him to leave, he said that I could just stay in his office as long as I needed so that I could calm down. I left his office as soon as I felt it was safe because he had left the building. I did not want to stay in there. The law clerks returned from lunch shortly after I was back at my desk and they could tell something was wrong. Catherine and Julie made inquiries, but I told them that I couldn't talk about it. I felt that if I discussed it at that time, I would experience another episode.

On May 30, I began experiencing severe pain in my left shoulder, which radiated into my back around my left shoulder blade, which lasted for about 45 minutes. The next day May 31, I again experienced the same pain, however, this time it began to radiate down my left arm and up my neck into my jaw. My chest felt tight and I was nauseated. My skin began to feel clammy and I did not feel well. I reached my husband to let him know what was going on and he was on his way to take me to our physician or the emergency room. Given the way I was feeling, the paramedics were called by my co-workers. I was taken to the emergency room and tests ruled out my problems being cardiac in nature. Before leaving the hospital, I spoke with my personal physician and he wanted to see me the next day.

The next day, I saw my personal physician. After going over my test results, he advised me that what I had experienced was due to work-related stress. My doctor was point blank and told me that I should get a different job. After considering the work environment in which I currently find myself, he strongly suggested that the best thing I could do for my health was to leave that situation.

When I returned to work the following Monday (June 5), the pain started again in my shoulder and back on my drive into the office. I knew that Justice Markman was going to be in the office Monday morning and I wasn't looking forward to going into work. I knew what was going to happen. He would ask me to come into his office first thing and ask me how I was doing. That is what happened. I told him that I was doing okay and was taking things day by day. He left the office later that morning and was out all day Tuesday (June 6). He was supposed to be out of the office on Wednesday; however, he changed his appointments without advising the individual in charge of his schedule and unexpectedly came into the office Wednesday morning. The pain almost immediately started again in my left shoulder and I felt tightness in my chest.

I do not feel that the work environment will change. From what I have seen since I started, when there is a confrontation with Justice Markman and a staff member, he sort of backs off of that particular individual and is pleasant to them for awhile. This lasts until he feels that the incident has blown over. It almost seems to be like a form of manipulation. And then we will wait for the next blow up.

Justice Markman has indicated to me that he is difficult to work with. I will not disagree with that. However, I don't feel that difficult is the correct word. The behavior exhibited at times can be interpreted as irrational by some who work for him. I was told about his reputation before I took this position. Everyone can be difficult to work with at times, but I truly felt that being the type of person that I am, that it could not really be that bad. I was so wrong. If I knew then what I know now, I never would have taken this position.

I am not comfortable working with an individual that I feel I can't speak with. Every time that I need to speak with him, the stress of wondering what type of reaction I will receive creates a dread that I just can no longer tolerate on a daily basis.

What I find most distressing is that this is otherwise a wonderful job. I felt truly fortunate that I was given the opportunity to work at the Supreme Court, but I cannot continue to work in the environment that exists. If I truly felt that things would change, I would find a way to stay. But based upon the reputation that apparently has preceded him for a significant portion of his career, I conclude that the changes that need to happen most likely never will.

It is because of the above that I am resigning effective immediately. I apologize for the inconvenience that my leaving will cause, but I need to consider my health first and foremost.

Gerri L. Kozachik [signed][382]

Attached to the letter was a note on a prescription pad, signed by her doctor, Geoffrey M. Linz, M.D., and dated June 13, 2000:

Chest pain, back pain since late May 2000. Physical exam—unremarkable. Symptoms correlate very closely with level of stress at work. Strongly suggest a different work setting if possible.[383]

She now could not work for him; and that we had a doctor's note explaining that she cannot work for him; that the atmosphere was.... This is a classic worker's comp. case.

Well, according to one attorney, maybe it was even more: unlawful detention. By denying her the opportunity to exit, by blocking her way, the justice might have been going way over the top.

Weaver's next stop was going to be the Governor's office.

Needless to say, I didn't talk to Jim Barrett or Justice Taylor. I went right to the person who was responsible for all this, who really probably knew Markman's history from day one.

My conclusion was that this man was appointed by the Governor, he had never been elected by the people, and it wasn't too late, in June of 2000, for him to step down, and for the Governor to appoint somebody else, and then that person could run as the incumbent.

There would be some little time for a new justice to become known, said Weaver, before the Republican nominating convention in the late summer.

Justice Markman needed to step down; he was unworthy of the position. And this lady didn't need any more grief.

So, she made an appointment with the Governor and off to the capitol she went.

Now, the meeting with the Governor and Lucille Taylor occurred in what is known as the Ceremonial Conference Room in the Capitol, which was the old conference room of the Governor, before the Governor moved across the street to the Romney Building, the old Hotel Olds.

---

382 Gerri L. Kozachik, "Memorandum, 15 June 2000," unpublished.
383 Geoffrey M. Linz, M.D., 13 June 2000, unpublished.

Governor Engler sat at the end of the table, and I sat at the side of him to the right, and Lucille sat on the other side to the left. And what I wanted the Governor to do was to get—to ask Markman—to have Markman resign and then get it taken care of.

They would have none of it. They hardly let me get it out. "But," I said, "This is not right for this woman. This woman doesn't deserve to lose her job. The person who deserves to lose his job is Steve Markman, because he's not up to the job."

And so they said, "Well, we'll get her a job. Don't you have a job?"

I said, "We don't have any jobs there. How can she work there with him there anyway? But there aren't any jobs, and I'm not going to create a job." And Engler said he would get her a job. And I said, "Okay. You get her a job. And," I said, "you better talk to Markman."

The Governor reached out.

He called or had someone call Rick Bandstra, who was chief judge in the Court of Appeals; a very decent fellow. And Rick Bandstra got her a job in the Court of Appeals.[384] *They just weren't going to get rid of Markman, but they would get the problem solved for this lady; this lady was going to have a job. And I believe that she worked there for years.*

Bandstra was in Grand Rapids, where Gerri Lynn Kozachik did indeed continue working for a time. She eventually transferred to the Michigan Court of Appeals offices back in Lansing, in the same building—the Hall of Justice—but on a different floor than Markman inhabited.

And my understanding is that she's now deceased.

She died June 22, 2009, at the age of 46 "after a courageously long battle with cancer, a wonderful wife, an amazing mother, and a friend to many...."[385]

Markman was staying. And the future, while unknowable, had intimations.

We've had, now, two incidences and, apparently, a history that I did not know about. My opposing his appointment was based just on my experiences and my intuition, that this was not a man for the job. He might be intellectually smart, smart, smart, but I didn't detect a lot of wisdom, and I didn't detect an ability to deal with people on a reasonable, normal level. No judicial temperament. Meek and mild until he turned abusive and into a raging tyrant as I and Gerri Kozachik had experienced.

With Markman, I went through disappointment, disgust, feeling almost revulsion to the situation, and I felt like it was somewhat of an immoral atmosphere. And one of my principles is this: "Don't

---

384 An internal memo after the event indicates that Sharon Rothwell, then Governor Engler's chief of staff, said to keep Kozachik on the payroll and then referred the matter to Bandstra, who referred the matter to Carl Gromek, then the chief clerk and research director of the Court of Appeals. Sharon Rothwell currently serves as a commissioner of the Michigan Department of Transportation, appointed by Governor Rick Snyder. [http://www.michigan.gov/mdot/0,4616,7-151-9623_31969_31970-271290--,00.html.] Gromek is retired.
385 "Obituary: Gerri Lynn Kozachik," *Lansing State Journal*, 24 June 2009, http://www.legacy.com/obituaries/lsj/obituary.aspx?n=gerri-lynn-kozachik&pid=128842154.

breathe an immoral atmosphere unless in an attempt to purify it." So I was in a position to try and purify it, and I would stay with it.

And there was some leverage with the Governor at that point:

The last thing that was needed during the 2000 campaign was to have a Republican chief justice say, "This whole place is a mess, and I'm not going to be the chief justice and, furthermore, I'm going to retire. And I'm here for reform, and none of these people want to reform; and they're all a bunch of cats fighting with each other; you can't trust any of them."

But that didn't mean she didn't consider speaking out, at least about the Markman excesses.

Now, the regret I had to deal with is this: I was certainly tempted to go to the public with this, vis-à-vis Justice Markman, but contrary to what some may think, I am known to give people more than one chance.

And my biggest priority was for this woman. I realized enough that if this went public—and I had a right to make it public because I was copied—she would be attacked. Right?

Whenever somebody comes out and says something, it's turned on them. She would become investigated and attacked. They'd say, "She's not normal and she can't take it." Not that there wasn't this long history of Markman's unacceptable behavior; I myself had experienced what was Markman's irrational response to somebody trying to help him .... And to have total denial, attacks on me personally, and his leaving the room! I thought he would be back shortly. Anybody can get mad and leave the room. It's what they do forever after it. And when you have no justification.

By the way, I never got an apology from him. I kept waiting for him to apologize. And I told Taylor about it, and I said, "You better straighten him out." I didn't need an apology; it didn't affect me. But apology is a step toward reform and often the easiest step.

She didn't get that, either.

But my judgment was that it was in the best interest of this woman and the people of Michigan not to make this public. Apparently, Markman was talked to; John Engler probably talked to him, because he somewhat behaved.

My judgment of Markman was this: anybody he saw as inferior to him, or that he could make inferior to him, he would treat one way.

And anyone he saw in a superior position would receive a different kind of response. His peers, though, were not immune. Weaver said that when the justices met in conference, things could set him off...not just things said or done by those he despised but those closest to him on the court, too.

You could tell it was coming; the table would just shake from the abnormal movement of his legs underneath. And it was a long, heavy table.

But, why his explosion with his chief justice?

Perhaps he had a problem with me when I, a woman and someone who had opposed his appointment, was his superior as chief justice. But he still had his connections.

And if Markman had been the only problem!

I was having to deal with the difficulty of the situation between the justices who were up for election or retention and the ones who wanted them defeated. I had reason to believe that Kelly and Cavanagh were leaking information—and there would be plenty to leak, the way Markman, Taylor, and Young behaved. I would always deal with everyone fairly. So I said very little to most of them, which they didn't like. I wasn't going to tell Kelly and Cavanagh things that they would take out and use against the rest of the court, and I wasn't going to tell [the Engler Four] things that I wasn't going to tell Kelly and Cavanagh.

Her reticence extended to the annual State of the Judiciary Address; she didn't share a draft of what she intended to say with her colleagues to prevent it from being leaked.

It was the tradition that the chief justice just prepared and delivered it, and it wasn't passed around ahead of time.

When I gave the State of the Judiciary Address, many legislators liked it and told me so, and it was well received by the public. The only complaints came from justices.

Her goals, she said, were reform, openness, better service.

At least the Englerites should have liked it because the court looked good; it looked what it should be, and it laid out what we were still working to do. In spite of whether some justices liked it or not, we were going ahead with the pilots; we were doing this. But they didn't like it a bit, because they didn't like those programs, necessarily. ...The drug courts, the pilot programs, and/or the Guardianship Ombudsman.

Weaver asked Don Owens to serve as ombudsman. He stepped down from case call but kept on with some other Court of Appeals duties in addition to his new duties.

There was no cost—I announced that. They hated that, and they later got rid of it. It was to protect the public; the program was to protect the adults that were abused and neglected, just as there was a Children's Ombudsman for abused and neglected children, but it wasn't Engler's idea.

The Governor even expressed his displeasure about some of her reforms.

He wasn't happy about it. Well, of course I didn't ask him; it wasn't his business to decide. It was the court's business. We can create that. We did it without it costing anything to the taxpayers. What's the problem?

Notes from the Boys on the Bench

The Supreme Court sometimes was asked to take part in special events. May 3, 2000, was to showcase one of them. The court was scheduled to do its regular business in the morning: talk about an appointment to the Attorney Grievance Commission during a court conference and then to hear oral arguments. In the afternoon—starting at 1 p.m.—the justices were scheduled to witness a moot court session in the Supreme Court courtroom presented by Kalamazoo Central High School students who had traveled to Lansing.

They were going to compete nationally, and we gave them the opportunity to present their case—a trial with a judge, prosecution, defense and witnesses.

As chief justice, Weaver was in the center.

Kelly and Cavanagh were not there for the afternoon session. Corrigan and Markman were to my left and Taylor and Young were to my right; Taylor had moved over to Cavanagh's seat and Young into Taylor's since Cavanagh was not there. They were quite close to me, and they were together and they were misbehaving.

In particular, they were writing notes to each other.

At the end of the day, the others left and Weaver—often the last to leave—was faced with some disorder: there were loose papers on the bench where her colleagues had sat. Either, she said, she just tidied up herself, or someone else did and presented her with the detritus. She glanced at the leavings and confirmed her fears about the level of maturity on the bench.

Here's what they wrote:

Taylor, about the moot court: "Were you as earnest as the defense counsel in HS?"

Young: "You have to stop the back and forth at the red light"

Taylor: "We can't help ourselves."

Young: "Another [...] Textualist!"

There upon followed several pages of traffic observations and directions for travelling to the Detroit area before an enigmatic question that normally would be related to morals.

Taylor: "How did the good folks of Kazoo learn that we had round heels?"

Young: "EAW of course!"

Taylor: "This is an extra-ordinary waste of time. Please note we don't even have the *Kazoo Gazette* here. Another David G [Gruber] triumph.[386] If notified, they would, I believe, have come eagerly. Alternatively, David could take pictures and send them. Again, they would run them."

Taylor: "We will leave at 2:00! EAW will make statement to cover, etc."

Taylor: "This is as close as I can stand to being a trial judge! At or about 2:00 we will take a break and we can leave."

Young: "This seems to make being a trial judge very tedious."

Taylor: "YES"

Taylor: "Good God, how did this happen to me!"

Young: "Remind me, why did I agree to do this?"

Taylor: "This is what I was thinking!"

Young, who could see Cavanagh's area of the bench because he'd moved into Taylor's seat: "Why do you think MFC [Michael F. Cavanagh] keeps a picture of himself on the bench?"

Young answering himself: "Fear of amnesia. I think we've finally discovered the Shrine of Humpty Dumpty."

This reminded me of third graders or maybe junior high school boys. In this case, it was just Taylor and Young. At other times, Markman joined in.

Mr. Justice Markman Packs Serious Heat

Dealings with Justice Markman never did reach a level of collegiality. While he no longer was driving his staff to leave their employment, episodes with him weren't quite over. He was difficult to deal with, Weaver said, often beside himself with anger during the business of the court. All he needed to complete his hair-trigger temper was a hair trigger...on a gun.

---

386 David Gruber was then the court's public information officer. He reappears in Chapter 10.

Chief Justice Elizabeth Weaver and Justice Maura Corrigan stand with Kalamazoo Central High School students who came to the Supreme Court to present a moot court session in preparation for a national contest. Weaver and Corrigan were the only two judges available to be photographed with them afterward. Justices Cavanagh and Kelly did not attend the session and Justices Taylor and Young were exchanging notes on what they found an onerous duty. They left even before the session ended. Weaver said she does not remember if Markman was there.

This story happened a long time after Mr. Markman drove Gerri Kozachik from her job. Perhaps it belongs as a footnote or should come later in the book, because it occurs in the last of Justice Weaver's tenure on the court, during the time Marilyn Kelly was chief justice, 2009-2010. But it makes sense to include it here because it completes an assessment of Markman's character, and it has to do with his behavior with Gerri Kozachik.

Unknown to most other justices, he used to bring a handgun up from his car in the secure parking garage of the Hall of Justice into his office. Weaver was unknowing about the weaponry as was, evidently, everyone else other than the former chief justice, Cliff Taylor.

How could he legally do that? Didn't public law forbid firearms in courts as well as schools and other gun-free zones?

Well, it depended on whether or not you were a judge and whether or not you had permission. And that was related to 2008 Public Act 407 that allowed state court judges who had concealed carry weapons (CCW) permits to carry them in most of the otherwise "pistol-free zones."[387]

Most, but not all:

> The passage of 2008 Public Act 407 has <u>no</u> effect on the court's long-standing policy (i.e. *Administrative Order No. 2001-1*) that prohibits weapons in any courtroom, office, or other space used for official court business or by judicial employees unless the chief judge or other person designated by the chief judge has given prior approval consistent with the court's written policy.[388]

So, Taylor had given Markman permission to bring his gun onto the floor. And after Taylor was off the court Markman needed to ask permission from the new chief justice, Marilyn Kelly.

All justices and the clerk and the administrative aide person received a memo from Justice Markman dated May 15, 2009, concerning the Administrative Order 2001-03, what he called the Concealed Weapons policy. Actually, it's the policy for not having weapons in the Hall of Justice. The Hall of Justice is similar to Fort Knox: very difficult to access and very difficult to get in and security checks all along the way. This is a very secure place. If you come as a public member, you're going to be extremely well screened to get in.

The security checkpoint for the general public is just inside the front doors. Visitors are asked to sign in, their belongings are X-rayed, and they pass through a metal detector. If the visitors are there to see judges or justices or anybody else behind a locked door, security personnel make phone calls to be sure the visitors are expected and welcome. Once admitted, they must be buzzed through a hallway door along the route to their destination, all the while under video observation. Additionally, in the past, chamber doors (judges' and justices' office doors) were closed and kept locked, a situation which led judges and justices to complain that it made it difficult for interoffice visits. Visitors who are coming to tour the Hall of Justice Learning Center, to attend a matter in a courtroom, or to go the public counters in either of the clerk's offices at the Court of Appeals or the Supreme Court are admitted without phone calls to those places from security personnel.

The entryway for judges and justices is also secure.

The justices and the Court of Appeals judges can drive in at specially paid-for parking spaces. And there are special elevators accessible to the justices and judges for one, and the court staff for the other.

---

387 "Gun-Free Zones: Judges Exempt, Senate Bill 505 (2008 session) 2008 Public Act 407, MCL 28.421 and 28.425o," http://www.legislature.mi.gov/(S(upb55t55olinylrv0gq2i2zy))/mileg.aspx?page=getobject&objectname=mcl-28-421 and http://www.legislature.mi.gov/(S(upb55t55olinylrv0gq2i2zy))/mileg.aspx?page=getobject&objectname=mcl-28-425o.
388 Ibid.

The elevator for the justices and judges goes directly into their parking garage, which is a separate parking area with a dedicated entrance and exit which only they can access. This area in the basement of the Hall of Justice is completely enclosed. In fact, the entrance for staff parking is on one side of the building and for the judges and justices, it is on another side. While the two elevators are side by side, staff cannot get to the judges' and justices' elevator in the basement because there is a wall in the basement that separates the judicial elevator from the staff elevators. While there is a door in the wall, that door is locked to staff.

Everyone at the court is issued a pass that has to be swiped in order to activate the elevator. The pass only gives employees access to the floors where they work and to common areas. And while judges and justices share an elevator, the judges' passes do not allow them to get off on the sixth floor where the justices have their offices.

But Justice Markman thought he needed additional personal protection.

This is his memo:

> Memorandum
>
> TO: The Justices, Corbin Davis, and [...]
> FROM: Justice Stephen J. Markman
> Re: ADM Order #2001-03, Concealed Weapons
> DATE: May 15, 2009
>
> This is to respectfully request that the chief justice's new policy prohibiting judges, whose offices are in the Hall of Justice and who possess an expanded CCW permit, for carrying concealed weapons in the chambers be addressed by the court at the earliest possible opportunity. It is my understanding that: (a) in a departure from the policy of her predecessor; (b) notwithstanding the language of 2008 Public Act 407, which now expands the venues in which a judge holding a CCW permit may carry a concealed weapon; and (c) contrary to the policy of most judicial district and circuits throughout this state, the chief justice is unwilling to authorize a judge with an expanded CCW permit to carry a concealed weapon in his or her chambers, at least absent some specifically articulated threat. Among other aspects of discussion, I would ask that we consider whether the authority should continue to be lodged in the chief justice, rather than in individual judges and justices, to render this determination.
>
> Because I believe the discussion I am requesting may be characterized as a "Discussion regarding court security plan," 6(f) of Draft Rules for MSC Administrative Conferences, I am initially seeking discussion of this matter outside of the public administration conference. However, if there is objection to this, I request that we consider this at our next public session. Thank you for your consideration.

I was surprised to receive this memo because it was very well understood that other than security personnel, there were to be no weapons in the Hall of Justice.[389] *He cites that Kelly has denied permission as it not being appropriate; and he's objecting; and he feels that his CCW rights are being reduced because he can't carry it in the building and carry it up to his chambers. He is asserting that he had apparently for two years—at least two years—that he had a concealed weapon permit, and that the former chief justice, Justice Taylor, had allowed him to have a concealed weapon, and carry it in his chambers on the sixth floor, across from me and another justice down the hall, and Young— next to Young. He apparently carried that gun on that floor and in the entire building.*

This was news to me; Taylor had not chosen to tell me. Whether he had chosen to tell anybody else, I don't know. Although, Taylor had reason to tell me because he knew I was not Justice Markman's favorite.

What followed was a series of memos. The first one came from the administrative counsel for the Supreme Court, giving the policy contained in the court's employment manual:

> No employee may possess a weapon on court property or while operating or riding in a state vehicle unless specific written permission is received from the chief justice or the chief judge. This policy includes weapons carried pursuant to a concealed weapons permit. Any employee who learns that an unauthorized weapon is at the work site must immediately contact court security staff.[390]

The counsel then went on to outline the Public Act 407 communiqué, a copy of which she included.

Then Justice Young got in the discussion:

> A couple of weeks ago, Justice Markman circulated the attached memo concerning your refusal to continue the policy of Chief Justice Taylor that allowed Justice Markman to bring his weapon into his chamber—event [sic.] though he has a CCW permit. He requested an opportunity to discuss your new policy that precludes him even from having his handgun in his car when he parks in the MSC garage.
>
> I am writing for two purposes. First I am unaware whether or when you have scheduled this matter for discussion. Second, I wish to let you know that, although Justice Markman wished to discuss this matter in executive session, I object to doing so for the reasons I have stated previously on the record: Since we do not have unanimity on confidentiality and its consistent

---

389 It's not uncommon for other judges in other Michigan courts—most usually a sitting district or circuit court judge—to have a gun stashed on the bench.
390 Unnamed administrative counsel, e-mail to justices, their secretaries, Corbin Davis and Michael Schmedlen, 18 May 2009.

observation, I will consent to no matter being discussed off the record and in executive session.[391]

Young is making reference to the fact that, by this time, Justice Weaver had refused to go along with what she calls the gag order of 2006, which was an unsuccessful attempt by the majority to silence her recent public dissents and ultimately to keep her from talking about anything that occurred at the court. She would not, as they wanted, simply sit down and shut up. In protest, she spoke out <u>more</u> when she thought there was something—ANYTHING— important the public should know.

Justice Maura Corrigan's judicial secretary sent out a memo from her boss:

> I concur with Justice Young that the question of Justice Markman's CCW permit needs to be public in the absence of unanimous rules on executive sessions.

> I hope Chief Justice Kelly has made some progress with Justice Weaver on this issue.

> If Chief Justice Kelly has any written background she can offer, I would appreciate seeing it.

> Thank you in advance.[392]

So, if there were not going to be an executive session about the matter that meant it would be in a public session. How would that play? Second Amendment rights supporters might rejoice. Many others, including those with a deep regard for the amendment, might view Markman's insistence as odd. Weaver, who also has a license for a handgun and who is a member of the Cedar Rod and Gun Club, found it that way.[393] But the matter was important if it was going to go ahead.

And, of course, this administrative matter is a public matter, as to whether you're going to have guns in the building or not, and the policy on 2001-03 had been set publicly.

Then we get another memo on the 29th from Justice Markman asserting, again, that he wants this matter expedited.

This was his memo to the justices:

---

391 Robert Young, e-mail to justices and their secretaries, 28 May 2009.
392 Maura D. Corrigan, e-mail to justices, their secretaries and the staff, 29 May 2009.
393 Unless somebody tells you s/he has a CCW you're not likely to know it. The Michigan Supreme Court has upheld state law—MCL 28.425e-4—that denies releasing that information publicly. So, if you have an odd—even a VERY odd—neighbor, and you'd like to know whether s/he represents a danger by carrying a concealed weapon, you are not entitled to find out. [http://www.legislature.mi.gov/(S(lms0mgmxjedptjzjreg14xah))/mileg.aspx?page=getobject&objectname=mcl-28-425e.]

I indicated in my original memorandum of May 15th that, although I thought it best to discuss this matter in executive session, I had no objection to discussing it at our public conference. In part, I believed that addressing this in executive session would allow its consideration to be expedited and, as a matter of personal security, I sought such expedition. However, in light of Justices Young's and Corrigan's memorandums, this is to reiterate that I have no objection to placing this on the public agenda. Most of all, I would appreciate it if the chief justice might expedite consideration of this matter by placing in on the court's agenda. Her present decision had deprived me of a considerable part of the value of an enhanced CCW license and taken away a right that I enjoyed under her predecessor. While I do not question the chief's present authority to undertake the action she has taken, I do question whether it was with the intention of ADM 2001-03 to invest authority in the chief justice to second-guess the judgement [sic] of individual justices concerning appropriate personal security precautions—in particular precautions that are available to most other judges throughout Michigan.[394]

So then, on June the 3rd, I sent a memo to Chief Justice Kelly,[395] and in it I say that I'm following up on a telephone conversation that I had with her on Monday, June 1st.

In that memo Weaver sent a shot across the bow of the U.S.S Markman, a clear warning that this should stop:

As I stated in our telephone conversation on Monday, June 1, 2009, I had no notice and did not know that Justice Markman had permission to have a gun in the Hall of Justice, including his chambers, until Justice Markman's memos to all justices of May 15th and May 29th, along with Justice Young's May 28th email and Justice Corrigan's May 29th e-mail concerning the Gun Policy in the Hall of Justice (ADM Order 2001-03). As you stated, former Chief Justice Taylor permitted Justice Markman to have a concealed weapon in the Hall of Justice and you have denied Justice Markman's request to have a gun in the Hall of Justice as you find no "appropriate circumstances" exist for him to do so.

I concur in your position that, except for as provided in the existing administrative order, 2001-03, there is no need for guns in the Hall of Justice. Further, in particular, I am concerned about Justice Markman having a gun in his chambers based in part on my knowledge of his previous conduct toward court employees as outlined in a copy of one of Justice Markman's former secretaries June 15, 2000, resignation memorandum about which I spoke with you.

---

394 Stephen J. Markman, "Memorandum," 29 May 2009.
395 It was Weaver's custom to copy in all the justices on memos dealing with substantive issues.

The resignation memorandum is addressed to Justice Markman and copied to me, then Chief Justice Elizabeth Weaver; Margaret Chiara, who was Policy and Planning Coordinator for the Supreme Court; and Ronald Stadnika, who was chief financial officer.

My request continues that you contact Mr. Stadnika, chief financial officer, and obtain a copy of the resignation memorandum for yourself from the Supreme Court records into which Mr. Stadnika should have filed his copy of the resignation memorandum he was copied. At the time, June 15, 2000, Mr. Stadnika was responsible for personnel files because the court did not have a human resources director or department.

Please let me know whether or not Mr. Stadnika was able to supply you a copy. If Mr. Stadnika is unable to supply a copy of the memorandum to you, I have a copy available at your request. Thank you.[396]

That e-mail had three or four purposes. The first was to alert Kelly that Weaver thought Markman was potentially dangerous with a concealed weapon on the sixth floor.

Second, it was to alert the justices that the paperwork existed to document Markman's tirade against and detention of Gerri Kozachik. Weaver had reason to believe that the memorandum outlined Kozachik's resignation might be no longer in the file.

Right after Maura Corrigan was elected chief justice in 2001, the first stop she made was Stadnika's office. I suspect she went there to purge Markman's file.

Suspicion, but not proof. But if Kelly went hunting for the memorandum and then couldn't find it—and if Weaver learned about it—there would be support for the hypothesis.

Third, Weaver was sure that her e-mail to Kelly would reach a wider audience, alerting the other justices that Weaver still had the memo and, fourth, would not hesitate to reveal it if the matter went forward at Markman's insistence.

The next and last communication that came Weaver's way was a copy of a letter from Kelly to Markman, June 10, 2009:

Dear Justice Markman:

Pursuant to Administrative Order 2001-03 of this court, this is to authorize you, so long as you maintain a current concealed pistol license in this state, to carry that pistol into and out of the judicial parking garage in the Hall of Justice in your motor vehicle. It is understood that this pistol will be used

396 Elizabeth A. Weaver, "Memorandum" to Chief Justice Marilyn Kelly, e-mail, 3 June 2009.

exclusively for personal protection and that you will not take it into any area of the Hall of Justice other than the judicial parking garage.

Yours sincerely,
Marilyn Kelly [signed][397]

There was not a further memo from Markman, Young, or Corrigan. They had been outflanked.

I never heard anything more from Justice Kelly about this except her letter to Justice Markman. I think that the letter that I suggested that she get [about Gerri Kozachik] would give her reason to be concerned. We talked about the letter on the telephone, but I never heard from her whether she found it.

I chose to let it be. I certainly didn't believe anybody in the parking garage potentially was in danger from the outside. Why would he need a gun in the parking garage? Maybe the need would be for him between his home or elsewhere and the parking garage. But at least the gun wasn't in the rest of the building, and it wasn't on the same floor, across the hall from me or any other justices, or anyone else in the building.

It's possible that with the election in early 2011 of Robert Young replacing Marilyn Kelly as chief justice, that Markman has again the full privileges of carrying his gun with him anywhere he wants. But you and I won't know about that unless somebody who knows that it's so speaks or writes about it. The records of the inner workings of the Supreme Court are protected—like access to the lists of those with CCW permits—from Freedom of Information Act (FOIA) provisions. The justices voted themselves that wall of concealment.[398]

In 1997, the court, under Conrad Mallett, proposed a series of changes that would have given more access to the workings of the court, still without making the court subject to FOIA. There had been a move afoot in the legislature to put the court system under the provisions of the act, and the new "openness" measures were to forestall that. The article in *Michigan Lawyers Weekly* was written by Marcia M. McBrien.[399] It's a name to watch; she will shortly move from outside to inside, from writing about the court to working FOR the court.

As for Justice Markman and his weaponry, things were left on simmer.

397 Marilyn Kelly, correspondence to Stephen Markman, 10 July 2009.
398 MCL Section 15.232 Freedom of Information Act (excerpt), Act 442 of 1976, http://www.legislature.mi.gov/(S(agmmdojqkkr02o55mbeyi1m2))/mileg.aspx?page=getObject&objectName=mcl-15-232.
399 Marcia M. McBrien, "High Court Issues Public Access Policy; Constitutional Changes Still Needed, Say Nye," *Michigan Lawyers Weekly*, 22 December 1997, http://milawyersweekly.com/news/1997/12/22/high-court-issues-public-access-policy/

The need for a gun in the Hall of Justice is not great. And even late at night, you're very secure. There are cameras all over the place, there are people there. And what good is it going to do you? And whether he needs one in other places, I don't know.

Not that judges aren't threatened.

It's likely that if you've been a judge for more than a few years that you'll have your life threatened. Trial judges deal directly with the public and are most likely to be threatened, in danger, and have need for a weapon in the courthouse, courtroom, and chambers; appellate judges and Supreme Court justices not nearly so much. We all potentially can be targeted for some reason by somebody. Some people are not happy; there are a lot of people in prison that don't like what we've done; but I don't know that having a concealed weapon in the supremely secure Hall of Justice, especially the top floor, is going to help. This is true even not considering the demonstrated intemperance of a justice beyond a reasonable response.

Markman would disagree, he did disagree; he said he wanted the exception to carry a weapon in the Hall of Justice including his 6th floor office, an exception that had been secretly granted him by Chief Justice Taylor.

Chapter 9

Put One on Your Finger
(Maybe) Not Your Father's Court,
Donut and a Half

Bling on the Bench

We've had a few grim stories, and there are a lot more to come. We offer this story... something that might seem like a brief respite: there are no briefs, plaintiffs or defendants, no legal opinions parsing fine points of law. But this story serves as a close up look—a micro examination—of how decisions were made. The process here was sometimes employed in the larger issues that faced the Michigan Supreme Court.

Whenever you have the opportunity, take a close look at the hands of Michigan's Supreme Court Justices—current and former. Do you see something that glitters that's not a wedding ring? Maybe a big-ol'-hunk o' gold with a representation of the seal of the court on it? What you're espying is one of THE RINGS.

They are not to be confused with Wagner's *Der Ring des Nibelungen* or the ring from Tolkien's trilogy, *The Lord of the Rings* ("One ring to rule them all"), nor the Papal ring.

This story starts about this time, during Elizabeth Weaver's stint as chief justice, but it goes on into the coming years, running in the background.

It started in the ground-floor hallway of Lansing's Kellogg Center, Weaver's home away from home.

I had met with the justices, or some of the justices, and Cliff Taylor and I were walking down in the lower area, and Cliff Taylor approached me. He said, "We need to get rings with the seal of the court," and I blew him off with "Are you nuts? That's just a preposterous idea. It sends the wrong message, because it will be perceived that we see ourselves as a club." This was not a long conversation with him. He was very interested in it, and it was so preposterous that I just put him off—I just said, "No. Not doing it. Bad idea."

And she heard no more about it for some time and thought the matter concluded.

It did go away. But it was a memorable experience because I had to tell him "No," and he didn't like that. He took it, but he apparently never forgot it.

The rings may have been off her radar but not that of her colleague Cliff's, and the next she heard of the rings—and that barely—was a mention years later—perhaps in 2002—at the conclusion of one of the court's regular weekly conferences. By this time, Maura Corrigan was nearing the end of her first term as chief justice. Taylor made a comment in passing that was directed to the other justices.

After conference one day as I was leaving, Cliff said that he wanted to have people have their fingers measured for rings. That was really odd, but I was busy and I didn't think much about it. At that time, I didn't bring it back to our conversation in the Kellogg or associate it with the historical society. That came later.

The matter would come up again, shortly before the dedication, Oct. 8, 2002, of the new Hall of Justice.

That was a huge undertaking Engler wanted done so that he could be at the dedication of the building. And it had to be expedited because he was going out in 2002.[400] And, by Jove, it got done, and we saved money, being under budget.

I was then running for re-election, as was Justice Young, and Justice Corrigan was supporting my re-election, had given money to it. One of the reasons I believed, although it was never discussed, was because she needed my vote to continue as chief justice. She didn't have Taylor, Markman, and Young, because Taylor wanted it [the chief justice post] at that time, and she was not willing to give it up.

The evening before the formal dedication there were plans for a big dinner (Oct. 7, 2002) that was going to be hosted by the Michigan Supreme Court Historical Society[401] at The English Inn (formerly Dusty's) in Eaton Rapids.

Corrigan had made a call to Weaver to talk about the historical society event and the dedication. Weaver wasn't there to catch the call.

And I returned her call and we got into discussing it. And I was saying, "Why is the historical society having this big celebration and all this, a big formal dinner for all current and former justices, when they have enough going on with the dedication?" The dedication by itself should be enough, but it wasn't.

And she said, "There is something special going to happen at the dinner." And I said, "What? What are you talking about?" And she might have said something about special gifts "The Historical Society's going to be doing rings...."

---

400 Groundbreaking for the new building was in 1999, said Weaver, and the building was nominally finished in time for Engler to participate in the dedication. The staff moved into the building in 2003.
401 That society was the special project of Dorothy Comstock Riley and her husband, Wally, both of whom Weaver cherished.

And so I said, "Wait a minute. Don't tell me this has to do with rings. Does Cliff Taylor have anything to do with this?" And it hit me, "Hey, was he talking about that after the conference? Now, is this going on?" It didn't mean much of anything to me until Maura called.

And that's when I asked her to check it out because I would have nothing to do with rings.

Corrigan, who had no knowledge of Taylor's earlier interaction with Weaver on the matter, had no idea that this thing was likely to blow up. She was concerned immediately; after all, she needed Weaver's vote. Corrigan made the inquiries Weaver had requested and confirmed Taylor was behind it.

She called me back and said that this was going to be a big surprise for the justices. The historical society had made, and was giving to each justice—current justices and retired justices— a gold ring, a $700 gold ring, with the seal of the court on it.

Corrigan presented the matter as a *fait accompli*.

And I said, "What?" I said, "I'm going to have nothing to do with this. This is insane. That's the wrong message. The historical society's job is not to be raising money for 700-dollar gold rings to give jewelry to the justices. The whole thing is symbolic of a secret club, a fraternity, and I don't want anything to do with it. If the rings are given out in my presence, I'm going to denounce them. I will report this stupid idea of Cliff Taylor's."

Oh-oh.

When I rejected Justice Taylor's approach to me about it, hands down, he had every right to bring it to the whole court. I would still feel, however, it was inappropriate and would express myself—but I was quite used to being voted down six-to-one—so that wasn't the issue. But instead, unbeknownst to me, he went to the Historical Society and got them involved.

There was a flurry of further phone calls trying to soothe Weaver's concerns.

So then Maura called me back again and she had by then talked to Wally Riley, the president of the historical society. And there was a new plan, and the plan was that the rings were going to be offered for sale to the justices. And at some point, I understand that Justice Riley had purchased one and that she would be wearing it that night. This conversation was on Monday, the 7th, and it was that night the dinner was going to occur. And I made it clear that if any of that went on while I was there, I was going to say what I thought about it.

So I sat with the Rileys at their table. I didn't notice whether Justice Riley had a ring on or not, and it was not mentioned. But I didn't stay the whole time. So what happened after I left, I don't know. It was not brought up while I was there.

But the matter was not left there, though it would take another two years to play out. During that time, a lot had become evident of the character, the administrative and judicial actions, and the philosophies of the Englerites. Weaver had found herself not in agreement.

A portion of the Michigan judiciary—some of the current and former Supreme Court justices, judges from the Court of Appeals, the circuit, district and probate courts assembled Oct. 8, 2002, to dedicate the newly constructed Hall of Justice in Lansing. This photo took place after the event. As a part of the dedication, the justices and judges processed from the Capitol Building to the new Hall. During the ceremony of all the honorees, Former Chief Justice Dorothy Comstock Riley was thanked first.[++] The night before the dedication, current and former justices met for a dinner where the gold rings were to have been presented. It didn't happen while Weaver was there, but it did happen at some subsequent time...some purchased and some accepted as gifts.

I could not agree with their increasing often unjust, unprofessional, disorderly, secretive and deceitful way the business of the court was administered and performed by them as a power block of four. The rings to me were a symbol of a very powerful secret club the Supreme Court should not be.

So, it was October 2004, and she received an invitation from the Rileys.

> Dorothy Comstock Riley invites the Michigan Supreme Court Justices of then and now, and their spouses, to a reception and dinner December the 3rd, 2004, 7:00 to 8:00 o'clock, at the Grosse Pointe Club.

Then at the bottom it read: "Toasts tolerated, rings worn, pictures posed, presents prohibited."

[++] Michigan Hall of Justice Dedication Ceremony, Michigan Supreme Court Historical Society, 8 October 2002, http://www.micourthistory.org/special_sessions.php?get_id=125.

Shortly after the invitation went out, Dorothy Comstock Riley died (October 23, 2004) as a result of Parkinson's disease. A follow-up notice came from Wallace Riley: "Dorothy wishes the gathering to be held. She will be there in spirit." Weaver hoped to go, certainly, but she didn't pay much mind to the invitation initially.

I think one of my clerks pointed out that it said "rings worn." So then, on November the 29th, I called Mr. Riley—Dorothy had already passed away, and I'd been to the funeral home and had written Mr. Riley a note.

The party was scheduled for a Friday evening and Weaver and the other justices would have been in the Detroit area for the better part of a week. That was no inconvenience for most of them because they lived there. But Weaver said she felt the need to return home.

I wasn't sure whether I could stay longer to go to this event. In the end I did, but I called Wally on the 29th to let him know two things: one, that I might not be able to attend; and two, I wanted to ask him what "rings worn" meant, to which he said, "Well, it's the rings from the historical society." And I had a discussion with him about the inappropriateness, in my opinion, of the rings and how I didn't want anything to do with them.

Weaver also wanted confirmation of Taylor's role in the forging of the rings.

Well, he evaded that it was Justice Taylor. He did mention that the board had voted on it. Now, this was different from what I was told by Justice Corrigan back in 2002, when they were first supposed to be given out.

...And when it was possible that some of them <u>were</u> given out.

I think that some people had rings and some people didn't. Mr. Riley, on November 29th, told me that of the justices, the Engler Four—only he didn't call them the Engler Four—had them, and the people who still didn't have them were Justice Cavanagh, Justice Kelly, and myself. And apparently, the idea was to give them out at this party, and maybe there was some thought that my refusal in 2002 had to do with my campaign. I made it very clear that I felt exactly the same way that I had ever felt about it, that I was not going to participate in such a thing.

But she did go to the party.

I was not overly popular with some of my colleagues—especially the four. I noticed there were several retired justices there, including Justice Fitzgerald, who is now deceased, and Justice Brennan, and I was talking with them. I saw that Justice Fitzgerald had a ring on, and I asked him how he got it. And he said it was sent to him in a box to his home. And I asked him if he paid for it, and he said "No." Brennan offered one had been sent to him in a box, and he was down in Florida. And he had not paid for it, either. But he wasn't wearing it. So that was of interest.

Now, on December 6th—this would be three days after the party—I got an e-mail from Justice Corrigan. And she asked, "Have you decided what you want the Supreme Court Historical Society to do about the ring?"

THE ring? HER ring!

Yes, there was a ring for me.

There was one waiting for her whether she wanted it or not.

Weaver pondered an answer to Corrigan but waited to send it. In the meanwhile, she noted that Michael Cavanaugh was wearing his.

As of December the 9th, Justice Kelly related that she had neither purchased nor accepted a ring.

But that still left Weaver's ring in the air...or in a box in a drawer.

I drafted a letter to Justice Corrigan dated January 13, 2005. January 13, 2005, is an important date because that is the date that I announced that I intended to leave the Supreme Court in October 2005.

So when I answered to Justice Corrigan I said this: "I was surprised by your inquiry to me last month: 'Have you decided what you want the Supreme Court Historical Society to do about the ring?'"

"I was not aware that there was an expectation that I had any further decision to make regarding that subject. My rejection of the idea of gold, seal-of-the-Supreme-Court rings has never changed."

And I told her in my letter, "It's a surprise to me because I made it clear from day one, and had made it clear to Mr. Riley, that I will not accept it, I will not buy it; it's inappropriate to say the least."

Weaver has the draft of the letter, but she is not sure she sent it. There was so much going on at the time. And so much of it was so very bad.

This was not the only issue. This was the smallest issue to me of what was going on.

So, where is the ring now?

I assume they have it, unless they've melted it down or given it to somebody else. I don't know whether they're inscribed or not; I suspect they might have been. I don't know.

So what is the big deal about the rings anyway? Might Weaver be over reacting?

It symbolizes the secrecy, the unnecessary secrecy, and the secret-club nature of the Supreme Court. The Supreme Court is not an elite club; it shouldn't be. This is a public office.

That didn't mean there couldn't be special gifts...but they had to be gifts among peers.

I understand Justice Soapy Williams, as chief justice, had gold cufflinks of the seal of the court for the men, and apparently pins for the ladies—lady. And I know Justice Cavanagh wore his with pride. I don't know if Brickley ever wore them. But the fact of the matter is, gifts from one justice to other justices is fine. Justice Williams paid for them and they were his gifts. The money for them was Williams', not raised through a 501(c)(3).

I don't see what getting gold jewelry for justices has to do with the purpose of the Michigan Supreme Court Historical Society. But if it had, then it should have been done openly: "We are starting a project for Supreme Court Justices to have gold seal rings, and you can contribute to this specific fund." That wasn't done at all.

And remember that the Supreme Court Historical Society Board is basically composed of lawyers, and those lawyers are giving gifts to the justices. They had spent $10,000 on these rings.

Actually, according to the year-end budget for 2002 of the Michigan Supreme Court Historical Society, Inc., the total was $10,500...$8,400 for the rings themselves and another $2,100 for management of the project.[402] At $700 a pop that would be 12 rings: seven for current justices and five for the formers.

There is another venture of the Michigan Supreme Court Historical Society that involves lawyers' money—seemingly small sums—but in this case for the privilege of dining with justices in the Hall of Justice. The lawyers are members of a select group, The Advocates Guild. Attorneys become eligible to join after they have argued a case in front of the Michigan Supreme Court. From these advocates, a select number are offered the opportunity to chat and chew with the justices. Here's the story on the Oct. 4, 2011 dinner held in the Hall of Justice:

> Chief Justice Robert P. Young, Jr. welcomed advocates to the dinner, noting that only that morning some of them had come before the court in oral arguments.
>
> The Advocates Guild Dinner was held on the first night of the court's new term. The fall date has been the time when the court and guild traditionally come together for the event. This is the fifth year the guild has hosted the dinner for its members.
>
> Because of the special nature of the dinner and the exclusivity of Advocates Guild membership, attendance was limited to 40 advocates. Each advocate was seated at a table with a Michigan Supreme Court Justice, and all of the tables were in the sixth floor rotunda outside the Supreme Court courtroom.[403]

---

402 "Statement of functional expenses—cash basis, year ended December 31, 2002," Michigan Historical Society.
403 *I questioned the appropriateness of holding the dinner in the building. You have* hors d'oeuvres *before hand in the conference room—and that's a restricted area—and dine at tables under the rotunda....*

The historical society has its offices on the first floor of the Hall of Justice, home base for the Supreme Court, Court of Appeals, Michigan Judicial Institute, Michigan Board of Law Examiners, the state court administrative offices, commissioners, officers, and the Supreme Court Learning Center.

The Advocates Guild has been "telling the history of the court from the other side of the bench" since 2007.[404]

There was even a piece of Pewabic pottery presented to each attendee.

That's Young's special interest.

Weaver has been a life member of the society since 1989, but she says she didn't give her money to personally benefit the past, present, and future justices or lawyers who want to associate with them. She went to at least one of those dinners and found it...

Well, if you want to just mix with the people who are going to argue in front of you, that's how I found it. It gives the advocates an exclusive access to the justices that nobody else has.

She had expressed her concerns for such dinners.

I objected, but it was not something I made a big deal about. If that was the worst thing the Supreme Court ever did, I'd have no problem at all. It's special access, and it reeks but....

Why the need for special access? Is the Supreme Court all that remote? Yes, but it wasn't always that way.

In times past, we used to go out and hold public hearings, meet with Bar associations and groups of lawyers. We weren't remote and we'd listen to what they had to say to us. But that changed when the Engler Four took over, they didn't want to go out and meet with rank and file.

And the historical society that organized it?

They really urged you to come. There is no way to make a command performance of a justice, but as much as they could, this was it. They put the dinner at a time when we were there for oral arguments, so the only way to avoid it was to just leave.

Too, Weaver held Wally Riley in high regard; in her view he is wrong on this issue and the issue of the rings, but correct in so much else, and very dear to her heart.

Initially, Weaver thought the event was a moneymaker for the historical society. It turns out it's not. One attorney who had sat with her related that the price of the dinner was under $100. At that price, could the society cover the cost of the dinner? ... The drinks, the *hors d'oeuvres*, the meal, the wages of the servers, the photos with the justices,[405] and the Pewabic?

---

404 "A Night for Traditions; 2011 Advocates Guild Dinner," *Society Update; The Official Publication of the Michigan Supreme Court Historical Society*, 8, Winter 2012, http://www.micourthistory.org/pdfs/newsletters/winter12.pdf.
405 The cutline for one of the photos in the historical society newsletter describes it this way:

> The court graciously posed for photos with individual advocates in front of the bench before the dinner. Shown here is Advocates Guild member John W. Allen who practices in the Kalamazoo office of the Varnum firm. The photos with the Court, which are taken every year, are a favorite memento of advocates who attend the dinner. [Ibid.]

Oh, sure. It's not that good a dinner.

And if it's not a fundraiser, what is it?

It's obvious access to the justices. And you get to hear some stories, depending on who you sit with.

For the justices, it's political, a free campaign event. This event is to give people—the "right" people—access to the justices. They control who gets there. It's typical. It's right that we communicate with people, but we should not have a way of controlling it. Everyone should have that opportunity.

Ah, but we started this section with rings. We should end it there, too.

I didn't give money to the Michigan Supreme Court Historical Society to buy rings for the justices. It's supposed to be for promotion of the history of the Supreme Court in Michigan. The Historical Society shouldn't be used as a vehicle for getting jewelry for the justices. It's just that simple.

For the rest of her time on the bench, some of her fellow justices wore their rings. Weaver observed that Justice Cavanagh often did. And, for the justice who thought up the whole thing:

Taylor always wore his with great pride. He made sure it was visible in his portrait.

An Agreeable, Independent, Influential Court?

At about the same time the ring escapade began, a trio of researchers was readying an examination of the Michigan Supreme Court. The project entailed measuring not just the Michigan Supreme Court but all the state supreme courts in the nation, and then comparing and ranking them.

Even though their paper didn't come out until 2008, the researchers, Stephen J. Choi, Mitu Gulati, and Eric A. Posner, gathered their data from the years 1998, 1999, and 2000, just about the time events in this chapter unfold.[406]

First, in their survey of prior efforts and the literature of the field, the three reviewed existing studies purporting to get at the same idea of the best and worst courts. They summarized and reported several academic studies (Dear and Jessen most prominently[407]) in detail. Of the academic papers, Choi, Gulati, and Posner remarked the researchers were "in general, focusing on the extent to which a state's high court is cited by out-of-state high courts.[408]" But far more influential than the academic reports

406 Stephen J. Choi, Mitu Gulati, and Eric A. Posner, "Which States Have The Best (And Worst) High Courts?," John M. Olin Law and Economic Working Paper No. 405
(2nd Series), The Law School, The University of Chicago, May 2008, http://www.law.uchicago.edu/files/files/405.pdf. PUBLIC LAW AND LEGAL THEORY WORKING PAPER NO. 217
407 Jake Dear and Edward Jessen, "'Followed' Cases and Leading State Cases, 1940-2005," 41 U.C. Davis L. Rev. 683. (2007), http://lawreview.law.ucdavis.edu/issues/41/2/essay/DavisVol41No2_Dear.pdf.
408 Stephen J. Choi, Mitu Gulati, and Eric A. Posner, 1.

were Chamber of Commerce studies in the various states. In particular, Choi, Gulati, and Posner said they were entirely subjective studies; there was no hard data.

> The U.S. Chamber of Commerce surveys ask senior lawyers at corporations that earn more than $100 million per year in revenues to grade state court systems, from A to F, and aggregate their responses.[409]

And those reports by senior lawyers were widely reported and put to use:

> It is sufficient to point out that U.S. Chamber of Commerce rankings have been more influential than Dear and Jessen's ranking, and much more so than those by academics. They have been cited by state legislators to criticize their judiciaries and ask for reform, by a judicial pay compensation commission as a justification for a salary increase, and by two governors to advertise the attractiveness of their states for big business. The U.S. Chamber of Commerce has used its annual survey of state court systems as a means to pressure state legislatures to improve their court systems. Academics have also used the rankings in empirical studies of the relationship between judicial quality and institutional design.[410]

All those earlier studies had ranked Michigan as an okay or better-than-okay state, sometimes with far-reaching results. But not everyone thought them suitable or complete:

> Groups like the Ralph Nader led organization, Public Citizen, have complained that these rankings are biased toward the interests of big business. But, in the absence of meaningful competitive rankings, this is the equivalent of law schools urging students to ignore the *U.S. News* rankings. It doesn't work. Rather than urge people to ignore imperfect rankings, we should develop better rankings.[411]

So they set out to do that. Choi, Gulati, and Posner set out to qualitatively measure three elements they thought would best tell the story of the courts: productivity, influence, and independence.

> We apply these measures to a data set consisting of the decisions of all the judges of the highest court of every state for the three years from 1998 to 2000. We exclude the District of Columbia, and we treat the separate civil and criminal high courts in Texas and Oklahoma as, in effect, separate states. We thus have 52 "states."[412]

They defined them this way:

---

409 Ibid., 1.
410 Ibid., 2.
411 Ibid., 2.
412 Ibid., 9.

Productivity—the numbers of opinions generated at each Court.

Influence—the numbers of out-of-state citations of opinions as a measure of the quality of the reasoning at each individual court.

Independence—the numbers of times justices crossed party or other affiliations lines to side with opposite parties as a measure of "the judge's ability to withstand partisan pressures, or disinclination to indulge partisan preferences, when deciding cases."

So, how did Michigan do? Not well, not well at all.

Productivity?

> Productivity refers to the number of opinions a judge publishes in a year. All else equal, a judge who publishes more opinions is better than a judge who publishes fewer opinions. There are two reasons for this. First, if all opinions are published, then a judge who publishes more opinions, decides more cases, thus resolving more disputes between people. Dispute resolution is the judge's core function, and the more disputes a judge resolves, the greater is the service that she is providing.[413]

Michigan ranked 40th with 389. Georgia claimed the top spot with 1225, New Mexico the bottom with 151.

Influence or opinion quality?

> We measure opinion quality by using a proxy: the number of out-of-state citations by state high courts defined to equal the sum of all citations to majority opinions published by the state high court in question from other state courts, federal courts (other than the home federal circuit), and the U.S. Supreme Court. (In other work, we use other proxies for quality as well, such as law review citations; these measures are highly correlated with out-of-state citations by state high courts.) We assume that a high-quality opinion is more likely to be useful for out-of-state courts, and therefore is more likely to be cited.[414]

Michigan ranked 42nd with 8.67 out-of-state citations/judge year. Top was California with 33.67 and bottom was Oklahoma (criminal) with 3.69.

Independence?

> Independence refers to the judge's ability to withstand partisan pressures, or disinclination to indulge partisan preferences, when deciding cases. Our measure of independence gives a judge a high score if he is more likely to

---

413 Ibid., 9.
414 Ibid., 10.

vote with opposite-party judges and a low score if he is more likely to vote with same-party judges. We focus on votes by judges in situations where the judge faces an opposing opinion, defined as either a majority opinion when the judge writes a dissent, or a dissent when the judge joins the majority. We assume that a judge exhibits independence when she writes an opposing opinion against a co-partisan. For each judge, we obtained information on the political affiliation of the judge. In a few states, all the high court judges belong to the same party in our data set, and so we cannot assign those judges an independence score. In our sample, 220 judges were classified as a Democrat and 170 as a Republican (with 16 no data or Independent party judges).[415]

Rhode Island's high court was most independent; Michigan's was least. That meant that partisan aggregation was prevalent; birds of a political feather, if you will, were flocking together.

That was no surprise to Weaver:

And I was even part of it to some degree because not everything that was done was always wrong. We often worked together. I still was sympathetic and thinking they were overreacting and reacting poorly to attacks—some of which were unfair and some of which weren't.

But that was when Weaver agreed with them about the law. Otherwise...

It was terribly politicized. You had Cavanagh and Kelly and you had the Four.

And for Choi, Gulati, and Posner and their study of the actions of the court at the end of the century, there was a grand summing up. Equally combining all three measures of productivity, influence, and independence, California claimed the pole position as the best and most effective court in the land. Michigan came out on the bottom.

Dead last.[416]

Weaver took exception with the conclusions of productivity and influence.

I didn't think their study was particularly useful. Granted it was more objective than the Chamber of Commerce surveys, but there was no way that they could account for the change that was taking place in the court during the span of their research. The court had three new justices arrive during that time and that changed the court completely. But we did the work of the court. In fact, under Mallett we probably took too many cases.

In 1999, Weaver's first year as chief justice, the court completed 2,571 cases. According to the court's annual report for that year:

---

415 Ibid., 10.
416 Stephen J. Choi, Mitu Gulati, and Eric A. Posner, 21.

In 1999, the Court issued 482 additional orders on motion matters as follows: 56 orders granting leave to appeal; 241 orders on motions for rehearing or reconsideration; 46 orders holding cases in abeyance, issued on the Court's own motion; 30 miscellaneous orders [...]; 95 orders issued by the Chief Justice—here commonly called "housekeeping orders"—including orders on motions to extend the time for filing briefs, to place on or withdraw a case from a session calendar, or for oral argument, etc.; and, 14 remands with jurisdiction retained.[417]

Believe me, we were not lazing about.

But the number was down from a high of 2,992 under Justice Mallett's leadership.[418]

Nor was Weaver at all concerned with the study's concept of influence.

Just because your decisions are not cited in the decisions of other states' supreme courts doesn't mean that the work isn't good. It may have been that the cases we were deciding were not the kinds of cases being handled by other courts at that time.

The one finding with which she concurred was that of the lack of independence on the court.

During the time of the study, the Engler Four took the field. But gradually I was realizing that I was being deceived, and I could not rely on their work. The study does accurately show that the court was very partisan.

The study also caught the attention of Todd C. Berg, reporting for *Michigan Lawyers Weekly*. Berg even updated the data from when the study left off. He also noted there were significant changes in personnel during the years of the study,[419] and that the court's productivity had actually improved...or declined—depending on how you looked at it—from the court measured in the research:

> That's because each of the justices, on average, is writing more opinions—majority, concurring and dissenting—than she or he used to. However, the productivity of the individual justices varies, and, the productivity of the court, as a whole, is declining, when measured in terms of cases decided by written opinion.[420]

---

417 Michigan Courts: Striving for Excellence; Michigan's One Court of Justice, 2000 Annual Report, Michigan Supreme Court, 9, http://courts.michigan.gov/Administration/SCAO/Resources/Documents/Publications/Statistics/1999/1999%20Michigan%20Supreme%20Court%20Annual%20Report.pdf.
418 Ibid.
419 Todd C. Berg, "Which court? U of C law school report, in which MSC ranked poorly, addresses cases decided by three court configurations," *Michigan Lawyers Weekly*, 30 June 2008, http://milawyersweekly.com/news/2008/06/30/which-court063/.
420 Todd C. Berg, "MSC justices more 'productive' than they used to be; Average opinion output per justice has increased, yet number of cases with written opinions has decreased," *Michigan Lawyers Weekly*, 30 June 2008, http://milawyersweekly.com/news/2008/06/30/msc-justices-more-productive-than-they-used-to-be/.

And the concept of independence took on a new importance with Berg's continuing assessment:

> For followers of the Michigan Supreme Court, however, the trend identified in the University of Chicago Law School report should come as no surprise.
>
> Similarly unsurprising should be the fact that the trend continues.
>
> Below is data gathered by *Michigan Lawyers Weekly* that shows the frequency with which justices of the same party affiliation have voted together during recent terms.
>
> • 2000-01 term—The Republican justices—Clifford W. Taylor, Elizabeth A. Weaver, Maura D. Corrigan, Robert P. Young Jr., Stephen J. Markman— voted together in approximately 89 percent of the cases. The Democratic justices—Michael F. Cavanagh and Marilyn Kelly—voted together in approximately 92 percent of the cases.
>
> • 2001-02 term—The Republican justices voted together approximately 93 percent of the time, whereas the Democratic justices voted together in 81 percent of cases.
>
> • 2002-03 term—Republican justices: 69 percent. Democratic justices: 69 percent.
>
> • 2003-04 term—Republican justices: 73 percent. Democratic justices: 87 percent.
>
> • 2004-05 term—Republican justices: 66 percent. Democratic justices: 77 percent.
>
> • 2005-06 term—Republican justices: 66 percent. Democratic justices: 52 percent.
>
> • 2006-07 term—Republican justices: 40 percent. Democratic justices: 53 percent.[421]

I am the one responsible for those Republican numbers heading down. It turned out that I was more and more independent. Now, I often was in agreement with them concerning how the law fell on an issue before us but there was more to it than that because of what would get written. In the end, after 2008, the vote often came down to 3-3-1...three Republicans, three Democrats, and me.

By then, there was much discord on the court. And, generally, as the discord increased through the decade the voting became less predictable.

---

421 Todd C. Berg, "Partisanship persists on MSC: Report gives high court low 'independence' rank for 1998-2000. Research shows things haven't changed," *Michigan Lawyers Weekly*, 30 June 2008, http://milawyersweekly.com/news/2008/06/30/partisanship-persists-on-msc/.

A Vote for Me Is a Vote for....

The 2000 election season was upon them and the Republicans had three seats on the Supreme Court to defend: those of Taylor, Young, and Markman. Taylor would be running for a full eight-year term, Young for the remainder of the two-year term to which he'd been appointed, and Markman for the rest of the four-year term to which he'd been appointed. The Michigan Campaign Finance Network reported the competition:

> The Democrats nominated Marietta Robinson for the eight-year term, Judge Edward Thomas of the Third Circuit Court (Wayne County) for the four-year term, and Court of Appeals Judge Thomas Fitzgerald for the two-year term. The Libertarians nominated Robert Roddis, David Raaflaub and Jerry Kaufman for the eight-, four-, and two-year terms, respectively.[422]

While the Libertarians—as usual—spent nothing to advance their candidates, only one of the major-party candidates was going to spend less than a million dollars. That would be Thomas Fitzgerald. Moreover, independent expenditures (IEs) totaled a million and a half.[423]

That meant the candidates were out fundraising. For the Supreme Court justices, that meant raising money when and where they could.

And we were having meetings around the state with the trial courts, and we had one in Marquette. So we had flown up there, just as we had done in times previous.

Taylor, Markman, and Young informed me that they had a scheduled event while in Marquette for the evening, a fundraiser with friends of theirs and they very much wanted me to come. Maura also was invited, but I doubt that Kelly and Cavanagh were invited. Anyway, Maura even asked me if she should go, and I said, "Well, it's perfectly all right to go and be supportive of them. There's nothing improper about that, and it's in no way a court activity." I don't remember whether she went or not. But I do remember distinctly her asking me whether it was okay to go.

So we went. And it was at a home, and it wasn't far from the Landmark Hotel where we stayed. And when we got there Taylor, Markman, and Young were introduced by whoever the host was, and each of them spoke.

And as silly as it may seem in this day of super PACs, there are rules and regulations about judges and justices raising money. It's an odd way to do things, but the judges aren't supposed to be there for the "ask."

422 Barbara Moorhouse and Richard Robinson with David Hogg, *Special Interests v Public Values—Funding Michigan Supreme Court Campaigns—1994-2000* "1996 Supreme Court Election" (Michigan Campaign Finance Network, Lansing, Mich.), 39-49, http://www.mcfn.org/pdfs/reports/SCAppendix.pdf.
423 Ibid., 39.

The Code of Judicial Conduct spells it out in Canon 7(B) conduct a judicial candidate must follow during the campaign:

(1) A candidate, including an incumbent judge, for a judicial office:

(a) should maintain the dignity appropriate to judicial office, and should encourage family members to adhere to the same standards of political conduct that apply to the judge;

(b) should prohibit public employees subject to the judge's direction or control from doing for the judge what the judge is prohibited from doing under this canon;

(c) *should not make pledges or promises of conduct in office other than the faithful and impartial performance of the duties of the office.* [Emphasis added]

(d) should not knowingly, or with reckless disregard, use or participate in the use of any form of public communication that is false.[424]

(2) These provisions govern a candidate, including an incumbent judge, for a judicial office:

(a) *A candidate should not personally solicit or accept campaign funds,* [Emphasis added] or solicit publicly stated support by improper use of the judicial office in violation of B(1)(c). A candidate may send a thank-you note to a contributor.

(b) A candidate may establish committees of responsible persons to secure and manage the expenditure of funds for the campaign and to obtain public statements of support for the candidacy.

(c) Such committees are prohibited from soliciting campaign contributions from lawyers in excess of $100 per lawyer, but may solicit public support from lawyers. It is not a violation of this provision for a committee, in undertaking solicitations that are not directed exclusively to lawyers but may in fact go to lawyers who are members of a group or found on a mailing list, to solicit more than $100 per person, provided that the following disclaimer appears on the letter or on a response card, in print that is at least the same size as the remainder of the print in the letter or the response card:

Canon 7 of the Michigan Code of Judicial Conduct prohibits a judicial campaign committee from soliciting more than $100 per lawyer. If you are a lawyer, please regard this as informative and not a solicitation for more than $100.[425]

---

424 This provision is the result of a decision by the Supreme Court that found an earlier version unconstitutional in its Chmura decision (*In re Chmura*). Subsequently, the court found that Judge John M. Chmura had not crossed a line in his attacks on his opponent, 37th District Court Administrator/Magistrate James P. Conrad. The decision was important because it opened rather than narrowed the scope of judicial campaign speech. Weaver signed on to this opinion by Maura Corrigan and was joined by the other Englerites. They were opposed by dissent from Cavanagh and Kelly. The case is well worth studying and deserves its own book, as so many of these cases do. [*In re Chmura*, No. 117565, Michigan Supreme Court, 30 May 2001, http://publicdocs.courts.mi.gov:81/OPINIONS/FINAL/SCT/20010530_S117565(12)_Chmura.10Dec00.PDF.]

425 Canon 7(B), Michigan Code of Judicial Conduct, http://coa.courts.mi.gov/rules/documents/8michigancodeofjudicialconduct.pdf.

That meant and means the candidate cannot solicit funds on their own and s/he should not make any promises—actual or implied.

Weaver says she had always told potential campaign donors pretty much the same thing:

The best thing I could ever say to people was "I may well rule against you." And that doesn't raise money. We're not supposed to solicit money in any way, which makes it very difficult to have money to run. But I could accept that. I always felt it was too bad that we couldn't get on television and say: "This is who I am. If you're interested in me, this is what I think. This is the kind of judge I am or I'll be. This is what I think needs to happen. And, if you're interested, send five dollars to my campaign." You can't do that.

So she grew alarmed when she heard her colleagues at the house gathering.

I was quite disturbed about it when they spoke because they referred to needing a donut-and-a-half. Now, at these fundraisers, a justice is never to ask for money.

But that's exactly what they were doing.
The fund raiser is there; the money is collected ahead of time, I guess; but it's supposed to be an opportunity to meet the candidates.

Asking for a donut-and-a-half clearly meant that they needed now not a hundred dollars but hundred-and-fifty dollars from each of the donors. I felt that was crossing the line. And I was not pleased about it and told them after that that was inappropriate, and they should not do that; it was soliciting.

There was also talk about the great amounts of money that was involved in the cases before the Supreme Court and their ways of dealing with that; that they [the donors] would elect them and they [the justices] would see that it was right—whatever that meant.

Sounds like an implied promise, a *quid pro quo.*

It never happened in front of me again, but it did then. And I remember it distinctly, and I was concerned about it because I wasn't with them at many of their fundraisers in the 2000 campaign.

I was willing to support them and show my support, but not to solicit money or to be a part of it by my presence there. But I felt it was a mistake. People make mistakes; let it go.

These three guys were a disappointment, to say the least, almost beyond that; but I attributed a lot of it just to the pressures of being up for re-election and wanting to get elected.

Their electioneering wasn't enough to keep them fully occupied.

During all of this time, they began to want me to get rid of staff because they weren't satisfied with them.

Top in their sights was David Gruber, the public information officer at the Supreme Court.

He wasn't defending them in their political problems. I never viewed the court—the institution and the staff—as working to take care of the political problems of the justices. The justices had their own problems—and they can be of their own making or not—but it isn't up to the staff to defend them. The staff is there to get information out to the public; that is true. And if the court as an institution is under attack, then the staff is there to give the public the right information. But they're not to be working for individual justices or all of the justices, to protect them or promote them, and to be their public relations people.

And our guy Gruber was not a PR flak. He was an experienced journalist; he had been there, certainly with Mallett and I think with Brickley, and he was a low-key guy, but he was not one to be involved in protecting the justices or promoting them, either way. That's not the way we're supposed to spend taxpayer money; there's no place for that. And interestingly enough, until the Englerites took over, we only had a person in public information as a half-time assignment. And Gruber spent much of the rest of his time on the new building [the Hall of Justice] that was going to be built. This building was 280,000 square feet.

Now I wasn't about to fire Gruber and get rid of him just because Young wanted him gone. I wouldn't have any of it. I would not do it.

Gruber wasn't the only one with a target on his back.

Likewise, there was a desire to get rid of the state court administrator John Ferry, and also the head of the commissioners Al Lynch. And I wouldn't do it. And that was it.

As long as she was chief justice, there was some protection for them, but Weaver's tenure in the position of chief was shortly to come to a conclusion.

And Gruber was top on the list to go. [426]

I thought it was very important not to eliminate staff people who are institutionally loyal and are not minions to protect and promote the justices. And that had been asked for, and that wasn't right. And I just hoped that it would work out and I would stick with it.

Without public relations operatives to deflect criticism, there was plenty of reason to think that the three incumbent justices might not remain on the court. The fight was, as C. Jesse Green described it, "bare knuckle politics":

> The fierce battle for the Supreme Court has also garnered unprecedented coverage in the general press, and has even been spotlighted by national publications like *The Wall Street Journal*.

---

426 And there would be others—so many others—who dared speak their minds...or who, Weaver said, simply knew too much or were harmless or innocent but simply in the way.

Some lawyers use words like "undignified" and "unjudicial" to describe the frenzy, which many observers fear will cause long-term damage to the Supreme Court as an institution, regardless of the election's outcome.

[...]

And the possibility of knocking one or more of the three Republicans off the bench and gaining a voting majority on the high court is a prospect that makes Democrats salivate.

Markman, Young and Taylor have the benefit on the campaign trail of being able to trumpet the title "justice" in front of their names. But that designation also comes with a voting record in cases, which makes them vulnerable to attacks.

Throughout the election, the incumbents have portrayed themselves as champions of "judicial restraint" who faithfully interpret statutes according to the intent of the legislature.

But labor, teachers and other groups traditionally aligned with the Democratic Party have unleashed an assault on Markman, Young and Taylor that has shown little restraint in attempting to package the incumbents as minions of big business, the insurance industry and others.
As a result, re-election—which has traditionally been a cakewalk for Michigan Supreme Court justices—has been an out-and-out brawl between the Republican incumbents and their Democratic opponents, Court of Appeals Judge E. Thomas Fitzgerald, attorney Marietta Robinson and Judge Edward Thomas.

And while Fitzgerald, Robinson and Thomas do not have the advantage of hanging "justice" in front of their names while campaigning, the challengers have positioned themselves as "pro-family" representatives of accessible justice for all.

But, just as traditional Democratic allies have gone after Markman, Taylor and Young, Republican constituencies have taken aim at Fitzgerald, Robinson and Thomas, calling them pro-trial lawyer and "judicial activists."[427]

Taylor, Markman, and Young still hadn't learned their lessons about being careful what they said, to whom, and when. As a result they came under additional fire, reported Green:

---

427 C. Jesse Green, "Battle for the High Court; Has The Infusion Of Politics Damages Michigan's Judiciary?," *Michigan Lawyers Weekly*, 30 October 2000, http://milawyersweekly.com/news/2000/10/30/battle-for-the-high-court/.

With the battle fully engaged, lawyers openly attacking sitting judges—something that was all but unheard of in years past—has become almost commonplace this election season.

In fact, *Lawyers Weekly* has received an unprecedented number of letters to the editor from attorneys regarding the Supreme Court race—and the lawyers putting in their 2 cents include some very heavy hitters.

For example, Eugene D. Mossner, a past president of the State Bar of Michigan, recently fired a salvo at Justice Markman.

Pointing out that the Michigan Code of Judicial Conduct provides guidelines and prohibitions regarding what is permissible in judicial elections, Mossner chastised Markman for allegedly telling the Michigan State Medical Society (MSMS) that plaintiffs' lawyers are "our enemies" and "our opponents," and for making comments regarding an avalanche of "frivolous litigation." (See, "Sitting Justices Should 'Know Better,'" Letters, Oct. 9, 2000.)

Mossner claimed such public statements by Markman have put his objectivity into question.

"Any fair minded reading of the text [of Markman's speech] leads to the inevitable conclusion that he and his colleagues will not be impartial when it comes to medical malpractice cases and other types of tort litigation," Mossner wrote.

In his letter, Mossner also criticized all three incumbent justices for radio ads declaring that they will be "tough on criminals."

"Can anyone representing a person accused of a crime hope to receive an impartial hearing from justices with that kind of mindset?" Mossner asked.

Similarly, Young has come under fire for claiming he and the Supreme Court's Federalist Society members were engaged in a "jihad," or holy war, against the media and the Democratic Party.[428]

Jef Mallett,[429] then an editorial cartoonist for Booth Newspapers, summed up what he saw going on.

Of all the races in 2000, the nastiest by far were for the Michigan Supreme Court. It got ugly. And they were the races that were supposed to be civil. They were supposed to be nonpartisan. They were supposed to be the high road all the way.[430]

---

428 Ibid.
429 Jef (yes, just one "f") Mallett is the creator and artist of "Frazz," a runaway cartoon favorite, especially of co-author Schock. Jef Mallett is no relation to Justice Conrad Mallett, Jr.
430 Jef Mallett quoted in Gleaves Whitney, *John Engler: The Man, the Leader and the Legacy*, (Chelsea, Mich.,

Cartoonist Jef Mallett said that this cartoon depicting the politicization of the Michigan Supreme Court was one of his favorite. In one panel, he captured the dynamics of the Englerites on the court. (*Booth Newspapers.*)

Jef Mallett had often drawn cartoons favorable to Governor Engler. Not this time, though, he reported of his art work associated with that election:

> The cartoon shows Governor Engler at his desk with three puppets. One puppet is Justice Markman; one puppet is Justice Young; one puppet is Justice Taylor. Governor Engler is holding one puppet on each of his hands and one on his foot. The puppets are talking to each other. Justice Markman asks Justice Young, "How did the Supreme Court race become so politicized?" "I don't know," answers Justice Taylor.
>
> The implication, of course, is that since all three justices were appointed by Engler, they not surprisingly followed Engler's line of thinking, and Engler's thinking, naturally made its way into the contest. I was happy with that cartoon—it is one of my favorites.[431]

The three were plenty worried.

When they wanted to talk to me, I knew they probably were desperate. And they were even desperate enough to talk about seeing if Justice Brickley would say something in their favor. I suggested to them that I didn't think so, but they would be willing to try that. I didn't think that was going to happen.

Among the state's attorneys, they were in deep trouble.

> If Michigan lawyers had their way, the three Republican incumbents on the state Supreme Court would be turned out of office, according to an exclusive survey conducted for *Michigan Lawyers Weekly*.

Sleeping Bear Press, 2002) 352.
431 Ibid.

All three Democratic candidates hold comfortable, if not commanding, leads among lawyers in their quest to unseat the GOP trio.

Justice Robert Young, Jr., appears to be lacking the most votes among attorneys in the state, with only 28 percent of the respondents in the poll saying they intend to vote for him. Meanwhile, 42 percent say they will vote for his Democratic challenger, Court of Appeals Judge E. Thomas Fitzgerald. Justice Clifford Taylor fares slightly better among attorneys in the *Lawyers Weekly* survey, getting the support of 29 percent of the state's practitioners. His challenger, Marietta Robinson, has 39 percent of the lawyer vote.

In what appears to be the closest race among attorneys, Justice Stephen Markman has 32 percent of lawyer-respondents saying they will vote for the incumbent, while 40 percent indicate they will cast their ballot for his challenger, Judge Edward Thomas.[432]

There was one point when Taylor came to Weaver for some advice.

Taylor was facing going on Off the Record[433]*, and he was going to be with Robinson [Democrat candidate Marietta Robinson[434]] who was sometimes described as The Banshee Woman. She was a very assertive and, perhaps, an aggressive woman, a trial lawyer. She was a pretty good candidate; she had qualifications. But she came across as beyond assertive. You know, women easily can be described as aggressive, and that's not good. So he was concerned about going on* Off the Record *with her.*

So I met with him and suggested that Taylor needed to just be calm, and if she became aggressive or assertive, he would come out fine as long as he was calm. And he took that advice, and that's exactly what happened. She went after him. So he survived her challenge.

For her part, Weaver supported the three with her financial support, too.

It came time to give them the contribution. My deal is, I give somebody a hundred dollars, and that's a lot of money as far as I'm concerned. I wrote the checks for Taylor and Young and Markman. I sent the checks for Taylor and Young. I sat on the check for Markman for at least another month or two. Finally I said, "He's going to run," and I sent it.

432 Traci R. Gentilozzi, "Incumbents Lag Behind in Supreme Court Race: Survey Shows Attorney's Voting for Change," *Michigan Lawyers Weekly*, 30 October 2000, http://milawyersweekly.com/news/2000/10/30/incumbents-lag-behindin-supreme-court-race/.
433 *Off the Record* is a weekly television program originating at Michigan State University's WKAR studio and is hosted by senior capitol correspondent Tim Skubik. [http://wkar.org/programs/record.] Justice Weaver was on the show in early 2007 in what was a pivotal interview...not so much for what she said, but what she chose to not say. There will be more about this.
434 Marietta "Marti" Robinson is a Lake Orion trial attorney specializing in medical malpractice. She was nominated in March of 2012 by President Barak Obama to serve on the Consumer Product Safety Commission, a nomination that was pending Senate approval. In 2011 she served "as independent legal counsel to the Chair of the United Nations Peacebuilding Commission in Liberia." [Lynn Monson, "Noted area attorney receives appointment to Safety Commission," *Detroit Legal News*, 7 February 2012, http://www.legalnews.com/detroit/1199586.]

That was my mistake. I was too willing to hope that it would be better and too naïve to realize that I was being deceived in some ways. I don't know if it's naïve, exactly; you just don't want to believe that people are deceiving you, so you always give people a chance. And there was nothing I could do about it, because Markman was nominated. They were not going to make him step down; and they could have made him step down, and they could have appointed Rick Bandstra or Nanci Grant.

Taylor, Markman, and Young did not lose.

For the eight-year term, Taylor bested Robinson, 1,675,147 to her 1,210,809 votes. Libertarian Roddis tallied 236,404 votes.[435]

And the money was huge, a record. Here is a report of the traceable money.

Taylor's campaign brought in $1,332,975.[436]
Robinson raised $1,195,683.[437]

With the independent expenditures, that worked out to almost $1.11 per vote for Taylor and nearly $1 per vote for Robinson.

For the four-year term, Markman outpolled Thomas 1,707,977 to 1,139,676. Raaflaub gathered 194,973 votes.

Markman raised $1,244,502.[438]

435 Barbara Moorhouse and Richard Robinson with David Hogg, *Special Interests v Public Values—Funding Michigan Supreme Court Campaigns—1994-2000* "2000 Supreme Court Election" (Michigan Campaign Finance Network, Lansing, Mich.), 39-49, http://www.mcfn.org/pdfs/reports/SCAppendix.pdf.
436 That came from 4,772 contributors (an average of $279 each), most of it from manufacturing and miscellaneous business. That was followed by contributions from finance, insurance, and real estate. "Unknown" was the third largest category. Of the top ten contributors, the Michigan Republican State Committee led the way with $67K. Following came Michigan Association of Realtors/REALTORS PAC $34,200; The Ann Arbor PAC $34K; Detroit Regional Chamber PAC $34K; Governor Engler Leadership Funds $34K; Michigan Association of Home Builders/Builders PAC $34K; Michigan Health and Hospital Association/Health PAC $34K; Posthumus Leadership Fund $34K; Associated Builders and Contractors of Michigan/ABC PAC ($20,400), and Michigan Farm Bureau PAC $20K. Still, those top ten accounted for only 26 percent of the contributions. Taylor also had independent expenditures (IEs) of $453,227 from the Michigan Republican State Committee and $69,400 from the Ann Arbor PAC. [Barbara Moorhouse and Richard Robinson with David Hogg, *Special Interests v Public Values—Funding Michigan Supreme Court Campaigns—1994-2000* "2000 Supreme Court Election" (Michigan Campaign Finance Network, Lansing, Mich.), 39-49, http://www.mcfn.org/pdfs/reports/SCAppendix.pdf.]
437 From 2,291 contributors (an average of $522 each). Far and away the bulk of that came from lawyers and lobbyists, followed by labor. The candidate herself was the third largest contributor ($152,240) and the top individual donor. The other nine included Sommers, Schwartz, Silver & Schwartz, P.C. $96,187; Michigan Democratic State Central Committee $44,693; Michigan Education Association/MEA PAC $34K; Michigan Trial Lawyers Association/Justice PAC $34K; United Auto Workers/UAW MI V PAC $34K; Honigman Miller Schwartz & Cohn, LLP. $21,094; Sachs, Waldman $20,217; International Brotherhood of Electrical Workers/IBEW COPE $17K; and AFSCME PAC $15K. Robinson had supporting IEs of $122 from the Michigan Democratic Central Committee and $9,626 from the Michigan Democratic Party Justice Caucus. [Ibid.]
438 From 4,437 contributors (averaging $280 each)And if you need to know from whence, just look at Taylor's support. It's identical at those levels with the exception of IE support from the Michigan Republican State Committee of $427,673.

Thomas raised $1,008,420 from 2,332 contributors (averaging $434 each). His money—as Robinson's—came in the main from lawyers and lobbyists and labor. His third top sector was the party. His top

For the two-year term, Young bested Fitzgerald 1,614,017 to 1,194,890. Libertarian Kaufman picked up 311,589 votes.

Young raised a total of $1,292,912.[439]

In addition to all the above, there was nearly as much spent for issue ads dealing with specific candidates: $7.5 million.[440] The Michigan Campaign Finance Network contacted television stations and added up all the money that went into the ads...ad spending that didn't have to be reported to the state:

> By carefully stopping short of using the "magic words" of express advocacy, such as "vote for" or "defeat," that subject electioneering ads to disclosure, the Chamber and the parties were able to provide political cover for the interest groups and individuals who paid for the attack advertising. Corporations and unions, which otherwise must conduct their political activity using segregated funds through fully disclosed PACs, were able to spend freely from their treasuries for these "non-election" communications. Neither the parties nor the Chamber of Commerce reported any Supreme Court opposition advertising in their respective campaign finance reports.[441]

Many observers were alarmed. This had been the state's most expensive Supreme Court campaign; it totaled nearly $16 million spread among candidate committees ($6.824 million), independent expenditures ($1.587 million), and electioneering television ads ($7.5 million).[442]

Even one of the participants—Justice Young—wondered aloud at the increase in the reported campaign spending—much less the unreported spending—and its

ten donors included Sommers, Schwartz, Silver & Schwartz, P.C. $99,851; Michigan Democratic State Central Committee $58,076; Michigan Education Association/MEA PAC $34K; Michigan Trial Lawyers Association/Justice $34K; United Auto Workers/UAW MI V PAC $34K; Thurswell, Chayet & Weiner $20,600; Sachs, Waldman $20,192; AFSCME PAC $15K; Michigan State Firefighters PAC $15K; and Michigan Laborers Political League $11,550. Thomas' IEs were the same as Robinsons. [Ibid.]
439 From 4,635 contributors (an average of $279 each). And, again, his top contributors mirror Markman's and Taylors, with the exception of the IEs from the Michigan Republican State Committee. He received the most of all the Republican candidates: $469,485.
Fitzgerald raised $750,539 from 1,350 contributors (an average of $556 each). Again, lawyers and lobbyists, labor, and the party were the largest sectors. His top ten individual contributors included Summers, Schwartz, Silver & Schwartz, P.C., $78,949; Michigan Democratic State Central Committee $46,011; Michigan Education Association/MEA PAC $35K; Michigan Trial Lawyers Association/Justice PAC $34K; United Auto Workers/UAW MI V PAC $34K; Sachs, Waldman $19,467; International Brotherhood of Electrical Workers/IBEW COPE $17K; Fieger, Fieger, Schwartz & Kenney, P.C. $16,500; United Food & Commercial Workers Local 951 $16K; and AFSCME PAC $15K. IE's to Fitzgerald's campaign were identical to Thomas and Robinson. [Ibid.]
440 Michigan Supreme Court Campaign Finance Summary, 1984-2010, Michigan Campaign Finance Reform, http://www.mcfn.org/pdfs/reports/MSC_table84_10.pdf.
441 Barbara Moorhouse and Richard Robinson with David Hogg, *Special Interests v Public Values—Funding Michigan Supreme Court Campaigns—1994-2000* "2000 Supreme Court Election" (Michigan Campaign Finance Network, Lansing, Mich.), 12, http://www.mcfn.org/pdfs/reports/SCreport.pdf.
442 Michigan Supreme Court Campaign Finance Summary, 1984-2010, Michigan Campaign Finance Reform, http://www.mcfn.org/pdfs/reports/MSC_00.pdf.

implications. He was quoted in the *George* magazine article that showed him standing behind what the magazine described as a "money tree":

> "My advisors tell me I'll have to raise $1 million or more to run a Supreme Court race," he told *George* in July. "How can this not be a problem? The public has the right to ask: 'If you have to raise $1 million, can you really be impartial?'"[443]

Governor Engler, too, would later express concern about the money, but at the time, he was very pleased with the results of the court election. Gleaves Whitney, the Governor's speechwriter, friend, and biographer, relayed the perspective of the executive office:

> Engler was extremely pleased with the Supreme Court races. All three of his recent appointees to the court won. Justices Clifford Taylor, Stephen Markman, and Robert Young added great depth to what was already the best Supreme Court in the United States.[444]

The public had spoken through the ballot box. As a result, the trio of Englerites was returned to the bench and the imprimatur of legitimacy settled over the court.

443 Nancy Perry Graham, "The Best Judges Money Can Buy," *George*, December/January 2001, 77.
444 Gleaves Whitney, *John Engler: The Man, the Leader and the Legacy*, (Chelsea, Mich., Sleeping Bear Press, 2002), 354.

Chapter 10

The Beginning of
Dark Days at the Court

A Looming Defeat

With the 2000 election in the rearview mirror, the Michigan Supreme Court looked inward. One of the top orders of business would be the approaching vote to either maintain Elizabeth Weaver as chief justice...or to pick another.

In the first place, Weaver said she thought she was under an obligation to continue.

I felt I needed to because I didn't think that Governor Engler should run the court, and I didn't think that anybody else was ready to do it in the sense that they would not use the court to fulfill agendas, be they Governor's agendas or party agendas, special interest agendas, or their own agendas.

It was an important institution, and we had important work to do to continue reforms, and it was more obvious to me that there was more need for reforms at the Supreme Court itself now that I saw the potential and some abuse and misuse of power.

Okay, the three boys—Taylor, Markman, and Young—couldn't be trusted to run it; and Kelly and Cavanagh weren't a solid choice—AND they were in the minority in terms of party affiliation. But what about Corrigan? Wasn't Corrigan still a Weaver supporter?

No. I had been warned as early as spring of 2000 that she had turned on me. But I still had hope that she would come around. Where Maura was concerned, I always had a hope that maybe she would be what I had thought she could be. That's why I had mentored and helped her, and why I had let her represent me on my campaigns.

So...?

So, she was then with the Governor and the other three.

And Weaver's fellow justices had made it clear that she was not going to be their first choice unless….

So, in November after the election, I understood that the Engler Four wanted control, and I had made it clear to them that I wasn't going there.

They made it very clear that unless Weaver would make a deal, she would no longer be chief justice.

It played out after a swearing-in ceremony for a new young lawyer, Matthew Schneider, a volunteer who worked for Cliff Taylor's election.[445]

And we had a big ceremony in the Supreme Court courtroom with all of the people that were supporting him (I don't believe Kelly and Cavanagh were there), and his family, and the Engler Four asked me to do it, even though, obviously, there were problems there. And so it was all very gracious. And after that was all completed then, the Four wanted to talk to me, and we went into a conference room. And they spoke to me about that, if I wanted to continue to be chief justice, there were things they wanted to do, which was still getting rid of the institutional staff, and that they would be in charge, but that I could have the title.

Another *quid pro quo.*

Wanna Go to Cincinnati?

They sweetened the pot a little, or so they thought.

So I was offered the chief justice post if I would do what they wanted, and that then I could soon leave to go to the Sixth Circuit Court of Appeals.

That was a federal court and the post was a federal appointment. How could members of the court make an offer like that?

They couldn't.

But the Governor more or less could. If this communication was coming from the Governor—either directly or through Lucille Taylor to Cliff—that meant that the Engler Four were in close communication with him and Weaver wasn't.

---

445 *This fellow was a Taylor protégé, and they have fast tracked him.*

Schneider is now legal counsel to the Michigan Supreme Court. That came after a series of related jobs starting as a senior advisor and assistant general counsel to the White House Budget Office. That was during President George W. Bush's first term. In 2003, he came back to Michigan as an assistant U.S. Attorney in Detroit, rising through the ranks before his appointment to the high court. He speaks with Chief Justice Robert P. Young, Jr. on a daily basis. [John Minnis, "Profile in brief: Matthew Schneider, supreme counsel," *Legal News*, 23 February 2011, http://www.legalnews.com/macomb/1004931.]

That's right. They had no authority on their own. But later in early 2001, Governor Engler directly indicated to me that he was quite interested in my going, and supportive and told me he'd talk to my Congressman Dave Camp about it. Camp indicated he supported me. In retrospect, it might have been a smart thing for them to send me off.

I was never keen to have to go to Cincinnati on a regular basis, but I was willing to—that would be a decent thing to do. I had many people urging me to be willing to go.

She even went through the motions of initial inquiry.

Alfred Hoffman [Jr.], the national finance chair for the national Republican Party, offered to and did write a letter of recommendation for me, amongst other things.[446]

Even if he was telling her a lie, could Engler have made such an offer? Did he have that much pull at the federal level? Part of that depended on his own political clout within his own state. And he had promised George W. Bush and the Republican faithful to deliver Michigan in the 2000 primary—what he called the firewall against John McCain—and failed to deliver.

Still, he had the juice with the new Republican president. How'd he get it? Well, he worked for it—and he worked hard—all through the preceding year.

He was, in fact, the first among equals when it came to access by governors during the 2000 campaign. When Bush was exploring his candidacy, Engler was the only governor on the committee. According to Jim Brandell, an aide in Engler's first gubernatorial run and an aide in his administration, "He was serving with George Schultz, Condoleezza Rice, Colin Powell, and others."[447] Brandell continued:

> Not only was Engler the only governor on Bush's exploratory committee. He was one of the lead governors making calls to other governors to engage their support. Engler the political animal was involved in the politics, constantly strategizing and identifying specific constituents to reach out to: "We really need to court the auto industry, or the farmers, or the homebuilders." Engler was one of the only governors involved in policy. He was constantly offering suggestions on issues like welfare and taxes and federalism. Engler was out there fundraising—really he was a lead fundraiser. And Engler was involved in communications. He was willing to appear anywhere and everywhere on the candidate's behalf.[448]

John Miller, who reported for *National Review*, wrote of Engler as a strong contender for a cabinet post and maybe even something higher:

446 *But I did learn that the Governor was not truthful with me about his support. He also told Hoffman a different story. So I did learn, point blank, that while Governor Engler could look you in the eye telling you one thing, he could be telling somebody else exactly the opposite.*
447 Jim Brandell quoted in Gleaves Whitney, *John: The Man, the Leader and the Legacy*, (Chelsea, Mich., Sleeping Bear Press, 2002), 340.
448 Ibid.

[T]he Bush campaign registered "bushengler.com" as a web domain name. It's easy to see why. As a longtime Bush loyalist—backing the father in 1980, doing so again in 1988, and endorsing the son in the current cycle—Engler is a known commodity in Austin. As a tax cutting Republican governor from a labor-union state in the Midwest, he brings experience to the ticket and helps deliver contested electoral votes. And as a pro-life Catholic conservative, he simultaneously satisfies the party base and reaches out to Reagan Democrats.

[...]

Engler is an unlikely success in the era of blow-dried politics. He's more a cloakroom arm-twister than a telegenic bully-pulpit man. In Lansing, he is known as a bruiser. "Win or lose, he will always take a pound of flesh from you," says one Michigan Republican. Yet there is very little turnover on his staff, and he can be strikingly loyal.

[...]

His record through nine years is impressive: some 26-tax cuts, saving the public some $11 billion; fewer state employees; and a plummeting abortion rate. Engler has also reshaped the state judiciary: Michigan may have the most conservative state supreme court in the nation. When the Cato Institute released its biennial report card on governors two years ago, it declared that "there is almost nothing not to admire," about Engler's work.[449]

His inability to deliver Michigan for Bush was a stunning setback. Rachel Siglow, his executive assistant, recalled his actions at the conclusion of the Republican primary:

> That evening when it was clear that George W. Bush would lose the primary, the Governor gave his speech down in Southfield. There must have been 50 or 60 news cameras, more than I've ever seen before. Then he went on CNN live and really showed the kind of leader he is. On national news he said, in effect, "This is not George Bush's loss. This is John Engler's loss. The votes for McCain were votes against me."

> On national TV, the Governor took all the blame. He emphasized that Bush was a great candidate who deserved to win, but that his [Engler's] enemies had come out and voted for McCain just to spite him.[450]

Those "enemies" could have been Democrats who voted in the Republican primary and Republicans who just liked John McCain better. He might be putting too much on himself, imagining that he was more important in all that than he really was. Or,

---

449 Ibid., 344-345, reprinted from John J. Miler, "W.'s Man in Michigan: The Story of John Engler," *National Review*, 21 February 2000, 18-20.
450 Ibid., 348.

maybe he was right; the man had created a lot of enemies, including many within his own party.

He deeply offended many Republicans along the way.

For all the love between and among the Bush camp and John Engler, he won neither the number-two spot nor a cabinet post.

Whatever else you say about the Bushes, they are honorable people and they pay off their political debts. Engler didn't deliver the Michigan "firewall," but they still owed him for his early support. And they owed him a serious appointment.

If he wasn't going to be vice president—and he wasn't—Engler decided to choose the route of making big money.

So he was destined to serve out his last term as Governor before taking on the presidency of Electronic Data Systems. He held that position for little more than a year before moving on as head of the National Association of Manufacturers, a much more lucrative position: $1 million in salary by 2008. He would jump, in 2010, to the presidency of Business Roundtable, an even higher paying lobbying concern.[451]

In addition to his own secured future, he snagged an appointment for Spencer Abraham, who had lost his re-election race to Debbie Stabenow. Abraham was named Bush's Secretary of Energy. And Michelle Engler was handed a political present that turned out to be ticking: appointment to Freddie Mac.[452]

Michelle getting Freddie Mac was VERY lucrative.

...All thanks to the Bushes?

While he served as Governor, he certainly had the clout to recommend appointments to the federal bench to a sympathetic president. Recommending Betty Weaver to the Sixth Circuit would be within his ambit; he would be heard by the President. So, if Weaver had been "offered" a seat on the Sixth Circuit Court of Appeals in Cincinnati just after Bush was elected, that was do-able.

But would he have the same kind of power later, once he left office Jan.1, 2003?

Don't you see that once he left office, he had greater influence than ever? He was a really influential lobbyist.

---

451 Dan Eggen, "CEO group picks Engler to be its new president," *The Washington Post*, 22 December 2010, http://www.washingtonpost.com/wp-dyn/content/article/2010/12/21/AR2010122105969.html.
452 She was aboard the good ship Freddie Mac as a governor (one of its many captains) in 2008 as it steered onto the rocks of subprime mortgages, sending the economy into a recession/depression. Her work and compensation (almost $277,000 in 2007) is covered in a later chapter and the blog of co-author Schock, http://www.mymicourt.com/?p=20.

So, Engler still had the regard of the Bush administration, and he would be heard beyond his time as Governor, as long as there was a Republican in the White House.

Whoever went on the federal bench had Engler's actual promotion or was somebody he allowed to go. And that was both while he was Governor and after.

And while the appointment that might have had Weaver's name on it was at the top of the federal heap—except the U.S. Supreme Court—there are lesser federal judgeships: federal magistrate judges, federal district judges, and federal bankruptcy judges. Weaver lists a whole gaggle of judges that were appointed during the Bush years.

Four went to Sixth Circuit: David McKeague[453], Richard Griffin[454], Raymond Kethledge[455] and Helene White.[456] They tried to get Stephen Murphy there, too, but it didn't work out.[457] David McKeague went to the Sixth Circuit, and he and his wife, Nancy, were VERY close with Engler and [Spencer] Abraham. And McKeague's wife for a time was the senior vice president of the Michigan Chamber of Commerce.

McKeague was appointed to the Western District of Michigan in 1991 by President George H. W. Bush, and then raised to the Sixth Circuit Court of Appeal in 2005 by George W. Bush.

Then Griffin went, but that wasn't so much Engler's doing as he didn't oppose it. It was [Vice President Dick] Cheney who made that happen.

Griffin also joined the court in 2005.

Then they put up Kethledge and Murphy at the same time in 2006. Raymond Kethledge...he's definitely an Engler favorite, and he had no judicial experience. And Murphy was important because as a federal prosecutor he went after Geoffrey Fieger in an election campaign prosecution.[458]

At the time of the nominations, the U.S. Senate was under Republican control. That would flip to the Democrats by the time it came to confirm Kethledge and Murphy. And the Democrats weren't going along.

They were still plenty aggrieved by the actions of former Senator Spencer Abraham, who in 1999 sat on the Judiciary Committee and blocked President Clinton's nominations of Helene White and Kathleen McCree Lewis.[459] Oh, yeah, the Dems had put White up once before. So in the late 1990s, there was an uneasy balance among Abraham, Michigan's other senator, Carl Levin, and President Bill Clinton concerning

453 "David McKeague," Judgepedia, http://judgepedia.org/index.php/David_McKeague.
454 "Richard Griffin," Judgepedia, http://judgepedia.org/index.php/Richard_Griffin.
455 "Raymond Kethledge," Judgepedia, http://judgepedia.org/index.php/Raymond_Kethledge.
456 "Helene White," Judgepedia, http://judgepedia.org/index.php/Helene_White.
457 "Report on the nomination of Stephen J. Murphy, III, to the Sixth Circuit," Alliance for Justice, 19 September 2006, http://www.afj.org/assets/resources/nominees/murphy-report.pdf.
458 That is a whole other story. Imagine 100 or so FBI agents raiding Fieger's office, his home, and the homes of his employees. We'll go there, too, later in the book.
459 Amy Steigerwalt, *Battle over the Bench: Senators, Interest Groups, and Lower Court Confirmations*, University of Virginia Press (Charlottesville, Virginia), 2010, 62.

the judiciary. And after Bush came in 2001, and Abraham was gone as Senator (replaced by Debbie Stabenow), there was a continued delicacy required to get any federal judge appointments through, much less at the Sixth Circuit Court of Appeals. The balance of parties shifted again in the U.S. Senate, and for a time the Republicans had enough power to work things out with the Democrats to the extent that McKeague and Griffin got through in 2005. But when the Dems resumed power in the Senate again, they were not going to forgive and forget. And they had more to remember including the recent actions of Senator Sam Brownback opposing the federal district court appointment of Janet Neff:

> In response to Brownback's hold, Michigan Senators Carl Levin and Debbie Stabenow retaliated by placing holds on two other Michigan district court nominees. When this tactic failed, Patrick Leahy placed a hold on all judicial nominations currently on the Senate floors, many of which Brownback strongly supported.[460]

President Bush renominated them again in 2007,[461] and they didn't fare much better. At that point, the Democrats had allowed some appointments to the federal district court and blocked others, but they stood fast on the Sixth Circuit Court of Appeals. They were waiting for something...a *quid pro quo*.

> The White House on Tuesday [April 15, 2008] nominated Michigan Appeals Court Judge Helene White to the U.S. 6th Circuit Court of Appeals and U.S. Attorney Stephen Murphy to U.S. District Court in eastern Michigan.
>
> Political observers described the arrangement as a deal between the White House and Michigan Sen. Carl Levin,[462] who for more than a decade has pushed White for a spot on the federal appeals bench.
>
> Her previous nomination was held up by partisan bickering over federal judicial appointments.
>
> The White House, which previously had nominated Murphy to the federal appeals bench only to see his confirmation stalled by Senate Democrats, withdrew Murphy's name for the 6th Circuit job on Tuesday and nominated him for federal district judge.
>
> "We are pleased that, after so many years of delay and frustration, a new willingness by the White House to engage in meaningful consultations with us has resulted in nominees who will hopefully have strong bipartisan support in the Senate," Levin and Michigan Sen. Debbie Stabenow, a fellow Democrat, said in a statement Tuesday.

460 Ibid., 82.
461 Ken Thomas, "Bush nominated five for federal judicial posts," *Michigan Lawyers Weekly*, 26 March 2007, http://milawyersweekly.com/news/2007/03/26/bush-nominates-five-for-federal-judicial-posts/.
462 White had clerked for Michigan Supreme Court Justice Charles Levin after she graduated from law school. They would later marry, and in 2006 they divorced. Justice Charles Levin is Carl Levin's cousin.

Observers said the deal also calls for confirmation of Raymond Kethledge, whom President George W. Bush nominated for the 6th Circuit bench along with Murphy in 2006.[463]

Carl Levin made a deal to get Helene White on and Bush would get Kethledge. ...And Stephen Murphy would go to the eastern district. He was a protégé of Markman and Engler.

In 2008, Stephen Murphy, III received a presidential appointment as a federal district judge for the Eastern District of Michigan.[464] In addition to Murphy at the Eastern District federal court, President Bush appointed others. Weaver recalls some of them.

Nancy Edmunds. Or was she Reagan appointed?

Nope. Nancy G. Edmunds was appointed by the first President Bush in 1992.[465]

He got one or two up in Midland, Congressman Camp's home territory. Robert Cleland is out of Midland, and he went to Eastern District. I think he also ran for Attorney General.

Cleland may have had Engler's approval, but he also was appointed by George H. W. Bush in June of 1990, a time before Engler's election to the Governor's office.[466]

The other judge from Midland was Ludington...Thomas Ludington.

Ludington spent a spell waiting between his nomination by President George W. Bush in 2002 and his commissioning in 2006.[467] He was one the Dems let slip through.

And let's see, who else did they get.... Well there was Sean Cox out of Livonia.

There was no waiting for Sean F. Cox[468] who was appointed United States District Court Judge on June 12, 2006, and immediately assumed duty.[469] Another pass from the Dems.

In the western district, President Bush appointed Paul Maloney, Robert Jonker, and Janet Neff. All three came in 2007 and were approved by Levin and Stabenow.

Paul Maloney was chair of the Sentencing Guidelines Commission. He was from Berrien County. I know him, he's a nice guy, very qualified, had some early D.C. federal experience, was a former county

463 David Ashenfelter, "White House nominates 2 for courts," *Detroit Free Press*, 16 April 2008, B5.
464 "Biography: Stephen J. Murphy," United States District Court, Eastern District of Michigan, http://www.mied.uscourts.gov/Judges/guidelines/topic.cfm?topic_id=387.
465 "Biography: Nancy G. Edmunds," United States District Court, Eastern District of Michigan, http://www.mied.uscourts.gov/Judges/guidelines/topic.cfm?topic_id=141.
466 "Biography: Robert H. Cleland," United States District Court, Eastern District of Michigan, http://www.mied.uscourts.gov/Judges/guidelines/topic.cfm?topic_id=85.
467 "Biography: Thomas L. Luddington, United States District Court, Eastern District of Michigan, http://www.mied.uscourts.gov/Judges/guidelines/topic.cfm?topic_id=185.
468 Yes, his brother Mike was Michigan's Attorney General.
469 "Biography: Sean F. Cox," United States District Court, Eastern District of Michigan, http://www.mied.uscourts.gov/Judges/guidelines/topic.cfm?topic_id=98.

prosecutor and circuit judge, worked to improve judicial services for Berrien County. He is a very good judge.

Maloney came to the court "on the recommendation of Congressman Fred Upton and U.S. Senator Carl Levin." He now serves as chief judge of the United States District Court for the Western District of Michigan.[470]

Robert J. Jonker was another who was in private practice.[471]

Janet Neff went on, put up by Bush. She was a staunch Democrat and there was a deal made for her.

She was nominated and confirmed in 2007. She took the seat vacated by David McKeague.[472] McKeague, of course, had gone on to the Sixth Circuit Court of Appeals.

Staying Power

Politics. It was just politics.

In one sense, John Engler's political staying power seems extraordinary.

Take a look at the appointments of Michigan's latest Governor, Rick Snyder. Much of his staff is made up of former Engler appointees and friends.[473] It begins to look like Engler redux. In one sense, it's natural: you need people of your own party who know how the state works. So, you reach back to a previous administration. In another sense, it's kind of creepy IF you believe that Engler exerted an oppressive political hand, now an oppressive political dead hand.

If John Engler had expressed more honesty and transparency, his administration would have been a model of good government. In that case, I'd have welcomed his continuing influence on the governing front. But his use of deception and misuse of power often attracted and encouraged just such activity. His legacy lingers, corrupting the democratic process.[474]

At the time they approached me about the federal bench, my eyes were pretty well opened to what was going on. ...Not fully, but pretty much.

And from her perspective, Cincinnati's Sixth Circuit really wasn't all that much a draw.

---

470 "Paul Maloney," Judgepedia, http://judgepedia.org/index.php/Paul_Maloney.
471 "Robert Jonker," Judgepedia, http://judgepedia.org/index.php/Robert_Jonker.
472 "Janet Neff," Judgepedia, http://judgepedia.org/index.php/Janet_Neff.
473 For an early list of recycled Englerites, see Tim Skubik, "When Johnny Comes Marching Home," Skoop's Blog, 7 January 2011, http://skoopsblog.blogspot.com/2011/01/when-johnny-comes-marching-home.html.
474 Weaver was an early and staunch Snyder supporter. She spent an hour or so with him before the Republican primary confirming her assessment, and she recommended his selection among her circle of friends.

It was my hope that Governor Snyder would see John Engler for all that he was and did, and would be extremely cautious of employing his associates and protégés. I have reservations about our current Governor and the influences working at him. And I don't think he knows much or enough about the judiciary and justice system, much to the detriment of the people of Michigan. Yet I believe he's a decent, intelligent, hardworking, well-intentioned, positive, honest leader, unafraid to do his highest sense of right and fear not. I still have hopes for him and pray.

I didn't need to go to the Sixth Circuit. And I didn't want to. I didn't want to be away from Glen Arbor that often, that far, or that long.

Another Carrot? Probate Court Reform?
Not Even That!

The continuing chief justice position and the subsequent appointment to the Sixth Circuit Court of Appeals were not the only enticements.

Also, they offered that they would see that the part-time probate judge bill got passed and signed.

That probate bill was near and dear to her heart. She had been one of those part-time probate judges, and she knew Michigan citizens deserved better. The bill would have seen to it that every county had at least one full-time probate judge.[475] This was a reform that had been high—very high—on her list. That might have made it tempting to sit down, shut up, and do what they wanted. But no...Weaver didn't do deals.[476]

But I would never go there at the betrayal of the people of Michigan and the judiciary. Just to go along to get along? I was a justice who had the confidence of a lot of people, and I couldn't do that. When it's principle—and this is principle when we're talking about separation of power—it was obvious everyone knew that the Governor rightfully controlled the executive branch, but he also controlled the legislature. He had a Republican House and Senate. The Governor had people very well placed over at the legislature and, if nothing else, monitoring it.

That was no secret. One of his most effective observers was Mike Gadola. From 1991 to 1995 and during 1997 and 1998, he was deputy legal counsel and counsel for executive organization to Governor John Engler (that would be right under Lucille Taylor). In 1999 and 2000, he was House majority counsel. He would subsequently come to the Supreme Court as Supreme Court counsel in 2001, and in 2003 move up to general counsel for the SCAO, the State Court Administrative Office.[477] He is now Governor Rick Snyder's legal affairs director.[478]

To add Engler's control of the judiciary to that of the legislature was too much, said Weaver.

So, no. It would be better to be ousted as chief justice than to assume the office with strings. She knew that Taylor, Markman, and Young were solidly against her; she was relatively certain Corrigan joined them.

475 *That would exclude a very few counties that had agreed to be districted together several decades before. There were only a handful that did it.*
476 *It would take the departure of Engler and two more years beyond that until Governor Granholm signed into law the conversion of the part-time probate judges to full time.*
477 Marcia McBrien, "Michael F. Gadola, Michigan Supreme Court Counsel and State Court Administrative Office General Counsel, Selected as 2003 Toll Fellow," Michigan Supreme Court, 17 September 2003.
478 Paul Jancsewski, "'Catholic kid from Flint' service as Snyder's Legal Affairs Director," *Legal News*, http://www.legalnews.com/jackson/1027551.

So now that I was going to not have the votes of my Republican colleagues that I had helped get elected....

That left Cavanagh and Kelly—not enough votes to carry the issue, but enough at least to make a point.

I still thought Cavanagh and Kelly would not go there, and that if Maura was going, it would be 4-3 against me. And so I sought out, eventually, Cavanagh and Kelly, to tell them that I was going to proceed with it.

Cavanagh did say that he was supportive of me, and he would support me, and then I talked to Kelly, and she was evasive which, to me, meant no. And then I really had the feeling, "Well, maybe, but probably not. But Cavanagh will support me and that's fine."

Cavanaugh had served his turn as chief justice. In their talk about her running again for the position, he lamented the demands of the job.

And Cavanagh acknowledged that we both understood the burdens of it to do it right. If you don't really care or you just want it to be show, and you'll let other people run it, it's supposedly all glory. But to really do the job it's 24-7, a lot of extra work. It's a service, as I had explained, that I never really yearned for.

And while Cavanagh was theoretically supportive in their conversation, Weaver learned subsequently through a letter that he had changed his mind.

I got this letter, dated December 28th, and he sent it confidentially to me. It says:

> Dear Betty:
> In our meeting last week I indicated that I was leaning to support you for another term as chief justice.[479]

I thought he had indicated he would, but regardless, he's acknowledging that.

> I so advised Maura. Since then, it has become apparent to me that neither Marilyn nor anyone else on the court is so inclined. I am concerned that a contested 5-2 vote, or even a 4-3 vote would serve no purpose other than to exacerbate the already existing hard feelings between you and a majority of the court. However, if you will insist upon calling the divisive roll, I will nominate you if you can indicate you have a vote, other than yourself, for a second.
>
> As we discussed, the "honor" of serving as chief justice soon wears thin for anyone who has shouldered those ever-present responsibilities. Having been there and done that, I can assure you that relief from those responsibilities is immeasurable. I would urge you not to call the question.[480]

479 Michael F. Cavanagh letter to Elizabeth A. Weaver, 28 December 2000, unpublished.
480 Ibid.

He didn't want blood on the floor.

And I think I had learned that Maura had talked to him and told him she wanted to be chief justice, and she had also talked to Kelly.

Well, I thought about it. I was surprised and not pleased, disappointed. And I knew that Maura was really wanting to take over. ...Ready was another matter. So, where would the votes be for me? They certainly wouldn't be from Taylor, Markman, and Young. So I thought a lot about it, and I talked to Justice Riley, amongst others. She urged me not to do it; not to be public about it and just to let it go.

And I talked to other people that would be in my kitchen cabinet and my friends and advisers, and decided that I could not be silent about it. I would let my name be there if there was only one vote. And, if that were the case, it would let people know there was something askew there.

The press had picked up on some of the discord.

Dawson Bell[481] had mentioned the selection of chief justice right before or after the November general election, and that—well, not in a friendly way. I could tell there was something going on; this was not straightforward. I was not close to Dawson Bell. But Justice Taylor was.

The matter came from somebody within the court, and I guessed it was Taylor. And the story was that maybe I wouldn't be the chief justice.

Others in the media picked up the story, and by the time it came for the conference to select the chief justice—retain or replace—the atmosphere was pretty well charged.

But in the end, I decided if I only had one vote, my own, I would go there, because I hoped that it would send a message.

And the conference when the vote was held was odd in itself, said Weaver.

I don't know that anybody wanted to discuss why I shouldn't do the job. But Maura gave us a long dissertation that was really quite bizarre about how she did have time to do it. You have to remember, at that time her husband [Joe Grano] was ill. I think it was Parkinson's, just as Justice Riley had.

The vote?

I did decide to go down to defeat even if it was 6-1. Frankly, I have no regrets.

Six-to-one against Weaver.

And the vote was taken, and then we left. This was in the old building. And Maura went down the hall, and that was it.[482]

---

481 Dawson Bell is a reporter and columnist for the *Detroit Free Press*.
482 Weaver theorizes she went down the hall and into the file room to purge from Markman's file the letter from Gerri Kozachik. *Maura was now theirs.*

As she envisioned, the vote sent a message, but not necessarily the one Weaver had hoped.

I didn't anticipate that they would really set up a PR scheme immediately. That was stupid on my part, naïve, or just, you know—I just didn't think it would go there. I was just hoping that the press and people would realize it was more important than that.

It was disappointing to me when they really had the PR machine ready to go that day.

But it couldn't have been the work of the public information officer, David Gruber.

He was not that kind of guy.

So, probably it was a result of one or more of the individual justices reaching out.

Michigan Lawyers Weekly covered the results of the vote:

> Michigan Supreme Court Justice Maura D. Corrigan has been elected to a two-year term as the court's 62nd chief justice. She replaces Elizabeth Weaver.
>
> In a Jan. 4 press conference attended by *Lawyers Weekly*, Corrigan stated that after the recent "incredibly bruising" Supreme Court elections, she believed her colleagues chose her as chief justice because it is important to achieve "more shared goals for the court."
>
> Corrigan said that she viewed her chief justice election as "an attempt to build consensus" on the high court.
>
> But while Corrigan acknowledged that it is typically a "tradition of sorts" to allow a serving chief justice to retain that position if desired, she indicated there is "no right to a second term."
>
> The new chief justice also pointed out that there was "an attempt to make the vote unanimous"—which is also traditional—but that it was ultimately a 6-1 split decision.
>
> Meanwhile, Weaver was conspicuously absent from the press conference. She arrived early to distribute a prepared statement and then left just before the conference began.
>
> "I was willing to serve a second two-year term but my colleagues have decided, by a 6 to 1 vote, to change leadership," she said in her prepared statement.
>
> Weaver also noted the progress made under her leadership, including "significant" trial court improvements and the development and acceleration of various other programs, including the construction of the Hall of Justice.

Further, Weaver praised those staff members who worked with her, saying, "I trust that the new leadership recognizes the contributions of court staff, both here at the Supreme Court and in the State Court Administrator's Office, and that they will not unjustly discipline or unfairly terminate these loyal employees."

Apparently in response to such concerns, Corrigan indicated there are no plans for any "widespread staffing changes." However, she said she will ask each staff member to assess what can be done to improve their own performance.

Despite not being re-elected chief justice, Weaver said she will continue to pursue "the one project which will most improve our 'one court of justice' the critical effort to reform Michigan's method of selecting Supreme Court justices."

Corrigan indicated that she intends to continue pursuing many of Weaver's plans, including the advocation of judicial appointments.[483]

Weaver had laid it out for everybody to see that Corrigan and the Engler Court intended to clean house.

George Weeks, a *Detroit News* columnist, followed up on the story, too.[484]

A big factor, as I noted in a previous column on the pending ouster, was Iron Betty's management style.

As noted by Secretary of State Candice Miller, Weaver is "a very independent person."

Weaver, unlike Corrigan, did not do a TV ad for the three Republican justices who were successful on the Nov. 7 "non-partisan" ballot.

In a Dec. 14 memo to the court members Weaver said: "I firmly believe that a change in leadership at this time would be detrimental to many works in progress which are designed to improve judicial services for the people of Michigan. Significant projects and programs initiated during my term as chief justice require continuing guidance and direction," particularly trial court improvements.

---

483 "Corrigan is new MSC Chief Justice," *Michigan Lawyers Weekly*, 8 January 2001, http://milawyersweekly.com/news/2001/01/08/corrigan-is-new-msc-chief-justice/.
484 George had reported, edited, and served as bureau chief, diplomatic correspondent, and Washington foreign editor for United Press International, served as Governor William Milliken's press secretary and chief of staff, and in 1983 began work as a political communist for *The Detroit News*. In retirement from the *News* he still writes a weekly column that appears in syndication. A native of Traverse City, he had by then returned to the area and also now lives in Glen Arbor. He is a friend of Weaver's. ["George Weeks (1996)," Michigan Journalism Hall of Fame, http://hof.jrn.msu.edu/bios/weeks.html.]

After Weaver's ouster Corrigan and Gov. John Engler praised her achievements as chief justice. But it remains to be seen how much support Weaver will get from Engler and the high court in her push for a constitutional
amendment to replace the election of justices with gubernatorial appointment of each justice for one non-renewable 14-year term.[485]

That was a short description of her plan for Supreme Court reform at the time. It's
changed substantially since then.[486] But any reform was in jeopardy, no matter what
the new chief justice said. Weaver told C. Jesse Green of the *Michigan Lawyers Weekly*
that

> [S]he is under no illusions regarding the chances of her proposal being im-
> plemented. "I'm sure that if the special interests want to throw money at it,
> they could see that it would be defeated," she said.

> However, Weaver was optimistic that with proper education "first of the
> legislature, then of the public" that the people of Michigan might see the
> benefits of appointing justices rather than voting for them.[487]

It seemed John Engler would support it. ...Well, he said he would in a most public
forum.

*Governor Engler gave the State of the State in 2001—in January or February—right after I had been
replaced, and he said positive things about me, and he agreed that we needed to look at judicial selection.*

This is the text of the Governor's speech that relates to court reform:

> Reform is also needed in the way Michigan chooses Supreme Court justices.
> In the past two elections, new highs in spending were reached as well as
> new lows in attacks against candidates and even the institution itself. And
> there is clear evidence that the attacks will be even nastier and the spending
> even higher in the years ahead. I have long believed there is a better way.

> Tonight, I endorse a proposal called the Modified Federal Plan, which is be-
> ing promoted by Justice Elizabeth Weaver. This reform would afford future
> Governors, with advice and consent of the Michigan Senate, one appoint-
> ment to the Supreme Court every two years. The appointed justice would
> serve only one 14-year term.

> I ask the legislature to study this issue, conduct hearings, and vote to place
> this reform plan for Supreme Court selection on the 2002 ballot.

485 George Weeks, "Democratic leaders would like to avoid ugly primary in 2002," *The Daily Globe*, 9 January 2001, 9.
486 She has since modified her position and supports a reformed dual system of election and appointment
of justices. See Appendix A for her plan for Supreme Court reform.
487 C. Jesse Green, "CJ Weaver calls for new method to pick justices; general election is no longer the best
way," *Michigan Lawyers Weekly*, 18 December 2000, http://milawyersweekly.com/news/2000/12/18/cj-weaver-
calls-for-new-method-to-pick-justices/.

Certainly, the filling of judicial vacancies by appointment is already one of the most important responsibilities of a Governor. During my tenure, I have made 171 appointments—more than one-quarter of the Michigan judiciary. The history of gubernatorial appointment demonstrates sensitivity to balance and diversity while providing ethical, competent, diligent jurists. A reformed appointment process would attract persons with outstanding professional credentials who otherwise would not subject themselves to the rigors of politics and fundraising.[488]

And he may have acknowledged that [Senator] Ken Sikkema had something on the reforms. He was proposing, and was going to go forward with the proposal. And I thought, "Well, that's good."

Sikkema was of a firm mind for reform, too. In December of 2000, he—with Weaver—had attended "a two-day summit in Chicago on 'Improving Judicial Selection,' which was coordinated by the National Center for State Courts."[489] Sikkema did introduce legislation in 2001.[490]

Great.

Except when I talked to Sikkema later, he told me that Engler told him not to move it. And Sikkema did not move it. There, again, is what you're dealing with: deceit from the Governor.

The reforms came to naught at that time.

But that's, again, the idea: Who really controlled the legislature?

"She's just bitter"

And the Engler Four were just warming up on her.

Part of what I had learned from Lucille—if you did not do what you're asked or expected to do, then you should be punished accordingly.

Nearly every time she wrote or said anything they disagreed with, they responded that she was a disappointed crank who was venting her spleen because she wasn't given a second two-year term as chief justice.

---

488 John Engler, "Building the Next Michigan; Governor John Engler 2001 State of the State Address," 31 January 2001, http://www.michigan.gov/formergovernors/0,1607,7-212-31303_31317-1931--,00.html.

489 C. Jesse Green, "CJ Weaver calls for new method to pick justices; general election is no longer the best way," *Michigan Lawyers Weekly*, 18 December 2000, http://milawyersweekly.com/news/2000/12/18/cj-weaver-calls-for-new-method-to-pick-justices/.

490 William Glaberson, "States Taking Steps to Rein In Excesses of Judicial Politicking, *New York Times*, 15 June 2001, http://www.nytimes.com/2001/06/15/us/states-taking-steps-to-rein-in-excesses-of-judicial-politicking.html?pagewanted=all&src=pm.

After the change in the leadership of the Michigan Supreme Court in 2001, Justices Cliff Taylor, Robert Young, Jr., Maura Corrigan, Stephen Markman, and Elizabeth Weaver stand with United States Supreme Court Justice Antonin Scalia. The occasion was a private reception before a dinner and speech at the Amway Grand in Grand Rapids. The event was hosted by the Economic Club of Grand Rapids, May 23, 2001. While most of the other justices talked with Scalia about his accomplishments, Weaver said she talked with him about New Orleans' cuisine, a topic dear to both their hearts.

They came out with the untruths about being a bitter person. And they began the idea that I was bitter because I didn't get a second term, and it was the tradition of the court to have a second term. And this is one of the lies that was put out, and the press didn't care. Obviously, it wasn't much of a tradition because Mallett had only served one term right before me; he had left. And then Brickley was eligible for another term, and he didn't serve a second term. Now prior to that, there had been two terms and what-have-you. I don't know where the real active tradition was, but it was irrelevant.

They would bring up the issue again and again. And the media reported it over and over, as if it were a new revelation each time.

Corrigan had become chief justice in 2001, and now she'd have the two years.

And the new chief justice wasn't wasting any time. Some of it was pure lip service, but this is what she told *Michigan Lawyers Weekly*'s C. Jesse Green:

[...] Corrigan emphasized that her perspective on the leadership transfer is "a change of style, not focus." For example, she referred to initiatives started by Weaver—such as the newly formed Chief Judges' Council and the advocation of Supreme Court appointments rather than elections—as "absolutely critical."

"Those [issues] will be coming to the conference table," she said. "Certainly, the question of judicial selection is front and center, and we will be working on that. And I think there has been a great interchange between the chief judges as a result of the council."[491]

Wheels In Motion

Although she has been chief justice for only a few weeks, Corrigan is already putting her administrative experience to work and trying to build consensus on the court.

In order to do this, Corrigan is establishing some priorities.

"First, you have to identify the fires," Corrigan said. "You need to decide what needs the most attention. The administrative agenda of the court is very, very long I think it is about nine pages. I've given an updated version to all the justices and asked them to give me their 'Letterman Top 5' of administrative priorities. We are then going to sit down together, alone, and figure out where we want to go—together."

The new chief acknowledged that she has no intention of "forcing an agenda" upon the high court. Instead, Corrigan said she hopes to plan an administrative retreat where "we try to figure out what our shared vision is. It doesn't have to be something on the list."

Meanwhile, Corrigan admitted that she has her own pet projects.

"You all know at *Lawyers Weekly* from dealing with me over the years that I love court rules," she said. "I'm interested in reform through rules. I'm interested in the Rules of Evidence project but that's just me."

As chief justice, "I want to advance the agenda as identified by the justices. I want to see what the other justices want to do. So we are starting that process. I am very serious about enlisting the help of all my fellow justices."

To this end, it was Weaver not Corrigan who swore in the House of Representatives members the week after Corrigan's election. "Where the former

---

491 *The question of judicial selection never came to the table. Proposals I circulated to the justices and the public over the years were never put on an agenda or discussed at conference.*

chief was invited to do things, she should do them," she said. "Then, as new things arise, I'll do those."

Corrigan said it's her intention to allow each member of the court to share their expertise. "I've asked the justices to designate and I'm starting to get responses from them in areas of their administrative interest for which they can delegate responsibilities."

For example, Weaver "has a huge interest in judicial selection," Corrigan noted. "That is one of the things she has identified on her list."

The chief justice indicated she hoped to have the allocations completed by the end of January.

Meanwhile, Corrigan isn't anticipating many staffing changes at the court only three. [Sic.] Two of those include naming Carl Gromek, court of appeals chief clerk and research director, and Michael Gadola, house majority counsel, to the court's staff.

The third change is likely to be a replacement, she said.

"I'm in negotiations with that person. I'd rather not talk about these personnel matters until they are completed."[492]

There it was: the start of a new kind of court, beginning with Carl Gromek and Mike Gadola. Weaver knew both of them, and she didn't like what she knew. She first met Gromek when she was sitting on the Court of Appeals.

I was initially supportive of him when he began as research director for the Court of Appeals. I thought he did a good job at first. As I worked with him for a while and came to know him, he appeared to me too quick to make up his mind then he'd take rigid positions. And he was too critical and disdainful of people. Even then it seemed he had a disdain for the judges, and he thought many judges were lazy or incompetent or both. It was like he believed himself smarter and superior. He began to get too authoritarian, in my opinion.

He was reaching for power, she said.

And he wanted to change the basic operations of the Court of Appeals in a way that would not be helpful or productive. In fact, they would be counterproductive.

Weaver said one effort Gromek proposed at the Court of Appeals was for the court to shed staff, specifically the research attorneys.

But that was not feasible. They were the core of the operations.

---

492 C. Jesse Green, "New chief justice brings administrative skills to job; Goal: build consensus on state Supreme Court," *Michigan Lawyers Weekly*, 22 January 2001, http://milawyersweekly.com/news/2001/01/22/new-chief-justice-brings-administrative-skills-to-job/.

Weaver and other judges blocked his efforts.

He aggressively pushed that, but he was unsuccessful.

With her move to the Supreme Court, Gromek was off her radar for a time.

But as chief justice at the Supreme Court, it was brought to my attention concerning the Court of Appeals budget that Carl Gromek was both head of research and then he was the chief clerk over there,[493] *and he was making more than the Court of Appeals judges. I responded that I felt that was wrong...that then-Chief Judge Corrigan and Carl should not have allowed that to happen, that was bad judgment on their parts, and that it needed to be corrected. I was told Carl was threatening to quit if correction was made.*

Before any final decisions were made, the Court of Appeals judges received a raise for 2001-02 (their last since then) and their salaries exceeded Gromek's. That corrected the imbalance, but Weaver said his difficult and oppressive tendencies and obstinate nature were revealed through it all.

So, I was not for Carl.

In his new position, Gromek was not assuming an existing post that had been vacated. This was a new job altogether.

> Upon becoming the new MSC chief justice in early January, Maura Corrigan contemplated creating a "chief of staff" position at the court. It was then decided that Gromek, who worked closely with Corrigan when she was chief judge at the Court of Appeals, was just the person for the job.
>
> "I was flattered, of course," Gromek said in discussing his new job. "A change is always energizing and I feel energized by this move."
>
> Moreover, Gromek said his specially-created role at the Supreme Court "definitely presents a new focus," though he emphasized that he enjoyed his stint at the Court of Appeals.
>
> "When [Corrigan] was elected chief justice and asked me if I'd be interested in coming over to the Supreme Court, I thought it would be a good idea, given the fact that the dual position [of chief clerk/research director] at the Court of Appeals had pretty much served its purpose," Gromek said.

---

493 From 1998 to 2001, Gromek served as chief clerk and research director of the Michigan Court of Appeals, where he was responsible for a staff of 80 research attorneys. He also directed the Court of Appeals clerk's offices, which processed over 7,000 filings each year. From 1988 to 1998, Gromek was the Court of Appeals' research director.

[Marcia McBrien, "Carl L. Gromek named State Court Administrator by Supreme Court, 14 December 2004.]

And while it's common knowledge that Corrigan and Gromek worked together at the Court of Appeals during the 1990s, some may not realize their "relationship" actually began in the 1970s, when they attended law school together at the University of Detroit.

In addition to Gromek, another new addition at the Supreme Court is the appointment of former House Majority Counsel Michael Gadola as the court's legal counsel.

Both Gromek and Gadola have been highly praised by Corrigan.

"The Supreme Court's growing responsibilities in the area of court system management require a high degree of organization and productive relations with the other branches of government," Corrigan said in a press release. "Carl and Mike are highly regarded for their administrative skills, knowledge of government, and cooperative working methods."

Corrigan added that the two staff additions will help the high court make "further gains in improving services to citizens."

New Responsibilities

Gromek's position at the Supreme Court is new and, as such, is "pretty flexible," he said.

"Right now, we're keeping it kind of loose," Gromek explained. "The chief justice and I are reviewing and evaluating the various structures and operations of the Supreme Court."

Gromek told *Lawyers Weekly* that Corrigan and the other justices will meet at an upcoming administrative retreat to discuss the evaluations and recommendations made by the chief justice and Gromek.

At that point, Gromek said, there will be "clearer definitions as to what actually will be implemented."

However, Gromek told *Lawyers Weekly* that practitioners need not be "anxious about pending or impending changes," as they [the justices] will be looking only at the "administrative aspects" of the court during their retreat.

Practitioners might not have had concerns, but the staff at the court surely did. And Weaver voiced her and their concerns that this was a return to some bad old days that presaged some bad new days.

I had objected to that because it was a complete changing of the way the court would do business. Members of the court should have learned never to give all the court's powers to one person who wasn't a justice by letting Gromek be the legal counsel and the chief of staff and [later] the State Court Administrator, as we had had happen in the past, before I was there.

And we had moderated that by letting the chief justice really be the chief justice. Why have a chief justice if you don't have them really knowing what's going on and having to report to the court, and not having one person underneath the chief justice, who has all the powers of the chief justice but no accountability whatsoever...which is what happened.

We had a group of top administrators at the court that included research, the clerk, the education branch, the legal counsel; and among other things Margaret Chiara was responsible for personnel matters and ultimately set up a human resources office. My last hire when I finished as chief justice was Michael Benedict to head HR.[494] (I never liked the term HR. I liked to call it personnel, but nobody wanted to call it universally that.) Margaret screened him, recommended him, and then I met with him and we hired him.

And so they all reported to the chief justice rather than one of them having several of those titles and being over everyone else. This way you had diversity of opinions and all these people not in competition with each other in one—maybe to some degree but, really, all working to report to the chief—and no one having power over the others, so that one couldn't destroy the other one in trying to advance. And there was no place to advance to.

This was a more democratic way of dealing with it, in one sense, because then you're more liable to get the good, diverse opinion on various important things that have to happen.

And immediately, by May 16 and 17 of 2001, we had a conference in Saginaw—one of these two-day things—where we met with the judges; but also, it was there to get all of the court and to announce the new structure. And that structure was to make Gromek the chief of staff and to have him over everyone, including the long-serving Supreme Court Clerk, Corbin Davis, who took it graciously anyway—because this was really a comedown for him. And, also, another one was [Ron] Stadnika, the finance guy. All these people had their areas of responsibility that the court's responsible for, but there was no valid reason to have any one person (i.e., a non-elected chief of staff) over those people, above the finance officer or above the clerk or above all of these vital operations and responsibilities of the court, which are ultimately the responsibility of the seven elected justices.[495]

As the court's legal counsel, Gadola was under Gromek.[496]

---

494 Benedict came from his post as the deputy city manager of East Lansing. He would serve at the Michigan Supreme Court until February of 2009 when he retired.

495 In a 2009 Supreme Court publication about him, Carl Gromek did indeed wield all that power, and then some:

> Mr. Gromek has served as the Michigan Supreme Court's Chief of Staff since February 2001. In that role, he supervises the Court's operational activities, including the Clerk's Office; the Commissioners' Office; and the offices of Human Resources, Finance, Security, Supreme Court Counsel, and Public Information.

And he would subsequently be given more power. [*Connections*, State Court Administrator's Office, Michigan Supreme Court, Winter 2008.]

496 And in 2003 Gadola would additionally be named as general counsel for the State Court Administrative Office. ["Newsmakers," *Michigan Lawyers Weekly*, 28 July 2003, http://milawyersweekly.com/

One of those under the new organization, Human Resources Director Michael Benedict, related what it was like to deal with the new chief justice and her staff:

> Carl [Gromek] asked me to prepare a list of goals and objectives for the HR function. He sent this to Chief Justice Corrigan and set up a meeting so we could discuss what I prepared. At our meeting, she began by saying she only read documents that were no longer than one page. Since mine was in the range of five pages, the meeting was ended and I was dismissed. I had no further direct dealings with Chief Justice Corrigan or any future chief justice without Carl being present. Everything that went to the justices from staff from that time forward was filtered through Carl.[497]

Gromek and Gadola were in place and exerting their influence. But Corrigan, in the *Michigan Lawyers Weekly* article, had mentioned a third change in personnel, one that was in tender negotiation.

That was referencing David Gruber who was holding down a half-time assignment of public information officer (in addition to other duties); he had to go.

So I had warned them—Gruber, Lynch, and Ferry—of the danger to them. And they all went, in varying times, because they were loyal to the institution of the Supreme Court and were not promoters or protectors of the justices. They were not public relations people for justices.

And in came his handpicked successor, Marcia McBrien.

They wanted Marcia McBrien, who is there today, who was, apparently, a very good friend of Maura Corrigan's.

She was an English graduate of Notre Dame, a law school graduate of the University of Michigan. She'd started her legal career as an associate at Miller, Canfield, then spent almost seven years reporting for *Michigan Lawyers Weekly*. She then worked a short stint for a public relations firm and then for herself for two and a half years before she was appointed to the Michigan Supreme Court in 2001.[498]

Human Resources Director Michael Benedict was there at her hiring:

> Corrigan wanted Carl to hire a PR person and he asked me to help. We worked hard on the selection process. It was very open and we had a lot of good candidates. Carl never pushed me to recommend Marcia and I did not know of her relationship with Corrigan. We recommended another candidate but she was nixed by Corrigan and Marcia subsequently was hired. I wasn't privy to the behind-the-scenes conversations between Corrigan and Carl so I can't say what was said. I did learn of the previous relationship of

Corrigan and Marcia at a later date, however, and I respected Carl for having made the recommendation he did (at least, I think he made the recommendation—no telling what happened behind closed doors). As an aside, I was never asked to again participate with Carl in hiring upper level positions, other than to advertise the positions, collect resumes, have them disbursed to those directly involved in the hiring process, and informing candidates of the results.[499]

Marcia McBrien's a smart gal and very smooth. She's a lawyer, she can write, and she works hard. And Marcia McBrien is very able.

She didn't come alone, either, at least not for long. Soon there were two others.

Instead of just having one person at $80,000 doing public information part time, we had Marcia McBrien now, full-time, for $108,000. Then McBrien needed to have help, so she needed another person and another person—a half person. So it grew into a three-person PR firm—and remember, these people all had salary plus benefits.

All of them to replace Gruber who had handled media duties part time in addition to his other work.

The court was converted into a major PR operation. And they fed stories.

And reporters liked McBrien and her colleagues, Weaver had been told.

So now we were spending hundreds of thousands of dollars on public information, and many of the press would say, "Oh, isn't this wonderful?" The press turned out that they liked PR operations because they didn't have to do all the work.

McBrien would respond to inquiries quickly, and pretty much always with something.

Yes, but in this era of declining news staffs, who is going to check to make sure she's telling the whole story? They certainly fed Dawson Bell a line. Marcia McBrien is very able, and she fed them stories. Or she didn't feed them, depending.

And the justices? The rest of them liked it better, Weaver said.

So now the justices don't have to speak for themselves or go out and hire some PR firm and pay for it themselves. The taxpayers get to pay except for additional PR obtained and paid for by each justice in his/her reelection campaign years.

Weaver never warmed up to McBrien's PR services.

I saw them as an unnecessary and expensive spin machine with too much potential to uninform and misinform the public with an ever-diminishing press corps not watching and checking on it. She was a

499 Michael Benedict, e-mail to co-author Schock, 1 June 2012.

spinner of information—sometimes accurate, sometimes incomplete, sometimes true, and sometimes untrue and deceitful. ...And sometimes there was no information.

Unlike most of the other justices, I didn't use her PR services, nor could I trust her to tell her what I was going to do before hand.

More Notes

As is customary in the court, there is a seating order based on seniority. At the time, Chief Justice Corrigan took her seat at the center of the bench. Weaver sat to her left, and Taylor and Markman sat to Weaver's left. To Corrigan's right were Cavanagh, Kelly, and Young.

As she had observed before, Weaver noticed that during hearings or oral arguments Taylor and Markman sometimes would write on the pads by their places and show each other what he'd written, in effect exchanging notes. It was obvious that they were distracted during their exchanges, but Weaver didn't really know to what extent until she lost a gold earring.

We were in a public hearing. I was wearing a pair of gold earrings and one of them had a penchant of falling off—I don't have pierced ears. Usually I was careful about making sure they were on as I moved from place to place. We had finished the hearing, and I realized that one of them was gone. So I got down on my hands and knees to look for it. At first I couldn't find it on the floor. Justice Taylor and I shared a wastebasket, and I turned it upside down thinking the earring might have fallen in there.

In pawing through the few sheets of paper that Justice Taylor had discarded, she didn't find her earring there,[500] but she did find the cause of his most recent amusement: side notes to Markman about the issues under consideration and observations about those were who were testifying before them.

In a public hearing these people have three minutes, and we are supposed to be giving them our complete attention.

Taylor had previously expressed his disdain for much of Weaver's court reforms, including the idea of family courts. On one of his notes he reiterated his thought, although it's a little confusing with the double negative: "I'm not at all sure that the Family Court isn't a bad idea."

It's reasonable to assume the Markman was responding, but Weaver hadn't gone to his wastebasket to find his notes, so she was reading one side of a conversation.

Taylor went on, each comment separated by time and, perhaps, Markman's response.

---

500 She eventually did find her earring and still wears the pair.

Taylor: "It is hot air to say it is pure coincidence that all the Family Court judges just happen to be junior?"

Taylor: "How much time do you think this woman expends in getting her hair set for the day?"

Taylor: "I'm guessing the time to, w/o combs, etc., to pull it back, i.e. about 10-15 seconds."

I remember the woman, but her appearance shouldn't have mattered to us. If that's your mentality when people are coming to talk with you about issues that are important to them, it was petty and mean. ...So despicable and sad. And it just got worse. They were having a jolly good time at others' expense.

Again, Taylor: "The Weasel is here! Skubick is in back."

Tim Skubick was—and is—the host of Off the Record *from WKAR.*

More from Taylor: "Note that EAW [Weaver] has lowered her mike [sic] and moved the water bottle so as to not impede the photographing of her."

Taylor: "She has, until now, had 0 [zero] interest in adhering to the Constitution."

Taylor, about a proposed reform: "These people are all here because of Lucille [Lucille Taylor, his wife, and then-Governor Engler's chief legal counsel]. They are very nervous about this."

And he had left this for the cleaning staff to take care of! What was he thinking?

A Little Trip to the Woodshed

Firmly entrenched in their newfound power, the Engler Four found the going a lot easier. There was even time for settling personal scores.

After they had taken over the court, Maura and Rippy[501] asked me to talk to Cliff. And I said, "Okay, I'll go talk to Cliff."

When I went in to his office he stood up, went to his desk, opened his desk drawer and pulled out a piece of paper before we sat down at the table in his office. And the piece of paper turned out to be a list, and he was holding it in front of him. And he proceeded with it, and it turned out to be a list of grievances.

The first one was that I had never supported him; that I didn't want him to be on the court. And that wasn't true. I said, "Well, Cliff, of course I had supported you...." He interrupted and maintained I

501 "Rippy" refers to the initials of Robert Preston Young, Jr.—RPY.

didn't. At that moment, I thought about saying, "Cliff, look, about that night when you first thought you were going to be appointed to the Supreme Court—Lucille called me the next morning and told me exactly what went on." And he could deny it, but how would I know what went on that night unless she told me? …Because she and I had been friends, you know? But I didn't say anything; I didn't want to potentially cause any trouble for the Taylor marriage. I just let him carry on because I realized this wasn't going to be a friendly discussion.

Well, then he started to go down the list. He was going to tell me all the things that he was mad at me about, and I gathered he was not going to be forgiving.

He conceded that I was smart but lazy. And that he really had considered me a sister; and he was so mad and was so disappointed because he had been so wrong about me. I mean, this went on, and finally, when he was finished, it was just like somebody was going to get it all out, and he had a list of it so he didn't miss anything. I don't remember all of them, but I've given you a few highlights that I do remember. And I made a dictation of it afterward.

So I was sitting there, you know how you're just going to listen? And I occasionally would say, "Well, you know, it really isn't…."—but he didn't want to hear anything. This was decided. So, finally, when it was over—because one venting displeasure just kind of gets exhausted, you know? And he did. So then I thought—I had been thinking: "What do I say about this?" So I finally said to him, "Well, Cliff, I am grateful that we've had this talk because I really now understand how you feel about me."

And that was the thing to say because it was the truth. I now understood what he had deceived himself into thinking now. And remember, this was after they were re-elected, after all of that stuff. …And all the times I could have exposed him to public criticism. I tried to tell him a couple times of how I'd helped him, but he would have none of it.

And we were no longer friends. I had been one, and he pushed me away. And that's the way it's been since. It's a disappointment.

On to the Future!

The Engler Court with the Engler Majority (sometimes called the Engler Four, the Gang of Four, or the Englerites) was in session. Each of the justices had been elected. Together they had, in turn, elected a new chief justice who was one of their own. And they had brought in staff that would extend the Governor's reach into the court. That same staff would usher in a new age at the court.

Gromek, Gadola, and McBrien were brought in to make the court look good. I wanted them gone.

In the end, she would leave before they would.

But that would be nine long years. And the court now had something it lacked before: top-level staff that would do the bidding of the majority justices.

And what I sensed about Gromek…he turned out to be much worse than I could have imagined.

Chapter 11

Reputations and Careers: Destroy Them!

Res ipsa loquitur

Res ipsa loquitur is one of the many Latin terms employed in the course of justice. As such, it is part of a linguistic heritage that stretches back to the *Magna Carta* and the beginnings of our common law. The term means, "The thing speaks for itself," and is commonly employed in negligence lawsuits. What is going to unfold here was not the result of negligence; it was fully intentional. And it DOES speak for itself.

There were within the court, employees who had targets on their backs. Some would be pushed out perhaps because of their independence, some because they knew too much, and others because they were too closely affiliated with Justice Weaver or were just in the way.

In the first year of Corrigan's reign as chief justice, one source put the total numbers of staffers who were shown the door at ten. In the case of part-time public information officer (but full-time employee) Dave Gruber,[502] it was because of what he wouldn't do: work as a PR-flak and spin the agendas of the justices. While he's been mentioned first in this account, he wasn't the first to go; there were others before him.

Two of them were Maria Candy[503] and Denise Koning.

Maria Candy

Maria Candy was someone Justice Weaver brought into the court during her time as chief justice. The nature of her entry may have assured her exit.

---

502 David A. Gruber was replaced in 2001 as the public information officer, but—by his own LinkedIn page—says he left the court in 2002 (perhaps as a result of those "negotiations" [read also severance pay]). He is now director at Dispute Resolution Education Resources in Lansing. [http://www.linkedin.com/pub/david-gruber/8/557/b75.]

503 She has since married and is now Maria Candy Weaver. She is no relation to Justice Elizabeth Weaver. To keep matters straight we'll refer to her as Maria Candy.

The two came to know each other when Weaver served as chair of the Governor's Task Force on Child Abuse and Neglect and Candy was a liaison from the Family Independence Agency [now the Department of Human Services] to that task force. The group was first convened as the Governor's Task Force on Children's Justice in 1991 by then-Governor Engler.[504] He picked Elizabeth Weaver to head the task force when she was still an appeals court judge. She also was appointed chair by Governor Granholm to a term that was to end in June 2014.[505]

> The charge of the Governor's Task Force on Child Abuse and Neglect is to review and evaluate Michigan's investigative, administrative and both civil and criminal judicial handling of cases of child abuse and neglect, particularly child sexual abuse and exploitation, as well as cases involving suspected child maltreatment related fatalities and cases involving a potential combination of jurisdictions, such as interstate, federal-state, and state-tribal.[506]

The group was composed of judges and attorneys, physical and mental health professionals, child advocates, law enforcement professionals, child protective service agency representatives, and parents. There were 34 members of the task force.

Maria was a very capable person with the Family Independence Agency. I had been the chair of the Task Force on Child Abuse and Neglect, and she had attended our meetings and was doing that kind of work as a legislative specialist for the Family Independence Agency so that the FIA would have as good a relationship as they could.

Her assignment to work with the Governor's Task Force was one of the highlights of Candy's career.

> It is the most productive group that I saw operating the entire time I was in state government, 25 years. It brought together judges, prosecutors, academics, county officials, state employees, and advocates to deal with issues around protective services for children. The names that were part of that task force are the names in the state that have done the most for children over the last 25 years. I was assigned to do legislation for them. As the task force met and if they decided that the law needed to be changed, I would help them get that done. So we worked very well together—it was effective and productive. We did get the law changed when we needed to.[507]

As an illustration of the kinds of things the group would accomplish, Candy and Weaver cite establishing protocols to interview victims of abuse. In prior days, a sexually abused child might have to repeat her or his story again and again…for the

---

504 About the Task Force, Governor's Task Force on Child Abuse and Neglect, http://www.michigan.gov/gtfcan/0,4588,7-195--155595--,00.html.
505 She served as the chair of the group for 22 years until February 12, 2013, when Governor Snyder ended her service.
506 "Governor's Task Force on Child Abuse and Neglect," http://www.michigan.gov/snyder/0,1607,7-277-57738_57679_57726-250286--,00.html.
507 Maria Candy Weaver, video interview with co-author Schock, 16 April 2012, Holt, Mich.

teacher, the school social worker, then for the police, then for other investigators and the prosecutors...each retelling and in effect re-traumatizing the child. With a new protocol in place, the child had to address the matter only once and that with a trained forensic interviewer. The telling would be video recorded so that if the testimony needed to be consulted, it could be viewed in its totality.

And there were other significant outcomes. Weaver and Candy connected over the need to help children. But they also shared a love of order and rightness in the process of law.

> Apparently the legislative person at the court was leaving, and I had, at that point, a really effective, good working relationship with Justice Weaver dealing with legislation. And so she came and said, "Why don't you come to the court?"[508]

We had perceived that there was a need to have somebody who understood how the legislature worked and would be able to keep us informed as to what was going on, where the court was concerned, and also, then truly and honestly to represent any positions the court had, if he or she were asked to do so. And there was other work involved.

> She wanted me to come to the court, basically, to do the same thing that I had done effectively at FIA. She stressed that she didn't want a lobbyist in the traditional sense or for the court to take positions on what the legislature was doing; she emphasized the separation of powers. The court's role with the legislature was to keep them informed about how what they were doing would affect the courts. So it was a perfect fit. What I was doing at FIA was exactly what she needed at the court, and she knew that I was effective at getting the things done that she needed. So she asked me if I was interested; I said yes.[509]

That was in October, November, or December of 2000, as Weaver was finishing her first (and only) two-year term as chief justice.

Maria was intelligent—not a lawyer—but very able. And she was very competent and very knowledgeable. She might not have been a lawyer, but she had been dealing with all kinds of legislative things for a long time.

> I had said to her "I'm not a lawyer." And she said, "Maria, <u>believe</u> me, we have plenty of those. We just want somebody to track things, to make sure everything is done."[510]

Anyway, I, and also Margaret Chiara, then policy and planning director, agreed that we would bring Maria over to be a proper liaison between the court and the legislature.

---

508 Ibid.
509 Ibid.
510 Ibid.

In one sense, Candy was taking a big risk. In moving from her legislative job, she was giving up her state civil service career.

> I had a very good position, a 15-level position, with the state civil service system, with all of the benefits and protections that go with that. Going to the court meant, while I could transfer all my service, I would not be in civil service anymore. And that was a huge decision for me, because I had seniority, I had a lot of protection, I had a successful job—people were happy with me. That's what I talked with Justice Weaver about.
>
> Justice Weaver said that she understood completely. And while the court was not civil service, that if something happened, I would not get fired. If they didn't want me to have this job, I would get moved to a different job in the court. And she told me, and other people told me, that the court at that point had never fired anybody—people were moved to a different job. The practice was that they only hired quality people and treated them as such.[511]

There was the opening, and then we had the FTE—the full-time employee spot, and it wasn't something that needed to be run past the justices. And at that point, Taylor, Markman, and Young were deeply involved in their own re-elections. She was hired and came over in the fall of 2000.

> ...And so I went to the court.[512]

Then, of course, the three Englerites got elected, and then, of course, they made it plain that they wanted me to do certain things, or I wouldn't be the chief justice.

> Right around the time I was coming to the court, apparently the whole dialogue with the Governor's office was going on. And Justice Weaver was very honest with me. She wanted me to understand what was going on because it could impact me, and she said that the Governor wasn't happy with her for some reason. He wanted her to do some things that she didn't want to do, and she felt it was inappropriate for the Governor to give direction to the Supreme Court.
>
> I could see that it was just agony for her. It was clear to me that she genuinely trusted and liked all of the people who were putting pressure on her; that she had a positive history with these people; and that she could not believe what was going on. I think she really, up until the end, did not think that they would follow through; she felt the separation of powers issue was really, really important, and that ultimately they would see that. I didn't say anything to Justice Weaver, but I knew—I knew that if they said, "You do this or you're gone," I knew she would be gone. ...Because I had been in politics long enough to know that if they said that, they meant it.

---

511 Ibid.
512 Ibid.

I also recognized that she didn't see it from a political perspective at all, that it was an issue of right and wrong and doing what she thought was wrong was not an option.

I knew this had turned entirely political if the discussions were even taking place.

She didn't believe that [Governor Engler] would actually do what he was threatening to do. But she was completely open with me and said, "If they do what they're threatening to do to me, it will affect you. You will get moved to a different position. You won't stay in this position, doing legislation; the Governor wants to bring his own person in."[513]

Candy was correct in her assessment: the Governor and his Four did what they threatened. And with Corrigan at the helm, the direction would change. First of all, the new chief justice wanted to meet her staff. It was an unsettling face-to-face for Candy.

I had a meeting with Maura Corrigan after she became chief justice. I was trying to be as professional as possible, but the entire time I felt like I was talking with someone who just wanted me gone. She could barely look at me.

I could tell that she just wanted me out of her sight. I could feel it, and a subsequent incident proved it. At the time, we both knew that I knew exactly what had happened. It was the elephant in the room.[514]

So, because Maria was brought in by me, she didn't fit their criteria because she was not going to be a political hack; she would be somebody, a loyal-to-the-institution person, who would be representing the Supreme Court and would not be taking positions that weren't necessarily true, or that were adverse to the institution, or doing anything but being a real liaison and communication person, and would not be acting outside the policies of the court.

Candy's replacement was already ready.

As it turned out, they had in mind letting Mike Gadola do that. He had been the chief deputy assistant to Lucille Taylor in the Governor's legal counsel office. Then they had sent him over to the House of Representatives in the legislature, and there he was legal counsel to the House, and now he was the liaison for the court. I was not pleased with his work to say the least.

I had not worked with Mike Gadola directly; I had worked with people who were on his staff for legislation, and they were excellent to work with. I didn't have any negative feeling about Mike; I didn't know him. But he was the person that the Governor wanted to come over to replace me...well, he was not going to replace me. He would have a different job, a much higher

---

513 Ibid.
514 Ibid.

level and power position. They were going to eliminate the legislative liaison position.

And I had worked in politics long enough....[515]

So that she understood she might be moved within the organization.

> Being the eternal optimist. I thought, okay, Mike Gadola—I had worked successfully with people who were on Mike's staff. I had worked successfully with everybody I had worked with in the Engler administration. I thought the people that he brought in were very good, I still do. And so I thought, okay, I'll just do a good job. If I have to do a good job for him instead of Justice Weaver or for Maura Corrigan, I will do that.

> So he came over. I do not remember how long he was there. I got along fine with him, I thought. Myself, and a colleague were working for him.

That was Denise Koning, who was brought in with Margaret Chiara two years earlier by Chief Justice Mallett with my approval.

And they were informed—I think it was within a month after Maura was made chief justice—that they would be gone and terminated. Either one of them can talk about the abruptness of that.

Yes...the "How" of it all. Maria Candy has the event indelibly etched in her memory:

> Denise Koning and I, after lunch one afternoon, out of the blue, were called in to an office. I don't remember whose office it was. Mike Gadola was in there, and Mike Benedict. He was the head of Human Services. And Mike Gadola just told me that we were going to be fired. And I was—we were both stunned. My colleague who was with me, she had two small children, she just burst into tears. She was very upset. I was upset too, but I just said, "Okay," and didn't say too much. After my years in politics, I'm not going to give anything away; I'm not going to let them know how I feel. I stayed very calm. Inside, I was destroyed.

> Mike Gadola, outwardly, was nervous. It appeared he did not want to do this. He said, "This is very difficult. I've never done this before." He thanked me for staying so calm and for handling it the way I did.

> I'm sitting there, and I'm stunned. I had given up a wonderful job to come to the court with the assurances that I would be fine, that I would be protected. As my mind moved from the initial stunned state, I was determined that what they were doing was not going to be the end for me. I knew right then, if they were going to do this, I would sue them; there was no question in my mind that I would fight.

515 Ibid.

But I didn't say anything. I felt like I had a stronger position than "You're fired. You're out the door." From a political perspective, from every perspective, I didn't believe at that point that I was helpless, but I believed I was going to have a huge fight. And I was upset. I can't remember exactly, but I think that right then they gave me a document that they wanted me to sign that basically said "You're fired and if you sign this document, we will give some severance pay."

Mike Gadola said to me, "This is not about your work. This has nothing to do with anything that you've done." They were clear that I hadn't done anything wrong.[516]

Then why fire her?

Politics—and this had turned into a political situation. You're either with me, or you're against me. I think because I was perceived as the person that Justice Weaver brought in, that I wasn't trustworthy. And I think I was just collateral. I knew politics well enough to know that I didn't matter as a person, only for how my role played out in the bigger picture.

And, in my opinion—and this is an opinion—I think it was to punish Justice Weaver. She did not behave; she didn't do as she was told. So when you don't behave, you get punished. And what are you going to do to a Supreme Court Justice? There was nothing that they could do, really, other than take away the chief justice position—she could deal with that. But they could hurt her by taking people that she had had a professional relationship with—people who might have loyalty to her—and hurt them. You know, that's the only thing that ever made sense to me. Because any of the other reasons just don't add up. What they did to us was completely unnecessary.[517]

So, the document Gadola and Benedict wanted her to sign...?

There was no way I was going to sign the document they gave me. They told us to go to our offices and get our things—this is having done nothing to deserve to be fired—and made us leave the building right then; had a guard escort us out. What was so nice during this nightmare was that all the people at the court had never seen anything like it and were so kind. They had worked with us, they knew us, and I felt they knew we didn't deserve this. Even as we're leaving, the guard is just, he's appalled. He didn't say anything inappropriate and did his job professionally, but you could tell that he's just appalled. He was very kind.

When we got fired, it was actually traumatic for everybody. There were people that just couldn't believe the way we were being treated. And there was

---

516 Ibid.
517 Ibid.

a woman there who clearly, to me, in the brief time that I had been there, was very, very respected. She was retiring in a very short period.

I was told she was so appalled at how we were treated that she went down to Maura Corrigan's office and expressed shame at the way we were treated. It was just so cruel what they had done to us she went and confronted Maura Corrigan.

So I left, and I begin looking at this document—and while I did stay very calm during the whole process, after I left, I was shaken. I had gone from having my pension, a very good, secure job—and I had nothing. I had lost everything. And while one part of my brain is saying, "I'm not going to let them get away with this," the other part of my brain was hysterical. Both things were going on at the same time.

I talked to Justice Weaver afterwards, and she was stunned. To the part of me that was hysterical, she said, "Maria, it will be okay. It will be okay." I believed her. That calmed me down.

And she told me that they had told her I was going back to my old job. I think that was the intent all along if either Justice Weaver or I created a problem. I think they fired me to get me to sign the document and to get to Justice Weaver.[518]

I felt very bad because I would never have asked her to come if I had thought that she would be vulnerable to being removed.

My next action was to redraft the entire document they had given to me. I changed it to state that they would give me my old job back with everything restored—seniority, pension, basically making me whole. I told them that I was willing to sign this document.

Because this agreement was with the court, they kept saying, "We can't give you your old job back." The court could not. But I knew and they knew that the Engler administration could, and that's really what we were dealing with; the Governor could make it happen. We just kept going back and forth until we both were happy. I wasn't real happy, ever, about it, but I certainly was relieved to get my job back, to get my pension back, and to get my seniority back. I do not know how the civil service process accommodated my return, but it did.

The ease with which I got my old job back is why I think that they always intended that as an option. Why they went through the firing, what they put us through, why they did that...?[519]

---

518 Ibid.
519 Ibid.

So she didn't just say, "Okay." She wanted to be able to go back to the FIA, back to her position. And that got arranged. And the way she was treated and how it got arranged, I think Governor Engler was involved in that. Not through my knowledge, because I was not involved in her going back.

The announcement to the justices of Candy and Koning leaving came from a memo by Carl Gromek:

> Mike Gadola, the new Supreme Court counsel, has restructured the staffing of his office. Solely due to the reorganization, and not because of any performance issues, two positions were eliminated. As a result, Maria Candy and Denise Koning left the court February 20. This was admittedly a difficult outcome, but an effort was made to soften the impact through the provision of a severance package and assistance in finding other employment.[520]

And then she also ended up back in the FIA or—and whether that could be accomplished or not remained to be seen—but it was accomplished.

It was accomplished because she wasn't going to take it without a fight.

As a part of her separation agreement, she was to receive eight weeks' pay in a lump sum, health care for the same eight weeks, and a promise for help in being reassigned to the FIA:

> Although the court can make no contractual agreements for or on behalf of the Family Independence Agency, it will work with you in your effort to transfer back to that agency.[521]

The cover letter from Mike Benedict, the human resources director, was more direct about her return to the FIA: "I also understand from the Family Independence Agency that you will be officially on their system in the next day or so. I hope everything goes well for you with them."[522]

Also as a part of her separation agreement was a letter of recommendation from Benedict:

> Dear _____:
>
> Ms. Maria Candy has applied for the position of _____. Ms. Candy worked for the Michigan Supreme Court, office of the chief justice, as a legislative liaison, having come to the court after a long and successful career in state government.

---

520 Carl L. Gromek, "Memorandum," 23 February 2001, unpublished.
521 "Separation Agreement and Release," Michigan Supreme Court, signed by Maria Candy 12 March 2001, and by Carl L. Gromek a day later, unpublished.
522 Michael Benedict, letter to Maria Candy, 13 March 2001, unpublished.

Ms. Candy has done very good work for the Michigan Supreme Court. Unfortunately and through no fault of her own, her employment was terminated for reasons of administrative restructuring and not for reasons of unsatisfactory job performance.

I would urge you to consider Ms. Candy for the position of _____. She not only has appropriate technical skills, but has the appropriate personality to work with people to accomplish the goals of your organization. Please give her every consideration and, if you would like to discuss this with me, please feel free to call at your convenience. My number is ***-****.

Sincerely,[523]

Candy refused to sign the agreement until she was back on the job at FIA, far more secure in her civil service position than ever she was at the court.

And there was at least one more significant prohibition in the agreement: she was supposed to keep silent about all of it.

From the beginning, I felt that I was being asked to sign something under duress. They had placed me in a position in which I had to give up my free speech and ability to tell the truth in order to survive. It made no sense, but especially so coming from the Supreme Court, who were supposed to protect the rights they were taking away from me.

I cannot imagine that they would have ever gone to court to stop me from speaking; that would have disclosed everything. I think they thought I would be so intimidated by the Supreme Court that I would not say anything. That I wouldn't figure out that what they did to me was unethical and unfair and that using their power to silence me was completely inappropriate. This was supposed to be a public institution representing the highest standards and the non-disclosure language made it clear to me that it was individuals using the lofty reputation of the institution to protect themselves. I always felt it hurt them more than helped them.

It reminded me of when I was a child; my brother Stephen constantly got into trouble, and I constantly helped him, being the good sister that I was (and am). Even after many warnings from my mother that he should not pee outside, he continued the practice. Unfortunately for him, I saw him one time and I immediately went to tell my mother. He knew I was going to tell, and he panicked. He kept saying, "Please don't tell. Please don't tell." And, of course, I was on a mission. As I went inside, he jumped in front of me and without thinking yelled, "Mum, Mum, please stop her. She's gonna tell on me!" It just wasn't an effective strategy for hiding a wrong.

523 Michael Benedict, letter of reference, undated but 13 March 2001 or before, unpublished.

I felt like the Supreme Court did exactly the same thing with that document—without the "please." They were doing something they didn't want anyone to know about, and they didn't want me to tell on them. The big difference was my brother didn't pee on me, we were children, and he didn't represent a public institution that should be entirely transparent.[524]

In the end, Candy had one more meeting with Corrigan. It might fall under the classification of bizarre.

After I went back to FIA, I went to a political fundraiser—there were many of those every week in Lansing—and this was a couple of months after I left the court. I was standing by a table, and Maura Corrigan came in. She saw me, and she walked right up to me. I'm at a fundraiser now, so I'm politically acceptable, and she walked up to me and said, "I think I know you." I just smiled and said, "You do. I used to be at the court." I could see recognition come over her face. She didn't say another word, and just walked away. She had attempted to destroy my life, and she didn't even remember who I was just a couple of months later. I knew I didn't exist as a person in this process, but it was still kind of unnerving to really know how little I mattered.[525]

But her life wasn't destroyed.

I was not destroyed because Justice Weaver protected me; and my colleagues from my previous job stood by me, I know that. ...And because I fought for myself. Had I just accepted the firing would I have stayed fired? Absolutely. Even though they gave assurances to Justice Weaver that they were sending me back, if I would have just caved, would I have mattered to them enough to do anything for me?—no. No.[526]

Maria's a very upbeat, happy person. She's just a very fine individual. It was unnecessary to get rid of her because she was highly competent, and she was going to be doing a lot of good work. It was going to be more than a very full-time job. And it wasn't just with the legislature. The state was lucky to have somebody that was as hardworking—there are a lot of good people like her in the system.

In the end, she worked as a civil servant until her retirement in 2011 and looking back on it now, Candy says she learned many lessons but one stands out.

I love histories; I read a lot of histories. And I like biographies. But, after my experience at the court, where I personally experienced what happened and then saw and heard what publicly came out, the discrepancy between the reality and what was being said amazed me. I realized that all of these histories that I'm reading, they are just one person's version of it, or the "winner's version" of it, as they say. Whenever I hear, "This is what happened," I

---

524 Maria Candy Weaver.
525 Ibid.
526 Ibid.

question it. I want to hear it from a few different people, and a few different perspectives, and then make my own decision.

That's a good thing.[527]

Denise Koning

Denise Koning was a legislative analyst for the chief justice of the Michigan Supreme Court. She had come to the court in 1999 from working with the Trial Court Assessment Commission with Margaret Chiara (who had hired her there) and was brought to the court by then-Chief Justice Conrad Mallett.

She shared the same firing as that of Maria Candy. But she had no other job to go back to. There was no Plan B for her:

> I had no option; I had always worked. This firing was the most shocking thing in my life to that point. I was a single parent with two children; they were five and eight. I really needed that job, and I never would have taken it if I didn't think it wasn't a good career move.
>
> They basically said the same thing to me that they did to Maria; although, she was at a different level than I was; she was both personally and professionally more aware. They told me it had nothing to do with my job performance; it was political. I wasn't a part of the plan for the court and the new direction it was going.
>
> I had always thought my job was <u>not</u> political. My responsibility was to the whole court and the system. I felt betrayed by what happened, but they made it very clear they did not need me.[528]

It took her five months to find her next job, working first as a county administrator in Wexford County and then Otsego County. Her experience at the Supreme Court helped in her new work: "The work I did with the trial court commission prepared me to work with county government. I had a very good introduction to how the courts worked."[529]

She worked for a time as human resources manager with the Nottawaseppi Huron Band of the Potawatomi. She is now the senior manager of human resources with Planned Parenthood, working with 18 sites in mid- and southern Michigan. She says she very much likes her present job. She also has remarried; her name is now Denise Sheneman.

---

527 Ibid.
528 Denise Konig Sheneman, telephone interview with co-author Schock, 4 June 2012.
529 Ibid.

She's stronger now.

> You learn to pick yourself back up and you learn to do what you need to do. I believe it all happens for a reason. I learned a tough lesson but I'm glad I learned.[530]

Survival at the court depended on falling into one of two camps:

> ...If you were a "yes" person and blindly dedicated, or so far down the line it didn't matter. Otherwise you were gone. Now, I was just a peon...I wasn't that important; I just worked for people who were. My loyalty to Margaret Chiara and Justice Weaver was the reason they felt uncomfortable with my being there.[531]

Justice Young Takes Action

Maura Corrigan was not the only one shaking out personnel. Michael Benedict, who had been the director of Human Resources at the Supreme Court, remembered another occasion, his first firing under the new regime.

> Soon after Chief Justice Corrigan was made chief justice, Justice Young and Carl [Gromek] came to see me. It seems Justice Young had a secretary he wanted to dismiss. This person was a long-time employee of the court who had worked for another justice who had recently left the court. She came to work for Justice Young in order that she could continue with the court. Justice Young told me he wanted to restructure his office, delete a secretary and add another law clerk, and asked that I prepare a severance agreement for his consideration.

> As I thought about it after our meeting, and realizing this person was an older, African American female, I wrote Justice Young a memo and outlined the court's statistics regarding demographics. Suffice it to say, the court was about 95 percent white at the time, and I was concerned that a jury looking at these statistics would conclude that the court was discriminatory in its approach to older, African American females, even though Justice Young was African American. When he got my memo, he went ballistic, came down to my office and asked me if I had ever been sued. Actually, because I had always been very careful while in my other jobs, and because, if necessary, I relied on an attorney for advice to make sure we were on solid legal grounds, I never had been sued. He then advised me he would have to respond back in writing, and that I should never put anything in writing in the future, unless it went through an attorney representing the court at which time it would be considered client-lawyer privileged information not subject to public

530 Ibid.
531 Ibid.

scrutiny. To an extent, I appreciated Justice Young's concerns. However, we did not have a labor attorney to advise on such matters at the time, and, frankly, employment statistics are public information and can be requested by a citizen (which includes someone suing the court for discrimination) at any time, regardless of whether they are funneled through an attorney who had the court as a client.

As I am sure you know, [employment at] the court is at will. But even as an at-will organization, no employer has a right to trample on the protected rights of employees based on race, sex, religion, etc. That is why it is important to show that the court acted fairly and with due diligence, which I was concerned had not been adequately done. Being new to the court (having been there about two months at this time), I did as I was asked, however, and we went forward with the termination. I will never forget, arriving at Justice Young's office, how happy the other secretary was. She and Justice Young had talked in the past, and she supported Justice Young's decision to fire the other secretary. Justice Young and I met with the [outgoing] secretary, gave her the severance agreement, and then, with the help of the security director who I had to bring with me from Lansing, got her things together and immediately took her out of the building. Because she was parked in a ramp some distance away, we drove her to her car and helped her get her things into the back of the car. I really felt bad because, as my first termination with the court, I thought this person was getting the shaft and was being treated poorly, particularly when considering how long she worked for the court. Fortunately, I learned soon after she did catch on with another state job and things worked out okay for her. But I can't imagine how difficult it was for her during the interim time when she lost her job at the court and had not yet started a new one. Oh, and by the way, a few years later the other secretary was terminated by Justice Young.[532]

Margaret Chiara

Margaret Mary Chiara came to the Supreme Court in 1999 as the policy and planning director. As such, she reported to and served at the pleasure of the chief justice, then Elizabeth Weaver. Weaver had known her for more than a decade.

In the '86 campaign, when I ran for Court of Appeals, a person I knew down in Berrien County, which is close to Cass, introduced me—I think it was Gloria Gillespie, who was a county commissioner down there. And I came to know Margaret Chiara.

Margaret Chiara had first trained as a teacher. She earned a bachelor's in education from Fordham University, her master's in education administration (with honors) from Pace University. She worked both as a teacher and an educational administrator before she went to earn her *juris doctor* from Rutgers.[533]

She was born and raised, I guess, in New York City—maybe Brooklyn—and maintains a New York accent. She is very well educated and was an able administrator.

Chiara began her career in Michigan as an assistant prosecutor in southwest Michigan's Cass County in 1982. She arrived in the office two years after Susan Dobrich[534] began her work there. In 1984, Dobrich was elected as the first woman prosecuting attorney in that county. Chiara then moved up to serve as her chief assistant in 1985. When Dobrich left the office for private practice in 1987, Chiara was first appointed as the county's prosecuting attorney and then elected in 1988 for the first of two four-year terms.

Margaret was not active politically at all. I guess when she ran, because as a prosecutor you have to run, she ran as a Republican. But she was not an active political party type, a party hack or anything like that, but she was highly qualified.

She was one of the few women ever elected as a prosecutor because most of the prosecutors in the 83 counties are men. And Margaret, while she was the prosecutor of Cass County, was elected the president of the prosecutors' association—the only woman ever to be elected at that time, and I think still.

She was elected as the president of the Prosecuting Attorneys Association of Michigan (PAAM) for 1993-1994.[535]

She was competent, a straight-arrow, and fair.

She also had served as her county's bar president in 1988-1989, was a member of the State Board of Community Corrections from 1992-1996, and served as a member of the Michigan Committee on Juvenile Justice from 1999-2001.[536]

Before her service with the court, she served in 1997 and 1998 as the administrator for the Trial Court Assessment Commission, a 23-member commission created by the Michigan legislature.

By the time the Trial Court Assessment Commission came into being, I was on the Supreme Court, and Engler appointed me in '96 to do that. And that ran until January 1, '99, as it turned out.

533 Margaret M. Chiara, resume, 2 February 2007, 248, http://judiciary.house.gov/hearings/pdf/EOU-SA209-253.pdf.
534 "MAC 2012 Legislative Conference Speaker Bios," 15, https://www.micounties.org/PDFs/events/SpeakerBios.pdf.
535 Margaret M. Chiara, resume.
536 Ibid.

The commission needed an administrator. Chiara applied.

So I knew Margaret well when she applied. She was one of the many applicants to be the executive director of the Trial Court Assessment Commission, which was an important commission created by the legislature to try and research and assess the needs of and for the trial courts and report on them.

In any case, when Margaret applied—and I think there were a hundred or so for this position—it occurred to me that she would be very good, from knowing her work.

Interestingly enough, the Governor's office was interested in this, because it wouldn't have gotten through the legislature and done if the Governor wasn't. And Lucille Taylor, the Governor's legal counsel, also, independently of me, spoke of how good she would be.

She made the cutoffs and eventually it was left to me to make the decision because the executive director would be working so closely with me; that was all quite legitimate. There were several good candidates, but in the end it seemed that Margaret would be the best. So she got it, and she did a marvelous job. She hired one assistant; that would be Denise Koning.

Both Margaret and Denise were brought over to the Supreme Court by Justice Mallett as the Trial Court Assessment Commission was ending. They were to come and work at our court in policy and planning. (Justice Mallett did run that by me, but that was before he announced that he was resigning.)

Chiara's initial assignment was to further judicial reforms recommended by the Trial Court Assessment Commission. She also helped with the planning of the new Hall of Justice, and she served as personnel director until Weaver hired Mike Benedict. It was during that time that Gerri Kozachik sent her letter of resignation, so Chiara knew all about the matter.

And so that letter, of course, became crucial with respect to Justice Markman and all that proceeded. It was going to bring problems for Margaret because when the Englerites did take over, Margaret, as I understand it, was informed that she was too loyal to me and that she would be moved.

Margaret was not <u>too</u> loyal to anything or anybody. She was loyal to the institution, to the court, to justice, to fairness, and—to the degree that I expressed that—she would be loyal to me. But Margaret was a prosecutor and a person of the highest integrity.[537]

Denise Koning supports Weaver's assessment of Chiara:

> ...Principled, bright, funny. A straight shooter. As honest as you can imagine. I learned so much from her. She and Justice Weaver were role models for me. I owe a lot to both of them.

---

[537] The alternate view was that the new chief justice selected her own staff and Chiara was merely being reassigned.

Not only do I consider Margaret as my mentor, but I made her the godmother of my children. That's how highly I think of Margaret.[538]

In addition to Denise Koning, Maria Candy also reported directly to Chiara. Candy described what it was like to work with her.

On a daily basis Margaret Chiara was my boss. ...The best boss I've ever had. You talk about competent? She required that you do your job, but she was so supportive. She required the work and supported you doing it. It was an ideal situation. And if you had a problem you could talk to her. In the brief time that I worked with her, I thought that she was the best.

Margaret Chiara always struck me as the same...that same ilk that I had come from: she wasn't political. You have a job to do, you get your direction about what you're supposed to do, and you get it done. There was nothing in my experience political about Margaret. Nothing.[539]

When Justice Corrigan became the chief justice, they didn't know what to do with Margaret, exactly, but she was told that she would not continue as policy and planning. And they were trying to figure out what to do with her. Her office was moved over to the State Court Administrator's Office, which at that time was in a different building several blocks away from the court.

According to Mike Benedict, Chiara knew her time at the court wouldn't be long: "Margaret and I were talking. She calmly yet clearly laid out some of the political issues in the court and indicated she and others would soon be gone."[540]
They just couldn't push her out the door immediately, because the prosecutors' association would really question it. She was highly regarded by them.

So eventually, she was given the task of implementing the federal Child Support Enforcement System. The state was in jeopardy of losing $40 million in federal money because the Family Independence Agency of the Engler administration had failed to achieve compliance of all counties to implement the computer system requirements for receiving the federal money.

That failure for compliance was a problem that had been growing but kept out of sight and hidden from Weaver through most of her tenure as chief justice, until October of 2000. And it was another little mess that Weaver learned more about with the help of Maria Candy.

The problem was of long standing and initially had been assigned to the judiciary—the Supreme Court—in the early '90s. Next it was transferred in 1995 or 1996 by the legislature to the executive branch and to the Family Independence Agency, and was going to be transferred back to the Supreme Court—with all the attendant blame for the delay.

---

538 Denise Koning Sheneman.
539 Maria Candy Weaver.
540 Michael Benedict, e-mail to co-author Schock, 6 June 2012.

If they had talked to me about it as chief justice, and if the state had been willing to pay for it, I would have implemented it. But that wasn't the issue, now. They needed somebody who would be more amenable to doing what they were told, like Maura Corrigan, because they knew that I would not just say "The courts are all to blame," you see. And they wanted to pull something.

Worse, the mandated system was inferior technology. Many of the counties had far superior systems in place and they balked. But $40 million was a lot of money. And the federal government was going to withhold the dough unless the courts in the various counties got on board with the federally mandated computer system.

Maura then decided to give Margaret this difficult thankless job of getting the refusing counties to convert to the inferior federally mandated computer system. If anybody could do it and still be respected, it would be Margaret. So, Margaret was given the task of having those big counties that wouldn't do it—Oakland, Kent, Grand Traverse, and a few others, that had better systems and weren't going to pay to get a worse system. But now she was empowered; I believe that it was going to be paid for by the state as opposed to early efforts requiring the counties to foot the costs, in which case, it was still not an easy job to get people to go to a worse system even if the state is going to pay for it. But she did accomplish that.

It was clear that when she had done that, there would be no place for her at the court; ultimately, she was going to lose her job. And so she was looking; she needed a job, as most people do. The Western District U.S. Attorney came open by Bush's election. And so by September of that year, Margaret did talk, as I recall, to Lucille Taylor (who, remember, had a great deal of admiration for Margaret). So Governor Engler and Lucille got behind Margaret to be appointed.

The reason stated publicly on several occasions was that the western district of Michigan needed a proven administrator to deal with numerous internal problems and the federal court and law enforcement's dissatisfaction with the district's performance. This was the rationale articulated when Governor Engler recommended her to the state selection committee and congressional nominating committee.

I do remember that she got recommendations, obviously from Governor Engler and Lucille. I remember her telling me that Justice Taylor did not—would not—recommend her, and I doubt that she asked Justice Markman. She did ask me, and—for whatever mine was worth—I recommended her, of course. She did get appointed, and she asked me to speak at her investiture. I did so with a sense of gratitude for her service and in recognition of her worthiness for the job.

Chiara was on the job as a U.S. Attorney in October of 2001, nominated by President George W. Bush.[541]

My understanding is that unknowingly she went into a real mess—that there were administrative and personnel problems there.

---

541 U.S. Department of Justice, *An Investigation into the Removal of Nine U.S. Attorneys in 2006*, Arc Manor, 237, http://books.google.com/books?id=PhHgyKwzrSUC&pg=PA237&lpg=PA237&dq=Chiara+appointed+federal+prosecutor+2001&source=bl&ots=szc9rlB8B-&sig=FHpPu2D2gj-cZrwRypAxLUgHZj0&hl=en&sa=X&ei=wAWPT6mSB_Cw0QH_vMiXDw&sqi=2&ved=0CGkQ6AEwBg#v=onepage&q=Chiara%20appointed%20federal%20prosecutor%202001&f=false.

...A real political mess that would grow into a personal mess.

And she went over there and did, actually, a very good job. But I think it was never forgotten that she had a copy—she was copied on that situation with Justice Markman and Gerri Kozachik.

Further, I later heard there were people working there with political clout who were wanting the U.S. attorney job, too, and I think Margaret went in to it not realizing that she had natural enemies that were in there. And then I think she held that position from 2001 until whenever they had the firing of the federal prosecutors, and she was added to the list of nine.

First there were no reasons given for her firing, as well as that of the others. Then it was necessary to supply some kind of reason. In Chaira's case, the Justice Department said there were reports of bad management, low office morale, and preferential treatment among the staff. Chiara was told in December of 2006 by officials at the Department of Justice to resign. She announced her resignation Feb. 23, 2007.[542]

Chiara was one of nine U.S. Attorneys targeted by high-level staffers in the Justice Department who were doing the work at the behest of the George W. Bush administration to get rid of "undesirables."

A *New York Times* article shortly after her leaving brought up the idea that what might have made her undesirable may have been that the Bush administration wanted someone else in the job. Chiara had kept silent all through her departure until the Justice Department began spinning her departure.

> The federal prosecutor, Margaret M. Chiara, 63, speaking publicly for the first time since leaving office last Friday, said in an interview that a senior Justice Department official had told her that her resignation was necessary to create a slot for "an individual they wanted to advance." The identity of the likely replacement was not disclosed, she said.
>
> Only after Justice Department officials attributed her firing to poor performance as a manager—even though her 2005 evaluation praised her management skills—did she decide to speak out, Ms. Chiara said.
>
> "To say it was about politics may not be pleasant, but at least it is truthful," she said, echoing an e-mail message she sent to a Justice Department official this month. "Poor performance was not a truthful explanation."
>
> Brian Roehrkasse, a Justice Department spokesman, declined to comment directly on Ms. Chiara's remarks, saying only that the reasons for the dismissals of all seven prosecutors fired in December "include policy and priority differences, failure to achieve results in priority areas, office management and a desire to see new energy and leadership in certain offices."[543]

---

542 Ibid.
543 The other two prosecutors would be fired later.

After the firings created a backlash, the Justice Department prepared statements justifying the dismissals. In Ms. Chiara's case, the agency said "the office has become fractured, morale has fallen" during her tenure, adding that "the problems here have required an on-site visit by management experts."

Ms. Chiara said that in 2005, the department sent an official from Washington at her request to mediate a disagreement she was having with another senior lawyer who has since left the office.

Last year, she said, she also asked the department for assistance in identifying who in her office wrote anonymous letters accusing her former deputy, Phillip J. Green, of improprieties. The accusations have stalled his nomination by President Bush to serve as the United States attorney in Southern Illinois.

Ms. Chiara said neither issue was raised when Michael Elston, the deputy attorney general's chief of staff, informed her that she would soon be asked to leave.

Instead, she said, according to a Nov. 5 e-mail message she wrote detailing the conversation, Mr. Elston told her that she had "erroneously assumed that good service guaranteed longevity," and noted that she and other prosecutors were "being asked for their resignations without good cause."

She defended her record on Thursday, saying her office increased felony convictions by 15 percent, nearly doubled the number of firearms cases and brought the first obscenity case under an initiative started by Attorney General Alberto R. Gonzales.

Her office also successfully prosecuted Michigan's first death-penalty case since 1938, even though she is personally opposed to capital punishment. She also complied with an order from the department's headquarters to pursue the death penalty in a drug-related murder case she believed did not merit it. Ms. Chiara said she had never received calls from elected officials or politicians asking about politically delicate matters before her office, as apparently happened with prosecutors in New Mexico and Washington State.

Robert Holmes Bell, the chief federal judge in the Western District of Michigan, praised Ms. Chiara as one of the most competent United States attorneys he had encountered in two decades on the federal bench, and said that the charges of poor management were unjustified.

"I feel a certain loss that someone of her caliber is leaving prematurely," Judge Bell said.

Mr. [sic] Chiara said she had intended to remain silent about her dismissal, but became distressed by the department's comments about her.

"There is irreparable professional damage here, unless it is corrected or retracted," she said.[544]

There was professional damage to her reputation at the time. And there would be more as the spin cycle sped up.

Jealous and vindictive subordinates—in particular Joan and Lloyd Meyer, husband and wife—spread rumors of her shortcomings and transgressions including alleging a lesbian relationship between Chiara and assistant U.S. Attorney Leslie Hagen.[545] This was front-page stuff and it went on and on.

But all that eventually followed showed that Chiara was not the problem.

So after Margaret was removed by the Bush Administration, by Bush, by this Alberto Gonzales, eventually he had to step down himself, if I'm not mistaken.

Oh, yes he did. Upon investigation, those staffers who had recommended the dismissal had been found overzealous in their actions against the nine. They stepped down, and the scandal tied back to U.S. Attorney General Alberto R. Gonzales, who also resigned.

What was really behind it all? Something that also had affected the Michigan Supreme Court: politicization. The *New York Times* reported:

Democrats, along with some Republicans and retired prosecutors, have charged that the Bush administration was attempting to politicize the justice system by infringing on the traditional autonomy accorded to United States attorneys, who are expected to act in a nonpartisan manner once they are confirmed.[546]

Only subsequently in the Department of Justice report, *An Investigation into the Removal of Nine U.S. Attorneys in 2006*,[547] would part of her side of the story come out...that the Meyers had poisonously and effectively conspired against her, and that she and Hagen

544 Eric Lipton, "U.S. Attorney in Michigan disputes reason for removal," *New York Times*, 22 March 2007, http://www.nytimes.com/2007/03/23/washington/23chiara.html?_r=1&ref=washington&pagewanted=print.
545 Ken Kolker, "Report: Margaret Chiara ousted over management not relationship concerns," *Grand Rapids Press*, 29 September 2008, http://www.mlive.com/news/grand-rapids/index.ssf/2008/09/report_margaret_chiara_ousted_1.html.
546 "United States Attorneys," *New York Times*, http://topics.nytimes.com/top/reference/timestopics/subjects/u/united_states_attorneys/index.html?inline=nyt-classifier.
547 U.S. Department of Justice, *An Investigation into the Removal of Nine U.S. Attorneys in 2006*, Arc Manor, 237-250, http://books.google.com/books?id=PhHgyKwzrSUC&pg=PA237&lpg=PA237&dq=Chiara+appointed+federal+prosecutor+2001&source=bl&ots=szc9rlB8B-&sig=FHpPu2D2gj-cZrwRypAxLUgHZj0&hl=en&sa=X&ei=wAWPT6mSB_Cw0QH_vMiXDw&sqi=2&ved=0CGkQ6AEwBg#v=onepage&q=Chiara%20appointed%20federal%20prosecutor%202001&f=false.

had never had a sexual relationship. Further, while others would agree that morale in her office was low, they admitted it was low long before she arrived; there had been significant and long-standing problems in the office. Even after Chiara had asked for help from her superiors to remedy the situation, she was left to twist in the wind. And, there was no preferential treatment among the staff.[548]

Oh, and all the foolishness, all those false accusations against her. There was nothing to criticize. They didn't have anything to complain about what she did. It was strictly politics at its worst in the federal government; that's it.

...And at the state level?

Same thing. And because she was a good public servant, and apparently was considered too loyal to me, you know? How ridiculous. Margaret is loyal to the truth. And maybe she knew too much of it, especially about Justice Markman and Gerri Kozachik.

Denise Koning agrees with the idea of where the trouble began: "I am absolutely convinced that what happened to Margaret got its start at the Michigan Supreme Court."[549]

As for Chiara, she now lives quietly, but not in Michigan.

Kevin Bowling

Kevin J. Bowling was—and is—independent. By his own description, he had grown up as a tough kid in Warwick, Rhode Island. If there was a fight (and there were plenty) he'd find it. By dint of intelligence and discipline he worked his way off the streets. He earned a bachelor's in political science from Providence College. Bowling moved to Denver and earned a master's in judicial administration from the University of Denver College of Law, and when he came to Michigan he earned his law degree at Thomas M. Cooley Law School.[550]

And by the spring of 2002, he'd spent 20 years of his professional life—almost all of it—as an employee of the Michigan Supreme Court.

Kevin Bowling <u>was</u> the Michigan Judicial Institute. That's the educational arm, a very important arm, of the court.

We've written about the MJI before in this book. In sum, "It is the training division of the State Court Administrative Office of the Michigan Supreme Court."[551] In addition to helping to train judges and other court personnel, the MJI operates the Michigan

548 Ibid.
549 Denise Koning Sheneman.
550 "Leadership: Board of Directors," National Association for Court Management, http://www.nacmnet.org/leadership/index.html.
551 "Welcome to MJI," Michigan Courts, http://courts.michigan.gov/mji/.

Supreme Court Learning Center, a series of rooms filled with educational displays in the Hall of Justice.[552] Bowling was in charge during its creation, and he oversaw the early part of the installation. He was the state judicial educator. He also had served as a regional court administrator, one of four.

He was already at the Supreme Court when Weaver arrived. In fact, in 1997, he had applied to serve as State Court Administrator (SCA), the top non-justice administrator in the court.

John D. Ferry, Jr., was the deputy at the time, so he applied. We had a national search as I recall, but it came down to a few. And in the end, I myself had opted to have Ferry, because he had more experience in the breadth of the court. But I felt that Kevin Bowling was very able and probably would follow Ferry, because Ferry was older than Kevin, anyway.

Weaver and Bowling got along even so, and he worked with her during her time as chief justice, in part because while he was under the SCAO, he reported to the chief justice.

I didn't always agree with him, and I think he's very forthright. I appreciated that. I always felt that you wanted staff to tell you what they thought, not what they think you think, because you'd rather hear it before you make a mistake as opposed to after. In the end, because you have the position, you make a decision, but you'd rather hear from staff, "Gee, this is what I think," and "I think you're wrong." It's nice if they'll say it in a nice way, but if they don't, it doesn't matter.

Bowling usually managed to say it in a nice way...but he'd say it in any event.

So then it was really shocking to me to find out, sometime shortly after March 22, 2002, that Bowling was gone.

Just like that; not even a "Goodbye. Nice workin' with you."

And the rumors had already spread. And we were told at a meeting of the justices that Bowling had been fired and terminated, rather abruptly—that he had been removed from the building precipitously, and he was not able to talk to any of the staff.

Justice Michael Cavanagh probably worked most closely with Bowling at the time.

Justice Cavanagh and Kevin had worked closely. Cavanagh was very interested from the time he was the chief justice—which was before Brickley—in Michigan judicial education and he led in that. And so he was the liaison from the court to the Michigan Judicial Institute.

But I remember him saying that he didn't know about Bowling's firing on the Friday [the 22nd]. I

---

552 Bowling has said that he and court employees Pam Creighton and Doug Van Epps came up with the idea. They shared it with Weaver and Margaret Chiara who then championed it. *The plan [for the building] had no Learning Center in it until I became chief justice, and Margaret Chiara and I—both with teaching backgrounds—were totally nonplussed by its lack, and I saw that it got in the plans. That's a feature of the building. This is where kids and adults will come, and they'll have an education about the courts.*

guess he was informed on the next day, Saturday. I don't remember whether we found out about it on Monday or Tuesday because there wasn't any agenda item, and what I remember is it was talked about at the next conference, because Cavanagh was told about it on Saturday.

Kelly and I wanted to know, "What's going on? Why? When was this done?" Kelly was, I believe, like me—out of the loop. I was totally out. As justices we were not informed anything about it happening before hand, no input.

And we were told that there was a sexual harassment allegation—unsupported—and that it could be in litigation and that we couldn't know. And eventually, we were told that there was an agreement, a settlement agreement made, and that he would be resigning, and that this was all secret, and that we justices couldn't see it. I know because I asked, I wanted to see it, and I believe so did Justice Kelly.

Sexual harassment? Did that strike her as reasonable?

No, frankly. I didn't think that about Kevin Bowling. I found Kevin Bowling to be a very straightforward and very moral, decent fellow, not crude in any way, and there was no sign of that. Now, anything can happen, but no, it was quite unbelievable to me.

However, there was a huge rumor mill running amongst staff because, even though this was all supposed to be secret, it apparently wasn't *really* secret. At some point, the name of the person that allegedly made the allegation came to my attention through, I assume, the rumor mill. She supposedly was the one. And I had come to know this young woman because I often would see her on the mornings before court, and I would stop and visit with her, and I got to know her.

And it was hard for me to see how this very nice person could have made such a charge when it seemed to me it couldn't have been true. And this was all in the rumor mill. I finally realized that maybe she didn't make the allegation, and that she didn't even know that she was identified as the person who made the allegation.

...That she or just her name might have been used without her knowledge?

...If, in fact, this was a sham to get rid of him. He was an independent person and would tell you what he thought...and, of course, that is not what the Englerites wanted. They wanted people that were under their thumb. So it's very possible that she never knew that the allegations had been attributed to her. But that was the rumor that I heard.

Why didn't Weaver investigate, follow up?

I don't believe in doing things that are pyrrhic; you always have to have the slimmest possibility that you will be successful, but there must be that. But if you perceive that there is no possibility, it is not to be attempted then.

And Bowling had not stood up at the time. Chances were that he didn't know there would be enough—or any—support among the justices. It was evident that he wanted it quiet at the time.

And so, as I had no denial from him, I had no knowledge for sure, just my belief, that the accusation against Kevin was not true. And Kevin was gone from the court and had not since contacted me. And it had been made clear at the conference that we out-of-the-loop justices were not to contact him and interfere, so I had to let it be for its own time.

And even if she'd have stood up and made a ruckus, what good would it have done?

The public would not have cared if I said I, as a justice, have a right to see what went on with Kevin Bowling. The public in 2002 was not prepared to think that the justices of the Supreme Court were not the most just, the most fair.

The chief justice then, Corrigan, had the votes: Taylor, Markman, Young, and herself. And I will ask you, what power does one justice have against four other justices if they say, "We're not telling you. That's it."? It wasn't something you could go to the press about. I didn't know facts. And it's just what I'm telling you. There was unsettlement about it, but I felt the Bowling matter had been grossly mishandled and it was an injustice.

And we were all told that this was bad, and that this is the way it had to be, and that it had to be secret, and we could never say anything. I gather, then, Bowling must have gotten attorneys and they had—yes, because we were informed that there was going to be, potentially, litigation and all that.

I didn't know the details, but having seen other injustices occur by the same people—that is the Engler Four and their chosen administrators—and we would see some more very shortly.

So, what would be the motivation to flush Bowling from the court? His independence? Yes. Anything else? Yes...maybe. He could have been in the way.

What was interesting is, that Kevin's assistant, Dawn McCarty, who, at some later time I came to know, was the wife of Larry Royster. Royster was the assistant in research to Gromek over at the Court of Appeals. Larry had been there when I was there as a Court of Appeals judge, and he was good; he had been put on the A-team (as my law clerk had been) when we worked to make efficiencies over there in order to help move the huge backlog that we had at the Court of Appeals.

Royster, then, I think, became the head of research for the Court of Appeals, and maybe still is.[553] And he was a capable fellow. In any case, Royster turned out to be the husband of Dawn McCarty, who was an assistant to Bowling.

Eight weeks later, after Kevin's settlement and all that, Dawn McCarty was made the head of the MJI. Kevin was just in the way, and he probably was perceived, quickly, as someone who was not going to just do whatever he was told if it wasn't in the best interest of the court and the people.

And so Bowling had to go.

---

553 He is, but like Gromek, he has added duties to his portfolio: he is now also the chief clerk. ["Larry Royster named chief clerk of the Michigan Court of Appeals," *Legal News*, 20 January 2011, http://www.legalnews.com/ingham/846067.] And on May 24, 2013, Royster moved to the Supreme Court as the clerk of the court. Like Gromek, he also was named as chief of staff [Marcia McBrien, "Larry Royster named Michigan Supreme Court Chief Clerk, Chief of Staff, 24 May 2013, Michigan Supreme Court, http://courts.mi.gov/News-Events/press_releases/Documents/Larry%20Royster%20New%20MSC%20Clerk_1.pdf].

Who had done this to Bowling?

The rumors were very clear on that. Carl Gromek. But he did it in front of John Ferry, the State Court Administrator, and Dawn Monk, Ferry's deputy administrator. The story was that Ferry and Monk were supposed to have a scheduled meeting with Bowling. They did, and once Bowling was there, Gromek came in and fired him. Gromek wasn't even Bowling's boss; Ferry was. But apparently neither Ferry nor Monk said a word.

The trial judges were furious about his departure, and they spoke up some, because Kevin Bowling was very good. He had been...let me put it this way: Before he was MJI, I think he had been a regional court administrator for what would cover Ottawa County and then all of southwest Michigan, and it would probably come up into mid-Michigan. There were four deputy court administrators. And he was beloved, because he was really good. There was no question in my mind that this was a very capable person, and we shouldn't have lost him.

He was outstanding, you know—judges stood up for him, and they even challenged Gromek. And my understanding is—and these rumors were all around—my understanding was, that at some of the meetings with Gromek and the trial judges, they were questioning him, and he refused to answer. And I heard that one time he even left, just left. Those are the rumors that were out there, and I knew—I had trial judges call me and complain about it, and I would say, "You know more about it than I do. I've been told I can't know."

And that, Weaver said, wasn't right.

This action was done in the name of the court. That means it was done in the name of justice and in the names of the justices. This was done in my name as one of the justices.

She said it seemed unreasonable that some of the justices, Chief Justice Corrigan at least, didn't know what was going on.

It <u>would</u> be unreasonable that she didn't know. It's just not believable that the action could have been taken without her knowing about it. She was the chief justice. If she hadn't known and she didn't approve, she was in a position to undo it. And when it was brought to our attention, she was the one who told us that we couldn't know about it.

Likely, the Four knew.

They had to have four approvers since they chose not to vote on these things. If you didn't have four, you could get caught out.

And by his own admission, Cavanagh knew by the day after Bowling's firing. As for Kelly's knowledge of the events, Weaver said she's not sure but didn't think Kelly knew.

And she couldn't be certain until later that the rumors surrounding Bowling's leaving were true.

There is no proof that Kevin did anything wrong, but I have proof that this happened to him and he was under threat.

This was the modus operandi they employed: aim for the lowest level. We saw it with Margaret Chiara on a national scale, and here it is with Kevin at the state scale.

It wasn't until years later that Bowling's side of all this was revealed to Weaver, confirming most of what she suspected. Most important, he asserted that the harassment claims against him were baseless. Weaver received a copy of a communication Bowling intended to send—but didn't—to John Ferry. Bowling wrote it shortly after he was shown the door:

> There is an interesting philosophic rule called Occam's Razor, which basically says when there are many competing theories or explanations, the simplest is preferred as being true. For me, that razor seemed helpful in cutting through the political nonsense related to my termination and Friday's announcement of a new interim director for MJI. I found it very enlightening on Friday when I received the news that Dawn McCarty (DFM) was appointed interim director.
>
> It was just eight brief weeks since Gromek announced, in your presence, that I was "terminated," that I was an "at-will employee," and that as an at-will employee he did not have to give me any reason for the termination. Of course eight weeks sounds like a brief time unless you are terminated with absolutely no warning, escorted out and locked out of your office like a criminal, cut off from your staff without opportunity for closure, attempting to support a family on one full time paycheck and set of benefits—which is suddenly eliminated; then eight weeks can seem like an eternity (you should try it sometime).
>
> During the last eight weeks I have thought a great deal about these events, trying to make some sense of them and finally, with Friday's announcement, many of the puzzle pieces began to fit together. By the way, if you do not like the reference to Occam's Razor you can play "connect the dots"—it gets you to the same place.
>
> March 22nd, Gromek fires me. Why Gromek? He was not my supervisor, nor did he supervise MJI. If there was a problem with my performance, why would you have not called me in to deal with it? Or, if it were more serious, why was Justice Cavanagh not involved as MJI's supervising justice? After being fired, I also learned that DFM led a group of MJI managers to a clandestine meeting with Gromek while I was at the Judicial College with Judge Bill Kelly, working on a distance-learning program for Michigan. If DFM had management concerns about MJI that she felt she could not bring to me, why is she going to Gromek—who has nothing to do with MJI and is

generally uninformed about the continuing education needs of trial judges and trial court personnel? Why not go to you as the State Court Administrator—you who are responsible for MJI and who are my supervisor? Or go to MJI's supervising justice?

As Occam's Razor suggests, the simple answer is likely the most accurate. More likely than not, DFM went to Gromek with the help and encouragement of her husband Larry Royster, who worked closely with Gromek for several years at the Court of Appeals and appears to still be on a friendly basis with him. More likely than not, it provided a twisted sort of "win-win" for both of them. DFM gets a convenient promotional/pay increase (even though as noted below she recognized she could not adequately perform her existing job duties—now she suddenly expects to be able to do the director's job...???) and less of the accountability she resisted from me. Gromek gets someone at MJI he feels he has control over. As for you and the SCAO, it is just one more example of the Office of Chief Justice making you irrelevant through fear and intimidation.

On March 22nd, when Gromek fired me and I pushed him for a reason, he eventually stumbled and came up with the patently false harassment allegation—which appeared to be nonsense then and seems to be even more so now. If anything, it seemed to be a smoke screen to divert attention from what was actually going on. In the 20 years I worked for the court, I harassed no one—and I believe in your heart you know that, regardless of whether you will ever admit it. The allegation was nonsense. That is why there was no investigation. That is why the SCAO's own mandatory harassment policy was violated and was blatantly disregarded—even after I requested an investigation. That is why there is no allegation in my personnel file[554]; there simply was no harassment.

---

554 Mike Benedict confirmed that he had never seen an allegation lodged against Bowling nor a settlement agreement between Bowling and the court. If such records existed, he said, they would have been maintained in the office of the State Court Administrator and not in the personnel records maintained in human resources:

> [T]heoretically, all files should flow through HR. However, when you consider that each justice has records of their staffs located in their offices and rarely pass these on to HR [...] some of their records are obviously being stored in some other location and not in HR, [and] you can see this policy is not something in which there is strict adherence. I believe that the justices and chief of staff/State Court Administrator [Carl Gromek and John Ferry] have felt that they wanted to maintain some files in strictest confidence and that they did not trust HR with those records. Other than being somewhere in their offices, I have no idea where those records may be.

> In regard to any sort of investigation of sexual harassment, etc., I always felt that HR should take a leading role in these matters. However, I know of circumstances where Carl did all the investigation and did not include our office [....] We had a situation where a woman filed a harassment claim with HR. I investigated the matter and then had a meeting with the woman, her boss, and Carl. Carl was very rough on the person filing the complaint and had her crying before the meeting was over. I talked with Carl after the meeting and discussed his behavior and he did say he felt bad that he came down so hard on the woman. The matter, by the way, was resolved in a fashion acceptable to the woman, but talk about an action that had a chilling effect on other women filing claims!!! [Michael Benedict, e-mail to co-author Schock, 6 June 2012.]

Yet after twenty years of unblemished service, a single controlling, vindictive individual is empowered by the court to end my career without justification (worse yet—with apparently manufactured information and with me being given no reasonable opportunity to respond). It is amazing to me that we pride ourselves in our system of justice, yet emerging democracies in third world countries provide criminal defendants with more notice, more courtesy, and more dignity than the Michigan Supreme Court offers to long term employees about to be terminated. It is not right, but at least the house of cards is now becoming more visible. Next the cards will begin to fall.

By the way, before DFM accepted her promotion did she bother to tell anyone that she was in my office 2-3 weeks before I was fired, dissolved in tears (a common occurrence when she was overwhelmed or felt pressured by the workload) requesting that I amend the MJI budget and reduce her work schedule from full time to 24 hours/week? She and her husband had come to the conclusion that she needs to spend more time with her children and she can no longer effectively balance motherhood and full time work. So she requested a schedule change as soon as possible, but no later than October 1st. I had agreed to "job share" to insure the judicial programs continued as needed and knowing of the current hiring freeze situation. Ironically, that was one of the agenda items I had planned to discuss with you on March 22nd. Now, it will be interesting to see how this impacts the house of cards.

I fully realize that none of this changes my status as a former "at will" employee or changes the fact that I was treated unjustly by the very organization that should be a guardian of justice, however, the clarity which was added by your announcement on Friday at least helps complete the puzzle and hopefully will provide some closure. Strange as it may seem, if the opportunity presented itself, I would continue my work at MJI because it would be a good thing to do; if done well—it is an important service for the judges, for court staff, and for the public; and the creative work is not yet complete.

At this point, it is simply time to move on. Obviously, if I were writing the script it would end much differently, however, I do not have the luxury of time nor money. You have a signed piece of paper that says I resigned; you know the truth. I did not resign. I was fired by Gromek, and I signed the paper under duress because it was the only way to get some money to feed my family while I look for work. Hopefully, for you and your family, you will never have to experience the humiliation and degradation of being treated in this fashion. If you ever are subjected to such a misfortune, however, I hope you at least have the benefit of having a supervisor with enough moral character to stand up and support you.

KJB[555]

---

555 Kevin J. Bowling, e-mail, 22 March 2002, unpublished.

After leaving the court, Bowling took refuge in service. He went to "western Africa as Deputy Chief of Party for the Nigeria Justice Sector Assistance Project."[556] He was working to bring the rule of law to a country in need of his expertise.

...Not that Michigan didn't need some of the same help, as he presciently noted in his e-mail.

Whatever else the rumors may have done, they didn't hold him back in the end. He is now the court administrator to the 20th Judicial Circuit Court (Ottawa County). He also serves as president of the National Association for Court Management.[557]

> He is a member of the State Bar of Michigan, the National Association of State Judicial Educators, the American Judicature Society, and the Ottawa County Bar Association. Mr. Bowling has served on the Board of Directors, National Association of State Judicial Educators; the Advisory Board of the Leadership Institute in Judicial Education, University of Memphis; the Advisory Board, National Judicial College - Courage to Live Program; and the Technology Law Advisory Board, Institute for Continuing Legal Education. Mr. Bowling is also a trained mediator and serves on the Board of Directors of the Ottawa/Allegan Center for Dispute Resolution. In addition to his service on the NACM Board of Directors as the General Jurisdiction Director, he is the Vice President of the Michigan Association of Circuit Court Administrators.[558]

The author has worked with Kevin Bowling on any number of projects. It was he who suggested asking Justice Weaver to take part in the *You and the Courts* video. Bowling had maintained a professional and personal relationship with Weaver, even arranging that she would speak at the 2010 dedication of the new Ottawa County courthouse.

About the closing of the longest chapter of his professional career, Bowling remains silent.

Now, Bowling had been an "at will" employee. All court employees are. That means their employment could be terminated at any time, for any reason. Or, no reason.

He may have been an at-will, but still, he's a human being, and if you're going to make a sexual harassment charge.... Policies that the court had were not followed in any way with respect to sexual harassment charges.

I'm not against the at-will policy for the court, but it should only exist because you can trust that the people at the top are the fairest. Here, there were no checks and balances. It was persecution,

---

556 "Leadership: Board of Directors," National Association for Court Management, http://www.nacmnet. org/leadership/index.html.
557 Ibid.
558 Ibid.

intimidation, bullying—tyranny and deceit. Yes, people work at your will, but you can treat them decently. Criminals get better treatment than some of these people got.

And I will tell you this: I think the Engler Four learned from some of those things, because I think they began to be more subtle in their executions—terminations, if you wish to call them that.

There Were Others: Aloysius J. Lynch

Another of those who was targeted even before Weaver was deposed as chief justice was Al Lynch, the court's chief commissioner. Weaver described his work as first rate.

He had been a real value to the court for 25 years as a commissioner.[559] He had tremendous knowledge and cared about the institution.

Justices Kelly and Cavanagh joined Weaver in her appreciation of his service.

They were promised that Al Lynch would not be removed when Maura became chief justice. I told them what I thought was going to happen. They didn't realize they were being deceived.

These people [the Engler Majority] were so mean spirited and on occasion just cruel, that it was unbelievable. I guess this happens in business, but this was the court, you know? It should be the most fair, the most just, the most professional and orderly of all organizations.

The Engler Four didn't want Lynch. They were ready to terminate him. But Lynch was willing to stand up, and because he was willing to stand up and not just fold, I was willing to join him. Kelly and Cavanagh were willing to stand up for him also.

The majority said there were reasons to get rid of him.

The Four were trumping up this, that, and other things. It was terrible. I stood and said, "How could one possibly treat somebody who has given us 25 years this way?"

They backed down and Lynch stayed...for a little while...a few months, until a new arrangement meant that he could retire.

That gave him an out. But I'm telling you, we were losing somebody very valuable to the court who might have stayed had things been different.

He left the court just after Kevin Bowling in 2002 to "retire" at age 54. In the press release announcing his departure, Maura Corrigan stated, "Over many years, Al Lynch has provided sound counsel and sage advice. I join my colleagues, past and present, in wishing him good fortune as he begins his next career."[560]

---

559 He had served under ten chief justices.
560 Marcia McBrien, "Supreme Court's longtime chief commissioner to retire; court names successor," Michigan Supreme Court Office of Public Information, 28 May 2002.

Here's your hat, what's your hurry?

His successor was Michael Murray.

He was the guy of the hour. He was a likeable, able commissioner and brother of Mark Murray the state Treasurer for Governor Engler.[561]

In addition to those staff members who had been terminated, there were any number of others who left either because they saw the handwriting on the wall or because they found the environment too toxic.

There would be one more notable departure at the court, someone who should have seen it coming, especially given Kevin Bowling's valedictory comment. And his replacement would drive a wedge between Weaver and the rest of her colleagues, not that they weren't already well separated by that time.

But first she would run for re-election.

---

561 Michael Murray would leave to serve as legal counsel for the Catholic Diocese of Lansing. He would be appointed by the Supreme Court to serve as vice-chair of the Attorney Grievance Commission in 2006. [Marcia McBrien, "Attorney Grievance Commission appointments, reappointments announced by Michigan Supreme Court," Michigan Supreme Court Office of Public Information, 13 June 2006.] He would later rise to chairman. He is no longer a member of that commission [http://www.agcmi.com/pages/TheCommission.html]. He is, however, still listed as the legal advisor to the diocese on its website: http://www.dioceseoflansing.org/staff_directory.html.

Michael's brother Mark Murray also had served as state budget director, director of the Management and Budget Department, and acting director of the Family Independence Agency. He would move from Governor Engler's administration to the presidency of Grand Valley State University, July 1, 2001. He left GVSU to assume the presidency of Meijer, Inc., in 2006. [Past Presidents, Grand Valley State University, http://www.gvsu.edu/administration/past-presidents-7.htm.] He also served (using personal time) on Governor Rick Snyder's transition team along with former Engler staffers Sharon (chief of staff) and Doug Rothwell (economic development chief). [Shandra Martinez, "Rick Snyder selects Meijer president Mark Murray as adviser," *Grand Rapids Press*, 3 November 2010, http://www.mlive.com/business/west-michigan/index.ssf/2010/11/rick_snyder_selects_meijer_pre.html.] More recently he was appointed by Governor Snyder as a member of the Education Achievement Authority Board, a "group charged with turning around Michigan's lowest-performing public schools." [Dave Murray, "Gov. Snyder taps Meijer President Mark Murray for authority overseeing struggling state schools," *Grand Rapids Press*, 3 August, 2011, http://www.mlive.com/news/grand-rapids/index.ssf/2011/08/gov_snyder_taps_meijer_preside.html.] In early 2013, Mark Murray moved from president of Meijer to co-chief executive officer with Hank Meijer. "[Murray] will share the position with Hank Meijer and serve as a partner to the development of future business strategy. He also will continue as vice-chairman of the Meijer board of directors, helmed by brothers Hank and Doug Meijer." [Shandra Martinez, "Meijer names new president as Mark Murray takes new role," *Grand Rapids Press*, 16 January 2013, http://www.mlive.com/business/west-michigan/index.ssf/2013/01/midwest_retailer_meijer_names.html.]

Chapter 12

Re-election
And One More to Go and Come,
And Time for Her to Go (or Maybe Not).

Governor John Engler was timed out. His third term, ending Jan. 1, 2003, was his last.[562] So the Republicans ran Lieutenant Governor Dick Posthumus against outgoing Attorney General Jennifer Granholm. And that's where the money went.

Both Weaver and Young were up for re-election, Weaver after completing her first term (elected in 1994), and Young after being appointed and then—in 2000—running in a hotly contested race to fill the remainder of the term for the seat he inherited from Conrad Mallett.

Reporting in the *Detroit Free Press*, Dawson Bell wrote:

> Norman Tucker, a past president of the Michigan Trial Lawyers Association, is a partner in a Southfield law firm long known for its generosity to Democratic judicial candidates. He shares the view that donations from those interested in the makeup of the court have been directed elsewhere, especially to Granholm.
>
> Experience has shown the trial bar that it is very difficult to unseat an incumbent, and that trying to motivates interest groups on the other side to spend more heavily, he said.
>
> Granholm "generates for the first time in a long time on the Democratic side a spirit of hope," Tucker said.
>
> For the plaintiffs' bar, that hope is focused on the Governor's authority to appoint judges to vacancies on the bench.
>
> [...]

---

562 And thereafter, Governors would only get two terms, a result of a 1992 ballot measure limiting tenure in the House, Senate, and Governor's office.

"I think John Engler has shown that if you want to affect the judiciary you can do it by appointment," Tucker said.[563]

Justice Robert Young agreed.

> Young, appointed to the court by Gov. John Engler in 1998, also isn't complaining.

> "It certainly is less ugly than it was two years ago. But I can't say I miss it," he said.

> Young became almost a household name during campaign 2000 as part of the trio "Markman, Taylor and Young, Oh, My!" who were vilified in Democratic Party campaign ads as tools of corporate and insurance company interests. Perhaps the most significant reason for the change in tenor and intensity this year is that all the effort two years ago appeared to have been wasted. Stephen Markman, Clifford Taylor and Young, benefiting from the ballot designation identifying them as incumbents, won easily.

> Young said he believes the interest groups that funded the 2000 campaigns of the Democratic nominees, principally plaintiffs' attorneys who objected to the rulings of a more conservative court, realized that their money would be better spent elsewhere—most notably in the campaign of Democratic gubernatorial candidate Jennifer Granholm.

> But that's a good thing, and not just because they aren't using the money to attack him, Young said.

> For too long, many special interests viewed court elections as the "cheapest political battleground...a place where they could legislate without having to go through the Legislature," he said.[564]

Weaver and Young were up against Democratic nominees Maggie Drake, a judge in the Third Circuit Court (Wayne County), and an Oakland County lawyer, J. Martin Brennan. The Libertarian Party put forward two: Michael Donahue of Detroit and Bruce Yuille of Clarkston. Donnelly Hadden of Ann Arbor ran on the Green Party ticket.

The Democrats were looking for issues. On Oct. 4, then-Democratic Party chairman Mark Brewer thought he found one in a comment Weaver had made about a proposed constitutional amendment. During a meeting, she said she thought the amendment idea was bad. When the state board of canvassers said that the proposal was improperly worded and the measure wouldn't go on the ballot, organizers appealed to the Court

563 Dawson Bell, "2 justices have the upper hand; unlike past contest, race is quiet, low key," *Detroit Free Press*, 31 October 2002, B.6.
564 Ibid.

of Appeals, where they were denied, and then sought leave at the Michigan Supreme Court. Brewer contended that Weaver should have kept silent in the first place because the matter was likely to end up before her. Or, he said, she should have stepped off the case, recused herself. He cited the Code of Judicial Conduct. Weaver also cited the code and suggested that Brewer didn't understand it; she'd made no mention of the ballot wording in her comments. The flap was dismissed as election-year politics.[565]

Perhaps the most interesting part of the campaign—at least from the outside—was the link between Weaver and a friend, a man by the name of Gregory Bruce Zolman. Weaver had known his family for years; Greg Zolman's parents lived just down the road at the river bend.

The Zolmans go back a long time in this area.

After high school, he went into the military and then came back to Michigan. He started working as a skilled tradesman—a carpenter, and eventually as a contractor. He had a reputation for doing good work.

Greg Zolman was very smart, so talented and really an artist. He could not only envision projects, he was able to do them, too. When there was a challenge, he'd figure it out. Every intricate puzzle that came along interested him.

He was Weaver's first choice when she remodeled her house along the Crystal River in Glen Arbor during the years from 1995 through 1998. Zolman added a large two-stall garage and storage space. He also remodeled Weaver's neighbor's house (Joy Taylor's) during the same time. The results were stunning, and the structure is still true and strong.

Weaver said she thought him an intelligent and interesting fellow, friendly. At the job site, he and Weaver often talked about social issues. Zolman may well have expressed his dislike of taxes. That much wasn't unusual; who does like 'em?

What Weaver didn't know was that Zolman had more than the average dislike of taxes. He was determined to avoid them. In fact, he hadn't paid them since 1991. Further, he asserted that he wasn't a U.S. citizen. When the I.R.S. contested his claims, he filed lawsuits that were deemed "frivolous." He wasn't hiding from them, really, and openly claimed citizenship in "the 'Michigan Republic,' and something he called the 'Unity States of Our World.'"[566] But he didn't tell Weaver any of that.

He was arrested in April 23, 2002, charged "with four counts of willfully failing to file tax returns from 1995 through 1998, despite gross income of $590,000 from his business, Glen Lake Construction. He faces up to one year on each count."[567]

565 AP, "State justice criticized for ballot stand; She says the complaint is politically motivated and the Democratic chairman misunderstands the code of conduct," *Grand Rapids Press,* 4 October 2002, D3.

566 Ed White, "'Betty, how did you get involved with this guy?': Judges payments turn up as evidence in tax rebel's case," *Grand Rapids Press,* 4 August 2002, A1, A20.

567 "Two men arrested on tax charges," *Traverse City Record-Eagle,* 24 April 2002, http://archives.record-

He pled guilty June 20, 2002, to a one-count misdemeanor charge of failing to file his taxes for 1997.[568] All that had been covered in the media. But the story of Zolman having anything to do with Weaver didn't break until Sunday, August 5, in the *Grand Rapids Press*.

And it broke at the top of page one:

> 'Betty, how did you get involved with this guy?'
> Judge's payment turns up as evidence in tax rebel's case[569]

The question in the kicker headline had been uttered by the federal district judge sitting on the case, Robert Holmes Bell, in response to reporter Ed White's[570] question about his thoughts seeing Weaver's name on the list of Zolman's customers.[571] It was the only customer's name that he raised in open court.[572] But she was a high-profile customer.[573]

> Weaver's role in the case came to light during Zolman's guilty plea hearing, when U.S. District Judge Robert Holmes Bell picked her name alone from a list of some 20 prospective witnesses and questioned Zolman.

> "Is she the justice on the Supreme Court?" Bell asked.[574]

Weaver was the largest paying customer. One of the issues was that she paid for the work while it went on, but in increments of less than $10,000. Zolman was under

---

eagle.com/2002/apr/24irs.htm.
568 Press release, Western District of Michigan, Department of Justice, 20 June 2002, http://www.justice.gov/tax/usaopress/2002/txdv02GZolman.html.
569 Ed White, "Betty, how…".
570 Ed White is a highly respected journalist who was writing for the *Press* at the time. He later moved to the Associated Press in Detroit and figures later in another chapter.
571 Ed White, "Betty, how…".
572 Bell also told the reporter during the subsequent interview that he doubted Weaver had anything to do with wrongdoing:

> Bell…said Weaver's role in Zolman's finances "Doesn't implicate her as a participant" in his crime. He suggested she may have been trying to change his views on the tax system—"bring him out of the rain."

> "She's a very nice lady, so sweet and kind. She's strait-laced," Bell said in an interview.
[Ibid.]
573 It is true that the Code of Judicial Conduct makes it clear that a justice's conduct is likely to be closely scrutinized:

> A judge should avoid impropriety and the appearance of impropriety in all activities.

> A. Public confidence in the judiciary is eroded by irresponsible or improper conduct by judges. A judge must avoid all impropriety and appearance of impropriety. *A judge must expect to be the subject of constant public scrutiny. A judge must therefore accept restrictions on conduct that might be viewed as burdensome by the ordinary citizen and should do so freely and willingly.* [Emphasis added.]
Canon 2A: http://coa.courts.mi.gov/rules/documents/8michigancodeofjudicialconduct.pdf.]
574 "Justices payments at heart of tax case," *Michigan Lawyers Weekly*, 30 September 2002, http://milawyersweekly.com/news/2002/09/30/justices-payments-at-heart-of-tax-case/.

the belief that the payments under ten grand were less likely to trigger automatic transaction reporting by banks to the government.

For a little while it didn't look good.

That was a year judges were doing a lot of bad things, and they thought in me they had a big fish.

First in order of events, she wouldn't speak with an Internal Revenue Service agent who came to her door in the spring of 2000.

Add to that, the *Grand Rapids Press* reported that in hearing the guilty plea, Bell asked Zolman:

> [H]ad he talked to Weaver "about this issue...about taxes?"
>
> "Yes. I have talked with her," Zolman said.
>
> The U.S. Attorney's Office said Weaver is simply a witness who is not ac-cused of doing anything illegal. Nonetheless, a member of the state highest court now is part of an unflattering case involving a 46-year-old tax rebel who was so brazen he filed a legal document stained with his own blood.[575]

Oh, and the U.S. Attorney's Office that pronounced her "simply a witness" was headed by Margaret Chiara. And Weaver said she wouldn't talk until Zolman had been sentenced.

"I have nothing to hide," she said in a *Michigan Lawyers Weekly* article. "I'd like to talk about it and get it behind me."[576] But reporters had heard that kind of rhetoric before.

The press really wanted to know if there was dirt here; it looked like there could have been. And she was a very big fish; her name would stick with the story. When Zolman was sentenced to a year's imprisonment Oct. 3, 2002, the headline read:

> Tax rebel linked to Justice Weaver gets prison time;
> Supreme Court Justice Elizabeth "Betty" Weaver says she didn't know of his anti-tax views when she paid him for work on her home.[577]

No specific mention of Zolman in the headline. But that story marked the end of the case, and it was at that point that Weaver could speak freely. And she did.

First, Weaver revealed she had paid every invoice by check. Further, she kept track of it all and would later supply those records. As for amounts under $10,000:

---

575 Ed White, "Betty, how...".
576 Ibid.
577 Ed White, "Tax rebel linked to Justice Weaver gets prison time;
Supreme Court Justice Elizabeth "Betty" Weaver says she didn't know of his anti-tax views when she paid him for work on her home.," *Grand Rapids Press*, 4 October 2002, D1.

You never pay more than they ask. This project went along and he'd bill me. I paid my bills.

Second, the reason she didn't speak with the IRS investigator was simple, according to what she told Ed White:

> "I do not talk to strangers who arrive unannounced at my door."

> Later she asked her accountant to contact the investigator to "find out what it was all about and why they wanted to talk to me."

> Weaver said she "promptly produced all the information asked for and sup-plied additional copies of checks...that the investigators did not have."[578]

I think I also called Greg soon after that guy showed up at my door, and I told him that he'd better talk with an accountant. He needed to get this sorted out. In the first place, I couldn't believe that he had done this...something so stupid.

How could somebody so smart be so dumb?

Exactly.

Third, while Zolman had talked with Weaver about his distaste for taxes, she said she had "absolutely no knowledge of Mr. Zolman's anti-tax beliefs or his failure to file and pay income taxes."[579]

And the idea that I'd be concerned about money laundering is so far from my thinking that it would never occur to me. I mean, I don't go around asking people if they are filing their taxes and behaving.[580]

Fourth, while Margaret Chiara was in charge of the office that conducted the investigation, she didn't have anything to do with it. That fell to assistant U.S. Attorney Phil Green. He said, "he supervised the case because there was 'something of a social relationship'" between Chiara and Weaver.[581]

Fifth, her silence had a reason: by her judgment, she <u>couldn't</u> talk about Zolman's case until the sentencing without breaking the code of judicial conduct. By her reckoning, if she had, she would have risked a trip to the Judicial Tenure Commission.

Finally, she said she urged Zolman to plead guilty to resolve the case as soon as possible:

> She said she urged him to "get his life back on the right path by admitting his wrongdoing, pleading guilty and accepting the penalties for his conduct."

---

578 Ed White, "Tax rebel...".
579 Ibid.
580 Weaver says that in working with her accountant, they are of a mind if ever there is ambiguity or doubt, it is resolved in the government's favor.
581 Ed White, "Betty, How...".

Appearing in federal court Thursday, Zolman said: "I realize I've been wrong. ... I want to get this behind me."[582]

Zolman was sentenced to a year in prison—the maximum sentence—in addition to paying his back taxes and fines.[583]

Once he was sentenced, Weaver put out a press release explaining her role,[584] and she drove down to the *Grand Rapids Press* and spent a session with the editors there.

I went down and talked with them. In the end, they saw it for what is was and got behind me in the election.

Weaver was no fair-weather friend to Zolman; she cared what happened to him. She certainly didn't approve of what he had done. While he caused her great distress and gave an issue to those who set themselves up as her enemies—in fact, he could have single-handedly sunk her re-election,[585] she has said that he did himself more harm.

I never abandoned him...then or now. I didn't talk or write to him while he was in prison or for a couple of years after he came out because it would not have been good for him or me. He had to come back into his own.

As for his beliefs, Weaver says those are his own business; it's his actions that count.

I suspect he still disagrees with the 13th Amendment, but that's his right. He pays his taxes; he's learned that lesson.

These days, he sometimes does work again for Weaver in her house along the river.

Yes, what he did was wrong. But just because Greg did something that was wrong was not reason enough to cross him off. The important thing was that he admitted his wrong, made his reparations and paid his due—including prison time, and that he has determined to live a better life in the future. My friends are not perfect. I don't ask or expect that of them.

That was the same reason she stuck by the Engler Four for so long, long beyond the dictates of pure reason.

I know people can change and I always have hope for them. Even now, even after all that has happened, they can do better. I believe Greg chose to do better.

---

582 Ed White, "Tax Rebel...".
583 AP, "Northern Michigan man sentenced in tax case," *Ludington Daily News*, 4 October 2002, A3, http://news.google.com/newspapers?nid=110&dat=20021004&id=OP9OAAAAIBAJ&sjid=DkwDAAAAIBAJ&pg=1838,3876477.
584 Elizabeth A. Weaver, press release, "Promised comment on the Zolman tax case," 3 October 2002, http://www.justiceweaver.com/zolmancomment.php.
585 Perhaps because they also saw it for what it was, the Democrats didn't jump on the issue. Or, perhaps they realized that Weaver was truly an independent and that could be good for them.

In the end, voters apparently didn't think the issue determinative; the election was a blowout. The Michigan Campaign Finance Network analyzed the results:

> The Supreme Court election was the least competitive statewide election in 2002, both in terms of votes and campaign fund raising. Incumbent Republican nominees Elizabeth Weaver and Robert Young, Jr. each had an overwhelming money advantage over the Democratic nominees, J. Martin Brennan and Maggie Drake. Weaver and Young also decisively won the election, each tallying more than two-to-one vote margins over both Brennan and Drake. Of the three minor-party nominees on the ballot, only Green candidate Donnelly Hadden raised money—$5,915. Libertarian nominee Michael Donahue was the top vote getter among the minor-party candidates with 329,587 votes.
>
> The 2002 campaigns ended a trend of dramatically increasing costs for winning Supreme Court campaigns. From 1994 to 2000, the average winning candidate campaign committee had more than quadrupled from $284,000 to $1.3 million.
>
> Party independent expenditures, which totaled $1.88 million in 2000, were much smaller this time—$1,943 each for the Republican nominees and $7,797 each for the Democratic nominees.
>
> While unreported "issue advertising" related to the campaigns dropped dramatically compared to 2000, when it probably topped $7 million, the Michigan Chamber of Commerce was again a major presence in the campaign. The Chamber spent roughly $840,000 extolling the qualities of the incumbents and their work on the bench, despite the candidates' own overwhelming financial advantage. That is nearly as much money as the Republican nominees raised, and more than ten times the amount raised by the Democrats. Neither of the parties engaged in issue advertising.[586]

Yes, about that Chamber of Commerce money and advertising.... As far as Weaver was concerned, it came as a surprise. She traveled throughout the state campaigning in her usual fashion. And she was startled at first when supporters told her how much they liked her TV ads with Justice Young. At the time, she had not made any TV ads. Yet there they were, courtesy of the Chamber of Commerce. She had no prior knowledge of them, no input, no participation. Even though they were "for" her, they were not hers.

The state Chamber of Commerce was carrying water for her, water she frankly didn't know about, in fact, COULD NOT know about.

---

586 Barbara R. Moorhouse and Richard L. Robinson with David Hogg and Christopher Moorhouse, "Appellate Judiciary: Supreme Court," *A Citizen's Guide to Michigan Campaign Finance 2002*, Michigan Campaign Finance Network (Lansing, Mich., June 2003), 14, http://www.mcfn.org/pdfs/reports/CG2002.pdf.

While I knew the state Chamber was supporting me, the campaign finance law prohibits any candidate from knowing of or participating in "the how much" and "the how" of independent expenditure or issue ad activities, and I did not know or participate in them.

Subsequently, Weaver's campaign did create and air her own advertisements, investing only about $40,000 in television ads...ten-second "pops" that reiterated her slogan from Michael Marontate: "Weaver, We Need Her."

Volunteer John Evans is at the wheel of the 2002 incarnation of the Weavermobile. John was yet another example of the ongoing and intergenerational friendships that Elizabeth Weaver enjoyed: both his mother, Liz Evans, and his grandmother Jane Martin had been longtime supporters and close associates. John had graduated that spring from Kalamazoo College and worked as driver, chief volunteer, and aide-de-camp, picking up his duties in September and staying with them through the election. Evans went on to earn a master's at Western Michigan University and then a doctorate in Kinesiology—Sport and Exercise Psychology at University of North Carolina at Greensboro. He is now employed by the U.S. Army as a performance enhancement specialist at Ft. Jackson in Greensboro.

The specifics of the spending and the vote totals showed the trend for that election.

Weaver received the top number of votes in the entire Supreme Court election: 1,376,180. Weaver spent a total of $282,383 (51 cents per vote). Of that total $280,440 came from her receipts. In addition, there were independent expenditures (IEs) of $1,943 from the Republican Party and $15 from an unnamed PAC.[587]

In contrast, the other victor, Robert Preston Young, Jr., spent more than twice as much money: $624,356. And he tallied fewer votes. His receipts totaled $622,413 with party independent expenditures also of $1,943, but other IEs totaling $8,899. [588] Young received 1,356,008 votes (78 cents per vote).

587 Her top ten contributors included: Michigan Association of Realtors/REALTORS PAC $17,100; Michigan Chamber of Commerce PAC $15,055; Michigan Health and Hospital Association/Health PAC $15,000; Michigan State Medical Society/Michigan Doctors PAC $8,000; C. Michael and Elizabeth Kojaian $6,800; Arnold and Janet Aronoff $6,000; Daniel and Nancy Aronoff $6,000; Michigan Education Association/MEA PAC $5,000; Michigan Bankers Association PAC/ Michigan Bank PAC $5,000; and Michigan Farm Bureau PAC $4,000. [Ibid. and "Appendix, I" to above, 57, http://www.mcfn.org/pdfs/reports/CG02append.pdf.]
588 Young's top ten donors included: Michigan Association of Realtors/REALTORS PAC $17,300; Michigan Chamber of Commerce PAC $15,390; Michigan Health and Hospital Association/Health PAC $15,000; Michigan State Medical Society/Michigan Doctors PAC $10,700; Michigan Bankers Association PAC/ Michigan Bank PAC $10,000; C. Michael and Elizabeth Kojaian $6,800; Robert and Ellen Thompson $6,800; William and Vivienne Young $6,800; COMM PAC $5,000; and Michigan Farm Bureau PAC $4,000. [Ibid.]

Judge Maggie Drake polled most votes for the Democrats, 617,858. Her campaign spent a total of $51,822, a far cry from the Republicans. Of that her receipts were $44,025 with Democrat Party IEs of $7,797. She spent the equivalent of eight cents a vote.

Fellow Democrat J. Martin Brennen received 522,426 votes and spent even less with total resources of $21,642, of which $11, 549 came from his receipts and party IEs of $7,797 and PAC IEs of $2,296. His cost per vote was four cents.

Libertarian Michael Donahue spent no money but garnered 329,587 votes.[589] Fellow Libertarian Bruce Yuille received 93,067 votes and spent no money. Green candidate Donnelly Hadden raised $5,915 and tallied 119,906 votes.

And Jennifer Granholm took over the executive office. As far as Weaver went, she would be a more benign presence, not reaching out and into the court in an attempt to control.

And I always remembered Engler, one time in his office, in what they called their ceremonial office over in the real Capitol Building as opposed to in the building across the street where they have their office, at some event—whether it was his farewell as the Governor or it could have been something other—but him talking about four votes; that's important: four votes. He understood it. He understood it after I got there really well. He may have always understood it.

Finally, Goodbye, John D. Ferry, Jr.

About the time of the conclusion of the ring debacle, there was one more personnel issue that completely tore the fabric of the court. Although he was acquiescent to the actions of the majority justices, John Ferry still was a target. He managed to hold on until late 2004.[590]

His replacement?

Carl Gromek.

He Didn't Apply for the Job

And this leads us to another story within the story. With John Ferry on the way out, there was need to launch a search for a suitable replacement.

The court invited three trial judges: Judge Freddie Burton, Jr., the president of the Probate Judges Association; Judge Tina Brooks Green, the president of the Michigan

---

589 "Election Results, General Election, November 05, 2002," Department of State, Bureau of Elections, 17 December 2002, http://miboecfr.nicusa.com/election/results/02GEN/13000000.html.
590 He is now the senior court administration consultant at the National Center for State Courts. [http://www.linkedin.com/pub/john-ferry/a/b76/8a2.]

District Judges Association; and then-Circuit Judge Alton Davis, the president of the Michigan Judges Association to serve on a committee to evaluate candidates. They would be joined by Chief Justice Maura Corrigan and Carl Gromek, the chief of staff in the office of the chief justice. Gromek, said Weaver, was supposed to gather all the materials from applicants and do the administrative work.

In all, there were 72 applicants for the position. Six of them made the cut for preliminary interviews. And of those six, one stood out: Ronnie L. Miller of Westfield, Indiana. He was serving as director of trial court management for the Indiana Supreme Court. In his application letter, he said he had not been searching for a job, but that his executive director had sought him out to tell him about the vacancy in Michigan, a definite step up. He was invited to interview.

I think Maura liked him, and I had hope....

She said to Weaver that she DID like him; Miller made a strongly positive impression on the selection committee and was asked to come and interview with the seven justices. He did, but not for long.

It's going along. I thought he would be good. All of sudden, Young called a halt in the middle of that interview: "Let's take a recess."

Could have been a natural need, and people got up and moved about.

Some people left. I wasn't really keeping track, but I know that Cavanagh, Kelly, and I didn't go down the hall to have a conference.

But did the others?

One assumes. And then we came back, and they were kind of polite, and that ended that...they came back and wrapped up quickly. It was obvious that it was over and that something was up.

Miller was out the door. And that was that. ...Except for the fault finding. The majority raised concerns: he was unfamiliar with Michigan courts, and for all of his experience, he had only overseen a small staff.

Was there perhaps something else? Did Miller telegraph that he was independent, his own man?

You got it. I knew what was happening.

And they decided that they would offer him to be the assistant. Well, why would he come to Michigan to be an assistant when that's what he was in Indiana; the only reason to come to Michigan was because it was an opportunity to be the full court administrator? And there was only one court administrator position.

A little time passed, and Weaver heard from Justice Cliff Taylor on the 1st of December, 2004.

Taylor called me and told me they decided they were giving it to Gromek as opposed to the guy that they brought up from Indiana. Gromek hadn't even applied for the position.

Weaver drafted a memo that outlined the reasons she thought choosing Gromek was a bad idea. She went into details and first wanted them to reconsider their course of action. When that failed, she wanted her memo—which was a dissent in an administrative matter—to be published or at least made available. That wasn't going to happen either.

Later, Maura told me that she wanted Miller, but the others told her it wasn't going to happen.

Corrigan called Weaver to her office on Dec. 10th and they had a long discussion about what was happening at the court. Corrigan agreed Miller was a sound candidate, and really couldn't find a reason to support Gromek...at least according to Weaver. It was too bad, a shame, really, said Corrigan, that all this was dividing the court.

On the 10th she's regretting that we're not closer...and on the 14th she's done with me.

And the 14th is the date the court was putting out the announcement of Gromek's appointment and promotion. Weaver revised her dissent, but she never made it public...until now.

Weaver drafted two documents that she circulated to the justices, Carl Gromek, Corbin Davis, the clerk of the court, Mike Gadola, Marcia McBrien, and Leslie Jenkins, McBrien's public information assistant. The first was an overview describing the situation at that time on the 14th:

> Attached is my <u>revised</u> dissenting statement to be included with the minutes of the court recording the appointment of Carl Gromek as State Court Administrator. Please note the revision includes the deletion of the paragraph on page 7 beginning "Fourth." I have circulated this revised statement to Carl Gromek so that, in fairness, he can know my position and communicate to me any thoughts he may have about it before it is released.
>
> Yesterday on the justices' telephone conference, the court denied my request to include in any statement of press release on the appointment of the new State Court Administrator my full dissenting statement (now revised). Alternatively, I asked that any statement or press release include the following information:
>
>> Justice Weaver dissented, saying she would not appoint Mr. Gromek, as she does not believe he is qualified for the position of State Court Administrator. Justice Weaver would instead appoint Mr. Miller to the po-

sition. Mr. Miller is highly qualified; the selection committee appointed by the chief justice (consisting of Chief Justice Corrigan, the presidents of the three trial judges associations, and Mr. Gromek) reviewed the 72 applicants for the position, and recommended Mr. Miller to the court for appointment. Justice Weaver's full dissenting statement is on the Supreme Court website with this press release.

The court decided that it would not include my full dissenting statement or my one paragraph summary dissent on any statement or press release on the appointment and that it would only include the statement "Justice Elizabeth A. Weaver dissents." Further, the court also rejected placing my full or any dissenting statement on the Supreme Court website.

The chief justice was to speak with the selection committee for the State Court Administrator this morning; in fairness to the selection committee I am distributing my revised dissenting statement to them shortly, so they will be informed when the press release comes out. I will of course request that they keep this confidential until the press release comes out. I would appreciate being informed of exactly when that will occur.

I plan to distribute my revised dissenting statement to the presidents and the executive committee of the Trial Judges Associations for the trial judges and to include it on my personal website—www.justiceweaver.com—for access for anyone interested.[591]

The second document, as she mentioned, was her revised dissent, seven pages in all:

The court has made a mistake in appointing Carl Gromek as the new State Court Administrator.

In July 2004, the Michigan Supreme Court began a nation-wide search for a new State Court Administrator to replace the current State Court Administrator, John Ferry. Mr. Ferry served this court and the trial courts well. His departure is a loss to Michigan.

When the application period ended on August 31, 2004, there were 72 applicants for the position, from 17 different states and India. A selection committee was appointed by Chief Justice Corrigan, consisting of herself; Judge Freddie Burton, Jr., the president of the Probate Judges Association; Judge Tina Brooks Green, the president of the Michigan District Judges Association; Judge Alton Davis, the president of the Michigan Judges Association; and Carl Gromek, the chief of staff in the office of the chief justice. Since the primary responsibility of the State Court Administrator is the administration of the trial courts, the chief justice rightly included on the selection committee the presidents of the three trial court associations, representing

---

591 Elizabeth A. Weaver, "Memorandum [1]," 14 December 2004. Unpublished.

the 580 trial judges. The selection committee screened the applicants and selected six applicants (three from Michigan and three from out of state) for preliminary interviews with the selection committee.

After conducting the preliminary interviews, the selection committee recommended one candidate, Ronnie L. Miller, the director of trial court management in the Indiana Supreme Court's Division of State Court Administration, to be interviewed by the seven justices.

Mr. Miller interviewed with the seven justices on November 18, 2004. During the interview, he showed himself to be intelligent, self-starting, able to communicate well, affable, competent, and informed. Mr. Miller's resume reflected hands-on experience in the administration of trial courts. In Indiana, he worked with 350 trial courts. He also came with outstanding references and the highest of recommendations from our neighboring state, Indiana. The Indiana courts would be sorry to lose Mr. Miller, but glad for him to have the opportunity of advancement, which would not be available to him in Indiana for some time.

Despite the excellent qualifications of Mr. Miller for the position of State Court Administrator, on December 1, 2004, I returned a phone call from Justice Taylor, who unexpectedly proposed the idea that the new State Court Administrator should be Carl Gromek. Mr. Gromek is currently serving as chief of staff in the office of the chief justice.

The next day, December 2, 2004, the court met for a regularly scheduled conference. Although the State Court Administrator appointment was not on the administrative agenda, the matter was raised during the executive update from Chief Justice Corrigan. At that time, it was suggested that Mr. Gromek could function as both State Court Administrator and chief of staff in the office of the chief justice. Given the unexpected consideration of Mr. Gromek for the appointment, I stated that I had concerns and would be preparing a memo for the court addressing those concerns.

A special executive conference was scheduled for December 9, 2004. At that conference, I provided the justices a memo laying out some of my concerns regarding the possible appointment of Mr. Gromek. As I stated in my December 9 memo, I have several serious objections to appointing Mr. Gromek as the State Court Administrator.

First, Mr. Gromek never submitted his resume for consideration by the selection committee; in fact he served on the selection committee. The excellent effort put forth by the members of the search committee was a waste of time. The committee's recommendations were rejected and an alternative, who was never even an applicant for the position, never interviewed with the selection committee or the justices, and who served on the selection committee, was appointed by the court.

The justices have every right to reject the recommendation of the selection committee. But fair and just process requires that the selection committee be reconvened and Mr. Gromek, without voting as a member of the selection committee, be interviewed for the position. The selection committee could then recommend Mr. Gromek or not. Informing and involving the selection committee would also allow the selection committee to recommend to the court another of the applicants that it had screened and interviewed, or re-start the process and put out a call for more applicants.

Second, the same person should not hold the positions of both State Court Administrator and chief of staff in the office of the chief justice. The State Court Administrator is a position created by the Michigan Constitution, 1963 Const. art 6, section 3:

> The Supreme Court shall appoint an administrator of the courts and other assistants of the Supreme Court as shall be necessary to aid in the administration of the courts of this state. The administrator shall per-form administrative duties assigned by the court.

Under the supervision of this court, the State Court Administrator assists in the administration of justice in Michigan's 250 trial courts. The State Court Administrator works directly with Michigan's 580 trial judges to, among other things, promote equity, efficiency, and accessibility to the courts. While the chief of staff position could easily become a part-time job, or be eliminated completely, be assured that the position of State Court Admin-istrator is not a part-time job. It is an office required by the Michigan Con-stitution.

Third, and most importantly, in my opinion Mr. Gromek is not qualified to take the position of State Court Administrator.

Mr. Gromek has no experience working with trial courts on his resume in his court file. His resume reflects that all of his experience is at the appellate level, primarily with the Court of Appeals. Mr. Gromek was a law clerk at the Court of Appeals, a partner in a Detroit law firm doing appellate work, director of research and clerk of court at the Michigan Court of Appeals, and chief of staff in the office of the chief justice. Mr. Gromek's appellate court experience has little if anything to do with the work of the State Court Ad-ministrator.

As detailed in the court's job description for the State Court Administrator, adopted by this court in July 2004, the duties of that office include:

> Develop, implement, and evaluate methods for overseeing operation of trial courts. Develop proposals for new rules and administrative orders relating to administration of courts for consideration by the Supreme

Court. Oversee work groups charged with developing administrative procedures for court improvement.

Advise the chief justice and justices regarding the development of goals, objectives, policies and procedures for the effective administration of justice in the trial courts. Interact with other executive staff of the court in goal setting and administrative efficiency efforts.

If Michigan work experience was a requirement of the State Court Administrator position, then there should not have been a *national* job search and this requirement should have been included in the job description. Moreover, given Mr. Gromek's exclusive focus on the appellate court, his resume exhibits no more familiarity with Michigan trial courts than did Mr. Miller's. Similarly, if it were a requirement of the position that an applicant have supervised a certain number of people, then that requirement should have been included in the job description. I note that many outstanding former chief justices such as Justice Cavanagh and Justice Riley had not supervised great numbers of people before they became chief justices.

After I presented my concerns, Chief Justice Corrigan and Justices Cavanagh, Kelly, Taylor, Young and Markman voted to appoint Mr. Gromek to the position of State Court Administrator and also to continue him in the position of chief of staff of the chief justice. Mr. Miller was to be offered the position of deputy State Court Administrator. Not surprisingly, Mr. Miller did not accept the offer to be a deputy to the position for which he had applied.

For the reasons stated above, I voted to appoint Mr. Miller as the State Court Administrator, and I dissent from the appointment of Mr. Gromek.[592]

The very idea of an open and published dissent in an administrative matter gave the other justices a bad case of the willies.

First, there was more memo traffic, this time from Corrigan. (December 14 would be a busy day for memo traffic and conversations.) This one went from Corrigan to all the justices:

I wanted to let you know that I just got off the phone with Judges Davis, Burton and Tina Brooks Green, who were our interview committee for the State Court Administrator search. Mike Gadola, as our legal counsel, was a witness on the call. I informed the judges regarding what had transpired in recent weeks. I indicated that the court had ultimately voted to select Carl Gromek by a 6 to 1 vote with Justice Weaver dissenting. I also informed them that we offered the position of chief deputy to Ronnie Miller and he rejected that offer. I told them, and they agreed, that we would keep confidential the objections voiced by Justice Weaver.

592 Elizabeth A. Weaver, "Memorandum [2]," 14 December 2004. Unpublished.

The judges all appreciated being participants in the process. They expressed their support for our decision[593] and appreciated being included in the selection process for the first time. In the words of Judge Freddie Burton "we were given a lemon and made lemonade."[594]

Second came a phone call later that day from Corrigan to Weaver. Mike Gadola also was on the line. Weaver taped it and then had it transcribed.

> EAW [Weaver]: Hello? Hello?
> Jan: Hi, I'm going to connect Mike Gadola to this.
> EAW: Mike Gadola?
> Jan: Uh-uh. Hang on. Mike, are you there?
> MG: Yeah.
> EAW: Is this Maura or Mike?
> CJ [chief justice]: Betty?
> EAW: Yes.
> CJ: Hi, I'm returning your call from earlier and I wanted...
> EAW: Yeah, I just wanted to let you all know that I have revised my statement.
> CJ: I saw that you did.
> EAW: I also question [Wayne County Probate Judge Freddie G.] Burton's statement, I wonder if that's going to be made public. You all making lemons out of lemonade?
> CJ: ...always not being made public.
> EAW: Who's the lemon? Miller?
> CJ: I believe he's describing the situation. I have a copy of your revised statement now. I've read it.
> EAW: Okay.
> CJ: Okay?
> EAW: Good!
> CJ: Is there anything...
> EAW: I'm sending another memo, I haven't sent, I haven't yet distributed to the selection committee because I'm quite objectionable-object to not receiving a copy of the press release in sufficient time to object to anything that might be said. I don't think that's fair process.
> CJ: Okay, well that's your...
> EAW: And, um, also it would be nice to know when it is planned.
> CJ: We'll be at 3 o'clock as I said yesterday.
> EAW: Yeah, okay.
> CJ: Your statement was due at noon and the press...
> EAW: Well, I got it out at noon.
> CJ: Pardon me?
> EAW: We got it out at noon.

---

593 Weaver contested Corrigan's claim concerning the judges: *Judge Tom Davis told me he did not endorse their decision but did tell Maura he believed the Supreme Court had the right to hire or choose somebody they were comfortable with.*
594 Maura Corrigan, "Confidential Memorandum," 14 December 2004. Unpublished.

CJ: I received it at 12:03…

EAW: Yeah, well, I think that's noon, isn't it?

CJ: Close Enough.

EAW: Yes, I would think so.

CJ: Okay, but…

EAW: We apparently had a computer glitch at 11:58.

CJ: All right, but, yeah, at 3 p.m. we're doing the press release here.

EAW: Okay. Well, it would be nice to have time to review it.

CJ: Pardon me? I want to make my position with you perfectly clear. That is, that I believe you're making an error by doing what you intend to do…

EAW: Which is what?

CJ: …Statement.

EAW: By making my statement public?

CJ: Violating the deliberative process privilege of our court, and I believe you are subjecting yourself to a defamation lawsuit. For your statement's not only about Carl Gromek but also about Ronnie Miller, because what you say in your statement is that by vote of six Ronnie Miller is unqualified.

EAW: No, I think I say that he was rejected. That doesn't make him unqualified.

CJ: You are showing that you are the only one who supported him and, ergo, saying that six people thought he was not qualified for the job. But, in my opinion, there is a slander suit available—or a defamation suit, rather— available on the basis of your statement and you don't have immunity for that according to my understanding of the law. You have only a good-faith immunity because you're acting in your administrative capacity and because of the fact…

EAW: Well, I'll see if Mr. Miller sues me, huh?

CJ: We will see if he does.

EAW: That's right.

CJ: Though he may not.

EAW: Yeah, he's probably finished with Michigan anyway.

CJ: I would counsel you that what you are doing is not a prudent or wise course of action and I counsel you in the strongest possible tone not to do what you are set out to do and, you, you…

EAW: You're trying to protect yourself.

CJ: Pardon me?

EAW: You're trying to protect yourself.

CJ: Trying to protect you and preserve your role as a justice of this court who deliberates with other justices on personnel matters…

EAW: And keep this matter secret, huh?

CJ: …is mistaken…

EAW: Who cannot know the history of how we come to conclusions? The public doesn't have a right to know how we made decisions?

CJ: The pub…

EAW: Is that your position?

CJ: Pardon me?

EAW: That we're supposed to have a secret deliberation about how we would appoint a constitutional office, something required by the constitution that the public is interested in, we're supposed to keep secret?

CJ: Betty.

EAW: That's what you're saying.

CJ: That...

EAW: That is an unfair process.

CJ: Okay.

EAW: If anybody can be sued maybe Mr. Miller will sue Young.

CJ: You like to speak about behaving lawfully and you are not in my judgment...

EAW: What is the law that I'm violating, Maura?

CJ: Pardon me?

EAW: What is the law that I'm violating?

CJ: The deliberative process privilege...

EAW: Is there a law and a deliberative process privilege?[595] Would you kindly send it to me?

CJ: Have you...?

EAW: I haven't seen any rules or any privilege about deliberative process.

CJ: Okay, Betty. I suggest you research the question. I am not researching the law for you.

EAW: Oh, thanks.

CJ: You may research it, and you will find that there is such a privilege for the decisions of the court for the process of the court before there is a decision. So, I want...

EAW: So the people can't know there was a selection committee and that it was, that the process was aborted?

CJ: The selection committee did not have the decision making power. They were advisory...

EAW: I never said they did.

CJ: Pardon me?

EAW: I never said they did. The court had every right to reject it.

CJ: Why do you...?

EAW: But in fair...and fair process...

CJ: Why do you call them the selection committee?

EAW: Hmmm?

CJ: Why do you call them the selection committee?

EAW: Because you call them the selection committee.

CJ: They were the advisory committee to us.

EAW: I think you called them the selection committee.

CJ: ...advise us.

EAW: Revised to say what they are. My understanding was the selection committee. If they are not the selection committee, I will certainly go back through my memos and see what they were ever called.

---

595 The concept of deliberative process privilege will come up again in Chapter 17 at the heart of heated debate.

CJ: Okay.

EAW: I'm not saying they're not even a selection committee.

CJ: But in any event, I, just so it's clear where I stand on this and why I believe you're mistaken.

EAW: Oh, and I appreciate that.

CJ: And I wish you would think through whether you wish to do this.

EAW: I continue to think through, but I do all the time.

CJ: All right. But then accept counsel on occasion from your colleagues. That's why we're here together.

EAW: If you want to give me counsel, you come up with the rules of where the deliberation rule that we're bound by. If you really want to help, do that.

CJ: I'm not doing your research...

EAW: You're not going to do that, no.

CJ: Ask Graham [Bateman, one of Weaver's clerks] to do research on the deliberative process.

EAW: I think that's something that the commissioners would do. I request a commissioner's report from the commissioners on the deliberative process rule that you're bringing up.

CJ: And I request you to...

EAW: I request that from the commissioners. That's something that every justice should have a right to know, and it should be very clear to every justice when they come on. If that exists, then they should know about it the minute they get there. And we've never been told anything like that, and so, therefore...

CJ: A lawyer, Betty. Hire a lawyer. The commissioners...

EAW: Well, we're all lawyers. But that's why we have commissioners, Maura. So I would...I request that. I will put that in a memo, too.

CJ: Request....

EAW: That you raise this. That may request...

CJ: I deny your request.

EAW: Well, I'm going to put it in writing so you can deny it in writing.

CJ: And say, you are making an error and making something public that is a confidential...

EAW: Well, put it down, put it all down.

CJ: Pardon me?

EAW: You've got a chance to put it all down in writing.

CJ: Well, we will certainly talk about this shortly, but at this juncture I have given you my best judgment about the error that you're making on two grounds...

EAW: Well, I don't think you have!

CJ: You do not have immunity for administrative acts when you're in violation of the deliberative process of the court and making something public that is secret and confidential, number one. Number two: you are slandering Carl Gromek and Ronnie Miller by your statement. Both of those things, Betty, put you outside, in my humble opinion, outside the scope of the immunity that you would enjoy in good faith and I have so advised you that you're making an error. As your colleague on the Supreme Court, I advise you.

EAW: Is Mr. Gadola there, your witness to this conversation? Is that the point for him?

CJ: Mr. Gadola is the Supreme Court counsel and I consulted with him on this score before we spoke.

EAW: And he's a witness, right? Mr. Gadola, do you agree with all of this?

MG: I do.

EAW: And you, too, would advise her to refuse to have the research done on this issue that she raises? And what about you, Mr. Gadola? You're counsel to the court. How come I don't see the research from you?

MG: To answer your question, there's nothing which says you have to release your statement today. You may conduct your research on these questions and come to your own conclusion.

EAW: I heard them say that I have to release it today, have I?

CJ: Pardon me?

EAW: I haven't said that I have to release it today.

CJ: No, you haven't.

MG: You have ample time, then, to conduct your own...

EAW: And I again request this court to give information that should be vital to every justice that we have some deliberative secret rule. And you and—Chief Justice Corrigan and Mr. Gadola—are refusing that.

CJ: I refuse to participate in...

EAW: You refuse to give me the information that you assert is true.

CJ: That's a tradition....

EAW: Did you do the research yourself?

CJ: Betty, the court has...

EAW: Is tradition a law at this court?

CJ: ...an executive session.

EAW: So, it's a tradition of an executive session now.

CJ: Has a right to have its deliberations regarding personnel matters kept confidential.

[BREAK IN RECORDING]

CJ: ...the court's search process. You're in error and in violating what goes on in executive session. I believe you're in error.

EAW: Well, Maura, you can put anything you want in executive session and make it secret, can't you!

CJ: Pardon me, Betty?

EAW: Uh, you and the chief justice, or four of you who vote, can put anything you want in executive session and make it a secret. That's your theory. And that's what you do anyway. And just drop it on us...

MG: When the court is in executive session, its deliberations are...

EAW: Well, and who brings up what's in executive session? The chief justice! Do we have any control or any notice about what's going to be on executive session?

MG: Of course...

EAW: No! We have no notice about what's going on until we get there and whatever the chief justice chooses to drop on us.

MG: These discussions were held in executive session and of course they are confidential. That is totally unremarkable.

EAW: Well, that's what you think!

MG: Well, it is what I think.

EAW: If that's the case, maybe it needs to change.

MG: I would hope not.

CJ: I don't [like it] when you go about changing it in this fashion, Betty. Because you're threatening the confidence of your colleagues by doing this.

EAW: I'm not threatening anybody.

MG: Prudential [shuffling of papers, can't discern] there's a legal concern in any of...

EAW: Well, that's interesting to know. And it would be well if this court got some prudence.

MG: Well, I think the court is exercising prudence. I question whether you're...whether the issue, the statement you've drafted would be prudent.

EAW: Well, I'll do what I feel I need to do and we'll see what happens.

CJ: Betty, what you might think about doing is putting your insurance carrier on notice that you're intending to do this. And maybe they'll help you with the research; you're covered by the court's policy.

EAW: Oh, now you say I'm covered by the policy? I thought you said I wasn't covered by the policy.

CJ: You have an insurance policy. I don't know the coverage question and I don't know that they'll decline to cover you or not. But you have an individual policy. Each one of us does; the court pays for it every year. And I'm, you know, concerned about what you're planning to do here and ask you to think it through. That's it.

EAW: Well, I continue to request what I did, that I think our commissioners and our legal counsel should give us information that you asserted were law, and you all are refusing to do it, no surprise to me.

CJ: You're behaving lawlessly, and the burden is on you...

EAW: I haven't. I have not behaved lawlessly. That will remain to be seen.

CJ: Pardon me?

EAW: You have no proof I have behaved lawlessly.

CJ: You haven't done anything yet. I'm cautioning you against what you plan, what you have told us you plan to do. You're right; you haven't done anything yet. You're just suggesting that you will do so. If you decide to do this it is my belief that it is one, lawless; and two, imprudent. And that's my position, Betty.

EAW: Well, I understand it.

CJ: All right. In any event...

EAW: I don't agree with it, but I understand it.
CJ: Okay. Thank you for your time this afternoon and...
EAW: I will be sending another memo.
CJ: Okay, fine.
EAW: Okay. Thank you. Bye-bye.
MG: Bye.
CJ: Bye.[596]

Well, it's like they're doing me a favor, you know?

It was evident to Weaver that Corrigan's verbal onslaught was bluster. But Weaver didn't learn until years later that Corrigan already knew the answer to the questions about deliberative process privilege and a justice revealing information—she suggested that Weaver and her law clerks do the research when Corrigan had done exactly that, but years earlier.

In July of 2001, Corrigan had her security director and also then-chief of staff Carl Gromek research the issue after there had been a leak at the court. The issue at hand may have been the hotly debated 2000 Public Act 381—the Carrying Concealed Weapon (CCW) law.

The Supreme Court majority overturned a Court of Appeals ruling that found the act was subject to public referendum.[597]

If this was the case in question, word of the Supreme Court ruling got out almost half a day before the planned release to the media. Reporter Tim Skubik detailed how he wound up with an exclusive based on a tip from an inside source:

> Bit by bit, the decision story started to fall into place for me. Remember, there are plenty of folks working at the court and while the security was tight, there were ways to get the information, if you made the right calls.[598]

The result was a scoop and a furious chief justice who threatened him:

> The chief justice said she was "angry and upset. This is the first time that had happened" and she took steps to make sure it didn't happen again. She warned if it occurred again, she would call in the state police to investigate.[599]

596 Transcript of telephone conversation among Elizabeth A. Weaver, Maura D. Corrigan, and Michael Gadola, 14 December 2004. Unpublished.
597 *Michigan United Conservation Clubs v Secretary of State*, No. 119274, Michigan Supreme Court, 29 June 2001, http://publicdocs.courts.mi.gov:81/OPINIONS/FINAL/SCT/20010629_S119274(61)_MUCC.JUN1.01.PDF.
598 Tim Skubick, *Off the Record*, University of Michigan Press (Ann Arbor, Michigan, 2003), 320.
599 Ibid., 321.

What Skubick didn't know was there was an investigation going on, and it was directed at the possibility that a justice had leaked the story, although it was possible that someone else, perhaps a high-ranking staffer, had spoken out of turn. In any event, Skubick reported the correct outcome but with the wrong vote. He had said it was 5-2[600] when in reality it was 4-3.

Why do we think that it was more likely a justice than a staffer? Because of the language of the memorandum to Corrigan from Gromek:

> Attached is _____'s investigation report. After reviewing it, I question whether a Supreme Court justice violates any constitutional statutory, court rule or ethical provision by disclosing the outcome of a court decision to a member of the press prior to the official release of the opinion.[601]

As it related to court rules and ethical standards, Gromek found no fault. It didn't rise to misconduct in office, nor did it violate the Code of Judicial Conduct. Gromek highlighted part of Canon 3A(6): "A judge should abstain for public comment about a pending or impending proceeding in any court."[602] That was as close as he could come, and the point in question didn't rise to crossing a line; the matter was neither pending nor impending—it was resolved. And, further, the rest of the Canon gave justices room to comment even during pending or impending proceedings:

> This subsection does not prohibit a judge from making public statements in the course of official duties or from explaining for public information the procedures of the court or the judge's holdings or actions.[603]

Gromek did let Corrigan know that the American Bar Association had a provision "which explicitly proscribes the disclosure of nonpublic information" that MIGHT have covered the situation, but Michigan had never adopted it. And Texas DID have a law that prohibited any outside discussion of events: appellate judges, including justices, could reveal information only through "a court's judgment, a written opinion or in accordance with Supreme Court guidelines for a court approved history project."[604]

When it came to considering a statutory violation, Gromek wrote:

> If the disclosure of nonpublic information is deemed misbehavior in office or violation of duty, then the conduct may seemingly be punished as a contempt of court. However, there are no published decisions from Michigan applying the contempt power in such a situation.[605]

---

600 Nor did he correct that in his book, still reporting the wrong number of votes for each side.
601 Carl L. Gromek, Memorandum to Chief Justice Maura D. Corrigan, 25 July 2001, unpublished.
602 Michigan Code of Judicial Conduct, http://jtc.courts.mi.gov/codeofconconduct.htm.
603 Ibid.
604 Gromek.
605 Ibid.

And, finally, when it came to any provisions under common law:

> Neither common-law offense—obstruction of justice or misconduct in office—applies neatly to the situation at hand. Disclosing the results of a Supreme Court decision to the press shortly before the official release of the case, although a breach of trust or confidence, does not seem to rise to the level of interfering with or impeding the decision-making process. Nor does it involve a criminal intent. Therefore it is doubtful that the conduct would constitute common-law obstruction of justice or misconduct in office.[606]

So, Chief Justice Corrigan was fulminating against Justice Weaver about an ill-defined deliberative process privilege in 2004, alleging things Corrigan knew weren't true as early as 2001.[607]

And by 2004, the end of December, Maura and Gadola were calling me. And they now were going to put Gromek in charge and they were going to deceive the public and to threaten me. ...The stupidity that I would be sued because I would put my dissent over the appointment of Gromek out to the public—which I had every right to do. When I realized they were that far off that they would call me and threaten me, and tell me they had reviewed my insurance, and I wouldn't be covered, and I would be sued...I knew that was all a bunch of baloney.

I had already had an attorney and had been talking to him for several years about the problems at the court and what they might try to do to me, and I knew that I would not be sued. I knew the court could be sued, but I also knew it was all baloney, because this gentleman from Indiana was no more going to sue the court or me—because I wasn't saying anything against him; I was speaking against Gromek's appointment. And Gromek would be the State Court Administrator, and he's a public official; it's in the Constitution.

They were just trying to intimidate me; that's where they're going to go. But if that's the depth to which they will go, it was useless. If this is where Maura really was...that she would fall and lower herself to that level....

As far as being given a copy of the press release, Weaver might as well have been pitching pennies into a fountain. But she sent one more message in the form of a memo:

> It is now 2:45 p.m. I understand that the press release for the appointment of the State Court Administrator will be released to the public at 3 p.m., and I have not received a copy of it. On important matters, such as the appointment of a constitutional position like the State Court Administrator, the press release should be made available to the justices in sufficient time (at least an hour) for the justices to comment on or object to it before it is released. Fair process requires this.

---

606 Ibid.
607 The issue of deliberative privilege comes up again later in the book. It turns out it was based solely on a supposed tradition, never codified, and not always adhered to.

For your information, at this time I have not distributed to the selection committee my revised dissenting statement.[608]

That would be "fair process" as Weaver understood and practiced it. Corrigan held to a different standard. The press release came out at its assigned time:

Attorney Carl L. Gromek of Lansing, who has served as Chief of Staff of the Michigan Supreme Court for the past four years, will also serve as State Court Administrator starting January 3, 2005, the Michigan Supreme Court announced today.

The Court voted 6-1 to appoint Gromek to the position. Justice Elizabeth A. Weaver dissents.

Representatives of the Michigan Judges Association, Michigan Probate Judges Association, and Michigan District Court Judges Association participated in the selection process for a new State Court Administrator.

Wayne County Probate Judge Freddie G. Burton, Jr., who represented the Michigan Probate Judges Association in the process, said "We are very pleased with the final product of the search and the selection of Carl Gromek as the State Court Administrator. We are also very pleased that the State Court Administrator's position is being merged with that of Supreme Court Chief of Staff. We look forward to working with Mr. Gromek as he goes forward in these dual duties."

Chief Judge Tina Brooks Green of the 34th District Court, who represented the District Court Judges Association in the selection process, agreed. "The position of State Court Administrator is obviously one of tremendous responsibility,"

she said. "The choice of Mr. Gromek is a wise one and will, we believe, reap future benefits for Michigan's justice system."[609]

Gromek will head the State Court Administrative Office (SCAO), the administrative arm of the Michigan Supreme Court. He will also continue to serve as the Court's Chief of Staff, said Chief Justice Maura D. Corrigan.

"The State Court Administrator must be a consummate manager, someone who is well versed in every aspect of administration, from budget issues to technology to human resource matters," said Corrigan. "Mr. Gromek has demonstrated, over a period of many years and in various positions of great responsibility, that he has a genius for administration. He has amply justified

---

608 Elizabeth A. Weaver, "Memorandum [3]" 14 December 2004.
609 Without an endorsement for Gromek, Court of Appeals Judge Alton "Tom" Davis was the only one of the three judges not mentioned in the press release.

the high confidence that this Court and the Court of Appeals have placed in him over the years. And indeed, as Chief of Staff, he has already made many improvements to the administration of Michigan's justice system."

Corrigan also thanked State Court Administrator John D. Ferry, who is stepping down at the end of the year.

"For seven years, Mr. Ferry has served the trial courts of this state faithfully and well," Corrigan said. "The Court thanks him for his dedication and his efforts to improve the administration of justice in Michigan, and we wish him all the best."

In addition to his Chief of Staff duties, Gromek will oversee administration of Michigan's 244 trial courts. His responsibilities will include supervising SCAO's four regional offices and all divisions of SCAO, including the Friend of the Court Bureau, Child Welfare Services, Office of Dispute Resolution, Judicial Information Systems, and Michigan Judicial Institute.[610]

The e-mail to the justices with the release attached came at 3:46:33 p.m. that afternoon. The communication was from Chief Justice Corrigan, and disseminated by Marcia McBrien.[611]

It was public and it was official, and the choice of Gromek could hardly have been worse, said Weaver:

That was my opinion, having known and worked with him at the Court of Appeals, and his obvious lack of any kind of qualification to be administering trial courts when he's had no trial court experience; his entire experience was at the Court of Appeals.

Furthermore, he didn't have the temperament to do the work and would be the worst kind of person to do the job. We already were living with him as chief of staff, and I had dealt with him at the Court of Appeals, and he's not a person that should have a lot of power.

She decided not to publish her dissent. That must have given her fellow justices great relief; from their perspective, their badgering had worked. So the matter was finished except for the fulminating animosity against her.

But, administrative things are never published—or, were never published then. I mean—unnecessary secrecy was the demand.

Why didn't Weaver go public, as she said she would?

610 Marcia McBrien, "Carl L. Gromek named State Court Administrator by supreme court," Michigan Supreme Court, 14 December 2004.
611 Maura Corrigan, "Announcement of Carl L. Gromek as State Court Administrator," e-mail, forwarded by Marcia McBrien, 14 December 2002, unpublished.

If, in fact, I had published my dissent, I concluded no one would care, and I knew they would lie about it all. I could put it out, but I felt it was useless because I had decided that it was an impossible situation; that there was so much deceit, so much going—that I could not do anything for. It didn't matter.

All the good she had seen in her colleague/friends on the court was negated by their ongoing deceit and bullying; Weaver realized that her efforts were futile. The betrayal of principles and the law was dismaying. Remember, this was the same time as that of the rings.

So, she determined that she would leave the court, resign. She would ponder the announcement, but she was pretty sure that's the way it would play out.

I made the decision at Christmas of 2004. I thought it over, during the holidays, and talked with those people close to me—not political people, and I realized this was an illustration of two of my principles: never try the impossible; and don't breathe an immoral atmosphere unless in an attempt to purify it.

She came back from her break and made her announcement.

On January 13th of 2005, having the day before given a speech at a swearing-in of an Oakland County judge at a big event down there (and where I came up with my first statements about what every judge and justice should be)—I announced that I intended to leave in October of 2005.

Only after she told the public via the media that she intended to depart did she talk with the Governor and others in political leadership.

I made the calls around out of courtesy and called Governor Granholm, and she said, "Well, I didn't want it to be you." That was the Governor who always wanted to get to appoint somebody to the Supreme Court and finally did, by the way, many years later.

So, it was time to leave. I hoped my leaving the court would be a serious message to people. Well, I only had stayed because I felt there was a possibility to reform from within. I figured the last thing I could do for the people was to say, "I'm out of here," and, hopefully, people would get the idea there was really something wrong, because I had just been elected two years before, and I had six more years— could have served another eight years after that. So I'm giving up this position; there must have been a reason why I was leaving.

And I got calls from some decent Republicans saying, just, "Oh, don't do this."

And there were others, Republicans and Democrats alike, people in the grocery store, in line at the bank, at the hairdressers. This unsettled and trying time was part of her growth, too. In the end, she didn't leave in 2005. But that was after an infusion of hope, hope that she needed to stay on the battlefield.

So, she announced that she had changed her mind. She was staying. Imagine the tooth grinding of the Engler Majority. They had been "this close" to being rid of her.

And at the time of the Gromek appointment, there were plenty of other issues confronting the court, issues that would determine the course of justice. And in following the personnel and personal stories we've jumped the time line again. We have to go back to look at some cases of just how justice was made at the court.

Chapter 13

Two Tokes over the Line
In re Gilbert

Some of the decisions being made at the court weren't faring much better than the decisions in personnel matters. And Justice Elizabeth Weaver's reservations of her colleagues' conduct weren't always just because of what they would do. Sometimes it was about what they wouldn't.

Enter the story of the toking judge.

The facts of the case were fairly simple: Thomas S. Gilbert was a district judge sitting at the 86th District Court for Antrim, Grand Traverse, and Leelanau counties. He was midway through a four-year term.

He made a trip downstate Oct. 12, 2002, to attend a Rolling Stones concert at Ford Field. While there, he took a few hits from a joint that was being passed along. Not surprisingly, somebody was watching, in this case a woman from Elk Rapids (in Antrim County). When she returned home and came forward, she was interviewed by Chief District Judge Michael Haley and Thomas Phillips, another of the district's judges. Here's the newspaper story that followed:

> Haley said he interviewed an unidentified Elk Rapids woman last week who reported she witnessed Gilbert twice take a drag from a marijuana cigarette as it was passed along a row of people at the concert.
>
> "She was concerned about it because she saw a judge smoking a joint and she was rightfully concerned," Haley said.
>
> Haley, Phillips and several other court staff members also happened to be at the Rolling Stones concert on Oct. 12, but they were seated in separate sections of the stadium and did not witness Gilbert smoke marijuana.
>
> Gilbert, a former Traverse City commissioner, was not available for comment, but Haley provided a written statement from Gilbert.

"I broke the law by twice puffing on a marijuana cigarette during a rock concert," Gilbert wrote. "I deeply regret this error in judgment, for I have let down my fellow judges, the court staff, my family, and the community."

Gilbert will be on voluntary leave until at least Nov. 15, pending a professional assessment for substance abuse. Gilbert can return to the bench upon recommendation of a substance abuse treatment provider, but he will be limited to hearing civil cases until further notice, Haley said.

"Based on what I know about Tom personally and professionally, I cannot believe that this is just a gross judgment error or a character flaw. I believe that this conduct is the result of substance abuse" that also involved alcohol, Haley said.

Haley, who in an interview was clearly troubled by the revelation, said he believes people, including judges, should get a second chance.

"Judges come in all shapes and sizes, they have all kinds of personal issues, problems, chemical dependency, and they're human beings," he said. "Judge Phillips and I and the staff would like to see him back on the bench, we're behind him, we believe he's a good man."

But he also said his concern for Gilbert is secondary to his concern for the integrity of the court.

"I will do everything I can do to ensure the integrity of the court, which I believe is very good at this time," he said.

Haley said he needs time to consider the implications of the incident for the court. For example, as chief judge, Haley may bar Gilbert from hearing certain criminal cases, such as marijuana cases.

Meanwhile, Gilbert, who is two years into a four-year term, has submitted a misconduct disclosure to the Michigan Judicial Tenure Commission.

According to Haley, after an investigation, the commission's options for Gilbert include a private censure, a public censure, a suspension with or without pay, limiting his judicial duties, such as precluding him from presiding over criminal cases, or removing him from the bench.[612]

In addition to the news story, there was a statement from Judge Gilbert acknowledging that he broke the law. In part, the statement read:

---

612 Patrick Sullivan, "Judge goes on leave for smoking joint at concert," *Traverse City Record-Eagle*, 8 November 2002, 1A-2A, http://archives.record-eagle.com/2002/nov/08gilber.htm.

I have a duty to uphold the integrity of the office of the district court, and I failed by making a thoughtless and irresponsible decision. I am reporting my misconduct, making a full disclosure, to the Michigan Judicial Tenure Commission. I will be seeking a professional assessment and will follow through with all recommendations made. I extend my deepest apologies, pledge that this will never happen again, and hope and pray the community will eventually forgive me for my reckless actions.[613]

Note that he refers to "a thoughtless and irresponsible decision" and that he's reporting his misconduct. Both are in the singular.

Traverse City is Weaver's home territory—that's where her Supreme Court office was—and it's not surprising that she knew Judge Thomas Gilbert. She had attended his swearing in. She knew his parents much better, though.

The irony of that is, I might have been with his parents in Saginaw at a fundraiser for myself on the night Tom Gilbert was is Detroit. I was up for re-election in November, and his parents and I were talking about the fact that he'd gotten elected and that was nice, and he seemed to be doing well.

And his father was a retired probate and circuit judge and a longtime supporter of me, and they were there at the fundraiser.

There would be more as the story of the judge's transgressions evolved. There was nationwide news coverage, even a joke by Jay Leno on *The Tonight Show*. Judge Gilbert had become the poster boy both for those who favored legalizing marijuana and those who found in him an example of what was wrong with society.

Letters to the editor both excoriated and exonerated Gilbert. The local bar association wanted him off the bench:

> The 12-member board, which represents about 300 attorneys who practice law in Grand Traverse, Antrim and Leelanau counties, drafted a three-page statement at a meeting Wednesday night calling for the judge's resignation.
>
> [...]
>
> Attorney Paul Jarboe, a member of the bar association's governing board and chairman of the association's district court judicial liaison committee, said he and other board members believed it was their responsibility to take a position on Gilbert in reaction to the impact Gilbert's admission has had on the 86th District Court.[614]

613 Thomas Gilbert, "Judge's statement," *Traverse City Record-Eagle*, 8 November 2002, 1A.
614 "Week in Review: Bar association board calls for Gilbert to resign," *Traverse City Record-Eagle*, 24 November 2002, http://archives.record-eagle.com/2002/nov/24week.htm

By that time in late November, Gilbert had been for an evaluation by the State Bar of Michigan Lawyers and Judges' Assistance Program and was off to Minnesota's Hazelden Foundation Center for nearly a month's worth of in-patient substance abuse treatment.[615]

He had come forward to the paper with a statement, that it had been the worst mistake of his life, and that he wouldn't have done it if he hadn't been drinking, and that he had an issue with alcohol; and so he was taking a 28-day paid leave and going for treatment; and the implication was that the drug thing was a one-time affair; that it was the dumbest thing or the worst thing he had done in his life.

...And this was the judge who handled the drug cases and was putting people in jail for the very thing that he had done and admitted that he had done downstate.[616]

All that was in her daily paper.

And what it meant to me was that we would probably be getting a JTC recommendation on this at some point unless he resigned before they acted.

He reported himself to the Judicial Tenure Commission, so we knew—assuming the Judicial Tenure Commission was going to operate and had a duty to investigate—it would. And it would appear, with somebody admitting it in a published statement, that the JTC should come to us with recommendation for either censure, suspension with or without pay, removal, or retirement. And retirement wouldn't be an issue because Gilbert had only been a judge two years, or less than two years, when he committed the offense.

Paul Fischer, the executive director of the JTC, handled the investigation. His recommendation came to the JTC, which handled it and made its recommendation to the Supreme Court. All this is ordinarily in secret for the protection of the process and integrity of the court, especially if the charges turn out to be unfounded. Only after the JTC makes its recommendation are matters supposed to be made public. The JTC cannot enact sanctions, but it can recommend that the Supreme Court do so.

And until the JTC makes an official recommendation, the JTC cannot respond or make public comment about anything and has to keep confidentiality. The Supreme Court has the ability to make confidentiality rules; it makes the rules for the JTC.

The confidentiality of what the JTC does, does not mean the Supreme Court needs to be confidential about such things, because any time it's going to make a decision, the Supreme Court is bound by Article 6, Section 6, that it has to have its decisions and its dissents in writing, with reasons, and obviously that must mean the public should be able to see it. So it should be published.

---

615 "Order 123270, *In re The Honorable Thomas S. Gilbert, Judge, 86th District Court*," Michigan Supreme Court, 25 September 2003.
616 Elizabeth A. Weaver writing in "Memorandum," [from a commissioner, 27 June 2003, 3, unpublished] added this: "A review of the court records of the 86th District Court would reveal that Judge Gilbert sentenced more than 50 defendants for controlled substances violations while serving as a judge."

The JTC reported to the Supreme Court its recommendation in a consent agreement on Feb. 12, 2003. It called for a public censure and a 90-day suspension (less the 28 days already served during residential treatment).

What we had here was a secret agreement. The JTC had no desire for it to go out. The desire was to keep this confidential, because they weren't giving us a regular recommendation—they didn't have a hearing, a public hearing. They made a deal with the judge and, I'm assuming, his attorney [Michael H. Dettmer]. They only wanted to recommend that he be suspended 90 days, with a public censure, and that he would get credit for his 28-paid-days of going to be treated, allegedly only for alcohol or whatever, because it was supposedly an alcohol problem. So, in essence, it was a 62-day recommendation, that would be with a public censure that he shouldn't have done what he admitted doing in the paper.

Except, there was more.

What was interesting in the matter was that there was a written statement published in the newspaper from the judge that implied he had not used marijuana regularly...just that one time.

Yet, Weaver noted, in Gilbert's signed "Stipulated Facts" to the JTC in the secret deal submitted to the Supreme Court, Gilbert subsequently admitted more marijuana use than just at the concert.

Now this is important—this is a statement of "Stipulated Facts" signed and submitted by Judge Gilbert confessing the use of marijuana at least twice a year for the two years that he had been on the court—not when he was a youth, not before he was a judge, but <u>while</u> he was a judge. And he had actually sentenced people to jail for the very thing that he now is confessing he did at least four times. There would be other questions: was it really only four times; how did he get it; did he grow it himself; was he doing it with anyone else...?

He had told the public in an interview in the paper that his real problem was alcohol rather than drug use.

Here's part of the continuing story from the *Traverse City Record-Eagle*:

> Gilbert's first step was to get a professional assessment for alcohol abuse and then get a second opinion. Both assessments, he said, determined he has an alcohol problem.

> Gilbert stressed that the assessments did not conclude that he has a drug problem or that he is an alcoholic.

> He says his problem is that he sometimes drinks to excess and his judgment becomes impaired.

> "The assessment says that I'm not an alcoholic, but I'm as close as you can get without being one and since it's a progressive disease I'm going to not let it progress any further," he said.

Gilbert has vowed [to] give up alcohol. He hopes that may lead him to avoid in the future something like what he did on Oct. 12.

"If I hadn't been drinking alcohol that night I wouldn't have done the most stupid thing I've done in my life, which was taking a couple of hits off a marijuana cigarette," Gilbert said. "Not only should I have known better, I did know better."[617]

There was no evidence that the reporter ever asked if his marijuana use was habitual. The implication that Gilbert let stand was that he was on the verge of becoming an alcoholic, and that the observed tokes were an isolated incident while under the influence.

But that's not what he admitted to the JTC.

So we had four times now. He had attempted to deceive the public that it was a one-time event of marijuana use and that he had only an alcohol problem.

And what was of concern, too, was the JTC was making a deal where it would be kept from the public. The deal was this would not be revealed. Although, interestingly enough, he was to be publicly censured, which would make one wonder: What would the court tell the public? It is publishing a public censure of a judge whose statements have led the public to think he only did it once, but he's telling the Supreme Court in his signed "Stipulated Facts" that he did it twice a year during two years. This would be deceitful.

The public would never know what he actually admitted to the court and to the JTC. This is not transparency, and it's actually hypocrisy and deceit. And, really, the JTC was asking the court to be a part of that.

Now, to me, it was a no-brainer case. The local bar association clearly saw it. Judge Gilbert was not worthy of the job. And once any kind of recommendation comes to us, we did have the power to reject the proposal, this consent agreement.

The judge would have to have been informed that we were not accepting it, and that he could withdraw his consent to the discipline. There was no rule, however, that we had to keep all that private.

On February 12th and thereafter, it became the subject of discussion: what were we going to do? There were those who simply wanted to accept it, and there were those who thought maybe 62 days wasn't enough, and there was me who said, "I will not accept it. We have to reject it," and that we should simply say, "We're going to remove you. If you want to withdraw your consent, then do so. But this will be published," and that would be the end of it.

Initially, Young and Corrigan did agree with me, briefly, that removal was the right course.

---

617 Patrick Sullivan, "Gilbert reveals private thoughts," *Traverse City Record-Eagle*, 17 November 2002, http://archives.record-eagle.com/2002/nov/17judge1.htm.

But they changed their minds.

And the argument came then, "We still have to keep it secret." Even a commissioner of ours wrote in a memo that we had cases where the court had kept such things secret.

So, this kind of thing had happened before? ...Maybe so, but not during Weaver's nine years at the court. And not about a case like this. It was already wide-open to the public; the news media were following it and would demand an explanation for whatever happened. After all, Gilbert was a laughing matter on the *Tonight Show*. Weaver didn't like anything about the proposal that would keep it quiet.

While Young and Corrigan had joined the others they had second thoughts. The justices had brought up the matter again in a March 6, 2003, conference. Corrigan said that 90 days was not enough of a penalty. In a March 11 memo, Markman said he agreed. In an e-mail from Young, also dated March 11, he began to see a looming problem of public perception.

> I am becoming increasingly uncomfortable with the so-called "confidentiality" of this process. The JTC has, in my view, produced a consent agreement that (1) adds surprising new allegations of misconduct; (2) failed adequately to explain the meaning of that new misconduct or its relation to the previously reported misconduct in its recommendation; and (3) has fostered, through this non-public sanctioning process, the impression that no action is being taken by this court even though Gilbert's attorney has told the news media that we have the case.
>
> I do not believe that this court is bound to maintain the confidentiality but am interested in knowing what other members of the court think about the possibility of our being maneuvered into what may look to the public as our failure to act on a high profile matter.
>
> Finally, I am becoming more persuaded that 90 days is not a sufficient sanction under these circumstances. In the event the court chooses to eliminate an express provision in the order stating that 90 days is insufficient, I may simply file a concurrence stating my own views.[618]

His views on the confidentiality of the matter were to change—or were to appear to change—when it came to his message to the public...but that came later. In the meantime, he had more thoughts about the matter and its resolution at an upcoming conference.

> I am unwilling to give the impression that I believe that 62 days of suspension (disguised as 90 days) is an adequate sanction when we have been provided new information that Gilbert's drug use is broader than that known to the public. Consequently, requiring Gilbert to appear at a session of the

618 Robert P. Young, Jr., e-mail, 11 March 2003, unpublished.

court for public rebuke would undoubtedly cause the public to question our judgment when it becomes known that Gilbert used drugs after he became a judge on occasions other than the one currently known.[619]

It is at that March 20th meeting that Weaver laid down the law, literally and figuratively.

The Constitution prevails. And when the court makes a decision, then you have to have a written order and the reasons for your decision and the reasons for your dissent. And I dissented, and there was a lot of argument because I then laid out what went on. And I wanted the thing to be published.

In her dissent, she not only listed the reasons why Gilbert should have been removed, but she also dissented from the "majority's failure to state what discipline it would impose."[620]

That dissent was revealing. Too revealing for her colleagues. The first response after the conference came from Maura Corrigan the next day:

> Betty, I wish to stress at the outset that I agree with you regarding the seriousness of Judge Gilbert's conduct. I believe that the ultimate result should be his removal from the bench for his acknowledged and repeated criminal conduct.[621]

Corrigan went on to lay out a way she thought she could do that under the court rules that would involve simply sending it back to the JTC for unspecified "further proceedings":

> Rather than further damaging the public's confidence in the judiciary, I believe this provision [MCR 9.225 as amended] helps to maintain and restore public confidence. In other words, the touchstone of our judicial (and disciplinary) system is that everyone, regardless of status or factual guilt, is entitled to due process. Although often not as swift as we would like, the individual stages of the discipline process assure the public that actions that impair confidence in the judiciary are not only disciplined, but disciplined in a fair and just manner.

> My concern is that summary action, without affording Judge Gilbert an opportunity to respond, would raise the appearance of denial of due process and risk further eroding public confidence in the judiciary. I believe, however, that it is possible to reject the recommended discipline as insufficient, give Judge Gilbert an opportunity to respond, *and* ensure that the Judicial Tenure Commission cannot quietly dismiss the case.[622]

619 Robert P. Young, Jr., e-mail, 19 March 2003, unpublished.
620 Elizabeth A. Weaver writing in "Second Memo," by an unnamed commissioner, 27 June 2003, unpublished.
621 Maura J. Corrigan, "Memorandum," 21 March 2003, unpublished.
622 Ibid.

Weaver's copy of the memorandum is covered in observations and analysis in her hand. Corrigan was providing eyewash to try to make something look better than it was. And under law, it wouldn't work. Beyond that, it made no sense. Judge Gilbert had publicly admitted at least enough of his bad behavior to open him to swift action.

Young wrote the next day about Weaver's dissent.

> ...I am writing to implore you to reconsider issuing your proposed statement in this matter.
>
> I know that you feel passionately about this case. Indeed, I have agreed with much of your counsel concerning how this court might protect itself from the public misperception that it might be engaged in a whitewash. In acknowledging this, I feel I must tell you as someone who cares about you that I believe your statement is "over the top" and unseemly insofar as it prejudges how the matter should ultimately be decided.
>
> I believe your strong beliefs have caused you to abandon your typically more restrained approach to the work of the court and blinded you to how your statement will be interpreted—as rank public grandstanding for your home community.
>
> Because of your counsel, the proposed rejection of the proposed consent recommended is being published—thus surely insulating this court from any public belief that we have taken no action in this JTC matter or merely "rolled over" in an effort to sweep this matter from the public stage. In so acting, I believe that, given the high profile of this case, the JTC cannot merely let it drop without further action. To do so would expose the JTC, not this court, to unusual public contempt and pressure.
>
> In short, I believe that our proposed order effectively accomplishes all of your stated goals, save your personal desire to express your contempt for Judge Gilbert. That, I submit, is both premature and inappropriate.
>
> For all these reasons, I hope that you will reconsider your position and join in the proposed order and forego a personal denunciation of Gilbert.[623]

I had no contempt for Gilbert. But how were you going to remove a judge who has violated the law and the public trust without denouncing his actions? As with so much else in his communication, Justice Young was wrong. In the end, he and the others allowed Gilbert to stay on the bench.

She would not join the proposed order; she would not delete her dissent.

But the majority could make sure that nobody knew about it. They suppressed it. In the process, they kept their own actions secret.

---

623 Robert P. Young, Jr., e-mail to Elizabeth Weaver, 22 March 2003, unpublished.

Come April 14th, they decide to remand it[624] for the first time. I felt they also should say what they would do; to tell the JTC how far off they are. But I know that I wrote that this is what should be done and detailed—to put the truth out there. We're supposed to be proceeding, and we're not supposed to hide it from the public.

The JTC came back May 21, 2003, with the same 62-day recommendation, but with news that Judge Gilbert "offered to consent to a public censure and a six-month suspension with credit for the 28 days he spent in drug treatment."[625]

So it was up to the court to accept, modify, or reject. Six of them voted to go with the public censure and six months off the bench.

By this point, I realized under the court's exercise of unnecessary secrecy in not publishing its order back to the JTC and my dissent, that the JTC could drop the matter and send no further recommendation to the court. And without a recommendation from the JTC, there would be nothing the Supreme Court could do, and Gilbert would have had no discipline at all.

Weaver prepared another dissent reiterating her desire to see Gilbert off the bench.

> Judicial disciplinary proceedings are civil, not criminal, in nature. Their primary purpose is to help repair the damage done to the public's trust and confidence in the judicial system by judicial misconduct. To that end, the decisions of this court must appropriately sanction and attempt to correct a judge's misconduct. Only the removal of Judge Gilbert from the bench for the remainder of his term will begin to repair the damage to the public's trust and confidence in the judiciary caused by his criminal misconduct and sufficiently sanction him for it.
>
> Therefore I dissent from the majority's six-month suspension without pay with credit for 28 days of paid leave (effectively a five month or 152 day unpaid suspension). I also dissent again from the order that "this court's file, including this order, be and remain confidential and not open to public inspection until entry of an order of discipline or until further order of the court." I concur in the order only to the extent that the majority concludes that the Judicial Tenure Commission's recommended 90-day suspension without pay with credit for 28 days of paid leave (effectively a 62-day unpaid suspension) is insufficient.
>
> [...]
>
> The majority of this court now suppresses its order and the file in this matter a second time. The suppression conceals indefinitely from the public the true extent of Judge Gilbert's misconduct and the misleading inconsisten-

---

624 A remand is a sending back of a case for further consideration because what has been advanced to the court is not considered by the court a sufficient solution.
625 Elizabeth A. Weaver writing in Order 123270, 8-9.

cies between his public statement and his admissions to the commission and this court.[626]

The commissioner was ready to let it go out—again without Weaver's latest dissent—unless there were some reason to hold it. That came from Cliff Taylor in an e-mail: "Please hold this case. Upon further consideration, I would simply state that the proposed discipline is inadequate without more."[627]

So the case hung around until the court responded Sept. 11, 2003.

> [T]he court unanimously rejected the commission's recommendation as "insufficient." A majority of six justices—Corrigan, Cavanagh, Kelly, Taylor, Young, and Markman—agreed that a six-month unpaid suspension would be appropriate and gave Judge Gilbert ten days to withdraw pursuant to MCR 9.225, or an order imposing a six-month unpaid suspension would enter on September 25.[628]

Weaver again wrote a dissent. And again the court...

> [S]upressed the order of decision and the file "until entry of an order of discipline or until further order of the court" over my dissent again objecting to the suppression.[629]

That meant nothing was coming out until Sept. 25. And what was coming out included the stipulated suspension time so that Judge Gilbert could withdraw from the agreement if he desired. He made no movement to withdraw, but he did notify the court that he had filed his petition to run for re-election. He had to do it before the secret-deal sanctions went into place or he'd miss the filing window.

Because once he was suspended, he would not be able to file while he was a suspended judge, or at least that would certainly be questionable. And then he lets us know that he's going to accept the deal.

...So, for him, better to file early than not at all. It was pretty clear that he didn't see his crimes as reason enough to leave the bench on a permanent basis.

By September the 25th, they realize they're going to answer me on the suppression, and claimed that they were always going to put my dissent out...it was just a matter of time. Baloney! They didn't intend to get it out. They just changed their minds and decided they'd better get it out, or I would after they released their order without my dissent.

But when it did get out, there was the order of public censure and the six-month suspension, less the 28 days. And there was a hot mess of an attack on Weaver and her

---

626 Elizabeth A. Weaver writing in "Second Memo," by unnamed commissioner, 27 June 2003, unpublished.
627 Clifford W. Taylor, e-mail to the justices, 27 June 2003, unpublished.
628 Elizabeth A. Weaver writing in Order 123270, 8-9.
629 Ibid.

dissent. Actually, there were two of them; the first written by Cliff Taylor and signed by the Engler Four:

> Justice Weaver is very critical of our "suppression" of her written opinion in this matter until the court's final order was ready for issuance. Yet it must not be forgotten that this settlement and consent process involving Judge Gilbert, the Judicial Tenure Commission, and this court, was understood by all to be entered into on the condition of confidentiality.[630]
>
> I thought we could not violate that understanding. Nor do I understand why it would have been a good idea to be public throughout. The reason is that this process, which resulted in Judge Gilbert's acceptance of the recommended discipline, could have required the Judicial Tenure Commission to adjudicate this matter had Judge Gilbert rejected the recommended discipline. Had the commission done so, it would have eventually made a discipline recommendation to this court.[631] If our views had been published, that would undoubtedly prejudice the commission proceedings and, importantly, be unfair to Judge Gilbert.
>
> While Justice Weaver would dismiss that concern, I cannot. Judge Gilbert has behaved unwisely and that has brought him before us, but he, even as any other litigant who seeks justice before this court, is entitled to a court that calmly, deliberately, and fairly decides his case. We have, to the best of our ability, done that. To have allowed Justice Weaver midstream in this process to announce her opinion would have compromised these judicial values. While some in the public may question as unnecessarily tedious the efforts of six members of this court to be judicious, I believe that when looked at from a longer perspective, as it, of course, some day will be, it will be seen as a situation in which mature guidance prevailed.[632]

Inexplicable at that time and of concern was that the Engler justices were attempting to create a due process issue to justify secrecy and suppression of dissent when Judge Gilbert had signed and submitted his "Stipulated Facts" admitting guilt to violating the prohibited use of marijuana law at least four times while a judge, and there was his statement published in the newspaper that was deceiving the public with the implication that he had broken that law only once while a judge, and there was a recommendation from the JTC to accept a secret agreement that we were free to reject and make our own decision including to remove him as a judge on the basis of the facts in the recommendation.

Even though Young had signed on to Taylor's statement, Young wanted to go further... and everybody else signed on against Weaver. Talk about a public censure!

---

630 Taylor again was in error. Weaver clearly had no such understanding.
631 *Taylor is not accurate here. The JTC was under no obligation to make another recommendation. It could have been dropped and that would be the end of it. We can't order them to make a recommendation. That would violate the Constitution.*
632 Clifford W. Taylor, writing in Order 123270, 5-6.

I write in concurrence because of the extraordinary character of the dissent. While I do not doubt the sincerity of my dissenting colleague's passionate feeling about this matter, I do believe that her statement, if left unanswered, is calculated to, and will, mislead the public about the nature of the judicial discipline process generally and the seriousness with which this court addressed the concerns of judicial misconduct raised in this case.

Contrary to what some members of the public may believe, the Michigan Constitution places in the hands of the Judicial Tenure Commission (JTC) the initial responsibility for investigating allegations of judicial misconduct and for recommending to this court a proposed sanction when misconduct has been established. Then, and only then, is this court authorized to act by accepting, rejecting, or modifying the JTC recommendation.

As happened in this case, in some cases of alleged judicial misconduct, rather than conducting a contested hearing to establish the misconduct, the accused judge and the JTC will negotiate a "consent agreement," which is akin to a plea agreement in the criminal system. Typically, in these consent agreements, the

accused judge admits to some form of unethical conduct in exchange for a negotiated and specific sanction. This court is not bound by such a consent agreement, but our rules permit them and the parties at the JTC level negotiate them with the knowledge that, until this court makes a final determination, these negotiated agreements will remain confidential. This is in recognition that no trial on the merits of the accusations has occurred. Also, because no trial has occurred, our rules permit an accused judge to withdraw from a consent agreement and proceed to trial if this court declines to accept the consent agreement.

As in this case, when this court renders a final determination, it publishes its decisions and the sanction it has imposed.

Until this case, our dissenting colleague has respected the confidentiality of this process and has seen no need to publish to the world her final judgment on the matter until the normal process had concluded. Consequently, I am shocked that our colleague has suggested that her fellow justices have engaged in a "cover up" when our suppression orders were necessary to prevent her from issuing a public denunciation of Judge Gilbert before the process outlined in our rules had been completed.

Even a judge who had failed to live up to the responsibilities of office is entitled to a fair process. Justice Weaver stands alone in her position that she is entitled to publish her conclusions in a case before the court itself has acted. In Michigan, an accused still has a right to a trial before an execution, not the other way around.[633]

---

633 Robert Preston Young, Jr., writing in ibid., 6-7.

And, actually, somehow I was the justice who was wrong for letting the public know this. It's all so absurd. It's kind of like Alice in Wonderland; you've just gone into an unreal world. Common sense did not prevail.

Weaver had two things going for her in the war of words: the Constitution and logic.

The 1963 Michigan Constitution—as she perhaps tired of repeating, but never failed to—stipulated that all decisions of the court would be made in writing and accompanied by reasons for those decisions, including dissents.[634] And the court's responses to the JTC <u>were</u> decisions.

Weaver responded to Young and Taylor:

> A fundamental reason for this requirement is to allow the people of this state to know and assess the decision and dissents of the Supreme Court and its justices. The publication of the decisions and dissents is absolutely necessary for the people to know them and to be able to assess the court's performance of its duties.

> This court is empowered by the Constitution to make rules that provide for "confidentiality and privilege of proceeding" within the judicial disciplinary process. The current court rules do provide that if the Judicial Tenure Commission does not file a formal complaint, its members and staff "may not disclose the existence or contents" of a judicial disciplinary investigation. But that confidentiality provision does not apply to the decisions of the Supreme Court. Thus, on April 14 and September 11, 2003, when each justice decided whether to accept, reject, or modify the recommended discipline, those decisions should not have been secreted from the public.

> Plainly, "confidentiality and privilege" of judicial disciplinary proceedings does not mean suppression of the decisions of the Supreme Court. The Supreme Court has a constitutional duty to provide the public its decisions and dissents in writing. What the majority, the Judicial Tenure Commission, and every judge needs to understand is that the Supreme Court neither should be nor is under any obligation to keep its decisions regarding a judge's confessions of criminal activity secret just because those confessions were made in the Judicial Tenure Commission's process of achieving a consent agreement.

> Once a recommendation for judicial discipline is before this court and this court renders its decisions, the public needs, and has a constitutional right, to know the whole truth about a judge's wrongdoing. This information is

---

634 "Decisions of the supreme court, including all decisions on prerogative writs, shall be in writing and shall contain a concise statement of the facts, and reasons for each decision and reasons for each denial of leave to appeal. When a judge dissents in whole or in part he shall give in writing the reasons for his dissents. [Michigan Constitution of 1963, Article 6, Section 6, http://www.legislature.mi.gov/(S(qzs2riubcusi0sv2ihrfem45))/mileg.aspx?page=getObject&objectName=mcl-Article-VI-6.]

especially vital to the public because judges are elected and may run for election again.[635]

Secondly, there was no doubt that the Supreme Court would determine the outcome
of the process. Gilbert had already admitted his misconduct, had said that his fate lay
in the hands of the court. What did it matter that he and others knew that the court
and the JTC were going back and forth and that one member of the court was standing
fast that he should be gone?

*Unfortunately, my other six colleagues, for varying reasons, in the end did not agree with that, and
from the beginning, some of them would have been happy to accept the deal—and it was a deal—to
keep the public uninformed.*

Her stand alone against her colleagues did not go unremarked when at last the case
came out. Franco Castalone, the pseudonymous author of the blog The LitiGator,
commented on Weaver's dissent:

> It is well understood in this state that Justice Weaver does not stand on the
> same ground as the rest of her "conservative" colleagues do, and that there is
> sometimes some friction between them arising from that fact. For this one
> justice, who has served for many years on this court, to stand alone against
> the remaining justices on this rather important though somewhat publicly
> obscure point of procedure is, to put it mildly, quite remarkable.[636]

Perhaps it's even more remarkable with the backstory revealed.

The next part of the story of Judge Gilbert came with the public's reaction to the
court's decision. For all their calculations of public perception and that Weaver would
be seen as grandstanding, the Engler Four badly missed the mark.

*The fact that he wasn't removed was out there. And it was an outrage to the citizens. After all this
was out there, I got letters from people telling me of the other times that he had been seen doing
it somewhere. This is all after October. And I could hardly go in the grocery store and not have
somebody say, "You were right, because he did it."*

And what the Supreme Court wouldn't do, the legislature might, under "a seldom-used
provision of the Michigan Constitution which permits the ouster of a sitting judge by
a two-thirds vote of both houses of the legislature."[637]

*The public didn't accept it well, and State Senator Michelle McManus went to the judiciary
committee in the Senate, and since the Supreme Court didn't do its job, as the general public felt that
it should, the state Senate and the legislature had the power to remove a judge.*

---

635 Weaver, writing in Order 123270, 11-12.
636 "The other Gilbert case," The LitiGator, 30 September 2003, http://radio-weblogs.
com/0110436/2003/09/30.html.
637 "The other Gilbert case."

McManus went to the Senate Judiciary Committee—Alan Cropsey was chairing it—and they knew the law, and this was an outrage to them, and they decided they were going to take up the power in the Constitution, because the Supreme Court obviously didn't do its job with respect to Judge Gilbert. But he could be removed. It would be tough; it would take a two-thirds majority. But they could have their own trial.

The attorney for Gilbert asserted that, "Ooh, the Senate will have to use the court rules, and all the things that will not let hardly any evidence in," you know—people are familiar with what happens in courts. Whereas the Senate would have had an open hearing and probably, then, the real questions would have been: When did he do it? Where did he do it? With whom did he do it? Was he growing it himself, therefore manufacturing, or was he actually buying it from somebody? Who was he buying it from? He would not want to testify, but all of that would be raised. And if, in fact, he was not doing it in his bathroom, in secret, even from his wife, then it might expose other people, and that could be serious. There were a lot of people who potentially could have gone down.

Judge Gilbert then decided that he would withdraw. He then had negotiations after the Senate refused to adopt the court rules as their rules, and he negotiated and decided that he would withdraw his filing that he was running for re-election; that he would serve out his term, but he would not run for re-election. And that is what happened. And they accepted that rather than going through the trial. And that was a wise decision on the part of the judge.

But it took too long, far too long.

This thing went on from 2002 to 2004 before it finally got settled.

There is more to the story...there is always more to the story. This time, though, it's not bitterly unpleasant.

At Christmas 2003, Gilbert sent a book about alcoholism and a note to Weaver. In the note he wrote: "I am sorry for the trouble I have caused. The disease of alcoholism/addiction is as pervasive in our profession as in our communities."[638]

And Weaver subsequently encountered him at a gathering.

I suspect it would have been in 2004, maybe, at the Chamber of Commerce annual January dinner, and his wife [Marsha Smith] was an executive director of the foundation for Rotary. The Chamber is a thousand-person dinner, and he approached me there and asked if he could talk to me, and I said he could. He apologized to me for what had gone on, and I simply said to him, "You don't owe me an apology. At least—let's put it this way—I don't need an apology. This wasn't easy. I had to do my duty, and you know how much I cared about your dad and your family. It cost me—your mother was not happy with me. But that's the way it is." And I said, "It is right for you to apologize, but I don't need it, because it wasn't personal to me."

But he then proceeded to say, "Well..." He was going into an excuse, and I said, "You deceived the public, and that was very important. And you violated the law, and you threw people in jail for

---

638 Thomas S. Gilbert, letter to Elizabeth A. Weaver, 2 December 2003, unpublished.

violating the same law. It's just that simple, and it was a no-brainer. You should have stepped down in the first place and spared us all this agony."

And he said something about the chief judge ordered him to go to the paper. And I said, "It was your decision. Quit making excuses. It doesn't excuse the chief judge if that was his advice, but you didn't have to take his advice on what you should do. You should have stepped down and that would have spared us all of this agony."

And he accepted it, and that was the end of it. Or at least he didn't get mad at me then. But, so be it.

These days Gilbert is presenting seminars about substance abuse. In a 2011 seminar on medical marijuana, he listed as one of his missions to "change state laws to reduce or eliminate penalties for the medical and non-medical use of marijuana."[639]

There is at least one unanswered question: why did the Engler Four—noted for their "conservative" stance—not want to drag Gilbert into the bright lights and have him hand over his robe?

Certainly, the court had done it to other bad judges, notably in 1998 to Andrea J. Ferrara, formerly a judge of the Third Circuit (Wayne County).[640] Of course, that was before the Engler Four had taken (and taken over) the bench. But there were other misbehaving judges, drunken (and driving) judges, thieving judges, incompetent judges. And in the years shortly after this case the Supreme Court had no trouble in giving them the heave-ho.[641] What was different about Gilbert?

The Judge Gilbert thing was for me. They thought they would make me look bad in my own home area.

And she really would have if she had signed on to their reasoning. And there was some muscle flexing, too, said Weaver.

They wanted to bully me into going along to get along. It was quite an example of tyranny, unnecessary secrecy, and judicial deceit. They wanted to prove they could suppress my dissents. The real thing going on was Fieger....

That's yet to come: this was overlapping what's known as the OTHER Gilbert case, *Gilbert v DaimlerChrysler*. And the Engler Four were just warming up. In this next case,

---

639 Thomas Gilbert, "Medical marijuana: The law and how it impacts your business and employees," presentation, 23 February 2011, Traverse City, Mich., Great Wolf Lodge, http://www.nwm.org/userfiles/filemanager/756/.

640 *In re Honorable Andrea J. Ferrara*, No. 109593, Michigan Supreme Court, 28 July 1998, http://caselaw.findlaw.com/mi-supreme-court/1168592.html.

641 One of the most egregious was the case of Judge James P. Noeker, 45th Circuit (St. Joseph County). The Supreme Court removed him from the bench Feb. 1, 2005, upon the recommendation of the JTC for being untruthful about a drinking and driving incident. The vote by the court was 6-to-1 with only Cavanagh dissenting. [John Eby, "Noeker removed as judge," *The Daily News*, 2 February 2005, http://www.dowagiacnews.com/2005/02/02/noecker-removed-as-judge/.]

they would be successful in keeping the sting of her dissent in the request for rehearing out of the public eyes.

But at the conclusion of *In re Gilbert*, Weaver felt the need to clean up the mess.

I had helped Corrigan and Taylor and Young come to the Supreme Court with the idea that we would reform, we would improve the judicial services of people, we would get transparency, we would be more open, we would reform how we select justices. And none of that was going to happen, and they weren't happy with me. So it wasn't a good situation.

I felt a duty to try to straighten it out. This case revealed earlier concerns about the JTC and about discipline. But this really revealed that there was something really wrong here—there were unwritten rules about what the JTC thought they were supposed to be doing. They were not supposed to be making secret deals and forever more hiding information from the public.

In this case, the JTC let us know what was going on; they had to, but they wanted to hide things from the public. But there would be other cases where they would take authority unto themselves to act to achieve discipline. The problem would become this: the JTC has no constitutional authority to discipline; it can investigate and then make recommendations to the Supreme Court to discipline. That's it. Later the JTC would reveal itself as an agency that could and would act in secret so not even the justices would know what it had done.

And the openness at this agency was important; it was important to have a judicial system and a Supreme Court that you can have trust and confidence in. We should be able to have trust and confidence in the court and its commissions and boards. In other words, the AGC, the JTC, the Board of Law Examiners....

Trust and confidence in the court, though, were in short supply for Weaver; she'd already seen more than enough to know the ongoing deceit.

Chapter 14

Evidence of?
Or Appearance of?
Bias and Prejudice
in
Gilbert v DaimlerChrysler

One of the cases that was badly mishandled by her colleagues—one of the very worst as far as Weaver was concerned—was their decision in *Gilbert v DaimlerChrysler*.

This was an auto industry-related case; an employee, Linda M. Gilbert, was suing then-DaimlerChrysler because it did little or nothing to stop the sexual harassment directed at her by other employees. The jury trial lasted six and a half weeks in the Third Circuit Court (Wayne County) under Judge John A. Murphy.

For the plaintiff, Linda Gilbert? None other than Geoffrey Nels Fieger, a prominent and provocative Detroit-area attorney, media personality, and one-time Democratic candidate for Governor. That's important.

Now, six weeks is a long time for a trial.

There are no perfect trials. You may not have a perfect trial if it only goes for an hour. But particularly if you had a six-week trial, it would not be perfect. Mistakes are made, usually on both sides.

So, when the jury found for the plaintiff and awarded her $21 million, defendant DaimlerChrysler appealed.

The real issue in appeal is, whether there is any serious mistake of law or fact. And that was the job of the Court of Appeals, to give it a thorough review, which they did, because they had oral argument on it, and they wrote a thorough opinion.

That opinion!

Legal writing need not always be dull, soporific. Some opinions are laced with erudition, clear insights, and even—on occasion—humor. There is nothing to laugh about in this Court of Appeals opinion, but it is a thorough statement of the facts. There is literary merit here...with one small deficiency: Fieger's name was misspelled throughout; we have corrected it. No one in particular on the three-member Court of Appeals claims primary ownership, that is the nature of a *per curiam* opinion.[642]

The three judges, William C. Whitbeck, chief judge, E. Thomas Fitzgerald, and Jane E. Markey were of one mind on this, or so we're led to believe. Whitbeck, however, had the literary chops to carry this off. In addition to his legal training, he also is a graduate of the Medill School of Journalism. He is the author of a mystery, *To Account for Murder*.[643] So, some—and maybe most—of the credit for this beautiful, lucid account of the facts goes to him. At the risk of boring the reader, I am using ALL of the section on the facts. On second thought, it won't be boring: it's graphic and nasty. And revealing.[644]

> A jury awarded plaintiff Linda M. Gilbert $21 million for her claim that defendant DaimlerChrysler, Inc.,[645] violated the Michigan Civil Rights Act (CRA), MCL 37.2102 et seq., when its agents, some of Gilbert's coworkers and supervisors, sexually harassed her for more than seven years. Chrysler now appeals as of right from the trial court's order denying its motion for an evidentiary hearing, judgment notwithstanding the verdict (JNOV), a new trial, and remittitur. We affirm.
>
> I. Basic Facts And Procedural History
>
> Following her graduation from high school in 1977, Gilbert held jobs at McDonald's and Comerica Bank before attempting to obtain a better job with Blue Cross and Blue Shield of Michigan. When the job with Blue Cross did not materialize, Gilbert decided to become a millwright. Millwrights are skilled tradespeople who work mainly with metals, installing, maintaining, and repairing machinery. This is heavy, dirty, and sometimes dangerous work, which interested Gilbert because of the combination of technical knowledge and athletic skills it requires. In the automobile industry, millwrights are considered among the elite skilled trades because they are responsible for keeping the assembly line moving. In 1986, Gilbert applied to the Millwrights Institute of Technology, where she was accepted and began her four-year millwright apprenticeship. In 1990, Gilbert became a journeyman millwright, having finished the apprenticeship and the many hours of work it required. She spent her first two years as a journeyman working as an independent contractor through her union.

---

642 Latin meaning by the court as a whole.
643 You can read more about the judge and his work at his website: http://williamcwhitbeck.com/.
644 The footnotes in the section of this chapter given over to the facts of the case are original to the document. We will render them in quotes to further clarify that.
645 "In order to be consistent with the majority of testimony and documentary evidence presented in this case, we refer to defendant as Chrysler."

Because of layoffs common to the trade, Gilbert worked very little during fall 1991 and winter 1992. At the same time, Gilbert, who had been abused as a child and had a history of alcoholism and cocaine use, began having personal problems. While details of this period in her life are not particularly clear, she was arrested for drunk driving and was involved in an altercation at a bar around this time. In early 1992, Gilbert sought treatment for her substance abuse problems from Steven Hnat, a psychiatric social worker who specializes in treating people with substance abuse problems. According to Hnat's evaluation, Gilbert had a substance abuse problem and the depression she was experiencing was a symptom of that substance abuse, not a separate condition. Despite Gilbert's history of abuse as a child and poor family support, Hnat thought that Gilbert was a resilient and motivated person with a good prognosis for recovery, in part because she had initiated treatment voluntarily. By the end of February or the beginning of March 1992, Hnat believed that Gilbert was clean and sober.

In March 1992, Chrysler hired Gilbert to work at its new Jefferson North Assembly Plant. Gilbert was the first female millwright in the plant; in fact, she was the only female skilled tradesperson for the first 1½ years she worked at the plant, and the only female millwright for her first two years there. According to Gilbert, her male coworkers immediately started harassing her because she was a woman. Gilbert spent her very first day working for Chrysler in training with other millwrights. One millwright remarked that they had finally been assigned a "bitch," and another made a comment suggesting that she should wear a dress to work and he would hold a ladder for her to climb so that he could look up her skirt.

These comments continued in the plant itself, where Gilbert was first assigned to work in the core assembly area on the second shift. In comments made directly to her, and made in reference to her among the men, the male millwrights, and some of her supervisors, called Gilbert "bitch," "whore," "cunt," "asshole," often adding "fucking" to these epithets.[646] Gilbert hoped that the male millwrights would accept her, or at least leave her alone, once they saw how competent she was; it is undisputed that Gilbert is skilled in her profession. Though she was friendly with a few other people in different trades, the millwrights did not change their response to her. The journeymen millwrights refused to be partnered with Gilbert, which left her to be partnered with apprentices. Gilbert did not mind working with apprentices generally, but she asked to be assigned to a journeyman millwright to benefit from his experience at Chrysler, noting that apprentices would also benefit from working with other experienced journeymen. Despite never formally declining to work with apprentices, Gilbert felt that always being assigned to work with apprentices forced her to assume a greater portion of the work because apprentices were not always able to help when dealing

---

646 "Throughout this opinion, we use very explicit language without resort to euphemisms or deletions. We do so advisedly."

with a problem. On occasion, she had to fix urgent problems by herself, and then explain to the apprentice what she had done.

Though millwrights must work in teams or small groups to perform certain types of work, some of the male millwrights refused to acknowledge Gilbert. On one occasion, a male millwright would not accept the tool that she tried to hand him until a supervisor made a comment. Despite the danger of trying to perform some repairs without assistance, some male millwrights would go to sleep or leave the area when they were supposed to help her. Two millwrights in particular, Jack Nigoshian and Gerry Ernat, disliked Gilbert, and on at least one occasion tried to get her in trouble by reporting to her supervisor that she was absent from her work area when she was actually there. Nigoshian and Gilbert also engaged in a very loud and public fight with each other at work once. For a two or three week period in her first year at Chrysler, unidentified individuals left pallets or other items in front of her large tool locker to block her from getting her tools, which she reported to her direct supervisor. The male apprentices working with her also received verbal harassment, with some millwrights suggesting that Gilbert was performing sexual favors for them.

During this first year of work, Gilbert said, she felt the stress of her working conditions even though she had made very good progress with Hnat. Her depression abated, but Gilbert had what Hnat deemed a "slip" in July 1992, when Gilbert was again arrested for drunk driving. Gilbert said that she felt the need to numb her emotions regarding her work environment and the constant harassment she experienced there. Hnat saw it as a good sign that Gilbert reported this slip to him and sought inpatient treatment at Sacred Heart Hospital in October 1992. Hnat thought that working remained an important component of Gilbert's recovery because it minimized her exposure to drinking and gave her something on which to focus, though working twelve hours a day, seven days a week was taxing on Gilbert. Additionally, he observed, Gilbert's success at work was tied to her recovery because of her strong identity as a millwright, her work ethic, and determination not to be forced to leave.

By 1993, one or more unidentified individuals at Chrysler had begun to leave lewd cartoons for Gilbert, sometimes posting them around the plant before leaving them for her to see. On May 22, 1993, Gilbert went to her tool box to retrieve a grinder, but found that someone had taken it. In searching through her toolbox drawers for the grinder, Gilbert discovered a cartoon entitled "Pecker Wrestling." In the cartoon, three men are watching a fourth man, who is sitting on a table with his pants around his ankles. A woman in the cartoon is grasping the seated man's penis and, from the expression on her face, appears to be exerting some effort to "wrestle" with his penis. A second woman is observing the action. Though difficult to discern from the photocopies in the record, the name "Linda" is written on the cartoon with an arrow to the woman who is "wrestling," the name "Bill Barr"—the name of a welder or millwright who worked with Gilbert—is written across the chest of the man seated on the table. Names of three other millwrights who worked with Gilbert and arrows pointing to the three other men in the cartoon are also visible. There is a question mark over the second woman in the cartoon.

Gilbert reported this incident to her supervisor, Harry Pilon, and in writing to Chrysler management, providing management with a copy of the cartoon.[647] She noted that she thought the cartoon was "obscene," citing the names written on the cartoon as names of people with whom she worked. As she saw it, the woman named "Linda" in the cartoon was "bare-breasted and about to perform fellatio." Gilbert stated that she was "extremely insulted and degraded. The insinuation that this happen[ed] between" her and a man with whom she worked "everyday" was "humiliating." Gilbert did not mention any earlier incidents of sexual harassment in her written report.

Two days later, Frank Battaglia, Sr., an employee in Chrysler's human resources department, discussed the situation with Pilon, Jerry Heikkila, who was Gilbert's union steward, Joe Christman, who was the area coordinator, and Dave Standen, who was the shift operations manager essentially in charge of the workforce in the entire plant. They agreed to talk to all thirty-six millwrights in the core area to explain that the matter was serious and to inform them of Chrysler's sexual harassment policy. Christman and Pilon apologized to Gilbert about the incident and reassured her that Chrysler did not condone this conduct. Though a memorandum indicates that Battaglia and others carried out their intentions to speak with the other millwrights, Gilbert said that no such thing happened. In fact, she said, she found a copy of Chrysler's sexual harassment policy and gave it to some of the other workers.

After Gilbert reported the wrestling cartoon to management, the other millwrights started making hushing noises in her presence and calling her a "snitch." About a week and a half after finding the wrestling cartoon, on June 5, 1993, Gilbert went to her toolbox, only to find that someone had taped a Polaroid photograph of male genitalia to the top of it. She reported this incident to Pilon and Battaglia. Battaglia spoke with Gilbert and Pilon about the Polaroid, but did not separately investigate it, partly because that was not his responsibility and partly because, he later claimed, the investigation into the wrestling cartoon was still underway. Chrysler never determined who had left this cartoon or photograph.

---

[647] "The record suggests that one of Gilbert's acquaintances may have seen her crying about the cartoon, and that acquaintance may have taken the cartoon to Pilon. In any event, Pilon directly knew of the cartoon."

Battaglia and Pilon decided that the best remedy to the problem would be to transfer Gilbert. When Gilbert consented, Chrysler assigned her to the third shift in the paint shop. Though a more favorable shift, this was not a favorable assignment because the paint shop had noxious fumes, which was of particular concern to Gilbert, an asthmatic. No one alerted Gilbert's supervisors in the paint shop that she was being transferred because of the sexual harassment that had occurred in the core area.

Gilbert apparently remained clean and sober until July or August 1993. Hnat, who continued to treat her, thought this was extraordinary given the pressure Gilbert had been under in June 1993, when Gilbert reported that her union representative was pressuring her to drop her complaint and the sexual harassment had continued. Gilbert, however, had developed a major depressive disorder, which was different from the depression symptomatic of alcoholism that Hnat had seen in Gilbert at the beginning of her treatment. This major depressive disorder was permanent, had affected Gilbert's mood, ability to move, articulate, think, and function. But Gilbert was still determined to prove that she could persevere at work, refusing to take time away from work even when she injured her back, fearing that she would be seen as weak.

Gilbert relapsed into alcoholism at the end of summer 1993, and her psychiatric situation had worsened by September 1993. As of November 1993, Gilbert was bingeing on alcohol after work. Throughout this time, though he was aware of Gilbert's other personal problems, Hnat remained convinced that the sexual harassment she was experiencing at work was the primary reason why she turned to alcohol. With her alcoholism spiraling out of control, Gilbert admitted herself to Sacred Heart Hospital in November 1993. This hospitalization may have coincided with her attempt to commit suicide by cutting her arm. Her Sacred Heart Hospital records noted that sexual harassment at work remained her greatest risk factor for future relapses.

Sacred Heart discharged Gilbert in December 1993. She remained sober for a few months. Hnat last saw her in January 1994. In March 1994, close to her second-year anniversary with Chrysler, Gilbert sued Chrysler for discrimination in the form of sexual harassment, as well as under a number of other theories. Though the chronology of events during this time is unclear, Gilbert claimed to continue to experience almost daily harassment even after filing suit. She had also lost a significant amount of weight, approximately fifty pounds. At about this time, more nonverbal incidents began occurring even though she moved from the paint shop back to the core assembly area. For instance, someone left a Penthouse magazine on her toolbox. Another day, Gilbert left her can of diet Pepsi on the table in a break area to respond to a repair call. When she returned, someone had placed a magazine next to her drink to make it look as if she had been reading an article entitled "Why Men Have So Many Sperm." That summer, in a separate incident, Gilbert returned to an area that she had blocked from public view to use as a changing area to find that someone had urinated on a chair on which she ordinarily sat to change her boots.[648] She did not report these incidents immediately, and Hnat thought Gilbert was doing "pretty well."

Some time in fall 1994, Gilbert found an article entitled "10 Times A Day Is Too Many" by Dr. Ruth Westheimer in her locker. Drafted in a question and answer format, the person requesting advice asked:

> Q: My girlfriend and I are very much in love and as we are both very highly sexed people, we make love often—up to 10 times in a day or night. However, we both find it very frustrating when my penis won't perform! Sometimes it gets too sore, or at other times after lots of sex it just won't rise no matter how much I want more. What can I do?

The response was straightforward:

> A: The first thing I [Dr. Westheimer] would suggest: Don't make love 10 times in a day or night. Make love only once a night and prolong it with foreplay, but don't put all that pressure on your penis to perform or you are going to get into trouble. Lovemaking can be holding hands, cuddling or having and intimate conversations, but it's not trying to get into the Guinness Book of World Records.

Chrysler was aware of this article no later than October 10, 1994. Again, though not clear on when this happened, Gilbert said that someone taped another lewd or derogatory cartoon to her toolbox or locker with the word "bitch" written on the tape. When she reported this incident, a supervisor, Richard Castleman, advised her to act like it did not bother her. Consequently, she left the cartoon taped to her toolbox or locker for two weeks, until someone else removed it.

On October 10, 1994, Gilbert returned to her locker only to find that it had been pried open and someone had left a cartoon entitled "Highway Signs You Should Know" in the locker. The cartoon had fourteen "signs" that used drawings of naked bodies or body parts engaged in sexual activity to illustrate the meaning of each "sign." For instance, for "men at work," the cartoon showed a man and woman having intercourse. Gilbert reported the cartoon to Pilon and to management. Maya Baker, a human resources employee, spoke with Gilbert. Baker suggested that Gilbert use a designated locker room, which was a relatively long distance from her work area, instead of her makeshift changing room, so she would draw less attention to herself. Baker also spoke to the union stewards on the three shifts and stopped by

---

648 "Apparently, the male workers changed into their clothes in the aisles and did not walk the distance to their designated locker rooms, so Gilbert had adopted a similar practice, fashioning a changing area that allowed only her feet to be visible to people in the vicinity."

Gilbert's work area several times before and after she reported to work to see if she could find anyone leaving the cartoons. Baker wanted to make it known to the workers that Chrysler was investigating Gilbert's allegations and that the person caught harassing Gilbert would be punished. Baker never caught the person who left the cartoon and lost touch with Gilbert because of Chrysler's policy of rotating human resources personnel through different shifts every few months.

In November 1994, Chrysler deposed Gilbert for the first time. In this deposition she detailed the comments and harassment, including some incidents she had not previously reported. Following this deposition, Gilbert indicated, no one from Chrysler approached her or attempted to investigate any of her complaints, though she continued working at the Jefferson North Assembly Plant as a millwright.

On March 12, 1995, Gilbert discovered an illustrated "poem" entitled "The Creation of a Pussy" that had evidently been posted in the carpenters' shop, about twenty yards from the millwrights' shop:

> Seven wise men with knowledge so fine,
> created a pussy to their design.
> First was a butcher, smart with wit,
> using a knive [sic], he gave it a slit.
> Second was a carpenter, strong and bold,
> with a hammer and chisel, he gave it a hole.
> Third was a tailor, tall and thin,
> by using red velvet, he lined it within.
> Fourth was a hunter, short and stout,
> with a piece of fox fur, he lined it without.
> Fifth was a fisherman, nasty as hell,
> threw in a fish and gave it a smell.
> Sixth was a preacher whose name was McGee,
> touched it and blessed it and said it could pee.
> Last came a sailor, dirty little runt,
> he sucked it and fucked it and called it a cunt.

Running around the border of the "poem" were caricatures of each of the seven "wise" men posed or brandishing an item that reflected each man's "skill;" the sailor, for example, was shown having intercourse with a woman. Gilbert reported this to Pilon and management. Tim Holland, a facilitator in the human resources department and member of Chrysler's new Civil Rights Committee, handled this complaint. Though he had not had any previous involvement with Gilbert's complaints, he was aware that she had been experiencing harassment. Holland took a photograph of the bulletin board with the "poem" and spoke with Gilbert, who said that she did not want anyone fired over the incident, she just wanted the harassment to stop. Chrysler then removed the bulletin board.

Almost immediately after seeing the "poem," Gilbert relapsed to a severe degree, expressing fear that men who were originally involved in the harassment, who had been off of work for some time for other reasons, were returning. Though the details, including the exact time, are sketchy, Gilbert evidently turned on the gas in her oven and tried to go to "sleep." She went through detoxification at Sacred Heart Hospital from April 11, 1995, through April 25, 1995. She was either rehospitalized or participated in an intensive outpatient therapy program from April 27, 1995, through May 4, 1995, at the Eastwood Clinic. She did not remain sober, and was admitted to Harper Hospital for detoxification on July 8, 1995. Her records indicated that she was no longer suicidal by July 18, 1995.

Gilbert returned to work again after this hospitalization. In March 1997, Gilbert encountered a male coworker who kept insisting over and over again to her that he had a "big meat." She reportedly responded "whip it out," and told her supervisor about this incident. This coworker was reprimanded. At another time, Gilbert asked her supervisor, Gordon Potempa, about the allowable variation or tolerance in an adjustment she had to make in a repair, to which he barked that she had to make the repair to within a "cunt's hair." She reported this incident, and Potempa—who had a history of being disciplined for inappropriate language—was reprimanded. On another occasion, Gilbert asked Herbert Hicks, her supervisor at the time, a question about work and he told her to "clean out" her "fucking ears." She did not report this comment at the time.

Even before Gilbert began drinking again, her new therapist, social worker Carol Katz, noticed that she was using food to replace her addiction to alcoholism, which was a warning sign of what was to come. In September or October 1997, Gilbert tried to commit suicide for a third time by cutting her wrists. She was admitted to St. John's Hospital. When she returned to work, she claimed, the harassment continued. She was readmitted to St. John's Hospital in 1998 and admitted to Bon Secours Hospital in 1999.

Gilbert's lawsuit went to trial in June 1999 while she continued to work for Chrysler. From the outset, Gilbert's attorney, Geoffrey Fieger, informed the jury that Gilbert had a longstanding substance abuse problem. However, his theory of the case was that Gilbert was in recovery by the time she started working for Chrysler, her prognosis was very good, her relatively lengthy sobriety demonstrated her motivation for and commitment to staying sober, and only the relentless sexual harassment pushed her back into alcoholism. Indeed, this alcoholism was more severe than what she had ever experienced in the past, and was accompanied by major depressive disorder, a new, permanent, and serious psychiatric condition that could lead to her death through suicide or the physical effects of continued alcoholism. Under this theory, Chrysler was legally responsible for Gilbert's damages, including future medical expenses, because she had reported the harassment as early as May 1993, and Chrysler never investigated the harassment nor stopped it.

Fieger laid the factual foundation for this theory that Gilbert worked in a hostile environment by having several of Gilbert's coworkers testify. Dennis Whitenight and Fred Lemmerz were both friendly with Gilbert. Though neither man was a millwright, they were able to observe her working, and considered her to be very good at her work. Both men corroborated Gilbert's claims of individual acts of sexual harassment. For instance, Whitenight saw that the other millwrights would not help Gilbert, but just watched her work. In his view, it was no secret that they did not like having a woman work with them. Whitenight saw cartoons left for Gilbert, and even removed some before she could see them because he knew how upset Gilbert was about the harassment. Lemmerz was with Gilbert when she discovered that someone had urinated on her chair, noting that the odor was unmistakable. Both Lemmerz and Whitenight commented that the male millwrights did not treat each other the way they treated Gilbert, the harassment was open and obvious, and the supervisors should have been aware of what was happening. In fact, in his thirty-one years working for Chrysler, Lemmerz had never seen anyone treated as badly as Gilbert had been treated. Lemmerz confirmed that, until he retired in 1999, he heard people make harassing comments toward Gilbert. Both men also observed the radical changes in Gilbert's weight, her crying at work, and depression. Robert Gupton, a tool and die maker, echoed Whitenight's and Lemmerz's testimony about Gilbert. Gupton was impressed at Gilbert's skills, but he had seen that the male millwrights did not like her. Further, though Pilon thought that some of the incidents that Gilbert detailed were more akin to rough "shop talk," even Pilon conceded that some of the incidents, like the Polaroid photograph of a penis, were unusual and "improper." Similarly, even though Standen viewed shop talk as a fact of life in the plant, he thought it was inappropriate. Fieger asked each Chrysler employee about what, if any, investigation or remedial action the company had taken in response to Gilbert's situation. Battaglia claimed to be responsible for investigating only the penis wrestling cartoon incident, and maintained that talking with the other supervisors and union representatives was an adequate response to Gilbert's complaint. He believed that these supervisors had talked with the people working with Gilbert and gave them a copy of the sexual harassment policy, though he had no documentation that they did so. Pilon suggested that someone had tracked who received the policies. However, unlike the circumstances when Chrysler handed out other policies to the workers, it did not have the individuals sign a form to confirm that they had received a copy of the policy. Chrysler did not attempt to compare the handwriting on the wrestling cartoon with any of the employee records, it did not set up cameras for surveillance, as it had done when there was a theft/sabotage problem in the plant, nor did it assign someone on the floor to report harassment directly to management. Neither Battaglia nor Pilon confronted any of the men named in the penis wrestling cartoon. On occasion, Pilon asked some of the men about the cartoons, but he never learned who was leaving them. However, Christman said that he had met with at least some of the men named in the penis wrestling cartoon, including Bill Barr, who had denied playing any role in leaving the cartoon for Gilbert.

Fieger attempted to underscore the inadequacy of Chrysler's response in general by asking Pilon, "If somebody peed on [former Chrysler Chairman] Lee Iacocca's chair, [do] you think he could find out who did it?" Pilon responded, "I believe so." Fieger then asked Pilon, who was seated with the defense as Chrysler's representative during the trial, whether Jurgen Schrempf was Chrysler's new chairman following its merger with Daimler. When Pilon responded affirmatively, Fieger asked, "If somebody peed on Mr. Schrempf's chair, do you think they would find out who did it?" Pilon again responded, "Yes, I believe if someone peed on his chair. If someone peed on my chair, I could find out who did it, sir." This prompted Fieger to ask, "Except nobody would find out who peed on Linda Gilbert's chair?" Pilon replied, "If I suspected someone, I would point them out." This last comment pointed to an overarching theme in the testimony of Battaglia, Pilon, and Baker. Namely, they claimed numerous times that it was Gilbert's responsibility to inform her supervisors or management of who was harassing her, and until she could identify her harasser or harassers, Chrysler could do nothing to stop the harassment—if it was actually harassment.

Hnat, who testified for four days as an expert, provided the most cohesive testimony at trial in terms of providing a timeline of Gilbert's improvement, relapses, short-term recoveries, and prognosis. Looking at Gilbert's sobriety between March 1992 and July or August 1993, including her "slip," Hnat concluded that she could be considered among a small group of people with the best prospect for lasting recovery. Studies he had read and his own experience as a therapist indicated that the majority of alcoholics—about seventy-two percent—relapsed within the first six months of recovery, which Gilbert did not do despite the stress of work. An even greater percentage of people relapsed within the first year of recovery, which Gilbert did not do. In his estimation, her likelihood for success was in the top ten percent of alcoholics who sought treatment from a professional. Hnat was aware of Gilbert's drunk driving arrests, but believed that, regardless of any court orders to seek treatment, she had actually sought treatment out of a personal desire to recover. He pointed out that the length of her treatment was unusual, especially because her insurance had stopped paying for treatment and she had to pay for it herself. Hnat was also fully aware of Gilbert's troubled past, including: physical and verbal abuse by family members when she was a child; sexual abuse by someone outside her family when she was a child; being forced to have an abortion as a teenager; involvement with a manipulative boyfriend who sold drugs; poor or nonexistent family support; and minimal opportunities for relaxation. Nevertheless, in his opinion: Gilbert had always complied with his treatment plan; she was dying from a combination of alcoholism and major depressive disorder, which had permanently changed the way her brain worked and would cause her physical pain from pancreatitis or other physical ailments she would likely suffer; the records by other individuals who treated Gilbert confirmed this grim prognosis; and Gilbert's poor prognosis was primarily because of the sexual harassment at work. He believed that for her to make any significant changes she would need at least six months of inpatient therapy, an additional six months in a half-way house, and ongoing treatment. Hnat added that inpatient treatment cost $2,000 per week, and therapists charged about $85 an hour for individual therapy and $45 for group therapy.

[Social worker Carol] Katz agreed with Hnat that Gilbert suffered from major depressive disorder, and that this was a serious, long-term problem. Katz had observed that Gilbert was also suffering from posttraumatic stress disorder in the form of dreams and flashbacks to her childhood abuse because of the harassment at work. Like Hnat, Katz saw the relatively direct relationship between incidents of harassment aimed at Gilbert and her relapses and suicide attempts. Katz also agreed that Gilbert had a strong work ethic, she wanted to persevere, and that she would have had a good prognosis without the harassment at work. Further, when cross-examined on the matter, Katz said that had Gilbert's only motivation for attending therapy been a court order related to a drunk driving arrest, Gilbert would not have attended therapy for so long. As Katz put it, there were far easier ways to satisfy the typical treatment required in court orders than the intensive and lengthy therapy in which Gilbert had engaged. Katz also had a long history of treating individuals who worked in the automobile industry, where substance abuse problems, even drinking on the job, was common in the assembly plants. Her experiences with these individuals led her to believe that Gilbert's coworkers would not ostracize her and treat her as badly as they had done and were doing just because she had a drinking problem. Moreover, Katz believed that harassment was a wellknown phenomenon for women who tried to break into a male-dominated workplace or career, irrespective of the individual's background.

Though denying that Gilbert had been sexually harassed, Chrysler posited numerous explanations for what had happened to Gilbert: the male millwrights did not like her because she had attended a formal apprenticeship program rather than rising through the ranks and being trained in the plant like the men; the men did not like to work with Gilbert because she drank on the job and had attendance problems; the comments and cartoons were commonplace shop talk not intended to be offensive, and which even Gilbert used; Gilbert was moody, difficult to work with, and provoked the men; if there had been harassment, Chrysler was blameless because Gilbert did not report the harassment or name her harassers to management under the open door policy used in the plant; Gilbert's relapses were attributable solely to the problems in her personal life and individual failings, including her failure to attend Alcoholics Anonymous (AA) consistently or follow a twelve-step program; and depression was commonly understood to be an ailment from which people recovered, not the fatal disease Hnat said it was. Chrysler also claimed that only the incidents Gilbert directly reported to management could be considered alleged harassment. From Chrysler's perspective, because there were long periods between Gilbert's formal reports to management, the harassment consisted of a few, isolated events and Chrysler effectively prevented harassment from happening in the time between the reports. Chrysler claimed that, having only reported six unrelated acts of alleged harassment, Gilbert could not prove that she had been subjected to a hostile work environment.

Chrysler had mixed success in providing evidentiary support for these theories. For instance, Gilbert's attendance problem was documented and she had once been disciplined for drinking on the job and being away from her work area. Her supervisors, including Pilon, indicated that they had given her the benefit of the doubt a number of times because they knew she was dealing with personal problems. Additionally, all new hires went through a probationary period, when it would have been fairly easy to get Gilbert fired had the men really desired that result. Some of the witnesses, like Danielson, also testified that Nigoshian and Ernat, two journeymen millwrights with whom Gilbert had had significant problems, had been at Chrysler for a long time and did not get along with most people. Nigoshian had also left Chrysler around 1995, eliminating the possibility that he had committed harassment later in Gilbert's employment with Chrysler.

On the other hand, though Potempa said that some men had asked not to work with Gilbert because they thought it was dangerous, he did not specifically say that any of the men had complained about her drinking. Though defense counsel, Johanna Armstrong, asked virtually all the Chrysler workers who testified whether they had seen Gilbert being moody, no one ever definitively replied that they had seen that behavior in Gilbert. Rather, some of the men had seen her try to act calmly in the face of offensive comments. At most, they had seen Gilbert cry after being harassed or reply when provoked. While some of the Chrysler workers recalled occasional incidents when Gilbert used a vulgar term, there was no evidence that she used shop talk regularly.

Armstrong pressed both Hnat and Katz about Gilbert's failure to attend AA consistently and whether Gilbert had been telling the truth in her therapy sessions. Hnat indicated that he believed that AA was generally beneficial to alcoholics, but to a lesser degree for women because of the dynamics of meetings and the difficulty in finding female sponsors. He also stressed that he did not think that AA or a similar program was an appropriate therapeutic approach for Gilbert—even if a court had ordered her to attend. In Hnat's opinion, AA helps people to deal with their emotions, but it was vital for Gilbert to minimize, not examine, the very strong emotions she was experiencing as a first step to her recovery. Only after she was sober and had some control over what she was experiencing could Gilbert begin to examine what was happening to her and attempt to develop coping strategies that did not involve alcohol or drugs. Additionally, Katz explained, Gilbert had tried to attend AA during their work with each other, but Gilbert's sponsor had not offered her the support she needed. Katz added that Gilbert had no reason to lie in therapy.

As for Chrysler's open door policy, which developed out of a new management plan negotiated with the union that was supposed to give workers more input into matters at the plant, Armstrong had a difficult time supporting the idea that Gilbert's failure to make formal reports more frequently prevented more action by Chrysler. For example, Michael Jessamy, a human resources manager who did not have specific knowledge of Gilbert's experiences, explained the complaint procedure available. Aside from recourse to the union, Chrysler encouraged employees to report harassment to their immediate supervisors, and if their supervisors were the harassers, to go to management. Jessamy did not indicate that Chrysler always required a written report to human resources, labor relations, or plant security. Holland also made this point, noting that the supervisors on the floor were often responsible for complaints and would remain involved in the matter even if the complaint was forwarded to management. There is no question from the record that Gilbert reported some incidents as they happened to Pilon and Potempa, even if she did not make a written report. The testimony of Lemmerz, Whitenight, and Gupton also suggested that the harassment was so open and obvious that it would have been impossible for Gilbert's supervisors not to know what was happening to her, even if they did not spend every minute of the shift with her. Even Holland, who did not know Gilbert and was only involved in investigating her complaint about the "poem," had heard about the harassment Gilbert was experiencing by March 1995. However, perhaps in Chrysler's favor, Gilbert did concede that she developed a suspicion about who had left the penis wrestling cartoon in her toolbox, but did not want to tell Chrysler because of a combination of her fear of reprisal and the lack of foundation for her suspicion.

The area in which the defense had the most success was discrediting or minimizing the effect some of the witnesses might have had on the jury. For instance, Fieger elicited testimony from Lemmerz, Whitenight, and others that they did not receive a copy of Chrysler's sexual harassment policy following the penis wrestling cartoon until Gilbert made the copies herself. However, Pilon, Battaglia, and Standen's testimony suggested that Chrysler had taken some steps to inform the millwrights about the sexual harassment policy, and none of these men testifying on behalf of Gilbert were millwrights. Armstrong also provided ample testimony that these individuals did not work directly with Gilbert, and they had only minimal opportunities to observe the quality of her work and the alleged harassment she experienced. Armstrong, who emphasized through her cross-examination of Hnat that he was not a medical doctor, also cast doubt on how well he understood what was happening to Gilbert, pointing out that he may not have understood that she was under court order to attend therapy, Gilbert may have been drinking without reporting that to him, and he never took any steps to verify that Gilbert was experiencing any alleged harassment at work. With respect to Gilbert's credibility and vulnerability, Armstrong questioned Gilbert, Hnat, Katz, and others about the many personal problems Gilbert had. Armstrong elicited information about Gilbert's troubled past, her history of treatment and hospitalization before 1992, her alcohol consumption and subsequent discipline at work, drunk driving arrests, home confinement coupled with drug testing, and loss of her driver's license, and the fact that she had been fired from her job at McDonald's. Armstrong also read part of Gilbert's deposition testimony to the jury in which she mentioned finding a liquid, not urine, on her chair in 1994.

At the close of proofs the trial court, with the explicit consent from Armstrong and Fieger, instructed the jury on the law before the attorneys made their closing arguments. After the attorneys gave lengthy closing arguments, the trial court submitted the case to the jury with a special verdict slip. In returning their verdict in favor of Gilbert, the jury indicated that it found that Gilbert had been "subjected to sexual harassment in violation of the Michigan Civil Rights Act," and Chrysler had notice of the harassment, but did not "adequately investigate and take prompt and appropriate remedial action." The jury awarded Gilbert $20 million for her emotional damages and $1 million for future medical expenses.[649]

One by one, the Court of Appeals took up and disposed of the issues relating to the jury trial, in the end affirming the lower court's finding of DaimlerChrysler's role in the matter.

One of the most important matters was the standing of Hnat, who had said he had a master's degree in psycho-biology and was the winner—as a graduate student—of the Pillsbury Award at the University of Michigan. The trial court had granted him authority as an expert witness. After the trial, the attorneys for DaimlerChrysler discovered that Hnat had not been granted the prize and never finished his master's. DaimlerChrysler had first sought a new trial, but Circuit Court Judge Murphy denied it at the lower court.

---

649 *Linda Gilbert v DaimlerChrysler Corp*, No. 227392, Michigan Court of Appeals, 30 July 2002, State of Michigan Court of Appeals, 30 July 2002, 1-11, http://publicdocs.courts.mi.gov:81/OPINIONS/FINAL/COA/20020730_C227392(124)_227392.OPN.PDF.

As the trial court indicated in its written order and opinion, the inaccuracies in Hnat's testimony were not "large." Though Hnat had not earned the master's degree in psycho-biology, he had completed the coursework, giving him a legitimate background in the subject. Additionally, Hnat had never claimed at trial that he was a psychiatrist or psychologist. Overall, the trial court did not think that the flaws in Hnat's testimony were substantial, much less that they amounted to fraud.[650]

The Court of Appeals also concurred with the lower court that the matter of Hnat and Fieger knowing each other, something Fieger admitted in opening arguments of the trial, had no importance. In fact, Hnat had worked on Fieger's ill-fated gubernatorial run in 1998.[651]

And the Court of Appeals dealt with the size of the jury award: $21 million. That was a matter for the jury and the jury had spoken (and Judge Murphy had confirmed it).

In the last of the opinion, the three Court of Appeals judges laid out the impossibility of coming to any other conclusion than that affirming the trial court.

> It certainly is possible that a different jury would have reacted differently to the evidence in this case and might have given Gilbert a smaller award. However, the jury in this case could have found compelling Gilbert's evidence that she would die an untimely death because of the effects of the harassment that Chrysler knew existed and did nothing to stop. Alternatively, the jury could have found persuasive Gilbert's evidence that her life was and would be completely joyless because the harassment had caused her to develop major depressive and post-traumatic stress disorders, changing the fundamental chemistry in her brain. Hnat also provided testimony explaining the high costs of treatment Gilbert is likely to incur in the future. All these factors, as well as the length of the harassment, might have contributed to the high award. The precise amount of appropriate damages is often an elusive figure that cannot be calculated with simple mathematical equations, which is why the law requires only a reasonable approximation by the jury. That the jury exercised its independence by awarding Gilbert only about fifteen percent of the $140,000,000 Fieger said was appropriate suggests that it decided the amount of the award on how it perceived the evidence the parties presented, not because of passion, bias, or misunderstanding. Like the jury, the trial court heard all the evidence and decided that it supported the jury's award. Giving the trial court the deference it is surely due, it is impossible to say that the trial court abused its discretion in reaching this conclusion.[652]

---

650 Ibid., 29.
651 Hnat and Fieger are again reunited these days according to Hnat's LinkedIn page: http://www.linkedin.com/pub/stephen-hnat/33/a02/318.
652 *Linda Gilbert v DaimlerChrysler Corp*, No. 227392, Michigan Court of Appeals.

There was a lot at stake in this verdict, and not just the money that had been awarded to Gilbert. DaimlerChrysler was understandably not pleased and sought redress at the court of last resort.

When the case came to the Supreme Court in the fall of 2002, Chrysler was not alone in asking that its voice be heard again in this matter. It seemed LOTS of people wanted a voice in the decision as *amicus curiae.* An *amicus curiae*—translated literally—is a "friend of the court." So, three outsiders, not parties directly involved, saw the case as an issue wherein they felt compelled to participate. It happens all the time. Sometimes they are denied, but this time, U.S. and Michigan Chambers of Commerce were going to be heard as was the Michigan Municipal League Liability and Property Pool. Their interests were in making or keeping Michigan a friendly state for business, especially the insurance business.

You don't think, do you, that all the $21 million would come out of DaimlerChrysler's cash reserves? Not likely. Odds were they had insurance for just such contingencies. Of course, their rates—like yours and mine—would go up if the award were granted. And such a verdict would set a precedent.

It took some time, but the Michigan Supreme Court unanimously granted leave April 8, 2003. The first thing Fieger (as Gilbert) did was to seek the removal of five of the justices from hearing it.

> On April 16, Gilbert filed a motion for recusal against Justices Corrigan, Taylor, Young, and Markman [and Weaver]. In a lengthy brief in support of her motion, Gilbert argued that recusal was necessary because the probability of actual bias on the part of the justices was too high to be constitutionally tolerable. Gilbert identified two sources of potential bias. First, she claimed that the justices had a pecuniary interest in the case because they had received large monetary donations and campaign support from the *amicus curiae.* Second, she asserted, the justices' public discourse revealed a deep-rooted animus toward Plaintiff Fieger. On September 17, 2003, the justices denied Gilbert's motion for recusal.[653]

Of the justices targeted for removal, only Weaver wrote about the reasons she was staying on the case. The others were silent. When Fieger asked again for the justices to remove themselves he listed only Markman, Taylor, Young and Corrigan; his request for Weaver to step off had been dropped. On October 30, again his motion was denied without reason.[654]

There was more than something to all of it.

---

653 *Gilbert, et al. v Ferry, et al.,* United States Court of Appeals of the Sixth Circuit, 10 March 2005, 2, http://www.ca6.uscourts.gov/opinions.pdf/05a0124p-06.pdf.
654 Elizabeth A. Weaver, "Memorandum," 28 September 2006, unpublished.

DaimlerChrysler had been a supporter of the Republican justices on the court, including me as it turned out; I think they gave me several thousand dollars. And Chrysler gave significant money to Taylor, Markman, and Young in 2000.

...And before. Direct money. The Michigan Campaign Finance Reform Network teased out totals from 1998 and 2000 elections:

> DaimlerChrysler's corporate PAC and its employees' PAC and employees made the following contributions to sitting justices in the last two elections:
>
> Justice Maura Corrigan $27,580
> Justice Clifford Taylor (1998) $30,950
> Justice Clifford Taylor (2000) $13,068
> Justice Stephen Markman $12,946
> Justice Robert Young, Jr. $13,862
> Total $98,676[655]

But in addition, there was hidden money, nearly untraceable, that went from DaimlerChrysler to the U.S. Chamber, in this case one of the *amicus curiae*. *The Wall Street Journal* had reported its investigation.

> Internal Chamber documents reviewed by *The Wall Street Journal* show that the organization has created several special accounts to take in money for projects on behalf of individual companies or groups of companies with a common policy goal.
>
> [...]
>
> Many companies are buying. Last fall, for example, Wal-Mart Stores Inc., DaimlerChrysler AG, Home Depot, Inc. and the American Council of Life Insurers all kicked in $1 million each for one of the Chamber's special projects: a TV and direct-mail advertising campaign aimed at helping elect business-friendly judges. The participants had all been targets of costly lawsuits, and the Chamber's campaign gave them a way to fight back—without disclosing their identities. That allowed them, among other things, to avoid attracting the attention of the nation's trial lawyers, who were spending millions of their own to help elect plaintiff-friendly judges.[656]

The news report didn't make much stir, and with understandable reason: it was issued early on the morning of Sept. 11, 2001. Suddenly we had other matters to tend to.

---

655 Includes contributions from the corporation's PAC, employees, retirees and spouses. Barbara Moorhouse and Richard Robinson with David Hogg, *Special Interests v Public Values: Funding Michigan Supreme Court Campaigns 1994-2000*, (Lansing, Michigan, 2002) 13, http://www.mcfn.org/pdfs/reports/SCreport.pdf.
656 Jim VandeHei, "Major Business Lobby wins back its clout by dispensing favors; some members can hide behind Chamber's name to pursue private ends, targeting 'Unfriendly judges,'" *Wall Street Journal* (Eastern Edition), 11 September 2001, A.1.

And, as we listed in the last chapter, the Michigan Chamber of Commerce underwrote—to the tune of $840,000—issue ads supporting Weaver and Young in the 2002 election.

Michigan Campaign Finance Reform Network, in analyzing the 2002 election, observed:

> The 2002 Supreme Court race was much less expensive than 2000, but still the average amount raised by a winner's campaign committee was $450,000. All told, the seven current justices have raised more than $8 million, and four of them have benefited from an additional $4 million of issue advertising sponsored by the Michigan Chamber of Commerce in the last two election cycles. There is no public record of who gave the Chamber that $4 million.
>
> Regardless of whether campaign contributions influence the decisions that judges make, and the data suggest that they do not, there is a perception problem. Faith in the rule of law depends on a shared belief in equal justice for all. Judicial campaign fund raising undermines that shared belief. Unlike legislators and elected executives, judges have no constituents. They serve only the law. No contributor has a right to expect a return on investment from a campaign contribution to a judge.[657]

There's no way of really knowing, for a lot of these groups, like Justice for All or something, who really put the money in there. It's a terrible system in Michigan.

Sometime before the case came to the Supreme Court in October for consideration, but after Justice Weaver launched her bid for re-election (late summer of 2002)...probably in September...Kienbaum, Opperwall, Hardy & Pelton, PLC, in Birmingham, hosted a fundraiser for Weaver. That law firm would subsequently represent DaimlerChrysler.

At the time, Weaver said she had no knowledge of the *Gilbert v DaimlerChrysler* suit headed for her court.

I had never heard of the case. I don't live downstate and this completely passed me by.

Had she known that the event was being hosted by those who would shortly appear before her, she would have made a different choice.

But the folks at Kienbaum, Opperwall, Hardy & Pelton, PLC, knew that they had a case they hoped would be heard by the court; they didn't gear up their defense against the appeal overnight. And with a retired justice "of counsel" to them (Justice Patricia Boyle), they certainly had a good idea of the Code of Judicial Conduct. And they probably could figure out what might constitute an appearance of conflict of interest. They could have placed Weaver in a most uncomfortable spot.

---

657 Barbara R. Moorhouse and Richard L. Robinson with David Hogg and Christopher Moorhouse, "Appellate Judiciary: Supreme Court," *A Citizen's Guide to Michigan Campaign Finance 2002*, Michigan Campaign Finance Network, (Lansing, Mich., June 2003) 23, http://www.mcfn.org/pdfs/reports/CG2002.pdf.

After Weaver checked her own fundraising she found the support not only from DaimlerChrysler, but also—to her relief—from Geoffrey Fieger.

My people found that I had received like $300 dollars from Fieger for my campaign—$200 or $300 dollars. And then he had asked for all of us to be disqualified. So I simply answered and said, "No," because his complaint was that I had gotten money from DaimlerChrysler in my 2002 campaign. My answer was "Well, yes, but I also received it from you." And I simply said, "No, I am not prejudiced for or against, biased or prejudiced with respect to either the plaintiff or the defense, and I will look at this fairly." I felt I had a duty to answer it.[658]

The other four had not had the balance of a Fieger donation but they also refused to step off, not answering the charge, merely dismissing it.

They just said "Deny." And they couldn't state that they had no bias or prejudice; they never were able to say that.

The tragedy of it is that this is an example of an agenda case, in my opinion. And the agenda involved was, I think, two-fold: one, get Fieger; and two, put a stop to these sexual harassment cases to some degree, or put a clamp down on them. This was not a bogus sexual harassment case; it was very clear.

I was very aware of their dislike—intense dislike—of Geoffrey Fieger, and had heard Justice Young talk about how proud he was that Fieger hated him.

Fieger agreed:

> There was no way that the plaintiff was going to be permitted to win by this four-judge majority in the Supreme Court, because one, Geoff Fieger was the attorney, and two, that DaimlerChrysler had to pay the money of a $30-million sex harassment judgment. Egregious! I mean, the facts in the case were truly, truly egregious.[659]

So, Fieger was stuck with the court Governor Engler dealt.[660] He summoned his work team: Tammy Reiss, Mark C. Smiley, and Mark. R. Bendure.

DaimlerChrysler hired the highest-powered attorneys it could find; it was not going to make the same mistake it made at trial by using in-house counsel. The author of the LitiGator observed:

> Daimler-Chrysler is apparently sparing no effort to use not-so-subtle politi-cal influence in the briefing of this case, having retained the law firm of for-

658 Elizabeth Weaver, Memo in response for request for recusal, 17 September 2003.
659 Geoffrey Fieger, video interview with co-author Schock, 12 March 2012, Southfield, Michigan. The $30 million he was referring to may include the original $21 million judgment plus interest, estimated to a total of $31 million in 1999 by *Automotive News*. [Robert Ankeny, "Lawyers feud over $21 million ver-dict against D/C," **Automotive News**, 29 November 1999, http://www.autonews.com/apps/pbcs.dll/article?AID=/19991129/ANA/911290717&template=printart.]
660 Governor Engler was no Fieger fan. When asked how to stop him from defending Dr. Jack Kevorkian, Engler suggested depriving Fieger of his law license. This would be a recurring theme in Fieger's future dealings with the courts.

mer Supreme Court Justice Patricia Boyle, and the Washington, D.C. firm
of Gibson, Dunn, & Crutcher, to handle the appeal, and prominently listing the names of both Boyle and Gibson's Eugene Scalia on its brief.[661]

With Justice Boyle from Kienbaum, Opperwall, Hardy & Pelton, PLC, was Elizabeth
P. Hardy.[662] They were joined by Thomas G. Kienbaum, Noel D. Massie, Theodore J.
Boutrous, Jr., Paul DeCamp, and Joanie L. Roeschlein. The court scheduled the case
for oral arguments, which were heard Dec. 10, 2003. The opinion was released July 22,
2004.

You'll note that we used the Court of Appeals facts of the case instead of those chronicled
by the Michigan Supreme Court. There is a reason. The author of the opinion at the
Michigan Supreme Court, ostensibly Robert Preston Young, Jr. made just a hash of it.
In the first place, he was writing "soft" to keep the graphic testimony from the trial out
of the "facts" section. Second, in the facts of the case, he almost couldn't help but start
where he oughtn't: he began by blaming the victim:

> It is undisputed that plaintiff, Linda Gilbert, has long waged a losing battle
> with substance abuse. Her personal struggles were thoroughly documented
> in medical records that plaintiff introduced at trial in order to establish dam-
> ages. According to those records, Ms. Gilbert began drinking at fourteen and
> began using cocaine at twenty years of age. Most of her adult life has since
> been marked by excessive drinking. At one point during her employment
> with defendant, she reported to her substance abuse counselors that she
> was consuming a pint to one-fifth gallon of alcohol a day. Her cocaine use
> also continued during her employment with defendant, as documented by
> records from St. John Hospital and Sacred Heart Rehabilitation Center.[663]

It's worth reading but likely won't give much clarity or pleasure. Young's argument is
deficient in something we've tried to avoid in writing this book. It's a logical fallacy
called card stacking...you advance only the facts that support your argument; you
ignore all others.

At issue were what the Engler Four called "an excessive verdict," describing it that
way in the first sentence of the opinion: "the largest recorded compensatory award for
a single-plaintiff sexual harassment suit in the history of the United States."[664] Then
Young laid out the other factors that would come into play:

661 "Upcoming case: Gilbert v DaimlerChrysler," The LitiGator, 28 December 2003, http://radio-weblogs.
com/0110436/2003/12/28.html.
662 Remember her? She was named as a possible Supreme Court Justice in Chapter 7. And for a look at
her opinion of how things went in this case, consult Lynn Patrick Ingram, "Lawyers of the Year: Elizabeth P. Hardy—Birmingham," *Michigan Lawyers Weekly*, 27 December 2004, http://milawyersweekly.com/
news/2004/12/27/lawyers-of-the-year-2004-82801/.
663 *Gilbert v DaimlerChrysler*, No. 122457, Michigan Supreme Court, 22 July 2004, 4, http://publicdocs.courts.
mi.gov:81/OPINIONS/FINAL/SCT/20040722_S122457_162_gilbert11dec03_op.pdf.
664 Ibid.

Not only does the verdict exceed verdicts in similar cases by leaps and bounds, but, as shown in this opinion, it was awarded by a jury inflamed by hyperbolic rhetoric, prejudice-baiting argument, and unscientific expert testimony.[665]

The hyperbole? According to Young, Fieger was likening Linda Gilbert to the Jews and DaimlerChrysler to the Third Reich.

> Plaintiff's counsel deliberately tried to provoke the jury by supplanting law, fact, and reason with prejudice, misleading arguments, and repeated *ad hominem* attacks against defendant based on its corporate status. Given the undeniable role of this inflammatory rhetoric, the trial court erred in denying defendant's motion for a new trial. [Footnote omitted.]

> One of counsel's tactics in this vein was his repeated attempt to equate plaintiff with the victims of the Holocaust. This association began during the testimony of plaintiff's expert, Steven Hnat, when Mr. Hnat testified that plaintiff's psychological state was akin to that of concentration camp survivors. Plaintiff's counsel further developed this theme during his closing argument:

> > Never again. Never again. That is a line now used by the sabreurs [sic.; sabras] in Israel, the land of Israel, to mean that the unspeakable horrors that were perpetrated on the people of Israel, on the Jews, must never be forgotten and must never happen again. Never again. Never again.

> Counsel also exhorted the jury to:

> > provide full and complete justice and thereby, as I indicated at the start of this trial, raise the roof of this courthouse so that justice will ring loud and clear. No more.

> > As those young [sabras] said in the land of Israel, no more. We will not let this stand. We will not allow this to pass. We will not allow you, you, an equal with all of us in this, the great equalizer, to crush the health and the dreams of a woman who simply had the American dream.

> Even the final sentence of plaintiff's closing argument referenced the Holocaust theme: "Let's bury this prejudice once and for all so that we may appropriately say, never again." [666]

As well, there was the issue of Hnat's qualifications and competence. First, wrote Young, Hnat had claimed expertise and a degree he didn't hold. In other words, he'd lied, and while the Court of Appeals didn't find his degree inflation an issue, instead calling it a misstatement, Young certainly did:

---

665 Ibid.
666 Ibid., 25-26.

We disagree with the Court of Appeals' suggestion that the trial court could have legitimately concluded that Mr. Hnat "had simply misspoken" when he said that he had a master's degree in psychobiology and had won the Pillsbury Prize. [...] We doubt that anyone could honestly misspeak about having a degree that he did not, in fact, possess, much less that he could "misspeak" in a written resume.[667]

Young determined that the trial court had erred in its "gatekeeping" function by allowing Gilbert's therapist, a social worker, to testify as a medical professional.

He speculated about plaintiff's impending physical inability to work, testified about the type of medical complications that plaintiff would soon experience, predicted the cause of her death, and gave testimony concerning plaintiff's life expectancy. Mr. Hnat expressed his "opinion" on physiological disease, cause of death, and plaintiff's lifespan. Yet there was no evidence or showing that Mr. Hnat was qualified by training, experience, or knowledge to render such opinions or interpret medical records that would arguably support such a diagnosis or prognosis. There was, in other words, no evidence that Mr. Hnat was qualified to testify that defendant's actions concerning workplace harassment caused neurological and physiological changes in plaintiff and shortened her life.[668]

And that's exactly what Hnat claimed...her life would be shortened and that she would die a painful death. The Supreme Court majority of four rejected his argument and the majority remanded the case to be retried.

[W]e conclude that the trial court abused its discretion in denying defendant's motion for a new trial under MCR 2.611. Once the jury issued its verdict, it should have been apparent to the trial court that the persistent and calculated efforts of plaintiff's trial counsel to thwart the jury's fact-finding role had borne fruit. The jury's deliberations had been palpably affected and this wrought substantial harm to defendant's right to a fair trial. This case is remanded to the Wayne Circuit Court for a new trial to be held consistently with this opinion.[669]

Justice Michael Cavanagh wrote the dissent for the minority. He agreed that the verdict was excessive, but about all else, he was rock steady: Fieger's conduct, Hnat's qualification to serve as an expert witness. The majority, he said, had cherry picked the facts to arrive at its conclusion.

Most serious, though, was evidence of bias and prejudice. In the opinion, the Four had characterized Fieger's conduct in other cases, at other times. Here's an example of what Young wrote:

---

667 Ibid., footnote, 44
668 Ibid., 47-48.
669 Ibid., 55.

Counsel's persistent and deliberate efforts to incite passion and prejudice distinguish this case from those in which inflammatory remarks were fleeting and unintentional. Plaintiff's counsel has been admonished in two published Court of Appeals opinions since this trial for precisely the same sort of hyperbolic and vitriolic argument he made on behalf of Linda Gilbert. Overreaching, prejudice-baiting rhetoric appears to be a calculated, routine feature of counsel's trial strategy. This deliberate use of improper argument, coupled with the astonishingly excessive verdict rendered against defendant, precludes us from concluding that counsel's misconduct was "innocuous" and "unintended."

In fact, plaintiff's counsel's behavior during trial is remarkably similar to what necessitated a new trial in *Reetz v Kinsman Marine Transit Co.*[670]

...And they were off and running to scold him soundly for his repeated acts of what they saw as bad behavior. That was bad judging, wrote Cavanagh:

This case is not about plaintiff's counsel's "routine" behavior, contrary to the assertions of the majority. Whatever plaintiff's counsel may have done in past cases is irrelevant to *this particular case*. In this case, an objective review of the evidence indicates that plaintiff overwhelmingly provided facts to prove that she was sexually harassed and that defendant conducted an inadequate investigation into this harassment.[671]

Cavanagh also brought in substantial language from trial that would more clearly reflect the degree of harassment that Gilbert suffered on a daily basis.

Weaver and Marilyn Kelly joined in the dissent.

In Cavanagh's dissent, three dissenters agreed the $21 million jury award was excessive in relation to similar one-victim cases and should be remitted for reduction. But we dissenters disagreed with the majority's reversal of the jury's verdict that defendant DaimlerChrysler be held liable for sexual harassment of plaintiff Gilbert.

DaimlerChrysler's behavior was so egregious that I believe that's why the jury granted an excessive award. This lady endured over ten years of grief—from 1992, including going through a gruesome and difficult trial until a verdict at the Court of Appeals in 2000, and then a decision from the Supreme Court at the end of 2003 and a final decision in 2004. So, regardless of Justice Young's creative writing that hyperbole by plaintiff's attorney Fieger was reversible error, there was a fair trial and just verdict, and the majority of four shouldn't have reversed the jury verdict of liability. They should have disqualified themselves and not sat on the case unless in accordance with the Michigan Constitution they put on record in writing with reasons in their denial decisions refusing to disqualify themselves that they had no bias or prejudice or appearance of bias or prejudice for or against attorney Fieger and DaimlerChrysler. They did not do that.

670 Ibid., 32-36.
671 Ibid., dissent 1.

Of course, even when it was over, it wasn't over. Fieger asked for reconsideration and the Supreme Court denied.

There is both a long and short version of what happened then and thereafter. Here's the short:

> In the process of denying the rehearing, Weaver wrote a dissent that assessed that the majority—and Young in particular as the author—was "biased and prejudiced" against Fieger. Young responded attacking Weaver... and the two went back and forth in memos, with Young finally imploring Weaver to say that she thought there was at most the "appearance of bias and prejudice." Weaver told him she wouldn't, but by the time her dissent to the order came out, Jan. 28, 2004, it was simple and not particularly pointed. That's the short version of the story.

> For those who want it all, here's the long:

Justice Weaver circulated her dissent to the denial of reconsideration Sept 20, 2004... in 14 pages. On page 6 she reiterated the criticism Michael Cavanagh leveled at the majority for bringing in Fieger's prior "bad behavior."

> Standing alone, the majority's reliance on other cases to support its conclusion in this case creates an appearance of bias and prejudice. Unfortunately, the majority's focus on plaintiff's attorney's argument style does not stand alone in the record of this case as evidence of the majority's bias and prejudice against plaintiff's attorney.[672]

The majority should have recused themselves, she argued, because they were not objective and could not fairly judge the matter.[673] She also began the argument that all decisions of the court should be in writing with reasons attached, citing the 1963 state Constitution.

The item was passed[674] *without discussion at the next scheduled conference on Sept. 23rd.*

But it wasn't finished. The next event in the sequel was a letter from Justice Young dated September 28, 2004.

> Dear Betty:

> I am writing concerning your circulating dissenting statement to the order denying rehearing in the Gilbert case.

---

672 Elizabeth Weaver, dissenting statement, 20 September 2004, unpublished.
673 Chapter 17 contains much more of the evidence Weaver would cite in subsequent matters involving Mr. Fieger.
674 When an item was "passed" by the court that meant it was carried over to a future time for consideration.

All seven members of this court agreed that the verdict rendered in Gilbert was excessive. As the majority and partial dissenting positions in the published case demonstrate, it is possible to have a principled disagreement as to why that verdict was excessive. Unlike Justice Cavanagh's partial dissent that you joined, your dissenting statement on rehearing abandons a critique of my majority opinion analysis in favor of an overt *ad hominem* assault of my professional ethics. I understand Mr. Fieger's tactical reasons for attempting to impugn my judicial ability impartially to evaluate this case; I do not understand your motivation for embracing and endorsing his assault.

That you would repeat and accept Mr. Fieger's accusation as your own is particularly troubling given to your historical opposition to the sharp exchanges that periodically occur between [sic] members of this court. However, your circulating dissenting statement is an *ad hominem* attack of high order. Not only do you repeat all of Mr. Fieger's imputations of bias, but you abandon any pretence that yours is merely a recapitulation of *his* charges; you specifically and personally endorse them as truthful *evidence* of actual bias in the following statement:

> Unfortunately, the majority's focus on plaintiff's argument style does not stand alone in the record of this case as *evidence of the majority's bias and prejudice against plaintiff's attorney.* (EAW Dissenting Statement at 6)

It is disturbing that you have abandoned your historical disdain for personal and vitriolic attacks by endorsing in your statement Mr. Fieger's assault instead of concentrating on the flaws you see in my argument. But it is especially troubling that *you*, a colleague, would publicly challenge my ethics. I have the luxury of ignoring Mr. Fieger's obvious strategic attempt to intimidate me to avoid doing my duty as a member of the court. However, when you, a colleague, publish a statement suggesting that I am, by virtue of bias and prejudice, unable to discharge my judicial duties, such an accusation requires, as I am attempting here, a frank exchange.

None of us is immune from having the most outrageous accusations leveled against us. So it is particularly noteworthy that, when charges of ethical impropriety have been leveled against you, no one on this court sought to republish them. Until your dissenting statement, no member of this court would have dreamed of exploiting such charges—publicly or privately—and I believe that I and all of your other colleagues on this court have been supportive of you in those several circumstances. I am frankly surprised that you have undertaken a contrary course in actively propagating such charges. Only Justice Black[675], to my knowledge, has so directly assailed a sitting colleague in a published opinion.

---

675 A member of the court from 1955 until 1972. He died in 1990. ["Eugene F. Black, 87, ex-justice in Michigan," *New York Times,* 9 August 1990, http://www.nytimes.com/1990/08/09/obituaries/eugene-f-black-87-ex-justice-in-michigan.html.]

Mr. Fieger's previous ethical entanglements are a matter of public record. That he has had documented professional ethical lapses, however, is entirely unrelated to the merits of *his client's* cause or my judicial assessment of that cause. Relatedly, the fact that Mr. Fieger is a political public figure has no bearing on his client's cases. When Mr. Fieger's clients have deserved to win in the court, they have. You will recall that I was the author and architect of the analysis in *Beaudrie v Henderson*, 465 Mich 124 (2001) that limited the application of the *White* common law government immunity doctrine. This opinion represented a significant win for Mr. Fieger's client. By my rough calculation, during my tenure, Mr. Fieger has won more cases in this court than he has lost, including one involving a claim against his law firm that appeared within the last two weeks on our conference agenda. I think it is worthy of your consideration to recall that *only* in Gilbert has Mr. Fieger chosen to seek my (or any other member of this court) removal from consideration of cases in which he was counsel. These all point to the tactical nature of his effort in the Gilbert case to which your dissenting statement gives unwarranted life.

My judgment in Gilbert is that Mr. Fieger inappropriately overplayed his hand in an otherwise exceedingly strong plaintiff's case. His "style of argument," as you put it in your dissenting statement, was only one of several critical problems that caused me to conclude that a fair trial had been denied. I spend a number of pages in the opinion addressing what I consider fatal evidentiary problems in the trial. As I noted in my memo voting to deny rehearing, I consider that these other issues provided a basis independent of his trial conduct for reversal.

I fully appreciate that you believe my majority opinion analysis flawed as Justice Cavanagh detailed in his partial dissenting opinion in which you joined. Wholly absent from Justice Cavanagh's partial dissenting opinion was any imputation of bias or prejudice to those of the majority who had opposing views about the merits of this appeal. Because you have now forcefully leveled such a charge, and apparently need assurance on the question, **I unequivocally state to you that I do not believe I harbor any bias or prejudice against Mr. Fieger that has ever precluded me from impartially assessing his clients' cases or that I have ever acted in any fashion to penalize any of his clients because of Mr. Fieger's conduct that was *unrelated* to issues actually extant in the case.** [Emphasis added.] I do not believe that holding attorneys accountable for their professional obligations at trial represents *bias or prejudice*.

Accordingly, I respectfully ask that you withdraw those portions of your dissenting statement that repeat Mr. Fieger's imputations of prejudice and bias as well as your apparent endorsement of his position.

Very truly yours,[676]

---

676 Robert P. Young, Jr., letter to Elizabeth Weaver, 28 September 2004, unpublished.

You'll note he doesn't assert that he has no bias or prejudice. Believe me, he did, and all you had to do was hear him going on during the campaigns about the ills Geoffrey Fieger was inflicting on our culture, and you'd know he had an animus. But here he says that his bias and prejudice didn't have any effect on his judgment. It doesn't work that way. If you have ANY bias or prejudice, you need to step off the case. And even if there is only the appearance of bias and prejudice, you need to step off. He refused and the majority opinion was the result. And he wasn't alone. By the time this letter was written, Justice Corrigan was running for re-election and running on a platform that highlighted her opposition to Fieger.

On October 13th, Weaver responded to Young, and circulated her response to the justices.

> Dear Bob:
>
> Contrary to your letter's suggestion, the justices do not have the "luxury of ignoring" any motion filed by any attorney or party in the court. Certainly, however, my dissenting statement to the order denying plaintiff's request for rehearing in this case is not about the conduct of plaintiff's attorney, Mr. Fieger, nor is it an endorsement of him. My dissent is about the performance in this case of the four-justice majority (you, Chief Justice Corrigan, and Justices Taylor and Markman).
>
> At its core, my dissent asks the four-justice majority to answer two questions, yes or no:
>
>> 1. Are the justices bound by the requirements of Art 6, section 6, of the 1963 Michigan Constitution that states, "Decisions of the Supreme Court...shall be in writing and shall contain a concise state of the facts and reasons for each decisions..."?
>> 2. Do the procedures regarding the disqualification of judges set forth in Michigan Court Rule 2.003 apply to Supreme Court justices?
>
> My dissenting statement answers "yes" to those questions and explains how the four-justice majority has failed in this case to abide by the rule of law. My dissenting statement explains how this failure has contributed to the unjust reversal of a jury verdict in this, as you described it, "exceedingly strong" sexual harassment case.
>
> At our September 30th conference, you and Justice Taylor questioned whether I meant what I said in my dissenting statement. As I stated at conference, my dissent reflects what I intend to write regarding this case at this time. The substance of my dissent is that the four majority justices' failures to abide by the constitutional requirement that the court state reasons for each decision (Const 1963 Article 6, Section 6), their failures to abide by the court rule procedures governing the disqualification of judges (MCR 2.003), and the irrelevant and improper reference in the majority opinion in this case to

the plaintiff's argument style in other cases, are evidence of and create an appearance of bias and prejudice in this case.

Instead of addressing my substantive and constructive reasons for criticizing the majority's performance in this case, your letter questions my motives. Baseless attacks on the messenger in order to avoid acknowledging and responding to the message are as old as human history and sadly continue today, particularly in government. Such attacks and methods are unworthy of any justice of the Michigan Supreme Court.

Your letter also seems to seek to convince me that you do not harbor any bias or prejudice against the plaintiff's attorney. As stated in my dissent, the reference by the majority on this case to plaintiff's attorney's style of argument in other cases is irrelevant and improper under the law, just as the references in your September 28 letter to how you have performed by affirming in other cases involving plaintiff's attorney is irrelevant to your performance as a justice in this case.

Thus, while I acknowledge your effort, you, Chief Justice Corrigan, and Justice Taylor and Markman should recognize the obvious appearance of bias and prejudice in this case, your explanations of your decisions and participation should be in writing in the order denying rehearing for the parties and public, who have a constitutional right to know under law.

At conference I invited, and I continue to await, constructive comments or suggestions that anyone might have regarding the substance of my dissent.

Sincerely,

Note: You handed me a copy of your personal letter minutes before the court's September 30, 2004 conference. During the conference, you mentioned to the justices that you had written me a letter regarding my dissent. Justice Kelly questioned, "What letter?" To that I commented that I had no objection to your sharing the letter with the justices. After conference, you circulated by e-mail to the justices a copy of your letter to me dated September 28. Therefore, I have similarly circulated by e-mail a copy of this, my responding letter.[677]

The item was again passed at the Oct. 14th conference.

And then, Oh, boy! When this majority of four didn't get its way, the response was usually to badger...to keep up the attack until it got what it wanted, most often by wearing down what it saw as the opposition.

---

677 Elizabeth Weaver, letter to Robert Young, 13 October 2004, unpublished.

On October 20 Young sent a letter to Weaver. It had come down to one word: "appearance."

> Dear Betty:
>
> As I did initially, I am writing directly to you about my concern about your proposed statement. Should you desire it, I will share it with our colleagues.
>
> I have reviewed your letter of October 13, 2004, responding to my earlier letter. I am disappointed that you considered my letter an attack rather than an appeal as I had intended. As I understand your letter, your statement is intended to force a response to your views on the proper disqualification procedure. While this may be a legitimate goal, I do not believe that it is necessary to that goal to suggest that the *Gilbert* majority harbors *actual* bias against plaintiff or her attorney as I believe that your current statement suggests.
>
> In particular, as I did in my original letter, I call to your attention the following sentence:
>
>> Unfortunately, the majority's focus on plaintiff's argument style does not stand alone in the record of this case as *evidence of the majority's bias and prejudice against plaintiff's attorney.* (EAW Dissenting Statement at 6).
>
> Unlike all other characterizations of the *Gilbert* majority in your statement, this sentence is unique in that it does not acknowledge, as your statement does elsewhere, that your concern is with the *appearance of bias.*
>
> Accordingly, I ask that you modify this sentence to make clear that you are not suggesting that the Gilbert majority is actually biased:
>
>> Unfortunately, the majority's focus on plaintiff's argument style does not stand alone in the record of this case as support for an appearance of the majority's bias and prejudice against plaintiff's attorney.
>
> I believe that this change is consonant with your statement and hope that you will be amenable to making this modest change.
>
> Very truly yours,[678]

No sale. Weaver responded October 27, 2004, both to all the justices and separately to Young. She included her revised dissent. Here's the memo:

---

678 Robert P. Young, Jr., letter, 20 October 2004, unpublished.

Plaintiff's request for rehearing was received by the court in mid-August and appeared on the first scheduled agenda thereafter on September 9. At that time, there were four votes to deny rehearing in the *Gilbert v DaimlerChrysler* case so I held it for a dissenting statement.

I circulated my dissenting statement on September 20, the Monday before our next scheduled Thursday conference on September 23. The item was passed without discussion. Shortly before the following conference on September 30, Justice Young gave me a letter regarding my dissent, which was shared with the other justices by e-mail after conference. On October 13, before the next scheduled conference on October 14, I responded by letter to Justice Young and copied by e-mail my response to the justices.

On October 14, the item was passed again. Before the next scheduled conference on October 21, I received a second letter dated October 20 from Justice Young requesting one change to my dissent that cannot be made. Although I was satisfied with my dissent, the few changes that have been made to my attached revised dissent are intended to further clarify, particularly for Justice Young, my position in this matter.

With the exception of Justice Young's letter and Justice Taylor's comments at the September conference, which I answered then and again in my October 13 letter, I have received no comments regarding my dissent from any other justice.

All the other motions for rehearing from our last term that appeared on the September 9 agenda have been resolved except for this motion in *Gilbert v DaimlerChrysler.* Unless there are further circulations in this case to which I may wish to respond, I am ready to release this case and my pen is down.[679]

In the letter to Young, she repeated the call for answers concerning the matter relating to the constitution and disqualification and concludes with:

Your letter of October 20 did not respond to my questions. Instead it requested a change to my dissent that cannot be made. That request revealed the need to further clarify for you the dissent. To that end I have made some changes to the dissent and have circulated today, October 27, my revised dissent to the court.

Sincerely,[680]

More or less "I'll see you and raise you...two." Seventeen pages worth.

---

679 Elizabeth A. Weaver, "Memorandum," 27 October 2004, unpublished.
680 Elizabeth A. Weaver, letter, 27 October 2004, unpublished.

Among other modifications, she called their denial of the request for rehearing,

> The final opportunity <u>for the four majority justices to respond to the evidence of bias and prejudice in this case</u> and to correct the appearance of bias and prejudice caused by the majority justices' <u>irrelevant and improper reference in their decision to plaintiff's attorney's argument style in other cases, and the majority justices'</u> failures in this case to abide by the Michigan Court Rule, MCR 2.003 that governs the disqualification of a judge, and their failures in this case to abide by the Michigan Constitution, article 6, section 6 that required that the court state "reasons for each decision," when considering the plaintiff's motion for disqualification.[681]

There was more, much more that directly impugned their actions, not merely the appearance of their actions.

But it all came to a halt. However much we might wish she'd gone ahead and published her full dissent, what showed up in the final order of denial was something much more abbreviated.

> January 28, 2005.

> In this cause, a motion for rehearing is considered, and it is DENIED.

> MICHAEL F. CAVANAGH and MARILYN J. KELLY, JJ., would grant rehearing for the reasons stated in the dissenting opinion by MICHAEL F. CAVANAGH, J.

> WEAVER, J. (dissenting).

> I dissent from the decision of the four-justice majority (Chief Justice Taylor and Justices Corrigan, Young, and Markman) to deny plaintiff's motion for rehearing. After six weeks of testimony and argument, a jury found defendant, DaimlerChrysler Corporation, liable for several years of sexual harassment suffered at work by plaintiff, Linda Gilbert. Tragically, four months after the four majority justices reversed the jury verdict, plaintiff, Linda Gilbert, died at age 45 of a heart attack.

> I would grant plaintiff's motion for rehearing, vacate the majority's reversal of a jury verdict in this exceedingly strong case of sexual harassment, and remand for remittitur.[682]

Oh, yes, Gilbert had died by that time.

681 Elizabeth A. Weaver, dissent draft, *Gilbert v DaimlerChrysler*, 27 October 2004, unpublished.
682 Order of denial, *Gilbert v DaimlerChrysler*, Michigan Supreme Court, 28 January 2005, http://www.leagle.com/xmlResult.aspx?xmldoc=20051127691NW2d436_11118.xml&docbase=CSLWAR2-1986-2006

She died four months after the majority of four reversed the case and sent it back for remittitur for a new trial. So she did die really fast. To me, it shows a great injustice. They had to reach and find a way to reverse that case because they wanted to reverse it.

The gal was dead; it was useless. And I was done; I was leaving the court.

The conclusion of this case and others were proximate with her announced intention to leave the court.

This case played a role, but it was not in itself determinative. There were the multiple tyrannies, the deceits, the unnecessary secrecy that had effectively controlled and determined both the administrative and case decisions of the court...in this case and In re Gilbert and others you'll learn about—particularly In re JK. Too, there was the treatment of the court staff and the Gromek appointment. I had come to the conclusion being there on the court was futile—that it was an immoral and impossible situation—that efforts to correct and improve it could not be successful by working from within. The best I could do was announce my intended departure and hope it would send the strong message that things were most seriously and terribly wrong at the Supreme Court.

For Fieger, too, there was nothing else to be done for Linda Gilbert, the matter was closed. There would be no retrial. But he said her death was tied to the Supreme Court's reversal:

> She killed herself. ... She was truly a victim. They mocked her. And specifically Young, because he wrote [the opinion]—although he got the other three to join along. He clearly had a role in her death, and the brutality that was inflicted upon her, in the name of protecting that corporation. ...Getting Geoff Fieger and protecting that corporation.
>
> Also, we'll never know the extent to which [...] Chrysler—DaimlerChrysler—shuffled millions of dollars through the Chamber of Commerce and it ended up in their campaign coffers, which is a significant possibility. But they never disclose that.[683]

As far as Weaver is concerned, it came down to numbers...11 and four.

Well, there are 11 judges. You start with the trial judge, and then there were three on the Court of Appeals, and there were seven on the Supreme Court making 11. Seven of the 11—plus the jury— got it right. But the unjust work of the power block of the majority of four, the Engler Four—that controlled the court—reversed it. ...A tragic irony—a tragic result of four trumping seven—plus the jury—when the four should not have participated in the case. It was an example of injustice and agenda pushing at the Supreme Court, agendas of apparent and actual bias and prejudice against an attorney and wanting to shut down plaintiffs' trial lawyer cases.

---

683 Geoffrey Fieger.

Plaintiffs' trial lawyers, I think, had their way earlier on with justices on previous Michigan Supreme Courts, and now the Engler Four were going to assert their own agenda and reverse it and let the opposite group, their financial supporters, have their way with the court. It's wrong. It's not justice; it's injustice.

Justices should look at these cases one at a time and not be driven to their decisions by their own agendas or by all these special interests, be it plaintiffs' trial lawyers, insurance companies, prosecutors, businesses, or doctors, or what-have-you. They all are important to the function of society, but none of them are always right. And we the people don't need justices with agendas who are dependent on one group or another set of groups to get the millions of dollars that now have gotten into the Supreme Court justices' campaigns.

If only the Four had been paying attention.

Chapter 15

The Forever Family?
In re JK

By the time a court steps in to remove a child from a parent's custody, things have come far down the road. There are reports and evaluations, files and recommendations. Along the way, there have to be a long series of failed attempts on the part of the parent to do the kind of rearing that will not actively harm the child.

That primal bond between parent and child—where it exists—should be sundered only with great care and oversight. And usually somebody is not happy with the result. This time it was the majority of the Michigan Supreme Court.

The case involved a young single mother, Melissa Kucharski, who was 16 years old when her first son, Jacob, was born Dec. 16, 1997.

Melissa's parental rights were terminated March 30, 2001, by Kent County Probate Judge Patricia Gardner. That was after two years trying to work through a series of issues that included marijuana use and lack of appropriate care by the mother for the child. The decision was upheld by the Court of Appeals March 1, 2002. Then Judge Gardner oversaw Jacob's adoption by Deb and John Wordhouse, May 8, 2002. The Wordhouses had previously fostered him under a contract with Catholic Social Services.

By the time the Supreme Court made its ruling to reverse the adoption more than a year later, May 20, 2003, the legal system had been involved in this child's life for four years and would continue to be so for some time after.

The Supreme Court opinion sending Jacob back to the custody of his mother began this way:

> A judge in the Family Division of the Kent Circuit Court terminated the respondent mother's parental rights to her three-year-old son after concluding that there were attachment and bonding problems between the respondent and the child.[684]

684 *In re JK, Minor*, No. 121410, Michigan Supreme Court, 20 May 2003, 1, http://publicdocs.courts.mi.gov:81/

Based on what we learned of the majority's writing style in *Gilbert v DaimlerChrysler*, what might we note? You will recall that Justice Robert Preston Young, Jr. began his recitation of facts in that case by putting the blame squarely on Linda M. Gilbert for being an alcoholic drug user. If there is anything to that analysis, who might have been the target for the wrath of court here?

The judge?

The opinion continued:

> Following an unsuccessful appeal to the Court of Appeals, respondent filed a timely application for leave to appeal in this court. While that application was pending, unknown to this court, the family division of the circuit court engaged in the apparently unprecedented and extraordinary action of allowing the foster parents to adopt the child. Again, unaware of this adoption, we remanded for additional findings.

> Because we find the evidence supporting termination to be insufficient, we vacate the order terminating the respondent's parental rights. We also take this opportunity to make clear what we believe to be obvious, that the circuit court is not permitted to proceed with an adoption following a termination of parental rights where the parent's appeal of that decision remains pending.[685]

Well, now you know who the Supreme Court held at fault. But all this is in the middle of things—a literary device known as *in media res*. We'll take it both ways from here, but we'll begin with much that led up to this opinion.

In Michigan, when a judge—usually a probate judge—permanently removes a child from his or her family of origin, there is a nearly automatic review launched at the Court of Appeals—all the parent or parents (well, probably the attorney) need to do is simply file. This is the kind of case that really needs an additional examination: was the law followed, were procedures observed, were all the reports in order, was anything overlooked?

This was a case of a very young mother, Melissa, and her son, Jacob.[686] By the time Kent County Family Independence Agency protective services worker Mona Norris petitioned the Kent County Circuit Court, Family Division, to take jurisdiction of Jacob, Melissa was 17 years old and Jacob was 14 months. That was Feb. 1, 1999. The reason? Melissa wasn't acting responsibly for her son, instead, leaving him in the care of whomever would watch him at her mother's home. As well, Melissa tested positive for—and admitted to using—marijuana.

OPINIONS/FINAL/SCT/20030520_S121410(49)_IN_RE_JK12APR03.OP.PDF.
685 Ibid.
686 Jacob's father Travis Englehart, had his parental rights terminated in the same process. He did not, however, contest the court's action.

Judge Patricia Gardner presided at the April 21 adjudication/disposition hearing that resulted a week later in both Jacob and his mother going to a foster care home. That began a long series of foster care placements, some with mother and child together, some apart. In all, Jacob would be separated from his mother five times as the system worked with her to get back in school, off drugs, and adequately caring for her son.

Judge Gardner was overseeing the case with reviews every three months.

There was pretty much every effort made: parenting lessons, substance abuse counseling, talk, talk, talk. And it didn't take, at least not enough to satisfy the court that would shortly decide Melissa was not ready to be Jacob's mother.

On June 15, 2000, the Kent County Prosecutor's Office petitioned to have Melissa's parental rights terminated. That petition, again before Judge Gardner, was scheduled for a hearing June 28, adjourned to Oct. 23, and again adjourned, this time to Dec. 14.

Along the way, the court determined on Dec. 4, 2000, the need for an attachment assessment. If Jacob was not attached to his mother, it might have some bearing on the case. If there were a lack of attachment, that might be enough reason to terminate Melissa's parental rights even though she had been making progress. At a certain point, the court has to step in and say "enough," considering especially the length of time the process had consumed.

Meanwhile, the foster mother—Deb Wordhouse—had on her own identified Yvwania Richardson, M.S.W., as a recognized expert in bonding and attachment.[687] Catholic Social Services set up and then paid for the assessment Richardson performed Dec. 5.

The records indicate Richardson spent 50 minutes observing mother and child. She would report and later testify that there were issues of concern. She was joined in her assessment by Lora Holewinski, the Catholic Social Services foster care case manager, who had carefully studied the relationship between Melissa and Jacob and had overseen Melissa's completion of her behavioral agreement with CSS. In many areas, Melissa had made progress: she had finished school, stayed off drugs, and spent time with Jacob. But there was the nagging concern over the degree of the bond between parent and child.

Contravening that assessment was that of Elaine Hoogeboom, a substance-abuse counselor from AO of Arbor Circle. She worked with Melissa under a contract through Catholic Social Services, first on the drug issues, and, later on

> ...[P]arenting instruction and an evaluation of Melissa's attachment to Jacob. Ms. Hoogeboom conducted six joint sessions with Jacob and Melissa beginning on November 9, 2000. Ms. Hoogeboom did not notice any attachment issues and recommend that Jacob be returned to Melissa's care. Ms.

---

687 Richardson is listed as chief executive officer of Alternatives for Children and Families in Burton, a community near Flint, Mich. [http://www.acfinc.org/.]

Hoogeboom has no special training or educational background in the area of attachment or bonding.[688]

The day of decision was March 30, 2001. During the termination hearings, January 22 and March 7, 2001, Judge Gardner heard on the one hand Hoogeboom, who said that she thought there were few problems...and those could be overcome. Richardson countered that the child would be better served separated from his biological mother; that if reunited with his mother, he was likely to regress on gains made with the foster family.

Judge Gardner had a thorny issue.

> Judge Gardner's opinion noted that although appellant's substance abuse issues during pregnancy and after Jacob's birth were the primary reason he was made a temporary ward of the court, substance abuse was no longer a barrier to reunification, and the primary reasons for the request for termination were bonding and attachment problems between the appellant and Jacob. Judge Gardner concluded that even though this was a difficult case because the appellant had in many respects made significant improvement, appellant had not rectified all of the conditions that caused the child to come within the jurisdiction of the court, and there was no reasonable likelihood that those conditions would be rectified within a reasonable time considering Jacob's age, which was between 3 and 3 ½ on the date of Judge Gardner's 3/30/01 decision.[689]

Gardner wrote in her opinion "Melissa Kucharski has been given more time and more chances than most parents based on her age and ability to make progress on some issues...."[690]

Gardner did what she thought she ought to do, first by terminating Melissa's parental rights, and—after an appeal at the Court of Appeals affirming her decision (March 1, 2002) and a denial of a request for rehearing at that court (April 4, 2002)—by allowing the foster parents to adopt Jacob. The adoption before Judge Gardner took place May 8, 2002.

Gardner based her decision to allow the adoption based on the law contained in Michigan Compiled Laws (MCL) 710.41 and 710.56.

In the first, MCL 710.41, the law said

> ...[A] child shall not be placed in a home for the purpose of adoption until an order terminating parental rights has been entered. [...] After an order

688 Mark T. VanSlooten, "Answer to application for leave to appeal, brief on appeal—appellee, Jacob Kucharski," 38 March 2003, 5.
689 Commissioner's report, "Recommended denial to be considered at conference," 10 June 2002, unpublished, 3.
690 Ibid., 11.

terminating parental right has been entered, the court shall enter any appropriate orders.... [...] Such orders shall not be withheld because the period specified for a rehearing or an appeal as of right has not expired, or because of the pendency of any rehearing or appeal as of right.[691]

That meant that once Melissa's parental rights were terminated, Gardner had the authority to place Jacob with the Wordhouses for a pre-adoptive placement. That's the language contained in the next part of MCL 710.41:

> If an order terminating parental rights is entered pursuant to this chapter or chapter XIIA, the child may be placed in a home for the purpose of adoption during the period specified for a rehearing or an appeal as of right and the period during which a rehearing or appeal as of right is pending.[692]

No adoption could be completed, though, until the Court of Appeals made its final ruling. That's the language both in MCL 710.41:

> ...[A]n adoption will not be ordered until 1 of the following occurs:
>
> [...]
>
> (c) There is a decision of the Court of Appeals affirming the order terminating parental rights.[693]

...and the language in MCL 710.56(2) (c) that allows an adoption to go ahead only when "the Court of Appeals affirms the order terminating parental rights."[694]

The adoptive placement was described to the parties as an "at-risk adoption," that is, it would stand unless it was reversed by the Court of Appeals, an extremely unlikely event. There also was a further possibility that if the Court of Appeals affirmed the lower court ruling that the matter could move to the Supreme Court. But it was even more unlikely that the high court would grant leave and even less likely that it might reverse. Weaver couldn't recall a case where that had ever happened while she was sitting on the court.

Both provisions of the law allow an adoption to occur once the Court of Appeals has affirmed the order terminating parental rights. In this case, this Court of Appeals affirmed the order terminating parental rights in a unanimous opinion on March 1, 2002, and the adoption by the foster parents, with whom the child had been living since May 2000, occurred on May 8, 2002. Judge Gardner should not be criticized for following the applicable adoption law as that law was written by the legislature.

---

691 Probate Code of 1939 (excerpt) Act 288 of 1939, MCL 710.41 (1) http://www.legislature.mi.gov/ (S(p4ltr0unuwhtjf45onbgqsne))/mileg.aspx?page=GetObject&objectname=mcl-710-41.
692 Ibid., (2).
693 Ibid.
694 Probate Code of 1939 (excerpt) Act 288 of 1939, MCL 710.56 (2) (c), http://www.legislature.mi.gov/ (S(p4ltr0unuwhtjf45onbgqsne))/mileg.aspx?page=getObject&objectName=mcl-710-56.

But that's eventually what the Supreme Court did...when it finally granted leave in the case. That leave almost didn't happen. In fact, the case was first sent back for additional fact-finding, and then it was unanimously denied.

The application came April 25, 2002, about two weeks before Jacob was adopted. (The matter of his adoption was not on the high court's radar until later; it was the element of surprise that kicked the majority into high dudgeon.) The first commissioner assigned to the case recommended in his "Greenie"[695] June 10, 2002, that the case be denied.

Justice Markman circulated a memo June 21 criticizing the actions at the trial court, concluding with "while I am not certain that reversal is the right course of action here, I do want to encourage the court to reflect further upon this case."[696]

July 23rd Justice Young circulated a memo suggesting peremptory reversal—if there were the votes—to avoid adding delay in resolving the matter. Otherwise, he wrote, let it go; deny it.

The court gathered at a July 25, 2002, conference and decided to send it back to Judge Gardner for additional fact-finding and an update from her court.

Weaver created a timeline of events that runs eight pages. And from that, she created a 35-page unpublished narrative of all that transpired. Here's her account of what happened:

> Over dissent from Justice Young and myself, on August 8, 2002, more than three months after the appeal was filed, the majority justices caused an order to enter remanding[697] the case to the family court for a supplemental hearing and "updated" findings on the present circumstances of the biological mother and the child. This was done despite the fact that any new information on the biological mother's and the child's present circumstances, including his adoption after the termination of the biological mother's parental rights, would be irrelevant in reviewing the trial judge's decision a year earlier to terminate the biological mother's parental rights.[698]

Judge Gardner did as the Supreme Court ordered, held a hearing and reported her findings to the high court on Sept. 9, 2002. Weaver noted:

> All seven justices then learned that the child had been adopted after the Court of Appeals opinion issued, as well as the fact that the biological mother remained unmarried but had had another child by a different father.[699]

Even Justice Markman, who had been leading the parade for reversal seemed resolved to the situation:

---

695 The commissioners' reports were printed on green paper.
696 Stephen J. Markman, "Memorandum," 21 June 2002, unpublished.
697 A remand is a sending back of a case, often for update and sometimes for "do overs."
698 Elizabeth A. Weaver, "Draft history and comments on *In re JK*," unpublished, 6 January 2006, 9.
699 Ibid., 10.

Although I previously favored reversal of the probate court's parental ter-mination decisions, on the basis of the updated information—in particular, Jacob's adoption and his apparently positive family life and personal devel-opment—I do see how this position can now be sustained.[700] Indeed, I am not even sure that reversal is now possible, given Jacob's adoption. Must we deny on the ground of mootness?

Although I have no reservations about denying leave at this juncture, I am nonetheless concerned that this court's review has apparently been ren-dered futile by the action of the probate court in allowing the adoption to proceed during the pendency of this appeal. It seems anomalous that the probate court, whose own decision was in the process of being appealed, could effectively thwart such appeal by its own actions. I look forward to discussing the merits of opening an administrative file on this matter at our conference.[701]

On Oct. 22, 2002, all seven justices joined in denying the appeal. Not all of them were satisfied, though. And over the winter, the issue of the case was raised several times. One of the reasons was because of new and inexperienced commissioners.

These were new people that were hired by the chief justice—essentially by the Engler Four.

The report we had from experienced staff all along was, "deny this case; and it's sad, and close, but not that close, and we're not the fact-finders. And so the trial judge is following the law." But we had new staff being brought in, and we had two new staff who didn't really know the law and failed to mention the adoption law in their reports, but who had sympathy for the biological mother.

One of them wrote urging the court to take up the case.

Justice Cavanagh favored reconsideration and granting leave. He joined Justice Kelly, Justice Taylor, and Justice Markman. Writing March 7, 2003, Justice Corrigan raised the issue of

The so-called "attachment problem" between Melissa and Jacob [that] was supported by only a single expert, who was paid approximately $500 for his [sic] testimony following a single interview lasting less than one hour. Virtually every other witness who interacted with Melissa and Jacob saw no attachment or bonding issues and thought the child should be returned to his mother's care.[702]

---

700 This is a footnote included in his document at this point:

> However, I am considerably less persuaded that the updated evidence of the respondent's conduct suggests the correctness of the termination of her parental rights. Had Jacob not already been adopted and faring well, I do not view such evidence as sufficiently strengthening the case for termination.

701 Stephen J. Markman, "Memorandum," unpublished, 11 October 2002.
702 Maura D. Corrigan, "Memorandum," unpublished, 7 March 2003.

Corrigan wanted to go back and retry the case, said Weaver, this time at the Supreme Court. But that's not where you try cases. Of note is the idea of a single expert. That will come up again. And for Corrigan the issue is one of jurisdiction:

> This case affords us an opportunity to explain that we are not ousted of jurisdiction where a trial court permits an adoption to proceed while the termination decision is still under review. We can also use this case to discuss the strictures of the Safe Families Act and the Binsfeld legislation. On the basis of what I now know, I would be prepared to undo the adoption and return Jacob to his mother. In light of the horrific circumstances, we should expedite our review.[703]

They just decided that they wanted to change the law because they were insulted that the trial judge had followed the legislature's law. The legislature had really seen the history of things, and had said that for the sake of the child's best interest, after the Court of Appeals case is over and that appeal period is gone, the trial judge, at her discretion, can go on and do the adoption so the child moves on. In the last ten years preceding the 2003 reversal decision in the JK case, the Michigan Supreme Court had 229 applications for leave to appeal in termination-of-parental-rights cases. During that time, the court issued orders addressing the merits of cases or opinions in only seven cases. In none— zero—of those cases did the justices reverse the termination on parental rights. The court had never reversed under those circumstances.

But there must have been some legal reason that would allow the majority to reverse.

There was. They had found a way through a court rule, MCR 7.215(F), tacking it on to the legislative adoption statutes. In essence, MCR 7.215(F) says that no ruling of the Court of Appeals is final until either the time for an appeal to the Supreme Court runs out, or the appeal is filed and the Supreme Court disposes of the matter...either denying leave on the case or resolving it. This is how the majority would swing it:

> While the statute refers to affirmance by the Court of Appeals, <u>it must be read in conjunction with MCR 7.215(F)</u> [emphasis added], which establishes the effective date of a Court of Appeals opinion:
> (1) Routine Issuance. Unless otherwise ordered by the Court of Appeals or the Supreme Court or as otherwise provided by these rules,
> (a) The Court of Appeals judgment is effective after the expiration of the time for filing a timely application for leave to appeal to the Supreme Court, or, if such an application is filed, after the disposition of the case by the Supreme Court.[704]

It was a matter of power and pride, too: How can it be that the legislature can say that we can't have the last word as the Supreme Court? And, so, we're going to change that. We'll do it by overruling the

---

703 Ibid.
704 *In re JK, Minor*, No. 121410, Michigan Supreme Court, 20 May 2003, 17, http://publicdocs.courts. mi.gov:81/OPINIONS/FINAL/SCT/20030520_S121410(49)_IN_RE_JK12APR03.OP.PDF.

statute with our court rule, which was exactly, for three of the Engler Four, what they had said courts <u>should not</u> *and* <u>could not</u> *do in* McDougall v Schanz.

McDougall v Schanz was important to this case because it made clear the precedence between enacted legislation and court rules.[705]

The important part of McDougall v Schanz was that it had made it clear that when the legislature has spoken on substantive law, and when the court rules have spoken on substantive law, the legislature prevails. McDougall v Schanz was over whether the legislature could put caps on the amount of damages that could be gotten in plaintiffs' trial lawyer suits. And our opinion determined "Yes, the legislature could." And in this child case, In re JK, the legislature's statute—the statute allowing the trial court to go ahead with an adoption after the Court of Appeals decision affirming termination of permanent rights was final—was substantive law.

Let the legislature's substantive statute prevail? No, not this time. On March 13, 2003, six of the seven justices voted to reconsider and grant leave. Weaver voted against it.

And I argued vigorously to not take it up, and I dissented on that, and then I argued vigorously that they look at the record here. This was folly as to what is going to happen to this child. In terms of the correctness of the adoption, you could possibly be right, but you could probably be wrong. It's always close. I mean, you don't know what people are going to do, whether they're really reformed or not. And this was causing extreme trauma in the child's life to not know who his permanent parents were.

I was looking for some common sense and some real caring about the child as opposed to proving legal points or creating new law or disliking the statute.

And she was outvoted. The court would grant leave and oral arguments were scheduled for April 9, 2003. There was a very busy time before those oral arguments were heard.

On April 1, one of the "new" commissioners delivered a three-page memorandum that served as a cover letter to a draft of what she suggested should be the court's opinion in the matter undoing the adoption and re-placing Jacob with Melissa Kucharski.

> The proposed opinion addresses both the lack of evidentiary support for the termination of respondent's parent rights and the invalid adoption which occurred while leave to appeal was pending in this court.[706]

That, of course, was not the determination under *McDougall v Schanz*. The commissioner wrote at length about the bonding assessment and Judge Gardner's comments from the bench:

> In the trial court's findings on remand from this court, the court portrayed seemingly innocuous circumstances in the worst possible light for respon-

705 *McDougall v Schanz*, Nos. 107956, 110707, Michigan Supreme Court, 30 July 1999, http://caselaw.findlaw.com/mi-supreme-court/1309783.html.
706 Unnamed commissioner, "Memorandum," 1 April 2003, unpublished, 2.

dent. For instance, the court disparaged respondent for purchasing a large-screen television despite her limited resources. The family court suggested that the television purchase illustrated that respondent's priorities were improper. The court also emphasized that respondent was not wearing an engagement ring, despite claiming she was engaged. If respondent had been wearing a diamond engagement ring, it is quite possible that the judge would have considered that an improper purchase in light of respondent's finances.

The trial court's findings on remand raise additional concerns. Throughout the discussion of the foster family, the court refers to the foster parents as "mom" and "dad." She refers to the extended foster family as the "grandparents," "aunts," "uncles," and "cousins." Conversely, the judge refers to the natural mother as Melissa or Ms. Kucharski. The phrasing of the entire written update suggests to me that the termination of respondent's rights and the subsequent adoption were foregone conclusions.[707]

The commissioner was writing about what occurred on remand...when the case had been sent back after the adoption for additional fact finding, none of which, according to Weaver, should have played into the Supreme Court's decision on the case. And of what followed in the memorandum, the commissioner additionally observed:

The draft opinion vacates the order terminating parental rights and orders Catholic Social Services commence reunification efforts. These reunification procedures are usually gradual ones, designed to prevent the child from being traumatized by the sudden change of homes.[708]

Well, the commissioner at least got that right: the justices thought they'd rule, and the child would go home with his natural mother. It wasn't going to work that way. I think they didn't know enough about the probate court to even realize that this child wasn't immediately going back to the parent, anyway, because when they reversed it, there had to be a period of transition. This was going to take longer, much longer. And these foster parents were so wonderful, because they didn't just throw up their hands in great dismay at the court's doing this; they went on and tried to work carefully with the transition.

What happened next was unprecedented in Weaver's experience. Two days before the oral arguments, Justice Taylor sent out a memo:

After getting ready for oral argument I remain convinced that we should reverse the trial court and Court of Appeals thus returning the child to his mother. I think the proposed [*per curiam*] prepared by commissioner [name excised] is well-done [sic] and can be adopted by the majority with few changes. I do urge two small changes [....]

707 Ibid., 3.
708 Ibid.

Given the lengthy delay that has already transpired in this case, I suggest we enter our opinion and judgment as soon as possible. I see three possible ways of proceeding. The first way would be for Justice Weaver to circulate her dissent taking less than the usual amount of time. The second way would be for us to enter our opinion this week with her dissent to follow. Or, third, we could enter an order this week with both opinions to follow.[709]

Chief Justice Corrigan chimed in with another memo:

I approve Justice Taylor's changes to the proposed *per curiam*, and I agree [name excised] did a fine job on the PC. I also agree that we need to expedite our opinion and await our conference discussion to decide how to proceed most expeditiously.[710]

It was not unusual for justices to talk about where they were on cases; vigorous debate was part of the process. Taylor knew well that Weaver was likely to dissent. But for Taylor and Chief Justice Corrigan to sign on to an opinion two days before the oral arguments was too much for Weaver. Writing in her history of the case she observed:

This case was "pre-decided." [...] Oral argument should be a time when justices are open-minded, willing to put aside their personal opinions and impressions about the case. It should not be a time when justices attempt to lay a foundation through their questioning to justify a pre-determined result for a decision already written, circulated, and signed on.[711]

Oral arguments take the form of pretty much whatever the court allows. The attorneys have already laid out their arguments in briefs supplied to the court. The oral portion gives them one more chance to say what's most important about the case, to make a reasoned argument before the court, and to respond to questions from the justices. Each side in a regular oral argument is given 30 minutes. In a tradition established by Weaver when she was chief justice, the attorneys before the bench have been given five uninterrupted minutes before they are engaged with questions or issues for clarification raised by the justices.

I established the five minutes for people to have an opportunity to speak without being interrupted. They pay thousands of dollars to get there. It shouldn't be used as an opportunity for justices to establish how smart they are, or that justices actually know the case or have read the case, or to promote justices' own agendas or ideas. At least give people five minutes to say why they are there, what they think their most important issues and arguments are before you start cross-examining or badgering them.

But when Justice Corrigan became the chief justice, she called it free-fire zone because she apparently looked at it as firing at these people.

---

709 Clifford W. Taylor, "Memorandum," 7 April 2003, unpublished, 1.
710 Maura D. Corrigan, "Memorandum," 7 April 2003, unpublished.
711 Elizabeth A. Weaver, "Draft history and comments on In re JK," unpublished, 29.

A video of the event is both compelling and disturbing.[712] There would be frequent interruptions from the bench, starting with a fusillade led by the chief justice.

Next, Taylor asked FIA attorney Quadiru Kent how many bonding experts there were in the state and why Yvwania Richardson had been picked. Kent didn't know why she was picked; it could have been coincidence. Taylor wanted to know more: "How many people in the state of Michigan are experts in the field? Would you be comfortable if the figure were, say, 10,000? Do you think there are 10,000 experts in the field?"

Kent responded: "I don't know, and I don't necessarily know the significance of it."

Taylor: "You're arguing coincidence; I'm just trying to test the probabilities of that."

Kent: "There may be just one in Michigan but there may be 10,000 nationwide."[713] Taylor kept on, wanting to know where Richardson had come from. Flint. Why? Had Kent ever seen a witness from that far away? He didn't know; he handled appeals, not the day-to-day work of the FIA.

Corrigan wanted to know why it was proper to have the foster mother identify the expert. Kent assured her that Richardson had not played any part in anything deceptive. Corrigan wanted to know if there shouldn't have been rules. Kent suggested that it was a matter for the legislature.

The justices kept on him, teaming up on occasion, not really allowing Kent to respond fully. At a little more than eight minutes in, Kent noted that he'd used his time. But no, the court would keep on with the matter. And there were Catch 22 questions far exceeding Kent's expertise as any kind of bonding and attachment expert.

Finally, Corrigan wanted to know if the FIA had knowledge that the adoption had no right to go ahead until the Supreme Court ruled. Young wanted to know how the adoption even occurred: "How is it that an adoption occurred during the pendency of an appeal to this court? Does the agency not recognize it cannot proceed while a termination is pending in this court?"[714]

For the first time, Weaver said something:

> Maybe the agency is relying on the statute.... Maybe the probate judge is relying on that.... Now, some may argue that one of our court rules that are not supposed to supersede the legislature enactments addresses this. But I think a study of that would find that it doesn't. So maybe that's what the judge was doing. It seemed to be legislative policy the judge was following.[715]

---

712 *In re JK,* video recording of oral arguments, Michigan Supreme Court, Michigan Government TV, 9 April 2003.
713 Ibid.
714 Ibid.
715 Ibid.

Kent agreed and stepped back after his time in the free-fire zone.

Next came Mark VanSlooten on Jacob's behalf. He related that instead of bonding and attachment surfacing as new issues late in the case, they were there from the start; even early on, Melissa was inattentive to Jacob and neglected her parenting role. VanSlooten was given far more time to answer questions without interruption than Kent, although Corrigan told him that Richardson's involvement "didn't smell right." Young again wanted to know why an "expert" had to come from outside the area and why the foster mother made the recommendation for her hiring by Catholic Social Services.[716]

More disturbing was the leading by the court of Melissa's attorney, Peter P. Walsh.

That guy took it and ran with it.

Smooth sailing.

At one point, Justice Markman slowed down the action. He wanted Walsh to deliver a message to his client:

> Mr. Walsh, I cannot let this hearing end without sharing one very personal thought to you. This is a remarkable case, as I think you know. There is no ideal resolution that's possible on this case. I don't know what this court's going to do on this case; it's a very difficult decision. But I'd like to say to you that if in the end you prevail and if the child is returned to Ms. Kucharski, I hope you'll communicate to her that this court has done a very remarkable thing on her behalf—a very unusual thing on her behalf—that this child has been subject to a remarkably wrenching experience—just as the adoptive parents have—and that she has at least the moral obligation to do everything in her power to understand what this court has done and to become the best possible mother she can; for it's her conduct that set this whole process in motion in the first place. And you don't have to answer me, I hope you won't answer me, but I hope you'll personally communicate this to her if, in the end, the child is returned to Ms. Kucharski.[717]

It was touching. And Ms. Kucharski was able to hear it first hand; she was there. And talk about playing to your audience!

But the fix was in. In fact, Weaver said she has reason to believe that the inexperienced commissioner had help from Markman in writing the draft opinion.

I mean, it was such a deceitful, dishonest presentation. We had a "pretend" fair hearing—there was nothing fair about it. It was a charade. And the four of them promoted this conspiracy theory, which, of course, the young birth mother's attorney picked up. I mean, he was being led by the court as to

716 Ibid.
717 Ibid.

what to argue, and the attorney for the child, as often is the case, and the agency, the FIA, were taken aback by the whole thing. But nevertheless, the attorney for the gal got it; that this is what to argue.

Chief Justice Corrigan was saying how she was really looking into this, while she had already signed on to an opinion about it.

And Taylor is then questioning this bonding. The "conspiracy" was that there had been a telephone call between the foster parents and the expert, which was short, but that was hiring, and they'd paid all of $500 to have this expert come ALL THE WAY from Flint to Grand Rapids. Anyone who knows Michigan, between Flint and Grand Rapids is not a HUGE amount; it's probably under a hundred miles.[718] It's not ALL THE WAY. Five hundred dollars for an expert is not an outrage. And it was like Taylor portrayed it as reaching out to get this particular expert, who the foster parents had gotten. In fact, it was the agency that really got her. The foster parents talked to her briefly by phone. And they were all made to look like a group of terrible conspirators, and the judge, of course, is this judge who, according to them, doesn't follow the law. And so all these people were being trashed...their reputations.

It was all made to appear that there had been a conspiracy to take this child away from the mother and not give her a chance. All the chances she'd had for two years didn't count. And supposedly, she had made all this progress. It was all there. She'd made some progress, but it wasn't enough; that was the judgment of the trial court. And the Supreme Court is risking this child's life. The law says that the court should get permanent placement for the child, that's important. It would be good for the Supreme Court to be thinking about the child and not be insulted because the legislature has allowed the trial court—that knows much more about these cases than the Supreme Court—to make an adoption decision for permanency for the child once the Court of Appeals affirmance of termination of parental rights decision is final, whether or not the Supreme Court reviews it.

Weaver was outvoted six to one. Nonetheless, she prepared a 50-page dissent listing all the missteps of the high court. It would never see the light of day. Instead, she would recuse herself. ...Something to do with the issue of the possibility of "10,000 experts" in bonding and attachment.

In the final opinion, she explained her stepping off the case:

> My decision not to participate in this case is based on a communication that I had on Monday, April 28, 2003, with the state's central Family Independence Agency office in Lansing regarding an issue raised by a justice at oral argument on April 9, concerning the number of attachment and bonding experts in Michigan—"Do you think there are 10,000 experts in this field?"
>
> The communication occurred at the end of a telephone conversation with a staff person to the Governor's Task Force on Juvenile Justice (Children's Justice Task Force), which I chair. This staff person is employed by the

---

718 It's about 115 miles.

state's central FIA office in Lansing with task force funds. The conversation dealt with matters pertaining only to task force business until the end, when, in passing, I asked the staff person how many experts on attachment and bonding there are in Michigan.

Although he did not know, he connected me to someone whom he thought might know, a person who is also employed by the state's central FIA office in Lansing. After checking, this person informed me that there may be two such experts in Michigan and certainly not 10,000. Late on Monday, April 28, I shared that information with the justices on the court, writing:

> In a preliminary contact with the Family Independence Agency in Lansing the agency indicated that it was aware of two Michigan experts on bonding and attachment. Ms. Richardson is one of those two experts.[719]

That was all the majority needed.

I get a call from the chief justice, and she said that if I didn't drop my dissent and get off of the case and disqualify myself that they'd turn me in to the Judicial Tenure Commission because I've had an ex parte[720] communication with the plaintiff, FIA.[721]

Well, to me this is ridiculous, and I say so. Because they just don't want my dissent; because it just laid out all the things that were wrong...about what the real law was and how the judge followed the law.

And I said, "Well what are the rules for disqualification? Why should I disqualify myself? Even if you think it was ex parte—what was the harm?"

I didn't believe it was ex parte. They could wink and argue all they wanted about it, but I didn't talk to the people who were <u>in the case</u>. I was talking to the central office to somebody that worked for my task force.

But the message was clear: they didn't like my dissent, and they weren't going to have it published, and they would squelch it. And the way to squelch it is to threaten me with the JTC.

Back to her recusal statement:

> Although I believed this communication was not an *ex parte* communication—that the state's central FIA office in Lansing is not a party in this case because the Kent County division of the FIA filed the petition and is a party in the case—as discussed below, I recognized that it is a question of law and fact which has not been decided by this court.

---

719 Elizabeth A. Weaver writing in dissent, *In re JK, Minor*, 3.
720 An *ex parte* communication refers to interaction with only one party to the action at court. In this case, Corrigan threatened action because the person Weaver consulted was from the FIA.
721 That's corroborated in a memo by Chief Justice Corrigan to Weaver, 16 May 2003, unpublished.

Because the chief justice raised the question whether it was an *ex parte* communication, and *ex parte* communications can be grounds for disqualification, I believed the parties and their attorneys had a right to know of the communication.[722]

So Weaver contacted them and let them know that, should they desire, she'd disqualify herself and step off. She assured them that the knowledge gained wouldn't give either side an advantage, nor would it influence her decision. The attorneys for the child and the FIA had no problems, but Melissa and her attorney did.

I continue to believe that the state's central FIA office in Lansing is not a party in a termination-of-parental-rights case brought by a county FIA office. Nevertheless, preliminary research does not reveal any decision by this Court regarding whether the state central FIA office in Lansing is a party in a case brought by a county FIA office.

This question is one of both law and fact. In order to resolve it, this court would need to hold an evidentiary hearing and make a finding on this point. Such a hearing and the time needed to make the legal decision would further delay this case.

Accordingly, for all the above reasons, I am not participating in this case.[723]

Weaver's operating maxim for disqualification has always been this: When in doubt, get out.

And if it went to the Judicial Tenure Commission—and I believed the justices would do it—then this would go on for years. The Judicial Tenure Commission didn't have any time rules for them as to when they have to act on anything. They could drag it on, sit on it, what-have-you.

And this poor child's life, where there are six votes that are going to do this no matter what, that this was now not a matter of good sense for this child. This was a matter of power and pride, agendas, and getting me in line. And so I weighed the cost to the child; that took precedence. I would have happily had it out, to have let everyone—the people—know what really went on here.

So she was off the case, and her dissenting opinion against reversing the trial court was effectively suppressed. And no one would know the "what" and "how" of the way the majority reached its decision.

When it came to me explaining in my dissent the process of achieving the decision, it was too much for the majority; the decision couldn't stand the scrutiny. And in this case, it was dilatory and really deceitful; that's not how you're supposed to make a decision. And people had a right to know.

---

722 Elizabeth A. Weaver writing in dissent, *In re JK, Minor*, 4.
723 Ibid., 7.

The *Grand Rapids Press* had been closely following the story:

> An adoption reversal ordered by the Michigan Supreme Court means joy for one family, tragedy for another and yet another life change for the little boy in the middle.
>
> "It's like a death in the family," said Franklin Wordhouse, the adoptive grandfather of 5-year-old Jacob, who Wednesday with his adoptive parents gathered at Wordhouse's home on Grand Rapid's Southeast Side.
>
> "In some ways it's worse than death because the child is still alive and we know what's coming."
>
> Caught in a legal tug-of-war won by his birth mother, the boy could have trouble rebuilding trust after spending nearly half his life with adoptive parents, therapists said.
>
> "Who are you going to trust?" asked Vic Steinbeck, a counselor for The Therapy Clinic in Cascade Township.
>
> "There are going to be a million issues going on," he said. "I think the mother needs to be strongly involved in therapy, too."[724]

The *Grand Rapids Press* editorialized about the lengthy process of the termination and appeals:

> Michigan's appellate courts must do a better job of moving quickly on cases involving adoptions of children and parental rights. The Supreme Court's reversal last week of a Kent County adoption order is an example of the problem.
>
> Because it took more than two years for this case to wend its way through the appeals process—in the state Court of Appeals and the Supreme Court—all the people involved have or will suffer: the birth mother, the adoptive parents and the 5-year-old boy at the center of the case.
>
> [...]
>
> Whether or not the Supreme Court is right in its assessment of the case, a clear wrong has been done in taking so long—more than two years—to get to the decision. Quicker decision at the appellate levels—in months, rather than years—could have avoided much of the heartbreak surrounding this case.

---

724 John Agar and Barton Deiters, "Difficult changes to follow adoption reversal," *Grand Rapids Press*, 22 May 2003.

[...]

With this case fresh in their minds, a task force already working on ways to reduce appellate delays involving termination of parental rights (TPR) must get the ball rolling on reforms. Justice Elizabeth Weaver, who did not participate in the Kucharski ruling due to a legal conflict, seems aware of that. Justice Weaver chairs the Governor's Task Force on Juvenile Justice. In a separate attachment to the Kucharski case she noted that a proposed court rule would eliminate appellate delays by mandating TPR cases take no more than 11 months (eight in the Court of Appeals, three in the Supreme Court) after an appeal is filed.

Even 11 months seems too long, but it's better than the two to three years the process now takes. When a child's future hinges on decisions coming from appellate courts, speed ought to [be] a paramount consideration. One reading of Jacob's story testifies to that.[725]

In a subsequent *Press* story, reporter John Agar noted the delays at the high court:

The Supreme Court initially refused to hear the case but later overturned the termination. [...]

A Supreme Court justice blamed her own court for leaving two families "in legal limbo." The court took far too long—13 months—to reach a decision, Justice Elizabeth Weaver said.

"This court should ensure that so excessive an appellate delay never happens again," she said in the opinion.

She noted that since the May 20 decision to overturn the termination was issued, the court has taken a "modest first step to reduce delay in termination of parental-rights cases" by speeding up the appeals process. But the steps were not significant, she said.

She blamed her own court for being the "real problem of this delay." She said that shortening the appeals process by requiring tighter deadlines for appellants would not have a big impact.

"The amendments impose time restrictions on the parties, but not the Supreme Court itself. These amendments would have no effect on the 13 months that this case, which was timely filed, spent in the Supreme Court."[726]

725 Editorial, "Adopting new rules: For children's sake the state's appeals courts must move faster," *Grand Rapids Press*, 31 May 2003, A12.
726 John Agar, "Court rejects appeal in adoption dispute," *Grand Rapids Press*, 20 June 2003, A1.

The Kent County Prosecutor's Office had asked for a rehearing by the Supreme Court June 12, 2003, and was denied later that month. *Michigan Lawyers Weekly* picked up on it making note of the underlying issue that Weaver had repeatedly raised:

> Assistant Kent County Prosecutor Timothy McMorrow said Gardner's termination of the now 21-year-old's parental right should not have been second-guessed by the high court.
>
> "It's not the Supreme Court's job to reweigh the evidence," McMorrow told the *Grand Rapids Press*. "They're not the trial court."[727]

Judge Gardner would continue to supervise the case as the reunification process commenced. There would be some detours:

> The reunification of Melissa Kucharski and her 5-year-old son will be de-layed because she did not disclose she and her fiancé lost their jobs, a judge said Wednesday.
>
> Kucharski wept when [acting] Kent Court Circuit Court Judge Patricia Gardener[728] said visits with Jacob would be suspended 30 days while the mother works to rebuild trust with the therapist overseeing the process.[729]

Kucharski had submitted a monthly budget that indicated employment income. The lack of disclosure was the issue, said Gardner.

Things got back on track, and by March 2004, Jacob was nearly ready to move back with his mother. A *Press* story indicated that Jacob was a bright, inquisitive kindergartener. He wanted to see where he was going to be living with his mother, his half-brother, and his mother's fiancé, Derrick Rademaker, and the court was going to allow extended and unsupervised visits.[730]

It would take three more months before the entire case unraveled. Here's part of the *Press* story that chronicled the devolution:

> Four more days.
>
> That's how much longer 6-year-old Jacob Kucharski must wait to find out who his parents will be, after a courtroom bombshell Wednesday delayed a decision on whether he will return to his birth mother.

---

727 "High court to reconsider adoption reversal?" *Michigan Lawyers Weekly*, 23 June 2003, http://milawyer-sweekly.com/news/2003/06/23/high-court-to-reconsider-adoption-reversal063/.
728 Gardner was a probate judge serving in the family division of the Circuit Court by assignment of the Supreme Court and, so, was an acting circuit judge.
729 John Agar, "Mom's reunion with son put off," *Grand Rapids Press*, 11 September 2003, A1.
730 John Agar, "Reunion of mom, son on track," *Grand Rapids Press*, 4 March 2004, A21.

Family Court Judge Patricia Gardner said she will decide Monday whether to again terminate Melissa Kucharski's parental rights, after the Wayland woman recently tested positive for marijuana use.

The latest twist came a year after the state's highest court criticized the judge's early handling of the case, in which Kucharski lost custody of her son partly because of drug use.

The ruling gave Kucharski the chance to regain custody, and social workers and court officials have since suggested the boy could be returned to her.

But new allegations of marijuana use, revealed during Wednesday's hearing to reunite the pair, will keep the boy in legal limbo through the weekend—a familiar yet potentially damaging place for a child who has spent most of his life in the heart of what the judge has called "an impossible case."

"He needs an answer," psychotherapist Thalia Ference said Wednesday. "He urgently needs resolution."

[...]

Witnesses said the process has increasingly troubled Jacob. His attorney and others say he wants to remain with the Wordhouses, where he has continued to [live] as the case resolved.

He has had supervised and unsupervised visits with his mother, in preparation for the change, but the stress and anxiety are taking a toll.
Jennifer Webb, a child-welfare specialist for Catholic Social Services, said Jacob is "experiencing increased anxiety."[731]

Melissa had flunked two hair-follicle drug tests in March. Nonetheless, she denied using drugs. That led the court again to question her truthfulness.

But the judge was in another sticky spot. If Judge Gardner terminated Melissa's parental rights, the whole thing could start all over again with appeals to the upper courts. It could have dragged on another bunch of years.

This time Melissa acted for what she could see was Jacob's best interest; she had matured that much. This is from the continuing coverage:

A custody dispute between a woman and a couple who adopted her son has ended with the birth mother surrendering her parental rights to the boy.

---

731 John Agar, "Drug test adds twist to custody battle," *Grand Rapids Press*, 3 June 2004.

Calling it the "ultimate act of love," Melissa Kucharski's attorney said that 6-year-old Jacob will stay with Deb and John Wordhouse, the Grand Rapids couple who adopted him in 2001.

Kucharski, 22, of Wayland, believes that Jacob has a "crucial need for permanence," said attorney Charlie Clapp.[732]

She was evidently back into drugs and decided to voluntarily give up her rights, so they were terminated. She had then done the unselfish, loving—though difficult—thing for her child.

The child was re-adopted by the foster parents. But he had that extra, unnecessary long period of time (almost a year of his young life) caused by the poor performance of the Michigan Supreme Court and the misuse and abuse of its power...of not having the stability to know that he was always going to be with his parents. They were trying to give him the life he deserved that, obviously, the young gal wasn't ready to do for him because she was on her own immature tear.

The child had to go through that extra year of being in jeopardy. If it had gone the other way, he would be dispossessed of the family association with the only people that he was bonded and attached to: the Wordhouses. They were those he knew and loved as his parents.

Melissa had her own pain, part of which was and is having to live with her choices and the results. She has posted a website, My Son Jacob.[733] In it, she acknowledges that the Wordhouses are a powerful force for good in Jacob's life. She continues to deny her drug use before the hearing, and she has some hard words for the judicial system. But most important, she wants to let her son know that she loves him and thinks of him always.

Not Done Yet

This story could have ended here, but it didn't.

The Supreme Court looked bad. Worse, Weaver's assessments and criticisms had been vindicated. In typical Engler-majority fashion, they cast about for someone to blame. But you already know where this is going; it's where we started: blame Judge Gardner.

Before the case had concluded, there had been a complaint to the JTC.

On Feb. 9, 2004, Chief Justice Maura Corrigan received an anonymous letter condemning Judge Gardner's conduct in two cases. The first dealt with another Kent County custody case, but this time involving a teen girl. That case was *Ryan v Ryan*. The second was *In re JK*.

732 "Birth mom gives up parental rights," *Michigan Lawyers Weekly*, 2 August 2004, http://milawyersweekly.com/news/2004/08/02/birth-mom-gives-up-parental-rights/.
733 http://mysonjacob.com/.

Here's the carefully written letter:

> Dear Ma'am,
>
> In the enclosed opinions, Judge Patricia Gardner of the Family Division of the Kent County Circuit Court has been reprimanded by the Michigan Supreme Court and the Michigan Court of Appeals for judicial misconduct and abuse of her authority.
>
> The young child in the Kucharski case remains with his adoptive parents at the direction of Judge Gardner in indefinite defiance of this Court's Order. Judge Gardner has suspended the biological mother's visitation with her son for 30 days on at least one occasion during this reunification process. Each family remains is [sic] in the same limbo in this situation. The Supreme Court might as well not have issued its Order.
>
> Judge Gardner's misconduct and abuse of her authority in the Ryan case has resulted in a federal lawsuit.
>
> These cases were published in Detroit and Grand Rapids area newspapers.
>
> The Michigan Court of Appeals and the Michigan Supreme Court and the public are all very well aware of Judge Gardner's flagrant and ongoing misconduct. The Kent County Judges, court staff, and attorneys who appear before her are afraid to complain for fear of publicity and retaliation.
>
> A Michigan judge was disciplined if not removed from the bench for smoking a marijuana cigarette at a concert. Ignoring Judge Gardner's far worse and continuing misconduct damages the bench, and the Bar, in the eyes of the public. Ignoring Judge Gardner's misconduct puts families at risk. Judge Gardner must be disciplined and removed from the bench to protect the public and restore some credibility to the bench and the judicial system in the eyes of the public.[734]

Enclosed with the poison-pen letter were what the writer thought were illustrative newspaper clippings.

Most often, anonymous letters receive the attention they are due: filed and forgotten. But this time it was different. First, said Judge Gardner, Corrigan had the matter investigated by James Hughes, one of the four regional court administrators. Gardner described his visit:

> He came to the courthouse, met with our court administrator and reviewed the file. He met with members of our permanency planning department and

---

734 Anonymous letter to Maura D. Corrigan, undated, received 9 February 2004.

was told that all was in order. He also learned that I was a well respected, hardworking judge. There were no skeletons or bad feelings about me at the courthouse. He was further told that there was nothing to refer ....[735]

"The file was in order and there was nothing amiss," said Gardner.[736] Gardner related that Hughes took his report back to the chief justice who decided, evidence notwithstanding, that the matter was worthy of sending on to the Judicial Tenure Commission: ["...]You see that he was directed to forward the anonymous letter to the JTC," wrote Gardner[737]

That was too much. The chief justice shouldn't be making the referral because she might be sitting on it in the end. But as with many things...there aren't any rules. And, obviously, Maura thought it was absolutely necessary to act on it.

Weaver's reaction when she later learned of the letter was that it deserved no attention.

You usually would throw away a "love letter" like this. It's unsigned, and if the person doesn't have enough courage to stand and be identified as the accuser, it's suspect. Anything that is anonymous raises questions. I wouldn't think you would send this to the JTC. You might turn it over perhaps to the State Court Administrator to find out about it...but Maura already knew all about it. She knew or should have known Gardner was not acting out of bounds in In re JK.

The JTC filed the complaint against Gardner on Feb. 18, 2004, dealing solely with the *Ryan* case. That complaint was amended and broadened March 9 to include *In re JK*. For Gardner, the complaint meant additional work. She had to file responses to the JTC, explaining and documenting exactly what she had done.

And the kinds of questions the JTC was asking were...interesting. Here's a sampling:

1) Please provide the reasons for your finalizing the adoption of the minor child by his foster parent in 2002, in light of the fact that the Supreme Court's decision regarding the termination of parental rights as to the mother was not final.
2) Please provide the legal authority upon which you relied to disregard state law that provides a parent, whose rights to her child have been terminated, the right to appeal that decision, and prohibits you from ordering an adoption until the finalization of the termination of parental rights.
3) Please comment on your apparent attempt to circumvent appropriate judicial process, including the Supreme Court's appellate jurisdiction, by finalizing an adoption before the appeal regarding the termination proceedings was final. Address in your response whether you determined the adoption was "at risk" merely because the Supreme Court might vacate the termination of parental rights.

735 Patti Gardner, e-mail with co-author Schock, 27 June 2012.
736 Patti Gardner, conversation with co-author Schock, 5 July 2012.
737 Patti Gardner, e-mail with co-author Schock, 27 June 2012.

4) Please comment on your apparent failure to consider the impact on the child and adoptive family if the adoption had to be vacated, due to the reversal of the termination of the mother's parental rights. Please include in your response a consideration of the fact that the law prohibiting an adoption until appeals on termination proceedings are finalized was implemented to prevent such a situation from occurring.[738]

And there was more, but you get the idea.

And then there was a six-month period of wondering and stomach-churning anxiety before she learned that all the complaints against her at the JTC were dismissed, Aug. 13, 2004.[739]

After Corrigan sent on the anonymous letter to the JTC and both the *Ryan* and *In re JK* matters had been dismissed by the JTC, Tim Ryan, the girl's father, also independently grieved Judge Gardner. He commenced that action Sept. 15, 2004, and it was dismissed Dec. 29 of that year. The JTC had not sought a response from Gardner, and the first she knew of the complaint was when she received its dismissal.[740]

Even though the questions it asked seemed loaded, the JTC got it right this time, said Weaver. But that didn't always happen. Part of it had to do with changes among the members of the commission as their terms ran.[741] And part of it had to do with the latitude granted its executive director and general counsel, Paul Fischer.[742]

And just because the JTC found no fault in Gardner's conduct didn't mean she got a pass from the majority justices at the Supreme Court. She wasn't out of mind there.

Move ahead a couple of years to 2006 when it came time to name the chief judges for the various courts across the state, something the Supreme Court manages: Patti Gardner—the choice among the probate court judges—was passed over in favor of the chief judge of the 17th (Kent County) Circuit Court, Paul J. Sullivan.[743]

It started with the retirement of Kent County Chief Probate Judge Janet Haynes, who, on June 8, 2006, alerted Chief Justice Taylor[744] that she had informed the Governor that she intended to step down.

738 Casimir J. Swastek, staff attorney, Judicial Tenure Commission, 9 March 2004, unpublished.
739 James Mick Middaugh, chairperson, JTC, letter to Judge Patricia Gardner, 13 August 2004, unpublished.
740 James Mick Middaugh, chairperson, JTC, letter to Judge Patricia Gardner, 29 December 2004, unpublished.
741 Michigan Judicial Tenure Commission, http://jtc.courts.mi.gov/commission.htm.
742 They had got it wrong in *Gilbert* and shortly would get it disastrously wrong when it came to the case of Kent County District Judge Steven Servaas.
743 Appointing a circuit judge as the chief judge of a probate court was highly unusual. Probate court is, after all, a separate court under the state's Constitution.
744 Oh, yes, by 2006 Taylor was chief justice; he had been since 2005.

The first paperwork that Weaver saw on the matter was a report making a recommendation for Haynes' replacement that was circulated at a June 28, 2006, conference. The report was from James P. Hughes, one of the four regional administrators under Carl Gromek. Hughes outlined what he saw as the various strengths of the three Kent probate judges for the job, Nanaruth Carpenter, Gardner, and G. Patrick Hillary:

> Kent Probate Judge Janet Haynes has submitted her resignation to the Governor effective August 1, 2006. This will create a vacancy in the office of chief judge. Judge Haynes has served as chief judge since January 1, 2002. She carried a docket of exclusively probate matters. The other three Kent Probate Judges, Nanaruth Carpenter, Patricia Gardner, and G. Patrick Hillary, work full time in the family division of the 17th Judicial Circuit Court. Judge Gardner has provided "back-up" on probate matters during Judge Haynes' vacations and when a conflict case has been identified. In a letter to the chief justice dated June 8, 2006, the probate judges recommended that Judge Gardner be appointed chief judge and Judge Carpenter chief judge pro tem.

> One logical choice for chief judge would appear to be Judge Carpenter. She has served as chief judge pro tem of this court since January 1, 2002. However, Judge Carpenter does not routinely hear probate cases and prefers to remain full time working in the family division. She would serve reluctantly if appointed, but prefers that Judge Gardner be appointed.

> Judge Patrick Hillary also serves full time in the family division of the 17th Circuit Court. He believes Judge Gardner is the logical choice for chief probate judge, since she currently serves as "back up" for probate matters to Judge Haynes. He would serve as chief judge if selected, but would not want to create a rift among his colleagues by seeking appointment.

> Judge Gardner is willing to serve as chief probate judge and has indicated a preference for moving to a 50 percent probate docket. Under this plan the incoming probate judge would also do 50 percent probate work and 50 percent family division work.

> She believes public service would be enhanced with two judges sharing the probate docket. Judge Gardner has served as probate judge since January 13, 1997. While primarily serving in the family division, she is knowledgeable about probate matters, as a judge, and, previously, as an attorney. She has worked closely with current Chief Judge Haynes to perform probate work during judicial vacations. She is well acquainted with the staff of the probate court.

> Judge Gardner has received significant attention in recent years due to her involvement in two high-profile family division cases—the Ryan case and the Kucharski case. A review of the opinions in these cases causes me to question the administrative skills of Judge Gardner. The judge bypassed

proper procedures and failed to fully consider due process in her decision making. Her attention to administrative detail and adherence to directives of SCAO might be lacking should she be selected as chief judge at this time.

I recommend that the 17th Judicial Circuit Chief Judge Paul Sullivan be appointed chief judge of the Kent County Probate Court for the balance of the term ending December 31, 2007. Judge Sullivan has not sought this appointment. His preference is that Judge Gardner be appointed. However, he would accept the appointment if asked. [...][745]

The matter was put off for further consideration by the justices. In the first place, using a circuit court judge as a chief judge in the probate court was a most unusual move.

And shortly after the conference where she received a copy of Hughes' recommendation, Weaver dictated in her notes that she wanted to know why Gardner was being passed over:

Allegedly there is something in the file, a report from Gromek. We need to get a report on it. I am going to call the Kent County judges and find out. Judge Gardner, Judge _____ [...] I think [the Engler Four] think they won't be able to control any of those people.[746]

And Weaver also noted that she had not been given a copy of Judge Haynes' retirement letter and the recommendation that Gardner take over the position as chief judge that was referenced in Hughes' recommendation. The next day, she sent a memo asking for a copy of Judge Haynes' letter.[747] It was supplied, and Weaver could read for herself what Judge Haynes said she and the other judges of the Kent County Probate Court thought should happen:

In preparation for this transition on my bench, I met with my fellow Kent County Probate Judges, and it is our collective desire that you appoint Judge Patricia Gardner as Chief Judge of Probate, and Judge Nanaruth Carpenter as Chief Judge pro tem, effective August 1, 2006.[748]

The next communication came from the leading contender for the chief judge of probate, Circuit Court Judge Paul Sullivan. It was addressed to Chief Justice Taylor:

Dear Chief:

I understand that you and your colleagues very soon may be appointing someone to succeed retiring Probate judge Janet Haynes as chief judge of the Kent County Probate Court. I also understand there is a possibility that

745 James P. Hughes, SCAO regional administrator, letter to Carl Gromek, 23 June 2006, unpublished.
746 Elizabeth A. Weaver, notes, 28 June 2006, unpublished.
747 Elizabeth A. Weaver, memorandum, 29 June 2006, unpublished.
748 Janet A. Haynes, letter to Clifford W. Taylor, 8 June 2006, unpublished.

administrative staff may recommend my appointment to this position. If I am appointed, I will do my best to carry out the responsibility appropriately. Respectfully, however, I believe my appointment as chief probate judge would not serve the best interests of our probate court here in Kent County.

Here are my thoughts:

1. As I understand it, our four probate judges here unanimously recommended that Judge Gardner be appointed chief judge of Kent Probate Court upon the retirement of Judge Haynes. If this is what they want, and Judge Gardner is willing to accept, I fully concur with and support their recommendation. Judge Gardner is a dedicated and hard-working judge.

2. If for whatever reasons the Supreme Court elects not to appoint Judge Gardner, I believe strongly that one of the two remaining probate judges ought to be appointed. Perhaps they don't want the job. If one of the other does, however, I'm having a difficult time understanding why he or she should not be appointed.

3. The newly appointed probate judge [replacing Judge Haynes], whoever it might be, is not likely to be a good candidate for appointment as chief judge.

4. All things being equal, I think the chief probate judge at the very least ought to be knowledgeable about probate law and procedures. Currently, three of the four probate judges are engaged almost entirely with family court duties. If appointed chief judge, Judge Gardner has indicated a willingness to take a shared probate/family docket with whomever is appointed to succeed Judge Haynes as probate judge. Of the three remaining probate judges, Judge Gardner I believe has far more experience both as a judge and a practitioner in the more traditional non-family probate arena. She would be a great asset to help orient the newly appointed judge. From a practical standpoint she will be sharing a judicial suite with the new judge.

5. If the Supreme Court contemplates naming the chief circuit judge as the chief probate judge, please know that I barely know how to find the probate court. There could be some administrative efficiencies with combining the two, but at what cost?

6. There are a variety of ways to "administer." At present, I believe I have the full support of all 12 judges (circuit and probate) assigned to our court. I believe our court functions better when we retain good collegiality. Appointment of a circuit judge (me, for example) as chief judge of probate, without first securing the support of the probate judges, jeopardizes this support and neutralizes any possible administrative advantage of having one judge administer both courts.

7. If a non-probate judge is appointed chief, I believe the probate judges will be offended. Historically, such appointments have evidenced the existence of serious problems within that particular court. I am unaware of any serious problems here. The local press likely will be "intrigued" with the decision, and the probate judges unduly embarrassed as a result.

In closing, I again wish to recommend Judge Gardner for appointment as chief probate judge. A pair of high-profile cases possibly has sullied Judge Gardner's reputation at the Hall of Justice. This is unfortunate. She has served with distinction for many years, and continues to do so.

It is much easier to carry out the duties of chief circuit judge when that judge has the support of the other judges. If I am appointed chief probate judge, I believe there will be dissention in the ranks, and any actual or perceived administrative benefits will be overshadowed by same. Simply stated, the benefit is simply not worth the cost.

Cliff, that's my two cents worth. Thanks for listening and all the best to you.[749]

It was pretty obvious that Sullivan didn't want the job, didn't think he had the requisite experience for the job, and thought it would cause far more problems than it would solve. So, why didn't he stand up about it?

He had that opportunity. But what do you imagine would have happened the next time it came to appoint the chief judge of the circuit? Or what if there were a federal judgeship that came open? If he stood up against the Supreme Court, do you think he'd have received a reappointment and/or a recommendation?

There was a conference for the justices to discuss the situation July 6th. Weaver's notes reflect her incredulity:

Incredibly, it has been voted 4-3 to appoint Sullivan. Can you believe it?!? And they had Gromek and this guy Hughes there. In my wildest dreams I couldn't have wanted to have this guy in front of everybody. [...] I did ask Carl if he agreed with the recommendation, since he sent it without comment, which he said that he did. [To] the chief justice, I said, "You sent it. Do you agree with it?" Yes, he does. That is Hughes's recommendation to appoint Judge Sullivan. And Hughes went on to made a big deal about how this would coordinate things.

[...]

So I said to Hughes "I'm going to ask you this question and I want you to think about it very carefully. Did you tell any judges in Grand Rapids that Judge Gardner was on our—the court's or justices'—radar screen?" And he said, "Yes." And I said, "Under what authority did you do that?" I said, "You're speaking for me. And she is not on my radar screen." So RPY [Young] spoke up and said "Well, she's on my radar screen, so he is speaking for me." And so did SJM [Markman]. [...] So I said he didn't have my authority and he couldn't speak for me that way.

---

749 Paul J. Sullivan, letter to Clifford W. Taylor, 5 July 2006, unpublished.

So, they will not appoint her. Interestingly enough, I hadn't talked with MFC [Cavanagh] of MK [Kelly] about this, but they voted for [Gardner], it was 4-3. And I held it for a statement.[750]

Weaver wrote a dissent:

> The majority's decision to appoint a circuit judge, Judge Sullivan, over the most logical candidate, Kent County Probate Judge Patricia D. Gardner, is unjustified and publicly unexplained. It deprives the people of Kent County of the best choice, Judge Gardner, for their next chief judge of probate.
>
> [...]
>
> Judge Gardner has the confidence and support of her Kent County Probate Court colleagues. Indeed, Judge Gardner has the confidence and support of Chief Circuit Court Judge Paul J. Sullivan.
>
> With all due respect to Chief Circuit Court Judge Sullivan, and with gratitude for his continuing service as the chief judge of the circuit court, he is not the correct choice for the job of chief judge of the Kent County Probate Court. The chief judge of the probate court should be a judge with significant probate court experience. Judge Sullivan admittedly does not have such experience.
>
> Probate Judge Gardner is the obvious choice....[751]

Weaver then raised the issues that the justices leveled against Gardner in *In re JK*. Since they had effectively silenced her at the time of the court decision, she was going to take the opportunity to chronicle some of the misdeeds and mistakes.

> The decision in *In re JK* changed the law by extending the period during which adoptions must remain pending to include any appeals to this court relating to the termination of parental rights.
>
> It was unreasonable for the *In re JK* majority to criticize Judge Gardner for failing to anticipate that this court was going to change the law.
>
> The Supreme Court's creation and imposition of new law in *In re JK* resulted in yet another year of turmoil and instability for the child, his mother, and his foster parents.
>
> If the law needed clarifying, the court could have made that clarification without engaging in an attack on Judge Gardner's well-reasoned decision to

---

750 Elizabeth A. Weaver, notes, 6 July 2006, unpublished.
751 Elizabeth A. Weaver, writing in "Order," 25 July 2006, 2, http://www.justiceweaver.com/pdfs/Final%20 order.pdf.

terminate the mother's rights. It could have acknowledged that the law, as it read, did not so "obviously" dictate the result the court wanted.

The majority's decision in *In re JK* received strong criticism in the press, especially in Kent County. Persons who watched this story unfold will remember the heart-wrenching efforts to reintroduce the child to his birth mother in the months that followed the *In re JK* decision, and the cooperation of the foster parents who stood by, willing and able to adopt the child. The press reported regularly on the efforts, which were overseen by Judge Gardner, to reintroduce the birth mother and the child, who had only lived with her for 16 months of his five years.

[...]

The history of the *In re JK* case provides no justification for this majority (Chief Justice Taylor and Justices Corrigan, Young, and Markman) to refuse to appoint Judge Gardner as chief probate judge.[752]

The Engler Four came off the rails. On July 17th, Taylor sent her an e-mail. He copied in all the justices and much of the court staff. This was NOT a secret communication only to justices:

I previously sent an e-mail indicating that we should discuss whether to allow Justice Weaver to file her statement that is so unfair to Judge Gardner. In the event that we do, here is my response to Justice Weaver's dissenting statement to be included with the order appointing 17th Circuit Court Chief Judge Paul J. Sullivan to the position of chief judge of the Kent County Probate Court.

Taylor, C.J. (concurring).

This court, by a vote of 4-3, has appointed Judge Paul J. Sullivan as chief judge of the Kent County Probate Court. Justice Weaver, having unsuccessfully urged that we appoint Judge Patricia Gardner, has filed a dissenting statement.

Behaving like a petulant "only child" Justice Weaver is, more or less, "holding her breath" until she gets her way: Judge Gardner as chief judge of the Kent County Probate Court. She hopes, as does the child engaging in a tantrum, that one of the adults will given [sic] in and allow her to dictate their chief judge vote to save Judge Gardner's reputation. While I would like to spare Judge Gardner from this (in fact, ever the conciliator, I even suggested Justice Weaver use a hunger strike as a vehicle as it seemed to have the potential for everyone to be a winner) we cannot give Justice Weaver this

752 Ibid., 3.

power to bludgeon her colleagues by threat of outrageous statements needlessly embarrassing to third parties.

It is a sad situation Justice Weaver has made here, but with apologies to
Judge Gardner, our decision to approve Judge Sullivan will go forward.[753]

Then came the responses from Justice Corrigan. In the first one, she "hoped" Weaver
would withdraw her dissent. In the conference, Weaver had revealed to the justices
that Gardner's trip to the JTC had resulted in nothing substantive. Corrigan said that
Weaver shouldn't have had access to those records. She cobbled together pieces of
the law that she thought would prohibit Weaver from any inquiry: "Plainly, Justice
Weaver is not permitted under the rule to disclose the confidential matter contained
in her statement."[754]

*And these people are lawyers! She didn't know the law, couldn't figure it out, but thought she had
what she wanted.*

There was another conference July 19th, and they all piled on, including Cavanagh
and Kelly, who—while they would join Weaver in dissent and vote for Gardner to
serve as chief justice—told Weaver they didn't think her comments about the JTC
were "necessary;" although, she had the right to say them. The Engler Four wanted to
know how she came by the JTC conclusions. They also disingenuously marveled that
Weaver couldn't see that she was impugning Gardner's name...at least that's what they
expressed. Weaver's notes after the conference reveal the next exchange:

MDC [Corrigan] stated that media could not corroborate JTC complaint.
But I said the judge can. And I have no doubt that the judge wants this in-
formation out. "Well, how do you know that? Have you spoken to her?" And
I said how I know that is my business. And to which nobody argued.[755]

The matter was left on the table. But Corrigan wasn't done. She sent another memo:

In her dissenting statement, Justice Weaver asserts that the JTC dismissed
the requests for investigation in the *In re JK* and *Ryan* cases. She implies that
the JTC cleared Judge Gardner in these cases. Apparently, Justice Weaver
has obtained inside information regarding the JTC's confidential review and
disposition of these matters. I hereby request that she share that information
with the other justices. I ask that she forward any JTC orders or documents
that she has in her possession, and that she permit us to determine whether
Judge Gardner actually received a clean bill of health or an admonishment
from the JTC. If Justice Weaver refuses to share her information, we may
need to consider requesting it directly from Judge Gardner, order the JTC to
forward its communication to us, or both.[756]

753 Clifford W. Taylor, "Memorandum," 17 July 2006, unpublished.
754 Maura D. Corrigan, "Memorandum," 18 July 2006, unpublished.
755 Elizabeth A. Weaver, notes, 19 July 2006, unpublished.
756 Maura D. Corrigan, "Memorandum," 20 July 2006, unpublished.

Wait! So, if it wasn't okay for Weaver to get documents from the JTC it WOULD be okay for other members of the court to do so?

You really have to wonder about the logic here.

It didn't dawn on any of them that Weaver might simply have asked Judge Gardner about it all.

I did ask her; I called her and asked her.

Gardner told her and agreed that Weaver could share the information about the JTC. And Gardner's reputation—while it had been marred—had not suffered that fate at the hands of Justice Weaver. Weaver had, in fact, urged her colleagues to contact Gardner themselves to see whether or not she wanted Weaver's dissent included. Not a one of them did, perhaps to give sustenance to their fiction of disdain, but they kept asserting that Weaver was, regrettably, doing harm to Gardner and a greater harm to the court.

Here is Taylor writing in the final order—from which, by the way, any reference to Weaver's behaving like a "petulant, 'only child'" and suggesting that she go on a "hunger strike" had been scrubbed clean. The rest of the vitriol was still there:

> I have, as I do roughly 260 times biennially as we pick chief judges, made my choice as to which of several candidates could, in my judgment, most satisfactorily serve. No aspersion as to any person is intended or should be imputed from my performance of my duty. Justice Weaver has done a disservice to Judge Gardner, by suggesting an antagonism toward Judge Gardner that does not exist. Sadly this was all so unnecessary. Justice Weaver should not resent her colleagues for simply seeing things differently than she does. Accordingly, I decline Justice Weaver's peculiar invitation to accept responsibility for the publication of the various matters in her statement. I hope that in the future judges who are willing to serve will not be reluctant to submit their names for fear of similar treatment as Justice Weaver scurries about to "help" them.[757]

Young chimed in, too:

> Until today, during my tenure on this court, no member has exposed the presumed shortcomings of a failed candidate who has been considered for an appointment by this court. For all of the reasons recited by the chief justice in his statement, I believe that Justice Weaver has injured our institutional interest in preserving the dignity of people who unsuccessfully seek appointments by this court. Equally significant, Justice Weaver may well have unwittingly injured Judge Gardner by recounting two very troubling cases in which Judge Gardner's rulings were overturned on appeal.

757 Clifford W. Taylor, writing in "Order; ADM file No. 2006-01," Michigan Supreme Court, 1, http://www.justiceweaver.com/pdfs/Final%20order.pdf.

In making her statement, Justice Weaver purports to speak with authority on behalf of Judge Gardner. Other than on the basis of Justice Weaver's assertion, no other member of this court knows whether this claimed authority is genuine.[758]

Young, ever the master of paralepsis,[759] continued:

Since Justice Weaver has chosen to make an issue of Judge Gardner's handling of *In re JK*, ... and *Ryan v Ryan* ... the public can satisfy itself whether these cases support or undermine the case for Judge Gardner that Justice Weaver advances. Judge Gardner's conduct in each of these two cases was particularly controversial, repudiated on appeal and led, in the Ryan case, to federal litigation against the court clerk for Kent County, where Judge Gardner presides.

These concerns point to the propriety of our traditional practice of not commenting on the failed candidacies of aspirants for Supreme Court appointment. It is my hope that Justice Weaver's deviation today will be the sole exception to that practice.[760]

Another trip to the woodshed for Weaver. Wouldn't be her last.

Columnist George Weeks picked up on the fray.

It was extraordinary last week when the Michigan Supreme Court issued five pages on what under normal circumstances would have been a one-line order appointing Chief 17th District Circuit Judge Paul Sullivan to also fill a vacancy as chief judge of the Kent County Probate Court. Such appointments usually are issued without a peep beyond the locality.

[...]

Supreme Court Public Information Officer Marcia McBrien said what happened on the Kent County order "was beyond unusual; it was unprecedented."[761]

Weeks drew quotes from the order by the chief justice and Young, and then he picked up with McBrien again:

758 Robert P. Young, Jr., writing in ibid., 1.
759 Paralepsis is a rhetorical strategy of emphasizing a point by seeming to pass it over. An example might be a hypothetical political candidate who refers to his hypothetical opponent's failings by indirection: "...But I will not talk today about my opponent being a target of a SEC investigation."
760 Robert P. Young, Jr.
761 George Weeks, "Discord erupts on Michigan Supreme Court," *Traverse City Record-Eagle*, 30 July 2006, http://static.record-eagle.com/2006/jul/30weeks.htm.

More opinions are in the mill. On Monday, according to spokeswoman Mc-Brien, the court will issue rulings on complaints against flamboyant attorney Geoffrey Fieger and Chief Judge Michael J. Haley of the 86th District Court, Traverse City.

Fellowship does not exist between Weaver and fellow Republicans on Michigan's splintered top bench.

Meanwhile, Weaver presses on with her idea of including terms limits on Supreme Court justices....
At one point, Weaver, who was elected to the Supreme Court and now has a term that doesn't expire until 2011, said she would leave the court last October. GOP lawmakers, concerned that this would allow Democratic Gov. Jennifer Granholm to appoint Weaver's replacement, started paying more favorable attention to her commendable ideas for court reform.

Right now, the attention she is getting from the other four Republicans on the Michigan Supreme Court is far from favorable.[762]

If he only knew the whole of it!

As for Judge Gardner, Weaver said Gardner called Taylor to find out the reason for being passed over as chief judge.

And he told her, as best I recall, that she would be okay if she changed her friends...that she should stop her communication and friendship with me, and she'd be all right. So that was the message.

That wasn't the only time that judges would be warned away from Weaver.

Justice Taylor, it was reported back to me as time went on, was known to tell one judge that, "I saw you talking to Justice Weaver. You better watch it." So, obviously, on these Patti Gardner issues, this matter was becoming personal with Justice Taylor, vis-à-vis me. But I knew when we had the meeting in 2002, that he wasn't fond of me at that point. But you always think that people get over these things. Some people don't.

At a 2012 law day gathering in Grand Rapids, former Justice Taylor was debating former mayor John Logie about merit selection (appointment) for Supreme Court justices in Michigan. Judge Gardner was in the audience, and when asked if Taylor was the same justice who suggested she find better associates, she replied: "The very same."[763]

---

762 Ibid.
763 In November of 2012, Judge Gardiner was elected by the people of Kent County to her third six-year term as a probate judge.

Chapter 16

No More Chief Judge
for You!
Did She Really Say,
'Make me look good'?

Judge Patricia Gardner was just one of the judges who felt the sting of the displeasure of the court and its officers. Under the leadership of Chief Justice Corrigan, Washtenaw County Probate Judge John Kirkendall was told in early 2004 to step down as chief judge after a badly flawed Office of Auditor General (OAG) report showed that conservatorship case files in his court—and in the probate courts of four other counties: Calhoun, Jackson, Wayne, and Huron—were not up to snuff. Further, the audit carried a list of recommendations where the State Court Administrative Office was coming up short on oversight, policy, and procedures. The audit report was scheduled to come to the whole court in the afternoon of Oct. 23, 2003, but the justices received this memo from Corrigan about it earlier in the day at conference:

> As of tomorrow, the Auditor General will release significant, adverse, and material findings based on an audit of conservatorships[764] in five probate courts. An advance copy of that report,[765] which includes responses from the State Court Administrative Office, will be delivered to the court by the Auditor General early this afternoon and distributed to each of you.
>
> The audit's stated objectives were to "determine the accuracy and validity of assertions contained in conservators' annual accountings filed with probate courts" and "assess the effectiveness and efficiency of probate courts' procedures and controls for administering and monitoring conservatorship cases." The report also states that "[p]robate courts' procedures and controls for administering and monitoring conservatorship cases were generally not effective." A further finding is that SCAO [State Court Administrative Office] needs to provide direction and guidance to probate courts to improve oversight of conservators.

764 Conservators are those appointed by the court to protect and guide the assets of those who are not able to manage their own affairs, either because of age (in the case of minors) or incapacity.
765 "Performance Audit of Selected Probate Court Conservatorship Cases, Office of the Auditor General," October 2003, http://audgen.michigan.gov/-audgenmi/finalpdfs/03_04/r0560501. pdf#search=Conservatorships.

The report cites many specific dramatic and troubling cases as examples of improper accounting and documentation, delinquent reporting, and other deficiencies. Some examples, on their face, suggest that protected individual's estates may have lost money, either through negligence or intentional wrongdoing.

We have directed the chief judges of the affected trial courts to respond to the charges made by the Auditor General's report. All the chief judges will review the files cited in the report to determine whether corrective action, including the possibility of referral for criminal prosecution, is warranted.

This court and the SCAO are examining each case and taking steps to improve oversight of conservatorships. One can criticize the report and its methodology, but I believe that public confidence in the probate courts is at stake. Accordingly, the SCAO response, which is included in the Auditor General's report, states that SCAO will be proactive in addressing the issues raised by the report. In addition to the action I have already described, SCAO will undertake random audits of other probate courts, in addition to intensifying training and oversight of probate court judges and staff. I ask you to review the audit and be prepared with your questions next week. In the meantime, should you receive any inquiries from media or the public, please feel free to refer them to Marcia McBrien or Jean Mahjoory.[766,767]

Of note in Corrigan's memo was the fact that the issue had not only been before her for some time, but that it was long enough for the SCAO to investigate and review the Auditor General's report, to have been in touch with the judges of the audited probate courts, demanded and had received their responses, and to evaluate them with an eye to criminal prosecution. This was plenty serious. And there was time also to prepare to deflect criticism: Marcia McBrien was at the ready to spin the story.

But it came as a complete surprise to Weaver.

We learned about it when the chief justice informed us and sent us a copy of the Auditor General's draft report a day before she said he was going to let it out; although, she had had it, apparently, for weeks or months but had not brought it to the attention of us justices, or at least not to my attention.

Weaver wouldn't know it for another month or so, but there were indications of serious flaws in the Auditor General's report AND in the subsequent investigation by the SCAO. She later on uncovered a message from Milton Mack, Jr., Chief Judge of Wayne County Probate Court. Mack had, in his late September response to the SCAO, let that office know that:

> While OAG has raised some genuine concerns, the judges [the judges of record in each case] have found that OAG made critical factual errors that are

766 Jean Mahjoory was a management analyst in the State Court Administrative Office.
767 Maura D. Corrigan, "Memorandum," 23 October 2003, unpublished.

contrary to the official record in many cases. After a detailed examination of each file, and the assertions of OAG, the judges have reported that they stand by their original decisions. Despite the fact that we have over 54,000 open files distributed among six judges, it is noteworthy that the judge of record in many of these cases was already personally aware of the issues raised and had already addressed them.[768]

Mack had been made aware of the audit long before, long enough to take in the report, call for an examination of the cited files and to speak with his judges. In fact, at the time it was laid before all the justices, the issue had been simmering for more than a year, but Corrigan apparently had elected to leave her court in the dark...or at least Justice Weaver. Chief Judge Mack noted that earlier corrections and comments to the SCAO's follow-up report had been unavailing:

In my letter to _____, dated March 22, 2002, [...] I noted other corrections and made several observations that seem to have been overlooked. In that letter I noted that it did not appear that any of the wards' substantive rights were affected, nor did any loss occur in any of the cases they had identified at that time. I informed _____ that many of the items raised could only have been discovered by a detailed site audit comparable to the audit by the OAG when they visited fiduciaries. I went on to write that many of the issues raised were matters of judicial discretion, and decision were made at duly noted hearings after notice to all interested persons, with everyone having the opportunity to testify in open court. The safeguards the court had in place appeared to be working and any mistakes were not the result of any systemic structural defect or flaw.

[...]

I would now suggest that the OAG's review of our files represents a nearly two-year-old snapshot of the past. Many of these cases involved decisions made many years ago.

[...]

If anyone has any questions about this court's response, I would urge that SCAO have a representative personally review any of these files, including transcripts of hearings, before reaching any conclusions.[769]

But the SCAO reached its conclusions. In the Auditor General's report of Oct. 23, 2003, it noted, "The agency's preliminary response indicated that the SCAO agrees with the findings."[770]

---

768 Milton L. Mack, Jr., letter to Jean Mahjoory, 29 September 2003, unpublished.
769 Ibid.
770 "Performance Audit of Selected Probate Court Conservatorship Cases, Office of the Auditor General," October 2003, 28, http://audgen.michigan.gov/-audgenmi/finalpdfs/03_04/r0560501.pdf#search=Conservatorships.

One of the problems that the SCAO didn't then recognize was the OAG's employment of a disused method for its evaluation.

The Michigan Probate Judges Association looked at the report, and the first point they had to make was that the Auditor General's report was based on the wrong law; that he was relying on pre-1978 [RPC—Revised Probate Code] and pre-EPIC [Estates and Protected Individuals Code, 1998] law, which required a lot more to be done.[771]

Judge Mack had also identified that the misuse of the pre-EPIC standards as a measure was an issue. And IF the OAG wanted those obviated measures used, it was going to cost more...a lot more:

> One of the fundamental problems facing probate courts is the fact that with every additional layer of process comes and additional layer of cost that is borne by the estate as well as the taxpayer. In fact, the costs of delivery of conservatorship services related to compliance with statute and Court Rule is a well-known consequence. In recognition of this problem, the Legislature made a policy to reduce the level of court supervision of decedents' estates by adopting EPIC. [...] EPIC recognizes that the cost of supervision by the court is steep. In supervising conservatorships, we must recognize that the cost of supervision is just as steep and that the cost is borne primarily by the ward's estate. The cost to estates and taxpayers would be very high if we were to reinstate the [pre-EPIC] audit program.[772]

The Probate Judges Association was not taking the matter lightly. Henry Grix, then the chairman of the State Bar of Michigan Probate and Estate Planning Section, later would write about what that association did next:

> The Michigan Probate Judges Association assembled an *ad hoc* committee that issued a strongly worded repudiation of the report of the Auditor General. The judges noted that the Auditor General failed to describe a single case in which a probate court failed to follow the requirements established by law or court rule. In a meeting with the chief justice of the Supreme Court in January, the probate judges disputed the findings of the Auditor General but reaffirmed their commitment to assure protection of Michigan's most vulnerable citizens through a system that operates in accordance with the law and with policy decisions regarding cost effective supervision of the estates of protected individuals.[773]

---

771 Richard C. Lowe, "Introduction: EPIC—new probate and trust legislation for the new millennium," *Michigan Bar Journal*, March 2000, Vol. 79, No. 3, http://www.michbar.org/journal/article.cfm?articleID=48&volumeID=6&viewType=archive.

772 Milton L. Mack, Jr.

773 Henry M. Grix, "The conservatorship controversy continues, key legislation is in the works, and our strategic planning bears fruit," *Michigan Probate and Estate Planning Journal*, Vol. 23, Spring 2004, No. 2, 1, http://www.michbar.org/probate/pdfs/Spring04.pdf.

In the cover summary of its report, the study group of the Probate Judges Association chastised the Supreme Court for buying into the study without...

> ...first determining the applicable law and the facts. This error, if left uncorrected, may undermine public confidence in the judiciary.

> • The reportable conditions found by the OAG were generally not accurate or valid.

> • No case has been identified where a probate court did not follow the monitoring requirements established by law.

> [...]

> • OAG's allegation, and SCAO's agreement, that conservators are prohibited by law from engaging in transactions with the estate they administer is wrong.

> • In no case has any financial loss to any estate been established.

> • The standards suggested for use by OAG, and concurred with by SCAO, would reverse 25 years of legislative direction and impose enormous cost on the estates of protected individuals, the taxpayers and the courts, with no measurable benefit.[774]

The report went deeper:

> As judges, we are required to find the facts and the applicable law before deciding a matter. It is for this reason that we are disappointed that the State Court Administrative Office (SCAO) agreed with the findings of the Office of the Auditor General (OAG) without first determining the facts or the law. What makes this failure so disturbing is that the conclusions of the OAG are contrary to Michigan law and are not supported by the facts.

> [...]

> OAG used an accounting standard for conservators that is not found in the case law, statutes or court rules and is far more stringent than required by law. [...]

> SCAO's conclusion that the standards used by the OAG are correct demonstrates a lack of knowledge of the law. Further, to impose these standards on conservators and probate courts would cause an immense increase in the cost to the estates of protected persons and taxpayers and clog the probate

---

774 Executive summary, "Michigan Probate Judges Association Response to report of Office of Auditor General and State Court Administrative Office; Executive summary," Oct. 28, 2003, unpublished.

court system without any measurable benefit. Such a radical change in public policy, including allocation of the cost and source of funding, should be left to the legislature.

> In their review of the cases cited by OAG, the audited courts found that the vast majority of the findings were not supported by the record. In fact, in one case, OAG claimed the court should have turned the minor's funds over to the mother, despite the fact that the mother was dead.[775]

And then, wrote the probate judges, there was the issue of the 18 months between the conclusion of data gathering by the OAG and its report coming out Oct. 23.

> At no time prior to release of the report were any of the affected courts made aware of any areas of weaknesses, any need for corrective action or any suggestions for remediation. The release of information to the media before informing the affected pubic institution of any perceived deficiency is puzzling and does not serve the generally recognized purpose for audits.[776]

The SCAO had been aware of the critical nature of the report for more than a year—by the accounting in Judge Milton L. Mack's September letter. It's logical and reasonable to assume that Corrigan also had been aware all that length of time and had allowed the probate courts to be blindsided.

It appears that the thing got out of hand, and that Maura wanted to just find a way to cover it over.

In responding to MPJA president Lowell R. Ulrich, Corrigan defended the SCAO, claiming it had not necessarily supported the OAG's findings (despite the OAG report saying that the SCAO indeed had done so) and calling the probate judges' report erroneous.[777] She closed with concerns of her own:

> I am also concerned that the MPJA response appears to have drawn premature conclusions concerning the particular cases at issue in the audit. For example, the executive summary states that "[n]o case has been identified where a probate court did not follow the monitoring requirements established by law." It then states that, "In no case has any financial loss to any estate been established." You told me in a recent telephone conversation that these statements are based upon preliminary findings of the judges involved in these cases. I hope that their conclusions will be confirmed by SCAO's own review of the files. However, until a thorough and independent review of all the files has taken place, I will make no conclusions about the facts. As

---

775 Preamble, "Michigan Probate Judges Association Response to report of Office of Auditor General and State Court Administrative Office; Executive summary," Oct. 28, 2003, 1-2, unpublished.
776 Ibid.
777 ["Interim report of the investigative follow-up review to the Michigan Office of the Auditor General 'Performance audit of selected probate court conservatorship cases', issued October 2003," Michigan Supreme Court, State Court Administrative Office, undated.] And the SCAO interim report that came out in the spring of 2004 did not wholesale accept the OAG's findings, but that was later.

I told you orally yesterday, I anticipate this process should be complete by the end of December. I also said twice previously during our telephone conversations that I stand ready to meet with the affected chief judges and the MPJA when our review is complete and before our "final agency response" to the audit is filed.

It is my earnest desire to work together with you to ensure public confidence in the probate courts. [...][778]

It's possible that she could have done that by giving the Probate Judges Association a head's up. By the time in the fall of 2003 that the Probate Judges Association had issued its statement, Weaver knew there was trouble.

That's when I knew that Maura had made another mess. It's really something that could have been avoided. Either Chief Justice Corrigan and/or whoever she had look over the report and advise her didn't perceive or chose to ignore the major flaws in the Auditor General's report.

But nobody was telling Weaver anything, much less asking for her input.

I was not in the loop on all this; I wasn't one of the people being informed. Maura kept us in the dark—or, at least me—about this. I don't' know if any of the others knew.

Weaver said Corrigan saw the problem as a potential scandal.

It was a long time before we were informed. Then, Maura's primary concern seemed to be how bad the Supreme Court might look and the leadership of the Supreme Court and SCAO, because they hadn't been supervising the probate courts.

In response, Corrigan needed to appear decisive in the crisis. She had aspirations to the U.S. Supreme Court,[779] and acting to root out corruption or ineptitude in her own state courts would position her as a leader, even if that meant that Corrigan had to go against what the probate court judges were telling her.

It didn't seem to matter that Corrigan herself had done away with a program designed to find and resolve just these kinds of problems. That was the guardian conservator ombudsman program that Weaver had put in place during her tenure as chief justice. (The first and only ombudsman had been Court of Appeals Judge Donald Owens.) The ombudsman program was intended to avoid just such a crisis that Corrigan faced.[780]

778 Maura D. Corrigan, letter to The Honorable Lowell Ulrich, 19 November 2003, unpublished.
779 In Chapter 17 we confirm Corrigan's hope of a seat on the U.S. Supreme Court. Her inclusion—twice—on the short list for the court by President George W. Bush was touted in a 2006 campaign letter from John Engler that supported re-election to the Michigan Supreme Court. The letter was distributed and paid for by Corrigan's campaign committee.
780 Press release, "Guardian ombudsman appointed by Supreme Court to strengthen system," 15 September 2000, http://www.justiceweaver.com/ombudsman.php.

As with so many of the courts, the opportunities for people in guardianships and conservatorships to not handle them right are always there. And there also are times when the laws change and some don't keep up.

Without an ombudsman at the state level, there was the possibility of more problems. But there wouldn't have to have been problems for an Office of the Auditor General review of court performance. The Office of Auditor General is authorized to investigate the inner workings of the various departments of state government; a performance audit would be the regular work of the OAG.

...To make suggestions of how things could be done better or criticisms of what's being done wrong, and try to prevent any kind of misdoing, wrongdoing, or fraud. The Auditor General picks and chooses what he wants to do at any given time.

That was a lot of discretionary power.

And this Auditor General thought he and his group had really found mistakes.

The Office of Auditor General was standing firm:

> Scott Strong, deputy Auditor General, said his office stands behind the report. The audit found that conservators who were family members, as well as professionals such as lawyers, engaged in self-dealing, paid bills late, borrowed money with interest-free loans and failed to account for how they spent the ward's money.[781]

And the proposed court response promised a lot.

> When the audit was released, the Michigan Supreme Court started a state review of every problematic case identified by the audit. It also promised to send staff to review probate cases statewide.[782]

Wayne County led with the greatest number of listed problems, "including several hundred open files for people who had either passed away or who had reached 18,"[783] said Bradley Geller, former judicial assistant/law clerk to Washtenaw Probate Court Judge John N. Kirkendall.[784] Geller would play a significant role in all that happened next: first, he knew how to read and analyze a report; then he'd serve as a chronicler of much that happened afterward.

---

781 Wendy Wendland-Bowyer, "Washtenaw court shake-up follows conservator report," *Detroit Free Press*, 13 February 2004.

782 Ibid.

783 The report's assessment of Wayne County follows: "In total, 995 (7.4 percent) of the court's 13,475 reported open case files should have received court action to resolve outstanding issues and/or close the cases." ["Performance Audit of Selected Probate Court Conservatorship Cases, Office of the Auditor General," October 2003, 28, http://audgen.michigan.gov/-audgenmi/finalpdfs/03_04/r0560501. pdf#search=Conservatorships.]

784 Bradley Geller, telephone conversation with co-author Schock, 26 June 2012.

Geller had come to the Washtenaw court in August 1993 and remained there—with sterling evaluations—until February 2004. During his tenure there, he had served on the Michigan Supreme Court's Task Force on Guardianships and Conservatorships.[785] Before his 11 years with Washtenaw County, Geller had worked for eight years as counsel to the Michigan House Judiciary Committee and was "known throughout the state for his advocacy work on guardianship and conservatorship issues."[786]

He is the author of *Changes and Choices, Legal Rights of Older People*[787] and *Handbook for Guardians of Adults.*[788] Early in his career, he had been counsel to the Age Discrimination Study conducted by the U.S. Commission of Civil Rights.[789]

Geller had been doing guardianship and conservatorship work for many years at a very high level, and he analyzed the OAG's report and the court's response. He found that even though Wayne had the greatest number of problems, attention settled on Washtenaw County early on. According to Geller,

> Justice Corrigan had to make a public splash and she chose Washtenaw County as the whipping boy. Washtenaw was not any worse than any of the other counties. She chose to go against Washtenaw County and she was very, very successful. In the news reports she was basically cleaning up Dodge City.[790]

The media reported that the OAG's report had "Found problems with more than 50 conservatorships in Washtenaw County alone."[791]

So Judge Kirkendall became the victim of some not-best handling of some activity by the Auditor General.

The State Court Administrative Office was reviewing each and every conservatorship case studied in the Auditor General's report. That meant gathering a lot of information very quickly and meeting with the various courts and staff. After conducting its own investigation, the SCAO was going to issue an interim report. That eventually would be followed by a final report.

One of the meetings focused on the Washtenaw Court. On Jan. 6, 2004, Judge Kirkendall and Circuit Court Judges Donald Shelton and Archie Brown (with various

785 Task Force on Guardianships and Conservatorships, *Final Report*, Michigan Supreme Court, State Court Administrative Office, 10 September 1998, B1, http://www.pekdadvocacy.com/documents/MI/TaskForceReport.pdf.
786 Liz Cobbs, "Probate judge expects to regain chief appointment after shuffle," *Ann Arbor News*, 14 February 2004.
787 Bradley Geller, *Changes and Choices: Legal Rights of Older People*, Michigan Legislative Service Bureau, (Lansing, Mich., 1989).
788 Bradley Geller, *Handbook for Guardians of Adults*, Tenth Edition, 2012, http://www.barrycounty.org/Courts/Guardian_Handbook.pdf.
789 *Bradley Geller v Washtenaw County, et al.*, Case No. 04-72947, Doc# 25-19, U.S. District Court for the Eastern District, Southern Division, filed 28 June 2005, 14 (Pg. ID 474).
790 Bradley Geller, telephone conversation with co-author Schock, 26 June 2012.
791 "Washtenaw Co. Court Shake-Up Follows Audit," *Michigan Lawyers Weekly*, 23 February 2004, http://mi-lawyersweekly.com/news/2004/02/23/washtenaw-co-court-shakeup-follows-audit/.

court staff, including Geller) met with John Ferry (who at that time still was the State Court Administrator), Deborah Green (a regional court administrator), Jean Mahjoory (a management analyst with the SCAO), and Barry Joseph (also of the SCAO's office).

I—and I believe the other justices—knew NOTHING about the Jan. 6 meeting. In fact, we—well, I for sure—knew nothing about the ongoing process and meetings with any of the probate courts.

Of the meeting, Judge Kirkendall was later to write (Feb. 2, 2004) in an e-mail to Chief Justice Corrigan:

> ...John [Ferry] reported that he was not concerned about the specific cases cited by the Auditor General. This was because either:
>
> > a) The Auditor General was incorrect, or
> > b) The deficiency cited had been or was being responsibly dealt with in a timely manner.
>
> He stated his concern was about systemic administrative issues. He inquired about Washtenaw County compared to other counties with respect to staff size. I indicated this was very much an issue:
>
> > a) Kalamazoo County, with whom we are often compared because of our similarities, has one staff person for each 260 cases filed in the court. Washtenaw County has one staff person for each 400 cases filed in the court.
>
> The quality assurance plan we have developed is designed to get at that and other issues. Very importantly, it will provide the substantiation we need to receive the staff necessary to perform our statutory and constitutional function.
>
> Most of the activities engaged in by the Washtenaw County Probate Court are of the highest quality. Jean, at our meeting, pointed out that the educational and training materials for fiduciaries we produce, for example, are "the best I have seen."
>
> We take this assessment very seriously and will implement remedies to any discovered defect promptly and completely.[792]
>
> That would seem to indicate that Kirkendall thought any problems his court faced could be worked through; in other words he perceived he was on solid ground with the Supreme Court.

---

[792] John N. Kirkendall, e-mail to Maura D. Corrigan, 2 February 2004, included in *Bradley Geller v Washtenaw County, et al.*, Case No. 04-72947, Doc# 10, U.S. District Court for the Eastern District, Southern Division, filed 27 October 2004, 22 (Pg. ID 92).

So by the last week of January 2004, Chief Justice Corrigan reports to us that these reports are coming in, and that the Supreme Court or the SCAO supposedly was going to respond.

There was an administrative conference for the Supreme Court Thursday, Jan. 29, 2004, following a morning of public hearings about court rules. On the agenda, according to Weaver's notes, was something to do with the Michigan Supreme Court Historical Society, a budget presentation, a staff transition matter, and the probate court audit.

That's when the chief justice told us she was going down to Washtenaw the next day, on Friday the 30th. She did not tell us that she was doing anything other than just to go down there and check it out and see what was going on.

By her own admission, Corrigan wrote that she didn't actually go to Washtenaw; she went instead to her Detroit office accompanied by Carl Gromek. There they met with Judge Kirkendall.[793]

It's possible Ferry wouldn't do it or he wasn't asked. Ferry's days at the court were numbered, and Gromek would take his job by year's end. She must have felt she had to have somebody there with her, and Gromek did it.

Imagine Weaver's surprise a few days later when she found out that Kirkendall—who had just been reappointed to his chief judgeship effective the month before—was stepping down as chief judge. The announcement came in a February 9 memo from State Court Administrator John Ferry.

> Washtenaw County Probate Court Chief Judge John N. Kirkendall has requested that the court accept his resignation as chief judge of that court effective immediately (letter attached).
>
> Chief Justice Corrigan met with Judge Kirkendall to review the results of the Auditor General's findings regarding sample conservatorship cases, and the SCAO's preliminary review of those cases and conservatorship management practices in the Washtenaw County Probate Court. She requested that Judge Kirkendall resign as chief judge, in light of the findings of those reports. [Emphasis added.]
>
> Chief Circuit Judge Archie Brown indicated his willingness to serve as chief judge of the probate court. Judge Donald Shelton has been assigned to directly oversee implementation of improvements in the management of the probate court.
>
> The Washtenaw County Probate Court is a two-judge court. Judge Nancy Francis, the other probate judge, is assigned full time to the family division

---

793 Maura D. Corrigan interrogatory, *Bradley Geller v Washtenaw County, et al.*, Case No. 04-72947, Doc# 10, U.S. District Court for the Eastern District, Southern Division, filed 27 October 2004, 27 (Pg. ID 97).

of the Circuit Court. During her tenure as judge, she has been almost exclusively assigned to family matters. [...]

We recommend that Judge Brown be appointed chief judge of the Washtenaw Probate Court, effective immediately.[794]

Judge Kirkendall's letter attached to Ferry's February 9 memo also was dated February 2, the same day Kirkendall had communicated with Corrigan via e-mail about the Jan. 6 meeting with Ferry and his staff. It may be that Corrigan responded promptly the same day to that February 2 e-mail reiterating her position that he needed to go, and prompted Kirkendall's February 2 letter stepping down as chief judge of probate.

In his letter indicating his intent to step down, Judge Kirkendall wrote that he thought it would be a temporary measure:

> Given my continuing desire to rigorously deal with any and all administrative issues that are brought to my attention, I have now concluded it would be prudent to request that you consider, for the time being, my declination to serve.[795]

Kirkendall also would explain to reporters that he thought his stepping down was for the short term: "'I view this as a temporary situation to give us an opportunity to implement this plan,' he said of <u>his removal</u> from the chief position."[796] [Emphasis added.]

She did not tell us that she would be suggesting to the chief probate judge there, or in any way raise it with him, that he should step down or resign as the chief judge. She did NOT raise that with us, and I for sure had no idea that such a thing was going to be done.

I knew that Judge Kirkendall, who had long been the chief probate judge there, deserved better than that kind of quick judgment about anything that was going on, because it already was becoming apparent that the Auditor General's report wasn't his best work.

And there were other casualties. The *Detroit Free Press* reported:

> Washtenaw County's chief probate judge was asked to step down and two longtime probate employees were fired in response to allegations that court conservators improperly spent money belonging to children under that care.

> Judge John Kirkendall was asked by Michigan Supreme Court Chief Justice Maura Corrigan to step down as chief probate judge two weeks ago. Circuit Court judge Donald Shelton is now chief judge *pro tem*.

---

794 John D. Ferry, Jr., "Personal and confidential memorandum," 9 February 2004, unpublished.
795 John N. Kirkendall, letter to Maura D. Corrigan, 2 February 2004, unpublished.
796 Liz Cobbs, "Probate judge expects to regain chief appointment after shuffle; Kirkendall says stepping aside is a 'temporary situation,'" *Ann Arbor News*, 14 February 2004.

Shelton said Corrigan suggested he look at reconfiguring his staff, so he asked court counselor Bradley Geller and probate register Hillary Muscato to step down last week. Shelton stressed Thursday that neither Geller, Muscato nor Kirkendall is being accused of wrongdoing.

[...]

Many probate court judges have been highly critical of the Auditor General's report, saying it unfairly held them up to accounting standards they aren't legally bound to follow. Michigan law does not require conservators' annual filings to be checked against things like receipts for accuracy.

[...]

Marcia McBrien, Supreme Court spokeswoman, said that to her knowledge, Washtenaw is the only county where the chief probate judge <u>was removed</u>. [Emphasis added.]

Kirkendall, who is continuing to hear probate cases, said he hopes the attention will bring more staff, which is the same size as it was when he arrived in 1986, despite a rising caseload.

Muscato, a 22-year probate court employee, said the staff was already making changes to conservatorship before the shake-up.

"We have already...been asking for bank statements with the accounts, tracking down fiduciaries," she said. "Now that the Supreme Court has come in, it appears to me somebody had to take the fall."

Geller, who is known throughout the state for advocating for guardianship and conservatorship changes, said he gave his heart to the counselor job and did the best he could.[797]

So what had transpired during that January 30 meeting among Corrigan, Gromek, and Kirkendall that would account for his stepping down as chief judge? Was he "removed" as McBrien reportedly said? Or was it simply a request that had been blown into an order in subsequent reporting? Weaver had heard rumors that Corrigan had not merely requested or suggested, but, in fact, demanded his resignation.

In any event, it wasn't just Kirkendall and his preferential appointment as a chief judge; this time it was jobs, too, paychecks. Kirkendall stepped down as chief judge on Monday, Feb. 2nd, and Muscato, a 22-year employee of the court, and Geller, an 11-year employee, were advised on Thursday, Feb. 5th, that they were being let go. Hillary

---

[797] Wendy Wendland-Bowyer, "Washtenaw court shake-up follows conservator report," *Detroit Free Press*, 13 February 2004.

Muscato would subsequently find employment elsewhere within the county. The same didn't hold true with Geller, and his last day was the 20th.

Corrigan had promised a complete response to the Auditor General's report from the Supreme Court. She disseminated a draft of the preliminary report to the justices February 25, preparatory to a meeting with the Auditor General. Weaver, in a memorandum, took issue with the language:

> I strongly object to the statement on page 2 of the "finalized preliminary response," that "the Supreme Court has ordered a change of leadership in the Washtenaw County Probate Court." The court did not discuss, vote on, or order this leadership change. It was reported without objection in the press that, "Judge John Kirkendall was asked by the Michigan Supreme Court Chief Justice Maura Corrigan to step down." (See *Detroit Free Press*, Feb. 13, 2004, among others.) Since no communication to the contrary has been received, apparently the press reports are accurate.[798]

Weaver went on to ask that the process be slowed down and the meeting be postponed until the issue and the language had been reviewed by the court.[799] Corrigan nixed it and clarified for Weaver's benefit exactly what she said she had told Judge Kirkendall:

> When I met with Judge Kirkendall, I did indeed tell him that, in my judgment, it would be best under the circumstances for him to resign. I never indicated, to him or the media, that the court was directing him to do so.[800]

Well, that's all fine and dandy, except she didn't tell us that she was going to give him her personal opinion.

It would fall to Brad Geller to bring it to light another version of her conversation when he subsequently filed a lawsuit against Corrigan, the probate *pro tem* chief, Donald Shelton, the Washtenaw trial court, and Washtenaw County in the U.S. Federal District Court, Eastern Division.[801] The suit ultimately was dismissed, but there are documents including e-mails and even an interrogatory response[802] from Chief Justice Corrigan.

---

798 Elizabeth A. Weaver, "Memorandum," 25 February 2004, unpublished.
799 Ultimately, though, the report would get some review and be published in both an interim and final form. ["Interim report on investigative follow-up review to the Michigan Office of Auditor General performance audit of Selected probate courts conservatorship cases, issued October 2003," State Court Administrative Office, Michigan Supreme Court, undated, http://courts.michigan.gov/Administration/SCAO/Resources/Documents/Publications/Reports/Interim-Conservatorship-Response.pdf, and "Final report on investigative follow-up review, statewide phase to the Michigan Office of Auditor General performance audit of Selected probate courts conservatorship cases, January 2005," State Court Administrative Office, Michigan Supreme Court, January 2005, http://courts.michigan.gov/Administration/SCAO/Resources/Documents/Publications/Reports/Final-Conservatorship-Response.pdf.]
800 Maura D. Corrigan, "Memorandum," 25 February 2004, unpublished.
801 *Bradley Geller v Washtenaw County, et al.*, Case No. 04-72947, 29 December 2005, http://www.gpo.gov/fdsys/pkg/USCOURTS-mied-2_04-cv-72947/pdf/USCOURTS-mied-2_04-cv-72947-1.pdf.
802 Interrogatories are questions posed by one party in a lawsuit to another. They are sworn for accuracy and truthfulness.

Writing in the third person in her answer to the federal lawsuit, this is how Corrigan described what she said during the meeting:

> Defendant Corrigan informed Judge Kirkendall that on the basis of SCAO's findings regarding Washtenaw County Probate Court, she felt compelled to recommend his removal as chief judge of the probate court to her colleagues on the Supreme Court. [...] Defendant Corrigan offered Judge Kirkendall the opportunity to consider resigning the position of chief judge.[803]

"Compelled to recommend his removal"? Those were Corrigan's own words—as were those to Weaver sharing her judgment that Kirkendall's stepping down would be "best," and the interim response to the Auditor General's report using this language: "the Supreme Court has ordered a change of leadership." [Emphasis added.] That's a wide range. But in the end, would it even matter exactly what she had said?

If a chief justice arrives at a judge's office and even "suggests" that he or she step down, the average judge believes that the chief justice has the votes for that to happen.

An example of *force majeure*.

And there may have been something in Kirkendall's demotion that might not have been readily apparent. In his suit against her, Geller contended that Corrigan was settling an old score because Kirkendall had been critical of the Unified Trial Courts. Washtenaw County had been one of the test sites for the reforms started under Justice Mallett and continued under Justices Weaver and Corrigan.[804]

> [O]ne underlying motivation [...] was her desire to punish Judge Kirkendall and Washtenaw County for the embarrassment of calling into question the viability of the unified trial court model, in the success of which defendant Corrigan is heavily invested.[805]

And the underlying reasons for firing Geller might not readily be apparent: Corrigan's reaction to Geller's previous criticisms of her leadership on the high court. Not only had Corrigan gutted the guardianship ombudsman program that Weaver had established, Geller asserted she also had resisted reforms that would have made available information about appointments made by trial judges (including conservators and guardians) to the general public. Geller said that he had communicated with Corrigan on several occasions: Feb. 25, 2000; Aug. 30, 2000; July 29, 2002; Jan. 20, 2003. In his last letter, he reported he wrote, "Please let me know how we can stiffen the spine of the Supreme Court to effectively regulate and monitor our One Court of Justice."[806]

803 Maura D. Corrigan interrogatory, *Bradley Geller v Washtenaw County, et al.*, Case No. 04-72947, Doc# 10, U.S. District Court for the Eastern District, Southern Division, filed 27 October 2004, 27 (Pg. ID 97).
804 The plan is outlined in the 2002 annual report of the Supreme Court: One Court of Justice, Michigan Supreme Court 2002 Annual Report, 1.http://courts.michigan.gov/Administration/SCAO/Resources/Documents/Publications/Statistics/2002/2002%20Michigan%20Supreme%20Court%20Annual%20Report.pdf.
805 *Bradley Geller v Washtenaw County, et al.*, Case No. 04-72947, Doc# 10, U.S. District Court for the Eastern District, Southern Division, filed 27 October 2004, 5 (Pg. ID 6).
806 Plaintiff's affidavit in response, *Bradley Geller v Washtenaw County, et al.*, Case No. 04-72947, Doc# 10, U.S.

That's just the kind of writing that would put him in her sights. Geller wrote that she responded, but Corrigan would deny it in her interrogatory.[807] And in his lawsuit, he claimed that one of the issues was his right to free speech.

In addition, Geller wrote that he believed that Corrigan wanted to keep him from talking:

> One underlying motivation [...] was to silence [Geller], as it was clear that he would not have remained quiet were the Supreme Court to issue an expected response to the Auditor General that was disingenuous in not acknowledging systemic problems in probate courts and the Supreme Court's failure to address these longstanding problems, despite its own Guardianship Task Force recommendations years ago.[808]

Geller was not afraid to criticize the court system and that may have been enough irritation. The only way to take a whack at Geller was through Kirkendall, so she may have had to swing at the judge first.

Geller, in his lawsuit, reported an event that supported the idea that Geller was a second intended target in addition to Judge Kirkendall:

> On February 18, 2004, I crossed the hall from my office and spoke with Judge Kirkendall in his chambers.

> I asked Judge Kirkendall whether it was Maura Corrigan or county judges who were behind my termination.

> Judge Kirkendall answered he couldn't tell me because to do so would breach a promise he had made not to tell.

> I went back to my office and e-mailed Judge Kirkendall. I said if I didn't hear back from him within ten minutes, I could assume she (Maura Corrigan) was behind my termination.

> Within two minutes, Judge Kirkendall was in my office. He asked, "Are you going to take her on?"

> I replied, "I am not afraid of her."

> Judge Kirkendall replied, "But I am. I'm afraid she will know I was the one who told you."

District Court for the Eastern District, Southern Division, filed 28 June 2005, 5 (Pg. ID 89).
807 Ibid.
808 *Bradley Geller v Washtenaw County, et al.*, Case No. 04-72947, Doc# 10, U.S. District Court for the Eastern District, Southern Division, filed 27 October 2004, 5 (Pg. ID 6).

This conversation confirmed in my mind that Judge Kirkendall had been told directly or indirectly by Maura Corrigan that I was no longer to work in the probate court and that he was not to speak about it.[809]

We do know that while she denied it[810]—and the two other Washtenaw Trial Court judges denied it in their interrogatories[811]—all other indications were that she reached into the inner workings of a probate court to tinker with its organization and operations. She admitted phone conversations with Shelton and Brown immediately after her meeting with Kirkendall, and later.[812] What did they discuss? Geller says he thinks the topic was court reorganization, including his removal.

> I believe she gave them marching orders about how to proceed. One thing I believe she suggested—and she denies this—was to restructure the staff. Again, that would make a bigger splash. Hillary and I were just pawns in this game of Maura Corrigan to establish how aggressive she was in addressing this problem the Auditor General had found. And I believe Corrigan was quite specific. She called both Judge Brown and Judge Shelton the very afternoon after meeting with Kirkendall. And she called Brown a few days later. This was all scripted by Corrigan. It was a brilliant political ploy, and it worked.[813]

It was a matter of appearances, said Geller. And that led back to Corrigan's desire to go on to the U.S. Supreme Court.

> You know who told us at a little staff meeting that Corrigan wanted to go to the U.S. Supreme Court? Don Shelton. Maura Corrigan and Don Shelton. I view them as strange bedfellows.[814]

Geller has a theory of the plan between then Republican Corrigan and the Democrat Shelton.

> If Corrigan was going to the U.S. Supreme Court and left a vacancy on Michigan Supreme Court, it was no secret [Shelton] wanted to be on the Michigan Supreme Court. Here we'd have a Democratic Governor and a vacancy on the Supreme Court.[815]

And we do know that Shelton ran for the Supreme Court in 1994 and lost to Mallett and Weaver.

809 Plaintiff's affidavit in response, *Bradley Geller v Washtenaw County, et al.*, Case No. 04-72947, Doc# 10, U.S. District Court for the Eastern District, Southern Division, filed 28 June 2005, 1 (Pg. ID 85).
810 Maura D. Corrigan, affidavit, *Bradley Geller v Washtenaw County, et al.*, Case No. 04-72947, Doc# 10, U.S. District Court for the Eastern District, Southern Division, filed 28 June 2005, 1 (Pg. ID 68).
811 Trial court interrogatory, *Bradley Geller v Washtenaw County, et al.*, Case No. 04-72947, Doc# 25-14, U.S. District Court for the Eastern District, Southern Division, filed 28 June 2005, 1 (Pg. ID 440).
812 Maura D. Corrigan interrogatory, *Bradley Geller v Washtenaw County, et al.*, Case No. 04-72947, Doc# 10, U.S. District Court for the Eastern District, Southern Division, filed 27 October 2004, 27 (Pg. ID 97).
813 Bradley Geller, telephone interview.
814 Ibid.
815 Ibid.

And that would account for Corrigan's allegedly delivering a mandate to Judge Shelton: "Make me look good." So, where did Geller hear that? From Washtenaw Prosecutor Brian Mackie. Where did Mackie hear it? Geller says from somebody at the Supreme Court.[816] Was it true?

At the remove of almost a decade now, Geller has some observations of what happened in Washtenaw County:

> Tip O'Neill said, "All politics are local." Wrong. What he should have said was, "All politics are personal."
> My view is all this was choreographed by Corrigan to be able to say: "When I see a problem I deal with it." This was all about power. It was nothing to do with justice. She was willing to step on anybody to get ahead. In the end, she ruined Judge Kirkendall's career for no reason except that people would think she was decisive.

> This was deeply humiliating to Judge Kirkendall. He was doing one-third of the domestic docket as well as the probate docket. He had bent over backward to do the work in this county. To be publicly humiliated that he had failed in his job as chief judge was a very, very, big blow. But he really was given no choice.[817]

Judge Kirkendall retired from the bench in late 2005. He is a past president of the National College of Probate Judges and serves on the faculties of The Institute of Continuing Legal Education (ICLE), the Michigan Judicial Institute, the National College of Probate Judges, and the National Judicial College. In addition:

> Judge Kirkendall serves on the Advisory Council for the Elder Law Center of the National Center for State Courts; on the Advisory Council for Elder Law Issues of the Stetson University College of Law; and on the Faculty Advisory Council on Elder Abuse for the National Council of Juvenile and Family Court Judges. He is a member of the advisory committee for "Michigan Family Law Benchbook" (ICLE) and writes and lectures periodically about issues affecting judges and others in family practice.[818]

And Judge Kirkendall deserved much, much better than he got. …A decent, honest, intelligent, hardworking, caring judge and two staff, unjustly blamed, trashed, and discarded. The entire Washtenaw episode is another example of misuse and abuse of judicial power to promote agendas of personal ambition and prejudice—another example of tyranny and unnecessary secrecy in government at work.

---

816 *Bradley Geller v Washtenaw County, et al.*, Case No. 04-72947, Doc# 10, U.S. District Court for the Eastern District, Southern Division, filed 27 October 2004, 6 (Pg. ID 90).
817 Bradley Geller. Geller, by the way, now works in the Long Term Care Ombudsman program within the Michigan Office of Services to the Aging.
818 ICLE Contributors: Hon. John N. Kirkendall, Institute for continuing Legal Education website, https://www.icle.org/modules/directories/speakerauthor/bio.aspx?Pnumber=p16010.

Chapter 17

Re-election
and the Mysterious
Citizens for Judicial Reform
Reprimand Time for Geoffrey Fieger

Re-elect Them

Just like clockwork, the fall of every even year brought an election for the Michigan Supreme Court. In 2004, Justices Stephen Markman and Marilyn Kelly were to face the voters. Not that there was much doubt about their re-election. According to Michigan Campaign Finance Network (MCFN):

> The incumbents [...] each had an overwhelming financial advantage over their challengers, even without the stealth spending. They also had the advantage of being identified as incumbents on the ballot.[819]

Nor, said MCFN, was the election likely to generate a lot of excitement: "For the second election in a row, the stakes were not high and the contest wasn't close."[820]

Marilyn Kelly had the most seniority and gathered far and away the most votes: 2,139,382. She had candidate receipts of $728,800, and independent expenditures (IEs) from her party of $18,445. In addition, the Democrats ponied up $186 in direct support.[821] Her per-vote expenditure was 35 cents.[822]

819 Rich Robinson and Barbara Moorehouse, *A citizen's guide to Michigan campaign finance, 2004,* Michigan Campaign Finance Network, (Lansing, Mich., 2005), 22, http://www.mcfn.org/pdfs/reports/CG05.pdf.
820 Ibid.
821 Her list of top contributors reads this way: candidate/spouse $118,002; Sommers, Schwartz, Silver & Schwartz $34,535; Michigan Education Assn./MEA PAC $34K; Michigan Trial Lawyers Assn./Justice PAC $34K; United Auto Workers/UAW Michigan Voluntary PAC $34K; Intl. Brotherhood of Electrical Workers/IBEW COPE $20K; Fieger, Fieger, Kenney & Johnson $14,050; Gursten & Koltonow $8,750; Sachs Waldman $6,875; and Bernstein, Samuel & Susan $6,800. [Ibid.]
822 Ibid., Appendix N, 68, http://www.mcfn.org/pdfs/reports/CG05Appendix.pdf.

Stephen Markman, facing his second election in as many years, tallied 1,674,354 votes, had candidate receipts of $721,978, party IEs of $89,074, PAC IEs of $19,595, and direct party support of $8,901. He spent 50 cents per vote.[823]

Next on the candidate list was Democrat Deborah Thomas with 1,261,635 votes. She had unsuccessfully sought a Supreme Court seat in 2000 (and would do so again in 2008). Her candidate receipts totaled $68,374 and she had party IEs of $18,445 and direct help from her party of $186. She spent seven cents per vote.

Republican newcomer Brian Zahra gathered 595,907 votes. He had $22,279 in candidate receipts, party IEs of $89,574 (a little more than Markman), PAC IEs of $19,595, and party resources of $2,551(somewhat less than Markman). He spent 22 cents per vote.[824]

Libertarian Leonard Schwartz took 438,348 votes, had candidate receipts of $2,847, at less than a penny a vote.

The clanger in the otherwise uneventful election was the appearance of two television campaigns.

> The Michigan Chamber of Commerce spent nearly $1.4 million for television advertising lauding the incumbent Republican nominee, Justice Stephen Markman, for "protecting victims and fighting for our values." The chamber's ads cleverly avoided any reference to voting for Markman, so they also avoided any requirement under Michigan's flaccid campaign finance law to disclose who gave the money to buy the ads.

> A PAC organized under the name of Citizens for Judicial Reform spent almost $400,000 for television advertising defaming the same justice and explicitly instructing viewers to "vote no on Markman." Even under Michigan's weak law, those advertisements should have been considered independent expenditures and the PAC's financial supporters should have been disclosed. However, more than six months after Election Day, Citizens for Judicial Reform hadn't bothered to file a campaign finance report.

> Spending, especially in these amounts, is particularly troublesome in judicial elections. Frequently campaign contributors end up as interested parties in cases decided by the same judges that they either supported or op-

---

823 His list of top contributors? Cox 5200 Club $34K; Michigan Chamber of Commerce PAC $30,375; Michigan State Medical Society/Michigan Doctors PAC $15,000; Michigan Farm Bureau PAC $13,500; Michigan Assn. of Realtors/REALTORS PAC $13,400; Dickinson Wright $11,780; Aronoff, Arnold Y. & Janet $6,800; Aronoff, Daniel J. & Nancy $6,800; Devos, Jr., Elizabeth & Richard $6,800; Devos, Sr., Helen & Richard $6,800; Fried, Harold S. & Sarah Deson $6,800; Goggins, John D. & Sally J. $6,800; Jandernoa, Michael & Sue $6,800; Thompson, Robert & Ellen Anne $6,800. [Rich Robinson and Barbara Moorehouse.]
824 Governor Rick Snyder appointed Zahra to the Supreme Court in 2011. Zahra retained his seat in the 2012 election for the remainder of Justice Corrigan's term following her departure from the court. He will be up for re-election for a full term in 2014.

posed. When the spending is secret, the public has no way of knowing the relationships between the judges and the judged.[825]

Uh, yes. That's what happened all right. According to Rich Robinson of Michigan Campaign Finance Reform, the Chamber ad came out first; the Citizens for Judicial Reform ad came out at the tail end of the election.[826] *Michigan Lawyers Weekly* followed the story:

> [I]t was not until June—seven months after the election—that trial attorney and former Democratic gubernatorial candidate Geoffrey Fieger, a multimillionaire, filed papers in Oakland County acknowledging he spent more than $450,000 on the anti-Markman ads.

> The type of independent expenditure report Fieger made is supposed to be filed months earlier than when he submitted the paperwork, county clerks say. The penalty for the violation is $1,000.[827]

Fieger was proving a point—and he had the money to do it; a $1,000 fine was nothing. The point was this: the Michigan Campaign law was worse than useless.

> Bill Ballenger, publisher of the newsletter "Inside Michigan Politics," said the inability to track down until now who paid for the anti-Markman ads is an example of broader disclosure problems.

> "People have been thumbing their nose at this for years," Ballenger said. "Reports have been late or noncompliant, a lot of them with no sanctions at all, showing a complete disregard of the law."[828]

Rich Robinson, the executive director of the Michigan Campaign Finance Network was also referenced in the *Michigan Lawyers Weekly* article:

> Robinson says Michigan's campaign finance laws are stuck in the dark ages.

> Reporting is too slow, standards too lax and penalties for violations too lenient, according to Robinson. [...] But he says he isn't getting much help in his quest to shine light on the process of discovering who gives money to political campaigns.

> "We've got real weakness in our campaign finance law," said Robinson, who released his group's analysis of the 2004 election cycle last month. "The lawmakers don't want the laws to come back on them. So the law is toothless."

---

825 Ibid., 22, http://www.mcfn.org/pdfs/reports/CG05.pdf.
826 Rich Robinson, telephone interview with co-author Schock, 4 June 2012.
827 "Reformer: Campaign laws need changes," *Michigan Lawyers Weekly*, 25 July 2005, http://milawyersweekly.com/news/2005/07/25/reformers-campaign-laws-need-changes/.
828 Ibid.

[...]

Robinson calculated that campaign donations and spending in Michigan reached $124 million in the 2004 election cycle. About $69 million was spent on state races; the rest was on federal races.

Besides the weakness of the disclosure laws, he said he's also concerned about a lack of restrictions on donations to political parties and political action committees, and on issue-related advertisements paid for by special interests.

He regrets that the results of this summer's campaign fund-raisers for lawmakers won't be reported to state election officials for several more months.

"We don't have any idea who gave what until after the fact," he said. "Thousands of dollars are disappearing into the vapors."[829]

As bad as it was for 2004, it was nowhere near the $7.5 million in undisclosed spending in 2000[830] and not even a patch on what it would become later in the decade.

For Geoffrey Fieger, it was personal as well as professional.

"It was a suicide mission," said Robinson. "But he wanted to throw some mud at Markman. There has been a long-standing animosity between them."[831]

In fact, Fieger said he and Markman had gone to high school together (Oak Park High School). He joked that if he had known what a problem Markman would become for him, he'd have taken him out behind the school, presumably for a serious drubbing.[832]

Someone would face a serious drubbing out of all this, but it wasn't going to be Markman, at least not at the outset.

AG v Fieger

With his nearly half-a-million-dollar foray into the 2004 election process, Geoffrey Fieger sent a very public message. And the Supreme Court was going to send one back. Nor was the court alone...Attorney General Mike Cox would get into the mix.

And what happened next is worthy of a whole season of reality television.

829 Ibid.
830 News release, "Judicial campaign 'whodunit,'" Michigan Campaign Finance Reform Network, 2 February 2005, http://www.mcfn.org/press.php?prId=5.
831 Rich Robinson, telephone interview with co-author Schock, 4 June 2012.
832 Geoffrey Fieger, comments preparatory to the video interview with co-author Schock, 12 March 2012, Southfield, Mich.

First of all, people wanted to know why in the world an attorney who practiced before the Supreme Court would spend that much money vilifying one of the deciding votes. As Rich Robinson said, it was a "suicide mission."

It had started a long time before the 2004 election, explained Fieger.

> This goes back to John Engler. He used to hold public forums. Like town meetings, almost—and he used to do it on WWJ. I still have the cassette tape of it, from the middle-'90s, and it was during the time that I was representing Kevorkian. And one of the calls was, "How do we stop Jack Kevorkian?"

> And Engler had a slip of his tongue. And this is the genesis of everything if you ask me, because Engler has his hands in the Supreme Court. He was directly responsible for these four judges. But he's responsible for this stuff, too; he's very adept. He's a very adept political animal. He said, "The way we stop Kevorkian is we get Geoffrey Fieger." His actual words: "We disbar Geoffrey Fieger."

> Very soon after that all the complaints started to roll in, okay? A long litany of complaints started to roll in from Engler surrogates about me and about things that I had said.[833]

Complaints had not and were not likely to silence him.

> Because, you see, first of all I'm not simply a lawyer or a trial lawyer. I ran for Governor of this state; I'm also a politician.

> And, therefore, I had an absolute right to make commentary on things that I see. Well, one of the things that I see is what Engler did with the judiciary, among other things. And so, I said that. So I was aware, from that time on, that I had a very, very large target on my back, and that they did want to personally destroy me. They desired to do it. And if they say otherwise, if Engler or Markman or Corrigan or Young or Taylor denies that they sought to personally destroy me, and used their offices politically, as judges and the Governor, to destroy me, they're liars. They engaged in that type of activity.[834]

Fieger had said lots of things in addition to the ads denigrating Markman. For instance, he described some appeals court judges as Hitler and his henchmen. And there had been other derisive terms. (More about those presently.) ...But his television ads against Markman calling him an extremist and "charging that with Markman on the Court, 'no woman is safe'"[835] were pretty serious stuff.

---

833 Fieger.
834 Ibid.
835 News release, "Judicial campaign 'whodunit,'" Michigan Campaign Finance Reform Network, 2 February 2005, http://www.mcfn.org/press.php?prId-5.

And Cox and Markman were very pissed off that I funded a campaign against Markman, and with very negative advertising. And so there was a secret investigation done of me—unknown to me—in which Cox—and I'm absolutely positive—at the behest of Markman and Engler—although Engler was no longer in office at that time, but for sure, Markman. And they went into my bank accounts and conducted search warrants, through a district judge in Lansing, without my knowledge whatsoever. And I finally found out about it. And I said, "What the hell did you think you were doing?" And that's when Cox accused me of blackmailing him.[836]

Fieger blackmailing Cox? Here's Fieger's explanation:

> Cox had been sleeping with women over in the Frank Murphy Hall of Justice; they had it on videotape—and he accused me of blackmailing him, although, of course, he had no proof of that, either.[837]

That's one version of the story, and it included the possibility that Fieger might run against Cox for Attorney General.

The Associated Press broke the story about Cox and his alleged infidelity, and pegged attorney Lee O'Brien as the go-between who delivered the purported threat to Cox, in front of Cox's wife, at a Livonia restaurant. Cox told Oakland County detectives that O'Brien told him that Fieger was upset about the investigation into the campaign spending, and that he might retaliate. That was in late summer. In October, Fieger would allude to the infidelity in a television show. After that, there would be reports of more threats, an operative with a wire who recorded conversations that would reveal that O'Brien had worked both for Cox's re-election but owed an allegiance to Fieger because Fieger directed cases his way.[838]

And then there was a tearful public admission. Cox admitted it was true: he had an adulterous affair...once. Here's the *Michigan Lawyers Weekly* story about what transpired:

> Geoffrey Fieger said backers of his bitter political rival, John Engler, pushed Attorney General Mike Cox to begin an investigation of campaign finance irregularities that Fieger is accused of trying to derail by blackmailing Cox.
>
> The fevered story, which recently broke when Cox tearfully acknowledged his infidelity and blamed Fieger and another lawyer for forcing his public admission, is detailed in documents released by Oakland County Prosecutor David Gorcyca under the Michigan Freedom of Information Act.

---

836 Geoffrey Fieger.
837 Ibid.
838 Associated Press, "AG Cox knew of Fieger's plans," *The Michigan Daily*, 18 November 2005, http://www.michigandaily.com/content/ag-cox-knew-fiegers-plans.

Gorcyca announced that, based on an investigation by the sheriff's department, he was not filing charges against Fieger, the high-profile Southfield trial attorney, or Grosse Pointe Farms attorney Lee O'Brien.

Gorcyca said he believed statements attributed to O'Brien indicated that Fieger intended to divulge Cox's improprieties. But the statements would not be admissible as evidence without independent proof of an alleged extortion conspiracy between O'Brien and Fieger, he said.[839]

[...]

According to the recently released documents, O'Brien delivered Fieger's purported threat to expose Cox's alleged sexual involvement with two women to Assistant Attorney General Stuart Sandler in meetings held Oct. 14 and 17.

According to a transcript of the Oct. 14 meeting secretly taped by Sandler, O'Brien tells Sandler, Cox's external affairs director, that Fieger gave him the "names of two broads" with whom Cox had sex "in the line of duty."

Sandler told sheriff's investigators O'Brien gave him a piece of paper bearing the two names on Oct. 17, before the two met Fieger at Morton's, a Southfield steakhouse.

Cox told the *Detroit Free Press* that he had an affair with one of the women named in the documents, but he said the second was "a complete fabrication."

Sandler also told investigators he told Fieger during the Oct. 17 meeting "that things have really gotten out of hand between him and our office," and Fieger responded that "[you] started it."

According to Sandler, Fieger went on to say, "'I always thought Mike Cox was his own guy. Why was Cox allowing Dan Pero and the Engler people

---

839 That didn't stop the Gorcya's railing against him, said Fieger: "Cox had his friend, Dave Gorcyca, go on TV and say, 'Well, we have no proof that Mr. Fieger actually did this, but he's a hundred-percent guilty of that.'" [Geoffrey Fieger, video interview.]

In fact, that is pretty much what Gorcya told *South Bend Tribune* reporter Tom Krishner:

> Prosecutor David Gorcyca said although a conspiracy probably did take place, he does not have sufficient evidence to prove it beyond a reasonable doubt. Gorcyca said, although he is not bringing criminal charges, he does plan to submit the matter to the Attorney Grievance Commission. "Neither Mr. Fieger or [sic] Mr. O'Brien should claim victory, act virtuous or gloat," Gorcyca said. "Far from it. In my opinion—and based upon my review of the facts—the evidence soundly convinces me that a severe and reprehensible ethical violation or violations were committed by both Mr. Fieger and Mr. O'Brien."

[Tom Krishner, "No charges in Cox-Fieger case," *South Bend Tribune*, 16 November 2005, http://articles.southbendtribune.com/2005-11-16/news/27000582_1_geoffrey-fieger-attorney-general-mike-cox-prosecutor-david-gorcyca.]

As it turned out, Gorcya would have to get in line to complain to the AGC.

to lead this investigation?' Geoff said he didn't understand how Cox let him do this."

Pero managed Engler's 1990 and 1994 gubernatorial campaigns and was his chief of staff during Engler's first term.

Days before the 2004 election, Pero filed a complaint with the Michigan Secretary of State over the anti-Markman TV ads aired by a group called Citizens for Judicial Reform. Fieger has since acknowledged bankrolling the campaign.

Reached at his Lansing-area home, Pero said Fieger's claim of a vendetta by Cox is misplaced. The Attorney General's office, he said, only investigates alleged violations of campaign finance laws referred to it by the Secretary of State—a point Sandler said he tried to make during his meeting with Fieger at Morton's.

"You'd think Geoffrey would know that if he wants to be Attorney General," Pero said. "It just shows Geoffrey's fast and loose with the facts, and he's always been this way."

Pero now heads the American Justice Partnership, a group formed to put more conservative judges on state courts and pass state laws aimed at reducing incentives for frivolous lawsuits.[840] He was tapped for the job in January by Engler, now president of the National Association of Manufacturers.[841]

The pressure for the investigation came not just from Pero, but also someone else very high in the Republican scheme of things. And the scuttlebutt, reported in *Michigan Lawyers Weekly*, was that it was mostly political:

The state's top two elected Republicans are denying charges that partisanship led them to investigate election ads placed by Geoffrey Fieger bashing a Supreme Court justice.

Rich Robinson, a campaign finance watchdog, says Secretary of State Terri Lynn Land's decision to ask Attorney General Mike Cox for help investigating a political action committee was a "radical" departure from normal procedure.

The Bureau of Elections, a part of the secretary of state's office, referred Citizens for Judicial Reform to Cox's office in March after it had trouble locating the group—which was listed on TV ads criticizing GOP-nominated Justice Stephen Markman in last year's state Supreme Court race.

840 Colleen Pero, who is married with Dan Pero, would subsequently go on to manage Cliff Taylor's 2008 unsuccessful campaign.
841 "Fieger blamed probe on Engler operatives," *Michigan Lawyers Weekly*, 21 November 2005, http://milawyersweekly.com/news/2005/11/21/fieger-blamed-probe-on-engler-operatives/.

The bureau sought to bring the group into compliance with reporting requirements.

The PAC appeared to have a phony address, phone number and treasurer. It also missed a January deadline to report its spending or disclose its financial backers. In June, Fieger acknowledged funding the $457,000 worth of ads. The wealthy trial lawyer and former Democratic gubernatorial candidate has accused Cox and Land of having a vendetta against him.

According to Robinson, election officials rarely refer campaign finance cases to the Attorney General for prosecution. The Secretary of State normally is supposed to use informal methods to bring a candidate or committee into compliance.

"Enforcement should be blind to whether you have political friends or enemies," said Robinson, executive of the nonpartisan Michigan Campaign Finance Network. "It should simply be a matter of the violation."

A Land spokeswoman said there was no way to negotiate a settlement with Citizens for Judicial Reform. The group's address turned out to be a burned-out tire store in Detroit and its purported treasurer likely is not a real person.

"Not only did we not know who they were but we had no information on their funding source or their expenditures," Kelly Chesney said. "This is a very unique situation. The whole point of campaign finance laws are to let voters know who is behind the expenditures in a political campaign."

Robinson points to the Greater Detroit Leadership PAC, which accepted an improper corporate donation in 2004. The PAC has given money to Cox, Land and Democratic Gov. Jennifer Granholm, among others.

Robinson, who filed a complaint against the PAC and says the illegal contribution was facilitated by a former Cox campaign worker, thinks Greater Detroit was treated differently than Citizens for Judicial Reform and Fieger. Greater Detroit's case was settled by conciliation in May and the improper $25,000 contribution was only partially returned, Robinson said.

But Chesney said the law lays out different procedures for handling cases where committees miss filing deadlines—like Citizens for Judicial Reform—and ones involving finances.

Cox has relinquished control of the investigation into Fieger. Last month, Cox acknowledged an affair and blamed Fieger and another lawyer for forcing his public admission.

Cox now is looking for an independent prosecutor to avoid any hint of impropriety, a spokesman said. He denies any partisan reasons for investigating Fieger.

"When we began an investigation, we did not know who was behind it," Cox spokesman Rusty Hills said.[842] "If you don't know who is behind it, how can the investigation be politically motivated? The answer is it can't."[843]

Yes, but...Fieger stepped out from the shadows in June to take ownership of his ads. This was December.

And Cox would find his independent prosecutor, Democrat Patrick Shannon, a former Upper Peninsula prosecutor. Fieger had asked then-Governor Jennifer Granholm to pick one. Cox's choice, said Fieger's attorney Richard Steinberg, didn't even the odds:

"It's like a tag-team wrestling match," Steinberg said. "You've got Fieger in one corner and Cox in another, and Cox gets to appoint the referee."[844]

There was more to come at Fieger. This was the ultimate paragraph in the story:

In a separate matter, federal investigators are looking into [...] campaign contributions Fieger's staff made to Democratic presidential candidates John Edwards and John Kerry. A lawyer fired from Fieger's law firm has said he was reimbursed by the firm for contributions he and his wife made to Edwards' 2004 campaign.[845]

This would lead to an interesting conclusion to the entire Fieger story. But, that's later.

And in that same edition of *Michigan Lawyers Weekly* was another story confirming everything Fieger had claimed concerning the search and seizure of his records:

State attorneys improperly seized tax documents and financial records of lawyer Geoffrey Fieger and should give them back immediately, an Ingham County judge ruled recently.

Circuit Judge James Giddings,[846] in a strongly worded order, said he was shocked that Attorney General Mike Cox's office sought and was granted a search warrant to obtain 2004 federal income tax returns and other infor-

---

842 Rusty Hills twice had been the chair of the Michigan Republican Party and had served as one of John Engler's chief lieutenants for ten years.
843 "Partisanship issues in Fieger investigation," *Michigan Lawyers Weekly*, 19 December 2005, http://milaw-yersweekly.com/news/2005/12/19/partisanship-issues-in-fieger-investigation/.
844 "Cox appoints counsel in Fieger case," *Michigan Lawyers Weekly*, 26 December 2005, http://milawyer-sweekly.com/news/2005/12/26/cox-appoints-counsel-in-fieger-case/.
845 Ibid.
846 Remember him? Engler called him a "lunatic."

mation from Fieger's accountant. Fieger is being investigated for running 2004 election ads—anonymously at the time—criticizing a state Supreme Court justice.

Earlier this month, East Lansing District Judge David Jordan allowed investigators to get the documents with a warrant after he had previously denied their request for the information through an investigative subpoena, Giddings said.

"The Attorney General has absolutely ... no right whatsoever to these documents," Giddings said. "For the district court to allow it, it's deeply troubling to me and stunningly surprising."

Giddings directed Jordan, within two days, to order Cox's office to return the documents to Fieger's accountant. He also barred Jordan from taking any other action until Jordan first rules on Fieger's request to disqualify him from the case.

The ruling came the same day Cox named an independent counsel to take over the campaign finance investigation into Fieger. Cox last month admitted having an affair and accused Fieger of threatening to disclose the indiscretion unless he stopped the probe. The Oakland County prosecutor said he did not have enough evidence to charge Fieger or an associate with a crime.

During a three-hour hearing, Fieger's attorneys and state attorneys sparred over what records can be taken from Fieger—particularly documents also kept by his accountant, Paul Evancho of Southfield-based Correll Associates.

Assistant Attorney General Margaret Nelson said Jordan's earlier decision and a separate order issued by the state Court of Appeals did not bar the state from getting a warrant to seize records from the accountant. But Fieger's lawyers said Jordan essentially allowed the state to get the records by going through the back door instead of the front.

Giddings agreed with the Fieger camp.

"I'm frankly taken aback that a search warrant occurred for the same identical records," he said. "Is it improper? I want to tell you it's a first for me having had the privilege of sitting in the courts of this state for over 33 years."[847]

847 "Judge tells AG to give back Fieger's records," *Michigan Lawyers Weekly*, 26 December 2005, http://milawyersweekly.com/news/2005/12/26/judge-tells-ag-to-give-back-fiegers-records/. Of note, in 2007, the Michigan Court of Appeals overruled Giddings' decision:

> A county judge improperly blocked the state Attorney General from investigating lawyer Geoffrey Fieger over election ads against a state Supreme Court justice, the Michigan Court of Appeals has ruled.

Fieger was fortunate that special prosecutor Shannon couldn't make the dots connect. There would be no criminal charges at the state level against him in his ads against Markman.[848] The federal level was another question, though.

And that really didn't mean he was off the hook, certainly not with the Michigan Supreme Court. In fact, that court came looking for him.

The COA as "Nazis"?

It had to do with another case he won at the trial level but had overturned on appeal. Observing what was occurring at the end of *Gilbert v DaimlerChrysler*, the author of The LitiGator observed: "Fieger holds the dubious record of having more money taken away in overturned verdicts than any other attorney in this state, and perhaps in the U.S."[849]

When he won at the trial courts, he sometimes won big. That was the case he waged on behalf of Salvatore Badalamenti in *Badalamenti v William Beaumont Hospital, Troy*.[850]

It wasn't an easy win, either, said Fieger:

> Robert Anderson was the judge, a very conservative judge, in one of the most conservative jurisdictions in Michigan, which is Oakland County. So I won a $15-million-dollar medical malpractice verdict against Beaumont Hospi-

---

The three-judge panel also said Fieger's attorneys wrongly "shopped" for Ingham County Circuit Judge James Giddings so he could obstruct warrants and subpoenas authorized by a lower judge.

The ruling stems from Republican Attorney General Mike Cox's 2005 campaign-finance probe of Fieger, who spent $457,000 on TV ads bashing GOP Justice Stephen Markman in the 2004 election. Cox later turned the investigation over to a special prosecutor, who said criminal charges weren't merited but civil fines could be warranted.

Cox had appointed the prosecutor after admitting an extramarital affair and accusing Fieger of blackmailing him over it unless he stopped the investigation.

Court of Appeals judges Henry Saad, Stephen Borrello and Kurtis Wilder said Fieger's attorneys improperly filed civil lawsuits against Cox and GOP Secretary of State Terri Lynn Land and instead should have appealed the issuance of the warrants.

The appellate court said Giddings should have thrown out the suits and faulted him for interfering with the case.

[David Eggert, "COA: judge interfered with Fieger probe," *Michigan Lawyers Weekly*, 5 March 2007, http://mi-lawyersweekly.com/news/2007/03/05/coa-judge-interfered-with-fieger-probe/.]

The matter would rise on an appeal from Fieger to the U.S. Sixth Circuit Court of Appeals, which also found against him. [*Fieger v Cox*, No. 07-1103, United States Sixth Circuit Court of Appeals, 6 May 2008, http://www.ca6.uscourts.gov/opinions.pdf/08a0172p-06.pdf.]

848 Joe Swickard, "Fieger: 'I expect to be indicted'; It's part of GOP attack, he says," *Detroit Free Press*, 17 January 2006, A.1.

849 "Upcoming case: *Gilbert v DaimlerChrysler*," 28 December 2003, http://radio-weblogs.com/0110436/2003/12/28.html.

850 *Badalamenti v William Beaumont Hospital Troy*, Nos. 207038, 207149, Michigan Court of Appeals, 20 August 1999, http://caselaw.findlaw.com/mi-court-of-appeals/1311989.html.

tal and a physician in what was, arguably (and still probably is) if not the, one of the most conservative jurisdictions in Michigan, with the person who was, arguably, the most conservative judge—Republican—on the circuit court bench. That's the backdrop of that case, so that no one thinks that Badalamenti was somehow an aberration. It was an aberration, but it was an aberration because I won it under the circumstances, not because that it somehow took place in a jurisdiction or in front of a judge that wasn't conservative.[851]

And he lost it all on the appeal. According to Fieger, it was Engler politics.

And you have to also understand that, as a setup to the Supreme Court, Mr. Engler put in place several judges in the Courts of Appeals, who acted as kind of the early-warning system to the later judges in the Supreme Court. Or a better way to think of it would be like a gauntlet: If these judges who are appointed, who are equally as radical and equally as politically motivated didn't get you, if somehow they were outvoted in a three-judge panel and somehow you got through that, then the [Supreme Court] was alerted, by way of either dissents or phone calls—and I'm not convinced they didn't make phone calls. There were backdoor channels to alert these people. And they were identifiable judges, who still sit on the Courts of Appeals, who would alert the four judges who I specifically identify as being the Engler Cabal—to take a verdict away, or to undo it, because it somehow got through the first gauntlet.[852]

That's his theory at any rate, one iterated by more than just trial lawyers.

According to the opinion at the Court of Appeals, this was the situation that played out in the trial court:

It was plaintiff's theory at trial that defendant Dr. David Forst, a cardiologist, negligently failed to diagnose and appropriately treat plaintiff for cardiogenic shock, particularly that he failed to appropriately treat plaintiff's low blood pressure between 4 p.m. and 6 p.m. following plaintiff's admission to defendant William Beaumont Hospital-Troy for a heart attack on March 16, 1993. Plaintiff contended that as a result of Dr. Forst's negligent treatment of plaintiff for cardiogenic shock, gangrene developed in plaintiff's extremities from loss of circulation to and oxygenation of the tissues in these areas, which ultimately resulted in amputation of plaintiff's fingers, thumbs, and both legs at the knee.

Defendants maintained below that plaintiff did not suffer from cardiogenic shock and that the conditions that ultimately required the amputation of his extremities resulted from an unexpected, rare, and severe sensitivity

---

851 Fieger.
852 Ibid.

reaction to the streptokinase that plaintiff received in the hospital's emergency center. It was defendants' position that once the reaction to streptokinase had set in, they were virtually powerless to stop the ensuing, cascading events.[853]

The trial jury had found for the plaintiff in the amount of $15 million. The hospital and others listed in the suit appealed. The Court of Appeals found grounds to reverse, noting first and foremost that the trial judge did not correctly handle a request from the defendant for a reversal of the jury's finding in a judgment notwithstanding the verdict (JNOV).[854]

> After thoroughly reviewing the entire record of this trial, and doing so in a light most favorable to plaintiff, we are compelled to conclude that plaintiff failed to present substantial, legally sufficient evidence to establish that he suffered from cardiogenic shock, the sole claim on which defendants' negligence was predicated. Defendants were entitled to entry of JNOV.[855]

Then it got personal.

> Because our resolution of the foregoing issue is dispositive of this case, we need not consider the parties' remaining issues on appeal except defendants' claim that they were denied a fair trial because of the persistently improper and highly prejudicial conduct of plaintiff's lead counsel at trial. We must agree that the conduct of plaintiff's lead counsel was truly egregious—far exceeding permissible bounds—and we will therefore address this issue. We hold that even if defendants were not entitled to JNOV, defendants would be entitled to a new trial because of pervasive misconduct by plaintiff's lead trial counsel that denied defendants a fair trial.[856]

What had Fieger done that so warranted this assessment? Judge Jane Markey, writing for the three-member panel, was not shy about laying it out:

> Throughout the entire trial, plaintiff's lead trial counsel completely tainted the proceedings by his misconduct. For example, through innuendo and direct attack, plaintiff's lead trial counsel repeatedly and with no basis in fact accused defendants and their witnesses of engaging in conspiracy, collusion, and perjury to cover up their alleged malpractice. Plaintiff's lead trial counsel continually accused defense witnesses of fabricating, in response to the instant litigation, the defense that plaintiff had a rare, severe reaction to streptokinase that caused his injuries. Indeed, this appeared to be his main theme. Plaintiff's lead trial counsel also repeatedly belittled defense witnesses and suggested, again, with no basis in fact, that they destroyed,

853 *Badalamenti v William Beaumont Hospital Troy*, Nos. 207038, 207149, Michigan Court of Appeals, 20 August 1999, http://caselaw.findlaw.com/mi-court-of-appeals/1311989.html.
854 Ibid.
855 Ibid.
856 Ibid.

altered, or suppressed evidence. Plaintiff's lead trial counsel further insinuated, relentlessly, outrageously, and with no supporting evidence, that while plaintiff lay "neglected" in the coronary care unit of the hospital, Dr. Forst "abandoned" plaintiff to engage in a sexual tryst with a nurse during the afternoon of March 16. Plaintiff's lead trial counsel repeatedly argued that money and greed were the defendants' prime motivation and the overriding interest guiding their treatment of plaintiff and their desire to cover up their "mistakes." Counsel in turn linked these concepts with references to Beaumont Hospital's corporate power and with defendants' ability to hire the "dream team" to defend them and to raise as many defenses as they wanted no matter how "preposterous." Plaintiff's lead trial counsel also inappropriately appealed to the jurors' self-interest as taxpayers where, in response to a defense witness' testimony regarding vocational rehabilitation services available to plaintiff through a state-funded agency, counsel lambasted the defense for suggesting that the "taxpayers" should pay for vocational rehabilitation services for plaintiff rather than the "wrongdoers." Again, we emphasize that these accusations, allegations, and insinuations had no reasonable basis in the evidence presented and were completely improper.[857]

And they'd noted it wasn't the first time he'd done something like this:

> Moreover, the conduct that occurred in this trial was at least as egregious, if not more so, than conduct of a similar nature in other cases that required reversal for a new trial.[858]

We've heard that kind of language before. So, the Court of Appeals had overturned the verdict and found for the defendants.

And Geoffrey Fieger was not happy about it. Three days after the verdict, August 23, 1999, he took to the airwaves in his daily *Fieger Time* show on WXYT-AM and blasted the three members of the appeals panel, Judges Richard Bandstra, Michael Talbot, and Jane Markey. Subsequent court documents reveal the tirade:

> "Hey Michael Talbot, and Bandstra, and Markey, I declare war on you. You declare it on me, I declare it on you. Kiss my ass, too." Mr. Fieger, referring to his client, then said, "He lost both his hands and both his legs, but according to the Court of Appeals, he lost a finger. Well, the finger he should keep is the one where he should shove it up their asses."[859]

Two days later, he renewed the attack.

> Mr. Fieger called these same judges "three jackass Court of Appeals judges." When another person involved in the broadcast used the word "innuendo,"

857 Ibid.
858 Ibid.
859 *Grievance Administrator v Geoffrey N. Fieger*, No. 127547, 31 July 2006, 3, http://courts.michigan.gov/supremecourt/clerk/Opinions-05-06-Term/127547.pdf

Mr. Fieger stated, "I know the only thing that's in their endo should be a large, you know, plunger about the size of, you know, my fist." Finally, Mr. Fieger said, "They say under their name, 'Court of Appeals judge,' so anybody that votes for them, they've changed their name from, you know, Adolf Hitler and Goebbels, and I think—what was Hitler's—Eva Braun, I think it was, is now Judge Markey, she's on the Court of Appeals."[860]

Fieger says that last comment was taken out of context and that the show was a comedy, but it really didn't seem to matter; what was in context would be more than enough to be insulting, comedy or not. And a lot of people in and out of court thought that he had gone too far:

[E]ven some of Fieger's allies in the trial bar suggest he can be his own worst enemy.

"There's no question he is much more outspoken in the courtroom than other attorneys," said Carol McNeilage, a Southfield lawyer and past president of the Michigan Trial Lawyers Association.

"And there's no question that it sometimes backfires."

While McNeilage said she shares Fieger's concern that Michigan appellate courts have become increasingly hostile to large jury verdicts, she said Fieger doesn't help himself or his clients by launching profane, personal attacks on appellate judges [....] "If you call a judge a jerk, you run the risk ...that it may affect outcomes," she said.

Fieger rejects that notion as well.

The standards by which Michigan appellate courts measure his conduct stand in stark contrast to those used in criminal cases, he said. Prosecutors, who represent the plaintiff in criminal trials, routinely suggest that witnesses are lying or that juries should act out of civic duty by punishing the accused, Fieger said.

But those tactics almost never result in a guilty verdict being overturned, he said.[861]

Undaunted by the reversal of fortune (literally and figuratively), Fieger filed a motion for reconsideration with the Court of Appeals. No dice.

Then he applied for leave at the Michigan Supreme Court. Again, no joy. The high court denied his application March 21, 2003. But the court wasn't done with Fieger. Could an attorney make the kinds of remarks he uttered on his radio show with impunity?

860 Ibid.
861 Dawson Bell, "Fieger's wins lose luster in appeals," *Detroit Free Press*, 29 May 2001, http://www.jpjpc.com/content/Fieger2.pdf.

The Grievance Administrator of the Attorney Grievance Commission didn't think so. (And he had dealt with Fieger before, starting in 1994, sometimes at the behest of judges who would later become justices.)

According to Fieger, the complaints were made:

> Engler would have people—I'm not kidding you—his surrogates would write the complaints, and I'm pretty sure his surrogate wrote the complaint in this case.[862]

The Supreme Court opinion on the subsequent discipline case covers the facts pretty well:

> On April 16, 2001, the attorney grievance commission (AGC), through its Grievance Administrator, filed a formal complaint with the ADB [attorney discipline board], alleging that Mr. Fieger's comments on August 23 and 25, 1999, were in violation of several provisions of the Michigan Rules of Professional Conduct, including MRPC 3.5(c), MRPC 6.5(a), and MRPC 8.4(a) and (c).[863]

Michigan Lawyers Weekly spelled out what the first two violations meant:

> A formal complaint was filed against the respondent accusing him of violating Michigan Rules of Professional Conduct 3.5(c) which provides that "[a] lawyer shall not engage in undignified or discourteous conduct toward the tribunal" and 6.5(a) which provides that "[a] lawyer shall treat with courtesy and respect all persons involved in the legal process."[864]

The last two charges were explained this way in the majority opinion:

> MRPC 8.4(a) provides that it is professional misconduct for a lawyer to "violate or attempt to violate the Rules of Professional Conduct, knowingly assist or induce another to do so, or do so through the acts of another[.]" MRPC 8.4(c) provides that it is professional misconduct for a lawyer to "engage in conduct that is prejudicial to the administration of justice[.]"[865]

According to Fieger, the rules are a singular anachronism:

> Michigan has a totally unique rule about courtesy to the court. It's called the courtesy provision. No other state has it. And I was alleged to have been

862 Fieger.
863 *Grievance Administrator v Geoffrey N. Fieger*, No. 127547, Michigan Supreme Court, 31 July 2006, 4, http://publicdocs.courts.mi.gov:81/OPINIONS/FINAL/SCT/20060731_S127547_23_fieger9mar06-op.pdf.
864 Todd C. Berg, "Attorney's reprimand for radio rant vacated; First Amendment trumps MTPC," *Michigan Lawyers Weekly*, 22 November 2004, http://milawyersweekly.com/news/2004/11/22/attorneys-reprimand-for-radio-rant-vacated/.
865 *Grievance Administrator v Geoffrey N. Fieger*, No. 127547, Michigan Supreme Court, 31 July 2006, footnote 4, http://publicdocs.courts.mi.gov:81/OPINIONS/FINAL/SCT/20060731_S127547_23_fieger9mar06-op.pdf.

discourteous to these people by saying this on a radio show, and my defense is First Amendment.[866]

The court record reveals that Fieger and the Grievance Administrator came to an understanding.

> While the complaint was pending, the parties entered into a stipulation. In return for Mr. Fieger's agreement not to contest that his remarks had violated MRPC 3.5(c) and MRPC 6.5(a), the charges alleging a violation of MRPC 8.4(a) and (c) would be dismissed. The parties further stipulated the sanction of a reprimand. The agreement was specifically conditioned on Mr. Fieger's being allowed to argue on appeal, while the discipline was stayed, both the applicability and the constitutionality of MRPC 3.5(c) and MRPC 6.5(a). Mr. Fieger maintained that the rules were inapplicable because his remarks were made after the case was completed and were not made in a courtroom. Further, he maintained that the two rules were unconstitutional because they infringed his First Amendment rights.[867]

Okay, so there would be a reprimand in Fieger's file...if he wasn't successful on his further appeals. According to Fieger, a reprimand wasn't much, and he'd agree to it for a reason.

> That was a strategic move on my part, just so I [didn't] have anybody holding anything over my head. A reprimand is the lowest form of discipline; it doesn't matter, it's a slap on the wrist and you go on. So I agreed to that.

> So I knew, no matter what happened they couldn't do anything worse to me, because I knew if those four guys got me, and I hadn't agreed to that, they'd try to disbar me. So as a tactical measure—everybody understood this was a minor offense, so I stipulated to that, only for the purposes of then appealing the First Amendment issues.

Fieger was going to make a big deal out of a reprimand, especially after the Attorney Discipline Board (ADP)—the board of the Attorney Grievance Commission that recommends penalties—worked the matter over and came up with three opinions, with the one that counted leaving Fieger free to go.

> The attorney argued that the rules were inapplicable because the comments dealt with a case that had already been decided and were not made in a court of law.

> Additionally, he claimed that even if the rules did apply, their application in his case would violate the First Amendment.

866 Fieger.
867 *Grievance Administrator v Geoffrey N. Fieger*, No. 127547, Michigan Supreme Court, 31 July 2006, 5.

The ADB agreed with the attorney's constitutional argument, vacating the order of reprimand and dismissing the formal complaint.

"We [...] believe an interpretation of these rules that would punish nonfactual utterances made about an appellate tribunal after issuance of its opinion would be unconstitutional," wrote board members Theodore J. St. Antoine, William P. Hampton, and George H. Lennon.

Board member Lori McAllister, joined by board member Billy Ben Baumann, concurred "that the comments at issue fall within the protection of the First Amendment and, therefore, cannot be the subject of disciplinary action in this particular case."

Meanwhile, board members Marie E. Martell, Ronald L. Steffens, and Rev. Ira Combs, Jr., dissented, stating that "we do not find a violation of either the First Amendment or of the Due Process Clause."

On the issue of the rules' applicability to the respondent's comments, St. Antoine, Hampton, and Lennon found the rules did not apply, while Martell, Steffens, Combs, McAllister, and Baumann concluded they did.[868]

In effect, the ADB had given Fieger a walk AND opined that the rule was unconstitutional. But the AGC Grievance Administrator wasn't going to allow the matter to drop there, so he sought leave to take up the matter at the Supreme Court.

Detroit attorney Robert E. Edick, who appeared for the Grievance Administrator, said he was in the process of preparing an application for leave to appeal to the Michigan Supreme Court.

"We intend to present to the Supreme Court the opportunity to rule definitively on the question of whether the board possesses the power to pronounce a Rule of Professional Conduct unconstitutional," Edick stated. "Our position is that the board lacks the authority. The rules are promulgated by the court which is also the entity that created the board and there is case law suggesting that a quasi-judicial body—which is what the board is—does not have the authority to pronounce the rules that it operates under as unconstitutional."

Edick explained that allowing the board's decision to stand could, if taken to its logical extreme, turn Michigan's legal system on its head.

"If the board could take a Rule of Professional Conduct—which has been approved and promulgated by the Supreme Court, who is also their boss—and declare it unconstitutional, then, at least theoretically, you could have a non-elected, five-member majority quorum, with as many as three non-

---

868 Todd C. Berg, "Attorney's reprimand for radio rant vacated...."

lawyers, telling the Michigan Supreme Court that their rule is unconstitutional."

However, Farmington Hills attorney Michael Alan Schwartz, who also represents the respondent, warned that what the grievance administrator's position really boils down to is foreclosing attorneys from raising any constitutional challenge to the rules of professional conduct.

[...]

"The effect of the commission's argument is to literally invite action by the federal district courts any time there is a federal constitutional claim," he observed, explaining that if attorneys have no vehicle for raising their constitutional claims in the state courts, then they will turn to the federal courts for relief.

[...]

"I do not believe the Michigan Supreme Court is going to want federal intervention in its disciplinary cases," Schwartz concluded.[869]

Nevertheless, the court granted. According to the majority opinion:

We granted leave to appeal to consider whether the remarks by Mr. Fieger, although uncontestedly discourteous, undignified, and disrespectful, nevertheless did not warrant professional discipline because they were made outside the courtroom and after the Court of Appeals had issued its opinion. We also granted leave to appeal to consider whether the ADB possesses the authority to decide issues of constitutionality and whether the two rules in question are constitutional.

Fieger asked the Engler Four—Justices Taylor, Markman, Corrigan, and Young—to recuse themselves Dec. 17, 2004. They declined the invitation.

And in the meanwhile, Fieger filed a notice to remove the case to federal district court, along the way seeking to have Justices Taylor, Markman, Young, and Corrigan blocked from hearing the case because of purported conflicts of interest. He wanted a temporary restraining order AND a preliminary injunction from the Michigan Supreme Court hearing the case. It didn't fly.[870] Fieger sought further relief at the federal level, but it wasn't going to come before the court took up the AGC's case against him.

The Supreme Court majority found against Fieger, but in so doing they had to split the decision into two parts, the first dealing with their interpretation of the law where

869 Todd C. Berg, "Attorney's reprimand for radio rant vacated...."
870 *Geoffrey Nels Fieger and Richard L. Steinberg v Michigan Supreme Court, et al.* Civil Action No. 06-11684, United States District Court, Easter Division, Michigan, 17 July 2006, 1, http://scholar.google.com/scholar_case?case=13306129417550722770&hl=en&as_sdt=2&as_vis=1&oi=scholarr.

it concerned Fieger. The second part was to respond to Weaver's assertion that they were not fit to sit on the case. That was because she had filed yet another dissent.

> With her dissent, Justice Weaver completes a transformation begun five years ago, when all six of her colleagues voted not to renew her tenure as chief justice of this court. This transformation is based neither on principle nor on "independent" views, but is rooted in personal resentment. This transformation culminates today in irresponsible and false charges that four of her colleagues are "bias[ed] and prejudice[d]" against attorney Geoffrey Fieger and therefore must be disqualified from hearing his cases—a call that Justice Weaver, who has received Mr. Fieger's political support, seems to believe that she is uniquely privileged to make. But just as troubling, Justice Weaver's personal agenda causes her to advance arguments—adopted wholesale from Mr. Fieger's past disqualification motions—that would lead to nonsensical results, affecting every judge in Michigan and throwing the justice system into chaos. We have addressed these arguments on a number of occasions, but we do so again here in light of Justice Weaver's unwarranted accusations.

> In essence, Justice Weaver would create an environment within this state that would affect every judge and that would prove utterly untenable. A judge could run for election, but could not campaign. A judge could be sued, but could not defend himself or herself. A judge could witness misconduct, but could not report it. Judges could be removed from cases at the option of attorneys and litigants, who could instigate public attacks and lawsuits against judges to force their disqualification. Judges would be intimidated, subtly and not so subtly, from carrying out their constitutionally ordained duties.

> [...]

> It is deeply troubling that a member of this court would undertake so gratuitously, and so falsely, to impugn her colleagues. This is a sad day in this court's history, for Justice Weaver inflicts damage not only on her colleagues, but also on this court as an institution. However, we do not intend to be deterred by false accusations from carrying out our constitutional duty to hear cases, including those in which Mr. Fieger is involved, and to decide these cases fairly and evenhandedly, as we have always done in the past. In particular, we invite public scrutiny of this court's record in cases in which Mr. Fieger, personally, and his clients have been involved.

> In making her charges of "bias and prejudice" Justice Weaver essentially adopts verbatim arguments made by Mr. Fieger in various disqualification motions that each of us has already considered and rejected.[871]

871 *Grievance Administrator v Geoffrey N. Fieger*, No. 127547, 31 July 2006, majority response 1-3, http://public-docs.courts.mi.gov:81/OPINIONS/FINAL/SCT/20060731_S127547_23_fieger9mar06-op.pdf.

They went on for 18 pages.

What had she said? First, she had joined Cavanagh in his 51-page dissent claiming the courtesy provision was unconstitutional and the majority's actions were unlawfully broadening the scope of the rules. (Justice Kelly filed her own dissent claiming the ADB had the authority to decide, but that the rules were not violated because Fieger's speech was not in a courtroom. Beyond that, she agreed the rules were vague and might infringe on the First Amendment.)

But Weaver also gave chapter and verse of reasons the majority should not have stayed on the case. In her words, the Engler Four were "enmeshed" with Geoffrey Fieger in such a way that they could not objectively render a verdict in a case against him, not simply one of his clients. Certainly Taylor, Markman, and Young had made derogatory comments about Fieger in their earlier elections. But what was new was Corrigan's ongoing election for the fall of 2006. In particular, less than six months previously, her campaign committee had mailed out a letter from former Governor John Engler that cast Geoffrey Fieger as the bogeyman:

> One of my proudest legacies as Governor was having the honor of first appointing, then supporting jurists like Justice Maura Corrigan. Justice Corrigan has worked to recast the Michigan Supreme Court into a nationally recognized court. Today, the MSC is one of the most important voices of judicial restraint and limited government. So esteemed is Justice Corrigan that she has twice been on President Bush's short list for the U.S. Supreme Court.
>
> Justice Corrigan was elected to the Michigan Supreme Court in 1998 and served two terms as chief justice from 2001-2004. This November, she is seeking reelection to another eight-year term. Justice Corrigan has proven unequivocally by her record that Michigan will benefit from her continuing service on our state's highest court. We must work to retain our best and brightest. In Michigan, we no longer have a court where judges think that it is their prerogative to decide important policy questions. The majority on the court understands the constitutional role of the judiciary.
>
> Naturally, judicial activists in Michigan have been unhappy with our Supreme Court. They had grown accustomed to winning court rulings that they couldn't achieve through the democratic and representative process of government. Every time there is a state Supreme Court election, these activists are on the prowl, seeking to restore those good old days. This year will be no exception! We cannot lower our guard should the Fiegers of the trial bar raise and spend large amounts of money in hopes of altering the election by an 11th hour sneak attack.
>
> I believe our Michigan Supreme Court is truly exceptional. We simply cannot risk a return to the days of legislating from the bench. The court needs

to keep Justice Corrigan, a proven, experienced, and thoughtful jurist. In the past you have contributed to the Supreme Court race. I ask that you consider making a similar contribution or as much of the maximum amount allowed by law for any individual which is $3,400. Please show your support by sending your contribution today.

Your help in returning Justice Maura Corrigan to the Michigan Supreme Court will protect the growing reputation of Michigan's highest court.[872]

That might qualify as enmeshed.

Further, Markman was listed as a defendant in a federal suit by Fieger.[873]

Weaver noted:

While Justice Markman did not instigate that suit, he did file the motion seeking Rule 11 sanctions, using as background the fact that Mr. Fieger had previously filed numerous "frivolous" motions against him. Given that fact, Justice Markman has become so "enmeshed" in controversial affairs with Mr. Fieger that due process requires that he not participate in this case, in which Mr. Fieger is a party.[874]

What she didn't mention then[875]—but that others had—was that in May 2004, Attorney General Mike Cox hired Lucille Taylor. He also hired Kathleen Markman, who was married to Stephen Markman, in October of 2005. Both women had previously worked in the executive office with John Engler.[876]

Given the role of Mike Cox in all of Fieger's dealings with the court, that might also classify as enmeshed.

And, of course, there was $34,000 from the Cox PAC to Markman's campaign in the 2004 election. Fieger's co-plaintiff at the federal level was Richard Steinberg who observed:

"It's a signal of solidarity. You have this whole incestuous thing where the Cox 5200 PAC gives money to Justice Markman, his wife gets a job in the Attorney General's office."[877]

---

872 John Engler quoted in ibid., 11-12.
873 *Fieger v Cox*, No. 07-1103, United States Sixth Circuit Court of Appeals, 6 May 2008, http://www.ca6.uscourts.gov/opinions.pdf/08a0172p-06.pdf.
874 *Grievance Administrator v Geoffrey N. Fieger*, No. 127547, 31 July 2006, Weaver response 14, http://courts.michigan.gov/supremecourt/clerk/Opinions-05-06-Term/127547.pdf.
875 She would subsequently include the information in her next dissent concerning Fieger.
876 Associate Press, "Hiring justices' wives beneficial, Cox argues," *The Blade*, 23 December 2005, http://news.google.com/newspapers?nid=1350&dat=20051223&id=q3ZhAAAAIBAJ&sjid=ZgQEAAAAIBAJ&pg=6825,1981643.
877 Ibid.

Incestuous? Cox argued it was relative; he noted that Markman had hired former Governor Granholm as a federal prosecutor when he was a U.S. attorney in Detroit. Was that a conflict?

The *Detroit Free Press* editorialized against the employment of the two women:

> The fact that the spouses work for Cox already has provoked a motion that both justices recuse themselves from a case the Attorney General's office is defending before the high court.
>
> [...]
>
> Certainly there's a legacy of GOP coziness here [....] Cox's apparent effort to pick up where Engler left off doesn't inspire confidence.
>
> Still, in the situation as described, conflicts affecting the justices should be rare. But the justices need to address them forthrightly if they occur—and neither they nor Cox can act surprised when they get challenged.[878]

Weaver also brought up the issue of recusal...when and how justices are disqualified or how and when they disqualify themselves. She chronicled that she had been working on the issue for some time.

> For more than three years, since May 2003, I have called for this court to recognize, publish for public comment, place on a public hearing agenda, and address the procedures concerning the participation or disqualification of justices in at least 11 published statements in cases. Since that time, when a motion has been filed asking for my recusal from a particular case, I have given detailed reasons for my decision whether or not to recuse myself.
>
> [...]
>
> Currently, justices of the Michigan Supreme Court sometimes follow un-written traditions when deciding a motion for disqualification. At other times, justices follow portions of the current court rule on disqualification, MCR 2.003.
>
> Mr. Fieger filed three motions for recusal of various justices in this case; the motions were decided by the individual justices, and there was no possibil-ity of review of that justice's individual decision not to recuse himself or herself.

---

878 Editorial "Justices wives: Questions about conflict of interest can't be ignored," *Detroit Free Press*, 25 January 2006, http://www.redorbit.com/news/technology/368976/editorial_justices_wives_questions_about_conflict_of_interest_cant_be/.

This helter-skelter approach of following "unwritten traditions" that are secret from the public is wrong. There should be clear, fair, orderly, and public procedures concerning the participation or disqualification of justices.[879]

The 4-3 opinion against Fieger stipulated that he had to take the reprimand. Fieger asked for a stay—a delay of the implementation of the penalty—pending the outcome at the federal court. The Michigan Supreme Court denied. That would lead to yet another donnybrook, but before that eventuated, two more justices had to face re-election: Corrigan and Cavanagh.

Election 2006

The field included incumbents Cavanagh and Corrigan, but added Democrat Jane Beckering, Republican Marc Shulman, and Libertarian Kerry L. Morgan. Each of the candidates was profiled in *Michigan Lawyers Weekly*.

Beckering was a Grand Rapids litigator who had worked for both plaintiffs and defendants. She had not so much as argued a case before the Supreme Court, but she was well aware of its actions and the impact of its decisions. The court, she said, favored insurance companies, not a new declaration:

> I believe that our current Supreme Court is engaging in selective strict constructionism—selective textualism. [The majority] gets out its dictionaries and looks at the words "the," "a," "and," "any." When the justices make rulings, they will apply strict constructionism when it benefits the insurance company or big business.
>
> But in other rulings—where that same strict constructionism would benefit the worker or the individual—the court has said, "Well, that couldn't have been what the legislature intended. They probably meant this."
> I have a major criticism with the way they claim to be applying the law.
>
> [...]
>
> I think the *stare decisis* doctrine is critical to the stability of our justice system. [...] If you have 30-year-old law that our Supreme Court—whatever its composition was—interpreted and, for 30 years, our legislature never changed the law, then they [have] implicitly blessed it. It creates stability in the system when everyone knows the rules of the game. But when you begin overturning precedent, nobody knows what the rules are anymore.

---

879 *Grievance Administrator v Geoffrey N. Fieger*, No. 127547, 31 July 2006, Weaver response 20, http://courts.michigan.gov/supremecourt/clerk/Opinions-05-06-Term/127547.pdf.

The majority is not just interpreting the law; it is changing the law as it goes. You can't sleep at night as a lawyer—plaintiff or defense—because you are always wondering what they are going to do tomorrow.[880]

Many of her criticisms had been voiced by Weaver as well.

For his part, Marc Shulman of West Bloomfield had served as the former chairman of the Michigan House Appropriation Committee. He had been a three-time representative and had worked for 25 years as a trial lawyer, including clerking for U.S. District Court Judge Richard Enslen, and also for a circuit court judge. Like Beckering, he had never tried a case before the Michigan Supreme Court. He portrayed himself as a strict textualist who was at odds with Michael Cavanagh's point of view:

Many of Justice Cavanagh's opinions, I believe, have ended up containing a lot of his own policy, as opposed to interpreting the law. I think if you look at certain decisions, there is talk about moral evolution. There is talk about some of the favorites such as "legislative acquiescence," and perhaps the legislature just didn't know what it was doing. I have a little bit of a different philosophy, and I truly believe that the court's role is not to make policy but to interpret the law.[881]

Journalist Melissa Stewart spent a large portion of her interview latched on to the language of Schulman's campaign speech and literature.

Q. In your July 17, 2006, press announcement on your website, you're quoted as stating, "We cannot lower our guard should the Fiegers of the trial bar raise and spend large amounts of money in hopes of altering the election by an 11th hour sneak attack." During your trial attorney days, didn't you work with or refer cases to Southfield attorney Geoffrey N. Fieger?
A. No, I never worked with Geoff Fieger.

[...]

Q. As far as that quote which includes the "Fiegers of the trial bar" remark, are those your words or did you get them from somewhere else?
A. If there's a quote [attributed] to me, I said it. The press release is prepared by someone for me, sure.
Q. Would it surprise you to know that exact same phrase, word for word, was in a fundraising letter authored by former Gov. John Engler and sent out by the Committee to Re-Elect Justice Corrigan?

880 Melissa P. Stewart, Lawyers' election guide (389251): Jane M. Beckering, *Michigan Lawyers Weekly*, 30 October 2006, http://milawyersweekly.com/news/2006/10/30/lawyers-election-guide-389251/
881 Melissa P. Stewart, Lawyers' election guide (389252): Marc I. Shulman, *Michigan Lawyers Weekly*, 30 October 2006, http://milawyersweekly.com/news/2006/10/30/lawyers-election-guide-389252/.

A. I can't speak to that because I don't know. I'd have to ask my press person.[882]

Corrigan, of course, had used the remark, arguably enmeshing her with Geoffrey
Fieger. Stewart, however, didn't raise the issue with her. There were other things to
talk about with Corrigan.

Q. Much has been made about the lack of civility among the justices, especially during the opinions released during the last week of this past term.
For instance, justices accused one another of bias, prejudice, personal resentment, false charges, vindictiveness, and rewriting the rules to protect
themselves. Did you or any of your colleagues cross the line?
A. With regard to [*Grievance Administrator v Fieger*], I will not comment on
that case because it is still under consideration. With regard to the civility
issues generally, are we in perfect harmony? Of course not. Do we get the job
done? We do. I think that we need to be judged by the results, and not by
whether we're getting along or not getting along. I think that is interesting
gossip, but I don't think it is what I am here to do. I am here to do the work
of the Supreme Court, everyday; to try to adhere to my oath, everyday, with
my colleagues; to get us to clear statements of law. To get us to four votes on
a position, at least. If we can get it to seven, that is wonderful. I think that
the civility issue is overblown, and disproportionately taken out of context.
Q. How do you feel it has been disproportionately taken out of context?
A. Because I believe, as I have indicated, that the vast majority of our cases
are unanimous. The orders are unanimous. Only a small percent of the cases
are cases that we take, and there, I believe we are doing what a Supreme
Court is to do. We engage in rational debate. That is what our democracy is
about, and I think that we do it.
Now, are there ways that we can tone down the rhetoric? Yes. Could we do
better? Yes.

[...]

Q. You mentioned that the "vast majority" of the Supreme Court's rulings are
unanimous. In terms of decisions, though, I have noticed that between 2001
and 2004, the number hovered around 45 to 48 percent of the written opinions
were unanimous. From 2004 to 2005, that number dropped to about 27 percent,
and now, in this past term, it is about 17 percent [based on opinions and orders
issued in cases that were argued before the Supreme Court]. What does that
trend mean?
A. I don't know, because we are not trying to hit a certain number of unanimous or not unanimous opinions. [...] I am really not willing to attribute
much significance to the percentage variation.

[...]

---

882 Ibid.

Q. One of the hot button issues this term—it seems to be evolving over the past few years—is the court's handling of disqualifications and recusal motions. Justice Weaver has been calling for reform in this area since 2003.
A. We have had ongoing files on this issue.
Q. Justice Cavanagh even mentioned in *Grievance Administrator v Fieger* that "...I take my colleagues at their word that the issue of disqualification will be handled in a prompt manner in the coming months." Has the issue of disqualification been handled and, if so, how?
A. The issue of disqualification is still under review in our court. We are still in the process of having statements written about it. It has been enormous—it is a huge file because there are very significant issues connected with disqualification. Is it still under consideration? Yes, it is.
Q. Do you have any idea when it will be up for comment at a public hearing?
A. This has been ongoing for so long that I cannot predict when the final [comment period] will be. We have had drafts of documents—you have seen some parts of these publicly. It came up in *Adair v State of Michigan, et al.*, and we have had internal discussions about the rules in our conferences. Michigan has followed the same rule as the U.S. Supreme Court, whereby the question of disqualification is an individual decision for the justices, and it is a rule that has worked for us. That is the rule we follow right now. It is very much still under consideration, though, and it is a topic at our conferences.
Q. In 2005, when President Bush was looking to fill vacancies left by former Chief Justice William H. Rehnquist and Justice Sandra Day O'Connor, your name came up several times. How far did those discussions go?
A. I must tell you that the White House asks you to keep your discussion there confidential, but I was on the President's short list. I will confirm that.
Q. That you were not the President's nominee, did that have anything to do with the fact that Gov. Jennifer Granholm, a Democrat, would have had the opportunity to fill your seat on the Michigan Supreme Court?
A. You will have to call President Bush about that.[883]

Cavanagh, whose candidacy for the court would be his last because of age, said he didn't take it personally that the Engler court was dismantling decisions he'd crafted early in his 24-year career on the court. He thought the rhetoric was overheated and even he might have crossed the line a time or two...and things could be better. The last question dealt with disqualification. Here's his answer:

It has only been in recent times—and granted, the majority of the motions tend to come from the Fieger cases—that we have had motions to disqualify the current majority.

Our practice, historically—for however many years, 140 years?—has been like the U.S. Supreme Court. The justice that is the target makes the call.

883 Melissa P. Stewart, Lawyers' election guide (389253): Justice Maura D. Corrigan, *Michigan Lawyers Weekly*, 30 October 2006, http://milawyersweekly.com/news/2006/10/30/lawyers-election-guide-389253/.

However, as I looked at things, I started to think that that cannot meet minimum due process requirements. We talked about this about a year ago, and we came up with three different versions, two of which were crafted by the majority.

One was the status quo. Another tracked the court rule [MCR 2.003(B)], and the third was kind of a hybrid, wherein, if the targeted justice denied the disqualification motion, it would go to the court and the court would make the call. All of these were suggested with the understanding that it ought to be a pretty serious, significant matter that takes one of the seven of us out of the equation. It ought not to be done lightly because there are only seven of us and there is no substitution provision.[884]

As for what's being done, the issue's come up in our administrative meetings, but there's nothing official to report yet.[885]

Kerry Morgan, the Libertarian offering, was from Wyandotte. Like the two other new faces, he had never tried a case before the Michigan Supreme Court, although he had been "on brief" for several cases at the U.S. Supreme Court. He found plenty to fault in the *Fieger* decision.

Q. On your website you criticized the *Fieger* decision for "sweeping aside the inalienable rights of free speech and to earn a living according to one's calling," as well as attacking citizens' "right to legal counsel." Given that Fieger, the respondent, suggested that the judges who ruled against his client should be sodomized, called them jackasses, and likened them to Adolf Hitler, Joseph Goebbels and Eva Braun, what should have been done in the way of discipline?
A. The court has no authority to impose, in my mind, any sanctions against him for any out of court statements. This is out of court. This is not the old, "You are an officer of the court, you are in my courtroom, I am God in my courtroom and you will not cause disruption." Even in the courtroom, the judge has to say, "If you keep it up, if you keep it up I will hold you in contempt and I will have you taken off and put in my little jail over here. Or, you can leave if you are so emphatic about it." You get an opportunity to get out of there.

Here, the guy is on the radio—*the radio*—where is the media? Why isn't the media screaming about this? No. They only reach in and grab him because of the license.

When you look at the whole basis of licensing, you will see that it has something to do with the practice of law. Now, how does this guy's opinions

---

884 Weaver disagreed with this conclusion.
885 Melissa P. Stewart, Lawyers' election guide (389254): Justice Michael F. Cavanagh, *Michigan Lawyers Weekly*, 30 October 2006, http://milawyersweekly.com/news/2006/10/30/lawyers-election-guide-389254/.

about a case that is not even before a judge, have something to do with his practice of law? I just don't see the nexus there.

[...]

Q. Much has been made recently about the lack of civility among the justices, especially in the opinions released during the last week of the last term. For instance, justices accused one another of bias, prejudice, personal resentment, false charges, vindictiveness, and rewriting the rules to protect themselves. Did any of the justices cross the line?
A. Who made up this line? They did, so it is all just academic. The biggest damage done to the courts in this country is not by lawyers, but by the judges themselves and the contempt that they heap on themselves by the people. There is this universal disrespect for judges, because judges are just doing whatever they want. To talk about lowering the quality and integrity of the bar and the bench, you only need read judicial opinions that are steeped in pure political analysis and reach politically correct results. So if they want to argue and complain about each other all day, it is perfectly fine with me, because that is life.[886]

What also was "life" was the result of the election:

The 2006 Michigan Supreme Court campaign was among the least costly in a decade, at roughly $944,000 per seat. Incumbent Justices Michael Cavanagh and Maura Corrigan each had a comfortable campaign finance advantage over the three challengers, and both coasted to easy victories on Election Day. Corrigan, who had 300,000 fewer votes than Cavanagh, had three-times as many votes as the next highest vote getter.[887]

Top vote getter Cavanagh polled at 1,984,137. He had candidate receipts of $316,799, $206 in party independent expenditures (IEs), and an additional $100 in party funds.[888] His cost per vote was 16 cents.

Corrigan tallied 1,691,443 votes. She had candidate receipts of $679,286, party IEs of $310, and party support of $2,953.[889] Her cost per vote was 40 cents, the highest of the field.

886 Melissa P. Stewart, Lawyers' election guide (389250): Kerry L. Morgan, *Michigan Lawyers Weekly*, 30 October 2006, http://milawyersweekly.com/news/2006/10/30/lawyers-election-guide-389250/
887 Rich Robinson and Barbara Moorehouse, *2006 Citizen's guide to Michigan campaign finance*, Michigan Campaign Finance Network, (Lansing, Mich., 2007), 22, http://www.mcfn.org/pdfs/reports/07_MCFN_Cit_Guide.pdf.
888 His top supporters included: United Auto Workers/UAW MI Voluntary PAC $34K; Michigan Education Assn./MEA PAC $33,900; Michigan Trial Lawyers Assn./Justice PAC $20K; Miller Canfield PLC + PAC $16,785; Michigan Regional Council of Carpenters PAC $10K; candidate $9,359; Comerica Inc. PAC $15,250; Honigman, Miller, Schwartz $7,298; Foster Swift Collins & Smith + PAC $6,150; Dykema Gossett PLLC + PAC $4,562; Plunkett & Cooney PC + PAC $4,225. [Ibid., 85.]
889 Her top ten supporters included: Michigan Chamber of Commerce PAC $20,125; Michigan Assn. of Realtors/Realtors PAC $20K; Michigan Bankers Assn. PAC/MI BANK PAC $20K; Michigan Health & Hospital Assn./Health PAC $20K; Michigan Restaurant Assn. PAC $20K; Michigan State Medical Society MI Doctors PAC $13,250; Miller Canfield PLC + PAC $9,625; Dykema Gossett PLLC + PAC $9,085; Dickinson Wright PLLC $8,490. [Ibid.]

Next of the list of vote recipients was Jane Beckering with 561,386 votes. She had candidate receipts of $61,269, party IEs of $206 (and other party expenditures). Her cost per vote was 11 cents.

Marc Shulman received 385,458 votes, with candidate receipts of $29,989, party IEs of $300, and additional party support of $2,979. His cost per vote was 8 cents.

Kerry Morgan received nearly as many votes as Shulman: 369,216. There were no costs associated with his campaign.

But in what has become the norm, there was a lot more invested in the election than just the money put up by the candidates and their parties.

> As has become customary since 2000, the Michigan Chamber of Commerce spent more than any candidate in the race for issue ads. The Chamber spent about $800,000 on television advertisements during the month before the election that praised Corrigan's virtues and instructed viewers to 'thank' Corrigan. The advertisements did not instruct viewers to vote for Corrigan, so, under Michigan's weak campaign finance law, those ads are not considered to be campaign expenditures. Therefore, there is nowhere in the public record that one can learn who gave the Chamber the money it used to pay for the advertisements. Since 2000, the Chamber has spent over $6 million on such advertisements, all in support of the five Republicans on the nominally nonpartisan Supreme Court.

> The fact that political financial supporters can spend millions of dollars without being identified converges with a major shortcoming of Michigan court administration to create a serious threat to judicial independence. That problem is the absence of standards for recusal. Even though an individual, a corporation or an interest group may spend hundreds of thousands of dollars to support a candidate for the judiciary, there is no standard that says the beneficiary of such largesse must disqualify himself from a court case involving his supporter. And because millions of dollars can be spent secretly, there is no public scrutiny of such conflicts of interest.[890]

It is untraceable, unidentifiable, unaccountable, deceitful spending.

---

890 Rich Robinson and Barbara Moorehouse, *2006 Citizen's guide to Michigan campaign finance*, Michigan Campaign Finance Network, (Lansing, Mich., 2007), 22, http://www.mcfn.org/pdfs/reports/07_MCFN_Cit_Guide.pdf.

Chapter 18

Disqualification
Deals for Decisions,
A Proposed "gag order,"
It All Flies Apart

Fieger, Part 2

Geoffrey Fieger had asked for a stay for imposing his reprimand pending an appeal to the U.S. Supreme Court. The request for a stay would be denied by the Michigan Supreme Court in what had become the usual 4-3 pattern. Getting that opinion out, Dec. 21, 2006, would lead to another move against Weaver by the Engler Four.

And, as might be anticipated, there was a Weaver dissent behind it. She asserted that Fieger was being denied due process under the 5th and 14th Amendments. She reiterated her observations of bias and prejudice against him by the four justices. Something in what she wrote got the wind up for the majority. And the wind kept rising until it was at gale force. In fact, the Engler Four were so outraged that they would pass first an internal operating procedure (IOP) and then an administrative order (AO)—what came to be known as the infamous "gag order" to block her discussion of any matters that had transpired in their deliberations. Chief Justice Taylor would even notify the court clerk that her dissent was NOT to be published when the court's order came out.

The majority would toss out any efforts to reform the rules for the disqualification of justices. They would vote, then dismiss the votes as mere "straw ballots," and would refuse to put out minutes of the meetings wherein they had done all these things. They would launch more personal attacks, write of what they said were the outrages Weaver was foisting upon them, and what they said was the ruin she was bringing to the court. Add to all that the business of the court and, in sum, there was quite a bit going on. *Sturm und Drang.* And there was a confluence of factors that had led up to this gusty fulmination.

First, there was Geoffrey Fieger and his repeated insistence that the Engler Four recuse themselves. They didn't much like that demand...or him.

Over the course, each one of the majority of four had indicated obvious appearances of bias and prejudice. And in my opinion, they were biased and prejudiced; I witnessed some of it. They claimed they were not prejudiced against him, but I think people oftentimes are maybe the last ones to see it, if they ever see it. Or, maybe they never admit it. It's not a very pleasant thing to face or admit or think about.

Second, there was the ongoing matter of the disqualification of justices, especially in cases where parties might not otherwise get a fair hearing. There was a Michigan Court Rule (MCR) that governed whether or not a justice (or judge) should withdraw from a case, MCR 2.003. It provided (as we have covered in Chapter 7) that either a party to the action or the judge her/himself may raise the issue of disqualification. Then,

> A judge is disqualified when the judge cannot impartially hear a case, including but not limited to instances in which:
>
> > (1) The judge is personally biased or prejudiced for or against a party or attorney.[891]

But how do justices get disqualified? Should the Engler Four be disqualified from this Grievance Administrator v Fieger case? We had no written rules other than MCR 2.003. I thought it applied. The position of the Engler Four in general was that it didn't, and that we were relying on 169-year-old rules that were unwritten. Exactly how one would know what rules existed 169 years or more ago unless they were in writing was unexplainable. And they thought that maybe various rules of the U.S. Supreme Court applied for them. Well, those rules applied for the federal judges, not the state judges. So it was a lot of debate, a lot of disagreement. And that started in 2003-2004, and it increased in 2005 and 2006.

And it would go into 2007 and beyond.

There was something special about the ongoing saga of the reprimand of *GA v Fieger*: there were no other outside parties to consider, just an attorney who was both a party and the primary target.

Now it was a direct attack on Fieger, a personal attack on him, as opposed to any appearance of bias and prejudice against an attorney for the party in, say, Gilbert v DaimlerChrysler. We were arguing over whether MCR 2.003 applied to the justices who obviously are judges. There were four votes (the Engler Four) that 2.003 didn't apply to justices. But now, in GA v Fieger, it was possible to address it, in my opinion, because now it was direct prejudice against one of the parties—Fieger—as opposed to prejudice with respect to an attorney for a party.

In addition to pondering MRC 2.003, Weaver again had taken special note of the Michigan Constitution:

---

891 Aaron D. Hanke, "An Extreme Makeover: Why Michigan's Judicial Recusal Standards Needed Reconstruction and Why More Work Remains to Be Done," *University of Detroit Mercy Law Review* [Vol. 88.97, Fall 2010], 104, http://www.law.udmercy.edu/udm/images/lawreview/v88/881Hanke.pdf, citations eliminated.

> Decisions of the Supreme Court, including all decisions on prerogative writs, <u>shall be</u> in writing and <u>shall</u> [emphasis added] contain a concise statement of the facts and reasons for each decision and reasons for each denial of leave to appeal. When a judge dissents in whole or in part he shall give in writing the reasons for his dissent.[892]

That doesn't mean maybe justices might want to do this. It says the decisions of the Supreme Court SHALL BE in writing and SHALL contain a concise statement of the facts and reasons for each decision. And when a judge dissents in whole or in part he SHALL give in writing the reasons for his dissent.

The important decision and any dissents of whether a justice should or should not be disqualified was obviously included in these Constitutional demands. The intention that justices explain their decisions is VERY clear.

That was the practice Weaver began in 2003 after she was challenged by Corrigan (then as chief justice) in the *In re JK* case. And Weaver subsequently followed the standard that emerged there whenever she would withdraw from a decision on a case... she would determine her own fitness to judge the case under MRC 2.003 and then she would state it in writing.

But just because Weaver followed it as a matter of obligation didn't mean that others would.

After the *In re JK* fiasco, at Weaver's request, the court opened an administrative file on disqualification—DQ—issues: ADM 2003-26.

I had been asking for us to open up an administrative file, which was opened up in 2003, but there was no action then. And repeatedly in a number of cases where justices were asked to be disqualified—and it became a laundry list of cases—I said that we needed to get this straight. We shouldn't have helter-skelter at the Supreme Court on the vital issue of whether a justice should sit or not on a case. And it did matter whether there would be an appearance of bias or prejudice in the case. And it became a huge argument. And the court, at that time, was 4-3, basically, on these issues; the Engler Four versus Kelly, Cavanagh, and myself.

Arguments or not, the justices eventually had come up with three proposals they were considering, although the specifics were not yet public. But the justices had spoken of them: in the fall of 2006 Corrigan had referred to the DQ reforms in her re-election interview with *Michigan Lawyers Weekly*, the Engler Four had promised Cavanaugh they were going to move on them.

---

892 Constitution of the State of Michigan of 1963, Article 6, Section 6 "Decisions and dissents; writing, contents," http://www.legislature.mi.gov/(S(w3lai5eigzkfxwqjqjntnr45))/mileg.aspx?page=getObject&objectName=mcl-Article-VI-6.

Adair v State Board of Education

This momentum to consider the DQ issue had to build...and as Weaver said, that came case by case. Finally, the Engler Four were driven to deal with reform proposals by their participation in *Adair v State Board of Education*.[893] In that ongoing case, Markman and Taylor in particular got themselves sidewise of a Nov. 23, 2005, recusal motion, refusing to step off after the issue of the Attorney General's employment of their spouses factored into the case. The Attorney General's office was defending for the State of Michigan.

In the fall of 2005, Justice Young circulated a draft of his proposal for disqualification of justices. The need, he wrote (perhaps making a virtue of necessity in the *Adair* case), was clear:

> In the face of the court's historical, but unstated, disqualification practices, Justice Weaver has appropriately urged this court to adopt a specific written disqualification policy. I believe is it time to adopt an explicit policy.[894]

He began by erroneously claiming there was no one else who could do the work of the justices:

> Unlike judges who serve on the other courts in this state, an absent justice cannot be replaced by another judge. Therefore, needless disqualification of a justice deprives litigants of the seven justices to which they are entitled, produces the possibility of an even division on the merits of the case, and distorts the Supreme Court decision-making process. Additionally, because the removal of even one justice can alter the disposition of a matter, there is reason to guard against incentivizing strategic or tactical efforts to disqualify justices. These circumstances, unique to the Supreme Court, necessitate participation of every justice in the cases before the court absent a showing that the justice cannot impartially hear a particular case.

> Accordingly, unless one of the conditions specified below is met, it is the duty of the justice to serve in every case and a justice is not mandatorily required to withdraw from serving on a case. Each justice shall, on motion or *sua sponte*,[895] decide whether grounds exist for his or her disqualification in a particular case.

> Disqualification of a justice is required if:

---

893 This was a case that began in 2000 and would continue through 2012, ultimately involving 940 parties. The appellate docket sheet is available at http://courts.michigan.gov/opinions_orders/case_search/pages/default.aspx?SearchType=1&CaseNumber=129467&CourtType_CaseNumber=1.
894 Robert P. Young, Jr., e-mail, 30 November 2005, unpublished.
895 The term means "on one's own, of one's own accord."

1) the justice is actually biased against or for a party in the proceeding.[896]

Young went on to list all the conditions that would apply to a justice's recusal.

Dec. 5, 2005: Justice Taylor responded with some modifications. To the paragraph about how a justice was disqualified, he added the underlined sentence

> Accordingly, unless one of the conditions specified below is met, it is the duty of the justice to serve in every case and a justice is not mandatorily required to withdraw from serving on a case. Each justice shall, on motion or *sua sponte*, decide whether grounds exist for his or her disqualification in a particular case. <u>That determination shall not be subject to review by the court.</u>[897]

So, for Taylor the matter still would rest with each justice.

December 7: Justice Young noted his approval of Taylor's changes and proposed that they be published. They weren't, and the matter lingered, perhaps as a result of Weaver's response, the next day.

December 8: Justice Weaver responded to the two proposals in eight pages citing chapter and verse, beginning with Young's idea that "an absent justice cannot be replaced by another judge."

The state Constitution, she noted, provided for just such exigency under Article 6, Section 23: "The Supreme Court may authorize persons who have been elected and served as judges to perform judicial duties for limited periods or specific assignments."[898] That would apply to all the state's courts, she argued, including the Supreme Court.

She also criticized Young's plan for lack of specificity.

> Although in large part it tracks the grounds for disqualification in MCR 2.003(B), it does not state whether the procedural provisions in MCR 2.003 apply to Michigan Supreme Court justices. Nor does it address whether a justice's decision whether or not to participate in a case when the issue of disqualification has been raised should be written and published in the record of the case.
>
> [...]
>
> [S]ome justices would find that MCR 2.003 does not apply to the justices of the Michigan Supreme Court.

---

896 Robert P. Young, Jr., e-mail, 30 November 2005.
897 Clifford W. Taylor, "Memorandum," 5 December 2005, unpublished.
898 Michigan Constitution of 1963, Article 6, Section 23, http://www.legislature.mi.gov/ (S(q4a3dq454jy1lb3mqb3mmo55))/mileg.aspx?page=getObject&objectName=mcl-Article-VI-23.

[...]

The court's eventual new policy on the disqualification of justices should be in the court rules, probably as part of MCR 2.003. Before adoption of a new policy, the proposal or proposals should be published for comment and placed on a public hearing agenda, as any new court rule would be.[899]

Weaver wanted clear rules, and her critique and her call for publication <u>and</u> public comment stalled the process.

Shortly before the court made its recusal decision in Adair, the *Detroit Free Press* opined in January 2006 that the issue of spouses working for one of the parties (covered in Chapter 17) didn't look good:

> By hiring the spouses of two Supreme Court justices, Attorney General Mike Cox has raised uncomfortable questions about the Michigan legal system. The fact that the spouses work for Cox already has provoked a motion that both justices recuse themselves from a case the Attorney General's office is defending before the high court.
>
> [...]
>
> Certainly there's a legacy of GOP coziness here, accentuated by the fact that Republican Cox's political action committee gave Markman $34,000 for his 2004 re-election campaign. Cox's apparent effort to pick up where Engler left off doesn't inspire confidence.
>
> Still, in the situation as described, conflicts affecting the justices should be rare. But the justices need to address them forthrightly if they occur—and neither they nor Cox can act surprised when they get challenged.[900]

When it came time for the decision, less than a week later, both Justices Taylor and Markman claimed adherence to MCR 2.003 as the guiding factor. And they wrote they would have stepped aside if their wives had worked directly on the case. But they hadn't, and so Taylor and Markman noted they also found they had a "duty to sit" on the case.[901] Young supported their analysis. And Corrigan was right with them.[902] And at that time and in that case, each one of the Engler Four stated that MCR 2.003 was THE rule of the court and was sufficient.

---

899 Elizabeth A. Weaver, "Memorandum," 8 December 2005, unpublished.

900 Editorial, "Justices' Wives: Questions about conflict of interest can't be ignored," *Detroit Free Press*, 25 January 2006, A.10.

901 Motion for recusal, *Adair v State Department of Education*, No. 129467, 31 January 2006, http://caselaw.findlaw.com/mi-supreme-court/1172184.html.

902 "Justices refuse to disqualify themselves," *Michigan Lawyers Weekly*, 6 February 2006, http://milawyersweekly.com/news/2006/02/06/justices-refuse-to-disqualify-themselves/.

While he did not participate in the *Adair* recusal decision, Justice Cavanagh set forth his disqualification proposal. And it had teeth: if a justice refused to step aside and there was a further request from one of the parties, it would go to a vote of the court, and the justice in question would not be allowed to vote in her or his own cause.[903]

That was bound not to please the majority. And while there were three proposals before the court, only Cavanagh's then was visible to the general public.[904]
The majority's refusal to disqualify themselves in *Adair* was yet another in a long list that showed compromised application of vague and uncertain principles. MCR 2.003 was not always THE rule and was by no means sufficient. And the media were paying attention. *Michigan Lawyers Weekly* reported it:

> Justice Michael Cavanagh proposed a court rule that would let other justices decide a disqualification motion and bar the challenged justice from participating in the ruling. Justices Elizabeth Weaver and Marilyn Kelly also criticized the tradition of letting a challenged justice decide whether to recuse himself or herself.

> But Justice Maura Corrigan agreed with Taylor and Markman, saying the school districts' argument [in Adair] would "impose a constraint on professional couples and most certainly on a married professional woman's ability to practice law."[905]

And in February 2006, the *Free Press* stepped up the call for action:

> Two state Supreme Court justices spewed out pages of reasons on Tuesday why they won't step down from a case defended by the state Attorney General's office, where both their wives work. Unfortunately, their defensiveness may raise even more hackles.

> They didn't quiet some of their own colleagues' concerns, for starters. In a rare act, all five of the other justices commented on the joint statement by Chief Justice Clifford Taylor and Justice Stephen Markman.

903 Motion for recusal, *Adair v State Department of Education*, No. 129467, 31 January 2006, http://caselaw.findlaw.com/mi-supreme-court/1172184.html.
904 Those same three proposals would ultimately be considered in 2009. N.B.: If you want to examine them now, you'll have to do some sleuthing because the court completely revamped its website. Despite the promise from the Marcia McBrien press release that "Content from the former 'One Court of Justice' site is still available on the new site," hundreds of documents are no longer there. [Marcia McBrien, press release, "Michigan state courts' new web site debuts today," Michigan Supreme Court, http://courts.michigan.gov/News-Events/press_releases/Documents/NewWebsiteAnnouncement.pdf.] Before the website reconstruction the documents were available for consideration here: http://courts.michigan.gov/supremecourt/Resources/Administrative/2009-04-DQ-Order.pdf. The three proposals have vanished from the site as a separate file. They are, however, available because Justice Weaver included them in their entirety in her dissent to *GA v Fieger*: Appendix A, "The abandoned proposals for new court rules governing justice disqualification," Order, *Grievance Administrator v Geoffrey N. Fieger*, No. 127547," Michigan Supreme Court, 21 December 2006, 41, http://publicdocs.courts.mi.gov:81/SCT/PUBLIC/ORDERS/20061221_S127547_28_127547.122106ORDER.PDF. They can also be found on Weaver's website: www.justiceweaver.com.
905 Ibid.

Justices Michael Cavanagh, Betty Weaver and Marilyn Kelly, in separate opinions, concluded that the court needs a formal rule on when justices should disqualify themselves. Cavanagh even proposed one for discussion that would move the decision to the full court and no longer leave it up to each judge individually.

Justice Robert Young provided a statement of support for Taylor and Markman. Justice Maura Corrigan made an eloquent argument against any regression that might diminish the participation of women in the legal profession.

Taylor and Markman say they replied at length because of "media accounts that may, unless they are subject of a response, produce recurrent motions for recusal on the same grounds." But it is not the media accounts that raise eyebrows, it is their spouses' jobs. And their most sympathetic, if informal, argument—"that a judge's spouse who is a lawyer will effectively become unemployable"—is reason enough to ensure that no one overreacts.

But Taylor and Markman are too dismissive of the concept of "appearance of impropriety."

"This standard," they wrote, "cannot be equated with any person's perception of impropriety, lest a judge find himself or herself subject to a barrage of recusal motions." Yet it does not seem too much to ask, even if requests are frequent, for the two justices to state for the record that their spouses did not work on cases before them involving the state attorney general—a fact they affirmed Tuesday in a footnote.

Appearances do matter, especially for the state's highest court. The court should open the discussion of whether it needs a new rule.[906]

All that was in a request for recusal in *Adair*.

And there was another case working its way through the court—*In re Haley*—where the issue of the appearance of impropriety came to the fore. The case involved another case of a judge doing something he shouldn't have done: this time during a criminal plea hearing accepting football tickets for a big game from one of the attorneys (a former judge) in the case. Judge Michael J. Haley of Traverse City's 86th District Court (and an actor in *In re Gilbert*) had been sent to the Supreme Court by the Judicial Tenure Commission for a reprimand.[907] That raised quite a stink.

And then there was request from Geoffrey Fieger for a stay of his reprimand under *GA v Fieger*.

---

906 Editorial, "State justices shouldn't be so dismissive of the 'Appearance of impropriety,'" *Detroit Free Press*, 1 February 2006, A.11.
907 *In re Haley*, No 127453, Michigan Supreme Court, 31 July 2006, http://publicdocs.courts.mi.gov:81/opinions/final/sct/20060731_s127453_13_haley1dec05-op.pdf.

The Engler Four were growing restive under what they saw as Weaver's continual reminders of their shortcomings in her dissents. From their point of view, she just wouldn't give it a rest. And consistently, Weaver had outlawyered the Engler Four, a matter she ascribes to some of the best legal clerks and secretaries at the court.

I had good instincts when something was right or wrong, but I had really good staff. Their devotion to the law, research, writing, candor, and tireless work made such an impact.

She wasn't entirely alone (although she would be later).

At that point, Cavanagh was clear about standing up. And, too, he had good law clerks at the time.

And, she had been guided on her journey through the morass with the help of her then-attorney, Jon Muth.

Disqualification by the Numbers (Dates)

Pushed by stinging criticism from the press and others, the majority justices agreed at a conference March 1, 2006, to put three DQ proposals that grew out of ADM 2003-26 on the conference agenda. They were titled proposals A, B, and C. The first two came from the Engler Four. Proposal C was Cavanagh's, articulated in *Adair*.[908] But the Engler Four decided that it would not publish Cavanagh's proposal for public comment just then.[909]

At the same conference, the Engler Four voted on and adopted Taylor's proposed disqualification criteria from the prior December as an internal operating procedure, an IOP. As such, it required no hearings.

But Weaver noted that an IOP—this one or any other—also had no authority. She wrote "Unlike Michigan Court Rules that are enforceable, IOPs are unenforceable guidelines. IOPs, like 'unwritten traditions,' provide no due process protections."[910]

The disclaimer at the court's website acknowledged as much:

> [T]he internal procedures outlined in this document are only general guide-lines and may be modified at any time without prior notice by a majority vote. These internal procedures create no enforceable rights in any litigant.[911]

So, why would the four justices pass such a weak policy?

---

908 Motion for recusal, *Adair v State Department of Education*, No. 129467, Michigan Supreme Court, 31 January 2006, http://caselaw.findlaw.com/mi-supreme-court/1172184.html.

909 Elizabeth A. Weaver, "Memorandum," 28 September 2006, unpublished.

910 Elizabeth A. Weaver, "Memorandum," 28 September 2006, unpublished, 11.

911 This file seems to be yet another victim of the Michigan Supreme Court's reorganized website. The document had been available at http://courts.michigan.gov/supremecourt/2003-48_02-03-05.pdf, but is no longer listed and a search yields no results.

They wanted to be able to say to the public they had a policy...and also because it was even weaker than somebody claiming to use 2.003. It was totally nothing, and that's exactly what they wanted.

Weaver analyzed that in fact, the IOP would hold the justices to a lesser standard than the state's other judges.

Weaver, Cavanagh, and Kelly voted against the proposal but they were outnumbered. They were given until March 15 to prepare statements for the March 1 minutes. Those minutes were scheduled to be finalized into the record March 22, in accordance with the procedures at the court. It didn't happen that way. And this began a period where minutes of anything critical of the majority went astray, either never to be seen or so altered as to be unrecognizable with relation to what actually happened in a meeting.[912] One reason may have been because the majority started an oddly limping dance of doing and undoing. Weaver noted:

> After the statements [relating to the March 1 meeting] were circulated, however, ADM 2003-26 was returned to the court's administrative agendas on March 29 and April 19, 2006. During that period, members of the majority of four indicated their intent to withdraw their support for the IOP. Nevertheless, the majority refused to vote to rescind the IOP when a motion to rescind [it] was made at the April 19 conference. Because the IOP had been adopted by a 4-3 vote on March 1, 2006, four votes were required under the courts' written rules to amend the IOP.[913]

The Engler Four would subsequently try to paint the vote for the IOP and several other proposals as "straw votes." As such, they reasoned, the balloting was "nonbinding." And without notes, there was no way for the courts or the public to know.

They were scrambling to do what they wanted to do.

Smoke and mirrors. Weaver tried to clear the smoke. Here she was writing to clarify matters ten months after the March 1 conference:

> The majority of four continues to effectively suppress my dissent to the majority's March 1, 2006, vote to adopt an Internal Operating Procedure (IOP). The majority intended for the still unpublished, secret IOP to govern justice disqualification decisions. Because the majority's March 1, 2006, vote was a final vote, and not a straw vote, my dissent to the adoption of the IOP by the majority of four should have been made publicly available attached to the minutes for the March 1, 2006, administrative conference. However, the March 1, 2006, minutes have never been approved, now over ten (10) months later. Thus, what occurred on March 1, 2006, during the court's conduct of

---

912 While minutes eventually were circulated and filed, they were incomplete, something that led Weaver to protest publicly.
913 Elizabeth A. Weaver, "Memorandum," 28 September 2006, unpublished, 12.

the people's business remains a secret from the public as it has yet, as of this writing, to be made available to the public in the Clerk of the Court's office.[914]

On April 19, there was a unanimous decision to publish for public comment the three DQ proposals relating to ADM 2003-26. The date set for publication was June 15.

June 9, Justice Weaver responded critically to the DQ proposals.

On June 14, Weaver announced that she would dissent in *Grievance Administrator v Geoffrey N. Fieger*. Justice Young put a hold (holding any movement on the matter) on the DQ issue for further consideration. Taylor announced that he was pulling the DQ proposal from publication.

Michigan Lawyers Weekly analyzed the hold this way:

> Instead of trying to maintain the status quo with her colleagues in the "majority"—whose support had been crucial to getting the disqualification issue off the ground—[Weaver] announced that her forthcoming dissent in *Grievance Administrator v Fieger* was going to be highly critical of the majority, especially with regard to its denial of the respondent's recusal motions.[915]

On June 28, the DQ proposals were on the administrative agenda. There was discussion but no action.

Justice Robert Young, Jr., circulated a memo July 5 with an objection to the language Weaver used in her DQ policy memo of June 9.

> I object to Justice Weaver's reference to our internal deliberations in her disqualification statement. On page 3-4 of her June 9 revised statement, Justice Weaver states:
>
>> A majority of the justices could adopt a proposal, either one of the three published today or some other proposal that was not published for comment, as an unenforceable guideline with the court's internal operating procedure (IOP), as occurred on March 1, 2006.
>
> Justice Weaver's reference to our administrative deliberations in a published order is consequential. I insist that she remove the offending reference before I release my hold.[916]

---

914 Elizabeth A. Weaver, "Memorandum," 5 January 9 2007, http://www.justiceweaver.com/pdfs/1-5-07_DissenttoCJ.pdf.
915 Todd C. Berg, "If it ain't broke...: MSC declares procedures for handling recusal motions don't need fixing," *Michigan Lawyers Weekly*, 15 January 2007, http://milawyersweekly.com/news/2007/01/15/if-it-aint-broke/.
916 Robert P. Young, Jr., "Memorandum," 5 July 2006, unpublished.

On July 6, Weaver circulated the first copy of her *Fieger* dissent at the conference. The DQ issue also was taken up again.

On July 11, Corrigan announced in a memo that—based on Weaver's proposed dissent in *Fieger*—she was going to withdraw her support for DQ work:

> After reviewing Justice Weaver's opinion in *Grievance Administrator v Fieger*, [...] I will need to amend my statement in this matter. In addition I am reconsidering my willingness to publish the aspect of the proposal that would allow all justices to vote on a motion for disqualification. In light of Justice Weaver's opinion in *Fieger*, I am no longer certain that it is wise to consider tampering with our 169-year tradition of allowing each justice alone to decide whether recusal is warranted.[917]

Later Weaver would write of that Corrigan memo:

> ...Justice Corrigan divulged that she would change her vote on the publication of the justice disqualification proposals because of my position on the merits of Mr. Fieger's motion for her disqualification in *Grievance Administrator v Fieger*. The memo reveals that improper, if not unethical, considerations motivated her decision to vote to close ADM 2003-26. Indeed, the memo could be seen as an attempt to persuade me to withdraw my dissent in *Grievance Administrator v Fieger* or risk abandonment of the progress that had apparently been made at that time on the ADM 2003-26 administrative file.[918]

July 12, in conference, the justices discussed a new date for publication of the DQ proposals. There was not much agreement; it was further held.

July 31 was a big day, the close of a work year with lots of cases coming out at the same time. The *Fieger* decision came out, and it included Weaver's dissent.

So did the appointment of 17th Circuit Court Judge Paul Sullivan to oversee the Kent County Probate Court. And Weaver's dissent—already revealed in Chapter 15—laid out more bad behavior of her colleagues.

July 31 was also the opinion date for *In re Haley*. While the decision of the court to discipline was correct, said Weaver, there was the opinion by the Engler Four, and then there were three separate concurrences, each one a little different. Weaver's noted the behavior of the majority justices in her concurrence. In his opinion, Cavanagh reiterated the need for DQ reform: "I take my colleagues at their word that the issue of disqualification will be handled in a prompt manner in the coming months."[919]

917 Maura D. Corrigan, "Memorandum," 11 July 2006, unpublished.
918 Elizabeth A. Weaver writing in dissent, Order, *Grievance Administrator v Geoffrey N. Fieger, No. 127547,*" Michigan Supreme Court, 21 December 2006, 11, http://publicdocs.courts.mi.gov:81/SCT/PUBLIC/ORDERS/20061221_S127547_28_127547.122106ORDER.PDF.
919 *In re Haley*, No 127453, Michigan Supreme Court, 31 July 2006, http://publicdocs.courts.mi.gov:81/opinions/final/sct/20060731_s127453_13_haley1dec05-op.pdf.

In each of the three cases "Weaver came out swinging," analyzed Todd C. Berg in *Michigan Lawyers Weekly*:

> In *Appointment of Chief Judge of the Kent County Probate Court*, ADM 2006-01, she accused Taylor, Corrigan, Young, and Markman of "attempt[ing][920] to undermine the career and reputation of a good, hardworking judge by [unjustifiably and inexplicably] not appointing [the "best choice" candidate] as chief judge of probate," implying this was punishment for the candidate's rulings in two "highly publicized" but "strongly criticized" cases.
>
> Additionally, Weaver upbraided her fellow jurists in *In re Haley* for allegedly rewriting "the rules of conduct that govern judges" so as to protect themselves from future disqualification motions, noting "[i]t is not expected that when the going gets tough, justices who so ardently and frequently claim to be champions of judicial restraint will conveniently change the manner in which the laws governing their own conduct are to be applied."
>
> Finally, in *Fieger*—after three years of silence on the subject—Weaver denounced the majority for refusing to recuse themselves despite their "bias and prejudice" against the respondent and, thus, for violating the respondent's "rights to due process under the Fifth and Fourteenth Amendment."[921]

The court was on its August break, but the decisions were receiving scrutiny. Attorney Robert F. Garvey, of Saint Clair Shores, was one who took Weaver's dissents as a warning that something wasn't right at the court:

> As lawyers and citizens of this great state, we ignore Justice Weaver's concerns at our peril. We need to be aware of what is going on in our highest court. We need to be sure that the power entrusted to our highest judicial officials is not abused for the benefit of a few special interests to the detriment of this state's citizenry.
>
> The four justices who regularly vote as a block have characterized Justice Weaver's attacks as purely personal in nature. However, as lawyers, schooled in the art of analysis and cognizant of the importance of precedent, we have the tools necessary to arrive at reasoned conclusions with respect to these serious allegations. The claims by Justice Weaver are serious and warrant follow up and analysis.
>
> In our system of government it is permissible and, in fact, expected that the legislature will have a political agenda. However, the only permissible "agenda" of our highest court is the adherence to precedent and the protection of constitutional rights of its citizens.

---

920 These amendments were in Berg's story.
921 Todd C. Berg, "If it ain't broke...: MSC declares procedures for handling recusal motions don't need fixing."

An analysis of the opinions of this court should put the issue to rest one way or another.

[...]

As lawyers, we have the intellectual tools and the public responsibility to investigate these serious charges.[922]

And on Aug. 21, 2006, Geoffrey Fieger filed a request for a stay of his reprimand from the Michigan Supreme Court in order to appeal to the U.S. Supreme Court.

Sept. 7: After the break, the court reconvened, and the majority indicated it was going to deny Fieger's motion. Weaver informed them that if they did, she was going to dissent again. That left the matter hanging. Then, writing in a memorandum, she turned to the matter of the DQ file.

> I moved to publish for public comment the three proposals that had been previously circulated regarding the rules for the disqualification of justices. That motion was seconded and supported by Justices Cavanagh and Kelly, but failed to obtain the support of any one justice of the majority of four.[923]

The Engler Four—led by Young—then voted to close ADM 2003-26, the disqualification file. Weaver, Cavanagh, and Kelly dissented and were given time to prepare their statements for the minutes. This is Weaver's description of the reasoning:

> The only explanation for the majority's decision to close the justice disqualification file, ADM 2003-26, was offered by Justice Young when the matter of ADM 2003-26 was discussed on September 7, 2006. During that conference, he verbally attacked my character, and with the concurrence of Chief Justice Taylor and Justices Corrigan and Markman, Justice Young continued that the majority of four would "never publish the proposals" on disqualification and would "not give [me] any more power." The majority of four have provided no rational reason to close ADM 2003-26.

> The majority's decision to close justice disqualification file, ADM 2003-26, is made more significant and problematic by the fact that the same majority of four has now lowered the standards governing justice disqualification decisions.[924]

Todd Berg of *Michigan Lawyers Weekly* looked at it this way:

---

922 Robert F. Garvey, letter to the editor, "Are justices' personal attacks meritless or well-founded?" *Michigan Lawyers Weekly*, 18 September 2006, http://milawyersweekly.com/news/2006/09/18/are-justices-personal-attacks-meritless-or-wellfounded063/.
923 Elizabeth A. Weaver, "Memorandum," 28 September 2006, unpublished, 15.
924 Ibid., 15.

Not surprisingly, by the time the Supreme Court met for its conference on Sept. 7, 2006, the majority's perspective on the future of Weaver's reform efforts had changed.

In a 4-3 vote, Taylor, Corrigan, Young, and Markman not only pulled their support for publishing the proposals, but they pulled their support for the entire disqualification issue, opting to close ADM 2003-26, once and for all.[925]

They were going to punish me, and they simply voted to close down the whole thing and close the file. And, all of a sudden now, this DQ file didn't exist, and we never did get the minutes for the meeting. So it's like Soviet Union type stuff, rewriting history; it didn't happen. It's perfectly all right for them to change their mind and to decide that we're not going forward with it, but there should be a record of that. And I made a dissent to that.

No matter how much Justice Cavanagh had hoped that the majority of four were as good as their word and would deliver on disqualification reform in "a prompt manner in the coming months" it was kaput. Well, it was done unless....

...Unless Weaver would do what they wanted. You'll recall that Corrigan had earlier threatened Weaver in Corrigan's July 11 memo that if Weaver didn't drop her dissent in *GA v Fieger*, Corrigan would pull the DQ proposals. It's reasonable to assume that if Weaver had backed off in her dissent, that Corrigan would have allowed the proposals to remain on the table for consideration.[926] That, of course, would not have happened. But there was another attempt to sway her.

On Oct. 23, Taylor communicated to the justices that he would change his vote on the Fieger request for the stay of his reprimand IF Weaver would drop her latest dissent:

> I am writing to hold this case [the Fieger stay] and may be prepared to change my vote to grant the stay, however I wish to discuss it at conference first.

> I consider what Justice Weaver wishes to do in her dissent to be a violation of the deliberative privilege of the court. Memo traffic between justices is divulged, as is the conference discussion and commissioner submissions to the court. I believe it is incontestable that this is at variance with our ancient deliberative privilege rule. I find it almost inconceivable that this court could function without a deliberative privilege of the sort we have customarily had. Indeed I know of no other multi-person court in the English-speaking world that does not have the deliberative privilege of the sort that we have enjoyed since the 1830s.

---

925 Todd C. Berg, "If it ain't broke...: MSC declares procedures for handling recusal motions don't need fixing."
926 Elizabeth A. Weaver writing in dissent, "Order, *Grievance Administrator v Geoffrey N. Fieger*, No. 127547," Michigan Supreme Court, 21 December 2006, 11, http://publicdocs.courts.mi.gov:81/SCT/PUBLIC/ORDERS/20061221_S127547_28_127547.122106ORDER.PDF.

Evidently Justice Weaver does not hold that view. I am unsure where Justices Cavanagh and Kelly come down on this, but my understanding is, given their indications as to minutes of administrative conferences, that they may be sympathetic to per [sic] position. I am also not sure if this self-imposed open meeting-freedom of information regime that Justice Weaver would have this court create is only for this case, only for Fieger cases, or if it would be for all matters that come before the court. Operating on the assumption that it is only for this case, and that there would be no reason to destroy the deliberative privilege, if indeed she "prevails" on the issue of the stay, I, for the good of the institution, am prepared to grant the stay on two conditions. They are that first, Justice Weaver's statement or something akin to it not be released; and second, that this never again be what she attempts to do [....] If there is not an agreement as to both of these conditions, then I believe we need to sit down and talk about how we should handle the new world Justice Weaver would create.

If memo traffic and conference discussions are no longer to be kept private, the first issue that comes to mind is why would it be fair to have casual note-taking of what is going on in conference be the record? Wouldn't it be better to have a verbatim transcript? Similarly, with selectively released memos from the memo traffic, wouldn't it be better to have all memos? Likewise, with commissioner reports and the like, rather than having a justice who wishes to divulge these and have the whole court at his or [her] mercy, wouldn't it be better to have all of these be released? It also seems to me that to be considered is whether these new rules should apply to the Court of Appeals. They are a multi-person deliberative court also and if it is proper for us to have these new rules, why not them? In short, if we are going to a new self-imposed open meetings-freedom of information regime, these, and the multitude of other difficult questions, need to be worked through.

I await, with interest, your thoughts so that our conference discussion can be fruitful.[927]

He may not have been able to comprehend that his suggestions—made tongue in cheek—were exactly the kinds of disclosures Weaver wanted to see...at least in opposition to the secrecy in which the court cloaked itself.

The business of the Michigan Supreme Court is NOT dealing with treason, sedition, national defense, or international diplomacy where permanent secrecy is sometimes (maybe even often) necessary. The court's work is basically dealing with people's lives—their property, businesses, families, and freedom. There is no need for forever secrecy.

Weaver took a day to think over Taylor's offer and then responded:

---

927 Clifford W. Taylor, "Memorandum," 23 October 2006, unpublished.

It is not wise to suggest a justice's vote on a pending case can be bargained for another justice's silence. Such deal-making would not further "the good of the institution," as suggested by Chief Justice Taylor's Oct. 23, 2006, memo. Such deal-making would be unethical and interfere with the fair and orderly decision-making of this court. Further, an efficient and impartial judiciary is "ill served by casting a cloak of secrecy around the operations of the courts."[928]

Chief Justice Taylor's memo [...] expresses concern regarding references in my dissent of "memo traffic" and "conference discussion." He suggests that such references violate our "ancient deliberative privilege rule." There is no rule, ancient or modern, that prohibits a public official from speaking out regarding matters of legitimate public concern. Moreover, the memo and conference discussion referenced in my dissent pertain to an administrative file, ADM 2003-26, not a pending or impending case.

Chief Justice Taylor also expresses concern regarding some references to "commissioner submissions to the court," but he does not identify what he thinks they are. The fact is, to my knowledge, there are none in my dissent.

As to the potential "new world" of openness and "freedom of information regime" that Chief Justice Taylor fears that my dissent may usher into this court, I must state that this court should not be a secret society. Openness and freedom of information should not be feared, but welcomed, because it is necessary for good government so that the people can be informed and thereby enabled to hold public officials accountable for their conduct of the people's business.

I note further that my dissent simply sets forth the truth regarding some of what has occurred in an administrative file, truth that I believe is relevant to the fair and impartial disposition of this case.

Moreover, it is incorrect to suggest that the limited reference in my dissent to internal communications regarding a Supreme Court administrative file compels opening the Court of Appeals' deliberations to public scrutiny. Unlike the Supreme Court, the Court of Appeals does not have administrative power and cannot promulgate court rules. The only deliberative process at the Court of Appeals involves pending or impending cases, and deliberations during that process, like deliberations on pending or impending cases here at the Supreme Court, cannot be revealed under the Code of Judicial Conduct, Canon 3(A)(6).[929]

---

928 Weaver noted the reference to her quotation, one that would show up with regularity: *Scott v Flowers*, 910 F2d 201, 213 (5th Cir 1990).
929 Elizabeth A. Weaver, "Memorandum," 25 October 2006, unpublished.

So there you have it. Justice Corrigan offered that if I would withdraw my dissent in Grievance Administrator v Fieger, that she would put the rules out. And then Justice Taylor said he would even change his vote on the stay if I would drop my dissent in Fieger's request for the stay and would promise never to write such a thing again. These were deals, and I wouldn't make the deals. The majority of four simply were not liking that I wouldn't be bullied. I was going to stand up, even alone. But what else can you do? Why was I there? My duty was to the public.

And disqualification would remain off the table until 2009.

Gag Her with an Order

Still stinging from Weaver's revelations, on Nov. 13, 2006, the Engler Four adopted an internal operating policy (IOP) to keep any discussions of the court from the public eye. Cavanagh and Kelly abstained, but Weaver voted against it. This is the language of that IOP:

> All memoranda and conference discussions regarding cases or controversies on the CR and opinion agendas are confidential. This obligation to honor confidentiality does not expire when a case is decided. The only exception to this obligation is that a justice may disclose any unethical or criminal conduct to the Judicial Tenure Commission or proper law enforcement authority.[930]

On Nov. 29, just after Weaver communicated to the Engler Four that their IOP had no authority, they proposed an administrative order, what she called the "gag order"— not just an IOP—to keep her from talking about anything occurring in the court. In conference, it was moved, seconded, and tabled.

On Dec. 5, Weaver filed with the court clerk her dissent in Fieger's request for a stay.

December 6: Without prior announcement that the matter would be taken up that day in conference, or any reason stated for its implementation, the majority voted on and adopted the gag order and voted to withhold Weaver's dissent from publication. The gag order was very close to the IOP, but slightly expanded:

> The following administrative order, supplemental to the provisions of Administrative Order No. 1997-10, is effective immediately.

> All correspondence, memoranda and discussions regarding cases or controversies are confidential. This obligation to honor confidentiality does not expire when a case is decided. The only exception to this obligation is that a justice may disclose any unethical, improper or criminal conduct to the JTC or proper authority.

---

930 Administrative Order No. 2006-8: Deliberative Privilege and Case Discussions in the Supreme Court, 6 December 2006, http://www.icle.org/contentfiles/milawnews/Rules/Ao/AO-2006-8.pdf.

Cavanagh, Weaver and Kelly, JJ., dissent.
Dissenting statements by Weaver and Kelly, JJ., to follow.[931]

In her dissent, Weaver characterized the order as a poorly disguised effort at a cover-up, and she let the majority know that their emergency order had limited—if any—effect:

> The majority's adoption of AO 2006-08 during an unrelated court conference, without public notice or opportunity for public comment, illustrates the majority of four's increasing advancement of a policy of greater secrecy and less accountability—a policy that wrongly casts "a cloak of secrecy around the operations" of the Michigan Supreme Court.

> Simply put, AO 2006-08 is a "gag order," poorly disguised and characterized by the majority of four as a judicial deliberative privilege. The fact is, no Michigan case establishes a "judicial deliberative privilege," nor does any Michigan statute, court rule, or the Michigan Constitution.

> AO 2006-08—the "gag order"—has been hastily created and adopted by the majority of four, without proper notice to the public, and without opportunity for public comment, despite such requirements directed by Administrative Order 1997-11.

> Administrative Order 1997-11(B)(2) states:

>> Unless immediate action is required, the adoption or amendment of rules or administrative orders that will significantly affect the administration of justice will be preceded by an administrative public hearing under subsection (1). If no public hearing has been held before a rule is adopted or amended, the matter will be placed on the agenda of the next public hearing, at which time the Supreme Court will hear public comment on whether the rule should be retained or amended.

> The adoption of AO 2006-08 was not preceded by an administrative public hearing. Further, AO 2006-08 was not shown on the notice of public administrative hearing scheduled for January 17, 2007, agenda that was circulated and published on December 14, 2006. After learning that AO 2006-08 was not placed on the next public administrative hearing agenda as required by AO 1997-11, I informed by memo of the same date (December 14) the justices and relevant staff, that AO 1997-11(B)(2) requires that AO 2006-08 be included in the notice for the next public administrative hearing on January 17, 2007. That AO 2006-08 significantly affects the administration of justice is obvious given that the majority of four relied on it to order on December 6, 2006, the suppression of my dissent in *Grievance Administrator v Fieger*,

---

931 Ibid. Her dissenting statement would arrive on Dec. 19, and would chronicle all that transpired since the majority passed the gag order.

#127547, motion to stay. As of today, December 19, 2006, AO 2006-08 has not been placed on the January 17, 2007, public hearing notice and agenda.

The majority has not publicly articulated any reason why AO 2006-08 should be adopted, nor any reason why immediate action without prior notice to the public or a public hearing was necessary. Article 6, Section 6 of the Michigan Constitution requires in writing reasons for decisions of the court. However, AO 2006-08 can be employed by any majority to impermissibly and unconstitutionally restrict the content of a justice's dissent or concurrence. Thus any present or future majority can in essence censor and suppress a dissenting or concurring justice's opinions.

The public has a vested, constitutional interest in knowing the reasons for a dissenting or concurring justice's divergence from a majority opinion. The majority of four's efforts to censor and suppress the opinions of other justices significantly affect the administration of justice and violate the Michigan Constitution Art 6, Section 6. The "gag order," AO 2006-08, is unconstitutional and unenforceable. As employed by the majority in *Grievance Administrator v Fieger*, #127547, the current majority is using AO 2006-08 to censor and suppress my dissent. I cannot and will not allow it to interfere with the performance of my duties as prescribed by the Michigan Constitution and with the exercise of my rights of free expression as guaranteed by both the Michigan Constitution and the United States Constitution.

The majority of four has adopted this "gag order" (AO 2006-08) in order to suppress my dissent in *Grievance Administrator v Fieger*, motion for stay, No. 127547. Finding no "gag rule" in the Michigan Constitution, statutes, case law, court rules and canons of judicial ethics, the majority of four has decided instead to legislate its own "gag order." The majority of four's "gag order" evidences an intent to silence me now, and to silence any future justice who believes it is his duty to inform the public of serious mishandling of the people's business.[932]

December 15: Taylor submitted his concurrence to the majority opinion in the stay request and noted that he was ordering the clerk to withhold Weaver's dissent from publication:

Please include following statement with the order denying the motion for stay:

In her dissent, Justice Weaver seeks to publish details of the justices' deliberations, including justices' conversations during the court conferences. Never before in this court's long history has a justice attempted to violate

---

932 Ibid.

the court's deliberative process.[933] Until now, there has been an unvarying consensus on this court, as well as all other appellate courts in the United Sates of which I am aware, that appellate court deliberations concerning cases and controversies must be confidential. The assurance of confidences being honored inspires frank and robust discussion among justices so as to reach consensus and result in more thoughtful opinions and orders. No appellate court of law can, or ever has, operated without such rules and it is strongly in the public's interest that the current deliberative process continue in Michigan as it does elsewhere.

Accordingly, with the concurrence of a majority of the court, I have directed the clerk not to include Justice Weaver's dissenting statement in the court's publications in this file. Portions of her dissent breached deliberative confidence and thus violated the court's orders (AO 1997-10 and AO 2006-8). She has refused to remove these portions voluntarily; thus no other means of vindicating these orders exists, other than to disallow their publication in our proceedings. The resolution of this institutional crisis, which Justice Weaver has precipitated, is within her control. If she removes references in her dissenting statement to the court's private deliberations, her dissent will be promptly published.

My first duty as chief justice is to preserve this court as a conscientiously deliberative body. Actions that would undermine our ability to deliberate in this fashion make it difficult to carry out our responsibilities under the constitution of our state. Justice Weaver apparently now believes that the traditional understanding of the appellate judicial process can be violated whenever she wishes. This would be the end of open discussion. She cannot be allowed to undermine the process that is necessary to the proper and efficient functioning of this court.[934]

So they weren't going to publish my dissent at all. They'd just hold it out, and I was supposed to… what? And the "institutional crisis" of which he speaks is of their own making. But to Taylor, it's, of course, my fault.

What was amazing was the Engler Four's fear of people knowing the way they were conducting business. I guess they should have been frightened, because it was so disorderly, so unfair.

December 20: Unannounced—to Weaver at least—at the weekly conference, Taylor took up the *Fieger* stay. He told Weaver the order was going out the next day.

Eventually, the Engler Four decided that they changed their minds, and Taylor is now going to publish my dissent, and they're going to get the case out the door. I guess they probably talked with either Lucille Taylor or John Engler, both far more adept at public relations than the Four. I'm thinking they probably were told that if they withheld my dissent, the public repercussions would be

---

933 That certainly was not so. Much was subsequently made by the Engler Four of Justice Eugene F. Black (1955-1972) and his independent actions.
934 Clifford W. Taylor, "Memorandum," 15 December 2006, unpublished.

far worse than if they included it. That would have been huge news. The danger of this is so apparent, and yet it was done over Christmas and New Year's. And in my opinion the press liked the conflict but was not serious about following the issues.

December 21: The order went out WITH all of Weaver's dissent, including all the proposals for DQ reform.

I wrote in this case the reasons for my dissent in Grievance v Fieger, and I attached all the work that we had done on DQ—the three proposals[935]—so that at least the public would know. It was 68 pages. I knew they didn't like it.

That may be an understatement. Here's Taylor writing in a separate concurrence to the majority, and he talks about the order:

> I concur in the order denying the stay. I write separately to state that I and my colleagues joining in this order cannot respond to Justice Weaver's selective and misleading disclosures of our conference deliberations and internal memorandums because we view her disclosure as a violation of Administrative Order No. 2006-8, and a breach of this court's deliberative process. We have struggled with this matter for months and, by order dated December 20, 2006, seek public comment on how the integrity of this court's deliberative process can be maintained in the light of a justice who feels no obligation to respect the confidentiality that has always characterized the deliberations of this court, the United States Supreme Court and every other appellate court of the United States. It must be noted that, despite the fact that a justice of this court has now engaged, and continues to engage, in the unprecedented act of revealing deliberative confidences, every word of every statement of hers has been made public exactly as she has written it.
>
> I repeat again the questions that the court has posed to the public for consideration at our public hearing on January 17, 2007: Should AO 2006-8, which formally establishes the deliberative privilege rule, be retained and, if it is retained, what means of enforcement or sanction, if any, are properly adopted in response if a justice violates it?[936]

Well, at least the Engler Four got the message that the public hearing would have to be held. But for the rest....

Apparently, they couldn't deliberate if they couldn't bully. This was just so preposterous, that they couldn't do the public's business publicly. ...And they didn't even have to do it publicly. They just had

---

935 Elizabeth A. Weaver, writing in dissent, Appendix A, "The abandoned proposals for new court rules governing justice disqualification," Order, *Grievance Administrator v Geoffrey N. Fieger*, No. 127547," Michigan Supreme Court, 21 December 2006, 41, http://publicdocs.courts.mi.gov:81/SCT/PUBLIC/ORDERS/20061221_S127547_28_127547.122106ORDER.PDF.

936 Clifford W. Taylor writing in concurrence, "Order, *Grievance Administrator v Geoffry N. Fieger*, No. 127547," Michigan Supreme Court, 21 December 2006, 3, http://publicdocs.courts.mi.gov:81/SCT/PUBLIC/ORDERS/20061221_S127547_28_127547.122106ORDER.PDF.

to be willing to be accountable for what they said in trying to persuade people to change, or bullying them into changing their minds. And they didn't want to be accountable for that, and they didn't want people to know that that's how they got a result. This was a great deal of pressure. But it was all so absurd, so disorderly, so unfair, that it wasn't hard to see through it for what it was. And I was just determined, right from the time as a child that I had the experience of my brothers' State of Tulane, that I was just going to do what I felt was right, and I'd see what happened.

Cavanagh also dissented (and Kelly joined him) and in their dissent, Cavanagh strongly objected to the closing of the DQ file. After the repeated promises to him by the Engler Four, the file closure was a matter of betrayal. The Engler Four had betrayed him. But more important, Cavanagh wrote, they breached their word with the people of Michigan:

> Because I believe that our current disqualification process does not afford parties adequate constitutional protections, I also write to express my extreme disapproval of the majority's decision to abandon this court's earlier determination that proposals for the disqualification of justices would be published for public comment. The closure of this administrative file without public comment is expressly contrary to the majority's earlier explicit guarantee that these proposals would indeed be published for public review and comment.
>
> [...]
>
> I am disturbed by attempts by the majority to keep the public from commenting on this issue. If my colleagues truly believe that our current practice is the best for Michigan's citizens, then they should have no problem explaining their rationale to the public and hearing the public's assessment of this rationale. However, I believe they know that there is no reasonable justification that can be proffered for allowing a justice accused of bias to be the only one who decides whether he should be disqualified. I can think of no reasonable explanation that would be acceptable to the public for maintaining this procedure because it is apparent that it is incongruous with reason. This is especially true in light of the fact that Michigan's own court rules—adopted by this court—govern disqualifications for all other judges and explicitly provide the recourse of having the denial of a disqualification motion reviewed by another judge. See MCR 2.003(C)(3). Remarkably, the majority believes that members of this court are above the same rules that it has adopted to apply to all other judges in the state.
>
> For our system of justice to continue to have any validity, our citizens must have faith in judges. My colleagues' unabashed embrace of a procedure that does not afford due process and fundamental fairness to all parties who appear before the court does nothing to instill confidence in an impartial judiciary. While the majority's willingness to breach its word does not bode well for the possibility that our disqualification procedure will be examined

at any point in the near future, I strongly urge my colleagues to reconsider and remember that a fair and balanced procedure, made known to the public, would benefit our citizens now and in the future. It would apply to all justices, no matter the composition of the court. This is not a partisan issue, but a matter of ensuring fundamental fairness and due process to all those who seek justice before this court now and long after my colleagues and I are gone.[937]

Cavanagh finished with a defense of Weaver's right to her dissent and its publication... her right to write:

> Finally, I disagree with Chief Justice Taylor's contention that Justice Weaver's statement violates deliberative privilege. I have reviewed every aspect of the dissenting statement and have extensively researched the applicable areas of the law, including deliberative privilege. While the statement is obviously discomforting for the majority, I believe that the statement does not run afoul of any law. The statement merely references past actions taken and voted on by members of this court on administrative matters. I further note that the statement does not contravene recent Administrative Order No. 2006-8, which the majority voted in favor of. The administrative order allows for the disclosure of any unethical, improper, or criminal conduct. While I do not believe that the administrative order is relevant to this case because no substantive information on a past or pending case is being disclosed, any arguably substantive information in the statement could reasonably be said to fall within the administrative order's parameters. Thus, I believe that Justice Weaver has done nothing improper by releasing her statement.[938]

The order went out and the public (and televised) hearing for the "gag order" was scheduled for January 17.

In between was another vote for chief justice. Taylor put himself up for another two-year term. Weaver could not in good conscience vote for him. The result was yet another groundbreaking published dissent.

> It is necessary that I dissent from the election of Chief Justice Clifford Taylor as chief justice of the Michigan Supreme Court. Chief Justice Taylor has proven that he cannot properly lead the Michigan Supreme Court at this time. The people of Michigan deserve to have a chief justice who will conduct the people's business in an orderly, professional, and fair manner.

---

937 Michael Cavanagh writing in dissent, "Order, *Grievance Administrator v Geoffrey N. Fieger*, No. 127547," Michigan Supreme Court, 21 December 2006, 3-5, http://publicdocs.courts.mi.gov:81/SCT/PUBLIC/ORDERS/20061221_S127547_28_127547.122106ORDER.PDF.
938 Ibid. Interestingly, while Cavanaugh would vote against the gag order in 2006, he would subsequently vote for it in 2010. But at that point he was voting against Weaver.

Let it be clear, my dissent is not motivated by ill will or resentment—I have none for any of my colleagues. Nor do I have any desire to serve again as chief justice myself. I strive to base in fact and truth my opinions—dissents and concurrences—and to state only what I believe is necessary that the public know. Facts and truth, and dissents and concurrences based on them, are not always pleasant information.

I dissent because the majority of four of this court has misused and abused the judicial power by suppressing, or attempting to suppress, dissent and has engaged in repeated disorderly, unprofessional and unfair conduct in the performance of the judicial business of the court.

Not one member of the majority of four has demonstrated an ability to lead this court at this time. Thus, it is in the best interest of the State of Michigan and the Michigan Supreme Court for either Justice Michael Cavanagh or Justice Marilyn Kelly to serve as this court's chief justice.[939]

And she again included chapter and verse of the excesses and deceptions of the majority.

That got some attention. Some few in the press were supportive, in news stories, editorials, and op-ed pieces. But there was a lot of head-in-the-sand commentary, too, especially at the bigger papers.

Ron Dzwonkowsi, then editor of the *Free Press* editorial page, tried on the blame both ways:

If Weaver is given a forum to air her charges against the court's philosophical majority, the judicial ethics of those four justices become suspect. If Weaver is discredited, somebody may have to figure out how to get her off the court before her term ends in four years, for she could not be this wrongheaded about something and still capable of deciding complex legal issues in the requisite collegiality with the other justices, could she?

[...]

What cannot happen, seems to me, is nothing. Weaver has laid out some serious issues. If these charges where made about any other court in the state, there would be at least an investigation. Either some justices of the Supreme Court have problems or Weaver does. Either way, something doesn't smell right.[940]

Dawson Bell fell in line with the Engler Four.

---

939 Elizabeth A. Weaver, "Memorandum," 5 January 2007, http://www.justiceweaver.com/pdfs/1-5-07_DissenttoCJ.pdf.
940 Ron Dzwonkowski, "Odor in the court: Fumigation can't come too soon after Justice Weaver's charges," *Detroit Free Press*, 7 January 2007, C.3

Michigan Supreme Court Chief Justice Clifford Taylor said Tuesday that he's offended and dismayed by Justice Elizabeth Weaver's extraordinary accusations that he and three other justices are guilty of improper conduct and abuse of power.

But, in a lengthy interview with *Free Press* reporters and editors, Taylor said he's at a loss to figure out what to do about it.

Weaver's complaints, expressed in three dissents to court actions released in the last month, are "sort of strange rantings...of an unhappy human being," Taylor said.

And her decision to air the grievances publicly is both unprecedented and damaging to the court, Taylor said.

If Weaver has evidence of actual impropriety by any member of the judiciary—an accusation Taylor vigorously denied—she should present it to the State Police, FBI or Judicial Tenure Commission, which investigates charges of improper conduct by judges, he said.

[...]

Taylor said Tuesday the allegations, to the extent to which he can understand them, are "totally unfair."

Weaver "is a capable lawyer," Taylor said. "But the current things she is doing are not the work of a lawyer. They're sort of strange rantings that are difficult to stand back and appreciate."

Later Tuesday, Weaver said in a telephone interview she has not taken her complaints to law enforcement authorities because she has not alleged the conduct involved criminal activity. Similarly, she said the Judicial Tenure Commission would be powerless to deal with complaints against members of the Supreme Court because the court renders final judgment on its recommendations.[941]

Columnist Brian Dickerson, also writing for the *Free Press*, followed up, but with a vengeance:

If you ran into Betty Weaver on a street corner and didn't know she was a Michigan Supreme Court justice, you might mistake her for a bag lady.

Dowdy and unbrushed, with a conversational style that might charitably be described as rambling, Weaver can, in her most distracted moments,

---

941 Dawson Bell, "Chief justice fires back at accuser: 'Strange rantings' untrue, improper," *Detroit Free Press*, 10 January 2007, B.1.

leave casual observers with the impression that she has temporarily lost her moorings in time and space.

So it is tempting for her embarrassed colleagues on the state's highest court to dismiss Weaver's latest criticism of that august institution as the ravings of a lunatic.

Chief Justice Cliff Taylor seemed to be experimenting with that approach Tuesday when I asked him straight out if Weaver was psychologically competent.

"I think I probably shouldn't answer that," Taylor responded. "I'm not a person with training in areas of diagnosing what is going on with her, and I probably shouldn't speculate."

[...]

In a telephone conversation late Tuesday afternoon, Weaver chuckled at Taylor's insinuation that she is not all there and repeated her assertion that she has been targeted for "bringing the majority's abuse of power to the public's attention."

"My written work is there for the public to see, and I think it's pretty rational," she said. "There are serious problems in how the court is being run, and I can document them and will at the appropriate time."

But Weaver agreed with Taylor that none of her allegations merit an investigation by the State Police or the FBI.

"This is about the abuse of power," Weaver said. "It's not criminal, in my judgment, and the only people who can correct what's wrong with the court are the voters."[942]

The lead of his story is perhaps the most glaring example of what was happening in the press. "Bag lady," "dowdy," "unbrushed," "rambling," "temporarily lost her moorings," "lunatic"??? What in the world was this columnist—who covered breaking news for the state's most widely circulated newspaper—doing in this report? It was hardly fair or accurate. There's little doubt Justice Weaver likely spent a lot more time and money on her wardrobe and hair than he did; she always dressed with care and in keeping with her very public work on the state's highest court. And she had never lost her moorings no matter how far the Engler Four pushed her.

Like many others reporting Weaver's struggles against the political and ideological takeover of the court, Dickerson very publicly displayed a personal contempt toward

942 Brian Dickerson, "Weaver renews attack on her GOP colleagues," *Detroit Free Press*, 10 January 2007, B.1.

her.[943] And Dickerson was supposed to be one of the best of what he called the "chattering classes."[944]

The reporting ran on. While Taylor said he didn't want to speculate to Dickerson about Weaver's mental state, the chief justice didn't hesitate to explain to *Michigan Lawyers Weekly* what he thought:

> "This is a very angry, sad woman," Taylor said of Weaver. "I think she has said things that are inaccurate and not fair."
>
> [...]
>
> Taylor said he wants to get the situation resolved.
>
> "I think this a very sad chapter," he said. "We've got to draw this to an end."
>
> Other Republican justices have said that Weaver's attitude may spring from personal resentment. She wanted to remain chief justice when Corrigan was picked for the job in 2001.[945]

There it is again. That was about the tenth article in a row that raised the issue of her not being re-elected to the position of chief justice in 2001. No matter how many times she'd said she didn't want the job in the first place, nobody in the media seemed to believe her.

What they accused me of publicly that the press liked was this false story promoted by the Englerites that my motive for my dissents and speaking about the abuse of power at the court was because I had not been elected chief justice for a second time. I never wanted to be chief justice in the first place. I didn't want Mallett to leave. I only was willing to continue to be chief justice for a second time because I thought it was necessary to do it. I put myself into contention for the post for the sake of the institution and for the people of Michigan. The Governor, through his Engler Four, should not be controlling and politicizing the court system. Had I not done it, then the false accusation story would have been the same but in reverse: "Well, she wanted to, but she didn't speak up then, and she hasn't gotten over it." I did have the courage to put my name forward even though I had been advised by some that it wasn't politically wise. In the end, I did do it, and I stood for transparency and what I believed was right. Obviously, it wasn't a happy event. It has cost me repeated false press reports, but it wasn't a mistake, and I have no regrets.

---

943 There is something to the "bag" comment. It was, however, not as he portrayed it. Weaver would come to the court with several bags, often designer bags, filled with case work. She would actually read the cases she'd be ruling on; it wasn't enough for her to routinely rely on her clerks and the commissioners' reports to learn about the matters coming to the court.

944 Brian Dickerson, "Brian Dickerson says change at the top can be the wrong Rx," *Detroit Free Press*, 6 October 2011, http://www.freep.com/article/20111006/COL04/110060469/Brian-Dickerson-says-change-at-the-top-can-be-the-wrong-Rx?odyssey=mod|newswell|text|FRONTPAGE|s.

945 Tim Martin, "Weaver levels more criticism at Republican court colleagues," *Michigan Lawyers Weekly*, 15 January 2007, http://milawyersweekly.com/news/2007/01/15/weaver-levels-more-criticism-at-republican-court-colleagues/.

Of that oft-repeated and illogical attack and all the rest that was a-swirl at the court, there were plenty of others who saw and understood—thanks to Weaver's revelations—what was going on behind the curtain. They could read between the lines of the press reports to take note that something was seriously wrong at the Supreme Court. Some would come to Weaver's defense to the extent that they would stand up—literally—to the majority of four at the public hearing. Eventually even *Free Press* columnist Brian Dickerson would set aside his hyperbole for a serious and more balanced assessment.

Chapter 19

Will They Gag her?
A Call for Investigation,
Minutes? What Minutes?
And Fieger, Part 3

Notes at the Hearing

The day of the scheduled Supreme Court hearing, Jan. 17, 2007, Brian Dickerson's pre-meeting account was perceptive but not sanguine:

> Michigan's courts are the talk of the nation this week—and that's not necessarily a good thing.
>
> [...]
>
> The majority's new approach has dramatically shifted power to lobbyists, who shape laws to the specification of their monied clients, and to prosecutors, who no longer worry that the court will strike down novel theories [....]
>
> Today's hearing in Lansing arises over Justice Elizabeth Weaver's efforts to discredit the Engler majority by describing behind-the-scenes machinations that led to some recent controversial rulings.
>
> The majority says Weaver's publication of the justices' private correspondence and conversations violates a centuries-old tradition of "deliberative privilege" and has asked for public comment on whether and how she can be punished. Weaver and the court's two remaining justices, Marilyn Kelly and Michael Cavanagh, argue that Weaver has a right to bring the majority's actions to the public's attention.
>
> [The controversy underlines] the fact of life that many Michiganders are just beginning to appreciate: more and more, their rights and liberties hang on the druthers of the Engler Majority—four little-known lawyers who thrive on secrecy and see the courts as servants of the legislature, not the voters.[946]

---

946 Brian Dickerson, "Life, liberty and Engler's high court," *Detroit Free Press*, 17 January 2007, B.1.

The hearing, one of four scheduled each year, would run about three hours. The portion that dealt with the "gag order" discussion took up the last half of the entire morning's hearing.

The whole thing was an unnecessary and absurd exercise. I'd recruited no one to come other than my attorney, Jon Muth, and he was there to protect me in case it was necessary. But they never had to do anything.

According to Muth, he was there for "what if":

> And it really dealt mostly with issues of "What if they really do try and are successful in stealing her voice? What then is her remedy?" And we talked about things such as filing a 1983 action in federal court, Federal Civil Rights Act; a deprivation of constitutional right of free speech by a governmental action.[947] And the idea, of course, would be to get that legal controversy out of the Michigan Courts, which is the last place you'd want to have them heard, knowing who was the ultimate arbiter of the result, and getting it into a Federal Court, where you would, at least theoretically, have a fair shake at getting the constitutional issues heard.[948]

Each speaker at the hearing was to be accorded three minutes. In this account, we're covering them in a laundry-list fashion.[949]

Senior Judge Richard F. Suhrheinrich of the Sixth U.S. Circuit Court of Appeals was first; he supported the order, citing the U.S. Supreme Court's traditional secrecy. That secrecy, he said, gave the court "substance, dignity, and caution that befits the nation's highest institution of law. [...] If that tradition is good enough for the Supreme Court it ought to be good enough for this court."[950]

Court of Appeals Judge Peter O'Connell was next, and was somewhat tongue tied when he articulated his support for the order.

Judge Michael Warren of Oakland's Sixth Circuit Court was next, likening the administrative order to resistance at the court early in the history of the Open Meetings Act. He favored openness for the court.

Next was one of the most articulate opponents of the "gag order," Patrick Clawson of Flint. Clawson was a former television reporter, investigative journalist, and private

947 42 U.S.C. § 1983: US Code—Section 1983: Civil action for deprivation of rights, http://codes.lp.findlaw.com/uscode/42/21/I/1983.
948 Jon R. Muth, video interview with co-author Schock, 17 January 2012, Grand Rapids. And, of course, Muth had received permission from Weaver to speak about this.
949 The complete text of the hearing is available at Public Hearing, Michigan Supreme Court, 17 January 2007, http://courts.michigan.gov/Courts/MichiganSupremeCourt/rules/court-rules-admin-matters/Documents/PublicHearingTranscript_2007-01-17.pdf. The portion of the hearing that deals with the "gag order" begins at the bottom of page 25.
950 Ibid., 26. Co-author Schock also viewed the video file of the meeting. The rest of the exchanges in this section are from that file.

detective. He began with a description of a corrupt court that had been behaving exactly as the Michigan Supreme Court, and then he noted that it was in China.

> My experience over 30 years has shown that openness is essential to public trust in the judiciary and public trust in justice. And without it, we have nothing. Rightly or wrongly, fairly or unfairly, the recent incidents at this court have created a public perception that there's a stench of corruption here. I hope that's not the case, but it must be removed; it cannot be covered up. All public officials—and you are elected public officials at the Michigan Supreme Court—all public officials have an obligation to speak to their constituency, to speak to the public, to explain why you're doing what you're doing. We have elected you to uphold the constitution, not to mug it.

He was interrupted by Justice Markman: "Mr. Clawson, are you aware of any appellate court outside of Communist China, say the United States of America, for example, which does not protect the confidentiality of its conferences and its deliberations?"

Clawson: "Your Honor, I recognize there is a valid need to protect confidentiality on discussions about pending cases. I have no argument on that at all. The proposed order of the court, however, creates that in perpetuity. I don't happen to think that's good for the American system of justice, and I don't happen to think it's good for the American people."

Markman: "What do you mean it creates it in perpetuity? I don't understand that."

Clawson: "The administrative order that's been issued by this court makes a flat, blanket ban, period, on the release of documents, memoranda, conversations."

Markman: "Mr. Clawson, let me ask you the same question. Are you aware of any appellate court in the United States of America today, yesterday, 1789, that has not protected the confidentiality of its conferences and deliberations?"

Clawson: "The courts have historically protected the confidentiality of their deliberations. However, it's not necessarily on a perpetual basis. I believe that the order issued by this court—while well intentioned—is overbroad. It will just further, further enhance a bad public perception that is developing in this state about the integrity of the court. And that should be an issue of concern to all of you. We must restore public confidence in the integrity of this court."

Justice Cavanagh jumped in: "You're talking about in perpetuity references the proposed rule's prohibition against disclosing anything even after an opinion is in the books and released...is that right?"

Clawson: "Well, the way I read the order, it's a blanket order and it goes in perpetuity. And, frankly, I think it would probably be a big hindrance to you justices writing your memoirs at some point in time, explaining to the public how you reached your decisions about some things. And I think I, as a taxpayer, as the person who pays your salary, I have a right to know how you reached certain decisions. And for purposes of justice and the administration of a case you may want to keep some of that information confidential for a specific period of time, so there is not a public perception of bias or the impropriety of judging in cases, but that's not something that should be locked up in the dustbins of history forever, or away from public sight."

Rita Jacobs suggested that the justices not shoot the messenger and that the court needed more media access. "Suppressing minority opinions only enhances public distrust." The order was, she said, an example of judicial activism. She cited Taylor's threat to withhold Weaver's dissent as an example of "attempted constructive removal of Justice Weaver, and you do not and should not have that power."

Dan Diebolt noted that there were at least a hundred people in the courtroom. He wanted to know if the justices were going to be voting during the public hearing. The answer was NO. Diebolt cited MCL 600.224 that any voting by the justices on the proposed policy (and any other) needed to be made in public.[951]

William C. Whitbeck, Chief Judge of the Michigan Court of Appeals was next, emphasizing that the communications at the Court of Appeals were confidential in nature. He likened the administrative order to the situation at the U.S. Supreme Court when Chief Justice Earl Warren brokered the "unanimous" *Brown v Board* decision. What might have happened, he asked, if Warren had labored under the threat of each of his words being revealed. It would not have worked, Whitbeck said.

Judge Joseph P. Swallow (retired from the 26th Circuit, Alpena) came, he said, to sympathize with Justice Weaver.

> Her claims of abusive treatment and this rule as a "gag order"...I want to say that as a retired trial judge, I can attest that many of the tactics she now complains of were in the past perpetrated against myself and other judges.
>
> The example I'd like to cite today is my dissent to the process by which Michigan trial courts were consolidated. To refresh the court's memory, the Supreme Court rather authored that consolidation plan, nursed it over many numbers of years by many and various trial court projects, publicized it with extensive public relations, and lobbied it through the legislature. By any objective standard this was the Supreme Court's baby.

---

951 Sec. 600.224 (1) of Michigan Compiled Statutes reads:

> The Supreme Court shall adopt procedures to ensure that, when a majority of the justices of the Supreme Court or of the judges of a multi-judge court meet to discuss or decide upon court rules or administrative orders, the meeting shall be open to the public.

[http://www.legislature.mi.gov/(S(qds4te3npuuid0mf2tlkbhfb))/mileg.aspx?page=getobject&objectname=mcl-600-224.]

Yet, despite its parentage, court consolidation was of such doubtful consti-tutionality, that the very legislature that passed the bill requested that this court render an advisory opinion. To which you replied, "Sorry, not now; maybe some time in the future."

It was during the early part of 2002—a legislative session—when the bill was pushed through the legislature with much political haste. But even the arm-twisting of then-Governor John Engler could not garner the necessary two-thirds vote for immediate effect. So, pursuant to the Constitution, the legal force of the bill—the bill becoming law—could not occur until 90 days after the adjournment[952] [sine die] in the legislature, in this case April 1st, 2003. Despite the doubtful constitutionality and in the absence of lawful authority, it did not deter the Supreme Court from directing the trial judges in this state to begin the process of consolidating trial courts forthwith.

When in July 2002, nearly nine months before the effective date of the bill, your minions arrived at the 26th Circuit, advised me, and started directing consolidation. And I questioned the lawful authority by which they were there, and I questioned the constitutionality.

Then Justice Corrigan, as you may remember, you hand-delivered a letter to me advising me that I'd better get with the program, or I would be removed as chief judge.

I advised you then by return letter that, "Hey, mechanically, we're doing this," but I held out the option of continuing to speak out about the un-constitutionality of the bill as well as the fact that there was no real, lawful authority to do what was happening.

Apparently, the intimidation of your letter not working, then-court admin-istrator John Ferry was directed to draft a letter and send it to the *Alpena News* claiming Judge Swallow is an obstructionist. And I'm sure, as calcu-lated, that resulted in a headline on the editorial page: "Swallow is an ob-structionist."

Now, any objective appraisal of your conduct....[953]

And then Chief Justice Taylor told him that his time had run.

Swallow said that he offered his full comments with all supporting documents for inclusion into the record. And then he noted: "Any society that suppresses its judges when things are seriously wrong is not going to be a free society very long."

---

952 The court transcript lists this word as "term" and Judge Swallow does not clearly articulate the word, but co-author Schock believes he said "adjournment." What he says sounds like "germ," and that would be more consistent with "adjourn."
953 Public Hearing, Michigan Supreme Court, 17 January 2007.

There was applause to his parting shot.

The response from Chief Justice Taylor: "We will have no more of that. It's unnecessary." Next came then-Court of Appeals Judge Bill Schuette, who warned that the integrity of the system was at stake. It might otherwise "disintegrate into chaos."

> The deliberations of Michigan judges, Michigan justices, their musings, their observations, their questions, their concerns, their frailties, their arguments, must be kept confidential or otherwise this whole system blows up in smithereens.
>
> [..]
>
> No one, no one is above the law. Whether that's a governor, a judge, a justice, president ... wherever you may be situated. And if we as a judge or a justice are aware of a misdeed or a violation of the law, we ought to report it to the FBI, the Michigan State Police, but you don't call the newspapers. Don't drag this judicial system through the mud. I would support and urge you that you adopt this rule of confidentiality, which is essential to the Michigan and the United States system of justice.

Attorney Devon Schindler lined up for dignity and honor in his support of the rule.

Tom Whitaker had spoken in another portion of the hearing and also came forward in this part, too. He rambled, but in the main, he said he thought the public needed to know. "But it's pretty complex."

Kurt Hansen (retired from the 55th Circuit Court, Gladwin) noted that there was a clear distinction between the U.S. and Michigan Supreme Courts; foremost the Michigan court is elected. "People have a right to know what you're doing and why you're doing it and how you're doing it." Hansen noted that during the decision-making process on a case, the deliberative process should be shielded. But once the decision was made, he said, all should be fair game.

> Once the decision is made, I believe that we are in a situation where any justice has the right and sometimes the obligation to explain what the decision was and explain all factors involved, including any of the communications that were done during the course of the deliberations.

And, said Hansen, when it came to administrative matters, the court should follow the legislature and its adherence to the Open Meetings Act.

> I can see no reason whatsoever why all the communications concerning administrative matters are not open to the public, and I believe you should separate those matters which are administrative, and you should have open meetings concerning those particular situations. When you're acting as ad-

ministrators, you aren't acting much different than a legislature would be acting. I see no reason for confidentiality whatsoever when you're dealing with administrative matters.

Court of Appeals Judge Christopher Murray joined the other Court of Appeals judges urging the adoption of the "gag order." Murray said as a judge and without secrecy— "the utmost confidentiality"—there could "never be a full, open and frank discussion of the issues involved" in cases.

Lansing Attorney Richard McLellan[954] also opted for secrecy: "What should count are your written decisions, concurrences, and dissents, and not the back and forth that we hope takes place as you come to a decision." Further, he said, the public needed clear rules about electronic communications. The circulation of e-mails and other records posed a grave danger: "We don't need partial records and e-mails that would really confuse the public."

Justice Cavanagh asked if McLellan saw a difference between administrative matters and substantive matters. Yes, McLellan said he did, and administrative matters should be far more open, he said, but he argued against complete transparency.

Gilbert Engels, from Grosse Pointe Farms, was concerned with public perception and he wanted things open.

> Confidence is going into negative numbers. This society is committing societal suicide. You people stand there and know what's right and what's wrong. Why is every public record of the citizens open to the public? But our public servants are secret. I don't have anything other to say than I am disgusted with much I've heard here today.

Attorney Scott Strattard stood "in strong support of" the administrative order. "A lack of confidentiality will stifle the frank exchange of ideas and mask the differences of opinions that should be exchanged and dealt with during deliberations."

In contrast, Traverse City attorney Cheryl Gore Follette noted:

> You are elected citizens in the State of Michigan. And as elected citizens, you should answer to those who elected you. The administrative issues this court has to deal with should be transparent. I'm not talking about the decisions; I'm talking about administrative issues. The administration of justice should be open. Let us talk about a malady known as Black Robe Disease.

954 McLellan had served as head of Governor Engler's 1990 transition team. He has a list of political accomplishments, including serving 20 years as a member or the chair of the Michigan Law Revision Commission. [McLellan Law Offices, Richard McLellan, Government service, http://richardmclellan.com/rdm/government_service%20.] Governor Rick Snyder appointed him July 16, 2012, to head the effort to redraft the school aid finance act. [Dave Murray, "Gov. Rick Snyder assembles panel to plan for sweeping changes to school funding," M-Live, 16 July 2012, http://www.mlive.com/education/index.ssf/2012/07/gov_rick_snyder_assembles_pane.html.]

It's an idea that when the robe goes on, the power becomes absolute. Michigan doesn't need a Star Chamber.[955]

Justice Markman wondered whether Follette would be satisfied if the proposed administrative order dealt solely with administrative matters.

She would be, she said. After a question from Justice Corrigan, Follette continued:

> My additional comments are with regard to Justice Elizabeth Weaver, whom I have known for almost 20 years. I would tell you that she has never been sad, and rarely angry. As a mentor and model to countless women, she has inspired many. She has always evidenced the highest ethical standards. The comments made about her by the Chief [Justice] are interesting. He apologized after they became public, but it seems more like a child who's sorry he was found out, as opposed to truly sorry for what he had said. The comments were mean-spirited and malicious and one can only wonder at the level of invective behind closed doors if these were stated publicly. Personally, as a citizen, I want to know what goes on behind those closed doors.
>
> [...]
>
> If you say what you mean and you mean what you say, you should stand behind it. Why should you be afraid? If you've changed your mind in the course of deliberations because someone has persuaded you otherwise, I want to know that. I want to know who you are and what you stand for. And when I vote for you, I want to know what I'm getting. And, so, I would like it all to be open, but at a minimum, the administration of justice; there's no basis for administrative rules not being open.

Michael E. Cavanaugh,[956] a Lansing attorney, favored the proposed rule, using many of the reasons of prior speakers. He could think of no court in the U.S. where confidentiality wasn't practiced. It was the dignity of the institution, though, that he saw most at stake.

Attorney and Thomas M. Cooley Law School professor Elliot B. Glicksman appeared as "a contrarian" to speak against the order. He was concerned that the order was universal.

> It states: "All correspondence and memoranda, and discussion regarding cases or controversies are confidential." [...] When we use the word "all correspondence" it obviously deals with—and perhaps is in conflict with—the Constitution of the State of Michigan, 1963, Article 6, Section 6, which requires that "justices shall write their decisions to explain in concise state-

---

955 The Star Chamber was a supplemental court that sat in England until 1641 ostensibly to make sure powerful people could be held accountable for their actions.
956 Weaver noted that he was one of Taylor's favorites.

ments of facts their reason for the decisions." Now, this is extremely important for the litigants who await their decisions if, in fact, [justices] cannot explain their decisions because they are controlled effectively by an administrative order which in essence precludes them from disclosing what [...] decisions are made.

Young and Corrigan took him on, and the seemingly frail Glicksman rose to the occasion with vigor:

If, in fact, we are talking about the great purpose of privilege—which I DO understand after teaching in this area, studying in this area, writing in this area—why it was, if it was so important—which in theory I understand, why was this not uniformly signed onto? Why do we have dissenting points of view? And this is something I took into consideration standing before you and making a dissenting argument.

The next speaker, Barbara Willing, argued that confidentially was important but found issue with the way the order came down. There was no reasonable notice "and any time you make decision under hysteria, you always make bad decisions."

Eric Odmark[957] welcomed openness as a counter force to public distrust.

I don't believe that any of the deliberations any of you have to talk about should be private regarding a court case. [...] I am really opposed to this gag rule, especially with the circumstances that led us here today. And I guess if you decide to pass it, from the standpoint as a private citizen, not an attorney, it will smell like a dead skunk in the middle of the road.

Finally, attorney Eugene Driker, a senior statesman who had practiced before the Supreme Court for 42 years, said he was most concerned that the public perception was that of a "court in turmoil." Further, the court was discourteous. Deliberative privilege is good, Driker said, but he noted that it had been violated at all levels without imposed disciplines. A rule to provide punishment "was not wise; it's not needed."

Justices Young and Markman queried what should be done with a justice who asserted that she had a right and a duty to reveal the inner workings of the court. Driker related that in 1874 Chief Justice Cooley said:

"All wrongs are not redressed by the judicial department." He didn't explicitly say that you leave it up to electorate to decide, but that's the implicit message of this opinion. [...] If there are justices who are subverting the system, it seems to me that the sanction is for good or bad the fact that we have an elected judiciary in this state and that the public will ultimately make the decision.

---

957 Weaver called him a friend.

What would they do in the meantime, asked Young?

Driker suggested even bringing in some outside people to facilitate conversation.

Young: "Do you think therapeutic intervention? So, let me just ask: Does the therapist get to participate in our cases?"

Driker: "I don't think that's the question. But I think there are some issues before the court—this one...the disqualification issue—where the court could benefit by having somebody outside of this system come in...a respected retired jurist, perhaps from another state, somebody out of this framework to come in and assist the court, because the public is quite skeptical about what is going on and is concerned...as is the bar. And this is subverting the institutional reputation of this court. And that's not what should happen."

With that it was over.

Weaver said not a word during the hearing. But she was listening and analyzing. It seemed that those with political ties and aspirations urged the adoption of the rule. And beginning commentary with Judge Suhrheinrich seemed an indication of what the Engler Four wanted to have happen. He was a heavy hitter, much revered by the majority.

I listened earnestly to every speaker. Of course there were the people who it appeared the majority lined up to make their comments. It was disappointing to hear a few appellate judges say that they couldn't possibly do their work without forever secrecy...how ridiculous.

But other speakers in the hearing left her encouraged.

There were all those people, few of whom I knew, who said what a bad idea the "gag order" was. Non-lawyer citizens as well as lawyers, judges, professors, and a journalist showed up to speak. They were standing up, and it was encouraging. There were people who got it, and they came and spoke.

Pat Clawson in particular brought a solid argument, and he was in no way intimidated by the court.

I thought what he had to say was wonderful.

When it came to Cheryl Follette, Weaver was particularly gratified. Yes, they'd known each other for 20 years...

...and Cheryl was my former law clerk. It was so good of her to come and speak. I didn't know she was going to do that.

Weaver was especially heartened by Judges Hansen and Swallow. Although she worked to bring the unified trial court to the state and they disagreed with her, their disagreement was civil.

And although they had disagreed with my position on unified trial courts, I thought it was remarkable for them to show up and speak against the tyranny of the gag order.

And, perhaps most important, Judge Swallow gave a clear voice in public to the machinations of the leadership of the court.

Here you have a judge standing up and saying it happened to him and others. Which others? How many? She was hand-delivering letters? She didn't deny it in the hearing. And this happened even before Corrigan paid her visit to Judge Kirkendall.

For Weaver's attorney, Jon Muth, things came to much of nothing:

> Now, what happened, of course, was that the majority of the Supreme Court backed off, and that challenge to their actions in the federal court was never filed.[958]

Muth was referring to filing a 1983 action in federal court alleging deprivation of constitutional right of free speech by a governmental action.

> That was a remedy that was available to her. I think that the majority on the court at the time knew that was a remedy that was available to her, and that they decided that that was not the way their interests led them to proceed.[959]

Weaver's assessment of the entire event also was that it was "a flop" for the majority. And before leaving the courtroom, she met members of the press for an informal conference.

Then came the reportage and analysis of the hearing.

Peter Luke, writing for the Booth chain of newspapers under mlive.com observed that the hearing didn't settle much.

> A new Michigan Supreme Court rule barring justices from revealing internal communication was designed to address conflict on the high court. But so far it's just revealing more of it.

> Testimony during Wednesday's public hearing on the rule, approved 4-3 on Dec. 6 was as divided as the court. Backers, among them other appellate judges, said the rule was necessary to preserve the court's integrity. Critics called it over broad and unnecessary.

> Left unresolved was how the rule should be applied and what the response should be to a justice who violates it.[960]

---

958 Jon R. Muth.
959 Ibid.
960 Peter Luke, "Battle on state's highest court continues," mlive.com, 18 January 2007, http://www.mlive.com/news/statewide/index.ssf?/base/news-8/1169082602102860.xml&coll-1.

Todd C. Berg, writing in *Michigan Lawyers Weekly* asked jurists their opinions of the matter. Retired Chief Justice Thomas E. Brennan analyzed the controversy and came down for the freedom to speak and write and against the "gag order":

> [T]he former justice observed that, as much as confidentiality may facilitate candor in the short run, it should not be used as a justification for keeping "deliberations" secret indefinitely.

> "As one of the founders and an emeritus board member of the Michigan Supreme Court Historical Society, I have long believed that the internal papers of the justices ought to be preserved and made available for scholars and historians, so I would not be in favor of a permanent gag rule," Brennan stated. "Besides, I think that there is a certain restraining influence if a justice knows that what he or she writes to colleagues may someday be available in the law library."[961]

In the Berg article that featured Brennan, the analysis moved to possible penalties for justices who would violate a "gag order" like ADM 2006-08:

> What can happen to a justice who violates the confidentiality requirement of AO 2006-8's "deliberative privilege" rule?

> According to Judge Avern L. Cohn of the U.S. District Court for the Eastern District of Michigan, there's not much.

> Stressing that each Supreme Court justice "is elected by the people and accountable to the people"—not to the other justices—the judge explained to *Lawyers Weekly* that the "only mechanisms currently available to discipline so-to-speak 'errant' Supreme Court justices" are the constitutional provisions for "impeachment and conviction by the legislature" and "removal by the legislature on a request by the governor."[962]

There was a danger, though, Cohn said, of the "freeze out."

> From a practicality standpoint, Cohn advised that "if a judge of a multi-judge court chooses to violate a tradition of confidentiality of discussions among the judges, the only way it can be properly dealt with is by isolating that judge from discussions which you want to be confidential."

> Detroit attorney Timothy A. Baughman[963]—who has frequently argued and won in the Supreme Court—agreed.

---

961 Todd C. Berg, "Supreme Court confidential: MSC's codification of unwritten 'deliberate process' draws on historical practices, raises enforcement questions," *Michigan Lawyers Weekly*, 5 February 2007, http://milawyersweekly.com/news/2007/02/05/supreme-court-confidential/.
962 Ibid.
963 Baughman is the chief of research, training and appeals for the Wayne County Prosecutor's office. He was, said Weaver, a close friend of Corrigan's; his daughter clerked for her. And he shows up again in the last chapter. [Timothy Baughman, Wayne County Prosecutor, http://www.waynecounty.com/wcpo_execoffice_timbaughman.htm]

"Though it seems unthinkable to exclude a justice from conference, one has to think the unthinkable to deal with a situation [that is] itself unthinkable," he told *Lawyers Weekly*. "The vote on opinions and applications and motions and the like could come at a full conference, but justices could certainly justifiably refrain from discussing their reasons for their votes before a justice who will not maintain confidentiality, and decline to exchange memoranda or draft opinions with that justice."[964]

That's exactly what had happened to Weaver and—to a lesser extent—Cavanagh and Kelly. In her dissent on the Fieger motion to stay the reprimand, Weaver had argued against the "judicial privilege" the Engler Four practiced—which evidently allowed them to avoid meeting with her. It's as if they were taking their direction from Baughman's "unthinkables." Weaver wrote describing some of the conduct of those who set themselves against her:

> [J]udicial privilege does not extend to repeated resort to personal slurs, name calling, and abuses of power, such as threats to exclude a justice from conference discussions, to ban a justice from the Hall of Justice, or to hold a dissenting justice in contempt. Nor should it extend to conduct such as refusing to meet with justices on the work of the court as the majority of four have now twice done on November 13 and November 29, 2006.[965]

First, Justice Taylor proposed that I not be let in the building unless I would agree to being gagged. Then I was not to be allowed at the conferences. And that soon was realized as preposterous, and that it wouldn't fly well in the press. And then for a couple of conferences the Engler Four decided that unless we agreed to being gagged and to these rules, that they would not meet with us. So they left the conference room, went down to Chief Justice Taylor's office, and we were invited to go there if we would agree to their terms...that everything was silent forever on everything. So they went down, and that was the end of that conference.

Then, the next time they left the room—I don't know where they went that time—Kelly, Cavanagh, and I decided to stay and continue the court's business with the clerk, and we did. Then we were later informed that without us being informed that they were meeting again, that they went back into the conference—I assume having thought it over that that might be wise—and they then did the court's business. So, actually, the court's business had to be done twice, and the clerk then had to collate all the votes and do that additional work. This is really childish, irresponsible activity, and what I characterize as unprofessional, unfair, disorderly business.

...And the justices had left a crucial bit of business unfinished in and after their public hearing where they hoped to provide the mechanism to silence Weaver.

---

964 Todd C. Berg, "Supreme Court confidential: MSC's codification of unwritten 'deliberate process' draws on historical practices, raises enforcement questions."

965 Elizabeth A. Weaver writing in *Grievance Administrator v Fieger*, No. 127547 (24), Michigan Supreme Court, 21 December 2006, 36, http://publicdocs.courts.mi.gov:81/SCT/PUBLIC/ORDERS/20061221_S127547_28_127547.122106ORDER.PDF. She also noted that the remaining three—Corrigan, Young, and Markman—did it again in April 2010.

Nothing got done about it. The "gag order" had been adopted on an emergency basis. In order to retain it, they had to have a hearing, which they did after I told them they had to do it. Then we were supposed to meet on it subsequently and vote. And we never met on it and voted. It wasn't retained; it was put over, and it was never brought up again until 2010.

On the Record with *Off the Record*

Two days after the hearing, Weaver appeared on WKAR's *Off the Record*.[966] The late Charlie Cain of the *Detroit News* wanted to know if Weaver thought the Engler Four had been committing offences worthy of impeachment. "That is not what I've been saying," Weaver responded.

After a spell she was asked: "Has there been corrupt conduct by any of the justices?"

Weaver: "Well, how do you define corrupt?" She laid out misconduct and lack of professionalism, threats to ban her from the building, and other disorderly conduct, including being excluded from conferences.

Michigan Public Radio's Rick Pluta sought elucidation. He didn't know about the IOP or what it meant.

Host Tim Skubick wanted to know how the court could do its business without confidentiality. "How can the court operate if there is not the sense that the stuff that is talked about in that room stays in that room?"

Weaver: "Fairly easily. People can have robust and frank discussions and remain professional and remain orderly and remain fair. They're doing it in Wisconsin...."

Skubick: "There are some in this town who say you can't have a robust discussion if somebody is going to go outside and tell the media all of the stuff that went on inside. You don't agree with that?"

Weaver: "No, as a matter of fact."

Weaver went on to separate the issue of pending and impending cases from any area of comment. But as for the rest...especially the administrative matters...it was all fair game.

"It isn't just what we decide, it's how we decide it. And for administrative matters we should be doing it openly."

Pluta wanted to know why the Judicial Tenure Commission wasn't sufficient for her complaints about the other justices.

---

966 All of the quoted material in this section is transcribed by co-author Schock from the video program, 19 January 2007. The archived show is available for viewing at http://archive.wkar.org/offtherecord/.

Weaver: "Because they have no power. All they can do is recommend [action] to the Supreme Court."

Skubick: "You want the legislature to look into it, don't you?"

Weaver agreed.

Peter Luke: "What authority would they have to do anything?

Weaver asserted the Governor and legislature do have authority to investigate, and that all she was after was to have an accountable court. An independent and objective investigation might reveal what's been going on. "I'd be happy to have an investigation. Such investigation should be short, so it doesn't drag on forever." Additionally, she said, court employees should be able to speak without fear of retribution. Some place along the line, she asserted that within an hour after taking over as chief justice, Maura Corrigan had two employees escorted out of the building. The implication was that the staff was expendable under the Engler Four.

Charlie Cain wanted to know if Weaver thought the court had become the laughing stock of the nation, given what had happened in the previous few months.

Weaver: "I don't believe the court is worthy of the public's trust and confidence at this time. It's true, it's getting national attention; I've been told it is."

Skubick wanted to know for the person at home—who was "not a student of the court: 'So what?'"

Weaver: "We make decisions that affect everybody's life, and they need to be able to have trust and confidence in the judiciary."

Skubick: "Why shouldn't they?"

Weaver explained it all again, but it didn't register.

Skubick: "What does that mean to the general public?"

Makes you wonder if he'd been paying attention.

Pluta: "Haven't all your dissents been released?"

No. Weaver tried to explain how the disorder at the court had led to a breach in the ethical administration of the court's business. She explained the Code of Judicial Conduct, the Constitution. They didn't get it.

Skubick: "The chief justice—and we asked him to do this program with you, and he declined—he suggested that you're an angry woman."

Weaver: "Do I look angry?"

Actually, she looked a little weary, but she was calmly and gamely explaining as much as they could understand and a little more.

Then Skubick asked the question that wouldn't die: "You're not upset about not getting chief justice for a second [two-year term]?"

Weaver: "Of course not. Do you know what it is to be the chief justice? It's a 24/7 if done correctly...."

Skubick's last question: "This is a yes or no question: Is this a style difference as some have suggested? Or does it go deeper than that in your mind."
Weaver: "The problems are abuse of power and misconduct in office."

Skubick should have known better. A "yes or no" answer for a question like that?

That same day, Chief Justice Taylor had Marcia McBrien put out a press release of his statement responding to Weaver's appearance on the show. It went out by e-mail to editors throughout the state.

> Today Justice Weaver simply repeated old allegations without offering any support for them. This is irresponsible, and I again call on her to apologize to all six of her fellow justices and the public, and to get back to the job she was elected to do.
>
> In today's *Off the Record* program, Justice Weaver got direct questions but offered only evasive answers. She admitted that her colleagues have not done anything that warrants their removal from office. Asked if there was "corrupt conduct" on the court, she demurred, claiming a "lack of professional conduct." She said she is reporting "abuse of power and misconduct in office," but again failed to offer evidence to back those extraordinary claims. And she continues to refuse to report any of her allegations to the Judicial Tenure Commission because, she says, the commission is "powerless."
>
> It is clear that the Tenure Commission does have jurisdiction over judges including the justices. Even if that were not so, there are plenty of other investigative bodies available to look into Justice Weaver's allegation. Her call for the legislature and Governor to investigate the court is not only unwarranted, but also unconstitutional. In effect, she wants two other branches of government to sit in judgment on the way the court makes decisions about cases and administrative matters.
>
> In addition to her unjustified misconduct claims, Justice Weaver made other inaccurate statements that I must correct:

• It is not true that other justices threatened to ban Justice Weaver from the Hall of Justice.

• It is not true that her dissent in the Gilbert case was suppressed. Justice Weaver admits that it was published.   ·

• It is not true that two employees were dismissed within an hour of Justice Maura Corrigan being elected as chief justice in 2001.

Justice Weaver has said that her accusations so far are just "the tip of the iceberg." Yet when questioned repeatedly by the media, she refuses to reveal anything more, saying that "there's so much to say I couldn't possibly do it." She calls for "sunshine on the court," but she herself is not being open. This is simply irresponsible.

Justice Weaver should either pursue her charges through the many avenues already available, or should end this controversy and get back to the job she was elected to do.[967]

In reading over the release, Weaver realized she was wrong about one thing: it took Corrigan longer than an hour to march Maria Candy and Denise Koning out of the building. It was days. But it wasn't very many days.

All the rest of what she had said was true. Because the JTC reported to the Supreme Court and only the justices could take action, the JTC wasn't the appropriate body to undertake a systematic and systemic investigation. The legislature was one of the remedies offered under the Constitution, contrary to what Taylor claimed, and it would be fully constitutional. As for laying out her proofs, all any of the members of the media had to do was read what she'd written and follow up on it. Not one did. But that didn't stop them from editorializing about the call for investigation.

The Dowagiac newspaper ran the Taylor/McBrien press release in full in an editorial and added to it:

Taylor and Justices Maura Corrigan, Stephen Markman and Robert Young, Jr. all said Weaver's "unprecedented" disclosures were "selective and misleading" and violated confidentiality that traditionally protects internal deliberations not only in Michigan, but courts nationally, including the U.S. Supreme Court.

Democratic Justice Marilyn Kelly suggested the appointment of a special three-member commission of two attorneys or judges and one non-lawyer to address Weaver's allegations "because I am gravely concerned that the public conflict among justices is damaging the court."

---

967 Clifford W. Taylor, press release, 22 January 2007.

Each appointee would need support from at least five of the court's seven justices. Findings would be reported to the court within 90 days. No action was taken.

It would seem a justice harboring complaints of impropriety should turn them over to some investigate [sic] body—perhaps the FBI—rather that dragging the judiciary through the mud.[968]

The FBI? *The Detroit News* was even less welcome to the idea of an investigation.

We are hearing entirely too much about the internal difficulties of the Michigan Supreme Court. New suggestions by two of the justices for outside investigations into the court would be extremely destructive to the court's independence and are a very bad idea.

It is now well known that Justice Elizabeth Weaver is feuding with four other members of the court, Chief Justice Clifford Taylor and Justices Maura Corrigan, Stephen Markman and Robert Young.

She has issued a blizzard of dissents and complaints about the four, but all they add up to are policy differences and personality clashes, though she has cloaked them in charges of "abuses of power." Weaver has now suggested an investigation of the court by a panel named by the Governor, Speaker of the House, and Senate Majority leader. Justice Marilyn Kelly has called for the court itself to appoint a three-person commission composed of "distinguished members of the community."

The sound of grinding axes is deafening.

Each member of the court, including the justices Weaver complains about, has been elected by the people to conduct the court's business; no one else—not a panel of distinguished citizens, and certainly not appointees named by the legislature and Governor, has been entrusted with that task.

To have an investigation of the court, as suggested by Weaver, by people named by the legislature and Governor, would weaken the court's status as a separate and co-equal branch of government. And is it accidental that two of the three investigators proposed by Weaver would come from parts of the government controlled by the other party than the four justices with whom she is unhappy?

Kelly is the ideological minority in the court and is asking the majority to voluntarily cede some control over the court to an outside group. If she were in the majority, would such a suggestion be as appealing?

---

968 "The Donald and Rosie got nothing on feudin' Supremes," *The Daily News*, Dowagiac, 22 January 2007.

One of Weaver's complaints about the court is that it has issued an order making the court's internal deliberations confidential.

But as Court of Appeals Judge Christopher Murray pointed out at a hearing on the rule last week, courts have always had a "deliberative judicial privilege."

Should there be some sort of official rule and a punishment for violation of this rule? We still don't believe so. But being spiteful and ungracious and venting one's spleen in written statements is injudicious and undignified and hurts the justice system.[969]

Another "Sit down and shut up!" No help there. One might believe that a newspaper might conclude that more information is better, and unfettered access is best.

The News *had always supported John Engler, and this was just a continuation of that support.*

An Appeal to the Governor and the Legislature

Convinced the court was completely out of control, on January 24, 2007, Weaver sent a formal proposal to Governor Jennifer Granholm and the legislature to investigate the disorder in the court.

> As I have indicated in previous dissents and statements, a majority of four justices, Chief Justice Taylor, and Justices Corrigan, Young and Markman, on the Michigan Supreme Court has misused and abused power and engaged in repeated disorderly, unprofessional, and unfair conduct in the performance of the judicial business of the court. Rather than responding with facts or reasoned arguments, the chief justice has chosen to attack me on a personal level, including a challenge to my honesty in reporting facts. Discord of this base nature cannot continue. Only a truly independent investigation can examine the issues and make fair evaluation of who is, or is not, telling the truth. The court does not now deserve the trust and confidence of the people of Michigan. Any investigation this court might create, conduct, or control will not be credible.
>
> In the interest of beginning to restore the people's trust and confidence, I propose and request a commission be established to investigate and report upon the controversy, with blue-ribbon members chosen by the Governor, the Michigan House of Representatives and the Michigan Senate. Our Constitution at Article 6, Section 25 gives authority to the Governor, supported by a two-thirds majority of each house of the legislature, to remove a member of the Supreme Court. The investigation I here propose and request is

---

969 Editorial, "Outside investigation would damage court; Unneeded probe could harm independence of state justices," *Detroit News*, 22 January 2007.

consistent with the Constitution and is a necessary first step in determining whether removal of any member of the court may be justified. I expect that my conduct and veracity, as well as that of all of the justices, will be fully explored. This independent investigation should be accomplished promptly, hopefully within the next 60 to 90 days.

The commission should be given unfettered access to internal court documents and staff, so long as there is no intrusion upon the deliberation concerning pending and impending cases protected by Judicial Canon 2A, and so long as all present and former staff are granted immunity from retribution or adverse job action. The testimony of principal witnesses, including the justices, must be under oath and subject to penalties of perjury. If the commission is created, I pledge my full cooperation.

The people of Michigan are owed the truth. With the truth in hand, I am confident that they will be able to make proper judgments about this court and its justices.[970]

Someone who received the letter suggested that the JTC would be the appropriate body to investigate. That occasioned another letter from Weaver, this one chronicling the deficiency of that plan:

A referral and request for investigation to the judicial tenure commission (JTC) of this current Michigan Supreme Court controversy among justices will allow the majority to investigate themselves.

Further it will not resolve the controversy but will continue and extend the controversy [....][971]

The section headings on the document revealed her reasoning: the JTC operated in secret; it had only the power to recommend a matter to the Supreme Court where it would be considered; that would create an impossible situation and would lead to the disqualification of all the justices; and, because the JTC was a commission of the court, there was an inherent conflict of interest.

Her message to the Governor got some responses, not all favorable:

[S]he may face a tough sell to get the other branches of state government involved in the dispute revolving around her allegations that the GOP majority had suppressed her dissent, excluded her from case conferences and called her names.

Matt Marsden, spokesman for Republican Senate Majority Leader Mike Bishop of Rochester, said Bishop would not explore Weaver's "unsubstanti-

970 Elizabeth A. Weaver, letter to Governor Jennifer Granholm, *et al.*, 24 January 2007, unpublished.
971 Elizabeth A. Weaver, letter to Governor Jennifer Granholm, *et al.*, 31 January 2007, unpublished.

ated claims" without her at least first going to the Judicial Tenure Commission, which he said has jurisdiction over the matter.

"There are proper channels that need to be followed," Marsden said. "Chief Justice Taylor asked that she come forward with some hard facts and evidence. To my knowledge, that hasn't happened."

House Speaker Andy Dillon, D-Redford, said the chair of the House Judiciary Committee should look into the matter.

"It depends on what we see," Dillon said when asked how far a review could go. "If it turns out that we think this could be as serious as she is claiming it is, it probably merits some further inquiry."

Granholm's office has received Weaver's letter and is reviewing it, spokeswoman Heidi Watson said.[972]

Upper Peninsula attorney and columnist Richard Clark had seen the effects of what Weaver was describing and called attention to a *Michigan Lawyers Weekly* survey:

Attorneys were surveyed. Half represent individuals and the other half represent insurance companies and corporations. Almost 80 percent of the attorneys answered "yes" to the question "[d]o you generally agree that the decisions and opinions of the Michigan Supreme Court majority suggest a pattern of bias that favors insurance companies and large corporate interests over those of ordinary citizens in civil litigation matters?"

The majority of four's ruling had led to absurd results. A blind woman injured in a handicap stall in a restroom was denied her day in court on the basis that the risk was open and obvious.

[...]

While he was Governor, John Engler—now CEO of the National Association of Manufacturers—announced war against lawyers who represent individuals against corporations and insurance companies. As part of his war he appointed and supported the election of judges that would rule against these lawyers.

Mr. Engler's strategy worked. [...] As a result of the court's bias, insurance companies contest claims that would have been paid promptly.

---

972 "Weaver formalizes request for MSC probe," *Michigan Lawyers Weekly*, 29 January 2007, http://milawyersweekly.com/news/2007/01/29/weaver-formalizes-request-for-msc-probe/.

Mr. Engler's strategy in the courts has engulfed the Michigan Supreme Court itself. Justice Weaver, a judge since 1975, claims the majority of four is harming the court. Justice Weaver objects to the politicization of the court.

[...]

Justice Weaver has called upon the legislature to investigate [...] the majority of four. Given the stern criticism by a justice with so much experience the legislature should grant her request.[973]

So, somebody <u>was</u> paying attention. And while most in the political arena didn't want to touch this issue with a 20-foot pole, Senate Judiciary Chairman Paul Condino (D-Southfield) thought otherwise.

Ever the wit, Brian Dickerson analyzed the impending situation:

When last we peeked in on the guardians of Michigan's judicial system, as I recall, they were rolling around on the floor of the state Supreme Court chamber, trading insults and eye-gouges in a disciplinary proceeding involving Geoffrey Fieger (who'd been hauled before them, ironically enough, for making unflattering remarks about judges).

Now the skirmishing has resumed, with Justice Elizabeth Weaver renewing accusations that her GOP colleagues are making mischief in secret conclaves and the targeted justices insinuating that Weaver's elevator no longer goes all the way to the top.

It would all be raucous good fun—if only the stakes in this ugly little hissing match were as small as the combatants waging it. But a meltdown in Michigan's court of last resort is no petty domestic dispute, however much it may resemble one. The judiciary's credibility is under siege, although that has less to do with the personalities of the incumbent justices than with the lingering legacy of former Govenor John Engler.

An arm of the party

The state Supreme Court was a creature of partisan politics long before Engler came along. But it wasn't until Engler's last term, when his appointees achieved majority control of the high court, that justices were explicitly enlisted as guarantors of one party's policy agenda.

In 1998, when he was hustling insurance industry support for Maura Corrigan's Supreme Court candidacy, Engler was candid about his objectives.

---

973 Richard Clark, "There is no order in this court," *Escanaba Daily Press*, 13 February 2007, 4A.

"We need to elect justices who will uphold the tort reforms adopted by Republican legislators," he told a fund-raising dinner I attended, referring to a controversial package of bills that had tipped the balance of power in liability cases in favor of deep-pocket defendants. It was a case of the state's most powerful politician promising what his judicial candidates were forbidden to—a specific judicial outcome in exchange for the financial support of a favored group of litigants.

In the nine years since, Corrigan and her GOP colleagues have more than delivered, systematically emasculating Supreme Court precedents that had protected insurance policyholders, accident victims and targets of discrimination.

Bolting the caucus

Weaver, the only Republican justice to reach judicial office without Engler's sponsorship, initially was a reliable ally of the new majority, but she soon came to resent[974] her GOP colleagues. In Weaver's view, the Engler justices were behaving more like a partisan legislative caucus than like members of a collegial court. Some critics charged that the new justices had an explicit agenda—a list of Supreme Court precedents marked for reversal.

Weaver's most recent critiques of her GOP colleagues are an odd grab bag of personal grievances and substantive allegations that go to the heart of the majority's impartiality.

The latter deserve serious public scrutiny, and the hearings Senate Judiciary Chairman Paul Condino has scheduled later this month are a good place to

start. This court's problems are bigger than Betty, and it will take more than family counseling to address them.[975]

There was going to be a hearing at some point. It seemed appropriate, but I wasn't holding my breath. Paul Condino had it scheduled, and then it all got cancelled. We were at some place on one of the dog-and-pony shows[976] and I heard that the hearing wasn't going to happen the next day. Condino felt bad about it, but other politics enter into those things in the legislature. In the end, the Dems didn't want to go there. I don't recall that I ever heard from Granholm, and certainly the Republicans weren't going to do anything. It was one of those side trips. It would have been good to have had the hearings but....

In retrospect, I suspect the Englerites got to House Speaker Andy Dillon, who was close to Engler and Englerites like Doug Rothwell. Obviously, Dillon wouldn't today be Treasurer in Governor Snyder's administration unless the Englerites gave the "okay" to Governor Snyder.

---

974 *Words matter. To "resent" means to harbor bitterness or to be indignant about or at someone. I never resented my colleagues—I was never bitter toward them nor indignant with them. But it is fair to say that I distrusted them.*
975 Brian Dickerson, "Behind the low comedy, high stakes," *Detroit Free Press*, 9 March 2007, B.1.
976 The justices of the court would go throughout the state to do the business of the court and to meet with local judges and attorneys.

So, with the second-longest serving justice on the court yelling "fire," the crew put the pumper back into the barn. But even if nobody came to at least see what was burning, she wasn't giving up on trying to alert the public to what was occurring.

Geoffrey Fieger, who had more than a passing interest in all that had transpired, agreed that Weaver was doing everything she could.

> She's calling out from the proverbial wilderness there, and they attacked her. But the big problem in Michigan was that no one was there. We had no press here, so no one was there. So then, all of a sudden, it's a personality dispute and they make her appear to be a clown or an outcast rather than say, "Wait a second, what's really going on here? Perhaps she's shedding some light on some really shady business," and that's the problem. And the only way some light has been shown on them is Elizabeth Weaver and— well, they've marginalized me because they've said, "Oh, Fieger! You understand him." I tried to do it, and Elizabeth Weaver had tried to do it, and a guy named Brian Dickerson, who has written in the paper, had tried to do it somewhat. But beyond that, there is no coverage of this, so they could do anything they wanted, because there was no coverage. Nobody knows how truly corrupt it was.[977]

Down the Memory Hole

In his best-known book, *1984*, George Orwell (Eric Blair) writes about oblong slits in the walls at the Ministry of Truth, the "memory holes." Workers would shove papers through the holes. Those papers would then travel to the furnaces below. They received waste paper, certainly, but more important, they were the destination for truthful but inconvenient documents and records.

The Michigan Supreme Court was in effect installing memory holes with its missing or woefully deficient minutes of conferences. Justice Weaver had already referenced them in relation to the DQ issue. But pretty much all the minutes in the court at that time were inaccurate, incomplete, and/or misleading.

This was the people's business, and they had a right to records that correctly reflected what went on.

Weaver insisted that the minutes were important public documents. So, she dissented when what passed for minutes finally came around for approval, some of them more than a year after the meetings they purported to chronicle. Here's an example of what she wrote:

> This dissent reveals another example of the misuse and abuse of power, and misconduct of the people's judicial business by the majority of four, Chief Justice Taylor and Justices Corrigan, Young and Markman. The majority of

---

977 Geoffrey N. Fieger, video interview with co-author Schock, 12 March 2012, Southfield, Mich.

four has used its power to secretly suppress and silence dissent. The deceptive and/or inaccurate, misleading, and incomplete minutes now approved by the majority illustrate the majority's attempt to deprive the people of Michigan of ever knowing, in a timely manner, what, when, and how decisions were made on court administrative matters. By their approval, they reveal the majority of four's willingness to change and revise history by not recording the whole truth, or recording untruth, of the majority's formal actions.

What is harmful and important to the people about this misuse and abuse of power in the disorderly way of conducting the court's administrative business is that it effectively can (and too often does) result in the following:

- Keeps secret from the people important information of what the justices are discussing and deciding on the court;

- Keeps secret from the people important information of how the justices conduct the people's judicial business; and

- Keeps secret from the people when the justices are conducting the people's judicial business.

This abuse of the minutes' process makes it possible to attempt to mislead the people, or to confuse, deceive, misinform or not inform the people, about the conduct of the business of the court, and thus deprive the people of sufficient, accurate information to judge the performance of the justices.

The minutes should be timely produced, acted upon, and made available to the public on the Supreme Court website. The minutes should memorialize this court's conduct of the people's judicial business. They should be a window for the people to learn what, when, and how the justices perform one of this court's core constitutional responsibilities, the supervision of the administration of the Michigan judiciary.

Because the approval of these minutes makes it possible for the majority to suppress dissent and revise history, and to keep people in the dark by depriving them of important information as to how the justices conduct the judicial business of Michigan, I dissent to these minutes and insist that our present traditional system of processing, approving and publishing minutes end now. An efficient and impartial judiciary is "ill served by casting a cloak of secrecy around the operations of the courts."[978]

And then she went through each of the eight conferences, from March 1 to Nov. 29, 2006, comparing the "official" version with her complete record of what actually occurred. There was a vast difference in the content.

---

978 Elizabeth A. Weaver, "Memorandum," 20 March 2007, http://www.justiceweaver.com/pdfs/minutes-Dissent_320_07.pdf.

Those minutes are not available on the Supreme Court website, but Weaver put them up at her own: www.justiceweaver.com.

...Otherwise, there was the memory hole.[979]

And Weaver continued her outspoken disagreement with the Engler Four over recusal and disqualification. In *People v Parsons* Justice Corrigan stepped off the case and Weaver wanted her reasons in writing:

> A justice's decision to participate or not participate (recuse himself or herself) in a case implicates a bedrock principle of our judicial system—the impartiality of the judiciary. Without a record of a justice's reasons to not participate in a case, how can future litigants be guaranteed that the same reasons are not present in their cases? Moreover, how can the people of Michigan be sure that a justice is not simply refusing to work on a case to avoid some controversy that the case might involve—for example, a controversy that might call into question his or her impartiality on an issue or make reelection more difficult?
>
> [...]
>
> [W]hile it appears to continue to be for some justices a "tradition" of this court for a justice who disqualifies himself or herself from a case to not give written reasons, it is a "tradition of secrecy" that must for all justices end now.[980]

In response, Justice Young wanted to relate—incorrectly—that Weaver's position was newly arrived at:

> It should be stressed that until recently, Justice Weaver never believed that this constitutional provision applied to recusal decisions. Justice Weaver's own longstanding practice (in which she declined to state her reasons for self-disqualification) was not only consistent with the court's historic disqualification practice but with the constitution as well.[981]

Ah, that may have been the case in her first years on the court, but she had been moving this way ever since 2003 and *In re JK*...and she had finally arrived. And it was Corrigan who had given her the impetus. Ironic perhaps.

Corrigan did respond, but she started with a bit of whimsy, the lyrics to "Comedy Tonight," a song by Stephen Sondheim from the play *A Funny Thing Happened on the Way to*

---

979 The memory hole theory was given new life in the Supreme Court's 2012 reorganization of its website. [Marcia McBrien, press release, "Michigan state courts' new web site debuts today," Michigan Supreme Court, http://courts.michigan.gov/News-Events/press_releases/Documents/NewWebsiteAnnouncement.pdf.]
980 Elizabeth A. Weaver writing in *People v Parsons*, No. 132975, 6 March 2007, 4-5, http://publicdocs.courts.mi.gov:81/SCT/PUBLIC/ORDERS/20070306_S132975_48_132975_2007-03-06_or.pdf.
981 Robert P. Young, writing in ibid., 5.

the Forum. Then Corrigan went on to disclose that she would provide reasons, but only because Weaver was going to issue a statement "opposing my decision not to furnish reasons; her doing so will delay the disposition of this case."[982]

Even with Weaver's statement, the opinion was not delayed.

Corrigan went on:

> Accordingly, I feel compelled to disclose my reasons for nonparticipation in the interest of a speedy disposition of this apparent emergency.
>
> My beloved son, Daniel Corrigan Grano, is a third-year law student and, at age 25, a city councilman who has, believe it or not, political aspirations. Dan also works as a law clerk at the small, excellent firm of Flood, Lanctot, & Connor, the lawyers who are defending the Parsons case. I do not know on what cases Dan performs legal research, nor am I aware that any screening is occurring in the law firm regarding his assignments. Thus, he may well have worked on this case, and we may well have discussed this very case at the dinner table, not realizing that it would ultimately come before this court. Thus, I am not comfortable in sitting in this case. Lest there be any doubt, however, I am totally, completely, 100 percent biased and prejudiced in favor of my son, Daniel. I have been since he was just a gleam in his father's eye, and I plan to hug him no matter how old he gets! (He is also very handsome!)
>
> I have not participated in the substantive merits of this case. I initially declined to furnish my reasons so as not to either embarrass my son or afford unearned publicity to him or his law firm. It does not take hundreds of pages or complex rules of disqualification to understand that a mother should not judge a case involving her son. And restraint of speech on the subject is just sensible. Justice Weaver has forced my hand in the interests of her own agenda. I now say to her, as she herself once liked to say, "Let's cut the comedy." Betty, can't we stop wasting the taxpayers' money on this frolic and detour? Or are you determined to continue these theatrics, hoping that public opinion will somehow support your desire to abolish our elective system for justices and judges? Whatever your goal, this low comedy of your making can only end in tragedy: the public's loss of respect for this court and for our state's judicial branch.[983]

All that could have been condensed into something like this: "My son works for the firm that is defending Parsons. We may have discussed this case before I realized it was impending. For those reasons I am stepping aside." Although, the gushing-mother aspect is a revelation.

982 Maura D. Corrigan, writing in ibid., 7-8.
983 Ibid.

For her part, Weaver, found no comedy in what was going on. And she suggested subsequently on Interlochen Public Radio that a better song to describe the operations at the Michigan Supreme Court might come from a different theatrical production, *Chicago*: "(Give 'em the Old) Razzle Dazzle."[984]

Fieger, once again.

It would take some time, but the federal district court found in Fieger's favor on the reprimand Sept. 4, 2007:

> The court finds the rules are unconstitutional on their face because they are both overly broad and vague. Thus, they violate the First Amendment right to free speech and the Fourteenth Amendment right to due process of law.
>
> As interpreted by the Michigan Supreme Court, the State of Michigan's effort to regulate unprotected speech through the courtesy provisions causes a substantial amount of protected speech to be regulated as well. In addition, the courtesy provisions are so imprecise that persons of ordinary intelligence must guess at their meaning.
>
> [...]
>
> This court finds there are no procedural bars to addressing the merits. Plaintiffs have standing to raise these challenges. Plaintiffs' claims are ripe for adjudication and are not barred by the doctrines of *res judicata* or claim preclusion. Finally, defendants are not shielded by any doctrine of immunity.[985]

Okay, but would Michigan let it rest there, or...? Well, no. There was too much invested to allow a federal district court to have the last word. The Michigan Supreme Court appealed and the matter went to the Sixth Circuit Court of Appeals in Cincinnati. There the matter was reversed to allow the reprimand to stand.

> We vacate the judgment of the district court and remand with instructions to dismiss the complaint for lack of jurisdiction. We hold that Fieger and Steinberg lack standing because they have failed to demonstrate actual present harm or a significant possibility of future harm based on a single, stipulated reprimand; they have not articulated, with any degree of specificity, their intended speech and conduct; and they have not sufficiently established a threat of future sanction under the narrow construction of the challenged provisions applied by the Michigan Supreme Court. For these same reasons, we also hold that the district court abused its discretion in entering declaratory relief.[986]

984 Music by John Kander, lyrics by Fred Ebb.
985 *Geoffrey Nels Fieger and Richard L. Steinberg v Michigan Supreme Court. et al.* Civil Action No. 06-11684, 4 September 2007, 2, http://jaablog.jaablaw.com/files/34726-32374/Fieger_v_Michigan_Supreme_Court.pdf.
986 *Fieger v Michigan Supreme Court*, No. 07-2213, U.S. Sixth Circuit Court of Appeals, 20 January 2009, http://

The opinion was a split decision among the three appeals judges. Writing the majority opinion was Judge Richard Allen Griffin, former candidate for Michigan's Supreme Court...you remember, the one Weaver defeated in 1994?

And it wasn't the first time Fieger and Griffin had met before a question of law. The previous occasion was when Griffin was on the Michigan Court of Appeals. Fieger described Griffin's action in that other case, a wrongful death suit for the family of murder victim Scott Amedure against the *Jenny Jones Show* in 1999, this way[987]: "He took away the Jenny Jones verdict from me. He said, 'There was no proximate cause.' He's the guy."[988]

But there was much more in store for Geoffrey Fieger than the figurative slap on the wrist of the reprimand by the Michigan Supreme. In one of the earlier stories of the Southfield attorney and Attorney General Mike Cox, there was made mention of Fieger reimbursing employees for their contributions to the presidential campaign of John Edwards. One former employee complained.

Game on.

Under a federal campaign law, the feds would next move to indict Fieger for directing a total of $127,000 to John Edwards' campaign. The individual maximum donation was $2,000. And Fieger reimbursed "firm lawyers, employees and a few family members, as well as [...] vendors doing business with the firm. The employees subsequently received bonuses that, after taxes, totaled the exact amounts of their contributions."[989]

The federal indictment would come after a failed attempt to indict him at the state level. And it was something that he'd seen heading his way as early as January 2007:

> Just two days after avoiding state criminal charges, attorney Geoffrey Fieger predicted Monday that a federal grand jury will indict him for illegal fund-raising on behalf of John Edwards' 2004 presidential bid.
>
> The federal charges would focus, Fieger said, on bonuses he gave to "civic-minded employees."
>
> "I fully expect that I will be indicted by a grand jury who will indict a bottle of beer if the Republican U.S. attorney told them to do it," Fieger said in a prepared statement at a news conference. Federal investigators are trying to determine whether he tried to skirt federal limits on campaign contributions by funneling money through his employees.

caselaw.findlaw.com/us-6th-circuit/1286451.html.
987 *Patricia Graves and Frank Amedure v Warner Bros., Jenny Jones Show*, No. 226645, Michigan Court of Appeals, 17 January 2003, http://publicdocs.courts.mi.gov:81/OPINIONS/FINAL/COA/20021022_C226645_64_2330.226645.OPN.COA.PDF.
988 Fieger.
989 Terry Carter, "Motormouth: Geoffrey Fieger's fiery tongue has earned him millions. Now it could cost the Detroit lawyer his career," *ABAJournal*, 1 December 2007, http://www.abajournal.com/magazine/article/motormouth/.

Fieger's preemptive strike against possible felony charges came as little surprise to people who have become accustomed to his brash, confrontational style during a meteoric career that has made him Michigan's best-known attorney, specializing in personal injury cases.

At stake now are his freedom and his multimillion-dollar law practice.[990]

The U.S. Attorney in charge of the eastern district at the time was Stephen J. Murphy, III, an Engler man, and now one of the 20 U.S. District Court Judges in Michigan's Eastern District.[991] The federal efforts had visibly begun with an FBI raid:

> Fieger had known for some time what was coming. Shortly before 7 p.m. on Nov. 30, 2005, about 80 federal agents, mostly FBI, raided Fieger's offices and visited the homes of 32 alleged straw donors. An FBI agent told one law firm employee he had been flown in from Iraq for the job, according to Fieger's lawyers.[992]

Fieger said agents also raided his home. And he puts the number above 80:

> They had a hundred—over a hundred FBI agents investigating me, conducting raids. They got more FBI agents to investigate me than they ever have gotten—as far as I'm aware of—in the history of the United States. If you walk into a bank and mowed down everybody in the bank, which is a federal crime, you maybe get six or seven federal officers looking for you. [993]

A raid of that size and scope took some juice. Fieger said he is convinced that it went all the way to the top. In a *Free Press* article the day after his indictment (August 24, 2007) with law partner Vernon Johnson, Fieger put the blame on the administration:

> In a prepared statement, Fieger unloaded on President George W. Bush and U.S. Attorney General Alberto Gonzales. He accused them of leading a witch hunt of a prominent Democrat.

> "The timing of these unprecedented charges that have no support in fact or law during the height of the presidential fund-raising campaign is solely intended to intimidate Democratic supporters around the country," Fieger said.

> Bryan Sierra, a spokesman for the U.S. Department of Justice, denied Fieger's claim that the prosecution was politically motivated.[994]

990 Joe Swickard, "Fieger: I expect to be indicted; it's part of GOP attack, he says," *Detroit Free Press*, 17 January 2007, A.1.

991 Murphy's career and ties to the Engler administration were discussed in Chapter 10.

992 Terry Carter, "Motormouth: Geoffrey Fieger's fiery tongue has earned him millions. Now it could cost the Detroit lawyer his career."

993 Geoffrey N. Fieger.

994 Zachary Gorhow (with Brian Dickerson), "U.S. vs. Fieger; Indicted: He's accused of illegal political donations; defiant attorney says he's a victim of witch hunt," *Detroit Free Press*, 25 August 2007, A.1.

In a subsequent interview, Fieger reiterated the authority that would have been required.

> In order to raid a lawyer's office, irrespective—I mean, even if a lawyer's, like, dealing drugs out of his office—you need on the federal level the direct approval of the Attorney General. You need the direct approval. There's a rule within the Justice Department. To get a hundred FBI agents it would have to go—I mean, Gonzales wasn't really making decisions; Rove was. So you know that these decisions were being made at the highest level.[995]

Shortly before Fieger's indictment, the *Detroit Free Press* reported that U.S. Attorney Murphy had by that time "recused himself from direct involvement in the case."[996] Prosecutorial duties during the trial would be led by Assistant U.S. Attorney Lynn A. Helland.[997] But what role had Murphy played early on? Was he in on the raid?

It took almost a year for the case to be resolved...ultimately to the chagrin of the prosecutors and the satisfaction of Fieger, his then-partner Johnson,[998] and their attorney, Gerry Spence.

> Attorney Geoffrey Fieger won a dramatic acquittal Monday [June 2, 2008] on federal charges of violating campaign-finance laws, saving his lucrative career and sending federal prosecutors in Detroit to yet another crushing defeat in a high-profile case.
>
> Jurors rejected each of the felony charges against Fieger and his law partner, Vernon (Ven) Johnson, and then eight to 10 of them went to a downtown Detroit hotel to hoist glasses of champagne with the two defendants and their legal team.
>
> "I want to thank the jury for listening," Fieger said after the jury announced its verdict. It came after nearly 20 hours of deliberations over four days and a 20-day trial in U.S. District Court. "I hope this puts an end to political prosecution in the age of Mr. Bush," referring to President George W. Bush's administration.
>
> Johnson and Fieger hugged family members, supporters and their lawyers after the jury cleared them. A conviction on any one of 10 felony counts against Fieger, and five against Johnson, could have sent them to prison and ended their legal careers.

995 Geoffrey N. Fieger.

996 Joe Swickard, "Fieger: I expect to be indicted; it's part of GOP attack, he says," *Detroit Free Press*, 17 January 2007, A.1.

997 David Ashenfelter (with Ben Schmitt), "Thank you, jurors, cleared Fieger says; campaign-finance charges lacked evidence and motive, jury decides," *Detroit Free Press*, 3 June 2008, A.3.

998 Johnson left the firm in 2011 and sued Fieger in 2012. [Douglas J. Levy, "Ex-partner suing Fieger Law for professional misconduct, 'intolerable behavior,'" The Michigan Lawyer, A blog from *Michigan Lawyers Weekly*, 6 June 2012, http://michiganlawyerblog.wordpress.com/2012/06/06/ex-partner-suing-fieger-law-for-professional-misconduct-intolerable-behavior/.

The verdict was a victory for famed Jackson, Wyo., lawyer Gerry Spence, 79, who told jurors in closing arguments that his defense of Fieger was the last trial of his career.

Spence called the verdict "one of the great moments in my life. ... This is a nice way to end a career—representing a great lawyer who represents ordinary people."

Jurors said they acquitted because prosecutors failed to prove that Fieger and Johnson illegally channeled money to the failed 2004 presidential campaign of Democrat John Edwards.[999]

Reflecting on the event, Fieger was grateful he still had his law license and his freedom; it could have worked out otherwise for any one of the total of 27 counts.

Fieger admitted [...] that he was scared during the trial, which featured 18 days of testimony.

A conviction, he said, "would have been the end of my career, the end of my family as I know it. It would have been the end of my firm and the 60 people who work for me."[1000]

And he still insists there was no crime:

I mean, you have to understand this wasn't secret. Giving people bonuses, reporting it to the Internal Revenue, taking tax out of it, and saying it's legitimate, and then coming up with...you see, this was the incredible thing: they came up with a crime that didn't exist. I mean, if you read the law that they were going under, it doesn't say what they say. The law says: you can't give in the name of another. That means, you don't want to go into a phonebook and start sending out contributions in other people's names. It's pretty clear. It doesn't say: "If you give a contribution to John Edwards, and I'm so happy about it I give you a bonus," that somehow that's a crime. They could easily make it a crime if they wanted to. But they didn't.

And I'm not a conspiratorialist; it's just—it is too much of a coincidence to spend that kind of money to get me for bonusing my employees for making contributions to John Edwards. Why would you spend that kind—I mean, they spent untold millions of dollars in the federal prosecution, and they were unsuccessful in that, too.

And that truly was a political hit. And all of that grew out of the Engler axis, too. I'm absolutely convinced of it.[1001]

999 David Ashenfelter (with Ben Schmitt), "Thank you, jurors, cleared Fieger says; campaign-finance charges lacked evidence and motive, jury decides," *Detroit Free Press*, 3 June 2008, A.3.
1000 Jim Irwin, "Jury Finds Fieger not guilty of campaign violations," *Grand Rapids Press*, 3 June 2008, A4.
1001 Geoffrey N. Fieger.

Fieger was grateful to Weaver for her efforts from which he stood to benefit.

> I don't think that she necessarily shares a lot of my political views, but I be-lieve that she actually believes in the law. I believe that she has a profound respect for the judiciary and the judicial process, and I believe that she saw true corruption at its core in the back rooms, and tried to expose it. And what they did then—because they were able to do it in Michigan—was at-tempt to make her out as some kind of kook, when she was really anything but a kook![1002]

All Weaver said was that she wanted openness to give the public a fair opportunity for justice.

You've got the 800-pound gorilla rule of the court, which is four votes, and you can say what anything means. So who's going to challenge that? And unless it's a federal issue, it can't even go to the federal courts. The interpretation of the Michigan Constitution falls to the Michigan Supreme Court. That's why it's so important to have people on the Supreme Court who are independent and are going to want to have things open and be accountable for how they do things; that's all. Let people judge on who says what, where, when, how, and why.

Fieger says he knows well that 800-pound gorilla:

> That's their method by which they operate. They're truly thugs, you know? And I don't have a problem mixing it up with thugs, but these thugs are the Supreme Court and the Governor [Engler] of the State of Michigan [....] These thugs have power.

Based on their statements, their behavior, Weaver said she believed her colleagues on the court were intent on using that power and had a future picked out just for Fieger:

Prison. Going to prison would mean his effective and meaningful life was over.

1002 Ibid.

Chapter 20

An Attack on Common Law
Common Sense and *Trentadue*,
More Chief Judge Meddling,
But, First....

Court watchers sometimes grow familiar enough with justices that they can make predications about which way decisions are likely to go. The watchers base their foretellings on the utterances, prior opinions and other writings of the justices. At issue is the matter of how the individual justices think and what they most highly value.

This chapter might seem a catchall. There are four independent stories beginning with a small matter of an e-mail exchange involving Chief Justice Taylor that—while not intended for wide dissemination—was shared with a select audience. Then there is the reasoning he and the others in the majority employed in overturning the common law. Next is a screed from Justice Young that elucidates his take on the tradition of that common law. And, finally, there is the relation of a sad tale of Chief Justice Taylor narrowing the field for the appointment of a chief judge of the 37th District Court in Warren and Centerline. What holds this chapter together is the revelations of how the justices in the majority saw their world and their work in it. It didn't always comport with objectivity and fairness. We begin with the little story of the email....

Chief Justice Cliff Taylor was quite the joker. He also was a loyal alumnus of the University of Michigan (Class of '64) and a devoted fraternity brother of the Sigma Zeta Chapter of Lambda Chi Alpha.[1003] He also served as Interfraternity Council president. And he liked to keep in touch.

One of his correspondents was Ron Modreski, of Grand Rapids. Modreski was a 1965 graduate of the University of Michigan engineering program. He is the principal at PM&I Consulting and is the owner of RAM Management Group. Formerly, he was employed for nearly 20 years by Vickers Incorporated Aerospace- Marine Defense Group.[1004]

1003 "Alumni: Cliff Taylor '69," Sigma Zeta of Lambda Chi Alpha, http://www.lcamichigan.com/alumni.html.
1004 "Alumni donors & friends," University of Michigan—Dearborn, http://www.umd.umich.edu/campleadership/.

Modreski started an exchange, sending a message to Taylor at his Supreme Court e-mail at 11:56 a.m., June 21, 2007. They had seemingly been carrying on some sort of conversation previously about an upcoming reunion.[1005]

> Cliff:
>
> On behalf of all "non state employees" who provide the capital and operating expenses through "taxes, taxes, and more taxes" we would like to see a smaller wheel, we would like you to actually look around the wheel to see where it is going (in Michigan it sure is confused), and perhaps let the wheel roll backwards for a while and maybe we will need 10-20 percent less people in the state employ who at times only know how to push a wheel rather than serve customers. Yes, I could also write a lot more but will save it for our reunion.
>
> Ron Modreski.

At 1:52 that afternoon, Taylor responded.

> Ron, be calm—as far as I know, I'm the only person at the head of a branch of government in this state that has proposed, more or less, what you have proposed. I've proposed to the Gov. and the legislature judge reductions at the Court of Appeals and that about half of the existing open but unfilled judgeships not be filled by the appointment of the executive. Those are in low growth areas where we are, our studies show, over-judged. She isn't happy and most likely will appoint notwithstanding the studies and request. The difficulty is that the leadership of the state, both parties, feels that Michigan's economy is in a blip. The fact is that our tax base is, I believe, permanently reduced, and will likely be further diminished in the days ahead, and the accommodations that suggests should be undertaken. It is good to recall that for our whole lifetimes in the state, Michigan has been a "big" services state for better or worse. Those days are most likely gone for the simple reason it can no longer be afforded. It is getting that internalized that is the hardest part of our current situation. Indeed, to get even our judges, a group of people that don't see themselves as "government workers" really, to understand that is plenty tough and these are the smartest guys in the state's employ. By the time we see each other next Fall, much more will be known on this score I imagine. Thanks for your thoughts, even though a bit agitated, and understand that many who serve in the government are aware and trying to move that particular "wheel" in a new direction.

Modreski to Taylor, 3:48 p.m.:

> Cliff:

1005 This e-mail skein was revealed to the public first in 2008 by attorney Mike Butler at his blog: http://www.attorneybutler.net/2008/10/if-cliff-taylor-loses-the-election-in-his-own-words.html.

Thanks for the response. I hope you understand I was being a little face-tious. I have heard about some of the suggestions and initiatives you are pro-moting for "downsizing" or the PC word, "rightsizing" our state government and I strongly encourage you to continue. Obvious the Governor and many in the state legislature don't understand there is a fundamental shift taking place globally driven by technology that is changing the way we do business and therefore the way we need to govern and provide state services. I spent over 35 years with a large global corporation in aerospace and defense and saw first hand the changes driving the old model of airline and global tech-nology. We had to go through a significant cultural change starting 20 years ago with a focus on total quality management, lean manufacturing, metrics, customer focus/service, and financial performance. Guess what? We got more and more productive, business revenues grew, we hired more people, learned the culture of continuous improvement and had fun.

I spent about 20 years outside of Michigan and returned in 1990 to the Grand Rapids area to run a portion of our global business. It was like most of Michigan was still in a time warp. The auto industry, union leaders, and elected state legislatures seem to be still living in the world we grew up in the '50s and '60s. Meanwhile, many other parts of the country (some of which I lived in) were moving ahead (such as the Southeast, Texas, Arizona, and some other Mid West states).

Keep up the good fight. If I can help, let me know. I also recognize that there are many good and smart people in the state's employ, but many are working on the wrong things with bad or poorly designed processes. I am involved with a number of organizations and boards in West Michigan focused on many of these issues. I look forward to seeing you this fall.

Ron Modreski

Taylor to Modreski, 4:01 p.m., June 21, 2007:

Ron, thanks for taking the time to lay all that out. You are right on target. That "flat earth" concept is going down slowly here, and it can be seen, as you have mentioned, on every front. One of the standing jokes here on the court with the conservatives (four of the seven) is that if the left manages to beat me when I am up in 2008, I will, implausible—even shocking—as its seems, run for Governor in 2010 and then bring John Engler back as my chief of staff—only this time, as the old saw goes, it will be personal with him. I will, of course, once John is in the saddle, de-camp for the Caymans and the down-sizing that only he could have the courage to undertake will commence. Good fun. I look forward to seeing you and the others soon.[1006]

1006 Cliff Taylor, e-mail to Ron Modreski, 21 June 2007, http://www.attorneybutler.net/2008/10/if-cliff-taylor-loses-the-election-in-his-own-words.html.

Good fun. The e-mail communication had gone out to a list of 85 recipients.

Trentadue and the Common Law

We move from the *quasi*-personal to an opinion, publicly rendered—by Justice Corrigan. Remember along that way that two of the majority—Chief Justice Taylor and Justice Young—had been appointed to the Court of Appeals and then to the Supreme Court by John Engler, that most pro-business Governor, and that both Taylor and Young had practiced a lot of law for insurance companies.

And this story revolves around this question: How long is too long?

For many reasons, there are limits on the time one can wait to bring a civil lawsuit. The state's black-letter law, arrived at legislatively, had determined that in general, three years was enough to bring a civil action.

This is what the law says: "Except as *otherwise expressly provided* [emphasis added], the period of limitations runs from the time the claim accrues."[1007] And in Michigan, that period of limitations was three years for death or injury.[1008]

But what if you'd been wronged, knew you'd been wronged, but didn't know to what degree or by whom? How can you quantify the harm? How do you sue someone you can't identify? Can you file suit against a person or persons unknown? Have there been any exceptions to the three-year period?

Our tradition of common law said yes, there were exceptions. That tradition reached back hundreds of years in Great Britain. Very early on and until the Limitation Acts of 1540 and 1623, there were more or less perpetual rights to seek redress.[1009] Over the centuries, that limitation and other accommodations worked their way into the common law. That law was an inheritance from our forebears. And because it was the result of evolving practice and standards, it wasn't always tidy; determining the outer limit of time on bringing a lawsuit might depend on any number of factors.

> Traditional statutes of limitations begin to run when a cause of action first could have been maintained by the plaintiff. Normally, the wrongful act and

---

1007 Michigan Compiled Laws, Section 600.5827, http://www.legislature.mi.gov/ (S(e24a0w55l1pkxwj3tincrm45))/mileg.aspx?page=getobject&objectname=mcl-600-5827.
1008 Michigan Compiled Laws, Section 600.5805(10), http://www.legislature.mi.gov/ (S(1l3gdy45qk2o5t55zq5h1f45))/mileg.aspx?page=getobject&objectname=mcl-600-5805.
1009 Steven L. White, "Toward a time-of-discovery rule for the statute of limitations in latent injury cases in New York State," *Fordham Urban Law Journal*, Vol. 13, Issue 1, 1984, Article 5, 116, http://ir.lawnet.fordham. edu/cgi/viewcontent.cgi?article=1251&context=ulj&sei-redir=1&referer=http%3A%2F%2Fwww.google. com%2Furl%3Fsa%3Dt%26rct%3Dj%26q%3Dcommon%2520law%2520discovery%2520rule%26source %3Dweb%26cd%3D9%26ved%3D0CGwQFjAI%26url%3Dhttp%253A%252F%252Fir.lawnet.fordham. edu%252Fcgi%252Fviewcontent.cgi%253Farticle%253D1251%2526context%253Dulj%26ei%3DKa_5T5- BH4jW6wGKtKHhBg%26usg%3DAFQjCNEkcmF7dZOTpSQFpC5vK6osNiguAg#search=%22comm on%20law%20discovery%20rule%22.

injury occur simultaneously. For example, if a defendant negligently slams a door on a plaintiff's hand, the plaintiff has a cause of action at the moment the door was slammed. However, when the wrongful act and injury do not occur simultaneously, as in the case of injury from inhalation of asbestos fibers, ingestion of carcinogenic drugs or absorption of a toxic substance into the body, an injured plaintiff is faced with a complex problem: if the toxic substance produces injury which manifests itself several years after plaintiff's initial exposure to the substance, when does the cause of action accrue? The various judicial and legislative responses include decisions that the statute of limitations accrues when the wrongful act occurs, when the plaintiff is actually injured, when the plaintiff discovers the injury, and when the plaintiff discovers the causal connection between the injury and the defendant's conduct.

[...]

Modern statutes of limitations in the United States generally begin to run, in personal injury actions, when an individual's right of action first accrues, but only a few of the state statutes define "accrual." The question of when a cause of action begins to accrue has been determined judicially due to the absence of legislative designation.[1010]

The Michigan Supreme Court had repeatedly upheld (*stare decisis*) that the clock would begin to run <u>only</u> when someone was identified as the direct cause or a contributing cause of an injury. The period of limitations would be tolled, that is, held in abeyance.

Until this case, *Trentadue v Buckler Automatic Lawn Sprinkler Company*, the common law and the legislative law were thought in accord. The common and legislative law were about to be set at odds by the Engler Four as the majority parsed this case about the permissibility of allowing a suit that exceeded their understanding of laws pertaining to the period of limitations. The plaintiff had filed a complaint, but before it could go forward, the courts would have to make a determination whether she would be allowed to undertake discovery, the revelation of facts that might, eventually, lead to civil verdict.

The story began with a murder.

In 1981, Dr. Margaret Eby moved to Flint, Michigan, and began leasing a two-story gatehouse located near the entrance to the Ruth R. Mott estate (Mott Estate). Evidently Mrs. Mott lived a hermitic lifestyle on the Mott Estate grounds known as "Applewood." Virtually all her personal dealings were handled by the Mott Family Office (MFO).[1011]

1010 Ibid., 113.
1011 MFO was formed in 1969 to attend to the financial and personal needs of Ruth Mott, her children, and her nieces and nephews.

The gatehouse was remotely located some distance from Mrs. Mott's home and the gatehouse basement contained the valves and piping that supported the sprinkler system for the entire Mott Estate grounds. In January 1985, Dr. Eby complained to Mrs. Mott about break-ins she experienced at the gatehouse, including an incident on January 23, 1985, during which Dr. Eby's compact disc player and purse were stolen. Paul Yager, then the chief executive officer of MFO, responded to Dr. Eby's complaint on behalf of Mrs. Mott. In response to Dr. Eby's complaint and her request for installation of a security alarm system, Mrs. Mott had new deadbolt locks installed. No alarm system was installed.

Nearly two years later, late in the evening on November 7, 1986, Dr. Eby returned to the gatehouse after a dinner party. Two friends accompanied her to the gatehouse door and waited until she was safely inside before departing. Two days later, Dr. Eby was found dead in her gatehouse. She had been attacked, raped, and knifed to death. The police investigation of Dr. Eby's death focused primarily on persons who might have been known to Dr. Eby because there appeared to be no sign of forced entry. Police interviewed a number of suspicious persons, but there was never any evidence developed that implicated those persons in Dr. Eby's death. The evidence collected included deoxyribonucleic acid (DNA) evidence (semen) from Dr. Eby's body, as well as a partial fingerprint from a faucet inside the gatehouse.[1012]

Five years later, in 1991, flight attendant Nancy Ludwig was attacked and murdered in a hotel near Detroit Metropolitan Airport. There were remarkable similarities between her murder and Eby's murder. At the urging of Eby's son, testing revealed that DNA and fingerprints at both crime scenes belonged to the same individual. But there was nothing in the fingerprint or then-fledgling DNA database to link the evidence to any known individual. That would come later when one Jeffrey Gorton was arrested in Florida for yet another attack on a woman. Then everything lined up...the fingerprints and the DNA. Gorton was arrested, tried and found guilty for Ludwig's murder.[1013] He also was arrested and later pled no contest to the murder of Margaret Eby January 6, 2003.[1014] He was sentenced to life in prison.[1015]

While Gorton was not necessarily known to Eby, he had a reason to be in her home.

1012 Elizabeth A. Weaver dissent in *Trentadue v Buckler Automatic Lawn Sprinkler Company*, No. 128579, Michigan Supreme Court, 25 July 2007, 3, http://publicdocs.courts.mi.gov:81/OPINIONS/FINAL/SCT/20070725_S128579_81_trentadue4dec06-op.pdf.

1013 Suzette Hackney, "Man guilty is 1991 killing; jury convicts him in flight attendant's death," *Detroit Free Press*, 23 August 2002, B1.

1014 Associate Press, "Man Pleads no contest in 1986 rape, murder of Flint provost," *The Michigan Daily*, 8 January 2003, http://www.michigandaily.com/content/man-pleads-no-contest-1986-rape-murder-flint-provost.

1015 Melissa Stewart, "By the book: Three-year SOL for wrongful death claim controls, even where the killer's identity went undiscovered for 16 years," *Michigan Lawyers Weekly*, 6 August 2007, http://milawyersweekly.com/news/2007/08/06/by-the-book/.

Before Dr. Eby's death in 1986, Jeffrey Gorton was an employee of Buckler Automatic Lawn Sprinkler Company (Buckler), which serviced the Mott Estate's sprinkler system. Buckler was owned by Jeffrey Gorton's parents, Laurence and Shirley Gorton. Jeffrey Gorton was provided access to the sprinkler system controls housed in the gatehouse basement through Mott Estate staff members Victor Nyberg and Todd Bakos, both allegedly employed by MFO.[1016]

Gorton had unsupervised access to the home just two days before Eby's murder. The theory was that he had unlocked a window or a door to allow him entry to the home on the night of the murder.[1017]

Well, then, this is when the daughter [Dayle Trentadue] of the deceased lady knew <u>how</u> the crime occurred. They knew it did occur. They knew she was raped and murdered. They knew when it occurred. They did not know who did it and how that was accomplished until they had the DNA, and Gorton confessed.

Jeffrey Gorton was not new to crime. He'd been in prison in Florida on an assault and was released in 1985, just a year before Eby's murder. This according to Weaver in her dissent:

> Evidently Jeffrey Gorton had a history of violence against women and his felony convictions in Florida involved physical assaults on women. His paternal grandparents even appeared for his sentencing in Florida and begged the judge to permit Gorton to get psychiatric help for his violent outbursts against women. Yet, despite this knowledge, the Gortons employed their son in the family business and sent him to service the sprinklers at the Mott Estate.[1018]

Since the parents knew this, should they be subject to a liability? And, also, what was the role of the management company? What was the role for a safe premises for this lady? So a civil suit was filed within six months of when they found out what had happened and who did it.

> On August 2, 2002, six months after discovering the identity of Dr. Eby's murderer through the arrest of Gorton, plaintiff Dayle Trentadue, daughter of Dr. Eby and personal representative for the estate of Margarette F. Eby (Estate of Eby), filed a wrongful death complaint against multiple defendants. The defendants included Buckler, its owners Laurence and Shirley Gorton, Jeffrey Gorton, Ruth Mott, MFO, and MFO employees Nyberg and Bakos. The complaint alleged, among other things, negligent hiring and negligent supervision of Dr. Eby's killer, Jeffrey Gorton.

> With regard to her claims against the Mott Estate, MFO, and Nyberg and Bakos for negligent hiring and negligent supervision, plaintiff alleges that

---

1016 Elizabeth A. Weaver dissent.
1017 Melissa Stewart.
1018 Elizabeth A. Weaver dissent, footnote 6, 5.

on November 5, 1986, MFO employees Nyberg and Bakos provided Gorton with unsupervised access to the gatehouse basement to winterize the sprinklers, and that it was by this means that Gorton was subsequently able to come back on November 7 to attack and kill Dr. Eby. Moreover, despite Dr. Eby's earlier and repeated requests to defendants Ruth Mott and MFO to improve the security of the gatehouse, plaintiff alleges that defendants were negligent in failing to provide adequate security, thereby permitting Jeffrey Gorton's access to the gatehouse.[1019]

The issue before the Genesee County trial court was the length of time between the murder and the civil suit, 16 years. That term would be well over the statute of limitations...unless the common law, the equitable discovery rule, would hold sway.

From time immemorial, the common law has allowed for exceptions through what they call equitable estoppel[1020] on the ability to toll or freeze the running of the statute for reasons that are fair and just. And one of them historically has been—and they've been recognized in the Michigan law as a court rule that allowed for equitable estoppel—it's called a discovery rule, the Equitable Discovery Rule.

That, according to Weaver's rationale, should have stopped the clock. The reasoning was this: While Eby's estate was well aware that she had been murdered, police pursued a theory that she had known and admitted her attacker into her residence; there was, after all, no evidence of forced entry. Jeffrey Gorton hadn't even come up on their radar. Consequently, neither had Mrs. Mott, her estate management company, Gorton's parents, and their company. All that was concealed, unavailable to Dayle Trentaue in her efforts to have criminal and, later, civil justice.

The trial court held that the common law did apply and denied the motions from the defendants that said the clock had run.

The trial court allowed the application of that rule with respect to all the defendants, except on the one count of a safe premises—as to Mrs. Mott, I believe, and to the management company. And that meant that they would all go to trial on this. And what liability would they have if they were found negligent? The issue is negligence—then what the damages would be?

The defendant attorneys were basically the insurance companies—you know insurance was behind all of this; the insurance companies weren't sued, but they're funding, and they're going to have to pay. Needless to say, the defendants appealed.

The matter of the civil suit was idling at the trial court until the discovery issue was settled at a higher court or courts. If the discovery were allowed, the suit would move forward. (This was the same thing that had happened in *Dart v Dart*.)

1019 Elizabeth A. Weaver dissent, 5.
1020 Equitable estoppel in this case means the clock is fairly stopped until the facts of the case are made known.

And the matter went to the Court of Appeals. Sitting on this case were Judges Donald Owens, David Sawyer, and Helene White. The defendants again raised the issue of the statute of limitations. But the court noted the crucial element raised by Trentadue.

> Plaintiff argues that the discovery rule should apply because until Jeffrey Gorton's culpability for Eby's murder was discovered, there was no basis to assert breach of duty claims against Mott and MFO. Plaintiff asserts that, without the identity of Eby's murderer, there was no basis to assert any type of claim against the remaining defendants, Buckler, the Gortons, Nyberg, and Bakos, because their culpability was solely based on their specific job responsibilities or employment relationship to the murderer, Jeffrey Gorton.[1021]

The Court of Appeals, taking note of the prior decisions of the high court, affirmed that the discovery rule applied, citing the high court itself:

> As noted by our Supreme Court in addressing cases involving repressed memory of assault:

>> In those instances in which we have applied the common-law discovery rule to extend the statute of limitations, the dispute between parties has been based on evaluation of a factual, tangible consequence of action by the defendant, measured against an objective external standard. The presence of this external standard addresses the concern for reliable fact finding that is the underlying rationale for precluding untimely claims. [Lemmerman, supra, p 68.]

> Plaintiff 's claims against Buckler, the Gortons, Nyberg, and Bakos are neither speculative nor incapable of proof. Records pertaining to Jeffrey Gorton's employment, his prior criminal history, fingerprint and DNA evidence placing him within Eby's residence, and records verifying ties involving Buckler with access to the gatehouse by Nyberg and Bakos within days of the murder all constitute objective and verifiable evidence to support application of the discovery rule. Thus, the discovery rule applied to plaintiff 's claims against Buckler, the Gortons, Nyberg, Bakos, and Jeffrey Gorton.[1022]

The Court of Appeals also reversed the trial court's summary disposition to Mrs. Mott and MFO. However, it also found that it SHOULD have granted summary disposition to Nyberg and Bakos.[1023] With those stipulations, the Court of Appeals remanded the case to the trial court.

1021 *Trentadue v Buckler Automatic Lawn Sprinkler Company*, Michigan Court of Appeals, 5 May 2005, 3, http://publicdocs.courts.mi.gov:81/OPINIONS/FINAL/COA/20050324_C252155_79_690.252155.OPN.COA.PDF.
1022 Ibid., 5.
1023 Ibid., 5.

There would likely be millions at stake, and the defendants were not about to let that stand if they could help it. They applied for hearing at the Supreme Court.

Michigan Lawyers Weekly analyzed the situation:

> [A]rmed with an argument that under the common-law discovery rule, her claims tolled[1024] until she became aware of Gorton's identity in 2002, Trentadue initially withstood challenges in both the trial court and the Michigan Court of Appeals.

> However, her luck would not hold out once she reached the high court.[1025]

Boy, did it ever. The bad luck started with the Supreme Court even considering the case.

Now, then, this came to us, as the cases come, by an appeal to the Supreme Court, for us to decide whether to take it, and as always, this case was simply processed as a deny.

The commissioner said, "Deny," but gave what is called an alternative recommended order, knowing that there were those on the court that were not fond of the discovery rule—or the common law— particularly Justice Young. But the recommendation was to deny. It obviously got held—by at least one justice, and I think it was held by the Engler Four, but I wouldn't swear to which ones held. It got held. It got on the conference.

We had conference, and it was four-to-three to grant it, with Cavanagh, Kelly, and I saying, "Deny." And my notes, from day one said—and here's the original report of 4/14/06 with my notes—"Deny. No need to go into this. Justice was done." In any case, then it went to deferred grant, and it was granted.

So, the case was coming to the Supreme Court with all the parties, including lawyers who filed *amici* briefs representing individuals suffering from asbestos-related diseases, the State Bar of Michigan Negligence section, the Michigan Electric and Gas Association, Iron Workers Local 25 Pension Fund, and one other seeking to uphold the common law discovery rule. There were a lot of people who had interests in just this type of case.

It came up for oral argument in December of '06. That's an interesting time because it was argued either the 8th, 9th, or 10th, or some time in that time,[1026] and we had already had the December 6th "gag order" against me, with respect to my dissent that they suppressed in the AG v Fieger, so things were not terribly harmonious or what one would call collegial amongst the various justices.

1024 A toll is a delay in starting the clock ticking in the three-year period allowed by Michigan law.
1025 Melissa Stewart.
1026 According to a press release from Marcia McBrien, the *Trentadue* case was scheduled for the last argument of the morning of Dec. 12, 2006. [Marcia McBrien, "Rape-murder of university provost in 1986 is basis for civil suit before Michigan Supreme Court in oral arguments this week," Michigan Supreme Court, 11 December 2006. This was yet another document not included in the court's new website. It had been at http://courts.michigan.gov/supremecourt/Press/December2006orals.pdf.]

So we heard the argument. I always dictated after a hearing or oral arguments as to what I voted, what other people voted, what my thought about it was. And I continued to believe that the Court of Appeals got it right; the case should be affirmed, and we should even throw this case out; that leave was improperly granted, it was a mistake to grant in the first place, and so we should not even have an opinion. Just let it be.

I listened to them and just really realized that the Engler Four had no sense about justice and fairness. They were possessed, in my opinion, to overrule this kind of common law discovery rule that has had its basis for hundreds of years and had even been—within the last decades—affirmed by the court. And, further, it was very clear from the oral argument that they didn't understand that there is a place for equity—that there isn't a set of rigid rules. And even though the legislature had the power to definitively say to the courts under McDougall v Schanz *that the courts cannot have a discovery rule and had done so explicitly with medical malpractice, the legislature had not forbidden the discovery rule of three years for the general negligence cases.*

And *Trentadue* fell into that category. But it didn't matter to the majority.

It took seven months from the argument in December until, gosh—it came out July 25th, 2007. It was so much longer than somewhat similar cases, but with this case, there was a lot of writing going back and forth.

And the majority said three years were enough. Justice Corrigan wrote for the majority:

> We conclude that MCL 600.5827 alone controls. Because the Court of Appeals held to the contrary, we reverse its judgment and remand the case to the Genesee Circuit Court for further proceedings consistent with this opinion.[1027]

I wrote a dissent. Justice Cavanagh signed my dissent. Justice Kelly wrote a dissent. I agreed with parts of her dissent, and I think Justice Cavanagh did, too. We gave all the reasons why—how absurd and ridiculous and unjust it was to think that the legislature meant that a daughter whose mother had been murdered could not proceed in a suit even when there was no way and no reason that the daughter could know who she could sue. And it wouldn't be out of negligence on her part or failure to follow through. Instead, she would actually be barred from suing before she could know whom to sue because she did not know who had killed her mother.

This kind of case is what equity is for, these unique situations. Equity isn't applied very often. But it's a matter of common sense. This was a case of determination by the Engler Four to change the law—which, by the way, certainly protected the insurance companies, who were vast supporters of the Four, and who also have a distaste for the common law. The common law certainly can be misused, and has been misused—it was before and maybe will be again—but that's why we need more openness and less secrecy on the Supreme Court: so that after all is said and done, justices can be held accountable for how they reached an absurd unjust decision overruling centuries of the common law discovery rule which the legislature had not forbidden for three-year general negligence cases.

1027 *Trentadue v Buckler Automatic Lawn Sprinkler Company*, Michigan Supreme Court, 25 July 2007, 1, http://publicdocs.courts.mi.gov:81/OPINIONS/FINAL/SCT/20070725_S128579_81_trentadue4dec06-op.pdf.

In her opinion, Corrigan noted what she and the others were doing in overturning previously decided cases:

> Overruling these cases is the most appropriate course of action because they run directly counter to the legislative scheme.[1028]

So, the majority had intuited the intent of the legislature and determined the law ran "directly counter to the legislative scheme"? An interesting presumption.

That's reaching out to get the result they wanted. And this was not based on fact; they were doing it by intuition and unjustified presumption.

In her opinion, Corrigan went on:

> We have already explained that the statutory law and its changes over time cause us to question the validity of court-imposed applications of the discovery rule. Most significantly, the nature of the discovery rule contravenes any argument that our decision affects plaintiffs' reliance interests. A plaintiff does not decide to postpone asserting a claim because he relies on the availability of extrastatutory discovery-based tolling.[1029] To the contrary, discovery-based tolling is a retroactive mechanism for relief to be used only when a plaintiff could not anticipate his claims. To the extent reliance interests figure into the analysis, it is the expectations of defendants—including those who, as here, may have had as little indication that a claim existed as did the plaintiff—that are harmed when a plaintiff brings claims long after an event occurred. Defendants must, at some point, be able to safely dispose of business records and other seemingly mundane evidence that they would have no reason to expect could exculpate them in litigation.[1030]

"Mundane evidence"? This had been an open murder case. The records would have been kept in any event until the case either was solved or the case was closed by extraordinary measures—such as at the direction of a prosecuting attorney in cases that are too old to further be prosecuted. And those documents and business records would have had to have been kept in any event.

To counter all of Corrigan's arguments, Weaver had even supplied a black-letter way for the common law discovery rule to stand. That rule, MCL 600.5855, states:

> If a person who is or may be liable for any claim fraudulently conceals the existence of the claim or the identity of any person who is liable for the claim from the knowledge of the person entitled to sue on the claim, the action may be commenced at any time within two years after the person who is en-

---

1028 Ibid., 14.
1029 *How would she know this? He or she postpones the claim because he or she doesn't know who to sue. What she had written was gobbledygook.*
1030 Ibid., 14.

titled to bring the action discovers, or should have discovered, the existence of the claim or the identity of the person who is liable for the claim, although the action would otherwise be barred by the period of limitations.[1031]

What had Jeffrey Gorton been doing if not committing a fraud? He was trying to avoid his ties to the crime and punishment. Weaver cited the law in her dissent and the majority overrode it. First, Corrigan had claimed it was related to medical malpractice. It wasn't. Then she asserted:

> If we may simply apply an extrastatutory discovery rule in any case not addressed by the statutory scheme, we will render § 5855 effectively meaningless. For, under a general extrastatutory discovery rule, a plaintiff could toll the limitations period simply by claiming that he reasonably had no knowledge of the tort or the identity of the tortfeasor.[1032] He would never need to establish that the claim or tortfeasor had been fraudulently concealed.[1033]

In assessing the situation, *Michigan Lawyers Weekly* added this dismal note:

> As a final blow to the common-law discovery rule, Corrigan concluded her analysis by applying her decision retroactively.
>
> In ruling that "prospective-only application is inappropriate," she said "the very purpose of our holding is to respect limits the legislature has placed on plaintiffs' abilities to revive suits relying on events occurring in the distant past[.]"[1034]

It was a tragedy. The trial court got it right, a very fine trial court; a very independent group on the Court of Appeals got it right. But there were four votes that were determined. It was just inexplicable to me—and I wonder if it was because none of them had any experience as trial court judges.

But was this a case of the high court making law?

Absolutely. For those people reaching out to change established law because they could and they wanted to, and they didn't see that there was nothing just or fair about it, and that the law had long been established. They just decided to stretch their interpretation of what the legislature meant in its language.

Naturally enough, the plaintiff asked for a rehearing just in case enlightenment might have settled over the court in the interim.

1031 Michigan Compiled Laws 600.5855, http://www.legislature.mi.gov/(S(lzph0euuok55r03ivpumph45))/mileg.aspx?page=getobject&objectname=mcl-600-5855.
1032 A tortfeasor is a person who commits a tort, a civil wrong.
1033 *Trentadue v Buckler Automatic Lawn Sprinkler Company*, 12.
1034 Melissa Stewart, "By the book: Three-year SOL for wrongful death claim controls, even where the killer's identity went undiscovered for 16 years," *Michigan Lawyers Weekly*, 6 August 2007, http://milawyer-sweekly.com/news/2007/08/06/by-the-book/.

I, Justice Cavanagh, and Justice Kelly said we would grant rehearing.

Denied.

In her dissent to the denial of rehearing, Weaver in part repeated the conclusion of her dissent to the opinion:

> I dissent from the majority of four's decision to deny plaintiffs' motion for a rehearing and repeat the concluding paragraph of my dissent from the majority's opinion in this case, issued July 25, 2007:
>
>> Because I disagree with the majority's conclusion that with the enactment of the Revised Judicature Act, the legislature sought to abrogate the discovery rule, I would affirm the Court of Appeals decision applying the common-law discovery rule and tolling the period of limitations where plaintiff could not have reasonably discovered the elements of a wrongful death cause of action within the limitations period. [*Trentadue v Buckler Automatic Lawn Sprinkler Co*, 479 Mich 378, 407 (2007) (Weaver, J., dissenting).]
>
> Clearly, the majority of four's decision in this case reaches an absurd and unjust result, and lacks common sense.[1035]

And that was my opinion on it, and that is my opinion on it still.

The result would be one of the court's most far-reaching decisions, both in terms of impact and by the stretch of the law to reach the decision. A shockwave went through the legal community.

In the case of the 1979 murder of Hope College student Janet Chandler,[1036] it meant that there was no opportunity to discover just what—if any—complicity Wackenhut Security played in the 27-year delay in solving her murder. All five men sent to prison for her abduction, beating, rape, and strangulation murder were Wackenhut guards. Carl Paiva was the head of the guard detail. He also planned the crime, and—claiming he "didn't want sloppy seconds"—led the assault. Once the criminal case was settled, Janet's parents, Jim and Glenna Chandler, through attorney Rob Gaecke, filed suit in federal district court. They were denied hearing there and appealed to the Sixth Circuit Court of Appeals. Judges R. Guy Cole, Jr., John M. Rogers, and Martha Craig Daughtrey heard the appeal in December of 2011. Judge Daughtrey saw her way to allow discovery, but the other two held sway in their denial. Judge Cole, however, noted his reservations:

1035 Denial of rehearing, *Trentadue v Buckler Automatic Lawn Sprinkler Company*, Michigan Supreme Court, 28 September 2007, http://coa.courts.mi.gov/documents/sct/public/orders/20070928_s128579_85_128579_2007-09-28_or.pdf.
1036 This was first mentioned in the Introduction.

When a federal court hears a case due to the diversity of the litigants, it must apply substantive state, not federal, law. As a general matter, this principle furthers justice by ensuring litigants the same outcome regardless of which court hears their claims. At times, however, this principle ties us to law we believe to be erroneous. Sadly, this is one such case.

Today, our hands are tied by a rope woven from the pages of the Michigan Supreme Court's decision in *Trentadue*. To give James and Glenna Chandler their day in court, as they surely deserve, Michigan law requires us to find that Arthur Paiva's actions were within the scope of his employment with Wackenhut. For the reasons stated in the majority opinion, I am unable to do so. I regretfully concur.[1037]

Only one case would thereafter surface to challenge the court's decision, that of Connie Colaianni in her suit against Stuart Frankel Development Corporation, et al. The case served as a direct challenge to the *Trentadue* decision.

In his dissent to granting leave in 2010, Justice Young wrote that *Trentadue* had settled the issue, and he saw no sense taking up the argument yet again:

I believe that case was correctly decided. While it is certainly the prerogative of the court to reconsider this case, this order is another instance where the majority seems to retreat from its previously stated fidelity to *stare decisis*.[1038]

He neglected to note that his earlier decision in *Trentadue* had turned the common law upside down. He was joined by Justice Corrigan. Somehow Justice Markman didn't sign on.

The votes were there—four votes to grant it—so he didn't need to sign on in the dissent. He's a very much behind-the-scenes kind of guy.

But it was accepted by the court 5-2 and then argued October 7, 2010.[1039] That was after the Engler Four had been reduced to the Engler Three (after Chief Justice Taylor was voted off the court). By the time the matter was to be decided, Alton "Tom" Davis had taken Weaver's spot on the court. It's likely the votes were there to overturn *Trentadue*, but the matter was settled out of court, and the appeal was dismissed before the decision was announced.[1040]

1037 R. Guy Cole, Jr., concurrence, *Chandler v Wackenhut Corp.*, No. 10-1211, U.S. Sixth Circuit Court of Appeals, 27, http://www.ca6.uscourts.gov/opinions.pdf/12a0200n-06.pdf.
1038 Robert P. Young, Jr. writing in dissent, Leave granted, *Connie Colaianni v Stuart Frankel Development Corp.*, No. 139350, 29 January 2010, http://publicdocs.courts.mi.gov:81/sct/public/orders/20100129_s139350_54_139350_2010-01-29_or.pdf.
1039 Marcia McBrien, "Father whose parental rights were terminated seeks ruling he is not liable for child support; Michigan Supreme Court to hear case next week during first oral arguments of 2010-2011 term," Michigan Supreme Court, 1 October 2010, 15. This is yet another document lost in the website reorganization. It was at http://courts.michigan.gov/supremecourt/Press/October2010orals.pdf.
1040 Order to dismiss, *Connie Colaianni v Stuart Frankel Development Corp.*, No. 139350 & (50), Michigan

Well, somehow it became clear to the defendants and their insurers that they might get a result that would not be favorable to them, not only to them individually in that case, but to all insurance companies, because potentially you would have the discovery rule, assuming there were four votes now that would uphold it. Then Trentadue would be reversed. It would put discovery back in, and it would allow for this fairness to the average citizen and to every person in Michigan, and to the system in these unique circumstances—of which there are not many—to allow the discovery rule to continue.

Attack on the Common Law

Justice Young, in joining the majority on *Trentadue*, didn't then and there publicly raise the issue of his take on the common law. He'd done that earlier in a speech to the Federalist Society that was later printed in the *Texas Review of Law and Politics*. The common law, he said and wrote, was a real problem, and he wanted to focus his remarks...

> [...] on the embarrassment that the common law presents—or ought to present—to a conscientious judicial traditionalist. This idea that the common law authorizes judicial law making—and I believe this to be a fairly uniform understanding in contemporary judicial circles in America—has been regnant in Michigan in fact, if not in self-description, since we entered the Union. Yet this so-called warrant to make law should make any self-confessed judicial traditionalist extremely uncomfortable.
>
> To give a graphic illustration of my feelings on the subject, I tend to think of the common law as a drunken, toothless ancient relative, sprawled prominently and in a state of nature on a settee in the middle of one's genteel garden party. Grandpa's presence is undoubtedly a cause of mortification to the host. But since only the most ill-bred of guests would be coarse enough to comment on Grandpa's presence and condition, all concerned simply try to ignore him.
>
> Like the attendees at my imaginary garden party, common-law apologists have spent centuries denying that Grandpa was actually in attendance or, if so acknowledged, vigorously asserting that he was actually clothed and sober. Indeed, some jurists like Justice Cardozo actually celebrate Grandpa and his condition and enthusiastically urge all of us to relax, undress, and join Grandpa in his inebriated communion with nature.
>
> As is the case with young children unschooled in social niceties, legal realists have been pointing and making a regular fuss about the fact that there is a frightening, drunken old man laying about with no clothes on. And like that

Supreme Court, 29 December 2010, http://publicdocs.courts.mi.gov:81/sct/public/orders/20101229_s139350_75_139350_2010-12-29_or.pdf.

child, I too acknowledge that this modern conception of the common law that authorizes jurists to discover, create, or modify common-law rules—or policy—is entirely inconsistent with normative constitutional policies and principles, according to which prerogatives of policymaking are given to other branches of government.[1041]

Young makes leaps of logic throughout the piece. Here's an example: "Indeed, it is hard for me, a jurist of the 21st Century, to consider that the common law is 'law' in any conventional sense."[1042] That's his dismissal of nearly a thousand years of convention.

He goes on. One of the problems, he wrote, was that common-law jurists have for centuries been finding fixed, natural principles. Further, he asserted the judiciary was "largely institutionally incompetent—or at the very least, severely 'challenged'—to make sound policy choices."[1043] That should be left, he wrote, to the legislatures or other rule-making bodies. Finally, he wrote, natural law actually goes so far as to undermine the courts' abilities to make those choices.

> Now, this screed from a jurist who obviously has participated in decisions altering Michigan's common law may seem surprising. But I believe that we jurists ought to be candid with the public about what we do and how we do it. The fact is, the common-law tradition I inherited provides my colleagues and me with little more than our own personal instincts and judgments about when, how, and how much to address common-law issues. This reality is—and should be—a profoundly unsettling thing to all but those who believe that judges should be our society's philosopher kings.[1044]

In the end, though, he did draw back a little.

> Among the principles of conservancy that my court is developing and following is the notion that, if the common law rule being challenged is one of long standing, and if that rule does not appear to be creating significant turbulence in the legal environment (e.g., difficulty of consistent application), one ought not make a change in the absence of the most Herculean showing of need.[1045]

The need in *Trentadue* must have been just that, Herculean. Or, perhaps, Sisyphean. Or, biblical.

Young's rhetoric, his choice of metaphor and mockery, may be more revealing than he realized. Before the fall 2010 election that saw Young returned to the bench and

---

1041 Robert P. Young, Jr., "State Jurisprudence, the role of the courts, and the rule of law: The Federalist Society: Panel II: A judicial traditionalist confronts the common law," *Texas Review of Law and Politics*, 2, Spring 2004, http://dignitas.typepad.com/Texas.Review.of.Law.and.Politics--Young.pdf.
1042 Ibid., 2.
1043 Ibid., 3.
1044 Ibid.
1045 Ibid., 4.

eventually in 2011 to achieve the position of chief justice, co-author Schock wrote about Young's rhetorical choices:

> It brings to mind a thought: who among us that professes filial piety—the respect for our parents, grandparents, ancestors—would leave our drunken Grandpa sprawled naked? Would we not try to clothe him in a blanket and cover his nakedness? Would we not do everything in our power to restore him to wholeness, even if it means waiting while he sobers? If we had any respect for him and all he represents would we not keep him from censure and mockery?[1046]

There were plenty of others who over the years have weighed in on Young's writing. Jules B. Olsman, writing in the *State Bar of Michigan Negligence Law Section Quarterly* claimed a 30-year friendship with Young, but said, notwithstanding, the common law issue needed to be aired:

> One might charitably suggest that Justice Young's comments in the *Texas Law Review* article represent little more than him "heaving a side of beef" to the carnivores at a Federalist Society convention. That would be arguable but for the fact that his comments have found their way into the *stare decisis* of Michigan Supreme Court cases.[1047]

They had.

Judge Jennifer Faunce

Here is the last of the four stories in this chapter of collected tales.

Like Maura Corrigan before him, Chief Justice Cliff Taylor could be heavy handed with trial court judges in order to get his way. This order from Oct. 18, 2008, tells its own complete story:

> On order of the Court, effective immediately, the Honorable John M. Chmura is appointed chief judge of the 37th District Court,[1048] for completion of a term ending December 31, 2009.

> Statement by Weaver, J. (dissenting). I dissent from the administrative order appointing Judge John Chmura as Chief Judge of the 37th District Court. I would appoint Judge Jennifer Faunce as chief judge. Former state Representative Judge Faunce is currently the chief judge pro tem and is best qualified to handle the responsibilities of chief judge.

1046 David B. Schock, "October 1, 2010—Justice Young: 'You're Done!,'" My MI Court, 1 October 2010, http://www.mymicourt.com/?p=7.
1047 Jules B. Olsman, "I went to a Garden Party," *State Bar of Michigan Negligence Law Section Quarterly*, Winter 2009, 1, http://www.michbar.org/negligence/pdfs/winter09.pdf.
1048 The 37th District Court included the cities of Warren and Centerline, Macomb County.

Initially, both Judge Chmura and Judge Faunce submitted their names for consideration for the chief judge position. On October 7, 2008, State Court Administrator Carl Gromek sent a copy of Judge Faunce's fax, dated October 7, withdrawing her name from consideration for the chief judge position. Based on this information, I telephoned Judge Faunce's office on October 7 in the late afternoon to inquire about her withdrawal. She was not available at that time, so I left a message for her to call me if she would like to discuss the matter.

The following morning, October 8, at approximately 9:15 a.m., Judge Faunce returned my call. When I inquired as to why she withdrew, she told me that she was informed that she did not have the votes to be appointed. Therefore, she withdrew her name from consideration. I expressed to her that I had planned to vote for her and would continue to do so at the administrative conference. She stated that she would appreciate my casting my vote for her and thanked me for my support.

At the October 8, 2008, administrative conference at approximately 10:20 a.m., Chief Justice Taylor announced that there was only one candidate remaining for the chief judge position. At that point, Justice Kelly asked if anyone knew why Judge Faunce had withdrawn. Chief Justice Taylor explained that he was of the view that there were four (4) votes for Judge Chmura, and that he had decided to call Judge Faunce to inform her that there were four votes for Judge Chmura and that Judge Faunce was welcome to withdraw or stay, but that he did not want her to be embarrassed because there were four votes for Judge Chmura and she would lose. Chief Justice Taylor related that Judge Faunce told him that she would withdraw her name and she did so.

Chief Justice Taylor's action of telling Judge Faunce that there were four votes for Judge Chmura and that Judge Faunce was welcome to withdraw or stay, before the justices had ever met to discuss and vote on the chief judge appointment, is another example of his unprofessional, improper, and unfair conduct as chief justice.

Chief Justice Taylor's actions effectively interfered with the chief judge appointment process because what he told Judge Faunce during his telephone call caused her to withdraw her name before the justices of this court had even met to discuss the appointment.

Chief Justice Taylor has too often mismanaged the business of this court. Harmful to the proper functioning of the justice system is Chief Justice Taylor's inclination to act secretly, not openly and transparently with respect to the administrative business of this court. Administrative appointments of chief judges—judges who are elected public officials—constitute public administrative business, not personnel matters. Judges are not employees of the Michigan Supreme Court. They are elected officials of their counties or jurisdictions and are effectively only employees of the people of their counties or jurisdictions within the state of Michigan. This inclination toward secrecy also deprives the people of the information they need to properly make judgments on the justices' performance of their duties. The Supreme Court should not be a secret club run for the benefit of justices and judges.[1049]

Oh, and Weaver said that the goal in every chief judge selection was always to have two people who were willing to serve. So, there would always be a winner and a loser. And in the various courts around the state, the judges who found themselves in the selection process somehow managed to work it out without a lot of rancor.

1049 "Appointment of Chief Judge of the 37th District Court," ADM File No. 2008-01, 14 October 2008, http://www.justiceweaver.com/pdfs/2008-01_10-14-08Chmura_order.pdf.

Chapter 21

Punish Another Judge!
Protecting the Inept

The Trials of Judge Pamela Gilbert O'Sullivan

The Engler majority was no place close to done messing about in local courts. They were, after all, supremely in charge. And this story is about corruption within the probate court in Macomb County.

It's a book itself: the failure to do right, covering up mistakes, wasting taxpayer money, the continuation of problems that could have been solved easily, and the willingness to make scapegoats and to place blame on people that aren't to blame. All because of wanting to keep from being known what really occurred.

And as a result, it mushroomed, and I'm not sure that it's been solved yet. It deals with judges and their performance or lack of performance. It's a very complicated story, but the bottom-line of it is, great injustice and very dastardly acts were done by people in authority, and not ultimately to solve the problem; and good people ended up doing bad things.

There also were enough bad people doing bad things, too, though.

It also involved the temptations to be enriched by having work to do—paid for by the taxpayers— that didn't need to be done.

Judge Pamela Gilbert O'Sullivan was first elected to the Macomb County Probate Court in 1994. Weaver met her on the campaign trail—Weaver, running for the Supreme Court and O'Sullivan for the probate court. The two really got to know each other when Governor John Engler appointed O'Sullivan to the Governor's Task Force on Child Abuse and Neglect that Weaver chaired.[1050]

So I saw her abilities there as an early member of the task force. We no longer serve, but Judge O'Sullivan had been limited in her activity on the task force for a number of years because she had such huge problems over at Macomb.

1050About the Task Force, Governor's Task Force on Child Abuse and Neglect, http://www.michigan.gov/gtfcan/0,4588,7-195--155595--,00.html.

In 2000, she was named the county's chief judge of probate, a post she would hold until 2007, when it would be taken from her.

Early on as chief judge, she found some things that shouldn't have been. In a Nov. 3, 2008 letter to then-Chief Justice Taylor, O'Sullivan laid out what had occurred:

> For example, in 2001 I learned of several issues regarding the probate court's prior practices that concerned me, including the prior judge's use of "referees" in a "quasi judicial" capacity without statutory authority. I requested a review of these practices by the State Court Administrator (then John D. Ferry) and received a report containing recommendations on February 13, 2002. We implemented each recommendation.
>
> In 2002 I suspected possible misappropriation of county funds by the then-court administrator, Leonard Reinowski and Probate Judge James F. Nowicki. I contacted [the] State Court Administrator's Office and Macomb County corporate counsel and asked for investigation and review. The Michigan Supreme Court audited the finances and the State Court Administrator's Office reviewed the court's practice of handling "petty cash." As a result of the investigation, administrator Leonard Reinowski was fired (he was later allowed to retire) and Judge Nowicki retired. Further, we implemented every recommendation of the State Court Administrator's Office and the Macomb County Finance Department.
>
> In 2003, I heard allegations of mishandling of court guardianship and conservatorship cases by a Macomb County agency assigned by the court to act as guardian and/or conservator of wards (Macomb County Department of Senior Services). I requested an investigation by the State Court Administrator's Office, Macomb County corporation counsel, the Michigan State Police, and the Macomb County prosecutor's office. As a result of this investigation, the agency was removed from every case and a Macomb County Department of Senior Services employee and another involved person were convicted of felony charges. The court implemented new practices and procedures to provide a more strict oversight.
>
> On September 5, 2003, I summarized the progress made by the Macomb County Probate Court in addressing the court's compliance with statutes and court rules. This progress report was provided to then-Chief Justice Maura Corrigan and was received without contradiction. Subsequent to these investigations I again requested an audit to verify that the court's practices and procedures were consistent with statutory and court rule requirements.[1051]

1051 Pamela Gilbert O'Sullivan, letter to Chief Justice Clifford W. Taylor, 3 November 2008, http://www.mymicourt.com/?p=27. And in the interest of full disclosure, the co-author acknowledges that he edited this letter for Judge O'Sullivan.

But there was big trouble ahead. Judge O'Sullivan resumed:

> In spite of all this progress, there were problems in the court. In particular, beginning in January 2003 when Judge Kathryn George took office, she was—in my assessment—not able to do the job. She referred to the job as "part-time" and asked when she had to be here. As chief judge, I tried to find ways to improve her performance. I continued to request the assistance of the State Court Administrator's Office in addressing these issues—and others—within the court. On numerous occasions I had conversations with, sent correspondence to, and relayed faxes to the State Court Administrator's Office in an effort to seek its assistance in addressing continuing problems regarding Judge George's failure or refusal to comply with the court's practices, policies, and procedures. Without State Court Administrator's Office support, the situation simply did not improve.
>
> In September, 2003, I sent a letter to Chief Justice Corrigan indicating that I was no longer requesting the chief judge appointment. Subsequently, Chief Justice Corrigan called to ask why I was withdrawing my request to be chief judge. I outlined in great detail the problems with Judge George. Chief Justice Corrigan requested time to look into the matter. She called back indicating that she was aware of the situation and asked that I reconsider accepting the chief judge appointment with her assurance that something be done about the problem. I agreed to do whatever she would request of me. Shortly after I received a call from [Regional Court Administrator] Ms. [Deborah] Green asking how soon I could be prepared for the assignment of Judge George to Wayne County.
>
> Ultimately Judge George was assigned to Genesee County. Judge George remained in Genesee County for approximately six (6) months while visiting judges (including retired Judge [Kenneth] Sanborn) were assigned to Macomb County to fill her absence. The Supreme Court reimbursed Macomb County over $30,000 for the compensation for the visiting judges. I was reappointed to serve as chief judge for 2004-2005. When Judge George returned from Genesee County, the situation grew worse.
>
> Once again, I contacted the State Court Administrator's Office for help in addressing the continuing problems with Judge George.[1052]

By that time, though, the mantle had passed from Ferry to Carl Gromek. Suddenly, things were different. In her recitation of further contacts with the SCAO, she found no ready help. "In particular," she wrote:

> • The State Court Administrator's Office was advised of concerns regarding Judge George's attendance as evidenced in the Judicial Absence Reports

---

1052 Ibid.

(which were filed annually). These reports showed excessive absences, yet the State Court Administrator's Office took no action.

• I contacted the State Court Administrator's Office regarding Judge George's excessive adjournments. I informed the State Court Administrator's Office that Judge George insisted on adjourning all of her cases when I would cover for her and would continue to adjourn her cases unless I brought in a visiting judge to cover. This made it difficult to provide coverage because she would not let me handle her cases.

The State Court Administrator's Office took no action.

• The State Court Administrator's Office was contacted on numerous occasions regarding Judge George's refusal to appoint *guardians ad litem* from the court's list and the excessive GAL appointments being made by Judge George on her files.

The State Court Administrator's Office took no action.

• I expressed on numerous occasions concerns regarding Judge George's appointment of ADDMS/Alan Polack on files and what appeared to be a mishandling of these files by ADDMS/Alan Polack.

The State Court Administrator's Office took no action.

It was clear to me that the State Court Administrator's Office was no longer going to provide assistance or support for the Macomb County Probate Court especially in addressing problems arising out of Judge George's actions. Still, I tried one more time. In January of 2006, I met with Mr. Gromek, Regional Court Administrator Ms. Deborah Green, Judge George and Macomb County Court Administrator Mr. Donald J. Housey.[1053] I had hoped the meeting would provide an opportunity to discuss the continuing problems of Judge George's performance and receive assistance from the State Court Administrator's Office.

What happened next was outside my expectations. At the meeting, Mr. Gromek yelled at me that "This is bullshit and you should be ashamed of yourself. If I hear any more of this, I'm going to remove you as chief judge. Am I clear?" He was very clear. It was very clear to me that the State Court Administrator did not want to hear of any more problems or my court's concerns. It was disheartening to conclude that he would be of no assistance. That was our last meeting. I did not hear again from the court's regional administrator for almost two years until December of 2007 when Ms. Green

---

1053 Donald J. Housey not only corroborated O'Sullivan's story but played an active role. He had run in the 2002 primary for probate judge and had lost to George. As the Macomb County Probate Court Administrator, he was responsible for documenting and reporting lapses in Judge George's conduct on the bench.

called to tell me that Judge George had been appointed as Chief Judge of Probate in Macomb County effective January 2008.[1054]

The Supreme Court had taken an action that would seem counterintuitive. They stripped O'Sullivan of the chief judgeship and gave it to the inept Kathryn George. As usual, Weaver didn't go along with the majority.

I didn't become aware of the situation in Macomb County until the 2007 appointments. We would appoint the chief judges for all of these courts in the state. Most of them were routine, but there would usually end up anywhere from five to twenty that would be called controversial. Macomb County was put aside as one of those.

The recommendations, Weaver said, were prepared by Carl Gromek's office.

There was a recommendation to the justices, and it said something about O'Sullivan having been there a long time, which was fine, but also that there had been some not getting along, supposedly, between these people.

I happened to see an article in the Detroit News that was saying that there was trouble over there about the administration of estates, and that Judge George was involved, and she was the one that was being recommended to be appointed the chief judge. What was really interesting to me was this information—this newspaper article—wasn't in the report to us about appointing her.

So it was of concern to me. And I raised it at the appointment conference, "Hey what about this article? We're appointing somebody that's being accused—at least reported that there are problems with her handling of these guardianships and conservatorships, and some group that is apparently profiting from being assigned to do the work involved but not doing it well."

By that time, Weaver had done some independent fact finding and also raised the issues of Judge George's transfer to other counties to learn her job, the expense to the state—some $30,000—reimbursing Macomb County while Judge George was learning in Genesee County. That plan had been arranged by the State Court Administrator's Office.[1055]

George's qualifications were fairly thin: she'd served on the Sterling Heights City Council for a time (1999-2000) and been appointed by Governor Blanchard to the Michigan Worker's Compensation Appeal Board in 1989. Prior to becoming an attorney, she'd worked as a critical care nurse in California, Michigan, and the U.S. Embassy in Kuwait. In 2007, she was inducted into the Macomb County Hall of Fame.[1056]

Contrasting all that was Weaver's summary of Judge O'Sullivan's qualifications:

1054 Pamela Gilbert O'Sullivan.
1055 Elizabeth A. Weaver writing in concurrence of Appointment of Chief Judge of Macomb County Probate County, ADM file No. 2008-01, Michigan Supreme Court, 11 June, 2008, http://www.justiceweaver.com/pdfs/2008-01-Macomb.pdf.
1056 "Judge Kathryn A. George," Macomb County website, http://macombcountymi.gov/probatecourt/george_bio.htm.

Judge O'Sullivan has served on the Macomb County Probate Court bench for nearly 13 years, and has also excellently served the past seven-plus years as chief judge, since her initial appointment as chief judge in 1999, and for successive appointments by this court as chief judge in 2001, 2003, and 2005.

In addition to her nearly 13 years of bench experience, Judge O'Sullivan is a member of the Michigan Judicial Institute faculty and also sits on the Institute's Academic Advisory Committee. Since 1999, she has served on the Governor's Task Force on Children's Justice, having been appointed to that position first by Governor Engler, and then by Governor Granholm. Also in 1999, Judge O'Sullivan established the second Juvenile Drug Court in the state of Michigan. In addition, she serves as a State Court Administrative Office-approved general civil mediator, and serves on various community boards of directors including: 1) Care house—Child Advocacy Center, 2) CARE—Community Assessment and Referral Education, 3) Human Services Coordinating Body, 4) Macomb County Traffic Safety Commission, and 5) Childhelp, USA.[1057]

Oh, and Judge O'Sullivan had never been sent for remedial training nor had she asked if her job were part time.

It didn't seem to matter; George was appointed chief judge. That appointment would prove temporary.

Returning to the letter O'Sullivan sent to Taylor laying out the course of events, she resumed that even though she was no longer chief judge, she was still striving for right conduct for her county:

That doesn't mean that I didn't continue to alert the State Court Administrator's Office of problems, issues, and concerns. I did so through Barry Joseph—who had become our contact person and who consistently assured us that "the matter will be discussed with Deb Green."

In early 2008, there was yet another Whall Group audit[1058] performed on the Macomb County Probate Court. The findings of the audit released in May of 2008 reported serious irregularities in Judge George's conduct, including those I had raised to the State Court Administrator's Office almost two years earlier. The report also said I should have provided better oversight as chief judge. How much more oversight could I have provided?[1059]

1057 Elizabeth A. Weaver, dissent to the Appointment of Kathryn A. George as chief judge of Macomb County Probate Court, Michigan Supreme Court, 20 November 2007, unpublished.
1058 An extensive 2005 audit by that group turned up no major problems and under O'Sullivan's leadership implemented almost all the suggestions. [Pamela Gilbert O'Sullivan.]
1059 Pamela Gilbert O'Sullivan.

The Whall Group report of 2008 made special note of the antipathy between Judges George and O'Sullivan. According to Jameson Cook of the *Macomb Daily*, the report, cited in a subsequent decision by U.S. District Judge Avern Cohn:

> ...found noncompliance with court rules and procedures in 75 percent of audited cases and that a "substantial number of cases handled by ADDMS lacked adequate accounting for assets and income," Cohn notes. The judges' animosity grew to "dysfunction," the Whall Group said.

> The state Attorney General investigated but did not pursue a case.[1060]

But this was plenty serious. The Engler Four realized they had made a big mistake, and they were going to have to undo it. That meant removing George as chief judge and putting a caretaker chief judge in her place. That occurred June 11, 2008. The Engler Four hated to admit any fallibility on their parts and would have done nearly anything to avoid this measure. They also knew there would be an "I told you so." Weaver wrote:

> I concur in the removal of Judge Kathryn A. George as Chief Judge of the Macomb County Probate Court, and I concur in the order appointing retired circuit and former probate Judge Kenneth N. Sanborn as acting Chief Judge of the Macomb County Probate Court. The damage that has occurred to the vulnerable Macomb County citizens needing guardian and conservator services to protect them and their property must cease and those responsible must be held accountable. With the removal of Judge George as chief judge and the appointment of Judge Sanborn, acting Chief Judge Sanborn can focus on protecting the most vulnerable citizens of Macomb County needing guardians and conservators, and focus on getting to the truth about the administration of the Macomb County Probate Court and how the damage occurred.

> At the time that this court first considered whether to appoint Judge George as chief judge during the November 14, 2007, administrative conference, the court lacked sufficient information about certain events and actions concerning Judge George. Consequently, the majority of four of this Court (Chief Justice Taylor, and Justices Corrigan, Young, and Markman) should have refrained from selecting her as chief judge. Like Justices Cavanagh and Kelly, I voted for Chief Judge Pamela O'Sullivan to continue serving as chief judge because she had served well as the chief judge for almost eight years and to allow for independent investigation of the cloud hanging over Judge George's performance as a probate judge and her appointments of ADDMS Guardianship, Inc. (ADDMS).

> [...]

1060 Jameson Cook, "Fired Macomb Probate Court official's lawsuit tossed by judge," *The Macomb Daily*, 17 May 2012, http://www.macombdaily.com/article/20120517/NEWS01/120519586/fired-macomb-probate-court-official-s-lawsuit-tossed-by-judge&pager=full_story.

And while I would agree that there appears to be an acrimonious relationship between Judge George and Judge O'Sullivan, I disagree with SCA Gromek's assertion that the report establishes that Judge O'Sullivan is at fault. On the contrary, the report confirms not only Judge George's apparent inappropriate involvement with ADDMS guardian services, but also her apparent failure to properly oversee numerous guardianship cases.

SCA Gromek, in his very conclusory cover memorandum to the audit report, makes broad assertions against Judge O'Sullivan that are not supported by the substance of the report. To support his assertions, SCA Gromek creates a page and a half worth of bullet points supposedly summarizing the conclusions reached by the Whall Group. His first bullet point states "Proper procedures for court operations were either ignored or circumvented; the responsibility lies with both judges and, to a lesser extent, the court administrator." However, of the nine bullet points that SCA Gromek presents, five of them concern Judge George's questionable use of ADDMS conservator services. Although Judge O'Sullivan is mentioned in these bullet points, a thorough review of the report, as well as the responses of Judge George and Judge O'Sullivan to the Whall Group Report including the documentation offered by Judge O'Sullivan in her response, belies involvement by either Judge O'Sullivan or the Macomb County Probate Court administrator. The majority of the report discusses the numerous problems in Judge George's oversight of her cases, as well as Judge George's questionable overuse of ADDMS. SCA Gromek's memorandum correctly recommends the removal of Judge George as chief judge, but it seems a skewed representation of what the auditors conclude about the dysfunction within the Macomb County Probate Court.[1061]

Weaver had initially thought Kenneth Sanborn a good choice to step in, although, she offered retired Livingston County Probate Judge Susan L. Reck as a possibility, especially because she was an outsider. Sanborn was a retired attorney and circuit court judge in Macomb County. He also had been the county's probate judge in the 1970s, and he had helped out as a visiting judge when George was away in Genesee County supposedly learning what she was supposed to be doing.

Sanborn started off by doing one good thing: he brought back Don Housey as administrator. Housey had complained to the State Court Administrator more than 20 times about Judge George's conduct, and George had placed him on administrative leave.[1062]

Weaver and Sanborn had a long acquaintance. And by happenstance, she met him after he had again taken up the work in Macomb County. Weaver and Sanborn were

1061 Elizabeth A. Weaver writing in concurrence of Appointment of Chief Judge of Macomb County Probate County, ADM file No. 2008-01, Michigan Supreme Court, 11 June, 2008, http://www.justiceweaver.com/pdfs/2008-01-Macomb.pdf.
1062 Jameson Cook, "Fired Macomb Probate Court official's lawsuit tossed by judge."

at a meeting of retired probate judges at the Doherty Hotel in Clare, Aug. 4, 2008. They had a sit-down conversation, and, according to Weaver, Sanborn related his concerns about George's "deficient judicial skills." He initially spoke candidly, said Weaver, specifically mentioning "her inability to make decisions, her inability to do her work properly, and her unprofessional attitude toward [Sanborn], her colleagues and the court staff."[1063]

At the time, Weaver told him that he needed to come forward and tell the other justices his observations. Sanborn, she said, began back peddling.

I wasn't sure he would do it. I don't remember being pleased at our conversation.

Sanborn had also told Gromek "it is no secret that our two judges [...] have a communication problem."[1064] One of the ways he was going to bring peace to the court was by separating the work into two sections under: "wills and estates," and the "mental division." The lion's share was in wills and estates and that he assigned to O'Sullivan. In a letter to Gromek, Sanborn put it this way:

> This was done only after consultation with and agreement by both judges. In the beginning, this will increase the workload for Judge O'Sullivan; however, that should level off. To assist Judge O'Sullivan I have hired both a paralegal for her division and a paralegal-attorney in the mental division who has been instructed to also assist Judge O'Sullivan.
>
> [...]
>
> In closing, I wish to point out that the wonderful staff appear to be very happy since I've been here, at least that is what they tell me. There may still be one dissident anonymous letter writer[1065]; however, this is more political. I have refused to be involved in the probate election race and have so advised the two candidates, as I feel that it would destroy my credibility.[1066]

This August 6th letter to Gromek made no mention of his expressed perceived shortcoming in George's work. That would give rise to a problem, but before it did, Sanborn received a letter from O'Sullivan:

> In early July, you discussed with me the possibility of assigning Judge George's cases to me. This was after you had been reviewing several of her

1063 Elizabeth A. Weaver, letter to Kenneth N. Sanborn, 19 September 2008, unpublished.
1064 Kenneth N. Sanborn, letter to Carl Gromek, 6 August 2008, unpublished.
1065 Sanborn may be have been referring to an anonymous letter from a probate court employee dated July 29th that asserted that Sanborn was giving George preferential treatment including help in her bid for re-election. The one item that could have been verified was the writer's calculation that in her nearly six years on the bench, George had taken off 374 days. Given that a work year is usually calculated at 260 work-days, and that holidays might reduce that calculation by another 11 to 14 days (depending on the court), George had scored the equivalent of an extra year and a half in time off. The letter had been sent to the seven justices, but had evidently found its way back to Sanborn.
1066 Kenneth N. Sanborn.

cases, particularly those involving ADDMS/Alan Polack. You told me Judge George was "not able to handle these cases" and "that these cases are what got her in trouble."

In an effort to assist you in addressing the problems with Judge George's handing of her cases, I agreed to help by taking them over.

I never thought you would be assigning her cases to me as your permanent solution to Judge George's inability to handle the work she was assigned to do. This is not a permanent solution to her inability or unwillingness to do her work.

When you leave this court in December, the problems will not only continue to exist, but will be compounded by the fact that Judge George will more likely be re-elected for another six year term with no greater ability or willingness to do the work of this court than when she was elected six years ago.

Although I deeply appreciate your respect and confidence in my ability to handle such a large caseload, I do not want to be your solution to the problem of Judge George not being able to handle her cases properly.

Judge George would have you and everyone believe that she and I not being friends is the reason she is unable to do her work. This has been nothing more than an excuse for her inability to handle the cases assigned to her.

When Administrative Order 2003-02 was executed on July 7, 2003, its purpose was to equalize the caseload of this court between judges. This was done so each judge would be responsible for an equal number of cases in both divisions of this court to provide a more efficient delivery of services to the public.

On July 11, 2008, you set aside LOA 2003-02 and as a result, I am now responsible for approximately 85 percent of the court's docket. Not only am I responsible for a grossly disproportionate number of the court's cases (approximately 5,400), but, as you know, these cases are far more complex and require a greater degree of expertise and preparation.

When I inquired as to when you would be returning to an equalized docket, you said you could not do that because Judge George couldn't handle those cases. You offered to take my docket one day a week, but that is also a temporary solution to the burden you have now placed on me.

When you leave in December, you will have achieved nothing. You will not have resolved any of the problems for which you were appointed as acting chief judge.

If you believe Judge George is incapable of handing the cases of the court to which she was elected judge, do something about it.

If you believe Judge George is qualified to handle the cases of the court to which she was elected, then set aside Administrative Order 2008-01 and assign each of the court's two judges an equal number of cases from each division immediately.[1067]

So, Sanborn had told Weaver <u>and</u> O'Sullivan about George's inabilities. He also told Don Housey. But it was evident from his response to O'Sullivan's letter that Sanborn had no intention of intervening. But it was quite a history lesson. The letter is abbreviated whenever he was heading down memory lane in an act of scenic avoidance (what you do when you don't like what you see).

I am in receipt of and saddened by your letter dated today which deserves an answer.

It is true that Judge George does not have as much experience as you do in the handling of wills and estates cases.

Although the amount of will and estates cases may be more than when I started in 1972, you have much more help. When I started [....]

I would like to remind you when I started in probate we had two judges [....]

I am also amazed at how much security you now have [....]

I know that you are upset that I won't openly criticize Judge George. This is one battle that I don't want to be involved in. Unfortunately, you two judges don't work well together.

I am very sorry that I am put in a position where I have to write this letter, as I am not this type of person. When I leave here as acting chief judge, if ever, I hope that we will have made some progress.[1068]

He was not going to act, but he was about to be put on the hot seat. Weaver took note of his letter to Gromek from August 6th. He had failed to tell the State Court Administrator what he had told her in Clare about George's shortcomings. She wrote to him and copied in the court.

Your letter fails to include the information you shared with me during our conversation at the Retired Probate Judges' meeting in Clare on August 4, 2008, about your concerns about Judge George's deficient judicial skills. Among the number of concerns you raised, you specifically mentioned her

1067 Pamela Gilbert O'Sullivan, letter to Kenneth N. Sanborn, 12 September 2008, unpublished.
1068 Kenneth N. Sanborn, letter to Pamela Gilbert O'Sullivan, 12 September 2008, unpublished.

inability to make decisions, her inability to do her work properly, and her unprofessional conduct toward you, her colleagues and the court staff.

Although you imply in your August 6 letter that the problems at the Macomb County Probate Court stem from discord between Judge O'Sullivan and Judge George, your conversation with me on August 4 painted a very different picture regarding the Macomb County Probate Court situation. You described the real root of the problem as Judge George's inability to do the wills and estates work properly (the overwhelming majority of the work of Macomb County Probate Court), and evidenced by your transference of all of the wills and estates files to Judge O'Sullivan. You stated to me that you would not let Judge George do that work and expressed your distress at what you were finding in your review of Judge George's files. I urged you to report this information to all of the justices of this court and to the citizens of Macomb County given the harm suffered by (and possible future harm to) the vulnerable citizens who needed guardian and conservator services.

Your letter of August 6, 2008, to Mr. Gromek failed to include the pertinent information that you shared with me concerning Judge George's performance. It failed to contain a candid and thorough update regarding the Macomb County Probate Court, including the results of your review and report on the probate files that you concluded were mishandled by Judge George, and apparently, as you state, also mishandled by a staff attorney of the Macomb County Probate Court.

[...]

It has become clear that since your appointment the problems at the Macomb Probate Court have not been solved. Although you stated to me that Judge George cannot do the work properly, you did not address her deficiency, but simply transferred Judge George's wills and estates caseload to Judge O'Sullivan, giving Judge O'Sullivan approximately 85 percent of the entire Macomb County Probate Court caseload. [...]

You stated to me that you did not want to interfere with the probate court election. The fact is, as acting chief judge, you are interfering in the election by failing to disclose to the voters of Macomb County information important and pertinent to their decisions. Only with full disclosure, including the disclosure of any mistakes and misdoings of the probate court, will the voters of Macomb County have sufficient information to properly evaluate Judge George's performance as a probate judge and the performance of the entire Macomb County Probate Court. The people of Macomb County should be trusted with the facts about their probate court and its judges.

It has been well over a month since we met and you have not, as I urged you to do during our August 4 meeting, let all the justices of this court and the people of Macomb County know what is really going on at the Macomb County Probate Court. It is unlike the Ken Sanborn that I knew as a judge in the past, and that I believed our court was appointing acting chief judge this June. As an acting chief judge, receiving $390 a day to do your work, and having already received $17,900 since your June appointment, it was and is your duty to share this vital information with this entire court, the Judicial Tenure Commission and, most importantly, the citizens of Macomb County.[1069]

Weaver went on to tell him the action she would seek at the next (Sept. 24th) Supreme Court administrative conference: first she would move to end Sanborn's appointment; second she would seek an order to the State Court Administrator to refer George to the Judicial Tenure Commission; third, she would recommend appointing O'Sullivan to again take over as chief judge. She closed noting that Judge George's inabilities have so far cost taxpayers better than an extra $150,000.

On Sept. 22, she shared her letter to Sanborn with the entire court and asked to schedule the matter for the conference two days later.[1070] Justices Taylor and Young demurred and pushed the matter back to October 1.

Weaver responded that there was no reason for a delay; there would be plenty of time during the meeting given the schedule. She also wanted Sanborn to respond:

> We should request acting Chief Judge Sanborn to respond to us in writing by the end of today whether or not he said to Justice Weaver, Judge O'Sullivan, and Macomb County Probate Court Administrator Don Housey that Judge George cannot do wills and estate work properly and that he will not allow her to do that work. Judge Sanborn does not need over a week to answer that question. He either admits that he said it or he denies it.[1071]

The delay, Weaver noted, would occasion the expenditure of an additional $1,950 in taxpayer money to pay Sanborn for another week.

The majority justices were not eager to face the fallout that would be coming their way. That also gave Sanborn an opportunity to respond. He noted that he and Weaver had known each other for 35 years. When he took the assignment as acting chief judge, he asked for her support. She told him he'd have it. Her letter to him, he said, was painful. "When I received and read Justice Weaver's letter, the first thought that came to my mind was 'Betty, that hurts.'"[1072]

And he went on to respond to what Weaver reported he'd said. In fact, he asserted that Weaver was trying to pressure him; it was all her fault:

1069 Elizabeth A. Weaver, letter to Kenneth N. Sanborn, 19 September 2008, unpublished.
1070 Elizabeth A. Weaver, "Memorandum," 22 September 2008, unpublished.
1071 Elizabeth A. Weaver, "Memorandum 2," 23 September 2008, unpublished.
1072 Kenneth N. Sanborn, letter to Carl Gromek, 23 September 2008, unpublished.

At the August 4th meeting, I was aghast at Justice Weaver's strong feeling against Judge George and her pressure on me to join in the criticism. When I informed her that I would not become involved in the probate election, Justice Weaver appeared to be very upset with me. My position is that this would destroy my credibility in correcting the problems.

Judge O'Sullivan has much more experience in handling wills and estates files than Judge George and this is the reason enough alone to let her handle these matters.[1073]

He denied that Judge George had ever treated him unprofessionally, but of the other "yes-no" questions put to him by Weaver, he was silent. In a response letter, Weaver put him on the spot:

As to your various accusations against me, including your allegations of strong feelings against Judge George and any pressure on you to criticize her are simply false. Your mischaracterizations of my urging you to tell the truth to this court and to Macomb County are simply wrong.

I note that you have not denied that you said to me, Judge O'Sullivan, and Macomb County Probate Administrator Don Housey that Judge George could not do wills and estate work properly and that you would not give that work to her. By your letter of yesterday, you have now passed the point of credibly doing so.[1074]

For all the fuss, Sanborn expressed his willingness to stay on.

I can't think of any circuit court judge that would want to step into this situation. One possibility would be for me to continue as acting chief judge and then come in as visiting judge during the absence of one of the others. We have in our county budget adequate funds to cover the same. [...] I would strongly recommend that neither of our current judges be so appointed. If Judge George is not re-elected, then you could cross that bridge when you get to it.[1075]

Was he seeking to bring an apparent calm to the court no matter what was beneath the surface? No, said Weaver. In his actions and his words, Sanborn showed what was really motivating him: his retirement job.

This is an example of "Peace, peace ... when there is no peace."[1076] He could have taken a stand and this could have been fixed...but he was earning $390 a day for each day that he appeared. And he could set his own schedule. This was a good deal for him, and he was eager to stay on.

1073 Ibid.
1074 Elizabeth A. Weaver, letter to Kenneth A. Sanborn, 24 September 2008, unpublished.
1075 Kenneth N. Sanborn, letter to Carl Gromek, 23 September 2008, unpublished.
1076 Jeremiah 6:14.

And his 35-year friendship with Weaver? She suggested that he was well aware of the majority direction at the Supreme Court.

He could read the tea leaves.

At the conference of the 24th, after a short session of public comment, Weaver again asked that the matter be taken up. It was 10:40 a.m. Chief Justice Taylor denied her motion and said he was leaving the administrative conference at 11:00, which he did, wrote Weaver. The meeting was adjourned at 11:25.[1077]

Weaver made good on her promise to introduce her resolutions on the Macomb County Probate Court in the next court conference, Oct. 1.

First she moved to end Sanborn's appointment. "The motion failed for want of a second."[1078]

Second, Weaver moved that the Supreme Court order its administrator to refer Judge George to the JTC. "The motion failed for want of a second."[1079]

Third, she moved that the Supreme Court itself refer George to the JTC. "The motion failed for want of a second."[1080]

There was no reasonable hope for her to introduce a motion to restore Judge O'Sullivan to the position of chief judge. She left it. Not one of her colleagues thought the matters dealing with the Macomb County Probate Court worth raising.

Concerning the Engler Four, that would be consistent: they didn't want to own this situation. For Cavanagh and Kelly, though, it marked a turning point in much of any support they'd evince for Weaver.

Cavanagh was getting tired of all of it; he was worn out. And Kelly, you never knew. They just didn't want to go any further. I don't know why people do what they do. I suspect it was not worth it to them; perhaps they were anticipating Cliff would win the election, and they're looking down the road having to live with these people.

There would be no help to O'Sullivan from the Supreme Court. In her letter to Chief Justice Taylor and the rest of the justices, O'Sullivan took stock of where things stood Nov. 3, 2008.

> The problems persist and we are no closer today to resolution than we were
> in 2006 when I appealed to State Court Administrator, Carl Gromek. So,

---

1077 Elizabeth A. Weaver writing in footnote 1, dissent, "Minutes of the conference on administrative matters," 1 October 2008.
1078 "Minutes of the conference on administrative matters," 1 October 2008.
1079 Ibid.
1080 Ibid.

why didn't I report Judge Kathryn George to the Judicial Tenure Commission, that body in the state where alleged unsatisfactory judicial performance or bad judicial conduct is to be investigated and evaluated?

First, despite my conviction that Judge George's performance has been unsatisfactory and at odds with court rules, practice and procedure, I was hesitant to put the mark of a potential judicial censure, suspension or removal on her record; this is no light matter for any colleague.

Second, at that juncture there were extraordinary demands on my time: my husband was dying.

Third, given the climate in the State Court Administrator's Office in Lansing I was sure that my complaint would be dismissed out of hand.

I've often worked with people in situations that are not cordial. And somehow—if we were committed to the job—we finished the work. I'm no frail reed and I can take the heat that may come out of this. What's important to remember is that when I've seen improper behavior I've tried to correct it. There is not much I could have done to correct the situation with Judge George if the State Court Administrator's Office and the Michigan Supreme Court chose to do nothing.

My focus and efforts are and have always been for the citizens of Macomb County who have elected me. I am committed to doing whatever I can to provide them with the justice they deserve even if I am the only one willing to do it.[1081]

Sanborn would keep on until January 2010 when Judge Mark S. Switalksi took the post as chief judge for both circuit and probate courts in Macomb County.[1082] Switalski would serve until January 2012 when the Supreme Court named David F. Viviano to the dual assignment as chief judge.[1083,1084,1085]

Of interest during Switakski's tenure was his firing of Don Housey. Housey, like Washtenaw's Brad Geller, went on to file suit against his court and its judges (Switalski and George). Housey died in February of 2012, and his suit at the Federal District Court was dismissed subsequently by Judge Avern Cohn.

1081 Pamela Gilbert O'Sullivan, letter to Chief Justice Clifford W. Taylor, 3 November 2008.
1082 "Honorable Mark S. Switalski," Macomb County website, http://www.macombcountymi.gov/circuit-court/mss_bio.htm.
1083 "The Honorable David F. Viviano," Macomb County website, http://www.macombcountymi.gov/circuitcourt/DavidF.Viviano.htm.
1084 Jameson Cook, "State Supreme Court makes chief judge change," *The Macomb Daily*, 18 November, 2011, http://www.sourcenewspapers.com/articles/2011/11/18/news/doc4ec66ac7e2229404650912.txt?viewmode=fullstory.
1085 Governer Rick Snyder would elevate him to the Supreme Court February 27, 2013. [Press release, "Snyder appoints David Viviano to Michigan Supreme Court," State of Michigan, 27 February 2013, http://www.michigan.gov/snyder/0,4668,7-277-57577_57657-295946--rss,00.html.]

Jameson Cook, in reporting the story, noted:

> The ruling is a blow to the legal efforts of Housey's survivors and other supporters who believe he was treated unfairly.
>
> [...]
>
> The state Judicial Tenure Commission, which monitors judges, in November 2009 issued a subpoena to Housey for 17 case files, Cohn says. Housey went to Switalski for guidance, and Switalski assigned the task of responding to his secretary. Housey met in secret three times with the JTC investigator.
>
> After he was fired, Housey sued, claiming the defendants violated the Whistleblower Protection Act, his free speech and due process, and breached a contract.
>
> But Cohn says that because Housey's complaints to the SCAO were part of his duties and were not a "public concern," they were not free speech.[1086]

This ongoing story would take one more very quirky turn. An expert witness, Gerald Terlep, Ph.D., had been most frequently employed in Judge George's court for mental examinations. Terlep was "a respected counselor with a long-standing Macomb County practice."[1087]

George was so impressed with his work that she made her favor known:

> Macomb Probate Judge Kathryn George wrote a letter two years ago recommending Terlep as an expert. "Dr. Terlep regularly testifies before this court as an expert witness," George wrote in the June 22, 2009, letter on Probate Court letterhead. "He is qualified by the court for each case and has been performing this work several times per month for over six years. I have no hesitation in recommending Dr. Terlep to you."[1088]

And that was fine except Dr. Terlep was not qualified to make determinations of mental competency. He had a doctorate in education, and a master's in social work. He never falsified his credentials or exaggerated them, but his qualifications did not

> meet the state's requirement to be an expert witness because he is not a medical doctor or a licensed psychologist, said Macomb County's counsel, George Brumbaugh, who is reviewing the issue.

1086 Jameson Cook, "Fired Macomb Probate Court official's lawsuit tossed by judge," *The Macomb Daily*, 17 May 2012.

1087 Peggy Walsh-Sarnecki, "Expert witness faces credibility questions," *Detroit Free Press*, 5 December 2011, A.6.

1088 George Hunter and Serena Maria Daniels, "Medical impostor roils Michigan Probate Court; for years, man testified as an expert doctor witness," *Detroit News*, 4 November 2011, A4.

Michigan law says court-ordered mental examinations must be done by a medical doctor, a psychiatrist or a psychologist; it does not include counselors.

Charges are unlikely, and there is no evidence that Terlep ever claimed to be a medical doctor, Brumbaugh said. Terlep has not been testifying while the issue is under review.

Brumbaugh also said it appears unlikely that the cases Terlep testified for will be reopened.

"Those cases are terminated. It's not like somebody's serving a sentence," Brumbaugh said.

It's not clear how Terlep's credentials got called into question.

"That's one of the things that's being reviewed," said Chief Probate Judge Mark Switalski. "Typically, this would come up in the courtroom, and the court would make a finding. So I'm not sure how this was even raised."

Nor is it clear how a court could allow him to testify if he wasn't qualified. Brumbaugh and Switalski agree that before Terlep could testify, both sides would have to agree he was qualified. And although the law says he's not qualified to testify in competency hearings, according to several professional associations, Terlep's credentials qualified him to testify within his area of expertise.[1089]

…Which was not mental competency.

And another black eye for Judge George.

Meanwhile, in the spring of 2012, Probate Court Judge Pamela Gilbert O'Sullivan announced that she would not run for another term. She'd had enough.

But when O'Sullivan sent her letter to Taylor, Nov. 3, 2008, she was counting on him to do something. And she sent the letter recognizing the probability that he would be re-elected in a few days' time for another term on the Supreme Court. All the polls put him in the lead, and he had plenty of money.[1090]

And then the unimagined happened: Chief Justice Taylor was voted off the bench.

1089 Peggy Walsh-Sarnecki.
1090 Ed Wesoloski, "MSC campaign cash: a bit short of $20M," the Michigan Lawyer, a blog from *Michigan Lawyers Weekly*, 8 October 2008, http://milawyersweekly.com/milwblog/2008/10/08/msc-campaign-cash-a-bit-short-of-20m/.

Chapter 22

The Sleeping (?) Judge
The Power of an Image,
A Complicit Press,
And the Un-election of a Chief Justice

Chief Justice Cliff Taylor was opposed in the 2008 election by Democrat-nominated Diane Marie Hathaway, a circuit court judge from Wayne County (Third Circuit). She had been first elected to that court in 1992 and re-elected in 1998 and 2004. She also had experience as a visiting judge on the Court of Appeals and in 2006 had run unsuccessfully for a seat on that court[1091] (more about that in Chapter 27). In the fall of 2008, she was partway through her third term when she ran for the Supreme Court. Here's a partial summary of her career that was posted at the Michigan Supreme Court website after her election:

> The daughter of a Detroit police officer, Justice Hathaway was born, raised, and educated in the city of Detroit. After graduating from high school, she attended Henry Ford Hospital School of Radiologic Technology and became an X-ray Technician. She also obtained her real estate broker's license and worked in both radiology and real estate while raising her children and attending college. Justice Hathaway graduated with honors from Madonna University and received a bachelor of science in Allied Health. She earned her law degree from the Detroit College of Law (now Michigan State University College of Law) in 1987. While in law school, she worked as a research clerk at the Wayne County Circuit Court and Detroit Recorder's Court. She also taught real estate law and continuing education classes to real estate brokers.[1092]

She had started her legal career in private practice and then moved to the Macomb County Prosecuting Attorney's office where she rose to the post of chief of the Drug Forfeiture Division. Hathaway lives in Grosse Pointe Park with her husband Michael

---

1091 "Cavanagh, Corrigan win re-election to MSC," *Michigan Lawyers Weekly*, 13 November 2006, http://mi-lawyersweekly.com/news/2006/11/13/cavanagh-corrigan-win-reelection-to-msc/.

1092 "Biographies of the Justices," Michigan Supreme Court website. Following her resignation from the court Jan. 21, 2013, the posting is no longer there but it is still at the website of the Michigan Supreme Court Historical Society: http://www.micourthistory.org/bios.php?id=115.

Kingsley. He also is an attorney, as was her first husband, Wayne County Circuit Court Judge Richard Hathaway.[1093] She has five children and three grandchildren. Taylor also faced competition from Libertarian Robert Roddis.

But Taylor was the odds-on favorite. He would have the endorsements of both *the Detroit News*[1094]—as might be expected—but also earlier even the *Detroit Free Press* in a backhanded sort of way:

> Taylor is enough of a problem on the high court to warrant endorsing nearly anyone as an alternative.
>
> Unfortunately, state Democrats have chosen Wayne County Circuit Judge Diane Hathaway as their candidate. Despite a solid record on the circuit court, Hathaway, 54, demonstrates no better grasp of the role of high court justice than Taylor, and can't even articulate a judicial philosophy that she'd bring to the court.
>
> Voters would get a different justice in Hathaway, but not a better one. For that reason, they ought to retain Clifford Taylor, despite his shortcomings.[1095]

Columnist Brian Dickerson described Taylor as "Michigan's most secure Republican."

> Taylor's path to a second 8-year term on the court seems unobstructed. To say that Democratic challenger Diane Hathaway faces an uphill climb in her bid to unseat him is a little like suggesting the Detroit Lions are a long shot to win this year's Super Bowl. It's not a mathematical impossibility, but you'd be hard-pressed to compute the odds on a standard calculator.[1096]

To that point of mid October, the television ads had been fairly predictable and partisan with Republicans and friends taking the lead. The Chamber of Commerce fielded one ad that pictured Hathaway as easy on crime, giving a short sentence to a sex offender. That same ad attempted to link her to a terrorist, portraying her as "out of touch."[1097] Hathaway's reputation was not someone who was soft on crime but the reality and the assertion didn't seem to matter to the Republicans. The Democrats linked Cliff Taylor to policies of the departing President.[1098] There were soon going to be lots more ads.

1093 Trevor Calero, "Democrat Hathaway unseats chief justice of Michigan Supreme Court," *The Michigan Daily*, 5 November 2008, http://www.michigandaily.com/content/2008-11-05/hathaway-pulls-upset.
1094 "Or endorsements in Tuesday's election," *Detroit News*, 3 November 2008, 14A.
1095 "Despite his agenda, retain Justice Taylor; His own version of judicial activism is troubling for court, but he's best choice for voters in this contest," *Detroit Free Press*, 14 October 2008, A.12.
1096 Brian Dickerson, "Michigan's most secure Republican," *Detroit Free Press*, 17 October 2008, B1.
1097 http://www.youtube.com/watch?feature=endscreen&NR=1&v=lJIM378R8LY.
1098 http://www.brennancenter.org/sites/default/files/legacy/video/Judicial%20Ads%2008/MI/Boards/10-20-08%20STSUPCT_MI_MIDSCC_TAYLOR_GEORGE_BUSH.pdf. There are other state Supreme Court ads chronicled at the Brennan Center for Justice website: http://www.brennancenter.org/analysis/buying-time-2008-michigan, but the list is not exhaustive.

And the ad that generated the most buzz was that from the Michigan Democratic Party portraying Justice Taylor as "The Sleeping Judge."[1099] The Supreme Court case retold in the ad dealt with the liability for the deaths of six children in a Dec. 1, 2000, fire at the Brewster-Douglas Housing Project—City of Detroit-owned public housing. The city was defending itself against an $800 million lawsuit brought by Geoffrey Fieger's firm five days after the fire. Initially, the Detroit Fire Commissioner reported the blaze was started by an untended cigarette or children playing with matches.[1100] Fieger's expert witness asserted that the fire originated within the walls as a result of faulty wiring.[1101] And the record showed that the tenants had previously complained of electrical malfunctions and had asked that the wiring be made safe. An employee of the Housing Commission had been to the apartment the day before the fire to "trouble shoot" circuitry.[1102] (And by the time the case made its way to the Supreme Court, the justices agreed that the cause was indisputably the wiring inside the walls.[1103])

The goal for the plaintiffs was to get the matter before a jury. The objective for the defendant, the city, was to have the matter shut down. But under what provisions could the matter go to trial and get before jurors? What laws, codes and provisions applied? That was a matter to be determined by the courts for each of the six counts.

And if the case were allowed to go to trial, there were questions to be answered in addition to the cause of the fire: was there negligence? Was the city responsible for maintaining a safe premises? Or did the city have governmental immunity?

The issue made its way through the Wayne County Circuit Court where both sides— the families of the dead children and the city—won and lost. Much the same happened at the Court of Appeals,[1104] different findings on different issues. In its conclusion, the Court of Appeals affirmed in part, reversed in part, and remanded, but with the judgment that the case could proceed to trial.[1105]

The plaintiffs were trying to go to trial on this, and they and the city had all these various appeals going back and forth.

When the case reached the Supreme Court, there was more parsing, but the result was resoundingly for the city on all issues and there would be no trial:

> On order of the court, leave to appeal having been granted, and the briefs and oral argument of the parties having been considered by the court, we

---

1099 http://www.youtube.com/watch?v=yMdoBAqAJ9U&feature=player_embedded.

1100 Ben Schmidt, "Fire theories in opposition: Official says kids' play possible; families disagree," *Detroit Free Press*, 4 December 2000, B.1.

1101 *McDowell v City of Detroit*, No. 246294, Court of Appeals, 9 November 2004, 5, http://publicdocs.courts.mi.gov:81/OPINIONS/FINAL/COA/20041109_C246294_69_217O.246294.OPN.COA.PDF.

1102 Ibid., 2.

1103 *McDowell v City of Detroit*, No. 127660, Michigan Supreme Court, 11 April 2007, 1, http://publicdocs.courts.mi.gov:81/sct/public/orders/20070411_s127660_99_127660_2007-04-11_or.pdf.

1104 The panel included Judges Pat M. Donofrio, Michael Talbot, and Helene White.

1105 *McDowell v City of Detroit*, No. 246294, Court of Appeals, 9 November 2004, 12, http://publicdocs.courts.mi.gov:81/OPINIONS/FINAL/COA/20041109_C246294_69_217O.246294.OPN.COA.PDF.

hereby reverse the judgment of the Court of Appeals and remand this case to the Wayne Circuit Court for entry of a judgment in favor of defendants.[1106]

The vote was the usual 4-3 with Cavanagh writing the lead dissent. This is his conclusion:

> The focus of the majority on who owned or controlled the walls or the space between the walls is gravely misplaced. The majority should acknowledge that the correct analysis asks who owned, controlled, and had a duty to maintain the electrical wiring. Here, the duty to maintain the wiring, as well as ownership and control over it, was unequivocally defendants'. Defendants failed abysmally in their obligations, and six children died. Accordingly, I would affirm the judgment of the Court of Appeals and let the victims of defendants' neglect have their day in court.[1107]

Weaver not only joined Cavanagh's dissent to both the reversal and remand but also to a stay Fieger and his firm had sought from the Supreme Court until the federal lawsuit against the members of the court was resolved.[1108] That also was denied. In her dissent, Weaver added—once again—her call for reform of disqualification standards.[1109]

With so much at stake—justice for the six children and their families and the possibility of millions in judgments against the city—it's no wonder that the case was hotly contested. The case made news at the time, but to a limited audience.[1110] But that changed when election season rolled around with the release of the famous ad. The script reads:

> **Announcer:** One story's a fairytale. The other a nightmare. The fairytale, Sleeping Beauty. The nightmare, the sleeping judge, Cliff Taylor.
>
> **Woman #1:** Judge Taylor fell asleep several times in the middle of our arguments. How could he judge based on the facts when he was asleep?
>
> **Announcer:** Taylor was voted the worst judge on the State Supreme Court. And fellow judges called for an investigation of Taylor for misconduct and abuse of power. The sleeping judge, Cliff Taylor, he needs a wake up call.
>
> Paid for by the Michigan Democratic State Central Committee.[1111]

1106 *McDowell v City of Detroit*, No. 127660, Michigan Supreme Court, 11 April 2007, 1, http://publicdocs. courts.mi.gov:81/sct/public/orders/20070411_s127660_99_127660_2007-04-11_or.pdf.

1107 Michael Cavanagh writing in dissent, *McDowell v City of Detroit*, No. 127660, Michigan Supreme Court, 11 April 2007, 7.

1108 That matter was covered in Chapter 18.

1109 Ibid.

1110 Karen M. Poole, "City may be held liable for fatal fire; Case filed before 'Pohutski' cut-off,' *Michigan Lawyers Weekly*, 22 November 2004, http://milawyersweekly.com/news/2004/11/22/city-may-be-held-liable-for-fatal-fire/.

1111 http://www.youtube.com/watch?v=yMdoBAqAJ9U&feature=player_embedded.

The ad begins and ends with an actor portraying a nodding-off Justice Taylor.

The press, of course, loves that kind of thing.

The reaction was rapid and David Eggert of the Associated Press got the story out the evening of the same day the ad appeared, October 21, 2008:

> The Michigan Supreme Court race was jolted out of a peaceful slumber today when Democrats rolled out a TV ad that accuses Chief Justice Clifford Taylor of nodding off during oral arguments.
>
> The ad being aired statewide two weeks before the Nov. 4 election says the veteran Republican justice "needs a wake-up call."
>
> Taylor's campaign and Republicans denounced the allegation as untrue and asked stations to stop running the ad.
>
> A lawyer who was present at the hearings on Dec. 15, 2005, and Nov. 13, 2006, said in a sworn affidavit that Taylor, 65, did not fall asleep during the case in question. During oral arguments, James Gross successfully defended the City of Detroit and the Detroit Housing Commission against a lawsuit involving the deaths of six children in a Detroit apartment fire.
>
> Juanita Fish, the mother of some of the dead children, says in the ad that Taylor fell asleep "several times" during oral arguments.
>
> Taylor was among four conservative justices to rule against Fish and her sister, dismissing their suit against the city and the Housing Commission, whose employees had visited the city-owned apartment at least twice to address electrical complaints.
>
> "How could he judge based on the facts when he was asleep?" Fish asks in the ad.
>
> Taylor campaign manager Colleen Pero said Democratic Party Chairman Mark Brewer "made up" the allegation.
>
> "It's just throwing anything out there to see what will get traction and trying to ruin the reputation of the chief justice in the meantime," she said.
>
> When pressed by reporters for more evidence corroborating the allegation, Brewer said no more proof was needed.
>
> "We have eyewitnesses. We don't need anything beyond eyewitnesses," he said. "I will stand with these two mothers of six dead children who are looking for justice in the Michigan Supreme Court."

[...]

Republicans said one reason Taylor could not have been asleep is because the plaintiffs' attorney was Geoffrey Fieger, a longtime nemesis of Taylor and other Republican justices.

"Given Fieger's open hostility to this court, if this allegation had been true, Fieger would have certainly mentioned it by now," state Republican Party Chairman Saul Anuzis said in a statement.[1112]

Fieger was put in an interesting situation. He wasn't quoted in Eggert's story, but he later said he responded to questions about what he saw on the bench concerning Taylor this way: "I never looked at the man."[1113]

Fieger, I felt, said the smartest thing of all about Taylor because he has such conflicts with Taylor. So Fieger didn't know. But he said, "My clients say it." Fieger believed his clients, but to his credibility, did not say he saw what he did not see. But because Fieger said he didn't see Taylor asleep; that doesn't mean it didn't happen. That's the most Gross credibly could say as well.

While reporter Eggert noted that Gross had sworn an affidavit, he neglected to report that Joanne Campbell, the mother of the other three children who died in the fire, the lessee of the apartment, and the sister of Juanita Fish, also attended the arguments and had given her sworn affidavit that that she DID see Taylor asleep.

And there were other problems in the news account, hurried as it may have been. The story used no primary sources. Eggert relied on reports from Taylor's campaign manager Colleen Pero, then-state Republican Party Chairman Saul Anuzis, and then-Democratic Party Chairman Mark Brewer. There is no report that he spoke directly with Justice Taylor or even tried to. Nor was there any evidence he spoke with either of the mothers, Fish and Campbell. ...Nor with their attorney Geoffrey Fieger. Nor was there any evidence that he spoke directly with Gross; he refers only to the affidavit. This is all second-hand reporting, and there is no evidence that he spoke with anybody who was in the courtroom when Taylor was alleged to have napped.

He just quoted those people who were speaking for Taylor. And the attorney for the defense— Gross—made an affidavit that day, Taylor could have made an affidavit. In fact, that was the easy answer: for Taylor immediately to say, "No, I didn't fall asleep, and I have made a sworn affidavit." They're using Gross instead of Taylor to deny it.

...And Pero, and Anuzis....

Even the possibility that there may be a videographic record of the hearing receives remote sourcing by Eggert:

1112 David Eggert, "Dems run negative ad against Michigan GOP justice," *Detroit Free Press*, 21 October 2008, http://www.freep.com/article/20081021/NEWS15/81021084?imw=Y.]
1113 Geoffrey Fieger, telephone interview, 4 February 2013.

Michigan Government Television broadcasts arguments held by the Supreme Court. But the camera often focuses on attorneys as they make their case. Justices are seen only when asking questions or from a wide-angle shot that makes it extremely difficult to see if any of them have their eyes closed.

Did he look at the video himself or rely on someone at the court? He doesn't say, and he only reports on what's "often" the case concerning video coverage at the court. It's even possible that if he did look at the video files that he wouldn't find any instance of Taylor asleep; there is the distinct possibility that if a justice ever had been caught napping, that the video technician would have moved off the shot immediately in preview; it would never have been carried live or recorded.

And none of the secondary-source reporting takes away from the sworn statement of Joanne Campbell who swore under oath she saw him asleep.

We finally learned of some of the language contained in the affidavits in a story from one of the stations asked by the Republicans to pull the ad, WZZM in Grand Rapids:

> Since the ads are running on WZZM 13 and the Committee to Re-elect Chief Justice Cliff Taylor charged that the ad was untrue, we were required to get substantiation on the claim that Judge Taylor had fallen asleep during the case. Jo-Ann [sic] Campbell, the sister of Juanita Fish who is in the ads making the claim, provided a sworn notarized affidavit that she "saw Justice Clifford Taylor fall asleep during the argument."

> But the legal counsel for the Committee to Re-elect Chief Justice Cliff Taylor has their own affidavit. This one comes from James G. Gross, an appellate attorney in the case where the alleged sleeping took place. In his statement he says:

>> As is my custom, during my opponent's presentation, I took notes and watched the reactions of the justices to my opponent's arguments. All seven justices were plainly visible to me throughout my opponent's argument, most prominently the chief justice, whose seat is in the center of the bench...If the chief justice or any other justice had fallen asleep, I would have noticed it and remembered it...I can therefore attest to a moral certainty that neither the chief justice nor any other justice fell asleep during either of the aforementioned oral arguments.

> [...]

> There have been no submissions of video or photographic proof of Taylor's sleeping or alertness. What we have is affidavit vs. affidavit—and one more week to fight it out.[1114]

1114 Stanton Tang and Bob Brensing, "Was the judge asleep?" WZZM, 28 October 2008, http://www.wzzm13.com/news/story.aspx?storyid=100707.

Did the reporters go to check out the Michigan Supreme Court footage themselves? Or were they content on reporting only what had been submitted to them? That was not active investigation and there was no follow-up. They did at least get the language of the affidavits.[1115]

Gross' affidavit is interesting in several particulars. If he was taking notes part of the time, he wasn't watching the bench the full time. When he addressed the court, he had to consult his notes and look elsewhere than at the chief justice. It would be reasonable to conclude it was a physical impossibility that Gross studied Taylor every second of the argument.

And, in fact, the oral arguments of November 13, 2006, showed that's exactly what occurred. But there was more, so much more in the videographic record. No one mentioned that this hearing, the second of the day, began in an unusual way. Chief Justice Taylor called the case of *McDowell v City of Detroit*...and then he left the bench. At the invitation of Justice Cavanagh, attorney Gross began his argument without the chief justice on the bench. It would seem logical that if someone from the media had watched the account that it might be mentioned that Taylor didn't return for nearly a minute and a half, by which time, Gross was well underway. This doesn't imply that Taylor was doing anything sinister; it may have been a call of nature or perhaps he needed something from his office. But his absence was remarkable. And no one in the press remarked it.

For the next 15 minutes Gross addressed the bench, most of the time with his head down, reading from his text. He consulted at least nine pages. He raised his head to scan the bench, usually from his right to his left, and his glance never lingered at the center of the bench; and that's where Chief Justice Taylor sat. Further, when he was challenged extensively by Justice Young during the argument Gross looked directly at Young for lengthy periods. Justice Corrigan also questioned him for a shorter time and he turned to her. Young was at the outside left (from Gross' perspective) and Corrigan was one in from the right. Thereafter, Gross spent most of his time looking at the extremes when he looked up. Taylor could have dropped off at any point in his argument and Gross might not have noticed; he was that intent on his argument. But his affidavit made no comment about his time at argument, only during Fieger's presentation.[1116]

When Gross sat down and Fieger addressed the court, Gross was sometimes partially visible. He was shuffling papers, opening files and binders, sometimes looking down. He was NOT watching all the justices all the time, and the proof came when he again stood before the justices to make his rebuttal. He consulted more pages of text, apparently notes he'd compiled during the less than 13 minutes that Fieger stood before the court. He'd been busy, but it wasn't solely in studying Justice Taylor.[1117]

1115 This is something we have not so far been able to do.
1116 Oral argument, *McDowell v City of Detroit*, No. 127660, videographic record, Michigan Supreme Court, 13 November 2006.
1117 Ibid.

Gross could not have been looking at Justice Taylor all the time; you just can't pay attention to one person all the time when you are arguing a case. The women could; they had no other responsibility than to watch. So you have two people who said it happened, one of whom gave an affidavit.

It would be a shame to say that Gross had overstated his "moral certainty" in his sworn statement, but it's either that or an untruth.

At no time in the recording was Justice Taylor shown in close-up. Those shots were reserved for Gross and Fieger, Young and Corrigan. There were a very few shots of the entire bench...at the beginning and the end and when the opposing council switched at the rostrum. At no time did Taylor appear to be dozing; he was busy with papers and otherwise engaged. But the total time he was visible on screen was perhaps two minutes out of 30.

And there was no subsequent discussion or any attempt at accountability from the press concerning the video. They seemed to accept Gross' account as gospel. After all, he was a respected attorney of long standing. And the counter claim was that of a black woman who lived in subsidized housing, and who was three months behind on her rent and was scheduled for eviction.[1118] And there might have been the suspicion that Fish and Campbell, who would not have been pleased by the decision of the court, might have wanted to settle a score.

But it was unlikely she and her sister would have made up this particular story. Would it even have occurred to them that it could even happen, having a justice fall asleep?

The story didn't immediately gain traction; perhaps the media didn't understand how it would resonate with the public. In fact, we've not been able to find where it shows up again until a second AP story (one source credits Eggert[1119]) on Oct. 30, and then describing the Republican responses to the ad.[1120] In one of them, Taylor's campaign team fielded an ad that later was described as " [...] feature[ing] a bikini-clad woman on a beach and said that Judge Hathaway had previously pursued a seat on the Court of Appeals so she could have an easy work schedule [....]"[1121]

Here's the entire text for the ad:

> **Announcer:** Top newspapers and police groups endorse Chief Justice Taylor over unqualified Hathaway. 'Detroit Judge Hathaway is not a reasonable or qualified alternative.' 'She is not well qualified for the high court.' 'No compelling reason to make a change.' 'Hathaway has done nothing to

1118 Jim Schaefer, Dan Shine, James Hill, Amber Arellano, Tamara Audi, Amy Klein, Laura Potts, Shawn Windsor, Jack Kresnak, Kim North Shine, and Jennifer Dixon, "Fire robs family of 6 young lives; relatives, fire crew, witnesses are scarred by devastating blaze," *Detroit Free Press,* 2 December 2000, A.1.
1119 http://www.mlive.com/news/kalamazoo/index.ssf/2008/10/26-week/.
1120 Associated Press, "High-stakes Mich. high court race heating up," mlive, 30 October 2008, http://www.mlive.com/news/index.ssf/2008/10/highstakes_mich_high_court_rac.html.
1121 George Weeks, "Op-Ed: Court nominations get second look," *Traverse City Record-Eagle,* 23 May 2009, http://record-eagle.com/opinion/x75074376/Op-Ed-Court-nominations-get-second-look/print.

distinguish herself.' She favored the proposal that was designed to tilt State government in favor of one political party. Hathaway campaigned for Court of Appeals so she could spend most of the winter in Florida. Re-elect Chief Justice Taylor.

Paid for by the Committee to Re-Elect Chief Justice Taylor.[1122]

The ad was egregious in its beach-blanket portrayal,[1123] but why was no one calling the Republicans to task?

It was only after the election that somebody DID pick up on the ad: Viveca Novak, analyzing selected state supreme court races where truth may have taken second place to partisanship politics. She was analyzing for the Annenberg Public Policy Center:

> One of Taylor's spots claimed that [Hathaway] tried to win a Court of Appeals seat in 2006 so she could hang out at a Florida beach in the winter. That's a claim built purely on hearsay evidence that would never be allowed in court.
> Its only basis was an editorial in the *Michigan Chronicle*, a Detroit weekly, endorsing Hathaway's opponent in the appeals court race. The sourcing for the allegation is extremely vague; this is the whole sentence from the article:
>
> > **Michigan Chronicle, Oct. 25-31, 2006:** A Detroit based minister said Judge Hathaway said that one of the reasons she is campaigning for a seat on the Court of Appeals is so that she would be able to spend most of the winter on the sunny beaches of Florida.[1124]
>
> Got that? The editorial writer may have heard it from the minister (or perhaps there was still another intermediary) who may or may not have heard it from Hathaway herself. Who is the Detroit-based minister? We have no idea, nor, we'd guess, does Hathaway.

We'd hope for better evidence than that in a judicial race.[1125]

1122 Storyboard, "Unqualified Hathaway," Brennan Center for Justice, 25 October, 2008, http://www.brennancenter.org/sites/default/files/legacy/video/Judicial%20Ads%202008/MI/Boards/10-25-08%20STSUPCT_MI_TAYLOR_UNQUALIFIED_HATHAWAY.pdf. It's also viewable here: http://www.youtube.com/watch?feature=endscreen&NR=1&v=anSfNylRBiU.
1123 Although given what transpired in Hathaway's career that was determined by her desire to maintain a Florida home at all costs, it's possible there was a kernel of truth in it.
1124 Novak quoting endorsement, "Chronicle endorses Judge Brian Zahra for state Court of Appeals," Michigan Chronicle, 25-31 October 2006, http://americancourthouse.com/wp-content/uploads/2008/09/michiganchronicle2006judgezahraendorsement.pdf. (Of real interest here is that American Courthouse is the on-line work of Dan Pero, the husband of Colleen Pero, who was at the time Taylor's campaign manager.)
1125 Viveca Novak, "The Case of the Sleeping Justice...and other late-breaking tales from 2008's judicial campaigns," FactCheck.org, A Project of the Annenberg Public Policy Center, 26 November 2008, http://www.factcheck.org/2008/11/the-case-of-the-sleeping-justice/.

Another of the response ads by the Taylor campaign to bolster the image of its candidate showed Taylor and his newspaper endorsements. Sixteen seconds into the ad, there's a shot, a mock scene of what purports to be a group of justices carrying on a collegial discussion on the bench.[1126] There sat the real Taylor (center stage and chief justice) and there were Justices Markman and Young flanking Taylor, a dark-haired woman standing in for Justice Corrigan....and somebody who was supposed to look like Weaver.

Definitely a woman, who was supposed to be me, because she had a hairstyle similar to mine, short bob and all that; but it wasn't me. But, of course, the average person would not know that. It was deceptive, inaccurate, and misleading.

The producers got some other details wrong. While there was an older, grey-haired man—turned away from the camera—who might have been supposed to be Michael Cavanagh, the actor portraying the only other justice—Marilyn Kelly—was a young man. Oops.

The announcer claimed that Taylor had never fallen asleep on the bench. And the ad implied through its use of a graphic that the *Wall Street Journal* had ranked the court as the finest in the nation.[1127] "What kind of a judge makes decisions without documented proof? Not one that belongs on the Supreme Court of Michigan" the announcer said while Diane Hathaway's face appeared behind text.

At its conclusion, the 51-second ad showed a slightly smiling but firm and resolute Cliff Taylor outside the Hall of Justice, a police officer in the background indicating support of law enforcement. Justice Young made a cameo appearance as he walked through behind, looking down at something he was holding in his hand, perhaps a pocket watch. The ad didn't play well and may have had some unintended consequences.

I only know that to a lot of the regular citizens, that ad didn't come across very well. Apparently, the ad conveyed to some a kind of haughty superiority or a certain amount of arrogance. And I think that didn't help him. So even though he wasn't attacking anybody—it was a law-and-order ad, and, you know he's for justice; he's got the policemen behind him—it didn't necessarily help him.

I was so used to Justice Taylor's way of being superior that I didn't pay much mind to the ad, but when I was in the grocery store in Traverse City, and, as people would do, they'd ask you who they should vote for. And one person said to me, "Anybody but that guy in front of the building."

1126 http://www.youtube.com/watch?feature=endscreen&v=P5OrncSegUA&NR=1.

1127 It hadn't, but Patrick J. Wright, a former Supreme Court Commissioner and then a staffer for Midland's Mackinac Center made the assertion in an op-ed piece in the paper. It was just opinion, not that of the editorial staff of the newspaper. [Patrick J. Wright, "The Finest Court in the Nation," *Wall Street Journal*, 13 October 2005, http://online.wsj.com/article/SB112917133552367462.html.] As a reminder from an earlier footnote, Taylor was named charman of the Mackinac Center board in early 2013. [Ted O'Neil, "Taylor Named New Chairman of Mackinac Center Board of Directors; Former Supreme Court Justice Replaces Olson," Mackinac Center for Public Policy, 14 January 2013, http://www.mackinac.org/18166.]

That would be ABC...Anybody But Cliff. And the grocery-story response to the ad?

That alerted me that, yes, voters had reservations.

It wasn't just the mainstream media that were analyzing the candidates. The week before the election, *Michigan Lawyers Weekly* didn't play nice with Taylor. For one thing, the publication had surveyed those who practiced before the high court.

> In a *Michigan Lawyers Weekly*'s survey published in January, Supreme Court litigators were not kind to Taylor.
>
> The survey asked lawyers to rank the court's seven justices in eight judicial characteristics.
>
> The participants (79 out of the 774 attorneys contacted) put Taylor at or near the bottom in several critical categories.
>
> For both "thoroughness of opinions" and "overall knowledge of the law," Taylor came in seventh based on all of the lawyers' responses. Among the lawyers with whom he agreed at least half of the time, he came in sixth. And, among the lawyers with whom he agreed rarely or never, he placed seventh.
>
> [...]
>
> Taylor said he was unfazed by the survey results.
>
> For starters, he said, "I don't look to *Michigan Lawyers Weekly* for vindication in how I do my job."[1128]

The publication was not much more welcoming to Hathaway, suggesting she was unprepared:

> The centerpiece of Hathaway's campaign against Taylor has been her claim that he rules against middle-class families and in favor of "big insurance companies and corporate special interests."
>
> But she admitted she didn't know how that claim squared with Taylor's votes during the court's 2007-08 term.
>
> According to the Supreme Court's Web site, Taylor voted eight times for insurance companies and four times for insureds.
>
> But he also voted against DaimlerChrysler one out of two times.

1128 Todd C. Berg, "Taylor defends: Defiant despite storm of criticism," *Michigan Lawyers Weekly*, 27 October 2008, http://milawyersweekly.com/news/2008/10/27/taylor-defends/.

And, in the four medical-malpractice cases before the court, Taylor voted for the plaintiff three times, one of which had the effect of shielding as many as 30 lawsuits from dismissal.

"I haven't scrutinized those cases," Hathaway said.

She added: "I haven't really studied the decisions he's authored himself."[1129]

But that's not necessarily the kind of analysis that would make the *Free Press* or the *News*. Following the money, however, would.

On October 31, Doug Guthrie filed a *Detroit News* story about the costs—to that point—of the campaign ads: Taylor's campaign had spent $1,265,000; Hathaway's campaign had not spent a dime. But

> [t]he Michigan Campaign Finance Network, which analyzes campaign spending, says that through Oct. 27, the Michigan Chamber of Commerce and the Michigan Democratic State Central Committee spent $1,783,000 for television advertisements on the two candidates' behalf.
>
> [...]
>
> The Chamber has blanketed airwaves statewide with image-building ads that tout Taylor as a former naval officer, tough on crime, and a proven reformer. The Narrator says," Cliff Taylor believes judges should apply existing law, not make new ones." The Democrats have countered with the "sleeping judge" ads that claim Taylor snoozes on the bench—a charge that rankles Republicans.[1130]

Dawson Bell picked up the story on November 2 (two days before the election) and wrote that the "Sleeping Judge" ad "touched off angry denials and denunciations from Taylor's Campaign and Republicans."[1131]

To that point no one had directly quoted Justice Taylor, and it seems that if anybody could have gotten a word out of the justice it would have been Dawson Bell.

Justice Taylor had access to all the resources of the court...every recording, every image. He had a staff that would do pretty much whatever he asked. Taylor was the best placed person to provide evidence and proof IF the ad were false. He failed to do that. And he never really responded to the allegation, at least that we know of from the news accounts. He let political surrogates do so.

1129 Todd C. Berg, "Hathaway attacks; But sketchy on incumbent's record," *Michigan Lawyers Weekly*, 27 October 2008, http://milawyersweekly.com/news/2008/10/27/hathaway-attacks/.
1130 Doug Guthrie, "Supreme Court: Clash of ideologies, *Detroit News*, 31 October 2008, 1B.
1131 Dawson Bell, "State Supreme Court Justice; politics weighs heavy in contest for top state court seat," *Detroit Free Press*, 2 November 2008, C.5.

And then Hathaway won. The image of a nodding justice was enough to have captured the public's imagination.[1132] "'That ad had enormous impact, not so much in the legal community but in the non-legal world,' said Todd Berg, the editor of *Michigan Lawyers Weekly*."[1133]

And it wasn't until AFTER the election that Taylor was quoted about the campaign:

> Chief Justice Clifford Taylor of the Michigan Supreme Court was defeated Tuesday by Democratic challenger Diane Hathaway, becoming what is believed to be the first sitting chief justice in Michigan history to lose at the polls.[1134]

> "It looks like she's won," Taylor told *the Detroit News* in a telephone interview about 11:30 p.m. Tuesday. "It looks pretty conclusive."

> [...]

> He said the Democrats politicized the contest and "turned it into not a judicial race, but a partisan race."

> A key plank of Hathaway's campaign was portraying Taylor as a friend of big corporations and other powerful interests and arguing that she would be impartial and stand up for middle-class families. Her TV ads also accused Taylor of sleeping on the bench.

1132 In a truly odd turn, the Democrats under former chairman Mark Brewer would try the sleeping judge approach again in 2010 against Justice Robert P. Young. It didn't gain any traction, but it did draw negative attention to the Democrats and their leadership. [Carol Lundberg, "Sleeping judge, the sequel," The Michigan Lawyer, a blog from *Michigan Lawyers Weekly*, 1 April 2010, http://michiganlawyerblog.wordpress.com/2010/04/01/sleeping-judge-the-sequel/.]

1133 Ibid.

1134 In an earlier version of his story, Egan would claim "He is the first sitting chief justice defeated at the polls since statehood." [Paul Egan, "Chief Justice Clifford Taylor," *Detroit News*, 5 November 2008, online edition, Metro Section.] This assertion would be frequently repeated. Even the co-author Schock took it as gospel until Justice Weaver said she wasn't sure about it.

Certainly, Egan was correct that Taylor's unelection was the first of a sitting justice since 1984 (Thomas G. Kavanagh's defeat by the returning Dorothy Comstock Riley); such is the power of incumbency. But it wasn't the first election loss of a sitting chief justice.

Excluding Taylor, Michigan has set aside eight serving chief justices in either non-reappointment, non-renomination (before and during the early years of statehood) or defeat at election. Taylor made number nine. The others were Sixth Territorial Justice Solomon Sibley in 1836, who was not reappointed; Ninth Justice George Morrell, who was not renominated to another term by Governor John S. Barry in 1843 after a legislative investigation; 11th Justice Abner Pratt in 1857; 25th Justice Thomas Cooley in 1885 (Cooley resigned after he was defeated); 28th Justice John Champlin in 1891; 33rd Justice John McGrath in 1895; 52nd Justice John McDonald in 1933; and 37th Justice Louis Fead in 1937. Identifying the members of this select group required a collation of information taken from "On and Off the Court," [http://www.micourthistory.org/on_and_off_the_court.php?on_off=1], and "The Michigan Supreme Court History Court Chart," [http://www.micourthistory.org/court_chart.php], both data sets compiled by the Michigan Supreme Court Historical Society.

"It wasn't true, but it was a compelling piece of political theater," Taylor said.[1135]

Too little and too late. And not sworn. There were other stories, some of which referred to what Taylor was supposed to have said and some that quoted him.

This is how Zachary Gorchow reported Taylor's defeat:

> The race exploded in the last two weeks when the Michigan Democratic Party funded scathing ads labeling Taylor "the Sleeping Judge," claiming he fell asleep during a case—a charge Taylor and Republicans denounced as a lie.
>
> Taylor said Democrats turned the race into a partisan contest, one his campaign staff said allowed President-elect Barack Obama's landslide to have a spillover effect.[1136]
>
> "I congratulate her on her victory," he said. "I'm surprised. ... I had not expected this to happen."[1137]

Taylor was not quoted in his denial; although, he was on his reaction to Hathaway's victory.

Dawson Bell covered it this way:

> [T]his year, Democrats unloaded heavy and late on Taylor, most devastatingly with TV ads attacking him for his links to unpopular President George W. Bush and for allegedly sleeping on the bench (a charge Taylor bitterly denied). The sleeping judge ad, coupled with multiple phone, mail and in-person voter contacts from party and interest group activists, appeared to have been particularly effective.

1135 Paul Egan, "Chief justice concedes defeat," *Detroit News*, 5 November 2008, 5S.
1136 Former journalist Jesse C. Green agreed that the presidential campaign played a crucial role, but so did a pro-marijuana proposal on the state ballot:

> The ad was not a magic bullet. That was the Taylor spin: he lost just because of this ("dishonest") ad. The elephant in the room was the Obama campaign. It was common knowledge that Obama turned loose a huge Michigan political machine and the decision was made to use his coattails to help get Diane Hathaway elected. Most of Obama's ads and mailers and flyers and door hangers featured Hathaway. Such material was targeted to likely Democrat drop-off voters (people who would vote Democratic but might forget to vote for the non-partisan, judicial part of the ballot) and it worked. They voted Obama then voted Hathaway. Also, there was a significant turnout in Democratic districts for the pro-marijuana proposal. Those people were overwhelmingly pro-Obama, many were first time voters, and they voted Hathaway. I recall that many people thought that Taylor was being lazy. He believed his own press releases and thought he was a sure win so he didn't really try. The sleeping judge ad was cute and memorable, but didn't stand alone.

[Jesse C. Green, e-mail to co-author Schock, 12 March 2013.]
1137 Zachary Gorchow, "State Supreme Court: Chief justice's challenger pulls off upset," *Detroit Free Press*, 5 November 2008, A.7.

One voter leaving the polls in West Bloomfield, 27-year-old Lynda Winslow, was asked how she had voted in the Taylor-Hathaway contest. Her reply: "Was that the sleeping judge? I voted against the sleeping judge."

Taylor said Wednesday he didn't know how he could have responded more effectively.

At least, he said, "if they're going to make up something about you, it's nice that it was something benign, like sleeping."[1138]

If your source were "bitterly" denying a charge, it would seem likely to be quoteworthy. Bell did include a direct quote, but of the non-denial denial variety.

Then Brian Dickerson analyzed how he could have been so wrong about the Supreme Court election: "OK—so a whole lot of us were wrong when we dismissed Diane Hathaway's challenge to Chief Justice Cliff Taylor as a remake of 'Bambi[1139] Meets Godzilla.'"[1140]

In his column, things got strange, starting with a subhead in his story:

Based on a spurious story?

Then there was the TV ad in which an actor made up to resemble Taylor was depicted nodding off during an insurance case arising from the deaths of six Detroit children.

Taylor's campaign vehemently denied the allegation that he had dozed on the bench and produced affidavits disputing it.

But the 30-second spot - bankrolled by unidentified Democratic donors and aired repeatedly in TV markets across the state - broke through the clutter in a way Taylor's own TV campaign failed to.

Wednesday morning, an exultant but exhausted Hathaway said she had been up for 72 hours straight.

"I just pray," she said, "that I don't fall asleep on the bench."[1141]

Why did he choose that particular subhead? And where did the plural affidavits supporting Taylor enter the narrative? Who besides Gross? No one. And again, no direct denial from Taylor.

1138 Dawson Bell," Balance tilts on state Supreme Court; chief justice's defeat, internal feud weaken GOP bloc," *Detroit Free Press*, 6 November 2008, A.4.
1139 If you'll recall, Bambi was a buck not a doe.
1140 Brian Dickerson, "How Dems took out a chief justice," *Detroit Free Press*, 7 November 2008, B.1.
1141 Ibid.

Finally, there was a piece by columnist Nolan Finley that made a further assertion based on no evidence:

> [The Democrats] unseated Michigan Supreme Court Justice Cliff Taylor, the first chief justice ever to lose re-election, with the devastating—and deceitful—"sleeping judge" ad that the GOP never really answered.[1142]

Deceitful? Finley had declared this an accepted fact. But he doesn't explain himself.

It looked like several things had happened. First, reporter Eggert hurried the story into print without primary sources.

This appeared to be a rushed piece of journalism. He was in a hurry to get a story out to give a defense to another story that wasn't even in the newspaper; it was about a television ad. If it was that important, why not do it right? But maybe he was pressured by his editors. Or maybe it was his reporter's instinct to get it out first.

Second, there was no second-day or "folo" story to back up the initial story with primary sources. Eggert was a prolific reporter and a fast writer, and in our on-line survey of his efforts, we found five major stories between his "Sleeping Judge" story and the election, stories dealing with topics as diverse as ads for stem cell research[1143] and Michigan's proposed medical marijuana law,[1144] but nothing the day after he broke the "Sleeping Judge" story. His story of the 30th concerning the Supreme Court represented only his second story about the high court, but it deals with a wide range of issues and doesn't further explicate the story of October 21.

Third, other journalists apparently were content to pick up and use details from previous stories as substantive, something that gave rise to compounding errors.

Fourth, there is no evidence that one of them asked the chief justice to take an oath of his alertness; an affidavit directly from Taylor, might have answered, at least partially.

Why didn't he deny it under oath? If he had, then it would have been his word against the woman's.

And finally, there was the appearance of an active bias against the possibility that the ad may have been correct.

These Detroit papers had proved that they were determined to support Taylor. None of them got to the bottom of the issue. They could have been skeptical about it, but they could have gotten to the bottom of it.

1142 Nolan Finley, "State GOP got outworked, outspent," *Detroit News*, 9 November 2008, 5C.
1143 David Eggert, "Michigan ad likens stem cell research to Tuskegee Experiments," CNS News, 23 October 2008, http://cnsnews.com/news/article/michigan-ad-likens-stem-cell-research-tuskegee-experiments.
1144 David Eggert, "Michigan's medical pot law prompts airwaves fight," Fox News, 30 October 2008, http://www.foxnews.com/printer_friendly_wires/2008Oct30/0,4675,MichiganMedicalMarijuana,00.html.

The story also had national exposure in a small way.

In her post-election analysis, Viveca Novak analyzed the competing claims surrounding the ad for the Annenberg Public Policy Center. She reported her doubts about the claims of the two mothers whose children died in the fire:

> [T]here are reasons to be skeptical about this claim.
>
> For one thing, their allegation didn't surface publicly until the month before the election, more than a year after the case was decided. Taylor says it's untrue, and a lawyer for the city of Detroit and its housing commission has sworn out an affidavit agreeing with the justice. [...] And perhaps most tellingly, the women's own attorney passed up an opportunity to back up their claim when we contacted him. We asked attorney Fieger if he observed any napping on the part of Justice Taylor. He didn't answer the question. Instead he sent us an email saying, "Cliff Taylor is the single worst judge in Michigan history. He could care less if six children burned to death." With such a low opinion of the justice, we wouldn't expect Fieger to be bashful about saying Taylor was sleeping if he had seen any evidence of it himself.
>
> Healthy skepticism is warranted here. Since witnesses on both sides give conflicting accounts under oath, the best that can be said of the claim is that it isn't proven.[1145]

But it wasn't disproven, either. It could have happened and two women said it did; one of them under oath.

And it's interesting that Novak does not directly quote Taylor; she quotes Fieger at some length from his e-mail. Did she speak with Taylor or rely only of press reports of his denial?

And the idea that the story didn't come out until the election...that's when stories come out. Who was paying any attention to these two women who lost their children to the fire in the City of Detroit Public Housing apartment after the case was argued before the Supreme Court? Apparently, not the press and no one else.

Fieger agreed that the issue was raised early on: "These women complained of what they saw at the oral arguments right from the beginning."[1146] But the matter lay dormant until the trial lawyers—not Fieger himself—brought the matter forward during the election.

And despite his volcanic e-mail reaction to Novak, Fieger had already said that he wasn't watching Taylor and in fact avoided watching Taylor; he wasn't going to swear to something he didn't see.

1145 Viveca Novak.
1146 Geoffrey Fieger.

So, what was Weaver's opinion on whether Taylor was caught napping?

The two women are more credible, and their evidence slightly outweighs Gross'. Taylor never even asserted that he denied it under oath and no Taylor affidavit of denial appeared. Such an affidavit would have counterbalanced the woman's affidavit. So there was more credible evidence that he did fall asleep than he didn't. Now, it's not evidence beyond a reasonable doubt nor clear and convincing. But the preponderance of the evidence, perhaps by one scintilla, was that Taylor did nod off.

If it happened, it likely would not have been the first time a justice dozed off during oral arguments. Justice Charles Levin denied it, but he was reported to have fallen asleep and tumbled backward out of his chair, hitting his head against the wall.[1147] But that was long before, and was not raised as an election issue. There are stories of other judges, who, when they felt Morpheus' tendrils, would stand behind their chairs to force themselves to attention.

If Justice Taylor had actually fallen asleep—for instance, if he had fallen over like Justice Levin, or was snoring obviously—I would have noticed it. And none of the justices said anything other than they didn't know. They tried to draw me into it, to enter into the discussion and defend him, and I chose not to do one or the other. I didn't attack, and I didn't say because I didn't know if he was sleeping. All I could say was the truth: I really wasn't paying attention to Justice Taylor; I was paying attention to the argument. The only thing I could have said was that I didn't hear him snoring.

Diane Hathaway won with 49.3 percent of the vote, a total of 1,852,950 ballots. Total contributions to her campaign were $752,736 with independent expenditures (IEs) from the Democrats of $522,203, and other party support of $164,592. Her cost per vote was 69 cents.[1148]

Cliff Taylor took 39.5 percent, with 1,483,668 votes, and had total contributions of $1,937,759, party IEs of $263,990 and additional party support of $72,370. As well he reported PAC IEs of $225K. His cost per vote was $1.48, more than twice Hathaway's.[1149]

The Libertarians, as is their wont, spent nothing on the campaign, but Robert Roddis still received 420,823 votes, 11.2 percent of the total.

1147 And at the next sitting of the Supreme Court, he found a crash helmet on his chair. "Society present portrait of Justice Charles L. Levin to Michigan Supreme Court," *Society Update*, Michigan Supreme Court Historical Society, Summer 1999, http://www.jillwrightwrites.com/uploads/levin-portrait-presentation.pdf.
1148 Rich Robinson and Barbara R. Moorhouse, *Citizen's Guide to Michigan Campaign Finance 2008*, Michigan Campaign Finance Network, (Lansing, Mich., April 2009), 14, http://www.mcfn.org/pdfs/reports/MCF-NCitGuide08.pdf. Top contributors to her campaign fund included: Michigan Democratic Party $64,259; (Andy) Dillon Leadership Fund $34K; Kalamazoo County Democratic Party $34K; Macomb County Democratic Party $34K; Michigan Assn. for Justice/Justice PAC $34K; United Auto Workers/UAW MI Voluntary PAC $34K; Michigan Education Assn./MEA PAC $30K; Teamsters 299 PAC $30K; Kent County Democratic Party $23K; Intl. Brotherhood of Electrical Workers/IBEW COPE $20K. [Ibid., 56.]
1149 Ibid., 14. Top contributors included: Michigan Republican Party $65K; Detroit Regional Chamber PAC $34K; Michigan Assn. of Realtors/REALTORS PAC $34K; Michigan Chamber of Commerce PAC $34K; Michigan Farm Bureau PAC $34K; Michigan Health & Hospital Assn./Health PAC $34K; Michigan Restaurant Assn. PAC $34K; Michigan Bankers Assn. PAC/MI BANK PAC $31K; Frankenmuth PAC $30K; and Michigan State Medical Society/MI Doctors PAC $428,703. [Ibid., 56.]

The court after Taylor, 2009, from left: Justice Stephen J. Markman, Justice Michael F. Cavanagh, Justice Maura D. Corrigan, Chief Justice Marilyn J. Kelly, Justice Robert P. Young, Jr., Justice Elizabeth A. Weaver, and Justice Diane Marie Hathaway.

Hathaway personally didn't have that much money, but Taylor had well over a million. He had quite a chest. And the Dems didn't spend that much money, but she won anyway because she was at the right place and right time and was the right person. She really went out and campaigned like crazy, and it was this woman versus this man who had been in controversy. That's my opinion of it.

This election set an all-time high for the price per seat: $7,505,811, two million dollars more than in the next highest race in 2000.[1150] And the Republicans set several records. Here's the analysis from the Michigan Campaign Finance Network:

> Chief Justice Taylor's campaign raised $1,937,759 and broke the previous Supreme Court fundraising record of $1,332,975, also held by Justice Taylor, by the time his pre-convention report was filed. In three campaigns within ten years, Justice Taylor's campaigns raised a total of $4,257,300.
>
> Judge Hathaway's campaign began from a standing start with no money raised at the time of the pre-convention report. As late as 16 days before Election Day, Judge Hathaway's campaign had raised barely $300,000.[1151]

There was money behind the candidates but not directly in their coffers, MCFN noted:

1150 Ibid., 15.
1151 Ibid., 14.

Third-parties were a dominant part of the campaigns with spending that was reported and unreported. The political parties reported $786,000 in independent expenditures, with the Democrats outspending the Republicans in this area by a margin of nearly two-to-one. The Great Lakes Education Project reported independent expenditures in the amount of $225,000, supporting Chief Justice Taylor.

The greatest portion of campaign spending was not disclosed in any campaign finance report. The political parties and the Michigan Chamber of Commerce spent $3.8 million on television issue advertisements[1152] that defined the character and qualifications of the candidates without explicitly exhorting a vote for or against either candidate. Under Michigan's weak campaign finance law, such communications are not considered to be campaign expenditures and the sources of money that paid for the ads are not required to be disclosed. The Michigan Campaign Finance Network collected issue ad spending data from the state's television broadcasters and cable systems. Since 2000, the sponsors of issue ads have spent more than the Supreme Court candidates [...] but they have disclosed nothing about the sources of their funds.[1153]

I didn't enter publicly in any way in that campaign. And I myself was amazed that it came out the way it did, but one knew that there was more opposition than the talking heads of the press who just listened to their "conventional wisdom" as they called it. But it was just a matter of some awakening of people, and Taylor and them being so confident; it would be called over-confident.

And then the actions of the press with respect to "the sleeping judge" advertisement?

They gave the Republicans a free answer to this TV ad.

Down the Rabbit Hole

Before Justice Hathaway's formal investiture Jan. 8, 2009,[1154] she had been sworn and seated to take part in the first business of the court, choosing a new chief justice. Weaver knew she could be chief justice again if she wanted it. The three Democrats didn't control enough votes for a majority; but neither did the remaining Engler Republicans. And she knew that the Democrats could not vote publicly for the remaining three Englerite Republicans (and the vote would be made public). The selection of the chief justice was in her hands. And Young wanted it desperately. How much?

1152 $1,671,085 from the Michigan Chamber of Commerce and $700,546 from the Michigan Republican Party to support Taylor/oppose Hathaway; $1,432,492 from the Michigan Democratic Party to support Hathaway/oppose Taylor.
1153 Rich Robinson and Barbara R. Moorhouse, 15.
1154 "Investiture ceremony for the Honorable Diane M. Hathaway, Michigan Supreme Court Historical Society, 8 January 2009, http://www.micourthistory.org/special_sessions.php?get_id=160.

Young called me and asked me for my vote. But his way of doing it was in an arrogant manner in that, "Well, I understand you want to be back in the fold." So being in the fold means you're like a sheep and you follow, which wasn't going to happen.

I said to him, "Well, Bob, why should I vote for you to be the chief justice? What do you intend to do in the way of leading the court?" And I said, "Would you be interested in moving forward with the disqualification issues?"

"Well, whatever the court wants to do," was his answer. So that's no answer at all. And I listed a couple of the crucial issues and finished with "Are we going to get back to being orderly and professional?"

"Well, whatever the court says." So there was no interest in that.

I then said, "Why shouldn't I vote for Marilyn Kelly?"

And at that point he said, "Well, I can see you're not going to vote for me," and he hung up. That was not the first time that Justice Young was unhappy with me. But he certainly was unhappy.

In the end, although Hathaway wanted Weaver to be chief justice, Weaver said that her significant work at the court was to work for reforms, not something she could handily accomplish while serving as chief justice. Weaver supported Kelly, but not altogether happily. The Engler Three publicly dissented.[1155]

Diane had just arrived, and she had immediately gotten a rude awakening. I had more than once described being on the Michigan Supreme Court as the Disney version of Alice in Wonderland. And Diane was the one opening the book, and I was just Alice-slide-down-the-hole. Everything was upside down and backwards, and that's just the way it was at the Michigan Supreme Court. Instead of the most orderly—as it should have been—it was the least orderly, the least professional, the least fair or just place that I've been. And, the most secret.

And so when Justice Hathaway came, she was a breath of fresh air, but probably what she found there was not what she expected.

She also didn't expect to be forced to resign from the court in disgrace and to plead guilty to federal fraud charges in 2013 as a result of a short sale of one of her properties. But all that was to come later.

This is yet another instance where things have gone badly wrong. Her fraudulent actions invite consideration of Lord Acton's observation that "Power tends to corrupt and absolute power corrupts absolutely." The power of a Supreme Court justice is very nearly absolute. Vigilance against corruption is always called for when one has authority.

Justice Hathaway's deceitful and criminal behavior is further discussed in the Epilogue.

1155 Marcia McBrien, "Marilyn Kelly is new Chief Justice of Michigan Supreme Court; fifth woman to serve as head of High Court," 8 January 2009, yet another misplaced file that had be available at http://courts.michigan.gov/supremecourt/Press/MKcj.pdf.

Chapter 23

Having His Cake
Water for All?,
A Judge Gone Wrong

Depending on your point of view, Mecosta County Circuit (49th) Court Judge Lawrence Root was either a neo-Luddite, an obscurant...or he was a conservationist of the highest order. And it fell to him to make a hard decision: whether a new $150-million investment in a water bottling plant with 240-plus jobs (and a $16 million annual payroll) attached—a favored project of former Governor John Engler[1156]—could keep pumping 400 gallons a minute from his county's aquifer, or whether a group challenging that, the Michigan Citizens for Water Conservation (MCCW), gave him reasons to twist the spigot.

This case originated before the events in the last few chapters, but it belongs here because the two major portions of this chapter and the next share a link, a concept.

Mecosta County is water rich. There are lakes by the hundreds, rivers big and small, even a hydroelectric facility at the Hardy Dam on the Muskegon River. Mecosta County straddles the state's watershed, and the headwaters for the Pine, Chippewa, and the Little Muskegon rivers originate there, the first two heading east and the other west.

Perrier Group of America, the predecessor to Nestlé Waters North America, Inc., was desirous of tapping some of that pure water that often rises up from springs. So, in December 2000, the company negotiated groundwater rights to 600 acres[1157] owned by

---

1156 In filing its *amicus curiae* brief in support of Nestlé, the Mecosta County Association for Economic Growth noted:

> In 2001, then-Governor John Engler, who was adamantly opposed to unreasonable diversions of water from the Great Lakes, reviewed defendant's scientific approach to groundwater management, enthusiastically supported the project, and awarded defendant $9.5 million in tax rebates to induce defendant to make this investment.

["Brief on behalf of *Amicus Curiae* Mecosta County Association for Economic Growth, in support of defendant-appellee Nestlé Waters North America," *Michigan Citizens of Water Conservation v Nestlé Waters North America, Inc.*, No. 130802, Michigan Supreme Court, 13 May 2006, 3. This is yet another document no longer retrievable online following the court's web reorganization. It had been listed as http://courts.michigan.gov/plc/curriculum/amicus_brief_def2.pdf.]

1157 In Michigan, that's a substantial piece of property. Six hundred forty acres in a square is known as a "section"—a mile on a side.

Donald Patrick and Nancy Bollman (doing business as Pat Bollman Enterprises). The property was a fenced hunting preserve known as Sanctuary Springs. So, there was controlled deer hunting above and there was to be water extracted from below. Nestlé sought and received permission to drill four wells. It then laid 12 miles of stainless steel water line, and began building a bottling facility on 8 Mile Road, close to the intersection with U.S. 31. The sprawling industrial site—white and grey, clean and tidy—is across the road from what appears to be an Amish farm; in mid summer there is hay in stooks, drying in the field.

The water for the bottling plant is taken from an aquifer that also feeds several small lakes—Osprey and Thompson—and Dead Stream, a small tributary that eventually finds its way into the Little Muskegon River.[1158]

Michigan Citizens for Water Conservation, a 1300-member non-profit that arose at the same time Governor Engler welcomed Perrier, filed suit in June of 2001, even before the water plant was finished. MCWC was seeking "temporary and permanent injunctive relieve against Nestlé."[1159] The relief was denied by Judge Lawrence Root, then the only judge in a two-county circuit that includes Mecosta and Osceola counties. At the time of the first filing, Root warned Nestlé that it was proceeding at its own risk, given the likelihood that further suits would arise.

MCWC filed an amended complaint in November of 2001, again still before the operation had permits to operate. MCWC was joined by four property owners— Jeffrey and Shelley Sapp, and R.J. and Barbara Doyle.

> R.J. and Barbara Doyle live on property that is riparian to the Dead Stream, approximately one-half mile below the Sanctuary property where the spring is located. Jeffery and Shelley Sapp own property on Round Lake and Thompson Lake, a small 20-acre lake next to Dead Stream, where they live with their children. The named plaintiffs, other riparian members of MCWC, and members of the public all use the Dead Stream for recreational purposes from the Tri-Lakes area up to the Doyle's home and the bridge on State Highway M-20.

> In 2001, over the objections by the riparians, Nestlé's predecessor began construction of four high-capacity wells on the Sanctuary property. The wells are capable of pumping 400 gallons of groundwater a minute, 500,000 gallons per day, and 210 million gallons per year. After it is pumped, the groundwater is transported 12 miles through a pipeline to a bottling plant in Stanwood, Michigan. The water is bottled at the plant and sold under the "Ice Mountain" brand. The bottling plant is outside of the watershed of the Dead Stream and outside of the source aquifer for the spring. Ice Mountain

---

1158 *Michigan Citizens of Water Conservation v Nestlé Waters North America, Inc.*, No. 130802, Michigan Supreme Court, 25 July 2007, http://publicdocs.courts.mi.gov:81/OPINIONS/FINAL/SCT/20070725_S130802_167_nestle130802-op.pdf.
1159 Ibid., 5.

water bottled at the plant is marketed throughout the Midwest, including to areas outside the Great Lakes basin.[1160]

The plaintiffs lodged six counts:

> In count I, the MCWC requested an injunction against defendant's construction of wells, well houses, and the pipeline for water extraction from Sanctuary Springs. Count II alleged that defendant's withdrawal of water would not be lawful under the common law applicable to riparian water rights. Count III alleged that defendant's withdrawal of water was unreasonable under the common law applicable to groundwater. Count IV alleged that the waters of Sanctuary Springs are subject to the public trust and, consequently, defendant is without the power to withdraw, divert, diminish, or use the water in a way that alienates or destroys the public's title. Count V alleged that defendant's use of the waters would constitute an unlawful taking of public resources. Finally, count VI alleged that defendant's withdrawals would violate the Michigan environmental protection act (MEPA).[1161]

MEPA was the Michigan Environmental Protection Act, the showcase of the Milliken Administration. And it was based on Article IV, Section 52, of the 1963 Michigan Constitution:

> The conservation and development of the natural resources of the state are hereby declared to be of paramount public concern in the interest of the health, safety and general welfare of the people. The legislature shall provide for the protection of the air, water and other natural resources of the state from pollution, impairment and destruction.[1162]

When the legislature enacted the Michigan Environmental Protection Act in 1970, the highlight of that legislation was that it gave any and every person the right to bring suit to stop environmental harm. That act gave each person standing.

The rule arising from the act read:

> The attorney general or any person may maintain an action in the circuit court having jurisdiction where the alleged violation occurred or is likely to occur for declaratory and equitable relief against any person for the protection of the air, water, and other natural resources and the public trust in these resources from pollution, impairment, or destruction.[1163]

1160 Appellants brief, Leave for appeal, *Michigan Citizens for Water Conservation v Nestlé Waters of North America, Inc.*, 28 March 2006, 2, http://courts.michigan.gov/Courts/MichiganSupremeCourt/Clerks/Oral-Arguments/Briefs/01-07/130802/130802-AppellantsApp.pdf.
1161 Michael R. Smolenski, *Michigan Citizens for Water Conservation v Nestlé Waters of North America, Inc.*, Nos. 254202 and 256153, Michigan Court of Appeals, 29 November 2005, 3, http://publicdocs.courts.mi.gov:81/opinions/final/coa/20051129_c254202_116_209o.254202.opn.coa.pdf.
1162 Constitution of Michigan of 1963, Article IV, Section 52, http://www.legislature.mi.gov/(S(oqduzia4i0mqdrix0eagnv45))/mileg.aspx?page=GetObject&objectname=mcl-Article-IV-52.
1163 Natural Resources and Environmental Protection Act, Act 451 of 1994, Section 324.1701(1), http://

It was really simple and really powerful and would soon figure at the center of the *Nestlé* case.

Governor Milliken and the legislature had very clearly intended that every individual have a voice when it came to protecting our rivers, lakes, streams, and wetlands. Standing determines who gets to court, who has a voice in the course of judgment and justice. If you have no standing you are not allowed to file and pursue a matter or a case or to join and participate in a matter or a case—your voice simply will not be heard. So the issue of standing—with reference to the environmental issues presented—mattered. Did every individual have a voice or only some people?

The water first flowed from the wells to the bottling plant in early 2002. And the matter went to court where, of the six counts the plaintiffs raised, only the third and sixth— the alleged violation of common-law rules that governed diversion of groundwater and Nestlé's alleged violation of the Michigan Environmental Protection Act—would survive to trial. But with motion after motion filed by each side, it took a long time for the matter to get there. Writing of the history of the case, Judge Lawrence Root described it this way:

> Numerous motions, many dispositive, were heard and decided during the case's pendency. Finally, the trial began on May 5, 2003, and continued for a total of nineteen days, over a disjointed schedule, ending on July 3, 2003. Two post-trial views were conducted. One by the court without counsel present, but with their consent, was conducted on July 5, 2003. Another, with counsel present, was conducted on July 9, 2003. Post-trial briefing, even more extensive than the trial briefing, was submitted by counsel. The case was finally argued to the court on September 9 and 10, 2003. This case is, undoubtedly, the most extensive and intensive in the history of the 49th Judicial Circuit.[1164]

The 19-day trial had been spread over four months (May 5, 2003–Sept 10, 2003), and on Nov. 25, 2003, Judge Root granted a permanent injunction against the water pumping. In doing so, he had to weigh the rights of the two sides, Nestlé's right to use the water it had bargained for, and the rights of the property owners along the water and the rights of citizens who made use of the streams or otherwise enjoyed them. He also had to evaluate the environmental impact of the operation.

His opinion is another masterful piece of writing. He had debated about delivering a bench or a written opinion, and came down on the issue of the latter because of the complexity of the case. But his writing was conversational, intentionally so.

> Since the reader is...well...reading, it is apparent that the written opinion format was settled on. However, to try to retain a degree of the conversa-

www.legislature.mi.gov/(S(s5il05rfk333am554t2zsn55))/mileg.aspx?page=GetObject&objectname=m cl-324-1701.
1164 Lawrence C. Root, Opinion, Case No. 01-14563-CE *Michigan Citizens for Water Conservation v Nestlé Waters of North America, Inc.*, 25 November 2003, 1, http://www.ecobizport.com/NestleRootOpinion.pdf.

tional tone, the opinion will often lapse into the writer "speaking" in the first person, a method often criticized in formal writing, but that has its place when appropriate. It is felt appropriate here.[1165]

And while he was very certain what the case covered, he also was clear to state what it didn't address:

> As I noted at the conclusion of the trial, this case has been referred to as a "tempest in a tea pot," and I live in, and am elected from, the area in which the tempest rages. As such, despite my efforts to avoid exposure to community sentiment and discussion regarding the case and its subject matter, I have heard enough to know that there are many misconceptions as to what this case is really about and what it is not about.
>
> This case is about the defendants' pumping operation in and from the Sanctuary Springs area in the shallow unconfined aquifer referred to in this case and nothing else. Realization of that is the beginning of understanding this case.
>
> This case is not about preserving the Great Lakes or allowing or prohibiting any diversion of water from them, either in the form of an absolute prohibition (which is unlikely) or in the form of restrictions on such. Those issues are deserving of discussion and resolution, but this case is not about those questions.
>
> This case is not a one-person "referendum" on the merits of the beverage bottled-water industry. This is an area of the world blessed with an abundance of good water, but such is not the situation in many other areas. Even in areas with good drinking water readily available from the "tap," it is apparent that many consumers choose to buy bottled water for drinking, at least for some of their hydration needs. The defendants are meeting a market for their product, and it is not the charge of this court to decide the merits of that market.
>
> This case is not about the re-distribution of wealth or the proceeds from the defendants' activities. Decisions about taxing defendants' activities and products are made in other branches of government, not the courts. There has even been some "chatter" in some circles that Michiganders, or perhaps those residing in the impacted watershed, should be directly paid for the taking of "their water," like Alaskans are paid for the taking of their petroleum resources. Such an analysis does not apply to water, a more transient resource than crude oil, and such policy decisions are not in the province of the courts to make. The plaintiffs have made a claim for the deposit of a portion of the proceeds from defendants' challenged activities, which claim will be dealt with below.

1165 Ibid., 2.

There is no claim made in this case that anyone's water wells will be impacted by defendants' activities, so that is not part of this case. Even plaintiffs' experts make no such claim. Likewise, there is no assertion that there will be any impact on water-bodies outside those in the West Branch of the Little Muskegon River watershed, and then only in its upper reaches. The claims presented are restricted to effects and impacts in that limited area.

This case has nothing to do with Nestlé's large bottling plant located in Mecosta County, remote from the well field but connected to it by an eleven-mile long pipeline. The factory is indeed very large, though not so huge as argued by plaintiffs' attorney. Early in the case I declined to restrain the building of the plant as its existence had, and has, nothing to do with plaintiffs' claims in this case. Defendant Nestlé was cautioned that it was proceeding in building a bottling plant at its own risk should I decide plaintiffs' claims have merit such that there might be no water to be bottled in the plant. However, the plant is not part of any analysis undertaken in this opinion, so nothing ruled on here has any effect on whether the plant may be used to bottle water and prepare it for shipment anywhere.

Sadly, some of the "chatter" has been personally directed at the Defendants Bollman. They, and their family, have succeeded financially from real estate holdings and developments in Mecosta County.[1166] Frankly, [I am] certain of the comments in circulation are founded in some of the more base elements of human nature: resentment and jealousy. Needless to say, this opinion has nothing to do with such sentiments. Those who hold and voice them should pause and reflect on themselves, rather than others, and focus on the real issues presented which are substantial enough on their own. If the court finds contrary to Bollmans' interests here, such findings will be based on the facts and the law that apply to this controversy.

Issues regarding the financial and other benefits of Defendant Nestlé's operations being here in Mecosta County are not directly part of any relevant analysis here. From a "business community" standpoint it is clear that an entity that brings jobs and economic activity to an area has much to stand in its favor. Also, many of the supporters of the Nestlé operation are local government officials. Generally, government favors operations that generate revenue for the local economy, and in the process generate tax revenue for the government. As but one example, I have been exposed to commentary by certain local county commissioners favoring Nestlé and critical of plaintiffs. In keeping with my ethical obligations, I would cut such off immediately, but such comments by the leaders of one of this court's funding units are noted, even if ignored.

1166 Interestingly, both the Bollmans and the Doyles have long-standing family real estate businesses. Pat's father, Don Bollman, created the 7000-acre Canadian Lakes development from a series of pothole lakes and swamps. R.J. Doyle Realty has sold a lot of that property as well as much else in the area.

This case is not about any opinions I, as an individual aside from my role as judge and fact finder, might have. There's an old saying to the effect that a good lawyer knows the law, but that a great lawyer knows the judge. At first blush that sounds like a cynical commentary on the "ole-boys' network," but really it is properly interpreted to mean that a great lawyer is one who has researched the judge to find out if she/he has any known predilections or philosophical nuances that might run for or against his client. Such research here would reveal me to have history and interests that could be interpreted as "cutting both ways." My family background is in business (manufacturing) and my undergraduate degree is in business administration. On the other hand, I am a hunter, fisherman and generally an "outdoorsman," which means I am interested in conservation and the management of renewable resources. In the final analysis I would hope that any such research would also have revealed that I value my integrity as a judge above any such personal predilections.

Neither is this case about whether Defendant Nestlé is a "good corporate citizen" in relation to matters outside the issues of this case. Their shipment of water to Detroit after the electricity "blackout" this year, their contributions to various charities and the like certainly are laudable, but they are not part of the court's consideration here.

Finally, the case is most certainly not about public opinion or political pressure. There is no doubt that just about everyone around here has some opinion about this case, informed or not, and most are not at all shy about sharing their feelings on the matter. Discussion of this case began even before there was a filed legal case. Once it became obvious that there would be a lawsuit that I, as the only circuit court judge in the 49th Judicial Circuit, would be presiding over and serving as fact finder in, I undertook to insulate myself from public commentary as much as possible. This has not been easy. Some of the plaintiffs, and/or those sympathetic to their cause, put up signs "Go Away Perrier" (there apparently not being any catchy rhyme for Nestlé) and generally "talk-up" their point of view. On the other hand, Nestlé, and Perrier before it, have waged a campaign of "hearts-and-minds" to generate positive public image and to counter negative opinions. The end result is that I have had to become a virtual social hermit to avoid the, at times, raging debate. I assure the parties, and the public generally, that this case is being decided on the merits and not improper external influences.[1167]

He would be, he promised, independent. And as far as Justice Weaver was concerned, she had known only good things about Judge Root to support that promise.

Judge Lawrence Root was a very good judge, quite capable, and had served a long time. I think he served as the president of all of the circuit judges.[1168]

1167 Lawrence C. Root, Opinion, 3.
1168 Root's on-line resume confirms that he had served as president of the Michigan Judges' Association in

If the Court of Appeals description of *Gilbert v DaimlerChrysler* is the "first best" piece of legal writing covered in this book, Judge Root's decision is easily second best and a close contender for the pole position. It's filled with puns, entertaining cultural references, and unpretentious country wisdom. What makes it all the more remarkable is that this nearly 70-page opinion was rendered by a trial court judge who was the sole judge in his two-county circuit; it took a lot of time to write that opinion. Further is the evidence of the great care Root took in coming to his decision. He discussed and weighed scientific evidence, the often-conflicting testimony of experts.

> I came to the conclusion that I could not blindly accept counsels' characterizations of the evidence and had to, on many occasions, personally check the record to verify a point being made that didn't seem consistent with my recollection of the proofs or that was obviously in contention between the sides. Both sides called their opponent on points of exaggeration or minimizing of the effects and impacts of pumping. I have concluded that neither side was 100 percent accurate in their rendition of the proofs, either in argument or in briefing.[1169]

In crafting his decision, Root broke the bodies of water into separate hydrological systems. He discussed Dead Stream first in his opinion. Twice during the trial, he took field trips to the source for a first-hand look.

> I noted above that Dead Stream is curiously named, and unfairly so. I grew up in this area and remember crossing the stream on highway M-20 too many times to count. The name of the stream was the cause of much dark humor to the uninformed, a group that included me back then. Its appearance, especially as one passes over it at highway speeds, is that it is flat and unmoving, more swamp than stream. It shows none of the riffles or other visual indicators of moving water. It's not until you get down and personal with the stream that its nature becomes apparent. This I had the opportunity to do during the two views [....]

> The first of these views was on July 5, 2003, when I canoed, with my wife and our dog Chuck (I just had to get his name in here for posterity, an honor my wife insisted I deny her), from the public landing at the south end of Lake Mecosta to the channel between Lake Mecosta and Blue Lake (dodging boaters and "personal watercraft" on that Independence Day weekend) to the opening that represents the end of Dead Stream where it joins the channel between Blue Lake and Lake Mecosta. There was sufficient opening to make the Dead Stream channel apparent.

2002. Among other honors and activities, he'd served as the Michigan Judges' Association's delegate to the court reform summit convened by the Michigan Supreme Court in 1998. He'd also been appointed by the chief justice to the Task Force on Court Reform in 1996. He was even the Big Rapids High School Alumnus of the year in 2003. [Curriculim {sic.} vitae, Judge Lawrence C. Root (retired), http://www.13thcircuitcourt. org/AssetFactory.aspx?did=8384.]
1169 Lawrence C. Root, Opinion, 9.

From there up into what was referred to at trial as the braided-channel section of Dead Stream (which also includes volume and flow from Gilbert Creek) there was an apparent current in the stream. Actually, this braided-channel section is part of a large marsh between the two lakes on the east and the west, with its northerly boundary apparently being what I came to call the Gilbert Creek delta and high ground south of M-20. We had one dead-end exploration before we found the main channel up to the area referred to at trial as Doyles', being the Mecosta County residence of Plaintiffs R.J. and Barbara Doyle located just south of M-20 on the east side of Dead Stream. This area is where the infamous mud flats so often referred to at trial are located. We tried to paddle into and around the flats, but could not because of the mud that falls into the category of "too thick to drink, too thin to plow." The nature of the mud as rotting organic matter becomes immediately apparent as its surface is disturbed, as with a canoe paddle. Stench is not too strong a word. We continued to paddle up Dead Stream to M-20, a short distance upstream from Doyles', where we stopped, shared a celebratory Pepsi and reversed our course as we were running out of daylight to safely make it back to the now-distant landing on Lake Mecosta. I noted a definite current in the channel of Dead Stream its entire distance as far as we made it that day.

The second view of Dead Stream was with counsel and Greg Foote on July 9, 2003, as part of our extensive view of the area in question. We walked in the area of the wetlands in controversy and walked the well field area and along part of the north shore of Osprey Lake. We then paddled the length and breadth of Osprey Lake. Finally, we paddled the length of Dead Stream from M-20 to the Osprey Lake dam, then back to Doyles'. My observation of Dead Stream was that it had a definite current throughout its entire length. Actually, the upper stretch of the stream I would characterize as a channel winding through a large wetland. At times the distinction between wetland and stream would be clearly apparent, but at other times the transition would be less sharp.

Based on the trial evidence, and reinforced by the views, Dead Stream is not dead, but rather is the moving-water component of a complex and beautiful ecosystem that has many variabilities affecting its stage and flow.[1170]

After sorting through the expert testimony and reviewing all the hydrological evidence introduced, Root's calculation was the Dead Stream would drop by two inches if Nestlé were allowed to continue pumping. In all, it would lose almost 30 percent of its flow.[1171]

Next he turned to what he classified as the wetlands.

1170 Ibid., 17.
1171 Ibid., 22.

Regarding the wetlands generally, it should be noted that the effects of pumping will reach the wetlands at differing times depending on how quickly the groundwater under them reacts to pumping. The experts use the concept of lag to explain this.[1172]

Still, some of the wetlands would see water levels drop six to eight inches, Root calculated, if the pumps were allowed unabated.

Finally he came to the two lakes. Both of them had dropped since pumping had commenced.

As noted above, Osprey Lake and Thompson Lake had dropped at the pump rates existing at the time of trial and will drop even more as the pump rates go up. The drops to date were testified to directly by lay witnesses and the experts. [...]

From the evidence I find that the two lakes will react similarly in level of drop. Dr. Hyndman estimated that drop to be in the area of three to six inches. Dr. Andrews opined that the drop will be more in the range of 2½-3½ inches. Shelly Sapp, a riparian on Thompson Lake and one of the named plaintiffs, testified that "her" lake had dropped notably since pumping started, while it hadn't done so since her family moved there in 1995.

Based on all the evidence I find that Osprey Lake and Thompson Lake will drop up to six inches as the result of pumping at 400 g.p.m. [gallons per minute].[1173]

Root treated each count separately and provided his legal analyses. For count III, the common law issue of groundwater and riparian rights, he wrote there was "no controlling Michigan Law directly on point to this case."[1174] But from four cases in particular,[1175] either addressed by the Michigan Court of Appeals or the Michigan Supreme Court, he found enough support to halt the extraction. Elsewise, he said, there would be harm to Dead Stream, the wetlands, and the two lakes.

In this case the defendants' water-extraction activities from the Sanctuary Springs wells run afoul [...] of the standards [...] by a comfortable margin. As such, they are hereby enjoined. In stating they are enjoined I am holding that Nestlé's pumping operations at the Sanctuary Springs must stop entirely. I realize this is a dramatic and drastic result, but from the evidence I accept I have made the findings spelled out above. Further, I am unable to find that a specific pumping rate lower than 400 g.p.m., or any rate to date, will reduce

---

1172 Ibid., 28.
1173 Ibid., 28.
1174 Ibid., 44.
1175 The cases were *John B. Dumont v John G. Kellogg*, 29 Mich. 420 (1874), *Schenk v City of Ann Arbor*, (1916) Mich. 75 (1916), *Hoover v Crane*, 362 Mich. 36 (1960), and *Donald Maerz and Frieda Maerz v United State Steel Corporation*, 116 Mich. App 710 (1982).

the effects and impacts to a level that is not harmful under the Count III analysis.[1176]

On the other count, that of violating Michigan Environmental Protection Act (MEPA), Root analyzed:

> MEPA is one of those (unfortunately) altogether too-rare instances in which the legislature in Michigan has specifically set only broad objectives and left the specifics of meeting those objectives to the courts. The genius of that approach is that it recognizes the many issues and variables that may exist and doesn't try to anticipate and resolve them legislatively. The end effect is that the law of environmental protection in Michigan is constantly evolving through the common law as developed by the judiciary in the crucible of the adjudication of actual cases and controversies. This case is obviously one such vehicle.

> In "broad-brush" terms, MEPA lets the Attorney General, or anyone else for that matter, bring an action in the appropriate circuit court "...for the protection of the air, water, and other natural resources and the public trust in these resources from pollution, impairment, or destruction."[1177] That section continues to instruct that if there is any existing standard designed to serve those ends in force under the authority of virtually any state agency or instrumentality, the court can either use that standard or direct another standard that is not a lesser protection of the environment. Once a plaintiff has made out a *prima facie* showing under the act, the defendant may rebut that showing and/or may, as an affirmative defense, show that there is no "feasible and prudent alternative and that his or her conduct" is essentially consistent with the purposes of the act.[1178]

There was no question that the act was crucial in his deliberations.

In addition, Root examined relevant cases that had appeals before the appellate courts, and the Inland Lakes and Streams Act, the Wetland Protection Act, and the Great Lakes Preservations Act.[1179] In the end, he found that the pumping violated the law.

> Having determined that Nestlé's pumping operations at the Sanctuary Springs violates a number of standards of environmental protection I have adopted in this opinion at any pumping rate experienced to date and up to

1176 Lawrence C. Root, Opinion,49.
1177 Natural Resources and Environmental Protection Act, Act 451 of 1994, Section 324.1701(1), http://www.legislature.mi.gov/(S(s5il05rfk333am554t2zsn55))/mileg.aspx?page=GetObject&objectname=mcl-324-1701.
1178 Lawrence C. Root, Opinion, 49.
1179 Other parts of the Natural Resources and Environmental Protection Act covered under Sections 324.301 [http://www.legislature.mi.gov/(S(20dctgjlj0kller5mkepk255))/mileg.aspx?page=getobject&objectname=mcl-451-1994-iii-1-inland-waters-301], 324.303 [http://www.legislature.mi.gov/(S(kxoec5qggvazkp45fdzowq45))/mileg.aspx?page=GetObject&objectname=mcl-324-30305], and 324.327 [http://www.legislature.mi.gov/(S(ysfxr4z5vxpf0x45qwv4zeuy))/mileg.aspx?page=GetObject&objectname=mcl-451-1994-III-1-THE-GREAT-LAKES-327].

the maximum permitted rate of 400 g.p.m., it is my decision that injunctive relief against all pumping operations at that site is appropriate, and such an order is hereby issued. I again note that I understand that injunctive relief is not the only form of relief a court can grant in MEPA cases and that I have inherent discretion to fashion any appropriate remedies tailored to the facts of this case. However, I am convinced on this record that the defendants' proposal that I consider alternatives, such as conditions, and/or convene further proceedings to consider such questions would lead to no conclusions that I have not already made and, therefore, I will not entertain such.[1180]

Judge Root, in his closing observations wrote about the trial, his ruling, and where things were likely to head. It was all a matter of balance:

As observed in the opening of this opinion, this case has been extensive and intensive. The efforts on both sides have been substantial, as has been mine. The exercise has been an interesting one, but it is one I am not anxious to revisit. In the words of The Grateful Dead, "what a long strange trip it's been."

This controversy has generated much heat, but little light for other than those of us directly involved in it. I am fully aware, as noted early in the opinion, that there has been, and likely still is, much passionate emotion on both sides of the issues, some of it the result of being informed on the issues but much of it not informed. The emotive side seems to arise largely from the perception that the defendants are taking for a purely private-profit motive a measurably large amount of a natural resource that is part of that which substantially defines the nature of our state: WATER. While both sides in this case agree that water is not subject to the commonly held concept of ownership, popular sentiment is not in accord with that notion. Michigan is a state in which tourism is a major part of the economy and many people who choose to live here do so because of the recreational opportunities in and natural beauty of the state, much of which has to do with our aquatic resources, of which many here feel very possessive. After all, Michigan is the "Great Lakes State" with a state motto or slogan of "Winter Water Wonderland."

Those on the other "side" of the issue are champions of the economy, jobs, community growth (and tax base). Their concerns are real and not without merit, in the abstract. This case, and particularly my decision, is not about anyone being anti-business or being "Green". It is a case about finding balance.

It is expected that appeals are a virtual certainty, so the matter is likely not over yet. The appellate courts will have the final "say" in this case, but I am confident that everyone involved in this process to date has made sure that

1180 Ibid., 65.

the appellate courts have a good record from which to reach their conclusions.[1181]

The order required the Sanctuary Springs pumps to shut down within 21 days.[1182]

This was the quality of judging that the late Michigan Supreme Court Justice John D. Voelker, fisherman and author of *Anatomy of a Murder*, might have entertained.

Lawrence Root paddles on Dead Stream southeast of Big Rapids in the *Grand Rapids Press* photograph that accompanied one of the stories about the judge's decision in the Nestlé case. (*Grand Rapids Press*/Landov.)

And as Root predicted, there would be further attempts to have the matter definitively settled. First, at the trial court, the defendants moved for a new trial and amendment of the judgment. Nope. Then the plaintiff moved for costs incurred in bringing the suit. Yep: $122,212.47.[1183]

COA Considers

There was a lot on the line, and BOTH Nestlé and MCWC appealed to the Court of Appeals. Nestlé wanted water to flow again and didn't want to have to pay for the legal fees of expert witnesses working for the other side; MCWC sought further clarification on the public trust issue, count IV, one of the arguments not taken up by the trial court.

First, the Court of Appeals looked at the issue and granted an immediate stay of the order of the circuit court. The tap was back on. In a report, Steven Chester, then director of the Department of Environmental Quality, talked about the situation and his agency joining in an *amicus* brief on the part of Nestlé.

1181 Ibid., 66.

1182 Nestlé also had rights to pump 175 g.p.m. from a well at the site of the bottling plant. The only drawback was the water could not be labeled "spring water." [Ibid., 64.]

1183 *Michigan Citizens of Water Conservation v Nestlé Waters North America, Inc.,* No. 254202, Michigan Court of Appeals, 5, http://publicdocs.courts.mi.gov:81/OPINIONS/FINAL/COA/20051129_C254202_116_2090.254202.OPN.COA.PDF.

[O]n Monday, December 15, 2003, Nestlé sought an emergency stay from the Michigan Court of Appeals to block shut down of the Mecosta County facility. Nestlé informed the Court of Appeals that, if it did not receive the stay, it would lay off approximately 120 employees on December 17 and discontinue their pay after January 31, 2004. On Tuesday afternoon, December 16, 2003, the DEQ and Department of Labor and Economic Growth (DLEG) filed an amicus brief asking the Court of Appeals to grant the stay. Prior to filing the *amicus*, I and Deputy Director Skip Pruss had several conversations with legal counsel for MCWC regarding DEQ support of the stay. On the evening of December 16, the Court of Appeals issued a stay of the injunctive relief granted by the circuit court.[1184]

Pumping could resume, but at a diminished flow, 250 g.p.m., pending the appeal. And the matter would be taken up by the Court of Appeals.

When it took up the case, each of the Court of Appeals three-member panel wrote an opinion. The lead opinion was delivered by the late Judge Michael R. Smolenski. The two much shorter concurrences (in part) were drafted by Judges Helene White and William B. Murphy.[1185]

First and most important, Smolenski found there were no factual errors that would warrant a new trial.[1186]

But Smolenski did have a bone or two to pick with Root's reasoning at the lower court concerning the groundwater claim (count III of the circuit court ruling):

In its opinion and order, the trial court applied a hybrid rule of its own making to plaintiffs' groundwater claim. This hybrid rule is not consistent with the reasonable use-balancing test we have determined to be applicable to this case. Therefore, the trial court erred in applying it. However, although the trial court applied the wrong law to the facts of this case, because the record on appeal and the trial court's findings are sufficient for our determination of this issue, we shall proceed to apply the balancing test to the facts of this case.[1187]

And Smolenski did just that:

1184 Steven Chester, "Director Chester on the Nestlé Ice Mountain Decision," undated, http://www.michigan.gov/deq/0,1607,7-135--83319--,00.html.
1185 Murphy had been on the Court of Appeals since 1988. He also was a Democrat contender for the Michigan Supreme Court in 1996. White began her judicial career as a Common Pleas Court judge for the City of Detroit in 1980. In 1981, that court would become the 36th District Court. From 1983 to 1993, she served on the Wayne County Circuit Court. In 1992, she was elected to the Court of Appeals where she remained until she was appointed to the U.S. Sixth Circuit Court of Appeals in 2008 under the auspices of George W. Bush. Smolenski had been a Kent County district and circuit judge before winning election to the Court of Appeals in 1994. He died in 2009.
1186 Michael R. Smolenski, *Michigan Citizens of Water Conservation v Nestlé Waters North America, Inc.*, No. 254202, Michigan Court of Appeals, 29 November 2005, 12.
1187 Ibid., 23.

When determining the purpose of the use, the court should consider whether the use is for an artificial or a natural purpose and whether the use benefits the land from which the water is extracted. [...]

In assessing the suitability of the use to the location, the court should examine the nature of the water source and its attributes. [...]

In assessing the harm and benefits, the court should examine not only the economic harm and benefits to the parties, but should also examine the social benefits and costs of the use, such as its effect on fishing, navigation, and conservation. [...]

The court should also examine the extent, duration, necessity, and application of the use, including any effects on the quantity, quality, and level of the water.[1188]

And the plaintiffs—the local water users—were to be given some preference in the matter.

In his conclusion about the riparian rights enjoyed by the plaintiffs, Smolenski agreed that the full flow from the wells of 400 g.p.m. would infringe on the rights of the plaintiffs. "Therefore, taking all the factors outlined into consideration, we determine that defendant's proposed withdrawal of 400 g.p.m. would be unreasonable under the circumstances."[1189]

So, in his judgment on count III, he was sending the matter back to the Circuit Court to find the right amount that could be withdrawn: "Therefore, we affirm the judgment in favor of plaintiffs on the groundwater claim, but remand to the trial court to determine the appropriate parameters of the injunction and modify it accordingly."[1190]

That still left count VI considerations, and they would be more complex and would involve new law. In the claim under MEPA, the Court of Appeals in part reversed the trial court.

Defendant first argues that plaintiffs lack standing to sue under MEPA for claims respecting the Osprey Lake impoundment and wetlands 112, 115, and 301 because any adverse effect on those areas from defendant's pumping activities does not affect plaintiffs in a manner different from the citizenry at large. We agree.[1191]

That was different from the law Root had used to determine the issue. The Court of Appeals cited a decision in a case that had been released by the Supreme Court after the trial court's verdict but before the conclusion of the appeal:

1188 Ibid., 25.
1189 Ibid., 29.
1190 Ibid., 31.
1191 Ibid., 32.

...because of our Supreme Court's decision in *Cleveland Cliffs*, which was re-leased after the release of the trial court's original opinion in this matter, there is doubt about the continuing validity of the standing conferred by MCL 324.1701(1).[1192]

So, the MEPA standard—

The attorney general or any person may maintain an action in the circuit court having jurisdiction where the alleged violation occurred or is likely to occur for declaratory and equitable relief against any person for the protec-tion of the air, water, and other natural resources and the public trust in these resources from pollution, impairment, or destruction.[1193]

—would no longer apply. How could this be? And what was this *Cleveland Cliffs* decision?

Gutting the Law

The *National Wildlife Federation v Cleveland Cliffs Iron Company* decision was one of two prior major decisions that had environmental impact that Weaver said the majority got wrong, wrong, wrong in reversing the state's standing rule.

The other—and the first of the two—was *Lee v Macomb County Board of Commissioners.*

Lee v Macomb County Board of Commissioners did not deal with environmental issues, but the implications were broad. In *Lee*, the Michigan Supreme Court majority took up the issue of standing and wrote that the state would henceforward make use of the standards that had arisen from a federal case: *Lujan v Defenders of Wildlife.*[1194]

The *Lujan* test required:

First, the plaintiff must have suffered an "injury in fact"—an invasion of a legally protected interest which is (a) concrete and particularized, and (b) "actual or imminent, not 'conjectural' or 'hypothetical.'" Second, there must be a causal connection between the injury and the conduct complained of— the injury has to be "fairly . . . trace[able] to the challenged action of the defendant, and not...th[e] result [of] the independent action of some third party not before the court." Third, it must be "likely," as opposed to merely "speculative," that the injury will be "redressed by a favorable decision."[1195]

1192 Ibid., footnote 65, 32.
1193 Natural Resources and Environmental Protection Act, Act 451 of 1994, Section 324.1701, http://www.legislature.mi.gov/(S(s5il05rfk333am554t2zsn55))/mileg.aspx?page=GetObject&objectname=mcl-324-1701
1194 *Lujan v Defenders of Wildlife*, 504 US 555; 112 S Ct 2130; 119 L Ed 2d 351 (1992).
1195 Ibid., 560.

The wholesale adoption of the federal case abrogated Michigan law and fundamentally changed the state's jurisprudence by limiting who could sue.

Kelly wrote a dissent in *Lee*, but she agreed with the majority's adoption of the *Lujan* standing rule. Cavanagh joined her.[1196] They would later have to deal with the recognition that signing on to *Lujan* had been a mistake (see Chapter 25).

In *Lee*, Weaver concurred with reversing the Court of Appeals finding that plaintiffs had standing but disagreed with adopting the *Lujan* standing requirements. And she asserted that adopting the federal standard was absolutely "unnecessary." Michigan's concept of standing, Weaver wrote, was based on the common law tradition: "Unlike constitutional cases in federal courts, the Michigan standing requirements have been based on prudential, rather than constitutional, concerns."[1197]

Under *Cleveland Cliffs*, Weaver said, the Supreme Court had moved further to gut the "everyman" standard and replaced it, making it applicable to those only who the court determined had standing, in other words, only those immediately affected.[1198] In the majority opinion in that case, the Engler Four set forth:

> Perhaps the most critical element of the "judicial power" has been its requirement of a genuine case or controversy between the parties, one in which there is a real, not a hypothetical, dispute, and one in which the plaintiff has suffered a "particularized" or personal injury. [...] Such a "particularized" injury has generally required that a plaintiff must have suffered an injury distinct from that of the public generally.

> Absent a "particularized" injury, there would be little that would stand in the way of the judicial branch becoming intertwined in every matter of public debate.[1199]

That meant that standing went only to the parties who have ownership interests. While Justice Weaver had concurred in the result of the majority opinion, she fought to have the MEPA provisions clearly set forth:

> Pursuant to this constitutional provision, the people of Michigan have required that the legislature provide for the protection of Michigan's natural resources. The legislature properly acted in fulfillment of its constitutional responsibility through enactment of MEPA's citizen-suit provision that provides:

1196 Marilyn J. Kelly, writing in dissent, *Lee v Macomb County Board of Commissioners*, No. 114700, Michigan Supreme Court, 17 July 2001, 6, http://publicdocs.courts.mi.gov:81/OPINIONS/FINAL/SCT/20010717_S114700(60)_lee-walker.Jul17.PDF.

1197 Elizabeth A. Weaver writing in concurrence, *Lee v Macomb County Board of Commissioners*, No. 114700, 3.

1198 *National Wildlife Federation v Cleveland Cliffs Iron Company*, No. 121890, 30 July 2004, 7, http://publicdocs.courts.mi.gov:81/OPINIONS/FINAL/SCT/20040730_S121890_83_national5jan04-op.pdf.]

1199 Ibid.

The attorney general or *any person* may maintain an action in the circuit court having jurisdiction where the alleged violation occurred or is likely to occur for declaratory and equitable relief against any person for the protection of the air, water, and other natural resources and the public trust in these resources from pollution, impairment, or destruction. [MCL324.1701(1)(emphasis added).]

The majority disregards the intent of the legislature, erodes the people's constitutional mandate, and overrules 30 years of Michigan case law that held that the legislature meant what it said when it allowed "any person" to bring an action in circuit court to protect natural resources from actual or likely harm.[1200]

In the end, Weaver agreed with the majority's result in *Cleveland Cliffs*—that the case should be remanded to the trial court, but she disagreed with the reasoning that would gut the established environmental law. It was clear and simple: "any person" meant "any person." Black-letter law.

But she, Cavanagh, and Kelly, each writing a separate dissent, were outvoted by the Engler Four in that 2004 decision.[1201]

COA Continued: Count VI

The Supreme Court, because of elections and other issues of timing, hadn't quite severed all ties to Michigan's regard for natural resources, said Weaver. But that would come, she said, with *Nestlé*. And to reach its decision, the Court of Appeals had to deal with newly established law when confronting and analyzing Judge Root's decision on count VI of *Nestlé*. In the end, it determined that the law he relied on had to go:

Consequently, we must hold that, to the extent that it confers standing broader than the limits imposed by Michigan's constitution, as determined by *Lee* and *Cleveland Cliffs*, MCL 324.1701(1) is unconstitutional.[1202]

And there went the standing of "everyman" when it came to environmental incursion. But Weaver had seen it coming like a freight train.

In the *Nestlé* case, it meant the plaintiffs didn't have standing to bring suit on SOME OF THE PROPERTIES because they didn't have riparian rights to them. But for those properties to which they did lay riparian claim, the Court of Appeals granted them

---

1200 Elizabeth A. Weaver writing in *Cleveland Cliffs* dissent, ibid., 2.
1201 For an early analysis of the impact of *Cleveland Cliffs* decision see "The Shifting Sands of 'Citizen Suit' Standing after *Cleveland Cliffs*," by Joseph E. Quandt, Gina M. Bozzer, and Jeffrey K. Haynes. [*Michigan Bar Journal*, November 2005, 32, http://www.michbar.org/journal/pdf/pdf4article931.pdf.]
1202 *Michigan Citizens for Water Conservation v Nestlé Waters of North America, Inc.*, Nos. 254202 and 256153, Michigan Court of Appeals, 29 November 2005, 34, http://publicdocs.courts.mi.gov:81/opinions/final/coa/20051129_c254202_116_209o.254202.opn.coa.pdf.

standing. Further, the Court of Appeals determined that while Root had got much right, he incorrectly applied MEPA standards.

> While the trial court improperly applied the wrong law to plaintiffs' groundwater claim, it correctly determined that defendant's water withdrawals from Sanctuary Springs violated plaintiffs' riparian rights in the Dead Stream. Therefore, we affirm the trial court's holding to that effect. However, we remand this issue to the trial court to determine what level of water extraction from Sanctuary Springs will provide defendant with a fair participation in the common water supply while maintaining an adequate supply for plaintiffs' water uses. After making its determination, the trial court shall modify its original injunction accordingly. The trial court improperly relied on defendant's purported violations of ILSA and the WPA to establish a *prima facie* violation of MEPA. Because these statutes do not contain pollution control standards, the violation of either of these statutes will not, by itself, establish a *prima facie* violation of MEPA. Therefore, in order to determine that plaintiffs had made out a *prima facie* case, the trial court needed to make specific findings that defendant's conduct would impair the resources in question, which it did not do. Consequently, the trial court erroneously determined that plaintiffs had met their *prima facie* burden. For these reasons, it is necessary to remand this issue to the trial court.

> On remand, the trial court shall determine the applicable standard for impairment of the resources at issue and shall determine, on the entire record and giving due respect to the trial court's earlier findings and credibility assessments, whether plaintiffs have established a *prima facie* violation of the standard with respect to Thompson Lake, the Dead Stream, and the Dead Stream's wetlands. If the trial court determines that plaintiffs have met their *prima facie* burden, the trial court shall determine whether the record supports the conclusion that defendant rebutted that *prima facie* case. If the trial court determines that defendant failed to rebut plaintiffs' *prima facie* case, it shall enter an appropriate remedy.[1203]

In the meantime, Nestlé would be allowed to pump only 200 g.p.m. from the Sanctuary Springs wells.

In his largely partial concurrence, Judge William Murphy would have granted plaintiffs standing with relation to all the wetlands, not just where they enjoyed riparian rights. But he wrote they did so still under the "general standing principle cited in *Cleveland Cliffs*, without the need to rely on MEPA's less demanding standing provisions, there is no need to determine the constitutionality of MCL 324.1701(1)."[1204] Judge Helene White agreed with Murphy that "the Legislature's grant of standing under the facts of the

---

1203 Ibid., 48.
1204 William B. Murphy, *Michigan Citizens of Water Conservation v Nestlé Waters North America, Inc.*, No. 254202, Michigan Court of Appeals, 29 November 2005, 2, http://publicdocs.courts.mi.gov:81/opinions/final/coa/20051129_c254202_117_209c.murphy.254202c.opn.coa.pdf.

instant case does not unconstitutionally expand the judicial power of the courts."[1205] She wanted an additional discussion of the "qualitative impairments" of water flow found by the trial courts.

At his conclusion, Smolenski, writing in footnote of the Court of Appeals' opinion reversing in part and remanding in part, made note of Judge Root's status on the bench:

> Because of the complexity of the evidence, issues, and procedural posture of this case, we strongly urge that Judge Root, who ably presided over the lower court proceedings, be brought out of retirement to preside over this case on remand.[1206]

That's right, Root had retired. He had stepped down February 11, 2005. His replacement: Scott Hill-Kennedy, who had "most recently served as chief governmental relations and legal officer for Ferris State University."[1207] He would serve until Jan. 1, 2007, when Root's term would have expired.[1208] Judge Root had served with distinction since 1977, coming to the court when he was only 28. At his retirement, he was still relatively young, only 57, and he again took up the private practice of law.[1209]

His retirement may have been very handy for those who favored the pumping operations. Having him off the bench might make a difference going forward. Even by his own admission in what the trial was NOT about, he had proven an obstruction to the pro-business community.

On to the MSC

And while Judge Root had retired, the *Nestlé* case had not, and it would shortly come before the Michigan Supreme Court, where the majority could finish the work it set out to do in *Lee* and *Cleveland Cliffs*.

The result there was predictable:

> In *Nat'l Wildlife Federation v Cleveland Cliffs Iron Co*, we noted that "'environ-mental plaintiffs adequately allege injury in fact when they aver that they use the affected area and are persons "for whom the aesthetic and recre-ational values of the area will be lessened" by the challenged activity.'"[1210]

1205 Helene N. White, *Michigan Citizens of Water Conservation v Nestlé Waters North America, Inc.*, No. 254202, Michigan Court of Appeals, 29 November 2005, 2, http://publicdocs.courts.mi.gov:81/opinions/final/coa/20051129_c254202_118_209c.white.254202c2.opn.coa.pdf.
1206 Ibid., 49.
1207 Heidi Hansen, "Granholm appoints Scott Hill-Kennedy judge of 49th Circuit Court," 28 April 2005, http://www.michigan.gov/granholm/0,4587,7-168-23442_21974-116734--,00.html.
1208 And he was subsequently elected. The circuit is now served by two judges, Hill-Kennedy and Ronald C. Nichols [Mecosta County Circuit Court, http://www.co.mecosta.mi.us/circuit.asp].
1209 "Curriculim [sic] vitae," Judge Lawrence C. Root (retired), http://www.13thcircuitcourt.org/AssetFactory.aspx?did=8384.
1210 Quoting from *Friends of the Earth, Inc. v Laidlaw Environmental Services (TOC), Inc.*, 528 US 167, 183; 120 S Ct 693; 145 L Ed 2d 610 (2000).

Plaintiffs indisputably have standing to bring a MEPA claim against Nestlé to protect their riparian property rights to Thompson Lake and the Dead Stream. However, plaintiffs have failed to demonstrate that they use the Osprey Lake Impoundment (Osprey Lake) and Wetlands 112, 115, and 301, and that, as a result, their recreational, aesthetic, or other interests have been impaired. Accordingly, pursuant to MCR 7.302(G)(1), in lieu of granting leave to appeal, we affirm the Court of Appeals in part, but we reverse the Court of Appeals holding that plaintiffs have standing to bring a MEPA claim regarding Osprey Lake and Wetlands 112, 115, and 301, and remand this case to the circuit court for further proceedings consistent with this opinion.[1211]

They were whittling down the application even further: basing their analysis on *Lee* and *Cleveland Cliffs,* "Environmental laws, such as MEPA (or any statutory law for that matter), may be vindicated by persons who have suffered a real injury in fact and thus have a stake in the controversy."[1212]

Weaver was not shy in stating her dissenting opinion:

> I dissent from the majority's reversal of the Court of Appeals holding that plaintiffs have standing to bring a claim under the Michigan Environmental Protection Act (MEPA) with respect to the Osprey Lake impoundment and wetlands 112, 115, and 301. I would hold that plaintiffs have standing under MCL 324.1701(1) to bring an action to enjoin water pumping and bottling production activities that plaintiffs allege will irreparably harm natural resources. I would therefore affirm the [...] decision holding that plaintiffs have standing with respect to all the affected properties at issue.
>
> The majority's holding in this case marks the culmination of a line of cases in which the same majority of four (Chief Justice Taylor and Justices Corrigan, Young, and Markman) has eroded Michigan's traditional rules of standing.[1213]

The Engler Four, she wrote, had erroneously adopted law that had no application for the cases at hand.

> Now, the majority of four has taken this case as the opportunity to finish what it started in *Nat'l Wildlife [Cleveland Cliffs]*: to deprive the people of Michigan of the ability to protect the natural resources of this state. I dissent because the Michigan Constitution does not restrict the ability of the Legislature to grant standing to the citizens of this state. Further, the Michigan Constitution places a broad duty on the Legislature to protect the environ-

---

1211 *Michigan Citizens of Water Conservation v Nestlé Waters North America, Inc.*, No. 130802, Michigan Supreme Court, 25 July 2007, 2, http://publicdocs.courts.mi.gov:81/OPINIONS/FINAL/SCT/20070725_S130802_167_nestle130802-op.pdf.
1212 Ibid., 30.
1213 Elizabeth A. Weaver, writing in dissent, *Michigan Citizens of Water Conservation v Nestlé Waters North America, Inc.*, 1.

ment, and the Legislature has properly fulfilled its constitutional mandate through its enactment of MEPA.

[...]

Before *Lee*, no Michigan case had held that the issue of standing posed a constitutional issue. Nor did any case hold that Michigan's judicial branch was subject to the same case-or-controversy limitation imposed on the federal judicial branch under Article III of the United States Constitution.[1214]

Both Cavanagh and Kelly filed separate dissents, but the deed was done: remanded to the circuit court to rerule in accordance with the Michigan Supreme Court, an appeal for reconsideration notwithstanding.

Nestlé had returned to pumping, but not at former levels:

The company will continue to withdraw an average of 218 gallons per minute of spring water (313,000 gallons per day), with rates varying depending on the time of the year and seasonal conditions at the site. The agreement makes the water withdrawal rates permanent.[1215]

It took them three cases, emboldened with their encroachment upon the law at each step, to undo Michigan's legislative mandate in favor of their own. This was a sequence of cases where these justices who very publicly stated they were intent only on following the letter of the law written by the Legislature, were revealed for what they truly were: judicial activists.

Exactly.

Eventually, with the ascent of Diane Hathaway to the Supreme Court, the *Nestlé* decision would be overturned in part when the court took up *Lansing School Education Ass'n v Lansing Board of Education*[1216] (the court would finish reversing it in *Anglers of the Au Sable, Inc. v Department of Environmental Quality*) in 2010.[1217] That didn't stop the pumps at Sanctuary Springs, but it kept a weather eye on the meter. Nestlé subsequently would turn north to Osceola County where, supplied by a city well, the City of Evart allowed the bottler to operate at the rate of 150 g.p.m.[1218]

1214 Ibid., 3.
1215 Press release, "Nestlé Waters North America reaches agreement ending Michigan legal case," Nestlé Waters North America, 7 July 2009, http://www.prnewswire.com/news-releases/nestle-waters-north-america-reaches-agreement-ending-michigan-legal-case-62137872.html.
1216 *Lansing School Education Ass'n v Lansing Board of Education*, No 138401, 31 July 2010, http://publicdocs.courts.mi.gov:81/opinions/final/sct/20100731_s138401_54_lsea-op.pdf.
1217 *Anglers of the AuSable, Inc. v Department of Environmental* Quality, Nos. 138863 to 138866, 29 December 2010, http://publicdocs.courts.mi.gov:81/opinions/final/sct/20101229_s138863_121_anglers-op.pdf.
1218 Ashley Box, "DEQ waves new Ice Mountain well online," *Cadillac News*, 29 August 2008, http://www.cadillacnews.com/news_story/?story_id=395548&year=2008&issue=20080829.

The role of Judge Lawrence Root in all this looms large. It was he who with a dispassionate eye to the law, but a love of the county's water resources, ruled in accord with established law at the time and as he understood it. In his opinion, he noted that he was likely to be an unpopular judge even among some of his supporters, and certainly he was at odds with those who favored the economic boon Nestlé could bring.

He was under a lot of pressure on the Nestlé case you can be sure because Nestlé is a big employer down there in a very small Mecosta County. And I wondered when he resigned, "Why?" Because he was relatively young, and he had made courageous decisions—I wondered why had he resigned and rather suddenly? But I didn't make much about it because I guess he was capable of doing it. He probably had his period of time in for his retirement, and he could—as people do. So, it was too bad in a sense that he was leaving because I admired his courage in the Nestlé case.

A Retirement?

There was more to the story.

Years after he resigned, I was told that the reason Judge Root had resigned was that he had been picked up for shoplifting in Traverse City—he lives in the Big Rapids area, about 80 to a 100 miles away from Traverse City—and that he had pled guilty and then that he had been apparently dealt with by the State Court Administrator and the JTC in some way—which had never come to our attention at all as justices—and that he had resigned. I was appalled and disappointed to hear it. My understanding was that he had the alternative to resign and that no one would ever know, or he would be proceeded upon, and it would be pretty obvious—well, you hope it would be obvious, although in Grand Traverse we had had a judge who had admitted using marijuana, and the Supreme Court didn't remove him. But in this case, this judge probably figured this was the best way to go.

It did explain why he resigned so quickly, but it was sad; the right result as far as him stepping down, but wrong to not have it admitted and for the public to not know why the judge left.

Who would want, after a lifetime of serving the law and the public, to be held up for the ridicule and scorn of breaking that same law? It would be understandable that a judge would want to avoid the public censure that was sure to come. But how could he pull that off? It would take the proverbial juice.

For seven years, that juice was enough to keep the matter out of the light of day. It would take a tip and then some determined digging to get at the matter.

As it turns out, if you know what you're looking for—and that's the key in this matter—the records are there, one of them even online. But they don't come up on a casual search. After poking about on the net, there it was in the 86th District Court's records: case number 042490SMI.[1219] The matter was closed. The charge had been one

---

1219 86th District Court Cases, Grand Traverse County, No. 042490SMI, http://districtcourt.co.grand-tra-verse.mi.us/c86_cases/. (It will be necessary to enter the case number to pull up the record.)

count of retail fraud, third degree. That might constitute shoplifting or price switching for an item under $200.[1220] This is what showed up:

> Root Lawrence
> Fines and costs: $345.
> 10/29/2004 Arraignment area
> 11/03/2004 Judgment entered
> Arraignment held
> Case on hold (until 05/02/2005)
> Fingerprint order
> Order for fingerprints
> 11/10/2004 Judgment entered
> Paid in full
> 04/18/2005 Judgment entered
> Case dismissed
> Case is closed

No jail time, a six-month probation. A minor infraction, a misdemeanor. But, for what? What had happened? Was this even the right Lawrence Root?

The answers would require an in-person visit to the court. After making the request, co-author Schock (hereafter "I") was notified that it would take time to bring the case file from storage, perhaps as much as a day. In the interim, there was an available print out of the case history, and I then had far more information than was furnished to the public online. For instance, the Grand Traverse Sheriff's Department was the agency that handled the arrest and investigation. There also was a complaint number. Further, when the matter came to the 86th District Court, Judge Thomas J. Phillips handled the matter. So, might the file be brought up later in the day, perhaps late afternoon? "Leave a number and we'll call you."

With directions from the court staff, the next stop was the sheriff's department to request a copy of the complaint. That would require filling out a Freedom of Information Act (FOIA) form, having it approved by the detective in charge, and then paying modest fee. But the detective in charge was out. "Leave a number and we'll call you."

I went about other business until the early afternoon when the sheriff's office called and wanted to make sure the file number given was for the right file; it didn't seem to have anything to do with the my name. Yes, it did deal with Lawrence Root, and if that was the right file, I could return and pick up a copy; it had been approved. But I needed to have exact change: $2.75.

With a copy of the report in hand, I sat down in the sheriff's office to read it.

1220 750.356d, Retail fraud in second or third degree, Michigan Penal Code, http://www.legislature.mi.gov/(S(l50zs355rlfh5i55olpyqrav))/mileg.aspx?page=GetObject&objectname=mcl-750-356d.

The arresting officer "was dispatched to Meijer for a report of retail fraud. Dispatch advised that Meijer loss prevention had a male adult in custody in the office and that he was being cooperative."[1221]

The stolen property consisted of four recovered DVDs: *The Last Samurai* ($14.44), *The Final Countdown* ($15.99), *The Day After Tomorrow* ($19.95), and *Underworld* ($25.49).

The loss prevention officers, S___ and H___ described to the officer what they'd observed. Here is the report:

> S___ stated to me on this date she and H___ had observed Root in the media/movie area. H___ stated that he recognized Root from a prior contact on 10/1 or 10/2/04. H___ stated to me that on that date he had observed Root in the DVD area and that he had selected two DVDs and that H___ believed root had concealed those DVDs and taken them from the store, although at that time had insufficient evidence to detain Root.
>
> They stated that after they saw Root back in the DVD area again on this date, they began watching him where he had selected four DVDs and carried two DVDs in each hand from the media area over to the grocery aisle. S___ stated to me that she observed him walking down the grocery aisle where he had selected some candy and concealed all the DVDs on the inside pockets of his jacket. She stated that she then followed him out of the door where he paid for the candy that he [had] taken off of the shelf although exited the north doors without making any attempt to pay for the DVDs, which were concealed inside of his jacket.
>
> S___ stated that she then stopped and detained Root identifying herself as Loss Prevention and had him come back to the Loss Prevention Office with she and H___.
>
> INTERVIEW ROOT
>
> On 10/16/04 at approximated 16:54, I read Root his Miranda rights verbatim from a Miranda card. Root agreed to waive his rights and agreed to speak with me in reference to this incident.
>
> As Root was present while S___ made her observations to me, I asked him if what she stated was correct with him stating, "it's accurate."
>
> I then asked Root about the incident in which H___ had informed me of that occurred on 10/1 or 10/2/04 in which H___ stated that he observed Root with two DVDs and believed that Root had taken those DVDs without paying for them as well. Root admitted to the offense stating that he believed he did take the two DVDs although he is unsure of what the titles were.

1221 Grand Traverse County Sheriff, Summary, No. 2004-00032102, 16 October 2004.

I asked Root if he had come to Meijer on this date with the intention to take these DVDs with him, stating that he was staying in the area for the week-end and that he had come initially with the intention to get movie candy and when he went back to the DVDs, he decided to take them.

I asked Root if he had money on his person to pay for the DVDs with him stating "yes." I asked Root if he did leave Meijer with the intention of taking the DVDs without paying for them with him stating, "I did."

ACTION TAKEN

Root was issued a misdemeanor appearance citation for retail fraud 3rd degree. He was issued misdemeanor appearance citation G145182 and in-structed to appear within the 86th District Court within ten days at 09:45.[1222]

His arraignment didn't work out quite that way, but that didn't come out until later, when I returned to the court to check on the progress of obtaining the court file. The court had tried unsuccessfully to contact me. Yes, someone had gone to find the file, but it was one of a batch of recently purged files. "We only keep files for six years," said the head clerk. "That's all we're required to keep them under state law."

The court administrator, Carol Stocking, came over to confirm the details of the file purge. She also responded to my assertion that the arraignment may not have happened during the usual course of business...that it might have been before or after hours in an effort to keep it unnoticed by the press and public. I said I'd bet it happened that way.

"I bet it didn't," responded Stocking. "We don't do that here."

I reminded her that such things had happened in the past.

"Such as...?" she asked.

Judge Gilbert, the marijuana-smoking judge.

"Point taken."

And, while there was no way just then for her to prove exactly what time of day the arraignment occurred, she said she had access to the audio recording of the event. Those recordings were required to be kept for ten years. And she would make the recording available the next day.

She was as good as her word. The next day, Sheila Hale, a Certified Electronic Recorder at the court, invited me to sit at her workstation. She had tried to copy the file so it could be carried away, but because of the complex nature of the software that enabled five-channel audio recording, it wouldn't copy, and even if it had, it might not have

---

1222 Ibid.

been usable outside the court. But I could listen and transcribe whatever I wished. Hale also said she would provide a complete transcription of the arraignment if I desired. I told her I did.

The audio of the arraignment carried far more freight than any paper file could have. There were only four people in the room: Judge Phillips, Prosecutor Dennis LaBelle, Mr. (Judge) Root, and Sheila Hale, the Certified Electronic Reporter. The arraignment was held late in the afternoon—beginning at 4:02 p.m.—of November 2, 2004. It was during business hours for the court, but out of the normal sequence of morning arraignments.

The first question before the court was how Root's guilty plea would be taken: as a plea under advisement or as a plea taken with delayed sentencing. A plea under advisement would mean at the conclusion of any probation, the matter would quietly disappear; there would be no conviction and no permanent record in the court. Delayed sentencing would mean that a conviction would enter as a part of the permanent record. It's evident that the Root and LaBelle had discussed the matter with the thought—on Root's part at least—that the court might take a plea under advisement. What follows is from Hale's transcription. I have checked it against my own and found it as complete as possible in every respect.

THE COURT: We'll call the case of Lawrence Charles Root. Hi, Mr. Root, how are you today?

THE DEFENDANT: Good.

THE COURT: You're here to be arraigned today. You're charged with retail fraud third degree. That's a misdemeanor with a maximum of 93 days in jail and a fine up to $500. You fully understand the charge, is that correct?

THE DEFENDANT: I do.

THE COURT: And were you given an advice of rights today? You probably weren't, were you?

THE DEFENDANT: Not formally, but I've read thoroughly MCR 6610.

THE COURT: Okay, so you—

THE DEFENDANT: I'll put that on the record if that satisfies your Honor.

THE COURT: Okay, I'm sure it does; so you're fully aware of your rights?

THE DEFENDANT: I am.

THE COURT: And you're a member of the bar?

THE DEFENDANT: Yes.

THE COURT: So, how do you plea?

THE DEFENDANT: The prosecutor and I have had discussions and pursuant to all of the terms of what I understand to be an agreement, the terminology of which we're working out, I'm willing to admit the offense, plead guilty on those terms which I understand. The terminology may differ, we were speaking in terms of a plea under advisement, not formally accepted similar to a delayed sentence, but the plea is not accepted up front. And if I satisfy the terms and conditions spelled out in the order by the prosecutor and myself, that at the end of the period, I would have the opportunity to have the matter dismissed on those terms.

MR. LABELLE: Your Honor, what I'm thinking of at this point is the question of a delayed sentence, so in our discussions—

THE COURT: If it's a delayed sentence then a conviction enters.

MR. LABELLE: Right, but then you don't sentence and then at the end of the period, if all the conditions and terms of the sentence are satisfied, what is essentially a probationary term, then we have the option to dismiss it at the end of the period.

THE COURT: That's correct.

MR. LABELLE: Yes, and that's what I'm thinking of, and I think what some of the clerks do is deal with a diversion, the plea's taken under advisement never entered as such; I'm not sure what this court's practice is at this point. My preference is, is to do a delayed sentence, and then the court would then proceed as if it was just a regular case with the conditions and terms of probation that would be standard. And at the end of the year or six months, whatever the court deems advisable, then evaluate the case. That's my understanding on how some of the third degree cases are coming through the court at this point on some of the minor offenders, they're doing a few of the delayed cases.

THE COURT: Well, we did two of those this morning—

MR. LABELLE: Right.

THE COURT: The difference between a deferred under some statutes or the court taking under advisement is that there's no conviction entered. In a delayed sentence a conviction is entered, it's public record and, obviously, if the terms and conditions of probation are fulfilled then there would be ultimately a dismissal. So, Mr. Root, do you want to talk to the prosecutor further about this?

THE DEFENDANT: If that's agreeable with your Honor.

MR. LABELLE: Okay, now let me get that—you're talking about taking it under advisement?

THE COURT: That's one of the things that Mr. Root has indicated, I think that's what he thought was going to happen, so I—it seems like there might be need for further discussion and—

MR. LABELLE: Well, let me ask the court this question, what were the two pleas that you took this morning, they were under advisement or they—

THE COURT: No, they were under the delayed sentencing statute, and they were convictions that entered in both cases for retail third degree.

MR. LABELLE: Okay, that would be our normal practice at this time, and I didn't want to depart from that, but as I understand that unless the sentence is entered, the case is dismissed, so there's no indication that, in fact, the conviction occurred then, even though the sentence is delayed. That's our understanding in our office at this point, and if we're misunderstanding that, then I think we better go back and look at that again, because if you had two defendants this morning on these minor offenses and, in fact, a conviction's going to get entered, I think the defense attorneys and defendants are being—are operating under the assumption that if the case is subsequently dismissed no conviction occurs.

THE COURT: When we go through a plea where there's a delayed sentence, I do tell the defendant that a conviction is going to enter—

MR. LABELLE: Okay.

THE COURT: So they fully understand that at the time of the plea. Then we indicate if they go through probation then in a case where the prosecutor has agreed in advance that the conviction would ultimately be dismissed if you fully comply with the terms of probation.

MR. LABELLE: Right, that's what I want to clear up and have it absolutely clear that if, in fact, we dismiss at the end of the period no conviction occurs.

THE COURT: The conviction will enter today—

MR. LABELLE: Right.

THE COURT: He just will not be sentencing—sentenced today.

MR. LABELLE: Right, but then it's subsequently dismissed at the end of the probationary period, the record is cleaned at that point.

THE COURT: Right—

MR. LABELLE: That's what I'm looking for.

THE COURT: In the interim, there's a conviction—

MR. LABELLE: Right.

THE COURT: And it's a public record. And, actually, there is sentencing done, probation sentencing done—

MR. LABELLE: Right.

THE COURT: And then at the end of that period is when, if the terms of probation are complied with, then the case is dismissed.

MR. LABELLE: Right. And that's why I want to be consistent with what the practice is in our office policy now. I mean, we're going into this transition and there's some issues about how they want to start looking at these and they've apparently started, and that's what I want to be consistent with, what they've been doing for the last month or so, is to do the delayed sentence rather than the plea under advisement.

THE COURT: Okay, and actually we, as a general rule, don't take pleas under advisement—

MR. LABELLE: Right. I informed Mr. Root of that, too.

THE COURT: Other than a deferral, which you know is basically a plea under advisement. So I think that the offer is going to be different than what you thought it was going to be. Do you want to take some time to think about that?

THE DEFENDANT: Could I have a few minutes to talk to the prosecutor off the record?

THE COURT: Okay, that would be fine. We'll be in recess. Just let us know when you're ready.

(At 4:09 p.m., court recessed.)[1223]

1223 Sheila Hale, transcription of arraignment of Judge Lawrence C. Root, 86th District Court, Grand Traverse County, 2 November 2004.

It wasn't going to work out quite the way Root had envisioned with no conviction entering on his record. Then they were again on the record at 4:14 p.m.:

> THE COURT: Okay, we're back on the record in the case of *People v Root*. And, Mr. LaBelle, what is the agreement—or what is the offer to the defendant?
>
> MR. LABELLE: It would be a delayed sentencing, your Honor, consistent with our current practice office policies regarding that; so the question comes up what would be an appropriate length of time—we're getting a little [ahead] of ourselves here, and I can address that in a few minutes with the court—likes to go—depending on which direction the court likes to go in terms of the sentencing on that, because I do have a few comments about that.
>
> THE COURT: Okay, fair enough. Sir, you understand what the offer is in your case?
>
> THE DEFENDANT: I do, yes.
>
> THE COURT: Okay. And so how do you plead?
>
> THE DEFENDANT: To be consistent with the local practice, I will plead guilty under the terms that the prosecutor's offered.
>
> THE COURT: Okay, so you—and the offer is to plead guilty, and then you would receive a delayed sentence, you would be placed on probation for a period of time. If you fully comply with the terms of probation, then the case would ultimately be dismissed, do you understand that?
>
> THE DEFENDANT: I understand.
>
> THE COURT: In the interim, a conviction would enter and that would be public record. You're aware of that?
>
> THE DEFENDANT: I understand that, yes.
>
> THE COURT: Has anything else been offered to you relative to your plea other than the delayed sentence treatment?
>
> THE DEFENDANT: No, they were talking about the duration of the probation in a six- to nine-month range, but other than that nothing.
>
> THE COURT: Okay. And you realize to plead guilty to the charge that you'd be waiving all the rights you have as a criminal defendant?

THE DEFENDANT: I do.

THE COURT: You realize you will not have a trial in this case, you waive the right to an attorney, including a court appointed attorney if you could not afford one?

THE DEFENDANT: Understood.

THE COURT: And you wish to plead guilty to the charge?

THE DEFENDANT: I do.

THE COURT: Directing your attention to on or about October 16th, of this year, on that day were you in a retail store in Grand Traverse County?

THE DEFENDANT: I was.

THE COURT: And what store were you in?

THE DEFENDANT: Meijer's.

THE COURT: And did you steal something from Meijer's?

THE DEFENDANT: I did.

THE COURT: And what did you steal?

THE DEFENDANT: Four DVDs.

THE COURT: And they were offered for sale by that store, is that correct?

THE DEFENDANT: They were.

THE COURT: And it was your intent to take them from Meijer's without paying for them?

THE DEFENDANT: Correct.

THE COURT: And by doing so permanently depriving Meijer's of the DVDs, is that correct?

THE DEFENDANT: Correct.

THE COURT: And I take it that other than what we talked about before, there have been no additional promises been made to you or any threats relative to your plea, is that correct?

THE DEFENDANT: That is correct.

THE COURT: You wish to plead guilty, then, to the charge?

THE DEFENDANT: I do.

THE COURT: We will accept your plea to the charge.[1224]

Thereafter, Prosecutor LaBelle laid out some suggestions for terms of Root's six-to-nine month probation including counseling, a review of medications, and reports to the court.

And then—at Judge Phillips' invitation—it was Root's turn to speak:

THE DEFENDANT: This whole case has given to me the real meaning of the expression cold terror, the feeling of ice water in your blood. I'm feeling it a bit at the moment so if I stumble, I apologize.

THE COURT: That's okay, go ahead.

THE DEFENDANT: I agree with the prosecutor that there are issues; work overload, high profile matters, stress, depression, things of that nature that are inherent from the work, and we're trying to get relief in various ways to that, but in terms of personal coping skills, I need some help in that regard and that deals with both work related as well as (inaudible) stress issues. I'm being a bit ambiguous in deference to my family. I have difficulty in terms of, you know, me making regular reports that sort of thing because of my schedule, it's difficult to get away, but to the extent that the court would go along with the recommendation of six to nine months' reports from a counselor, I think that's entirely appropriate. That gives you an opportunity to see where I'm at; I am mortified to be here.

THE COURT: I can tell that.

THE DEFENDANT: And I want to put this behind me. My family's unaware of this; I don't want to burden them with it. I may deserve it whatever I get here; they do not. So I appreciate the court being discreet with the hour of the arraignment and the sentencing. (Inaudible) long afternoon, but I recognize the time.

THE COURT: Okay. Well, Mr. Labelle suggested the arraignment should probably take place out of the normal course of time; he was concerned about your wellbeing and—

THE DEFENDANT: Thank you.

1224 Ibid.

THE COURT: And, obviously, I am as well, and that relates not to your status in the community or the state, but just anybody [...] either the prosecutor or I would have concerns about, we would arraign out of the normal sequence. And you probably don't remember, but as an attorney, I was in front of you once upon a time, and I found you to be an excellent judge, and I've been a judge probably for I guess a little bit less than four years, and you have an excellent reputation as a judge—

THE DEFENDANT: I'm sorry to have tarnished it.

THE COURT: Well, I understand that; it's hard for me to have you in front of me today as well, but I do appreciate who you are and what you've done for the state of Michigan—

THE DEFENDANT: Thank you.

THE COURT: And obviously this is a total aberration from who you are in my mind—

THE DEFENDANT: And in mine as well, your Honor.

THE COURT: I'm going to place you on probation for six months, with the understanding this is a delayed—is taken under the delayed sentence statute. There will be $45 under the state fee and $300 local court costs; we are going to require that you obtain a counselor and provide the probation department with information as to counseling, and we don't need detailed reports, but we need confirmation that you are seeing a counselor and a status report as to how that's going—

THE DEFENDANT: (Inaudible) working with—the State Bar has an attorney's and judge's assistance program—

THE COURT: That would be fine. And, again, we don't need detailed information, but we need information showing that you are getting some help and that it's ongoing. The court—I don't know if you reported this to the Judicial Tenure Commission, but you need to do that as well.

THE DEFENDANT: I have not. I didn't know if that would be a condition, or it would be under advisement—

THE COURT: I understand.

THE DEFENDANT: So I obviously had hoped another disposition, but I understand the local practice.

THE COURT: Okay. And the court is going to require proof of self-reporting within seven days.

THE DEFENDANT: And for clarification in terms of terminology: self-reporting?

THE COURT: Just—

MR. LABELLE: Just a letter—

THE COURT: A letter to the Judicial Tenure commission indicating—

THE DEFENDANT: Okay, I see what you mean.

THE COURT: That there's a conviction for this; a copy of that letter would suffice.

MR. LABELLE: Yeah, and it may be helpful if—if any confirmation on any information they can contact me, or I can advise them of some of the details in this, if that would be appropriate.

THE COURT: Okay, well I'm sure if they want information, they will contact you. And I think that that's, you know, something that I'm going to have to require. I'm sure that's something you were planning to do anyways.

THE DEFENDANT: Well—(inaudible) conviction, that's why I was hoping for the plea under advisement procedure.

THE COURT: I understand.

THE DEFENDANT: I would still welcome if the court would—

THE COURT: Okay, other than the counseling information and the self-reporting confirmation, the court's not going to require any additional terms and conditions of probation other than the ones that are normal. And P__ B__ is our chief probation officer and will be your probation officer. And we're not going to require you reporting in person, and she will meet with you today and outline some information for you; she has a background as a counselor, actually substance abuse counselor mainly, but she will—I have confidence in her that things will work out today, and I will make sure that she's aware that this is not a reporting probation.

THE DEFENDANT: Thank you, your Honor.

THE COURT: Okay, well, Judge Root, I'm sorry you're here today, I'm sure things will get better for you, too.

THE DEFENDANT: Everything's up from this point.

THE COURT: Okay, I do wish you well, sir.

THE DEFENDANT: Thank you, Judge.

MR. LABELLE: Do I take him to see Ms. B___, Judge?

THE COURT: Yeah, we can do that. We'll give—if you just want to stay in the courtroom, I'll take you over to see Ms. B___.

THE DEFENDANT: Okay.

THE COURT: Thank you. We're in recess.

(At 4:26 p.m., court proceeding concluded.)[1225]

My understanding was that the plea was taken, not just as usual, but at some odd time, when no one else was there. And it may have been in the courtroom, technically in open court, but maybe no one else would be there if it was done early or late. And it never made the paper.

Court reporter Hale, who had worked with Judge Phillips for some time, agreed that the time was not the normal for arraignments...but it wasn't unusual for Judge Phillips to hear a matter at that time of day.

Especially in the "old" building—where this matter was heard, she said Phillips would do whatever he could to make arraignments convenient to out-of-town lawyers or for defendants who had to juggle work schedules. It may have been out of the usual sequence, she said, but it wasn't abnormal. In fact, when the court moved into its current building, the court staff had a little sit-down with Judge Phillips to help him learn new habits, a measure Hale said he adopted but didn't enthusiastically welcome. Judge Phillips was in her estimation both a wonderful judge and supervisor.

Weaver agrees.

I've known him to be a very good judge. I think very highly of him. And he did the right thing here in taking this plea as a delayed sentence.

Yes. If he'd allowed the plea under advisement, there would be no conviction and no record within the court. (It's likely there still would be an arrest record at the sheriff's

---

1225 Ibid.

department, but you'd have to know what to look for. Too, it might have been available only to law-enforcement personnel; otherwise, it would stay conveniently buried.[1226])

Court administrator Carol Stocking says it is NOT the policy of the court to keep things quiet: "We have any number of high profile cases come through here; they are not unusual for us. The newspaper knows when our morning arraignments are scheduled, and when we have anything outside of that, it's our normal process to alert the media."[1227]

That wouldn't necessarily mean that a reporter would show up, but it would seem likely in the case against a sitting and highly respected circuit judge. Did she have any record of contacting the media on that date?

"I cannot tell you that. I don't know," she said. "But we try to be conscientious. I do not want to give anyone any reason to question the integrity of this court."[1228]

Then, too, it really is the business of the news media to ask if anything news-worthy was going on.

A search of the *Traverse City Record-Eagle* in the week following the arraignment didn't reveal any report of the matter. And it didn't show up in the Big Rapids *Pioneer*, either. That's the home-town paper for Judge Root. What <u>did</u> show up on the top of page 1, Dec. 29, 2004, *Pioneer* was a story of Root's intention to retire:

> The man once hailed as the "youngest circuit judge in the country" will remove his judicial robes Feb. 11, and won't be putting them on again.
>
> Judge Lawrence C. Root, Chief Judge of the 49th Judicial Circuit of the State of Michigan, will, after 28 years on the bench, retire.
>
> Root's announcement came as a surprise to many throughout the community.
>
> In a written statement, Root explained his decision, saying, "It has been my privilege and honor to serve the citizens of Mecosta and Osceola counties... since Jan. 1, 1977. After over 28 very active years on the bench, I feel it is time to move on."
>
> Privately, Root says his reasons for stepping down are many.
>
> "To be honest, I'm not getting any younger, obviously," he said. "I turned 57 last Wednesday. (Retirement) is something you think about doing over time.

1226 Robert Gaecke, attorney, e-mail to co-author Schock, 18 September 2012.
1227 Carol Stocking, conversation with co-author Schock, 6 September 2012.
1228 Ibid.

"The balance sheet contains reasons to stay and reasons to go. The balance shifted."

Root was only 28 when elected to his post Nov. 2, 1976, and has served continuously since then.

He also served the judiciary in many state-level capacities including being a long-standing member of the executive board of the Michigan Judges' Association, and serving as president of that association in 2002.

Root says he's especially proud at that distinction.

"That was one of my proudest moments," he said. "The time I was selected by my peers to serve as president of the Judges' Association. For someone from a rural county, that was pretty remarkable."

Root intends to go on working in the private sector in mediation and arbitration.

"I believe I have skills to offer there," he said. "I look forward to serving in that type of role."

Looking back over nearly three decades on the bench, Root says many cases stand out, but that he considers each to be important.

"Every case is important to the people," he said. "There were some that caught the headlines and some that didn't."

Despite looking forward to this new chapter in his life, Root admits there are things he'll miss about being a judge. "Oh, sure, there are things I'll miss," he said. "It'll be a real change in mind set; I've been a public servant for so long."

That "public" part of the job also is the part Root says he'll miss the least.

"There are problems with being a public person," said Root. "The politics and everything. You sometimes get the feeling you're living in a fish bowl. I'm really a private person. I look forward to living a life without regard for political considerations."

Root adds he's grateful for his time in the court.

"Being a judge has been a wonderful experience," he said. "It's been good to be able to use the talents God gave me to their best advantage."

Root will finish his time in office by concentrating on civil cases and leave the criminal cases to visiting judges.

"I'd like to clean some of these civil cases before I leave," he said. "I think February is enough time to wrap them up."

Gov. Jennifer Granholm will appoint an interim judge to fill the remainder of Root's term.[1229]

Weaver was particularly concerned that it seemed that the Judicial Tenure Commission had something to do with this soft landing; after all, we know from Judge Phillips' mandate that the matter had been referred to them.

If a judge has done something sufficiently wrong that it is believed by the JTC that there ought to be an investigation, that's one thing. But, remember: it is not their right to remove the judge. They're supposed to recommend it to us and not use an intimidating, bullying way of doing it. Yes, you may get a wrongdoer to decide to get off or you may not.

So, should the JTC have communicated Judge Root's guilty plea to Weaver and her colleagues?

If you were on the Supreme Court, wouldn't you want to know what your judges were doing, especially if it involved breaking the law? Of course it should have come to us! And it did NOT.

Keeping us in the dark isn't the way the system should work. And if he wasn't a judge...well, the average citizen doesn't get the opportunity to not have it known. It gets printed in the paper, and they don't have special treatment. And there should not be special treatment for judges who do serious violations.

No, again, this criminal action wasn't printed in the paper.

The problem was the public should have known that it was cleaned up and that he did go. I think the majority of the people believe they should know. Overall, he did have a good record, but this was a serious mistake and disqualified him from being a judge. But it didn't mean that he hadn't done many good, courageous cases, but this is a serious problem.

So the public, to have trust and confidence in the judiciary, doesn't have to have the truth about why people leave hidden from them. And if judges have fallen, okay, they take their penalty, and if they deserve to be off the courts and not be judges anymore, so be it. And that should give you confidence that the system does work, and that it is cleaned up.

But to hide what's gone on is a wrong policy that goes on with the JTC and one that I had hoped to get reformed from within.

1229 Michael Taylor, "Judge Root to retire," *Pioneer*, 29 December 2004, 1A.

Reform is hard, especially when people want things hidden.

And Root's conviction was staying well hidden. In a Jan. 22, 2005 news account, Root was again on the front page of the *Pioneer*, this time offering to stay on to help his replacement get up to speed:

> In all likelihood that replacement will be new to the bench and a little "green" with regard to the finer points of the local judicial system. Realizing this, Root has offered his services—on a temporary basis—as a "coach."
>
> In a recent proposal to the Mecosta County Commission, Root says, "On a daily basis I am asked questions by the staff, the clerks, and others.... Fielding those questions after Feb. 1 would be part of my contract.
>
> "I would also review the mail ... that comes into court offices and see to their routing and, when appropriate, suggest replies."
> Root said he would also help select potential candidates for the position, assuming the Governor had not appointed a new judge within the allotted time frame.
>
> "If the vacancy remains after the interviews are all done, I would be willing to suggest a candidate to the board to be hired," Root added.
>
> "Basically, I am offering to cover the administrative operations of the court as I have for 28 years."
>
> Once a new judge is appointed or hired, Root said he would be willing to provide pointers as needed. "While the state offers a 'new judges' school,'" he said, "no such sessions are scheduled that will be of much use for my successor for some time. Part of my offer is to help my successor, as much as I ethically and reasonably can, understand and adapt to his or her new environment.
>
> In exchange for these services, Root requested only the laptop, printer and associated computer supplies he has used the past few years in office.
>
> Most commissioners were amenable to Root's offer. "That laptop is about two and a half years old," said commissioner Bill Routley. "I see this as the most reasonable offer we're going to get."
>
> With commissioner Norm Turner the sole dissenting vote, the commission voted to accept Root's offer.[1230]

So, he was kind of staying and kind of leaving, but he was scheduled to receive his retirement "cake" courtesy of the Mecosta Osceola Bar Association, which invited the

---

1230 Michael Taylor, "Root offers to 'coach' new judge; Retiring judge will help replacement settle in the job," *Pioneer*, 22 January 2005, 1A.

community to a big shindig Feb. 12, 2005, at the Holiday Inn Conference Center in Big Rapids. Cost: only $20 per person.[1231]

A capacity crowd turned out: the celebration in Judge Root's honor was complete.[1232]

But why would the JTC have allowed him to go quietly? Wouldn't it have better suited the pro-Nestlé forces at the state level to have Root revealed and then dragged through the mud?

Well, no. I think the pro-Nestlé forces would have been quite glad to have him resign and off the bench. That's an easy way to achieve what they wanted to achieve without a lot of work or trouble. His rulings were ones that they wanted reversed. If he got off the bench, he wouldn't make adverse decisions in the Nestlé remand. Why care whether he gets glory or not? Why care that the public is deceived and deprived of the truth about the judge's resignation?

As to the JTC, no one from the JTC ever told me of Judge Root's shoplifting conviction, nor did anyone from the State Court Administrative Office, nor any justice or anyone connected with the Michigan Supreme Court. I believe the same is true for Justices Cavanagh and Marilyn Kelly but do not know so as I have never discussed it with them. As to the Engler Four, I do not know if they were told. It would not surprise me if departing Chief Justice Corrigan and/or incoming Chief Justice Taylor and/or one or both of Justices Young and Markman did know.

Years later, I was reliably informed that a State Court Deputy Administrator did meet with Judge Root about the shoplifting conviction and his resignation.

Other unanswered questions are: Did chief of staff/incoming State Court Administrator Gromek know of Judge Root's shoplifting conviction and/or deceiving and depriving the public from knowing about it by keeping it secret? Did the whole JTC know about and/or act upon Judge Root's shoplifting conviction and/or deceiving the public of knowing about it by keeping it secret? Or was it handled only by JTC Executive Director Paul Fischer?

But would the JTC really do something like that, move in secret, not even allowing the Supreme Court to know what was going on?

1231 "Bar Association to host retirement reception for Root," *Pioneer*, 14 January 2005, 1A.
1232 Michael Taylor, "Reception held in outgoing circuit Judge Root's honor," *Pioneer*, 14 February 2005, 1A.

Chapter 24

Dragged Through the Mud
Assaulting Judge Servaas,
Justice Weaver Sent to the JTC

Attacking the State's Longest-serving District Judge

Sixty-third District Court Judge Steven Servaas sits on the bench in northeastern Kent County. His courthouse is new and very tidy. As one of his distinctions, Servaas—first elected in 1972—is currently the longest-serving district court judge in Michigan. Formerly the chief judge of the district, he serves with Sara J. Smolenski, who was elected in 1990 and now has the designation as chief judge.[1233] There is an uneasy relationship between them.

Of much of their time, they were separated: he in the northern division of the district in a courthouse in Rockford; she in the southern division. Kent County's Four Mile Road was the dividing line. Now they share the new building closer to the center of the district but south of Four Mile.

While Justice Elizabeth A. Weaver tells his story when she goes about the state giving speeches on the need for court reform, Servaas has even appeared in person as "Exhibit A" when she was speechifying in Western Michigan.

So, what happened to Judge Servaas that allowed him to serve as an exemplar? ...An encounter with the Judicial Tenure Commission that nearly cost him his judgeship.

It's kind of hard to tell exactly where this story begins, but one logical place was the meeting between Judge Servaas and a screaming Carl Gromek, the State Court Administrator. And that came about because Judge Servaas had been used to either signing or using a signature stamp on large volumes of documents that he thought needed his John Hancock, a time-consuming duty at the end of each day. According to Judge Servaas:

1233 Judge Sara J. Smolenski is the sister of the late Judge Michael Smolenski, referenced in the previous chapter as one of the three Court of Appeals judges who ruled on *Nestlé*.

In district court, you have tons and tons of files and orders and stuff you have to sign. Most of them aren't things that go through your court; they're just people plead to this, or traffic tickets, and you end up with these big piles of things that you have to sign.

And, you know, one day Dennis Kolenda came in. He was a good friend of mine, and he was the 17th Circuit Court Chief Judge. And I had these stacks on my desk, and he said, "What are you doing with all that stuff?"

And I said, "I've got to sign all these things."

And he said, "You know, we had the same sort of thing that they said we had to sign in terms of our divorce cases, and we talked to Kevin Bowling"[1234]—who was a great guy [....] He was trying to solve problems; he wasn't threatening you or doing anything. And Dennis said, "You know, we told him what the deal was, and cited him the law. And Kevin said, 'No, you don't have to sign them.'"

And I said, "Take a look at some of these things."

And he said, "I don't think you've got to sign them because you didn't have anything to do with them." You know, it was true because I didn't handle it.

So I said, "Would you send me the law?" So he sent me the cases, and, you know, Dennis graduated from Harvard Law School, and Dennis is a really bright guy. And I had sent a letter to Gromek with the research that Dennis had done and said, you know, "This is kind of a pain to sit there for 20 or 30 minutes after the day is over, signing or stamping these things, and I don't really think I have to, because I talked to Dennis, who is my chief appellate judge." You know, the first layer of appeals for District Court is Dennis, so he's a guy who has some sway and who I have a lot of faith in.

And then, I just got this call from Judge Smolenski, who is now the chief judge because she was appointed the chief judge, saying, "You've got to do this."

And I said, "You know, in the first place, you shouldn't get in between us. This is a dispute between me and Carl Gromek. But," I said, "the other thing is, I think it's a legal question, it's not an administrative question."

So one day Carl Gromek shows up with [Region II Administrator] Jim Hughes,[1235] and he's sitting in the court, and [District Court Administrator]

1234 At the time of Kolenda's discussion with Servaas, Bowling was regional court administrator and the state judicial educator at the Michigan Supreme Court. He would later become the 20th Circuit Court Administrator in Ottawa County, a story related in Chapter 11.
1235 Hughes played a significant role in launching the JTC investigation Kent County Probate Judge Patricia Gardner referenced in Chapter 15.

Donna Gilson comes in and says, "Well, they want to see you, and I think you're gonna like him. He's a good guy."

Well, they come in my office and they close the door, and he starts screaming about, "We're going to the mat. You're going to the Judicial Tenure Commission."

And I said, "About what?"

And he said, "About this signing thing. You're not doing what we tell you."

And I said, "It's a legal question, in my opinion. I've got Dennis Kolenda, a Harvard graduate, who is my first layer of appeals, who I have a lot of respect for, telling me that, legally, it doesn't have to..."

"I don't care!"

And he's actually screaming. So Gilson runs out, and she's closing the doors because everybody hears it. Bruce Horling, who was a retired Grand Rapids police officer that was the bailiff, he came running back and, you know, you could hear it all over the courthouse.

And then [Gromek] accused me of not following rules of about three other situations that Donna Gilson apparently had told him about, one of which was, we were having the magistrate hear summary proceedings in real estate. I said, "We aren't." I said, "He takes defaults, and when two parties agree, he takes the judgment, gives it to us, and we sign it."

And he said, "That's a lie."

And I said, "Wait a sec." And then I said, "He's here now."

So he said, "I don't want to talk to him."

And so I said, "I'm going to bring him in anyway." So Varis Klavins comes in, and he's been a prosecutor for like 35 years. He retired, and now he came back, a couple years later, as our magistrate. And I said, "V, this is Carl Gromek and Jim Hughes." And I said, "How do we do our summary proceedings in real estate?"

And he said, "Well, you know, I call off the names. If it's a default, I enter the judgment. If the two parties agree that one owes the other, I enter the judgment. We give them to you and you sign them."

I said, "Do you ever make any findings of fact? Ever have a hearing?"

He said, "No."

And I'm looking at Gromek, and V leaves and closes the door, and right after he leaves, Gromek says, "He's lying."

I said—you know, he called me a liar about what we were doing, then he called V a liar. In any event, I said, you know, "This isn't worth my time." I said, "If you want me to stamp these things, I'll stamp them."

And then we got into a little heated discussion and Jim Hughes said, "You've got a place in the Keys."

And I said, "I don't live there, either." And it was—you know, it was almost like a jealous thing. I don't even know why he brought it up. So they leave, and that's my introduction to Carl Gromek and, you know, obviously, I don't have any respect for him. I don't like him; he obviously doesn't like me.[1236]

And we learned from Macomb County Probate Judge Pam Gilbert O'Sullivan's encounter with Carl Gromek that when he yelled there were repercussions.

Time passed, Kent County leaders announced they wanted to build a new courthouse to replace the one Servaas used in Rockford and to get out of what Servaas called a bad building it was leasing in the southern division of the district for Judge Smolenski's chambers and courtroom. The idea was one courthouse, roughly in the middle in terms of north/south.

Servaas thought it an ill-considered proposal that had its genesis long before.

And as it was, nobody ever was for that to start with. That includes Judge Smolenski and myself. They asked us a number of times, you know, "What if we build a single courthouse?" and nobody wanted it.

So years went by, and they'd ask us, and, in my opinion, it wasn't worth the cost. It would detract from where the courts were, because we were—you know, we had the northern half of Kent County, and Rockford's pretty much in the middle of it, and there were just a bunch of reasons not to do it.

The 63rd District Court is one of the busiest district courts in the state, in terms of cases per judge, and they were always asking us, "Do we need a new judge?" for like five or ten years, and we were always saying "No," just because we could do it. And there is a problem of having a new judge come in. You don't know the chemistry.

And then, finally, it was to the point where I was thinking about retiring, and I was thinking that the county was saying that we'll get a third judge and "We want to build just one courthouse for three judges." And you know, I said, "I can't argue too much against that. I don't see how you should have three courthouses." And I said, "If that's the case, if we get another judge, I don't have a problem with it." And Judge Smolenski didn't have a problem with it, and so that was what was going to happen.

Then I found out—because I check in with the court administrator and also the county—we're not getting a third judge. And so I say, "Wait a second." And I call up Daryl Delabbio who used to be the manager in Rockford. I knew him real well, and he's the county administrator. And I say, "Daryl, they say we're not getting a third judge."

And he says, "Well, it doesn't look like it."

And I said, "Well, why are we spending this money to build this big courthouse for just two of us?" I know they're renting a place for Sara, and they got an extraordinarily bad deal. I don't know how much they were paying, but it was a lot. But in Rockford we were set. We paid $450,000, and the city had condemned part of a block, and they put the city building there, and they put the court there. And I said, "We're in the right place. Our costs are almost zero compared to this new place." And I said, "It's got enough space for the next 10 or 15 years."

What I was saying was, we're losing population. Maybe not exactly in western Michigan, but the state of Michigan is losing population, and so we're not going up the way we used to. And they were saying, well, not in western Michigan. And our caseload wasn't going up, either, anymore. You know, it was kind of leveling off.

So their position was we didn't have enough room. It's the only time in my life I've ever heard a county board of commission arguing that a judge needed a new courthouse for $8 million, when the judge was saying, "Hey, we've got plenty of room. It will be good for another 10 or 15 years without any additional space." And I just thought it was really kind of an odd thing. Because usually it's the other way around: the judge is saying, "Oh, we desperately need the space. Spend the money." Here I was saying, "Don't spend the money. We don't need the space," and they totally disregarded that.

But as soon as I had said, "I'm not for it," there was a statute that indicated that, in our type of district, you had to have a majority of judges agree before you could move a court that affected both judges. And so when I said, "No," that messed them all up because, for some reason the county really wanted to spend the money, and they really wanted to build this courthouse. And Smolenski apparently really wanted it. So what you have is all of these people that are all fired up for this idea, and it doesn't legally look like they can do it because they don't have a majority of judges.[1237]

1237 Ibid.

In the end, the county moved to do it anyway, but his disparagement of the building project may have reached Carl Gromek's ears, too. Ten months or a year after his initial interaction with Gromek, Servaas received another visitor from an agency of the Supreme Court. The date was Jan 16, 2008. Servaas described the encounter:

> I was in my office. I was talking to a lawyer named Martin Mead, and we were, you know, not talking about law, we were just talking about things. And a State Police Lieutenant, who I didn't really recognize—and I know most the guys at Rockford—came in and introduced himself; that was a Det. Lt. [Curt] Schram. I said, "How are you doing?" And he said, "Well, I met you some time ago," and I said, "Yeah?" And then he had this other guy with him, who I didn't know at all. And Marty left, and I said, "Have a seat." They sat down, and the other guy introduced himself as Paul Fischer, who was the chief counsel for the Judicial Tenure Commission. And he gave me a card, and I had no real idea, frankly, what they were there for or why. You know, he had an armed State Police Lieutenant with him at the time, and so I was somewhat joking and said, "Oh, am I being relieved?"
>
> And it turns out that was the whole idea, that he'd come to tell me that I had until 9 a.m. the next morning to resign and get all my things and, you know, leave this place that I've been for 35 years. And, of course, I was thinking that this was Halloween or some sort of joke, and it turns out that they were both dead serious. It also turned out to be, to my advantage, that they were recording this whole meeting; they never told me. I had no idea that it was being recorded. But Lt. Schram was recording it.[1238]

That recording would prove invaluable later when things got really ugly.

> And it all of a sudden got serious, and he informed me that, you know, I needed to leave tomorrow, by 9 o'clock, and if I didn't .... And Fischer basically accused me of—didn't accuse me of, he stated that I was living in my district but, apparently, outside my election division, which I knew. And I'd been living there for a period of time, and my phone number—my phone number was always in the phonebook; my address was in the phonebook; when you pulled up my name on the web, that was listed as my address, so it wasn't any real secret. I knew that I was outside my voting district, but I intended to—I was thinking about retiring and not running again. When I looked at the law, I thought there was no problem with it, and I still think there is no problem with it. And, actually, there doesn't seem to be any problem with it. I mean, it turns out to be nothing in retrospect.
>
> So at that point, he's telling me I'd given up my judgeship as soon as I moved out of there, the judgeship was now vacant and, therefore, you know, I was to leave and nobody will find out about it.[1239]

1238 Ibid.
1239 Ibid.

Judge Steve R. Servaas is the state's longest serving district judge. But his career was in jeopardy as a result of an attack by the executive director of the Judicial Tenure Commission, Paul J. Fischer. Why? Had Fischer been aided in his attack on Servaas by State Court Administrator Carl Gromek and/or his regional administrators and/or staff? In the end, Servaas remained on the bench by one vote when the matter came before the Michigan Supreme Court.

Fischer also accused him of perjury, living at one address and renewing a gun permit giving the address of another of his properties; Servaas had several homes and made a practice of buying properties and fixing them up. He didn't always sell them afterward.

At any rate, Fischer was there to either collect Servaas' resignation letter or to deliver several documents, the first a 28-day letter, a preliminary step before the Judicial Tenure Commission issued a complaint. The second was a petition for interim suspension without pay and a motion for immediate consideration by the Supreme Court. That, said Fischer, was based on Servaas' affidavit of where he was living, found on the gun permit renewal. The narrative picks up from the recording made by Schram:

F (FISCHER): And based on your affidavit, your affidavit, I have every reason to believe that it will be granted.
S (SERVAAS): Um hum.
F: Now this puts everybody in a bad situation.
S: Right
F: Including the judicial system, but especially you. The commission is offering you this opportunity to resolve this matter as quickly as possible and not bring shame, proceedings, accusations of perjury against you. You can resign immediately. And, immediately means immediately. I have a letter right here you can sign. The commission has said that I can give you until tomorrow morning. I prefer to take the letter with me right now.
S: Well, I...
F: I know that I'm springing an awful lot on you.
S: I was going to say.... You know, I'd like to talk obviously with somebody who knows this area much better than I do.
F: Yeah. So, here's a letter already prepared for you. If I have that letter faxed to me—my fax number is on that card I just gave you. If I have that letter faxed to my office by 9 a.m., and I mean 9 a.m. ....

S: Tomorrow?

F: Tomorrow.

S: I don't think I can do that by then.

F: Then I'll be filing the petition for interim suspension tomorrow and you will be suspended in a matter of days. And a formal complaint will issue with this. So, this will all.... You're up for election this year. So, this is all going to become public no later than March. You'll be off the bench before then. Nobody will know why, because the investigations are done under the rules of confidentiality. The motion for the petition for interim suspension is filed still under a sealed document because it hasn't been made public. But it will be public by March.

S: Well, you know I understand that you have to do what you have to do, but it still seems to me that I should at least have time to talk to somebody....

F: You have until tomorrow morning at 9. And I haven't even touched...I haven't even touched the sexual harassment...the little notes that you draw, the comments you make to the staff. I mean, we haven't even gotten...oh, yeah. We haven't even gotten there. And that's really....

S: You know, I'm not....that's bullshit.

F: No, it's not. No, it's not. It's a very serious matter.

S: Somebody's made a complaint?

F: You may think because you were born in 19-whatever it was...40-something or other...that you're from an old enough generation that can get away with saying certain things, but that's just not true.

S: May I ask you...?

F: Your comments...your comments about the lady with the "Go Blue" and filling up the Alma shirt.

S: Yeah?[1240]

According to our interview with Servaas:

> As we got into it, the next thing he said was, "And that doesn't even get into the sexual harassment." And I said, "Sexual harassment? What is that about?"
>
> And he said, "Well, you know, you basically harass your employees." We had probably, I think, 16 female employees. I mean all the people who do the work are usually female clerks, and if they don't do the work, your court doesn't run very well. They're really the heart of the place. And he was telling me that I was sexually harassing them, apparently, for 36 years, and it just now came out.
>
> And I said, "What are you talking about?"[1241]

1240 Transcription of meeting with Hon. Steven R. Servaas, 16 January 2008.
1241 Steven R. Servaas, video interview with co-author Schock.

All this went back to a comment Servaas made to a court staff member. This is Servaas' explanation of the background of what occurred. It was a Friday "casual" day at the southern division of the court that coincided with a retirement party for one of the probation clerks, so there were people from both the northern and southern courts:

> And the complaint was based on one of Judge Smolenski's female employees [Becky Andrus], who we didn't have a very good relationship with. [...] I made a joke about the size of her sweatshirt and, basically, she should get one that had a smaller college name, and it wasn't—I'm sure it wasn't the best taste, but it was not maliciously made.[1242]

She was wearing a sweatshirt with "Michigan" printed across it. Servaas suggested that she needed a school with a shorter name, say, Alma, if she was going to fill out the shirt. ...A dumb thing to say, in poor taste. And he knew it when he said it. He told the people nearby that he'd better get out of there before he got sued.

> There were a bunch of people around, and she was with a group of like four female employees. A couple of them were from my court and a couple of them were from Judge Smolenski's court.[1243]

Servaas said he didn't think much more about his comment until a court employee came to him and told him his comment REALLY didn't go over well.

> And then my secretary said, "You know, they said she took offense at this?" And I said, "Well, I certainly didn't mean it."

> So I called, and she didn't answer, and I asked her to return my call, which she didn't. And I left—I said, "Gee, if I offended you I didn't mean to," on her answering machine. That was the last I heard about it. Never heard another thing until Paul Fischer came in.[1244]

Back in the judge's chambers with Fischer, who was in full spate, we pick up the verbatim discussion about the sweatshirt comment:

> F: I'd get you thrown off just for that. But it goes beyond that. Well, you'll see in your 28-day letter. We've got one of your little doodles and we'll see what you think of that. I'd like to hear what you have to explain.
> S: Where's the little doodle?
> F: It's in the envelope.[1245]

Doodle? Subsequently, they talk a lot about the doodle, an allegedly obscene doodle. Two obscene doodles. Here's Servaas recollection:

1242 Ibid.
1243 Ibid.
1244 Ibid.
1245 Transcription of meeting with Hon. Steven R. Servaas, 16 January 2008.

And I said, "Obscene cartoon? What on earth?"

So he said, "Well, you doodle, and you doodle on the bench, and you have some obscene doodles that you use to harass the female employees."

And I said, "What on earth are you talking about?"

And he said, "Well, you know, you doodle."

And I said, "There are 26,000 files out here stored now, or more, and probably a third of them I've handled." I said, "Go get one and show me."

He said, "I don't have to."

And I said, "What are you talking about?"

So he came up with this yellow sticky that was about an inch—you know, a typical sticky thing, and there was kind of a phallic thing that was maybe half-an-inch tall in the corner of it. And I said, "What on earth is that?"

And he says, "Well, you tell me."

So, apparently, that was the obscene doodle, or whatever he was accusing me of. There was another mention during the hearing of another, supposed doodle of women's breasts, in a general thing, which I never found—I mean they never showed me, they never had, they never found anything else whatsoever and, frankly, I don't think I did that, but even if I did, you know, it was never intended to harass anybody. And it came out of a wastebasket. When a pile of files came out, apparently it was on the floor and one of the employees picked it up, and Donna Gilson, who was the Court Administrator at the time—and we had a tough relationship; you know, I didn't agree with the way she handled the employees—and she had taken it from the ladies and it was gone. And that was—I never heard anything about it whatsoever.

I asked Fischer, "What file did this come from?"

And he said, "Well, that's none of your business."

And I said, "What do you mean 'it's none of my business'? If it was on a file, if I look at the file, you know, I take all of my notes on the back of a file," I said, "maybe I can tell you what it is or if I did it."

"Well, I'm not here to debate with you. I'm not going to show you."

Of course, he never had a file, never showed me a file. The only thing they ever had was this sticky, that was evidence of my obscene doodling, for 36 years. They never found anything else whatsoever.[1246]

It might have taken a graphoanalyst to determine whether the doodles were the work of Judge Servaas; certainly they weren't signed. There was no direct evidence that he made them, but he was adjudged the most likely; only he and the court staff handled the files. But Fischer didn't need direct evidence in presenting the 28-day letter to Servaas. We resume from the transcript.

S: Let me ask you this: did someone make a complaint about sexual harassment?
F: Those are the documents that you have, as I've explained. If I have.... If the commission has your letter of resignation by 9 a.m., this matter will be gone. Nobody will ever hear about it. You'll have a retirement party. Everyone will go home happy. And if you choose....
S: I doubt it. I know I won't go home happy.
F: And if you choose to fight it, you'll be even less happy. So, those will be the options you'll have. Fight it, which you are certainly entitled to do. I almost welcome the opportunity. Or you can take the easy way out and take a resignation.
S: I would never take the easy way out.[1247]

Throughout the meeting, Fischer kept telling Judge Servaas what was going to happen to him, what he was so "kindly" attempting to save him from.

F: I've come here personally to give you this to perhaps avoid any embarrassing situations. I've come here to perhaps avoid having to drag your name through the mud with what is going to come out at a formal hearing and to give you an opportunity to obviate all that and retire quietly. I'm not here to discuss the matter with you. [...] If you choose to continue the matter, which is your right, you can do whatever it is that you think is appropriate and we'll, I guarantee you, engage you to the fullest. You also now have the opportunity, which not everybody gets, to just resign and not fight the matter.
S: And just sort of roll over on the sexual harassment?
F: The sexual harassment part is not going to be known to anybody. The petition for interim....
S: It's not true. I mean....
F: Then you don't have to worry about it.
S: Well, I have to worry about this because the allegations are here, don't I?
F: You have to worry about it if you choose to fight it. If you choose to resign, that's the end of it. Our file gets closed and that's the end. Nobody will know that I was here. You just decided to resign.

1246 Steven R. Servaas.
1247 Transcription of meeting with Hon. Steven R. Servaas, 16 January 2008.

S: Then people are going to ask me why.

F: Why? Because you've reached an age. You reflected on life. You took a vacation. You decided to move on to different avenues. Anything is possible. That's your choice. You get to frame it that way.

S: Do you work for Carl Gromek?

F: No. If we push this all the way, everybody's going to know why you left because you got thrown off the bench.

S: Well, they're going to know anyway.

F: Nobody is going to know anything.

S: I mean, I'm going to tell them if I decide to resign, I'm going to tell them why.

F: Oh, well, that's your choice, too. [...] They won't hear it from us. That will be under your control. If you choose to leave it as "I've decided to take a change in life and move on to other things" that's your business and nobody will say anything. Our file will be closed. That's the end of it. Now, the Judicial Tenure Commission is a separate agency from the Supreme Court.[1248] We don't work for Carl Gromek. I know who he is.[1249]

Servaas' question about Gromek was, perhaps, inspired. He could draw a line from the shouting match to Fischer's appearance in his office even though ten months had elapsed.

> Frankly, you know, I was so upset about that meeting that I figured—I had no idea who brought all this stuff—that Gromek was probably involved just because of our run-in.[1250]

The question would surface later, too, when Fischer was questioned by members of the Supreme Court.

And the letter that Servaas was to sign? It was all nicely typed out, said Servaas.

> He pushed over a letter of resignation that was on MY court stationery, my name, my private stationery.

> I said, "Where'd you get this?"

> He said, "You know, that's really nothing. I'm just here to tell you what the charges are."

> And I said, "Well, this is my stationery." I found out at the hearing later that Donna Gilson testified that Fischer had asked for two pages of my stationery, and Judge Smolenski had directed her to send it to him, so he could pre-type my letter of resignation on MY stationery. So when I'd sign it ev-

1248 Justice Weaver would remind readers that the JTC is a constitutionally created commission of the court. *And the court makes the JTC's rules and sets its budget.*
1249 Transcription of meeting with Hon. Steven R. Servaas, 16 January 2008.
1250 Steven R. Servaas.

erything would look like it was done properly, and I'd made the decision without any sort of extortion or pressure that he was exerting.[1251]

Everything that Servaas says squared with the recording and the transcript of the event. He is dead on. Of course, he experienced the event and then relived it about a million times, listening both to the recording and reading the transcript.[1252]

Fischer and Schramm left as quickly as they could, but inadvertently or not, Schram left the recording running and it captured all that was said immediately afterward. Servaas recounts what was said next:

> As he goes out of the office, there's a conversation between Schram and Fischer, and then they immediately call Judge Smolenski, because Fischer wants to talk to her; and then there's a recording of Schram, and it didn't— you know, it had to be amplified. So we amplified it, and it comes out... Fischer comes out and Schram is asking him some questions, and he's telling him, "You know, it looks like the judge is more upset with this harassment of his employees, and if you hadn't said that, that maybe he would have just stepped down, because he's agreeing that he lives out of his district."
>
> And Fischer replies, "You know, he'd have ceded anyway," and then he looks at him and says, on the transcript, "Like shooting ducks in a barrel." Like some people golf for pleasure, he apparently extorts judges out of their job for pleasure..."like shooting ducks in a barrel." He got the wrong animal. I think it's fish in a barrel. But their idea was, "Hey, this is real easy." You know, "We just threaten the crap out of these judges and they'll either leave or we'll bring this."
>
> So they start talking, and they get into the phone call with Judge Smolenski, who tells them, "Go ahead and take the gun, not because I think he'll shoot anybody, not because I think he'll shoot himself, [...] but just because I don't want it in the courtroom."[1253]

Oh, yes, Judge Servaas was one of those judges who kept a gun under the bench. There was far less security in his courtroom than at the Hall of Justice. And this would be a problem. Judge Smolenski, as the chief judge, had ordered that no weapons be allowed in the courthouse, much in the same way that Chief Justice Kelly banned Justice Markman from packing. She did not grant Servaas an exception. What kind of an offense it would be would remain to be seen. According to Servaas:

> So Schram comes back and takes the gun, and I say, "Whatever you're gonna do." But the conversation with Schram is interesting because he's talking to Donna Gilson and she says, "Well, is he gonna be gone?" because Gilson

1251 Ibid.
1252 Readers can listen to the recording here: http://www.mymicourt.com/wp/wp-content/uploads/2011/01/Paul_Fischer.mp3.
1253 Steven R. Servaas.

didn't want me around, and she was fired up to find out like, "Oh, he left like right now." And Schram says, "Well, no. We gave him until 9 a.m. tomorrow. So he'll be gone by tomorrow or the Supreme Court will boot him out by tomorrow." And she says, "Oh."

And then Schram says, "While we were in there, he admitted to the felony of not living in his district." And he said, "I didn't arrest him right then, and I'll probably hold off until they tell me."

When I read that on the transcript I'm thinking, you bring this guy, who is armed, in with you for whatever reason—maybe to make the threat more impressive—and this guy thinks that I committed a felony by moving south of my election line, like anybody in the country can do, move anyplace they want. It's not any kind of crime.
It's still in the district, and if there's anything wrong with it, it means maybe there's a problem with the job. But this guy has a gun, and he thinks that he can arrest me for a felony any time he wants because I admitted and stated that I'd moved out of my election division. And I'm thinking, is this like World War II Germany? They don't even tell this guy [State Police Lieutenant Curtis Schram] that it's not a felony? And I'm thinking, you know, this is scarier than I originally thought. And it got pretty bad as we went through it.[1254]

...Right through the mud. There would be no way Servaas would either go along with Fischer's demands or keep quiet about what had happened. One of his first moves was to consult those he trusted.

Right after this meeting, Dennis Kolenda just out of the blue calls me. And I said, "Dennis, you wouldn't believe what just happened to me," and I tell him.

He said, "Hey, this is something political. You need to talk to somebody with some stroke." You know, somebody that has—he said, "Why don't you call Bruce Neckers?" Bruce is a friend of mine. He was the President of the State Bar. So I call Bruce and tell him. I said, "I don't know what is going on."

And he said, "They gave you till like 9 a.m. tomorrow?"

And I said, "Yeah."

And he says, "Well, you know, I can't do anything by 9, but what I can do is, I can call this Fischer and see if we can get you a couple days."

And so Neckers calls, and then I find out later—all this—when I talked to Bruce, basically Fischer is telling him, calling me names. Like he said I'm a

1254 Ibid.

pig; I horribly abuse my female employees; I mean, he's just—it's like a gut-ter sort of thing, where you're thinking of names to call somebody who you don't like, one way or the other, and, of course, Bruce is appalled. He calls me back and he said, you know, "You've got to get a lawyer, and why don't you go to Jon Muth?"

So I go to Jon Muth, and that's how I ended up getting represented.[1255] And then, on the way home from that day, I'm in my car and my cell phone goes off. I answer it and it's Judge Smolenski and she's crying. And I said, "What's the matter with you?" because I hadn't figured out anything.

And she said, "Well, I'm just so sorry about that horrible thing."

And I said, "What are you talking about?"

And she said, "Well, didn't that Fischer come to"—

And I said, "Yeah." And then I said, "How did you know that?" because she wasn't in Rockford.

And, "Well, you know, I just heard from the employees."[1256]

And I said, "Oh."

And she's saying—finally she ends up saying, "But you did it yourself."

And I said, "What are you talking about? I did what myself?"

And she said, "Well, you brought it on yourself."

And I said, "What are you talking about?"

And she said, "You know, that horrible thing."

And I said, "What are you talking about?" And she was talking about the obscene doodle.

And she finally said, "You know, that penis. That thing, that penis that you drew."

And I said, "How did you know about it?"

1255 While Jon Muth would appear for him at the Judicial Tenure Commission and at the Supreme Court, James Brady would handle Servaas' first appearance when he was examined before a special master (who was usually a retired judge appointed by the Supreme Court who would determine if there was cause to send the matter before the JTC and then perhaps on to the Supreme Court).
1256 And we know from the recording transcript that she was in telephone communication with D.Lt. Curt Schram.

And she said, "I had it on my desk for three months."

And I said, "Wait a second.... You had it on your desk for three months, and you thought I drew it, and you never called me and asked me if I drew it or what it was?"

And, all of a sudden, I'm starting to figure out that all three of these things, if she's the chief judge, would have been things that any normal chief judge would have come and said, "Steve, you've got to move back north of Four Mile." "Steve, you've got to apologize." "Steve, you can't doodle." And I've never had anybody tell me anything.

So after I hung up on that, the light's starting to go on, and I'm starting to figure this out, but I still didn't figure out how far it went. I mean, the whole county commission is involved, and Morgan, Roger Morgan, is our [county commission] representative in Rockford, and I thought we were friends for years, but it turns out that Morgan is in on this, and that all the county commissioners are in on this in terms of, "Hey, we've got to get this building built, and it looks like we've got to get rid of Judge Servaas." So then I'm starting to find out how this is going, but I still can't figure out why Fischer and the state—you know, I don't figure out exactly what that's about. And, frankly, I really, to this day—if you said a hundred-percent "Do you know?"—I have a pretty good idea, but I don't know to a hundred percent.[1257]

And though he didn't know it until later that the recording of the event had been made, it would prove pivotal.

So the amazing thing was, these guys had recorded it and didn't tell me about it, and what it turned out to be was the best thing that ever happened to my side, because when I went to talk to Jon Muth and Brady, I was telling them all this, and they were going, "I don't believe it." I don't think they— "This guy's not dumb enough, or he's not bad enough to try to extort you out of office like this."

And I said, "Hey, that's what happened."

And then, in discovery, [Fischer] turns over this disk, and [Brady and Muth] play it, and they go, "Are you kidding me?" You know, everything I told them was right on the disk, including this 20-year felony by Fischer, who represents the Judicial Tenure Commission. And in one of his pleadings, he said, "They sent me to do what I did." Now, if that meant to extort me off the bench, which is what he did, that isn't so good for them because, you know, you aid and abet a felony, you're just as guilty as someone else.[1258]

1257 Steven R. Servaas.
1258 Ibid.

The matter was going forward. But, counter to Fischer's threat/promise that Servaas would be off the bench the next day, it didn't play out that way.

> Yeah, my name was in the paper, all these allegations were in the paper before anybody had any proof. It got to be a publicity battle, where they were telling everybody in the paper how bad I was, plus they made a motion in front of the Supreme Court to immediately suspend me without pay. That's the first time, and that's a really dramatic remedy, where you have some reason that the judge is totally incompetent, or totally offensive, and, you know, the Supreme Court denied that. That was the first time.[1259]

We got not an emergency, but a "right-away" request to remove Judge Servaas, to suspend him without pay from the bench. And we just don't do that as a rule. To suspend somebody without a hearing and without anything—just on a claim from the JTC in an emergency way until they proceed with it—is reserved for instances when the judge has been caught shooting somebody, or caught robbing a bank or something.

But to remove him because he allegedly had vacated his office? He is not a danger to the public. He was a judge in his 36th year of service, and had been elected and re-elected, unopposed, and had this huge reputation of being a wonderful district court judge. And this idea of vacating his office just seemed a little bit much—the JTC needed to follow the usual procedures.

Now, at that time, nobody particularly on our staff looked up what the statute says about the vacation of office—who is supposed to be involved with it and whether the JTC should be or not. But we didn't have to go very far because we weren't suspending anybody, period, much less suspending anybody without pay. And this was the whole court—all the justices. Nobody objected as I recall. And, simply, we sent it back and said, "No. Follow the usual procedures."

There would be a second time when Fischer sought another extraordinary suspension, said Servaas.

> Then the second time Fischer made a motion in which he alleged that I had a handgun, which is true. We've always had a handgun—well, since 1972—in Rockford, because [at that time] we had no bailiff or anything, and the county furnished us with a gun first, and then, later on, I had replaced it, after that one was stolen in a break-in, with my own gun. And I went down, took all the courses and, you know, I had a permit for the gun.[1260]

Fischer was trying to make a case that Judge Servaas posed an immediate threat to the court staff. After all, said Fischer, he had attempted suicide. That was true.[1261] But there was no evidence he ever threatened anybody else.

1259 Ibid.
1260 Ibid.
1261 Judge Servaas had been prone to depression. In 2004, after an injury that left him in near-constant pain, he did attempt to take his own life using Ambien and a razor blade. At the time, sheriff deputies removed from his residences and logged into property 13 firearms, "a razor blade, a set of keys to the gun vault and several letters left at the home." [Supplemental information dictated by Deputy Hooker on 37797-04, 24 June 2004, unpublished.] The pain has since resolved, and Servaas said he has made no other attempt on his life.

What [Fischer] said, is "On information and belief..."—which means, "Oh, I heard this," not that he investigated it—"...the judge has said, you know, 'If it hits the fan and I consider any of my employees the enemy....' And 'You guys better get out of the way because, you know, you might get shot.'" And I looked at this, and I'm just incredulous. Just a flat-out lie. I mean, it was just a lie to try to make them think that, you know, "He's so dangerous that he might go off the deep end and start shooting people." And, I mean, it was just a flat-out lie by this guy.

So the Supreme Court, thank God, looks at it, and they toss it out and deny it.[1262]

From Justice Weaver's perspective, this is what occurred:

This, again, did not seem to us meriting of emergency actions that were a threat to employees or the public, or any kind of thing that would demand immediately removing a judge even with pay, much less without pay—"without salary" I think the Constitution says—because we're supposed to have a recommendation, and we've made rules to the JTC as to what they're supposed to—the due process issues they're supposed to do, like notice to the judge and such things, before they make a recommendation—they have no power to decide what we should do. They can recommend that we censure, suspend with or without salary, remove, or retire the judge. Those are the limitations. And we can't do that unless we get a recommendation. There are supposed to be some checks and balances, and in the Constitution—this is all Section 30 of Article 6 for the Judiciary—the Supreme Court makes the rules for the JTC.[1263]

So it went back a second time, and so then we figured we'd either hear of this again or we wouldn't.

In his next step, Fischer requested a session before a special master, someone who would determine if there was cause to go forward. This time, he was following the usual steps in the rules. The Supreme Court appointed the Hon. Casper Grathwohl. A retired judge from Niles, Grathwohl had been in practice with his father for 21 years before being appointed to the circuit bench in 1986. In all, he served 16 years in the courts, with his court one of the early demonstration courts in the state. He had experience across the board of family and criminal law.

There were three counts to be considered: Did the judge vacate his office when he moved into the southern division of his district? Did he fail to comply with statutory

1262 Steven R. Servaas.
1263 This is the language of the Constitution:

> On recommendation of the Judicial Tenure Commission, the Supreme Court may censure, suspend with or without salary, retire or remove a judge for conviction of a felony, physical or mental disability which prevents the performance of judicial duties, misconduct in office, persistent failure to perform his duties, habitual intemperance or conduct that is clearly prejudicial to the administration of justice. The Supreme Court shall make rules implementing this section and providing for confidentiality and privilege of proceedings.

[State Constitution of Michigan of 1963, Article VI, Section 30, http://www.legislature.mi.gov/ (S(krlueum2i3l5ebfthudahzyr))/mileg.aspx?page=getobject&objectname=mcl-Article-VI-30.] Readers will find it again in Chapter 26.

notification requirement in his failure to change both his driver's license and voter registration information to show that he'd moved? And, did he engage in inappropriate conduct toward female employees of the court? For the latter, three examples were offered: a doodle of breasts, a drawing that might be a penis, and his comments to Becky Andrus about her choice of sweatshirt. The hearing was set for March 28, 2008. But before then, there was plenty of news to flow.

Among other events, Servaas moved back to his home in the northern division of the district, a move Fischer called a "sham."[1264] Then, the Rockford City Council voted to sue the county if necessary to keep the court there.

> City officials claim the move would breach state law about the location of district courts, especially since Servaas is elected by voters north of Four Mile Road. The 63rd District is divided into two sections, with Servaas presiding over the northern portion and Judge Sara Smolenski elected by voters south of Four Mile.

> The new 41,000-square-foot courthouse would sit about two miles south of that boundary.

> Some other northern Kent County communities, including Sparta, Cedar Springs, and Solon Township, last month passed resolutions opposing the court's move. Officials have said the extra distance to the new courthouse, about 10 miles each way, would pose a hardship to court users in the northern half of the county.[1265]

At the same time, support for Judge Servaas was overwhelming in the community. Letter after letter in the newspaper praised his honesty, integrity, and independence. Even 12 past presidents of the Grand Rapids Bar signed on to support him:

> We are all acquainted with Judge Steven R. Servaas in his judicial capacity. We write to express our deep dismay and disappointment about the manner in which the Judicial Tenure Commission has proceeded in its inquiry about the fitness of Judge Servaas to serve as a judge of the 63rd District Court.

> At the outset we think it extremely important to characterize Judge Servaas's judicial service over 35 years on the bench. All of us believe he has been a fair minded and reasonable jurist with a fine judicial temperament. Without fail he has treated lawyers and litigants in his court with the utmost respect. These qualities are all the hallmarks of a highly qualified judge. They have earned him a "highly qualified" rating from the Grand Rapids Bar Associations Judicial Candidates Qualification Committees.

1264 Nate Reems, "Servaas foes call move 'sham'; Tenure Commission Boss presses fight to remove judge," *Grand Rapids Press*, 6 March 2008, B2.
1265 Matt Vande Bunte, "Rockford sues to keep court in city; officials want a declaratory judgment from Kent County circuit judge," *Grand Rapids Press*, 11 March 2008, B1.

Given his performance as a judge we believe that the allegations against him as they appear in the newspaper seem to lack that degree of severity which rises to the level of public disclosure. For both lawyers and judges there are procedures to deal with such matters in a nonpublic fashion which have proven effective. Regardless of the reason that the Judicial Tenure Commission has undertaken to attack Judge Servaas, it has seemingly done so in a reckless manner. In our judgment it would to reconsider this issue in its entirety.[1266]

This is the new 63rd District Court building in western Kent County. The cost of the building was initially projected to be $8 million, but was delivered instead for $6.5 million. Even with a total of 39,000 square feet in the new structure, Judge Steven Servaas said his staffers have less individual work space and he has less office room than in the prior Rockford courthouse. [Barton Deiters, "Judges Servaas, Smolenski move into new 63rd District Court building, still disagree whether they should," *Grand Rapids Press*, 12 November 2009, http://www. mlive.com/news/grand-rapids/index.ssf/2009/11/judges_servaas_smolenski_move.html.]

And Judge Servaas, who had considered retiring, expressed a different sentiment:

"I was leaning toward not running, but now, I'm so damn mad," Servaas, 62, said Friday. "After 35 years, I'm not leaving because some punk told me to leave."[1267]

1266 Frederick D. Dilley, Stephen R. Drew, Robert J. Dugan, Hon. Janet A. Haynes, William W. Jack, Jr., Robert L Lalley, Jr., Bruce W. Neckers, H. Rhett Pinsky, Paul T. Sorensen, Joseph M. Sweeney, John D. Tully, Michael C. Walton, Letter to the Editor, 28 February 2008. It's interesting that the letter as sent was not exactly the way it was published in the next day's Public Pulse of the newspaper ["Past bar leaders express dismay," *Grand Rapids Press*, 1 March 2008, A10.]
1267 Barton Dieters and Tom Rademacher, "Servaas battles to stay on bench; State denies squabble over court move was factor," *Grand Rapids Press*, 16 February 2008, A1.

And he took a shot of his own at his chief judge. He also connected two other dots for the reading public.

> Servaas said Friday he blames some of the information contained in the complaints on his boss, Chief District Judge Sara Smolenski. Servaas has been at odds with Smolenski over his opposition to the proposed $7 million relocation of his courthouse from Rockford to a parcel on East Beltline, something Smolenski supports.
>
> Servaas said Fischer visited his courthouse one day after Servaas publicly expressed the opinion that moving the courthouse would require his approval as well as Smolenski's.
>
> "The next day, (Fischer) comes up and tries to extort me out of my job," Servaas said. "So it looks like they're related."[1268]

On March 28, 2008, Judge Servaas found himself before special master Grathwohl in a Grand Rapids courtroom. With Servaas were attorneys James Brady, Andrew Portinga, and Monica Inhulsen. Opposing him were Paul Fischer and Thomas Prowse.[1269] And in the gallery were the media. In testimony that filled 887 pages, Paul Fischer started with the worst of what he saw as Servaas' crimes: pride. "The Greeks had a term for it. It was *hubris*, unmitigated arrogance."[1270]

Judge Grathwohl would hear from a limited variety of witnesses, including supporters and detractors, even Becky Andrus who had worn the "Michigan" sweatshirt. And she had something new to add: when Judge Servaas showed up at a Christmas party at Judge Smolenski's more than a month after the sweatshirt comment, he had just come from a game of racquetball. He was dressed in shorts and a T-shirt. Andrus said when he was seated the judge exposed himself—his jockstrap was showing. Further, during a present exchange, Andrus said he grabbed her wrists and yanked her to him.[1271] Now, none of the other witnesses before the hearing master would corroborate her testimony. One, in fact countered it, saying the judge put a hand on her shoulder and wished her a Merry Christmas.[1272]

Interestingly, Andrus was once temporarily assigned—at Judge Smolenski's order—at Servaas' court, and Andrus admitted in her testimony that Servaas had "banished" her again to the southern division for causing "too much havoc." She was returned to Smolenski's court with instructions to not return.[1273] There may have been wounded pride on her part.

1268 Ibid.
1269 Hearing—Volume I, Formal Complaint No. 84, Michigan Judicial Tenure Commission, 28 March 2008, 5, unpublished.
1270 Ibid., 7.
1271 Ibid., 42.
1272 Ibid., 224.
1273 Ibid., 48

Servaas noted that things didn't go particularly well at the master's hearing.

> It was like the fix was in. We were there for four days. He let us call only
> three witnesses from our staff about this sexual harassment. And even that
> is crazy because, you know, if you have people working for you, and you
> call them as a witness and say, "Is your boss bad for you?" They're thinking,
> "God, if my boss wins, he's gonna fire me." So those aren't the people to talk
> to.
>
> We had a list of like ten employees, who had worked for a long time and
> then retired. And we had that list of people that didn't—you know, they
> weren't in the line of fire or anything. And we couldn't call any of those
> people. It was just like, you know, the writing was on the wall.[1274]

And—for whatever reason—Attorney Brady didn't raise the issue of Fischer's conduct.
That was inexplicable, said Servaas.

> He didn't even move into evidence the disk of this extortion. It's a felony
> for someone to come in to threaten you and say, "Hey, you perjured yourself
> on the witness stand and if you don't give me your car by tomorrow, I'm
> gonna go to the police and make a complaint of your perjury." Even if you
> did perjure yourself, it's extortion to demand the car. And if it's a lie—you
> didn't perjure yourself—obviously, it's even worse. But extortion is a 20-
> year felony in Michigan.[1275]

After the hearing but before the report from the master, the *Grand Rapids Press*
editorialized for Judge Servaas, called the case against him "paper-thin."

> The outcome should be a quick dismissal of any action against Judge Servaas
> and an immediate investigation into the conduct of Mr. Fischer. His work
> warrants scrutiny, no matter how the Servaas case ends.[1276]

In the end, the master upheld two of the counts:

> The master's report, issued on May 12, 2008, concluded that respondent va-
> cated his judicial office in violation of Const. 1963, Article 6, Section 20, when
> he changed his principal residence from the 1st division to the 2nd division
> of the 63rd District Court in August 2005. The master recommended that
> the second count of the complaint be dismissed. The master further con-
> cluded that respondent's "sexual doodles and sexual communication" con-
> stituted judicial misconduct and compromised the integrity of the court.[1277]

1274 Steven R. Servaas.
1275 Ibid.
1276 Editorial, "Quick judgment in misconduct case; There is no reason to let Rockford judge twist in the
wind awaiting a ruling on such flimsy evidence," *Grand Rapids Press*, 13 April 2008, A22.
1277 Elizabeth A. Weaver writing for the majority, *In re Honorable Steven R. Servaas*, No. 137633, Michigan
Supreme Court, 31 July 2009, 6, http://jtc.courts.mi.gov/downloads/FC84.SupremeCourtOpinion.pdf.

If you were Steven R. Servaas that would not be what you wanted to hear:

> Then you can either accept what he says, or you can appeal to the Judicial Tenure Commission. And we talked it over and said, "This is crazy." I'm still thinking it's crazy because there is not much to litigate. I agree that I live where I live. It's just my position that I can do that. And I agree that I told that joke, but there's not sexual harassment or any pattern of anything, and she's not my employee. And the only thing I disagreed with is whether I did that yellow sticky. And maybe I did and maybe I didn't. But even if I did, I can doodle like anybody else, and there's no intent to harass anybody. And so there really wasn't any dispute about the facts. This is just—I can move. I can live there and legally—if you don't like the joke, sorry about that, but there's no pattern of any sexual harassment. And I'd been there for 35 years. So if they had a pattern of sexual harassment, it wasn't going to be hard for them to find out, because we had ladies that had retired, we had ladies that worked there in our court, and they never bothered to interview any of them.

> In the meantime, Jon Muth files a [AGC] complaint against Fischer because he's not only committed extortion, which is a 20-year felony, but in the original complaint against me he has mis-cited the statute about where you can live. The statute he cited was basically amended like in 1983. And the reason I think he did it, the reason Jon thought he did it, was because back then, it looked like I was doing something that was wrong until they amended the statute.

> Now when they pointed that out in the pleadings, Fischer has this—writes this little thing to the Judicial Tenure Commission and says, "You know, it's human frailty. I guess I'm incompetent" —he didn't say that. I'm just—his defense was, "I'm incompetent and it's just a mistake. So just because I made a mistake, don't hold that against the case."

The complaint against Fischer[1278] was filed with the AGC July 3, 2008, said Jon Muth, and while he was the author...

> It was signed by, in addition to me, I think almost every living former president of the Grand Rapids Bar Association. It was signed by the former United States Attorney. It was signed by the former chief judge of Kent County Circuit Court. It was signed by the former chief judge of Kent County Probate Court.[1279]

1278 For relevant coverage see Nate Reems, "Local lawyers file grievance against court official investigating Servaas," *Grand Rapids Press*, 4 July 2008, http://blog.mlive.com/grpress/2008/07/local_lawyers_file_grievance_a.html, and Barton Dieters, "Failed effort to remove Judge Steven Servaas now puts former state Supreme Court justice in hot seat," *Grand Rapids Press*, 9 April 2011, http://www.mlive.com/news/grand-rapids/index.ssf/2011/04/the_long_shadow_of_the_judge_s.html.
1279 Jon R. Muth, video interview with co-author Schock, 17 January 2012, Grand Rapids. Muth had received permission from Servaas and Weaver to speak with the co-author Schock about this.

Fifteen signatories in all.

With the master's finding and the determination to fight it, next came a trip to the JTC in Detroit. And there on July 14, 2008,[1280] Jon Muth, Weaver's sometime attorney, would lead the effort:

> My active role began after the hearing with the hearing officer. My partner at that time, Jim Brady, handled that hearing. I argued the case at the Michigan Judicial Tenure Commission, which is like sort of a first appellate court, and then I argued the case in the Michigan Supreme Court. I had no contact with Betty Weaver for almost, perhaps, two years while that was pending. It was intentional on my part and I'm sure it was intentional on her part, because we knew—I knew—where that case was headed, and the last thing I wanted to do was create any impression of impropriety from me talking to Betty about anything. We didn't even talk; didn't have a phone conversation.[1281]

The defendant and his team didn't have a particularly warm reception at the JTC, something that took Servaas aback.

> I've never been in front of a more hostile group of people in my life. It was 30 minutes for Fischer to give his side, and it was 30 minutes for Jon to give my side. And we're in there, and they had this guy that was the representative of the Court of Appeals, this Talbot, he was just malignant.[1282] I mean, they were all over—first they were saying things like, "Well, you know, obviously the Judge lied here." And "he did this there." And I'm sitting there and I can't say anything. And I'm saying to myself, "Who are these people? I've never met any of them." And they're treating it not like I had moved two miles or four miles over into another district; they're treating me like I was Adolph Hitler. I mean, just this palpable animosity from this whole group of people who I've never met before.
>
> And then Jon starts to make his closing statement, and one of them—they're all from the eastern side of the state; that's why I don't know them—jumps on Jon and says, "You're supposed to be one of ten-best attorneys in this state. Why don't you just cut this out and get to the chase."
>
> It was like, you know, Jon Muth IS one of the ten-best attorneys in the state. And they're treating him like some tramp that wandered in off the street who doesn't know what he's doing. And it was, like, whatever is going to

1280 Brief in support of the Commission's decision and recommendation for order of discipline, Michigan Judicial Tenure Commission, *In re Honorable Steven R. Servaas*, No. 13763347, 26 December 2008, 47, http://www.courts.mi.gov/Courts/MichiganSupremeCourt/Clerks/Oral-Arguments/Briefs/03-09/137633/137633-JTCBriefinSupport.pdf.
1281 Ibid.
1282 We had covered Judge Michael J. Talbot's rise to the Court of Appeals as an Engler appointee in Chapter 4.

happen, it isn't going to be good for me. I mean, there just was no way from the questions and the way that they treated us, and this Talbot, I thought, was the most offensive. Some of them didn't say anything. I don't want to paint them all with the same brush, but there were quite a few of them. You know, there were four or five of them.[1283]

Muth agreed that his reception was hostile:[1284]

> I've argued cases in a lot of courts. I have never been more rudely treated as a lawyer than I was by the Judicial Tenure Commission. And it had nothing to do with the position; it was that they understood that I was after their boy, Paul Fischer. And there was palpable animosity toward me personally from certain of the people on the Judicial Tenure Commission. And the tone of the argument was very, very interesting. There was a nastiness there that you don't often see, and there was a real refusal on their part to focus on what the fundamental issues were. I mean, they went off on this, that, and the other thing, but I walked out of there saying, "That's a kangaroo court." And I've never walked out of any other appellate hearing in my career with that same feeling, ever. But it _was_ a kangaroo court. [...] They weren't interested in looking at the issues. They were interested in protecting Paul Fischer.[1285]

There was no joy from the JTC; one of the things it sought to punish Servaas for was what it called his lack of remorse.[1286] And the JTC struck any use of the recording that featured Fischer's tactics. On October 17, 2008, it upheld the findings of the master in its decision and recommendation for order of discipline. The JTC recommended removal for "judicial misconduct" alleging that Servaas was "unfit to sit as a judge."[1287] The matter would head to the Supreme Court.

Judge Servaas:

> The JTC says, you know, "We recommend that the Supreme Court boot him out." Well, the other interesting thing that's going on is this is right in the middle of an election year for me, and so I'm thinking, now, even if they say that I was wrong, and I shouldn't have moved into my district but over my election line, that's not anything that involves moral turpitude or anything where you'd say, "Oh, he can't ever be on the bench again."

1283 Steven R. Servaas.

1284 Reporter Barton Dieters also chronicled the hostility in his account: "Judicial tenure panelist criticizes approach of Steven Servaas' lawyer," *Grand Rapids Press*, 15 July 2008, http://blog.mlive.com/grpress/2008/07/judicial_tenure_panelist_criti.html.

1285 Jon R. Muth.

1286 Brief in support of the Commission's decision and recommendation for order of discipline, Michigan Judicial Tenure Commission, *In re Honorable Steven R. Servaas*, No. 13763347, 26 December 2008, 47, http://www.courts.mi.gov/Courts/MichiganSupremeCourt/Clerks/Oral-Arguments/Briefs/03-09/137633/137633-JTCBriefinSupport.pdf.

1287 "Judicial Tenure Commission rules Servaas should be removed from bench," *Grand Rapids Press*, 20 October 2008, http://blog.mlive.com/chronicle/2008/10/judicial_tenure_commission_rul.html.

So I decide, if you're an incumbent, you can file an affidavit of incumbency [to get on the ballot]. But if the Supreme Court finds that they should kick me out, that would have happened before the election. So I decide that I'm also going to get signatures, which you can do even if you're not a judge. That's how you get on the ballot. And it was unbelievable the people that northern Kent County were just—you know!

I had two advantages that judges that aren't there for 36 years don't have. One is, I was not overly-wealthy, but I had money that I could use to defend myself and was willing to use it.

And, two, I've been here for 36 years, so I knew all the people from northern Kent County, you know, maybe not personally, but I just lived there. I lived there, I was a judge there, I ran there, I went door-to-door, and so I knew all these people. And it was like, I know them by Bob; "Nice to see you, Bob." I know them by Tom. "Nice to see you, Tom." I played softball in the leagues with them. I played basketball in the leagues with them. You know, that's my home, really. So they knew this was all just garbage.

They'd seen me not only in court, but I lived most of the time within a four- or five-block area from the court; and my daughter grew up in Rockford. So I had the advantage of—this Fischer could come in and say all these lies and character assassinations that he wanted to and he could put them in the Grand Rapids newspaper. And I grew up in Grand Rapids, so people knew me, and they knew my dad, and they knew my mom. You know, my dad was president of the Bar, and he was a B-29 pilot, and my mom was president of the Humane Society. I had that advantage that they knew Fischer was lying and they knew the stuff he said about me was absolutely false.

I still get a little misty when I think about how good they've been. They've just been tremendous. So those were two advantages that younger judges or judges that have only been on the bench for four or five years, and they don't have the money, they have kids in school, and this guy comes in and threatens them and says, "Get out by tomorrow or we're going to charge you with perjury," or tries to extort them out. They don't have the money to defend, and some places like Kent County, we had insurance for a hundred-thousand, but it also cost me another $56,000 myself to defend this. And, you know, people don't have that kind of money to throw around, plus if they hadn't been on the bench that long, the people in the area, when Fischer starts assassinating their character, they don't have the personal knowledge of the judge to say, "Hey, that just isn't true." So I was just real fortunate in that respect.

But the bottom-line was, I got twice as many signatures as I ever needed to get on the ballot, and I went down and I filed them, and my name got on the ballot. So I'm thinking, regardless of what happens here, what are they gonna do? All this stuff they said about me, nobody ran against me, so I was the only one on the ballot. So I was going to win. So after this was over, and they had the election—it wasn't really after, it was during—there were 43,000 votes, the most by 10,000-people that I ever had in my life.

There were days when I was really down, and this was a huge upper.[1288]

So, even before the Supreme Court heard arguments, Servaas had been re-elected. He won; he was living in the proper northern division within his district; he was minding his manners. At this point, the matter was more or less moot.

The Supreme Court heard oral arguments in the case March 4, 2009. It was quite a show according to Muth:

> So it's not a system in which you have any checks or balances. You don't have an independent prosecutor; you don't have an independent decision-maker; you don't have an independent final arbiter of the result. And you've got a setting in which the whole fabric of judicial politics can play out. I'm not saying it does in every instance, but I think in Judge Servaas' case it did. It was political at the start, it was political throughout, and it was political at the end. And I'm not talking Republican-Democrat politics; I'm talking small "p" politics—who likes whom, how are you going to react, who are you gonna support, who are you gonna defend?[1289,1290]

The Supreme Court arguments began with Jon Muth giving his 15 minutes of facts and reasons. Then Fischer came to rostrum. There would be 40 or more minutes of hard questioning by six assertive justices as they peppered Fischer.

And so at the hearing, we start questioning the JTC director, who is presenting the case against Servaas—not just me, the other justices, too.

It was clear that with the exception of Justice Stephen Markman, Fischer's work was not well thought of.

Justice Young joined in. He was appalled just as were Corrigan, Justice Hathaway, myself, Cavanagh, and Kelly. We all had questions, because this was not just.

Here are some of the exchanges transcribed from a DVD of the oral arguments:

> CORRIGAN: I am very concerned, sir, to understand what the commission and you were thinking when you made that swoop-down visit and demand-ed his immediate resignation.

1288 Steven R. Servaas.
1289 Jon R. Muth.
1290 *In retrospect, Jon's not complete. He's right it was "politics" with a small "p" with respect to the Engler's Four's dislike and desire to show Servaas, me, and others wrong at any cost. But also it did come down to partisan politics for the Engler Four.*

YOUNG: I want you to understand how troubling it is for an agent of this court to go and simply threaten horrible things. The judge said he was less well treated than a criminal defendant. I agree with that.

FISCHER: About five times a year we will even have judges just quietly re-tire or resign rather than have anything come up.

YOUNG: Is this how you accomplish it?

FISCHER: The Commission does not send me to discuss it with them.[1291]

That would be a yes. Five times a year?

Weaver wanted to be certain it was the entire commission who was making the offer for Judge Servaas to resign.

FISCHER: Yes, the commission...was giving him the opportunity to re-sign.[1292]

Fischer also said that Servaas' attorneys had lodged a complaint against him with the AGC.

CORRIGAN: I am very concerned that there is an abuse of power going on here [...] Mr. Fischer.[1293]

Fischer said that the points she was raising weren't in the record referred by the JTC.

CORRIGAN: This court decides what's in the record.[1294]

Among other things, Weaver wanted to know exactly how Fischer got the stationary for Servaas' resignation letter. He wouldn't tell exactly who supplied it to him.

WEAVER: You're keeping this confidential from the court?[1295]

Fischer was dancing as fast as he could, and it wasn't enough to keep the justices attention away from the sticky points. Finally, Weaver burrowed in on the Gromek connection. Did Gromek know this was going to happen?

FISCHER: It's possible I told Jim Hughes [the SCA regional director who reports directly to Gromek], but I can't say that for sure. If a formal com-

---

1291 Transcription from oral arguments, 4 March 2009, in *In re Honorable Steven R. Servaas*, No. 13763347, DVD from Michigan Supreme Court.
1292 Ibid.
1293 Ibid.
1294 Ibid.
1295 Ibid.

plaint is going to issue on a judge sometimes we'll tell the regional, but I can't say for sure that happened.[1296]

He did admit that he'd spoken with Judge Smolenski ahead of his visit.

No one asked him if perhaps Carl Gromek had originated the matter with the JTC.

I let it go at that. In fact, I didn't make him answer because, okay, fine enough. But I also wanted to know if our State Court Administrator was involved in this. And it did later come out that the State Court Administrator, two years before, had raised this vacation of office issue and done nothing about it. In the original request from the JTC, as I said, our staff—our 18 experienced lawyers—had not looked up the law on what happens, the statute on vacation of office. But certainly by the time it came to us for this hearing, we had read and knew the law, which is a statute that says vacation of office is not a crime; it's simply an act that causes severe consequences to officeholders because they leave it. And there is a way to handle it, and it doesn't involve the JTC.

It says that if somebody believes a judge, or any kind of public official, has vacated their office, they go to the Attorney General, and the Attorney General is to take it to the Court of Appeals to hear it. ... Not the Supreme Court; the Court of Appeals. And only after the Court of Appeals would hear it, then it could it be appealed up to the Supreme Court. That's the procedure. It has nothing to do with the JTC. And if the Attorney General wouldn't take it, the person had a right to take it on to the Court of Appeals directly. And, of course, if the Court of Appeals had refused to take it, they could appeal it to us. So eventually it would get to us, but not through the discipline procedure of the JTC. The law wasn't very clear—but Judge Servaas hadn't moved out of the district, and he wasn't a division judge, he was a district judge for that district, which was in two divisions.

So the question really is this: What is the JTC doing making this decision? Because they sent it to us saying THEY had determined after having a hearing on it that he had vacated his office. Well, since when are they supposed to do that? It would be, as I put in my opinion in this case, as if a judge is accused of armed robbery. Is it up to the JTC to decide that the judge has committed armed robbery, or is that why we have the criminal justice system? ...Where you go through the courts, and then, if you're found guilty, then the JTC could take it up as a fact that you'd committed armed robbery. Even if you had a video of them committing it, it still would go through the criminal justice system. It's called due process and fairness.

So what was revealed here is, really, that the JTC was taking power it didn't have in this case. And perhaps it had taken power earlier in other cases, like In re Gilbert, *and tried to make a deal there. If Servaas had resigned, then it would have all been hidden, and we justices and the public would never have known why he resigned or when he resigned, necessarily, unless we happened to live in the area and see that there was some publicity. It would all be done in unnecessary secrecy, and the public would never know the truth about the matter. ...Much like Judge Root's resignation.*

It was clear from their comments and questions, said Weaver, which positions the justices would take.

1296 Ibid.

It was apparent to the watchers—it was going to be 6-to-1, because Markman was the only one that wasn't questioning and made some sort of opposite point of view comments. Markman was never appalled, and I would say that you could characterize most of the questioning by the other justices as: "WHAT? YOU DID THIS? IT'S BEEN DONE OTHER TIMES?"

Muth had been before the court enough times to get a sense of where the justices were headed:

> Yeah. I really thought they did get it. And if you listened to the give and take of the oral argument, it was apparent that they got it. And then you've got Justice Corrigan talking about how, while she wasn't sure we quite got there on our argument, that there was a deprivation of due process, and this is the closest she had ever seen it come to a situation where perhaps they ought to revisit the issue of whether there's no independence within the system, there's no independent prosecutor. I mean, she's on record saying that, and she's dead right.
>
> And Justice Young was appalled by Fischer's conduct.[1297]

So after we met, after this case, we voted 6-to-1, and in the process of the way cases are assigned—it's supposed to be by lot, and pulling a number out of a box, and then recognizing who had the last case that was assigned to them if they were in the majority—and Justice Young was in the majority and it was assigned to him.

Most times a draft of an opinion will require four to six weeks of preparation. There is a tremendous amount of research that goes into most opinions, much of it the work of commissioners and clerks.

So I did receive Justice Young's initial draft opinion. And, by the way, you can always change your mind, change your vote, but my contention is that you need always to be able to explain how you got where you are so it's not just secret at the end.

So I got this opinion draft April 27, 2009. It says, this is from Justice Young to all the justices, and the clerk and the research director and our reporter (who gets things in right English, supposedly): "Attached is my draft opinion in the matter. I welcome your comments and suggestions."

And Justice Young had written that six people had decided at that point that the whole thing should be dismissed because it was such an injustice, and there was no vacation of office. The whole procedure of the JTC was moot for two reasons: first, by this time Judge Servaas had been overwhelmingly re-elected in November of 2008, so even while he was up for re-election, all of this press went on, and he was still overwhelmingly elected. But the equally important reason would be that the JTC didn't follow the right procedure, the matter didn't go to the Court of Appeals. The JTC doesn't have any power to do what it did. And so that was it. And, that even though under normal circumstances, we totally disapproved of these sexual comments and what-have-you, but that they were basically an

---

1297 Jon R. Muth.

aberration because Judge Servaas had more than a 36 year career now, and it's one time. And he had been publicly censured. Good grief! It was while he was up for re-election, all over the pages of the Grand Rapids paper many, many times. And so it would be just a folly to have to do that per se. I mean, it would just be what? Carrying sand to the beach? ...Piling on when he'd been publicly censured in the press for a long time. So that was the text of the opinion. And I was prepared to sign it.

It was a very strong opinion, well written. Justice Young is a smart fellow, and he can write well, and he had gotten, in my opinion, that right, and I was grateful.

Then the next step would be this circulates, and it's supposed to wait two weeks—and it probably waited at least two weeks—before it came up on our regular, weekly conference where we would see where people were. Well, that conference I remember distinctly because it was in Detroit, and in the offices up in the former GM Building and in a conference room; it was very dreary looking out of the window. I remember being there so distinctly, and I remember it because of the discussion about this case. And Justice Young said something about that Gromek had had some involvement, and then I picked up on that, because I had picked up on it from what Servaas had said when he was surprised at Fischer's visit—"What? Does Gromek have anything to do with this?" And that was the question I had asked and then never got answers. And I think on the tape, Fischer either avoided it or said, "No." But in my questioning he said, "Oh, I'm subject to an AGC grievance," the Attorney Grievance Commission, which is the discipline arm of the Supreme Court and the Bar Association with respect to attorneys.

So what happens is this: Young then said that he was changing his vote, which was shocking to me. I didn't know why. Well, somehow—it wasn't particularly explained then—they began to talk—and Corrigan said she's changing her vote, too. And Markman had always been a "Remove him." And I was incredulous and wanted to know why, but I don't remember getting any specific answer other than they began to talk about, "Well, he hadn't told the truth. He lied." Well, what was this about? I don't know if it came up right then, but that was eventually where it went.

So, the justice who had drafted the majority opinion was changing his mind on the issue. But the question of "why?" remained. There had to be a reason, a real reason.

Justices Young and Corrigan had expressed their righteous indignation from the bench...it's on record. They were appalled at the unjust actions of Paul Fischer and they questioned whether the JTC was involved. And for a time, they were willing to stand up to do the right thing. And then I believe their agendas took precedence.

And the vote was 4-3. So only somebody in the majority could author the majority opinion. Who was going to write it? It could have been anybody. I think I might have even offered to write it. And in the end, I said that I would. I was somewhat incredulous and said to Young "I thought your opinion was so good, and so can I use whatever I need of it?" And that's usually what somebody does; if they change their mind—and it's perfectly all right to change your mind, it's just you better be able to explain, really, why you changed your mind. He agreed, so I took the opinion. In other words, it then fell to me, the opinion came to me, and I could use what I wanted or needed out of it.

Well, the very first sentence of my opinion and Justice Young's opinion were exactly the same, which is:

The Judicial Tenure Commission recommended that this court remove Respondent 63rd District Court Judge Servaas from office for vacating his office as well as for Judicial Misconduct involving a comment and two drawings of a sexual nature.[1298]

And the rest of his first paragraph just said:

We conclude that the appropriate proceeding to determine whether Respondent vacated his Judicial Office was a *quo warranto*[1299] action filed by the Attorney General in the Court of Appeals. However, we believe this issue is now moot as respondent was re-elected to a new term of office in 2008. Additionally, while respondent's comment and the two drawings was unquestionably inappropriate, we believe that no additional public censure is required in the light of the punitive tactics directed against the respondent by the executive director of the JTC in this matter. Accordingly, the petition is dismissed.[1300]

The rest of Weaver's first paragraph didn't come out exactly that way. Here is the entire first paragraph of her final opinion:

The Judicial Tenure Commission (JTC) recommended that this Court remove 63rd District Court Judge Steven Servaas (respondent) from office for vacating his office, as well as for judicial misconduct involving a comment and two drawings of a sexual nature. Because we conclude that the only appropriate forum to determine whether respondent vacated his judicial office is a *quo warranto* action filed by the Attorney General in the Court of Appeals, we reject the JTC's recommendation as to the vacation of office claim. Respondent's conduct concerning the comment and two drawings was unquestionably inappropriate; however, a majority of this Court concludes that respondent's conduct did not rise to the level of blatant judicial misconduct requiring the most severe sanction: removal from office. In this respect, we view respondent's actions as an aberration given his [36] years of apparent unblemished service as Judge of the 63rd District Court. Accordingly we impose public censure only.[1301]

Weaver, Cavanagh, and Hathaway signed on but Kelly offered her own concurrence, sort of. It was short but confusing:

1298 Elizabeth A. Weaver writing for the majority, *In re Honorable Steven R. Servaas*, No. 137633, Michigan Supreme Court, 31 July 2009, 1, http://publicdocs.courts.mi.gov:81/opinions/final/sct/20090731_s137633_9_servaas10mar_09-op.pdf
1299 *Quo warranto* means "by what warrant, law, or authority?"
1300 Robert P. Young, Jr., draft of majority opinion, *In re Honorable Steven R. Servaas*, No. 137633, Michigan Supreme Court, 10 March 2009, 1, unpublished
1301 Elizabeth A. Weaver writing for the majority, *In re Honorable Steven R. Servaas*, No. 137633, Michigan Supreme Court, 31 July 2009, 1, http://jtc.courts.mi.gov/downloads/FC84.SupremeCourtOpinion.pdf.

KELLY, C.J. (concurring in part and dissenting in part).

> I concur in Justice Weaver's opinion except for part II(A) and the portions of the introduction and conclusion discussing *quo warranto*. I agree with Justice Markman that the existence of an action for *quo warranto* does not prevent the JTC from assessing respondent's misconduct, regardless of whether that conduct happens to involve the improper exercise of a title to office. Accordingly, I concur in part II of Justice Markman's opinion.

So, which way was she going?

Justice Kelly wasn't quite clear. She signed my opinion only to parts, and she said that she believed that the JTC could do the quo warranto, *but it wasn't in this case deserving of removal—she kind of said that. And then she agreed with the censure [proposed by Corrigan, Markman, and Young in their dissent]. So it was not real clear what she said. There was a request by the parties for clarification for what she had written, which I guess she gave. It didn't make any difference. It was 4-3, he wasn't removed, and I think she said that she didn't believe that he should be removed. That's the crux of it.*

So, in the end, Servaas received a formal censure from the court. And the minority of the Engler three wrote that he not only deserved censure but to be thrown off the bench for lying and a pattern of deception.[1302] That was a change for Young and Corrigan from their comments from the bench and initially in conference, but for Young, in particular as the first author of the opinion giving Servaas a pass.

That was quite a change, but Justice Young had the right to change his mind. But then he was obligated to give his reasons why he's made the change. And, of course, in this opinion, nobody knows that he made such a dramatic change because the final opinion was the only thing that went out.

In my opinion, people needed to know how the justices came to this decision and to be able to judge for themselves whether the justices were fulfilling their responsibility.

Finally, in the opinion, Weaver filed a separate statement, joined by Hathaway, to launch an investigation:

> I authored and join the majority opinion; however, I write separately to request that this court open an administrative file to investigate how this matter unfolded, including the events and actions of the Judicial Tenure Commission (JTC) and/or others responsible leading up to the JTC's recommendation of this case to this court.[1303]

It had taken a long time to get the opinion out the door. For Servaas, it was a small eternity:

1302 Stephen J. Markman, writing in dissent, ibid., 1.
1303 Weaver, writing in ibid., following the majority opinion.

Well, you know, actually you just wait. It's not like it's the next day or from the bench they make any kind of decision. You wait and wait and wait; and I didn't feel bad about waiting, I felt good. You know, I thought that they had figured it out, and they'd figured out what [Fischer] had done, and so I wasn't apprehensive. And one night—I don't know whether it was on the radio or TV; I think it was the radio—and they came in and they had a news thing, and they just said that they'd come back 4-to-3 in my favor. And then I started getting calls from all my friends saying congratulations.

And I was saying, "4-to-3?" I'm glad I won after all this, but how could it be 4-to-3? You know, I just didn't think, from the nature of their questions, that Fischer had anybody, really, on his side. But if he had anybody, it was just Markman.

Well, it turned out Markman was on [Fischer's] side. He wrote a 59-page opinion that I couldn't understand. But he came out and said I should be kicked off the bench.[1304]

He wasn't...but by only one vote in his favor.

In my opinion, if Cliff Taylor wasn't the sleeping justice [and Diane Hathaway elected instead], I would be retired, or I'd be plumbing; I wouldn't be a district judge, not because of anything, in my opinion, that I did or didn't do, but because they would have had four people that were concerned about not investigating Carl Gromek and Fischer, even though, in my opinion, both of them should have been investigated based on what happened to me. Frankly, they would have booted me out.[1305]

And he knew the threat was good: Servaas said during and after his ordeal, he had heard from several other judges who had "retired." In the end, he called it a victory.[1306] After a request for rehearing by the JTC that was denied by the court, the matter for Servaas was legally concluded.[1307]

Young: "You're unethical!" Off to the JTC with You!

But the matter was hardly at an end for Weaver and Servaas' lead attorney, Jon Muth. And all that started with a simple question by Muth: "What happened?"

1304 Steven R. Servaas.
1305 Ibid.
1306 "Judge Steven Servaas views state Supreme Court's ruling as victory," *Grand Rapids Press*, 1 August 2009, http://www.mlive.com/news/grand-rapids/index.ssf/2009/08/judge_steven_servaas_views_sta.html.
1307 Order denying rehearing, *In re Honorable Steven R. Servaas*, No. 137633, Michigan Supreme Court, 11 September 2009, http://publicdocs.courts.mi.gov:81/sct/public/orders/20090911_s137633_12_rehg_561_10_mar_137633_09-11-09.pdf.

Because he's curious as to how it came out the way it came out because everyone thought it would be 6-1 and all of a sudden it's a confused opinion, to say the least—not my opinion, but the votes, 4-3 or 3 and a half or something.

Muth had encountered Weaver at a downstate event and the two agreed to talk over a lunch Oct. 1, 2009, when Muth was north in Traverse City.[1308]

There were a couple of reasons he looked forward to the meeting, said Muth: "One, was to sort of renew our acquaintance and friendship; but, number two, I was really curious about what had happened."[1309]

And we had lunch in Traverse City. And by then, the Servaas case was closed. I could talk about the case because it was not pending or impending. And as far as I was concerned, the "gag order" was unconstitutional and had not been retained. So I told Jon that there was just a change of opinions and votes for various reasons; that he was correct, after the hearing it was 6-1. But I believed that Corrigan and Young had become worried that the State Court Administrator had been involved— that was my thought because what had been said already, and that in my concurrence, I and Hathaway had asked for an investigation. But nothing had come of it.

According to Muth:

> So at lunch, you know, she told me how Young had written the initial major-ity decision, then decided he couldn't support it, and it had fallen to her, she used his opinion, and that Young and Corrigan flipped their votes and wrote opinions that were quite contrary to what I understood their feelings to be at the time of the oral argument.
>
> And Justice Weaver's view was that, somehow—and I don't understand how this was the case—the people on the court flopped their vote because of concern that if they didn't, that there was going to be some sort of an attack made upon the State Court Administrator who, according to Jus-tice Weaver, was kind of their stooge or acolyte, and to protect him, they switched their vote on Servaas. I don't know whether that's true. It seems to be kind of incredible. I don't understand why, but that was her view.
>
> And I passed that on to Judge Servaas, because he was feeling pretty blue about the fact that he only won by one vote. And so I said, "Well, Steve, you know it really was a little better than that. You really had six of them, except you had two of them who decided they couldn't vote that way." And I passed that on to him.[1310]

Well, that would be in October and, as I said, I had forgotten that Fischer, in answer to my question, "Did Gromek know about this?" had said, "Well, I'm under investigation by the AGC." Well, I don't

1308 Of note, while Muth had previously represented Weaver, he was not then or subsequently acting as her attorney.
1309 Jon R. Muth.
1310 Ibid.

know when they did it, whether they did anything or not, because nothing ever came to me, and I didn't know. Of course, their rules are they can have people on investigation for as long as they want. There's no time limit like there is on criminals. And it passed me by because the real thing was the injustices in this case.

In this opinion, we didn't address Fischer's conduct; we would leave that. ...Well, I assumed somebody would make a complaint. And a complaint had already been made when they came in front of us on March 4th, but that had passed me by.

I did NOT talk about Fischer with Muth. NOT! And there wasn't a case pending in front of us.

That fall, the AGC was at last taking up the case against Fischer. It had lingered: the AGC hadn't moved on it until the Servaas case was concluded. As a part of the investigation, AGC associate counsel Patrick K. McGlinn spoke with Judge Servaas after he spoke with Muth about what had happened on the court. Muth describes the Servaas-McGlinn meeting this way.

> So, McGlinn interviews Servaas, and I don't know how the conversation got to the Supreme Court decision, but Judge Servaas said, "Well, I was told that two of the votes flipped; that it originally was a 6-1." McGlinn didn't do anything with that; he just made a note of it. Well, then what happened was that report found its way into the Fischer investigation file. And when the Attorney Grievance Commission basically decided that it was not going to proceed with the Fisher grievance, for whatever reasons. They weren't going to do anything...they just weren't going to do anything.[1311]

In fact, in the end, the AGC did exactly nothing about it, and dismissed the complaint against Fischer.

That had been Nov. 17, 2009. Barton Dieters, reporting for the *Grand Rapids Press* started his account this way:

> The state Attorney Grievance Commission has ruled that Judicial Tenure Commission Executive Director Paul Fischer does not have to face a disciplinary panel for his investigation of Kent County District Judge Steven Servaas.

> In a terse pronouncement Nov. 17, the grievance commission reviewing a complaint against Fischer ruled, "no further action is warranted." As required in such cases, it gave no indication why.[1312]

The initial complaint of July 3, 2008, had been very carefully crafted, said Muth, but that didn't seem to matter. Muth analyzed the situation on the complaint at the AGC:

1311 Ibid.
1312 Barton Dieters, "Attorney who investigated Judge Steven Servaas will not face Discipline Board, grievance panel rules," *Grand Rapids Press*, 25 November 2009, http://www.mlive.com/news/grand-rapids/index.ssf/2009/11/attorney_who_investigated_judg.html.

And it went nowhere. Now ask yourself why?

Okay. Why?

> Who runs the attorney discipline system? The court. The Attorney Griev-
> ance Commission is a body of the Supreme Court. The Attorney Grievance
> Commissioner is an employee of the Supreme Court. So you run into the
> same group of people who made whatever critical decisions had to be made
> to prosecute Judge Servaas, and they're making the decisions as to whether
> or not Paul Fischer deserves to be charged, much less convicted.

> But I have a fair amount of experience with the Attorney Grievance Com-
> mission, and I can assure you that they have gone hell-bent-for-election to
> prosecute attorneys who have done far less wrong than what Paul Fischer
> did.[1313]

Did Muth agree with Servaas that Fischer had committed extortion?

> Yeah. I think he committed extortion. And it wasn't just the extortion; it
> was the fact that he made good on his threat to drag Judge Servaas through
> the mud.[1314]

When the decision by the AGC dismissing the complaint against Fischer came down
Nov. 17, 2009, as was their right, the group of Grand Rapids attorneys asked the
Supreme Court to take superintending control of the AGC on or about January 28,
2010.[1315] According to Muth:

> The only remedy at that point was a special petition to the Supreme Court,
> in hopes that the same people on the Supreme Court that were so critical of
> Fischer the first time around at the hearing on the *Servaas* case would at least
> ask the Attorney Grievance Commission to proceed with it.[1316]

The attorneys seeking corrective action were James S. Brady, Bruce Neckers, Michael
A. Walton, Robert J. Dugan, L. Roland Roegge, William W. Jack, Jr., H. Rhett Pinsky,
John D. Tully, Joseph M. Sweeney, Paul T. Sorensen, Frederick D. Dilley, Janet A.
Haynes, Dennis C. Kolenda, Robert L. Lalley, Jr., William S. Farr, Diann J. Landers....
and Jon Muth, two more than had signed the first request for investigation. Many of
them also had signed the letter to the *Grand Rapids Press* supporting Servaas.

1313 Jon R. Muth.
1314 Ibid.
1315 Ibid., but you can read more about it here: Ed Wesoloski, "Weaver, Corrigan, Young, and Markman:
Supreme Court potboiler," The Michigan Lawyer, a blog of *Michigan Lawyers Weekly*, 25 June 2010, http://
michiganlawyerblog.wordpress.com/2010/06/25/weaver-corrigan-young-and-markman-supreme-court-
potboiler/.
1316 Jon R. Muth.

When Weaver realized that Muth was one of the appellants seeking redress at the court, she alerted all parties on April 20, 2010, that she had spoken with Muth about the closed Servaas matter, not any matter concerning Fischer, the previous fall, but was willing to step off the Fischer matter because Muth was a party in the Fischer matter.[1317] The Brady bunch wrote back to express its willingness for her to continue, but there was no response from the AGC, so Weaver stepped off anyway following her mantra "When in doubt, get out!"

The AGC sent over its file to the Supreme Court. Included was the report by Patrick McGlinn of his conversation with Judge Servaas. That created a problem, said Muth:

> Well, included in that, Judge Servaas' comments about how votes had flipped, and there had been extraneous influences. And that was what she expressed to me, that's what I relayed to Judge Servaas, that's what found its way into the Fischer investigation file, and that's what ultimately ended up on the desk of every justice of the Supreme Court. And they were upset.[1318]

For three of them, it was more like livid.

So in April, I was at an appointment in Traverse City, and I got this call from the chief justice that there was this emergency. Kelly had to speak to me and to say that there was this charge against me that was coming, that I had violated confidentiality rules of the court with a communication. And I said, "I don't know what you're talking about, and I haven't done anything wrong. So when I'm finished with this, we'll get in touch."

And then I received this complaint that was characterized as a request—not quite a request—signed by Markman, Corrigan, and Young, that my meeting with Muth was a violation of the—I guess an ex parte *communication or something, on the AGC case, which we didn't have at that time. Anyway, it was a whole bunch of trumped up stuff. The AGC Investigator had talked to Servaas, and he reported things that Servaas has said he didn't say, but somehow that I had said things to Muth that I hadn't said, and it wasn't accurate.*

Weaver then knew there was extra trouble brewing, and she had a good idea of how they'd try to go after her: AO 2006-8, the non-retained and unconstitutional "gag order."

It hit the fan at the May 12, 2010 public administrative conference.[1319] Weaver herself raised the specter of the "gag order." She went through the history detailing that it had never been retained, and she proposed a motion to have it formally discarded; Hathaway supported it.

1317 Elizabeth A. Weaver writing in her recusal in *Brady, et al. v AGC*, No. 140409, Michigan Supreme Court, 23 June 2010, http://publicdocs.courts.mi.gov:81/SCT/PUBLIC/ORDERS/20100623_S140409_9_140409_2010-06-23_or.pdf.
1318 Ibid.
1319 Subsequent discussion is taken from the video recording of the Michigan Supreme Court and is viewable on Weaver's website: http://www.justiceweaver.com/.

That didn't go over well. The Engler Three maintained it <u>was</u> in effect. No, said Weaver, it was never subsequently retained or amended after the 2007 public hearing. She read the law aloud to them. Instead of adopting it, they had passed off the matter until a later time or occasion. The later time or occasion never came and the file was closed on Feb. 27, 2007.

The video of what happens is more than fascinating. There are vitriolic exchanges directed at Weaver. She remains apparently unruffled, unharried.

> MARKMAN (to Kelly as chief justice): Why today are we considering this proposal? What is different about things today [...] causing us to consider it today?[1320]

Well, said Kelly, Justice Weaver brought it up. Markman asserted that the confidentiality provision of AO 2006-8 was in the law books.

It wasn't, argued Hathaway, jumping in. She agreed with Weaver that the court didn't vote on it, and AO 2006-8 was not in effect. She said what while she wasn't on the court when the matter originated, if the Englerites could show her where it was in the law, she'd salute it.[1321]

> MARKMAN: Well, Justice Hathaway you sound exactly like the people whom Justice Corrigan and I used to deal with in the United States' Attorney's Office who insisted they didn't have to pay taxes because the 16th Amendment was improperly adopted a hundred years earlier. This has been on the law books....

> HATHAWAY: You sound exactly like my children when they were in kindergarten.[1322]

Silence.

And then Corrigan picked up the thread:

> CORRIGAN: I believe we know why, now, she wants this rule eradicated. She wants to kill this order retroactively and act as if it never existed because she broke the rule.[1323]

And then she broke the news:

1320 Public administrative conference, Michigan Supreme Court, 12 May 2010, DVD, Michigan Supreme Court.
1321 Ibid.
1322 Ibid.
1323 Ibid.

CORRIGAN: This is the subject of a recent referral of her to the Judicial Tenure Commission. And what she is doing today is part of a cover up plain and simple. She wants to avoid any attempt to enforce this rule against her.[1324]

Markman and Young also took their turns to boast of sending her to the JTC (they also sent her to the AGC, both on April 28, 2010[1325]), never mind that MCR 9.221[1326] indicates that the matter should be confidential unless or until there is a recommendation to the Supreme Court from the AGC to take up the matter of discipline.

YOUNG: I referred you because you are unethical. You have destroyed the confidentiality of this court. You have revealed our deliberations to a party in a closely related suit that gave them intelligence to support a motion that they filed in this court. You have compromised the integrity of this court and made it impossible to have deliberations without the fear that you at your whim will allow people who should not hear what this court is deliberating about that you will tell them.[1327]

Weaver allowed that Justice Young had a right to his opinion, but she didn't agree with him. There was more she had to report...that the Engler Three had stopped attending conferences in a protest against her; they were refusing to do the assigned work of the court, but they were still picking up their paychecks.[1328]

The discussion finally got to the point where the Engler Three, Cavanagh, and Kelly agreed that there needed to be another meeting to adopt the "gag order." Hathaway noted there would need to be yet another public hearing. Kelly moved to adopt an emergency order to implement an emergency order. They went on and on, Cavanagh calling what he saw as the rule's "wishy-washy language."[1329]

"Is there a rule on the books?" asked Young. For him that was the issue. He, Corrigan and Markman agreed there was. Markman was concerned that Weaver and Hathaway were "making clever arguments," and they didn't want her to have the chance in five years to make another "clever argument" and bring it all to naught.

"I disagree with much of what has been said here today," said Weaver. "This order [2006-8] was used to suppress a dissent, so it was unconstitutional." It also violated the Canon of Judicial Conduct. Weaver said she was willing to do the public's business openly. "What we have here is a secret club."[1330]

1324 Ibid.
1325 David B. Schock, "What Dat? Incompetence or Malice? Both?," 5 April 2011, http://www.mymicourt.com/?p=101.
1326 Michigan Court Rules of 1985, Chapter 9, Professional Disciplinary Proceedings, 9.221, http://courts.mi.gov/Courts/MichiganSupremeCourt/CurrentCourtRules/1Chapter9ProfessionalDisciplinaryProceedings.pdf.
1327 Public administrative conference, Michigan Supreme Court, 12 May 2010.
1328 Young thereafter refused to sign minutes until she was gone. Further, in the election of 2010, the Republicans could nominate her or him, but he vowed he was refusing to run with her.
1329 Public administrative conference, Michigan Supreme Court, 12 May 2010.
1330 Ibid.

There was more, including Weaver's pledge to put out even more information.

In the end, Kelly promoted yet another emergency "gag order" but one that would make an allowance to reveal "unethical, improper, or criminal" behavior at the court. That wasn't good enough. Kelly and Cavanagh voted for it, but everybody else voted against it, but probably for different reasons.

In closing, Chief Justice Kelly wanted to assure the public that even though the Engler Three were not attending conferences, the work of the court was getting done, and she was hopeful that all would be well in the end.[1331]

The *Michigan Lawyers Weekly* blog reported what it called the "Supreme Spat," first citing Markman:

> There was no choice but to stop attending the judicial conferences, Markman said because Weaver "has flagrantly breached rules of confidentiality, and promises to do so again, by revealing interim positions of justices as to their votes in conference, as well as their other privately expressed opinions concerning cases before this court.
>
> "I do not wish to continue to place myself in a position by which Justice Weaver can abuse the deliberative process, while taking out of context statements made by justices in the course of their deliberative discussions."
>
> Weaver fired back that when she was elected, she never "said I was joining a secret club."
>
> Further, she said, justices are required by Cannon 3 B of the Michigan Code of Judicial Conduct to "facilitate the work of the court," which the absent justices have not been doing.[1332]

It wasn't just their bad behavior, said Weaver, that was concerning.

Chief Justice Kelly allowed them to continue and did not early on expose their misconduct. When judging the performance of the justices, the public had a right to know of their unwillingness to facilitate the work of the court and their obstructive behavior in order to achieve their demand for unnecessary secrecy. Had she done so, it might have had an effect on Justice Young's subsequent re-election.

And Justice Weaver, in writing her statement for recusal in the matter of *Brady et al. v AGC* characterized the move by the Engler Three:

1331 Ibid.
1332 Carol Lundberg, "Supreme Spat," The Michigan Lawyer, a blog of *Michigan Lawyers Weekly*, 12 May 2010, http://michiganlawyerblog.wordpress.com/2010/05/12/supreme-spat/.

I have done nothing unethical, and the actions of Justices Corrigan, Young, and Markman amount to nothing more than political maneuvering in this Supreme Court Justice election year. [...]

Once again, Justices Corrigan, Young, and Markman are attempting to confuse the public by distracting attention from the true reasons for my non-participation. I spoke with an attorney regarding a *closed* case. Our conversation was limited to that *closed* case, and we did not discuss the subject of the attorney grievance referral that arose from that *closed* case. Nevertheless, I recused myself from participation in this court's review of the attorney grievance referral that arose from that *closed* case because these circumstances could have raised an appearance of impropriety had I participated. As this statement and its attachments show, I did not provide any information to a party which could give that party a "strategic advantage" in the Attorney Grievance referral that arose from the *closed* case.

In their statement to this order, Justices Corrigan, Young, and Markman continue to misstate the facts surrounding this matter. While they are entitled to their opinion, their opinions are incorrect and based on their continued misstatement of facts and vague, inaccurate allegations. Justices Corrigan, Young, and Markman assert that I provided information to a party that could be used as a "strategic advantage" in a related case, however, they fail to explain what this "information" is.[1333]

As well, she noted that as of the date of her writing, June 22, 2010, the JTC had neither contacted her nor taken any action of which she was aware.

And the Grand Rapids attorneys' request for the Supreme Court to take superintending control of the AGC? In the end, the court decided not to take up the matter, denying it in an order that came down June 23, 2010:

> On order of the court, the complaint for superintending control is considered, and relief is DENIED, because the court is not persuaded that it would grant the requested relief.[1334]

Weaver had, of course, recused herself, and only Hathaway would have granted.

Reflecting on the arc of the story of the case against Steven R. Servaas, Muth reflected:

> The writ that we asked for from the Supreme Court was never issued. They declined. They simply said, "We aren't going to instruct the Attorney Grievance Commission to proceed against Fischer." And why the decision was

---

1333 Elizabeth A. Weaver writing in her recusal in *Brady, et al. v AGC*, No. 140409, 8.
1334 The majority of five writing in *Brady, et al. v AGC*, No. 140409, 1.

made, they don't—maybe they don't have to say. They just said, "We're not going to do anything."[1335]

Ed Wesoloski, writing for the *Michigan Lawyers Weekly* blog reported the incident and asked a really good question:

> The whole affair raises a very interesting question: If either the JTC or the AGC or both initiate proceedings against Weaver and issue an adjudication, who will conduct the judicial review?[1336]

Yes, if the JTC agreed with the complainants, what would have happened? The matter would have been sent back to the Supreme Court for disposal. What would the justices do? What COULD they do given that Weaver could show a pattern of behavior they employed against her? Who COULD objectively have heard the case? A federal court?

Relating to his conversation with McGlinn, Servaas expressed his sorrow that Weaver had to go through extra innings:

> I've always felt terrible because I thought that the reason they turned on Justice Weaver like a pack of piranhas after this happened was because of my statement to him. But when I talked to Jon—I'm real careful about—you know, after this happened—what I say, and I said, "There are a lot of people that ask me all the time about what's going on, why this happened, why that happened." Most of the time I didn't really know until I started asking—and I said, "Is this public knowledge? Is this something that, when I talk to people, I can use to explain why it was four-to-three instead of what I thought should have been 7-0 or 6-1 at the very least?"
>
> And he said, "Yeah, I don't think there's any problem with it being public."
>
> [...]
>
> But I really feel bad because after that poor Justice Weaver, who's the epitome of a fair judge, a knowledgeable judge, a smart judge, someone who can't be threatened...it was just like blood in the water.[1337]

The JTC dismissed the complaint against Weaver in September of 2010. But that wasn't the end of the matter. The complaint against her that the three also had sent to the AGC lingered, later to be resurrected. And this time, it involved Jon Muth, too.

1335 Jon R. Muth.
1336 Ed Wesoloski, "Weaver, Corrigan, Young, and Markman: Supreme Court potboiler," The Michigan Lawyer, a blog from *Michigan Lawyers Weekly*, 25 June 2010, http://michiganlawyerblog.wordpress.com/2010/06/25/weaver-corrigan-young-and-markman-supreme-court-potboiler/. Carol Lundberg also covered the issue for the print version of the publication and reached the same conclusion. [Carol Lundberg, "Weaver issue has nowhere to go," *Michigan Lawyers Weekly*, 25 June 2010, http://milawyersweekly.com/news/2010/06/25/weaver-issue-has-nowhere-to-go/.]
1337 Steven R. Servaas.

According to Muth:

> [T]hree members of the court (Markman, Young and Corrigan) wrote the AGC saying that maybe Weaver and I had done something wrong by having our discussion. They made no specific allegations—just said the AGC should look into it. The AGC sat on that for a long time—months—then finally asked for a response from the two of us. Weaver made hers public; I did not. At this time, only Corrigan was pushing the issue. Markman and Young appear to have dropped it. I wrote a response; the AGC considered the matter; and I was informed that they determined not to proceed further for the reason that they were satisfied that I had done nothing that was contrary to the Rules of Professional Conduct.[1338]

So, the AGC would dismiss the matter against them both in June of 2011. But that's part of the story in the next chapter.

And as far as the Engler Three were concerned—and now joined by Cavanagh and Kelly—something of the "gag order" was in effect, probably, maybe....even though it had never been adopted, and it was still unconstitutional.

No matter what they thought or said, it wasn't law or a valid rule.

And Cavanagh's and Kelly's change in position was disheartening, Cavanagh's especially.

He was tired of all the conflict, and I think it wore him out. But he also liked the unnecessary secrecy, as did Kelly.

Weaver's only ally on the court when it came to matters of principle was Diane Hathaway. And as far as the Engler Three, in standing up for Weaver, Hathaway had enlarged the target on her own back. She would stand up again at a crucial time in the near future.

Weaver was left with several questions: what exactly—if anything—did Markman have to do with the Servaas incident, the State Court Administrator, and the JTC? After all, at that time, Markman was the liaison from the Supreme Court to the JTC. And was it possible that Corrigan also entered that mix? There was something about it all that didn't add up unless she accounted for the Supreme Court's influence. It's a question for future court historians.

This episode with Judge Servaas might do much to explain what had happened oh-so-quietly with Judge Lawrence Root in Mecosta. Maybe.

As for judges who have displeased the Judicial Tenure Commission, there seem to be two possibilities: if the judges go along, they get the retirement cake, the honors, and a cover up. If they don't, they are dragged through the mud.

1338 John R. Muth, e-mail to co-author Schock, 10 August 2012.

As far as Judge Servaas, things have gone well since his encounter with the JTC, for the most part uneventfully. ...With one small exception: he was selected by members of the Police Officers Association of Michigan as their 2012 "Jurist of the Year."[1339]

That had to feel a little better. Cake at last.

But not for the taxpayers of Kent County and the people of the State of Michigan. They had paid for a very nice $6.5 million dollar building they didn't need. Ironically, the new building is located in the southern division of the district court. Judge Servaas now holds court in the same southern division in which he sometimes lived and for which the director of a state government commission, the JTC of the Supreme Court, unjustly and cruelly sought to have him removed from office. More tyranny and unnecessary secrecy.

1339 Barton Dieters, "Michigan's police union names Judge Steven Servaas 'Justice of the Year,'" *Grand Rapids Press*, 24 May 2012, http://www.mlive.com/news/grand-rapids/index.ssf/2012/05/michigans_police_union_names_j.html.

Chapter 25

Time to Go
Opinions in the Wind,
Making up Her Mind,
Picking a Successor,
On the Campaign Trail

Between 2008 and 2010, with Diane Hathaway on the court and the balance of power at three Democrats and three Englerites, Weaver's vote became the deciding factor again and again during the next two years. And there were plenty of signs that a change was in the wind.

Shortly after Justice Taylor's 2008 defeat, Marilyn Kelly was reported to have promised to reverse direction at the court, including some recent decisions:

> We, the new majority, will get the ship off the shoals and back on course, and we will undo a great deal of the damage that the Republican-dominated court has done. Not only will we not neglect our duties, we will not sleep on the bench.[1340]

While the court had the authority to reach back and revisit cases, usually the method to make adjustments and restorations was to take up pertinent cases that came. And they came.

Most of the cases for the spring of 2009 would have been in the hopper from the court under Taylor.

Once those cases were cleared, other cases would come forward later in 2009 and 2010.

1340 This is taken from Robert P. Young's, dissent in *Regents of the University of Michigan and University of Michigan Health System v Titan Insurance Co.*, No. 136905, Michigan Supreme Court, 31 July 2010, 4, http://publicdocs. courts.mi.gov:81/OPINIONS/FINAL/SCT/20100731_S136905_70_uofm-op.pdf. Young cited it as having appeared as "She Said It," *Detroit Free Press*, 10 December 2008, 2.A, but co-author Schock has not been able to verify it. Neither has the staff of the Detroit Public Library. Neither does it show up in *the Detroit News* of that date. Weaver observed: *What's interesting about that is that at that point—Dec. 10, 2008—it hasn't been decided yet who is going to be chief justice.* In fact, the first mention of the quote appears to be in a Jan. 9, 2009, news story, uttered by Stephen Markman who ascribes the comment to Marilyn Kelly and referencing a Democratic Party event. All that was quoted in a story by Dawson Bell. [Dawson Bell, "Statewide: After 10 years of the GOP, Dem to lead high court, *Detroit Free Press*, 9 January, 2009, B.3.] Kelly has not denied that she said it, but it seems unlikely it appears as Justice Young asserted.

One of the significant cases that worked against the Supreme Court majority's crippling of the state's environmental standards in the *Nestlé* decision was *Lansing School Education Ass'n v Lansing Board of Education*.[1341] The case involved teacher safety in the face of student violence. The opinion moved the state back from the federal concept of standing adopted in *Lee/Cleveland Cliffs*.

In the *Lansing School Education Ass'n* majority opinion, Justice Cavanagh wrote that the court had earlier ignored established law. *Lee/Cleveland Cliffs* had gone too far.

> The flaws in the *Lee/Cleveland Cliffs* approach are many. Perhaps most egregiously, however, the *Lee/Cleveland Cliffs* majority dramatically distorted Michigan jurisprudence to invent out of whole cloth a constitutional basis for the standing doctrine and then, perplexingly, determined that Michigan's standing doctrine should be essentially coterminous with the federal doctrine, despite the significant differences between the two constitutions and the powers held by the respective court systems. There is no support in either the text of the Michigan Constitution or in Michigan jurisprudence, however, for recognizing standing as a constitutional requirement or for adopting the federal standing doctrine.[1342]

Cavanagh had come to this realization a little late. He had signed onto the *Lujan* standing concept adopted in *Lee/Cleveland Cliffs* and had to backtrack on his own position. To do that, he dedicated a large portion of his opinion to the implications of aligning a verdict with all that had been decided before. He had to find a way to turn away from his position in the earlier decision without abjuring the concept of *stare decisis*. This would take some fine parsing:

> In light of the fact that the Michigan Constitution's reference to the judicial power does not inherently incorporate the federal case-or-controversy requirement, and, in fact, importing this requirement is inconsistent with this court's historical view of its own powers and the scope of the standing doctrine, the question arises as to whether this court should continue to apply the *Lee/Cleveland Cliffs* doctrine. Under the longstanding doctrine of *stare decisis*, "principles of law deliberately examined and decided by a court of competent jurisdiction should not be lightly departed." [Citations omitted]. The importance of the *stare decisis* doctrine is well-established, for, as Alexander Hamilton stated, to "avoid an arbitrary discretion in the courts, it is indispensable that [courts] should be bound down by strict rules and precedents which serve to define and point out their duty in every particular case that comes before them...." As the United States Supreme Court has stated, the doctrine "promotes the evenhanded, predictable, and consistent development of legal principles, fosters reliance on judicial decisions, and contributes to the actual and perceived integrity of the judicial process." De-

---

1341 *Lansing School Education Ass'n v Lansing Board of Education*, No 138401, Michigan Supreme Court, 31 July 2010, http://publicdocs.courts.mi.gov:81/OPINIONS/FINAL/SCT/20100731_S138401_54_lsea-op.pdf.
1342 Ibid., 11.

spite its importance, *stare decisis* is neither an "inexorable command," nor "a mechanical formula of adherence to the latest decision...." Ultimately, it "attempts to balance two competing considerations: the need of the community for stability in legal rules and decisions and the need of courts to correct past errors." To reflect this balance, while there is a presumption in favor of upholding precedent, this presumption may be rebutted if there is a special or compelling justification to overturn precedent. In determining whether a special or compelling justification exists, a number of evaluative criteria may be relevant, but overturning precedent requires more than a mere belief that a case was wrongly decided.[1343]

In a footnote, Cavanagh took on those who dissented:

Contrary to the mewling of the dissenters, who would enshrine their disembowelment of 10 to 50 years of this court's jurisprudence, in *Lee* and many other cases, this majority's reversal of their recent activist efforts simply brings this court back to the *status quo ante*. Indeed, the dissenters' *stare decisis* protestations should taste like ashes in their mouths. Although the dissenters paid absolutely no heed to *stare decisis* as they denigrated the wisdom of innumerable predecessors, the dissenters would now wrap themselves in its benefits to save their recent precedent.[1344]

Weaver concurred with the opinion but dissented with the *stare decisis* implications. *Stare decisis* was indeed a "policy," she said, not an "immutable doctrine":

With regard to the policy of *stare decisis*, my view is that past precedent should generally be followed but that to serve the rule of law, in deciding whether wrongly decided precedent should be overruled, each case should be looked at individually on its facts and merits through the lens of judicial restraint, common sense, and fairness.[1345]

All three of those elements, she asserted, had been lacking in the *Lee/Cleveland Cliffs* decisions.

And, in addition to *Lansing School Education Ass'n v Lansing Board of Education*, there were other cases that reversed Engler Four decisions or parts of their decisions—thanks to a list compiled and lamented over by Justice Young—including: *People v Feezel* (reversing *People v Derror*), *McCormick v Carrier* (overruling *Kreiner v Fischer*), *Bezeau v Palace Sports &*

1343 Ibid., 16.
1344 Ibid., footnote 15, 19. Justice Corrigan responded to her colleague Cavanagh and his footnoted comment with this revealing rejoinder:

Rather than ash, the majority's *stare decisis* analysis should taste like bile in their mouths: like a bulimic after a three day bender, the majority justices now purge a decade's worth of vigorous protestations that they are committed to the principle of *stare decisis*. [Ibid., Corrigan writing in dissent, 64.]

1345 Elizabeth A. Weaver, writing in concurrence, ibid., 4.

Entertainment, Inc, (overruling parts of *Karaczewski v Farbman Stein & Co*), and *Regents of the University of Michigan and University of Michigan Health System v Titan Insurance Co* (overruling *Cameron v Auto Club*).[1346]

Even *Trentadue* was under review with a grant for *Colaianni v Stuart Frankel Development Corp.*[1347] *Colaianni* could have reinstated the common law discovery rule.[1348] Oral arguments had been heard, and it was likely the votes were there to reverse *Trentadue.* In the end, however, the *Colaianni* participants reached a settlement and *Trentadue* is still on the books.

More definitive—at least for a very short time—was *Anglers of the AuSable v Michigan Department of Environmental Quality and Merit Energy Company,*[1349] a case to restore the everyman standing in reporting and filing suit against environmental abuse.[1350] Young's "strenuous" dissent was joined by Corrigan and Markman.

Running?

As well, 2010 was another election year. Both Weaver and Young were up, she for her third full term and he for his second.

There was the possibility that they would not run together, especially if Young had anything to say about it. Young had appeared on WKAR's *Off the Record* with Tim Skubick, Jan. 9, 2009, shortly after Justice Hathaway had taken the bench and a day after the first televised selection of Marilyn Kelly as chief justice (to which Young, Corrigan, and Markman dissented). The topic of Betty Weaver WAS the agenda for the interview.

First Young was asked if Justice Weaver had "problems."

1346 Robert P. Young, J., dissent in *Regents of the University of Michigan and University of Michigan Health System v Titan Insurance Co.,* No. 136905, Michigan Supreme Court, 31 July 2010, 4, http://publicdocs.courts.mi.gov:81/OPINIONS/FINAL/SCT/20100731_S136905_70_uofm-op.pdf.
1347 Order to grant, *Colaianni v Stuart Frankel Development Corp.,* No. 139350, Michigan Supreme Court, 29 January 2010, http://publicdocs.courts.mi.gov:81/sct/public/orders/20100129_s139350_54_139350_2010-01-29_or.pdf.
1348 Carol Lundberg, "MSC to hear case that could reinstate common law discovery," *Michigan Lawyers Weekly,* 6 October 2010, http://milawyersweekly.com/news/2010/10/06/msc-to-hear-case-that-could-reinstate-common-law-discovery/.
1349 *Anglers of the AuSable v Michigan Department of Environmental Quality and Merit Energy Company,* Nos. 138863 to 138866, Michigan Supreme Court, 29 December 2010,.
1350 The victory was short lived. On a request for rehearing, that Dec. 29, 2010, decision was vacated four months after it was ordered [*Anglers of the AuSable v Michigan Department of Environmental Quality and Merit Energy Company,* Rehearing Nos. 576, 578, Michigan Supreme Court, 25 April 2011, http://publicdocs.courts.mi.gov:81/sct/public/orders/20110425_s138863_131_138863_2011-04-25_or.pdf], a result of new Republican majority and Young being selected chief justice. For a treatment of the reversal, see Noah Hall, "Michigan Supreme Court vacates *Anglers of the Au Sable* decision, reversing a legal victory for environmentalists." [Great Lakes Law; A blog about all things wet and legal in the Great Lakes region by Professor Noah Hall, 26 April 2011, http://www.greatlakeslaw.org/blog/2011/04/michigan-supreme-court-vacates-anglers-of-the-ausable-decision-reversing-a-legal-victory-for-environ.html.]

YOUNG: I think she does. She's made accusations against the majority of four that were completely baseless; they've never been substantiated. [...] It is very hard now.

SKUBICK: She has poisoned the water. (Not a question.)

YOUNG: Absolutely.[1351]

The issue was her ongoing release of information Young wanted kept secret: the inner workings of the court.

Rick Pluta, Michigan Public Radio Network, actually asked what harm there might be with letting people know what was going on. He kept on the issue and repeated the question.

At one point the media representatives actually suggested Young was whining, although he claimed that he was "a big boy."[1352]

Susan Demas, Michigan Information and Research Service, looked ahead a year and better: "So, in 2010 would you like to see the Republican Party not renominate Elizabeth Weaver?"

YOUNG: I'll put it to you this way: they can nominate her or they can nominate me.

CHRIS CHRISTOFF, *Detroit Free Press*: I don't think she's eligible.

YOUNG: She says she is. When was she born? No one knows?[1353]

...Ah, "no one knows."

Young knew very well because in my many efforts on reforming how we select justices, I had put in front of them various proposals, that the justices would have one term, and how this would affect everybody. And I had everybody's birthday down on a chart and so he had the record of everybody's birthday and how no one would really be harmed if they served and finished. So he knew precisely that I was qualified to run again, or he should have known.

To be qualified a justice cannot be 70 or older on the day of taking office; 69 years and 364 days (not counting a leap year) was okay. And, while Weaver now says

---

1351 *Off the Record*, WKAR, 9 January 2009, http://archive.wkar.org/offtherecord/.
1352 Young also admitted on the show that he'd asked Weaver for her vote for him to become chief justice in 2009.
YOUNG: "I asked Betty for her vote."
SKUBICK: "What did she tell you?"
YOUNG: "No."
1353 *Off the Record*, WKAR, 9 January 2009, http://archive.wkar.org/offtherecord/.

it's nobody's business just how old she is—she doesn't celebrate birthdays or other anniversaries—her birth date was on many documents at the court.

It was all on record. How many times have I filled out forms for my retirement and all of that? So either you think I somehow, since having been a judge almost 36 years, that from day one—when I was elected in '74—I had decided to change my birth date in order that I could run in 2010. I mean, how preposterous can something be? ...That somehow I would know that I would serve as a probate judge, and then become a Court of Appeals judge, and then to the Supreme Court, and just be there at the right time so I would not be 70 at the time? This is a little ridiculous. But that's what went on.

It grew even a little more ridiculous: field operatives.

And that 2009 statement would lay the surface the next year as to somebody checking the records in New Orleans of when I was born. This was more than interesting to me to find out. Somebody went down to New Orleans, checked it out, and then it was brought to me by the press—and it wasn't the press who checked it out. They'd been given the information that my birth records had been lost in the Katrina flood, in the basement of the Baptist Hospital, on Napoleon Avenue, where I was born. That hospital had flooded immensely.

Evidently somebody didn't do a very complete job. There also was a central repository of all birth records in the state but they remained unconsulted.

Those birth records were there the whole time in the records of the State of Louisiana. So if you're going to start talking about things like that—it was very offhanded. But Justice Young was frustrated and unhappy.

But who would have commissioned such an errand? The Republicans?

I don't know if the Republicans did. It could have been just somebody from the Engler Four or one of their supporters, because many Republicans still wanted me to run.

And Young had every ability to know my age. It probably would have been professional and appropriate, or collegial, to check with me before he talked about it, so he didn't make those mistakes.

Young's ultimatum of the Republicans nominating either Weaver or him was somewhat disingenuous. All justices had to do as incumbents was simply file for re-election.

Neither one of us had to be nominated by the parties anyway, so it was irrelevant. But he needed the party money.

That Republican Party affiliation would bring huge support, millions of dollars. Weaver had far less desire for the money that would come with any party-endorsed campaign.

The fact of the matter is, the records show that I was eligible to run, and I did file to run, and I was accepted. I would have been accepted for the ballot. There was not any challenge to that.

Weaver filed as an incumbent candidate, keeping her options open. This is her press release about running again:

> I have filed to place my name on the November 2nd ballot as an incumbent candidate for the Michigan Supreme Court. I need no nomination of any political party to be on the ballot and seek none. In doing so I strive to continue my efforts to bring openness to the court and to advance what I see are critical needs for reform in the court system.
>
> The system—as it stands on how we elect and appoint Supreme Court justices—is deeply flawed and in need of an overhaul. We find ourselves with a high court that is split along party and ideological lines. And this does not benefit the people of Michigan. Any time the court locks up independent thinking will suffer.
>
> [...]
>
> My commitment to you, the people of Michigan, is to remain independent, impartial, fair, and orderly; exercise judicial restraint and common sense; promote transparency, decrease secrecy; and to encourage the same in others at our Supreme Court.[1354]

But she was not enthusiastic about serving another term. So, she thought about leaving; she pondered all the possibilities open to her:

- She could stay and run again with the endorsement of the Republicans.

...Although Justice Young would have been unhappy.

- She could run as an independent. Her incumbency filing had already secured her name for the ballot, and she had pledged to BE independent (although that was not the same as running as an independent). In the event of running as an independent, she might or might not also have run with a party nomination from either the Republicans OR the Democrats.

I would have been happy to run as an independent.

But the election would be brutal. She would not dodge the truth about Young, and he would have taken every opportunity to savage her. So, they'd be facing off against each other AND taking on the Democratic contenders.

I think it would have been a bloodbath. I still considered staying, and I always kept all my options open. Most believed that I would win if I ran, and I had led Young the last time. I had support and plenty of it. In 2002, I had wondered why I had to run, because I felt I had been there and done

---

1354 Elizabeth A. Weaver, press release, "Re-elect Justice Elizabeth Weaver; We need her for Supreme Court," 30 June 2010.

that. Now, in 2010, I'd really been there and done that. But if there had been hope to achieve the reforms that I had stayed so long to try to implement, I would have been willing to do it. And I had Republicans who urged, "Oh, just stay, run, and you can make the reforms."

Ultimately, I realized that I could achieve no more from within the Supreme Court with respect to its reform and to achieve the reform of how we select justices; that is, reform of how we elect them, and to get checks and balances, rotation in office, get transparency, and get out the unnecessary secrecy that existed there. It had become more and more secret, not less secret, since I had gotten there.

My duty to the public was to do everything I could, and that was how I reasoned it through, and I'd had no duty to stay if it was an impossible situation. And it just became—it was useless, because Cavanagh and Kelly, now, had favored a new "gag order" on May 12th. It didn't pass, and there still is no legally adopted "gag order." And even if they followed procedures to adopt one, it would be unconstitutional.

That was when the Engler Three revealed they were sending Weaver to the JTC.

So she really didn't want to stay. But, if she ran and was elected, she could step down after she took office—as some Republicans urged. That would deliver the appointment to the Governor after the first of the year. But running and then stepping down was NEVER an option for her.

I couldn't deceive the people of Michigan by running for something I didn't intend to do. It's one thing to change your mind after you get there, as I did in 2005 after I had been there two years in my second term, but it's another thing to run knowing you were just going to step down.

• She could have served out without running. Her term would have ended with the New Year, at noon Jan. 1, 2011. If she announced she was serving out long enough before the election, it would have been possible the parties could have nominated candidates to take her spot. If she announced too short a time before the election (or after the election) that she was serving out, the incoming Governor would have made an appointment after the first of the year.

And it was that incoming Governor that concerned her. Governor Jennifer Granholm was term-limited; she wouldn't be there after the first of the year to make any appointment. So, who might the new Governor be?

The Democratic nominee was going to be one of these three: Lieutenant Governor John Cherry; Lansing Mayor Verge Bernero, a former state Representative and Senator; or Speaker of the House, Andy Dillon. Not one of them polled strong.

So, it looked like the Republicans had the best chance. But which Republican? Outgoing Attorney General Mike Cox? U.S. Representative Pete Hoekstra? Oakland County Sheriff Mike Bouchard? Rick Snyder? Or, Senator Tom George? (Secretary of

State Terri Lynn Land had entered and then withdrawn and was running as Bouchard's Lieutenant Governor.)[1355]

Several of the Republican candidates did not inspire her trust: Cox, Hoekstra, and Bouchard. George, in her opinion, had no chance.

Cox was a political player with a personal history that in Weaver's eyes disqualified him from public service. Hoekstra had a reputation as intelligent but aloof as a communicator, and his campaign spokesman, John Truscott, had been Governor Engler's communications director. And Bouchard promised "I'm John Engler with a smile."[1356] Weaver had already had too much experience with Engler, smiling or otherwise.

That left Snyder as the most inspiriting of the field. After the early August primary, he was left standing when he took the Republican spot, outdistancing second-place finisher Pete Hoekstra by 12 percentage points. On the Democratic side, Cherry dropped out and Bernero, a particularly inept choice, won the primary by a 20 percent margin over Dillon.

And I did support Snyder. I met privately with him and Chuck Yob for almost an hour in June of 2010 in Traverse City in his travel van. That was before his winning the August primary. I assessed him, and felt that he was the best hope we had for Michigan. I believed him decent and capable and not an Englerite (I still do even though now he has many Englerites in his administration and advisory circle. At that time, it did not appear he had any.) At the meeting, I showed them my campaign brochure and shared that I would be filing for re-election as an incumbent before the deadline in July—which I did. For the November election, I even put up a yard sign for Snyder.

But, even as an odds-on favorite, there was no guarantee that as a new Governor, Snyder would be able to pick a good justice; he simply didn't know enough about the court system.[1357]

• Finally, Weaver could step down, retire. Then Governor Granholm would appoint someone to serve who would have the advantage of "incumbent" on the ballot. If she did it early enough, that is before the parties held their nominating conventions in late August, the person taking her seat also could have had a party nomination...or not if he or she chose to run as an independent. However, if Weaver waited too long, there could be problems: The Governor might still make the appointment but that appointment might be challenged by the incoming Governor, a scenario reminiscent of the removal of Dorothy Comstock Riley. Timing would be crucial with this option.

1355 And despite his assertion to Ron Modreski that he WOULD run, Cliff Taylor also wasn't on the list of candidates.

1356 Kristin Longley, "Profile: Republican Mike Bouchard is a cop first, but believes politics can fix problems," *Grand Rapids Press*, 20 June 2010, http://www.mlive.com/politics/index.ssf/2010/06/mike_bouchard_republican_oakla.html.

1357 And this was borne out with the selection of Brian K. Zahra. That story is told in Chapter 26.

Out of all the possibilities, Weaver decided she would retire in a timely way and allow Governor Granholm to make the appointment before the parties' nominating conventions. This meant she'd have a voice in the selection of her successor.

This also meant hardcore and control-at-any-cost Republicans and other Republicans deceived and blinded by the Englerite justices and Republican top leaders would be furious and vindictive with me.

Nevertheless, she knew it would be fair to the Republicans since they would have the opportunity to choose their nominee for Weaver's spot without having Weaver's name along with its incumbency designation on the ballot; Weaver still had substantial grassroots Republican and other support. So for Weaver, it all had to do with a person she saw as a worthy replacement to occupy her seat.

And I felt there was an opportunity to have a justice from the north—not from the Lansing-Detroit Beltway.[1358]

Geographic diversity matters to Weaver. She links it to a diversity of thought and an understanding of the whole diverse state.

And the Governor was open to making an appointment of a really qualified independent justice. And Judge Alton "Tom" Davis was willing to take it on.[1359]

Weaver had seen him in action.

He had stood up with respect to the Gromek appointment; he was on the committee, and he dissented to the way it was handled.

Tom Davis had a lot going for him, but he was not particularly well known, nor was he a party apparatchik. And he was a Democrat, something essential for Granholm, but equally harmful in the Republicans' eyes—or at least some Republicans—when it came to Weaver.

Davis had been a prosecutor, then a judge and chief judge of the 46th Judicial Circuit (Crawford, Kalkaska, and Otsego Counties). Governor Granholm appointed him to the Court of Appeals in 2005. He ran successfully for the remainder of the term in 2006

1358 After the 2010 election, Weaver noted: *All seven justices were from three counties out of the state's 83: Wayne, Oakland, and Ingham. Those three counties are home to a third of the state's population. But that left two-thirds of us without proximity to a justice.* And over time, that number is still about right. In the wake of Bridget Mary McCormack's taking office in January of 2013, Washtenaw County was represented but Oakland—the state's second largest county—no longer was. At that time, those three counties represented only 24 percent of the state's population. But with Governor Snyder's appointment of 16th Circuit Judge David Viviano, Feb. 27, 2013, Macomb County was then represented. All the justices still come from the Detroit-Lansing Beltway, four counties that represent only 33.26 percent of the state's population.
1359 In nominating him, Governor Granholm delivered a paean to Weaver and her long career of working for justice and doing right and fearing not. She also outlined Davis' background. [Jennifer Granholm, "Remarks on Justice Weaver's Resignation and Justice Davis' appointment," Facebook, 26 August 2010, http://www.facebook.com/notes/jennifer-granholm/remarks-on-justice-weavers-resignation-and-justice-davis-appointment/481994140608.]

and again in 2008 for a full term. He lived in Grayling, some 50 or so miles east of the Supreme Court regional office in Traverse City.

He had not been active in party politics since he took the bench in 1984.[1360] But earlier, he had served as the Crawford County Democratic Party chairman and "northern Michigan coordinator" of Jim Blanchard's 1982 gubernatorial campaign.

In her resignation announcement, Weaver took the opportunity to let the public know that things were not going well at the court. Had a departing justice ever sounded such a warning? Certainly, not in recent history. In video of the event, she and Governor Granholm walked to a rostrum, and Weaver began her remarks after a welcome.

> [...] I formally notified Governor Granholm of my resignation as a justice of the Michigan Supreme Court, effective at 11 a.m., this morning, August 26, 2010. I also notified the State Court Administrator and the Secretary of State in accordance with the law.
>
> In my almost 36 years as a judge and justice—always elected by Michigan voters (12 years as a trial judge, eight years as a Court of Appeals judge, almost 16 years as a justice of the Supreme Court including two years as chief justice)—I have continuously endeavored to act and perform in the best interests of the people of Michigan.
>
> In June, when I filed my affidavit of candidacy to put my name on the November ballot for re-election, I believed that doing so would be in the best interest of the people.
>
> I am deeply grateful to all my many supporters throughout the state who have urged me to run again. "Justice Weaver, we need her," they say, offering every kind of support. I am aware that the pundits believe I would be re-elected even as "the independent candidate" without party nomination and special-interest funding. But that is not the point.
>
> After considerable deliberation, thought, and prayer, I have concluded that I have done all that I can do as a justice and now believe that I can be of most use as a citizen in helping further the critically needed reforms of the justice system.
>
> The present system of dual processes by which we elect and appoint Supreme Court justices is deeply flawed and in need of an overhaul. Specifically, we need to promptly reform the process of how we select justices and we need transparency and accountability in the administration of the people's judicial business by the Michigan Supreme Court.

1360 Brian McGillivary, "Local Judge to replace Weaver on Court," *Traverse City Record-Eagle*, 27 August 2010, http://record-eagle.com/local/x654499428/Local-judge-to-replace-Weaver-on-court/print.

The open discord on this court over the last 10 years is not really so much about clashes of strong personalities, but rather is the result of the formation of power blocks of justices usually joining together with a majority of four votes to promote agendas. ...Agendas of political parties and special interests. ...Agendas of personal interests, philosophies, and ideologies. ...And agendas of biases and prejudices.

Any time power blocks form and the court locks up, independent thinking and the interests of the people of Michigan suffer.

It is that independent-thinking judge who should be the most highly valued member of any court. That independent-thinking judge is not agenda driven and does not hold to political party lines, philosophies, or ideologies. We need justices and judges who are dedicated to the rule of law, who are independent, impartial, exercise judicial restraint, apply common sense, and who are wise, honest, orderly, competent, fair, civil and professional, open—not secretive, and are non-partisan. The current system of political party nominations does not advance those qualities.

Nor does the current system prize the diversity and independence of thought that come from geographic separation. The overwhelming majority of justices on this court come from the Detroit/Lansing beltway. Of the seven justices, four are from Southeast Michigan (Grosse Pointe Park and Bloomfield Hills), two are from the Lansing area, and after my resignation none were from northern Michigan until, thankfully, the Governor remedied this by the appointment of a justice from northern Michigan.

Independent justices cannot "go along to get along" when doing the people's judicial business. Supreme Court justices must fulfill their duty to the people to inform them of what they need to know—no more or no less—about not only *what* the Supreme Court does and decides, but *how*, *when* and *where*. The Michigan Supreme Court should not be a secret club, but should instead act in a transparent, open, and accountable manner.

To be absolutely clear, when I say "reform," I do not mean the elimination of election of justices. I mean specific reforms of the election and appointment processes in Michigan's dual system for selection of justices.

In the last election of a Supreme Court justice in 2008, $7.5 million dollars was spent for one open spot on the Michigan Supreme Court.

It appears that in this year, 2010, there'll likely be spent even more millions of dollars—closer to the $15 million that was spent in the 2000 election for three spots on the court. The many millions of dollars spent will be untimely reported, if reported at all.

This type of unseemly, exorbitant, and unhinged spending, and untimely reporting—or no reporting at all—for Supreme Court justice elections needs to be reformed before the 2012 election.

Millions of dollars are spent in Supreme Court justice elections by political parties and special interests for TV ads filled with some true, some untrue information, misinformation, incorrect information, and incomplete and misleading information. It's absurd, illogical, and irrational to believe that these expenditures will likely result in the election of justices that are dedicated to the rule of law, independent, impartial, exercise judicial restraint, apply common sense, and are wise, honest, orderly, competent, fair, civil and professional, open—not secretive, and are non-partisan.

My six specific proposals for reform of the system for selection of justices appear on my personally-funded website: www.justiceweaver.com.[1361]

The top two proposals are currently before the legislature in Senate committee and do not require Constitutional amendment. They are:

(1) Electing justices by district; and
(2) Removing the political party nomination for justice candidates.

I strongly urge the legislature—and the people to tell them—to enact these reforms before year's end so that the Michigan Supreme Court can move forward with transparency and accountability in 2011.

The remaining four proposals for reform are:

• End the Governor's unchecked appointment power;
• End lack of rotation in office;
• Reform campaign finance reporting requirements; and
• Implement public financing requirements.

I remain committed—as a citizen now—to actively help to reform Michigan's judicial system, specifically, again, including prompt reform of the selection process for justices and the administration of the people's judicial business by the Michigan Supreme Court with needed transparency and accountability.

Finally, I am most grateful to the people of Michigan for electing me as a justice and trusting me with the privilege of serving them on the Michigan Supreme Court for nearly 16 years.[1362]

1361 At this point in the evolution of her thought, Weaver had a six-point plan. It now has seven points and you can read the plan in Appendix A.
1362 Elizabeth A. Weaver, Resignation statement, 26 August 2010. To view the video of her statement see "Press Conference on the Michigan Supreme Court," govgranholm, 26 August 2010, http://www.youtube.com/watch?v=16yMFAhjlQU.

Granholm moved to the microphone and described Weaver as "an incredible servant of justice," Granholm noted that her ruling principle of "Do Right and Fear Not," could not be more apt for an independent justice:

> You have dedicated your career to doing what is right for Michigan's vulnerable children and their families, doing right for those who were pleading their cases before you, doing right for those who needed an independent judiciary to assure balance and fairness. Your commitment to doing what's right for people in need never wavered for fear of personal or political fallout. We appreciate your courage.[1363]

And then the Governor introduced Weaver's replacement, Alton "Tom" Davis.

Weaver's resignation and subsequent appointment of Davis made news. Here's that day's report in the *Traverse City Record-Eagle*:

> Granholm announced Davis' appointment shortly after noon today, fulfilling her pledge to replace Weaver with a judge from northern Michigan.
>
> "I'm pleased to replace one great northern Michigan Justice with another great northern Michigan Justice," Granholm said, during a noon press conference.
>
> Weaver said Granholm "picked the right person."
>
> "It's just perfect; it puts a new soldier on the field fighting for reform," Weaver said. "He's a judge that is really qualified, judicially qualified, to carry on with reforming the system."[1364]

The next day's paper, Aug. 27, carried some of the reaction. The reportage from the *Traverse City Record-Eagle* was more moderate than elsewhere in the state; after all, they knew her well:

> Republican leaders lashed out at Weaver's decision to let Granholm appoint her replacement, a move that presently gives the court a 4 to 3 Democratic edge and attaches "Supreme Court Justice" to Davis's name on the November ballot.
>
> Some called her actions a betrayal, but local party leaders, while "shocked" by her resignation, expressed continued support for Weaver. They also were relieved they won't have to choose between her and Republican-backed nominees.
>
> "I think 'betrayed' is a little bit of a harsh word for someone who has represented the party at all levels of the judiciary for the last 30 years," said Dave Barr, chairman of the Grand Traverse County Republican Party.

1363 Governor Jennifer Granholm, Weaver Thanks and Davis Appointment, ibid.
1364 Brian McGillivary, "Alton Davis picked to succeed Weaver," *Traverse City Record-Eagle*, 26 August 2010, http://record-eagle.com/archive/x1489516927/Alton-Davis-picked-to-succeed-Weaver.

Both Barr and Lance Roman, Leelanau County Republican Party chair-man, said many delegates were torn because Weaver announced in June she would run as an independent,[1365] and they would have been asked Saturday to support a Republican nominee to run against her.

"That was a little bit of (a) dilemma, but now that problem for a lot of local Republicans has gone away," Roman said. "Betty has enjoyed great support from throughout the county here; she attends all of our events."

Weaver dismissed complaints that she orchestrated a political deal.

"I raised it with Judge Davis and he was willing to step up to the challenge, and I raised it with Governor Granholm and she saw the wisdom of it," Weaver said. "Some top people in the Republican Party are complaining, and they have a right to their opinion, but I don't agree with them."

Weaver, who strongly believes in geographic representation, said none of the candidates seeking their party's nomination are from northern Michigan.

She called Davis "a perfect" choice to replace her.

"Now there's another independent judge on the court," Weaver said. "The public can judge his record. He has made courageous decisions and stood up to give the people good judicial services."

Davis said he appreciated both Weaver's words of support and Granholm's confidence in him.

"At some point every lawyer thinks of the Supreme Court, but as a realistic possibility, it's like going down to the store and buying a lottery ticket: The chance that it occurs is remote," he said.[1366]

Perhaps the most strident complaint came from Dan Pero, president of American Justice Partnership, John Engler's former chief of staff and campaign manager, and husband of Colleen Pero, Taylor's former campaign manager. Here's his take from his blog:

Democrats have seized control of the Michigan Supreme Court as a result of a politically-rigged, backroom deal hatched months ago by Governor Jen-nifer Granholm and former Justice Betty Weaver.

In a surprise move, Weaver has stepped down from the bench, allowing Granholm a clear path to appoint handpicked, trial-lawyer-friendly judge, Alton Davis. Granholm's appointment goes into effect immediately and does not require approval by the state legislature.

1365 This was an error. Reporters and others confused running as an incumbent and running as an independent.
1366 Brian McGillivary, "Local Judge to replace Weaver on Court."

Now, don't get me wrong, I'm not shedding a single tear in saying *adios* to Weaver. She has been an embarrassment to the bench for years. [...]

A well-known perk-grubber, she fought tooth-and nail to cling to a tax-payer funded car and a $60,000/year personal office.[1367] To top it all off, some of her fellow justices filed a complaint against her with the Judicial Tenure Commission earlier this year.

But this latest sleazeball move is an historic low, even for the likes of Weaver.[1368]

Another illustrative comment came from Michigan Republican Party staffer Jennifer Hoff in a press release of her own making:

"Michigan residents deserve a qualified judge, not a politician in a robe," said Michigan Republican Party Director of Communications Jennifer Hoff. "The Supreme Court is supposed to act as an objective observer and defend-er of the Constitution. Packing the court with partisan hacks to support her own radical, failed agenda on her way out the door is contradictory to Granholm's role as governor."

[...]

"Jennifer Granholm is pushing her ideology on Michigan residents," Hoff continued. "Justice Weaver's resignation offered her an opportunity to ap-point a bipartisan judge to finish the last few months of the term and to look classy doing it. Instead, the Governor and the Democrat Party are trying to pack the court and control it for the next decade."[1369]

"Partisan hack"? "Pack the court"? Hoff was not a deep well, certainly not deep enough to understand the history of her own party.[1370]

Other news outlets had other reactions to Weaver's resignation. The *Detroit Free Press* editorial started this way:

1367 *These were campaign issues raised by Taylor in 2008. He made no mention of the costs to the state of the other justices' Detroit offices, and there was no indication that justices driving their own cars and charging mileage had saved the court anything. Taylor had gone to great lengths to stress that his proposed economies at the court would go a long way to balancing the state's budget.*

1368 Dan Pero, "Judicial Coup D'état on Michigan Supreme Court; Weaver the Deceiver Plays 'Politics at its Worst,'" *American Courthouse*, 27 August 2010, http://americancourthouse.com/2010/08/27/judicial-coup-detat-on-michigan-supreme-court-weaver-the-deceiver-plays-politics-at-its-worst.html.

1369 "Granholm politicizes Supreme Court," Michigan Republican Party, 26 August 2010, http://www.migop.org/index.php/details/news/granholm-politicizes-supreme-court/.

1370 Jennifer Hoff's LinkedIn page indicates that in 2012 she served as the Grassroots Action Coordinator for the Michigan Chamber of Commerce. She had worked for either the Republicans or Republican candidate Dick DeVos from 2003 into 2011. ["Jennifer Hoff," LinkedIn, http://www.linkedin.com/pub/jennifer-hoff/4/892/3b3.]

That's some exit wound Justice Elizabeth Weaver left in Michigan's Republican establishment when she resigned her seat Thursday after nearly 16 years on the state's highest court. Her surprise announcement threw this weekend's party nominating conventions into turmoil and raises the stakes in November's contest for two Supreme Court seats.[1371]

That same piece, though, ended with some benefit that could come from her move:

> If it brings the importance of judicial independence into sharper focus and accelerates reform of the judicial selection process, Weaver's melodramatic departure from the court may leave a legacy as enduring as her tenure there.[1372]

The *Detroit News* was less sanguine headlining her resignation as, "Action by justice, Granholm is disdainful ploy."[1373]

Weaver had known that she wasn't going to please everyone, but figured the outcome was worth it.

I wanted to make sure that I did the very best I could as I left.

And in her view, Davis was the best choice of all.

Things were bound to happen fast once Weaver stepped down and Davis stepped in. Only three days after his appointment, the Democrats nominated him, along with Oakland Circuit Court Judge Denise Langford Morris to go up against Republican-nominated Young and Wayne County (3rd) Circuit Court Judge Mary Beth Kelly.[1374]

And that was a contest Weaver was destined to influence. The Republicans' uncritical acceptance of Young and Kelly didn't reflect Weaver's understanding of their characters.

Mary Beth Kelly, yet another Engler appointee (1999), was named chief judge at the Third Circuit Court only two years after she joined the bench. And she created some problems there when she refused to follow a Court of Appeals mandate that was related to a change she made as chief judge of court. Here's how that transpired, according to a source that studied what happened:

> During her term as chief judge, Mary Beth Kelly experienced some conflict when she attempted to privatize the Friend of the Court system, which

1371 Editorial, "Diminished court should take Weaver's warning to heart," *Detroit Free Press*, 27 August 2010, Opinion, A.14.
1372 Ibid.
1373 Peter Hardin, "Weaver resigns, shakes up Michigan high court," blog of Justice at Stake, 30 August 2010, http://www.gavelgrab.org/?p=13345.
1374 AP, "Michigan Democrats nominate Alton Thomas Davis, Judge Denise Langford Morris for court," *Crain's Detroit Business*, 29 August 2010, http://www.crainsdetroit.com/article/20100829/free/100829890/michigan-democrats-nominate-alton-thomas-davis-judge-denise-langford-morris-for-court.

brought protests from labor. She also instituted a new system for assigning attorneys for runaway children that resulted in far fewer attorneys representing more child-clients. A lawsuit filed against her [by the Judicial Attorneys Association] alleged that the new system violated the children's right to counsel and effective representation when she removed hundreds of individual attorneys and replaced them with handpicked attorney groups being paid a fixed fee. Judge Kelly stated that the moves were motivated by budget concerns and were not political.[1375]

The lawsuit was filed after an arbitrator's ruling that went against Kelly and her court. She and the court appealed at the trial court level. The trial court found against her and the court. In 2001, after an appeal, the parties reached an agreement that stipulated, among other things, that the appeal would be dismissed as long as Kelly followed the ruling. In 2004—with openings for attorneys at the court—the issue was revived. Kelly and her court were violating what had been laid down. The Judicial Attorneys Association (JAA) asked for relief and an issuance of a contempt of court citation against Kelly and the court. That suit was brought at the trial court level. And according to the subsequent Court of Appeals order:

> In April 2005, the trial court issued an order and memorandum of law denying plaintiff's request for relief and granting defendant's motion for an order to show cause why plaintiff should not be held in contempt.[1376]

There was more back and forth between the Court of Appeals and the Supreme Court. First, Sept 29, 2005, the Supreme Court granted immediate consideration and issued a stay of the trial court proceedings.[1377]

There were additional requests for a grant at the high court and by January 13, 2006, the case was again remanded to the Court of Appeals:

> [I]n lieu of granting leave to appeal, we remand this case to the Court of Appeals for consideration as on leave granted. We further order that the stay entered by this Court on September 29, 2005, remains in effect until completion of this appeal. The motion to vacate or reconsider is denied as moot.[1378]

1375 David Christensen, "What are Justice Mary Beth Kelly's beliefs on Personal Injury Law," Michigan Auto Law blog, 11 January 2011, http://www.michiganautolaw.com/auto-lawyers-blog/2011/01/11/what-are-justice-mary-beth-kellys-beliefs-on-personal-injury-law/.
1376 *Third Circuit Court v Judicial Attorneys Association*, No. 267785, Michigan Court of Appeals, 2 August 2007, http://publicdocs.courts.mi.gov:81/OPINIONS/FINAL/COA/20070802_C267785_63_267785.OPN.PDF.
1377 Stay, *Third Circuit Court v Judicial Attorneys Association*, No. 129500-1 & (30)(31) Michigan Supreme Court, 29 September 2005, http://publicdocs.courts.mi.gov:81/sct/public/orders/20050929_s129500_36_129500_2005-09-29_or.pdf.
1378 Remand, *Third Circuit Court v Judicial Attorneys Association*, No. 129500-1 & (31)(33)(35)(41), Michigan Supreme Court, 13 January 2006, http://publicdocs.courts.mi.gov:81/sct/public/orders/20060113_s129500_46_129500_2006-01-13_or.pdf.

On Aug. 2, 2007, the Court of Appeals panel of three judges[1379] affirmed the decisions of the trial court. Mary Beth Kelly and her court were on the hook to abide by their arbitration agreement AND the contempt and fine were upheld.

When the Supreme Court was asked again to reconsider the matter, it denied leave—the case was not going to be heard—but the majority did give Kelly a pass on the penalties: "the sanctions ordered by the trial court at the September 28, 2005, contempt hearing shall not be imposed if the plaintiff initiates compliance with its obligations under the July 17, 2000 order of the trial court by April 15, 2008."[1380]

In the denial of leave, Weaver concurred in part (denying the grant) and then set out the dissent in relation to what the then-Engler Four were doing:

> In effect, years after the plaintiff was found in contempt of court and sanctions were ordered, this court is providing the plaintiff with yet another chance to avoid sanctions for its deliberate disobedience in refusing to abide by the arbitration agreement and a court order to do so.
>
> [...]
>
> The trial court did not abuse its discretion in finding the plaintiff, the Third Judicial Circuit Court, in contempt because of the deliberate actions of Chief Judge Mary Beth Kelly. The material facts and law in this case are not in dispute. As chief judge, Judge Kelly violated the arbitration award in November 2004 and has knowingly continued to do so since March 2005. In June 2001, almost five years earlier, the Third Judicial Circuit Court, through the actions of its then-chief judge, had stipulated with prejudice, in writing, to the dismissal of its appeal regarding the validity of the arbitration order. The arbitration award and stipulation order had been *res judicata* for almost five years.
>
> [...]
>
> Chief Judge Kelly admitted at the September 28, 2005, hearing in front of the trial judge that the Third Judicial Circuit Court was not in compliance with the arbitration award and that she, as chief judge acting for the Third Judicial Circuit Court, had not followed the trial court's previous contempt order. The trial court ordered sanctions against the plaintiff because the plaintiff, through Chief Judge Kelly, had expressly refused to comply with the trial court's previous order. This court did not issue a stay of proceedings until after the trial court had ordered sanctions against the plaintiff. This court should not interfere with a trial court's execution of its judicial power

---

1379 The senior of the three Court of Appeals judges on the case was Alton "Tom" Davis.
1380 *Third Circuit Court v Judicial Attorneys Association*, No. 129500-1 & (31)(48), Michigan Supreme Court, 21 December 2007, http://publicdocs.courts.mi.gov:81/sct/public/orders/20071221_s129500_52_129500_2007-12-21_or.pdf.

and overturn a contempt order and sanctions imposed unless the trial court abused its discretion in ordering the sanctions. The trial court did not abuse its discretion in exercising its inherent authority to hold parties in contempt for not following a court order, and the trial court was correct to subsequently order sanctions for noncompliance with its order.

The majority's arbitrary decision not to impose the trial court's sanctions as long as the plaintiff initiates compliance by April 15, 2008, does not provide an explanation of whether the trial court abused its discretion in ordering the sanctions. [1381]

So, by election time in 2010, Weaver had memories—and not particularly fond ones—of Mary Beth Kelly. There was no way she'd endorse such a candidate. Nor could she support Young. Tom Davis was her choice, and she figured Denise Langford Morris was a less likely candidate but better than Young or Kelly.

What they should have done was found another candidate named Kelly...and they could have; there was another Kelly willing to run. Well, it was K-E-L-L-E-Y.

She was referring to Connie Kelley.[1382] If Connie Kelley had run and won, and Mary Beth Kelly had won, and with Marilyn Kelly still on the bench there could have been an interesting situation.

And they'd had three of one name many years before, three Kavanaghs: two with a "K" and one with a "C." And both Kavanaghs' names were Thomas, so you had to know whether it was Thomas G. or Thomas M. I mean, this is the ridiculousness of the Kelly name. When people start voting just for the last names you don't necessarily get good people.

And Weaver was keeping track of the messages the candidates and parties delivered through their ad campaigns.

From the point of view of the Republicans, it was brilliant, except it wasn't honest. It portrayed Justice Young as fair and just—from my experience he was not. And it portrayed this Judge Mary Beth Kelly—and using the Kelly name—as fair and just and all that.

Well, good grief! She had actually been found in contempt, even by our court, and even before, and her mentors—Justice Young and the other Englerite justices—could not get her out of that one. Yet the press paid no attention to it. It was a terrible affair, and the Democrats ran the stupidest campaign known because they did not put out the truths about Justice Davis and how fine, qualified and good he was. And they had made Young a target from early 2009, and they were not prepared to make the case of why he should not be reelected.

1381 Elizabeth A. Weaver writing in ibid.
1382 Connie Kelley was one of the three Democratic nominees for the Supreme Court in 2012. She was not successful. The 2013 court will have just one of the name: Mary Beth Kelly.

A JTC Dismissal Arrives Late

In mid October, Weaver received news that the JTC had dismissed the complaint against her September 27, 2010.[1383]

I didn't receive that letter until two weeks after it was dated.

Of particular interest to Weaver was the phrasing of the letter.

> Following a preliminary investigation and evaluation, the Commission has dismissed this Request for Investigation as you have retired from the judiciary. A letter of dismissal has also been forwarded to the Grievants.[1384]

...Dismissing any action against her just because she was off the court? What did that mean? Had she still been on the court would the answer have been different? But it was a dismissal nonetheless.

Weaver said she later learned that was NOT the message the majority of the JTC had voted to send. The letter was supposed to convey a simple dismissal without mention of retirement. Weaver wondered if someone had gone a little further than authorized and with specific intent. Then, too, the letter was so long delayed in reaching her.

Also in September, Weaver had heard that Young, in giving his stump speeches, was employing half-truths. This was something she wanted to hear for herself. So, with me (co-author Schock) accompanying her, she went to a Muskegon Tea Party meeting where Justice Young was scheduled to speak. The Sept. 28, 2010 encounter was memorable. Weaver and I had arrived far in advance of Young, and we'd sat through the presentation of local candidates and appeals for poll watchers. When Young walked in and saw Weaver, he stood still and looked at her a long while.

I wrote about Young's appearance and our interaction over the course of two days:

> In Muskegon, Supreme Court Justice Robert Preston Young, Jr. stood before the group of Tea Partiers this week, laying out his lament of justice gone wrong.
>
> First, he lauded fellow Republican nominee for the high court, Judge Mary Beth Kelly, Chief Judge for the Third (Wayne County) Circuit Court. She is without doubt, he said, the best-qualified candidate (we're assuming outside of himself) for the Supreme Court. He characterized Alton Thomas Davis—the newly appointed Justice who is filling out the last four months of

---

1383 The JTC also dismissed a complaint that had been lodged by Mark Brewer of the Democratic Party against Young.
1384 Kathleen J. McCann, letter to Elizabeth A. Weaver, 27 September 2010, http://www.justiceweaver.com/pdfs/combinedjune11.pdf.

Elizabeth Weaver's term—as a partisan judge given to agenda-driven decisions. And that's bad, very bad.

Then he went on to speak about the dangers of Rogue Judges: "Rogues do not find themselves bound by the law." The framers of the Constitution intended, he said, for the judiciary to have no real power. Further, he said, it's only been during the last 50 years that courts have taken on power, cloaked in the robes of interpretation...and enough power to control social, political, and economic direction. (We dispute his legal history. Take for example, Wilson's appointment of Louis Brandeis to the U.S. Supreme Court in 1916. Or Grant's of Morrison Waite in 1874. This really has been going on a lot longer than 50 years. Each judge, each justice tempers the law.)

He went on to speak about what the Framers had in mind...the sanctity of our tradition of law and the dangers of neologists who interpret black as white, red as green: "That's the power of the court." The best court, he said—the court Ronald Reagan would have liked best, anyway—was the court headed by Cliff Taylor, the court with a solid Republican majority... not counting Elizabeth Weaver. (Of her he said: "She was a conservative justice until she veered off the path." More about that soon.)

The bulk of his hour-long talk was questions and answers. This audience was instinctively conservative...the three guiding principles of the Tea Party movement are these: fiscal responsibility, constitutionally limited government, and free markets. Overall, that makes sense to me, too; but then, I'm an instinctual conservative as well. But not a member of the Tea Party. The questions and the answers were important to this audience, and Justice Young was telling them what they wanted to hear.

But I really wanted to know something. So I asked a question. (Now, understand I did not have a recorder going so this cannot be guaranteed as a verbatim record. But as a former reporter and editor, I think it's pretty darned close.) I started off by making sure I'd understood his definition of a Rogue Judge:

> DBS (me): "'Rogues do not find themselves bound by the law.' Do I have that right?"

> RPY (him) "They don't _feel_ themselves bound by the law," he said.

> DBS: "And it's a serious matter when they don't?"

> RPY: "Very serious."

I went on to posit some of the bad things that judges could do and what the sanctions might be...when judges don't rule according to the law they might be found in contempt? "And would this be a serious matter, to be found in contempt?"

RPY: "It could be."

DBS: "Just 'could be'?"

And then the penny dropped:

RPY: "This is about Mary Beth Kelly, isn't it?"

DBS: "It is. Here you have someone the Republicans have nominated for the Supreme Court and someone you have lauded in this meeting, and yet she's someone who fits your very definition of a Rogue Judge...she was found in contempt of court in her work as a judge, appealed that decision against her at the appeals court, had it denied, and then appealed to the Supreme Court where YOU and the other members of your court upheld the Court of Appeals' decision by denying leave to hear the case. In effect, you found her guilty of contempt of court."

[...]

Now, this denial to hear her case took place under the Taylor Court, December 2007. So, while they upheld the lower courts' decisions, the majority did manage to set aside the penalties; they more or less took the sting out of the judgment. Justices Cavanagh and Kelly also dissented but Justice Elizabeth Weaver not only agreed wholly with the denial, but also wrote to explain why she didn't see how Judge Mary Beth Kelly could get a pass on the penalties.

[...]

The majority ruled. The finding of contempt stood but the penalties could be waived.

And now Mary Beth Kelly was a judge Justice Young thought fit to sit along side him?

RPY: "She made a mistake."

She did that all right.

Tomorrow: The NEXT (and last) question.[1385]

1385 David B. Schock, "September 30, 2010—Justice Young at the Tea Party: "She made a mistake," My MI Court, 30 September 2010, http://www.mymicourt.com/?p=5.

And it really WAS to be a last question he'd take from me, as I was shortly to find out:

> This column picks up where yesterday's leaves off: with Michigan Supreme Court Justice Robert P. Young, Jr. at a Q&A session of the Muskegon Tea Party meeting, September 28, 2010.
>
> Others asked questions about ways he'd suggest to vet lawyers with ACLU leanings, his stand on gun laws, and his thoughts on the U.S. Supreme Court. Justice Young answered with care, and, for the most part, to the approbation of his audience.
>
> Then, I was accorded the opportunity to query the justice one more time.
>
> > DBS: "You've gathered that I'm somewhat critical of your practice."
> >
> > RPY: "Well, I figured as much. You're sitting next to my severest critic."
>
> Oh, did I mention that I was seated next to newly retired Justice Elizabeth Weaver? She was just sitting, observing, taking notes. At no time did she say anything to Justice Young or the group at large. But that didn't hold Justice Young back from repeated castigations of her work. And at no point in the evening did anyone in the audience or at the leadership table think to ask her if all he was saying was true.
>
> But back to my one more question. Justice Young had been speaking at length about the sanctity of the law, how its foundations are being eroded. I just could not square all that with something he'd written in 2004 concerning our tradition of common law. Now, that law is what's been handed down to us. Most often we cite the English Common Law as the beginnings of our own. And always, it's based on precedence...what's gone before. Oliver Wendell Holmes, Jr., (later Justice) in his *The Common Law* (1881) put it this way:
>
> > The life of the law has not been logic: it has been experience. The felt necessities of the time, the prevalent moral and political theories, institutions of public policy, avowed or unconscious, even the prejudices which judges share with their fellowmen, have had a good deal more to do than the syllogism in determining the rule by which men should be governed. The law embodies the story of a nation's development through many centuries, and it cannot be dealt with as if it contained only the axioms and corollaries of a book of mathematics.[1386]
>
> This is common law, and the law of other wrongs including fraud, acts of malice, contracts, successions...pretty much of what our courts deal with on a day-to-day basis.

1386 Oliver Wendell Holmes, Jr., *The Common Law* (Boston: Little Brown and Company, 1881), 1.

At any rate, Justice Young in an article published in the *Texas Review of Law and Politics*[1387] had much to say about our common law. I want to make sure I haven't taken things out of context [....][1388]

There followed a recap of Young's take on the common law that he expressed in the *Texas Review of Law and Politics* that already appeared in Chapter 20. I then resumed:

So, does the rhetoric really matter all that much? I THINK so, but I wanted to clarify it with the author of the screed.

> DBS: You have talked about the importance of the tradition of law, yet didn't you write a passage about the common law? Something characterizing it as a drunken grandfather lying sprawled naked...?
>
> RPY: "'...in the middle of one's genteel garden party.'"

He actually picked up the quote and finished the phrase. He knows these words.

And he explained there have been many cases where he has found the common law worth upholding. It was a lengthy answer. But what I was driving at and what I really wanted to know was the motivation for such disdain for this unwieldy common law. It's problematic to be sure, but drunken naked? Well.

So I raised my hand again and the Justice turned toward me and said something. Because of a slight defect in my hearing I thought he said "Your turn." Wow!" I thought, "maybe he <u>will</u> enter into a discussion about this."

I started to respond and was stopped. Arm extended and finger pointed at me, he thundered: "You're DONE!"

> DBS: I am?

He nodded and asked for other questions. Well, I suppose he's correct that we could have stayed at it for a little while, and he had to leave to get to another event. So, while I continued to raise my hand, I wasn't picked.

Today, I again went over his 2004 article. I find his writing lucid, persuasive, grandiloquent. There is no doubt at all that he has a tremendous intellect and many gifts. But, I pause when he writes:

1387 Robert P. Young, Jr., "State Jurisprudence, the role of the courts, and the rule of law: The Federalist Society: Panel II: A judicial traditionalist confronts the common law," *Texas Review of Law and Politics*, Spring 2004, http://dignitas.typepad.com/Texas.Review.of.Law.and.Politics--Young.pdf.
1388 David B. Schock, "October 1, 2010—Justice Young: 'You're done!,'" My MI Court, 1 October 2010, http://www.mymicourt.com/?p-7.

Indeed, it is hard for me, a jurist of the 21st Century, to consider that the common law is "law" in any conventional sense.[1389]

In what sense could common law be law of any sort <u>other</u> than by convention?

At any rate, his talk ended, he was thanked mightily, and he exited to a standing ovation.

Note to Harvard: Even though Justice Young attended there as both an outstanding undergraduate and a law student, you might want to hold off on funding appeals; I don't think you're going to get anything. Of you he said: "I am a recovering Harvard Law student. That's ground zero Sodom and Gomorrah." I sure hope he wasn't there on a scholarship; "How sharper than a serpent's tooth...."[1390]

I had intended to attend the meeting and sit quietly; after all I didn't want to embarrass Justice Weaver. And it was only midway through Young's opening remarks that I asked her if she'd mind if I asked a question. Her response: *You do as you see fit.*

1389 Robert P. Young, Jr., "State Jurisprudence, the role of the courts, and the rule of law: The Federalist Society: Panel II: A judicial traditionalist confronts the common law," 2.
1390 David B. Schock, "October 1, 2010—Justice Young: "You're done!," My MI Court, 1 October 2010, http://www.mymicourt.com/?p=7.

Chapter 26

He Said What?
Two Gatherings,
A Bitter and Expensive Election

A Celebration and a Revelation

After stepping down from the court, Weaver was the recipient of a surprise retirement party on Oct. 16, 2010. Hundreds of people came, including friends from high school and college in New Orleans, Glen Arbor friends, court friends from her nearly 36 years on the bench, church friends, new friends, her former first grade students, their parents and grandparents. Among the attendees were former interns—including one who flew in from Germany just for the occasion—and law clerks and associates from Michigan and throughout the U.S. Both the east and west coasts were represented. There was a band, a vocal number by The Subpremes—a one-off performance by a "girl" group that included Justice Diane Hathaway and Weaver's former law clerks singing a parody of "Johnny Be Good"—including the refrain "Go, Betty, go, go, go," food, a film, food, speeches (short), food, and talk, talk, talk. Everyone lauded Weaver's steadfast dedication to principle, her "Do-right-and-fear-not" attitude, and her devotion to friends. It was a love fest.

In a matter of days, Weaver would stand before a less adoring audience in Traverse City, where she'd been asked to give a speech on the upcoming election to a new group affiliated with something called the 9/12 Project.[1391]

It really was a simple matter. Weaver didn't think Young and Mary Beth Kelly worthy of election. Would she say something or wouldn't she? And, if she did, how much? And how much could the public apprehend? Talking only about a justice's bad decisions wouldn't necessarily connect with an audience, nor would his positions on the common law. After all, most people don't know about the courts, cases, or policy and procedure unless they have had a first-hand connection.

What else was there?

1391The 9/12 Project, http://the912-project.com/.

Bad behavior. In Kelly's case it would be clear: she had been found in contempt of court. That should matter.

And for Young? In addition to the things he'd done, he had a habit of saying things of others that weren't respectful, said Weaver. She agreed that it was a shame that probably the only thing the media would pick up on was his inflammatory language.

Her speech was short and very pointed:

> Because Mary Beth Kelly and Bob Young and their media supporters are repeatedly misleading the voting public with incorrect assertions about their performance, temperament, and character as judges, regretfully it is necessary that I share with the public facts—and not fictions—that I learned while serving as a Justice of the Michigan Supreme Court during the last 15-plus years. I ask that you listen and then decide for yourselves whether Bob Young and Mary Beth Kelly are fit to serve as Justices of the Michigan Supreme Court.[1392]

She started with Young, in particular his use of racist and sexual language during conferences while doing the business of the court. Weaver illustrated the point with a memo she'd felt compelled to send to her fellow justices in 2006:

> This court should maintain the highest level of professionalism, decorum, and dignity in conducting the public's business.

> Immediately after the April 19, 2006, conference, I had drafted the memo below. I spent some time deciding whether to send the memo.

> At the May 10, 2006, conference, Justice Young's use of the "N" word ("n---s") when commenting on an announced candidacy for a judgeship during court's discussion of Commissioner Report cases confirmed the need to share the following:

>> The business of the court should be conducted in the professional, respectful and dignified manner. But during the conference of April 19, 2006, there were two instances of unprofessional and offensive conduct. Such instances of unprofessional, disrespectful and undignified behavior, almost juvenile or locker-room behavior, occur much too often. My concerns voiced over the years have not succeeded in improving the situation, so I feel the need to write to you on this matter.

>> Justice Young's suggestion, in jest or not, that Justice Markman begin his proposed response to the State Appellate Defender Commission with the

---

1392 Elizabeth A. Weaver, speech to 9/12 Meeting in Traverse City, My MI Court, 19 October 2010, http://www.mymicourt.com/?p=9. In addition to her entire speech, readers can watch the video of her delivery.

phrase "you ignorant slut," was crude, offensive, inappropriate, and unprofessional.[1393]

Similarly, the comments at the April 19, 2006, conference characterizing the trial judges as "whining" about the proposals in ADM 2004-28 (sick leave and vacation for trial judges) were cavalier and unprofessional.

Further, in the morning before the May 17, 2006, conference there was another example of the unprofessional behavior that occurs on this court. In confirming his support for Justice Young's response to a dissent, Chief Justice Taylor wrote in an e-mail which was, accidently or not, distributed to the entire court:

Evidently MK [Marilyn Kelly] has missed the thrust of you [sic] opinion. How surprising. I think the response is fine.

At the May 17 conference Chief Justice Taylor was pushed to apologize and technically did apologize. Yet remarkably there was debate concerning the appropriateness of the e-mail. It (seemed to have been forgotten) (should be remembered that) there is an important difference between insulting a person's intelligence and engaging in principled, strong and direct debate on substantive issues.

This type of conduct is unworthy of the justices who engage in it and of the offices they hold. I ask that all the justices thoughtfully and carefully reflect on the standards of behavior to which this court should hold itself. Perhaps everyone should imagine that the court's conferences are being televised. The public would be appalled at how the court's business is often conducted.[1394]

And THEN she went on to outline his other excesses: support for the "gag order," his refusal to do the work of the court by not signing minutes, his ignoring newly passed DQ policies, his overturning of established law, especially in the cases leading up to and including *Nestlé*.

In her speech to the 9/12 Project members, Weaver next laid out Kelly's contempt of court situation and ended with this:

I share these facts with you as you decide whether these are the kinds of Justices you want to sit on the Michigan Supreme Court, our state's highest court—the one that should be the most professional, the most trustworthy, the most open, the most fair, the most dignified. Will they fulfill your expectations of an open and fair court? Would they fulfill the intentions,

---

1393 In a footnote, Weaver wrote: "I am aware that this language was part of a regular skit on *Saturday Night Live*, but such language does not belong at a court conference."
1394 Elizabeth A. Weaver, "Memorandum," 19 May 2006, My MI Court, http://www.mymicourt.com/?p=9.

expectations, and the hopes and faith of our Founding Fathers? That's for you to decide.[1395]

It took me a day to get back from Traverse City, to edit the video and to compose and post the entry.[1396]

And, then, BAM! Suddenly there was news. And we were correct in our prediction that of all the elements of excess it would be the "N" word that caught the attention of the media. Ed White, who had by then moved from the *Grand Rapids Press* (where, among many other things, he had covered the Greg Zolman incident) to the Associated Press, picked up the story and interviewed Young:

> DETROIT—A Michigan Supreme Court justice running for re-election acknowledged Friday that he used the N-word during a private conference with other justices in 2006.
>
> Robert Young, Jr. responded after former Justice Elizabeth Weaver gave a speech this week saying he used the racial slur and that it shows why he doesn't deserve another eight-year term on the court.
>
> Young, who is black, told [t]he Associated Press that he used the word during an "impassioned plea" to emphasize how someone was being treated "without rights, without dignity."
>
> "I'm sorry that I used the term. ... Obviously I was very hot about this. That's why I used the word," Young said. "I remember the heat and the purpose for using it."
>
> When pressed for details, he couldn't recall the case.
>
> Young said Weaver's actions were an "outrage."[1397]

He was not telling the truth, said Weaver.

He made that up; that wasn't what went on. He certainly didn't tell the truth. And there's a difference between lying and telling the truth. But I think he knew the truth, and I had it.

Contrary to what he told Ed White, he was not defending anybody's rights, and there was no impassioned response at an injustice. Instead, Young was making fun of a former judge, Andrea J. Ferrara, whom the Supreme Court had removed from the

---

1395 Elizabeth A. Weaver, speech to 9/12 Meeting in Traverse City.
1396 Her speech is viewable on YouTube: http://www.youtube.com/watch?v=Lzr_SoCP0sY.
1397 Ed White, "Up for re-election, Michigan Supreme Court Justice Robert Young, Jr., explains the use of N-Word," *Grand Rapids Press*, 23 October 2010, http://www.mlive.com/politics/index.ssf/2010/10/up_for_re-election_michigan_su.html.

bench in 1998 for lying to the justices.[1398] Certainly, Weaver recalled hearing Young use the language in the 2006 conference, but she had more than just her memory to back up her assertion.

When I was on the telephone for a conference from my office in Traverse, I would record it so that I could really know what happened because we had denials too often of what did happen. I wanted to know what really did occur. So I would have a recording, transcribe it, and then know exactly what our votes were. I didn't know that Justice Young would go there at all. But, as I said, it was a disorderly, unprofessional, unfair way of doing the business. So then when he denied the truth of that, I came up with the transcript.

Here was her formal response:

> Justice Young, in an interview with Associated Press reporter Ed White, confirmed that he had used the "N" word. Unfortunately, he didn't stop there. He attempted to deceive the reporter and the public by saying that he used it "during an 'impassioned plea' to emphasize how someone was being treated 'without rights, without dignity.'" Justice Young continued that "Obviously I was very hot about this. That's why I used the word. ... I remember the heat and the purpose for using it."

> The article stated that, "When pressed for details, he [Justice Young] couldn't recall the case."

> Below are the details and the truth—not the fiction—about the case and the conduct of Justice Young during the case while the court was holding its regular weekly conference to discuss the status of pending cases. He used the "N" word with disdain and jocularity...he was laughing. And so were others. His statement was made during the business of the court. The justices were in the middle of item number seven (7) on the May 10, 2006, court conference agenda: 130592 *Moxon v Moxon*. The trial judge in the case was Judge Antonio "Tony" Viviano. The justices had been discussing whether to deny appeal in the case, hear it, or remand it.[1399] The justices turned from the case before them to bring up that Judge Tony Viviano's son, David, might run for a judgeship in Macomb County and that might put him in the running against a former judge, Andrea Ferrara. The Supreme Court had removed Judge Ferrara from office in Wayne County in 1998 but there was talk of her running for another judgeship in Macomb County in the 2006 election.

1398 Weaver had written the Supreme Court opinion in this case. And that was BEFORE Young took the bench there. Ferrara had also used some pretty vile language, including the "N" word, in conversations that had been made available to the court and were included in the opinion. As unsavory as those were and as worthy of rebuke, she was kicked to the curb for her untruths under oath. [Opinion, *In re Ferrara,* No. 109593, Michigan Supreme Court, 28 July 1998, http://caselaw.findlaw.com/mi-supreme-court/1168592.html.]
1399 The Supreme Court remanded the matter. *This was an important case. We were dealing with the education and welfare of children in modifying a divorce agreement. This was NOT a casual matter.* [*Stella A. Moxon v Jack R. Moxon,* No. 130592, Michigan Supreme Court, 25 May 2006, http://publicdocs.courts.mi.gov:81/SCT/PUBLIC/ORDERS/20060525_S130592_23_130592_2006-05-25_or.pdf.]

Below is exactly what the justices said, from my notes and from a transcript of a recording I made of that conference. I share these facts for the voting public to judge for themselves whether Justice Young is fit to continue to serve on the Michigan Supreme Court:

7.130952 STELLA A MOXON V JACK R MOXON -

Chief Justice Clifford W. Taylor (CWT): "I'M QUICK TO SAY THE JUDGE ALWAYS HAS THE RIGHT TO CHANGE THINGS WITH REGARDS TO THESE KIDS."

Justice Marilyn Kelly (MK): "I THINK SO TOO EVEN THOUGH THAT WAS A SEPARATE..."

Chief Justice Clifford W. Taylor (CWT): "...BUT I JUST WANT TO RE- MAND THIS FOR FURTHER FACT FINDING CAUSE I DON'T THINK HE HAD ENOUGH IN THERE TO JUSTIFY DOING WHAT HE DID."

Justice Robert P. Young (RPY): "THE SALE WAS PENDING..."

Justice Michael F. Cavanagh (MFC): "VIVIANO'S SON WAS RUNNING..."

Chief Justice Clifford W. Taylor (CWT): "...ANDREA FERRARA. ISN'T THAT A SCREAM? ... YES, THAT'S WHAT SHE SAID. MOVING ON..."

Justice Robert P. Young (RPY): "WATCH OUT FOR THOSE N—-S OUT THERE. (Laughter) REALLY . . ."

Chief Justice Clifford W. Taylor (CWT): "...WE DIDN'T DO THE DEATH PENALTY..."

Justice Michael F. Cavanagh (MFC): "SHE HAS TO MOVE FROM DOWN RIVER OUT TO MACOMB."

Justice Robert P. Young (RPY): "SHE DID."

Chief Justice Clifford W. Taylor (CWT): "OH, I'M SURE SHE DID."

Justice Robert P. Young (RPY): "I THOUGHT SHE LIVED IN..."

Chief Justice Clifford W. Taylor (CWT): "SHE MOVED ACROSS 8 MILE, BOB."

Justice Robert P. Young (RPY): "I THOUGHT SHE LIVED IN THE POINTES. HER FAMILY LIVES OVER THERE. MAYBE THERE'S A FER- RARA DOCTOR THAT'S HER DAD I THINK..."

Chief Justice Clifford W. Taylor (CWT): "...LET'S SEE WHERE WE ARE HERE."

Justice Robert P. Young (RPY): "ALL RIGHT (laughs). I'M A DENY. STEVE, I DIDN'T HEAR FROM YOU."

Justice Stephen J. Markman (SJM): "I DON'T THINK TONY (Judge Antonio Viviano) EVEN INVOKED MCR 2.612. I'D FEEL A LOT MORE COMFORTABLE IF WE REMANDED, HAD THEM AT LEAST GO THROUGH THE STEPS."

Chief Justice Clifford W. Taylor (CWT): "I GUESS MAURA (Justice Maura D. Corrigan (MDC)) ..."

Justice Elizabeth A. Weaver (EAW): "WHAT WAS MAURA'S VOTE?"

Chief Justice Clifford W. Taylor (CWT): "SHE WAS A DENY."

Justice Elizabeth A. Weaver (EAW): "SO, THAT'S FOUR, RIGHT?"

Identity of speaker unclear: "THERES A SPECIFIC COURT RULE AND THE COURT JUST TOTALLY IGNORED IT, MARILYN."

Justice Marilyn Kelly (MK): "I'M WILLING TO DO THIS . . ."

Chief Justice Clifford W. Taylor (CWT): "IT'S A FACT QUESTION. I MEAN THE FEDERAL..."

Justice Elizabeth A. Weaver (EAW): "RIPPY (RPY), I THOUGHT YOU WERE A DENY."

Justice Robert P. Young (RPY): "I AM."

Justice Elizabeth A. Weaver (EAW): "SO, IT'S YOU, MYSELF, MK, AND MDC, RIGHT?"

Justice Robert P. Young (RPY): "RIGHT."

Chief Justice Clifford W. Taylor (CWT): "BUT I THINK PEOPLE ARE STILL THINKING ABOUT IT."

Justice Elizabeth A. Weaver (EAW): "I DIDN'T KNOW."

Chief Justice Clifford W. Taylor (CWT): "SO, DO YOU WANT TO TALK ABOUT IT ANYMORE?"

Justice Marilyn Kelly (MK): "I'M DONE."

Chief Justice Clifford W. Taylor (CWT): "SO IT'S A DENY."

Justice Robert P. Young (RPY): "I'LL REMAND."

Justice Elizabeth A. Weaver (EAW): "3-4 TO DENY."[1400]

That was Justice Young's idea of a joke; but it was a demeaning joke with respect to the situation. And as I gave more information, he kept changing his story. But I felt the public had a right to know.

And, of course, nobody looks particularly good there—the thing was so disorderly, they talked over each other—but only Justice Young had taken it to that degree. But the truth is the truth, and that's the way the business was done, and that wasn't the first or only time. I just happened to transcribe it—it was SO OFFENSIVE that I had made a note of it.

The next morning after I had published Weaver's response, I called Ed White at Associated Press. There was something I wanted to know. We had a short conversation and hung up. And then I started writing about our encounter:

> With yesterday's revelation through a transcript by Justice Weaver (retired) that Justice Young was laughing and joking about the bad acts and misfortunes of another judge when the phrase dropped from his lips I wondered if the reporter had any sense that he'd been misused. So, I called Mr. White. I told him I wanted to interview him. He was unaware of the further revelation [the transcript] that I had posted last night, had no idea who I was, or why I was calling. "I have no response," he said. "My reporting speaks for itself." I wonder if he thought I was being critical. I agreed his reporting DID speak for itself. I thought it first rate. But I was inquiring about this further revelation. "I have nothing to say about anything. Who are you?" Mind you, I had given him my name and said "How do you do?" It's true I had not identified Delayed Justice.[1401] Sometimes I'm not good at this...and what's Delayed Justice anyway that anybody would know of it? I clumsily rectified my affiliation. He went on to explain: "When I interview people I tell them I'm Ed White and I'm a reporter and then they tell me...." Uh-huh. I heard a click on the line and wondered aloud if I was being recorded. "This is a newsroom. There's lots of noise. ... I don't record my telephone conversations." Just wondered. Didn't object if he wanted to, although I don't think I'm necessarily worth all that bother. And in retrospect it's a little humorous considering the nature of the transcript. Anyway, he said he doesn't do that. I assured him that neither do I. Pretty close to the end of the conversation he reiterated that he didn't have anything to offer, but by that time he'd hit the website. Our conversation was concluded.

1400 Elizabeth A Weaver, "Statement," 25 October 2010, My MI Court, http://www.mymicourt.com/?p=13.
1401 This material was first posted at DelayedJustice.com, a site I use for my work in telling the stories of unsolved homicides. The court work threatened to take over the site, so I moved it to mymicourt.com, a site dedicated just to the workings of the court.

Still, I wonder what his internal reaction to all that might be. I'll probably never know. But I do wish him well.

Later: Mr. White called me this time. I told him I'd appreciate a *quid pro quo*. I'd answer his questions and he would at least consider answering mine. Nope, he said: "I am a reporter and not a participant in this story. I have nothing to say to you." I tried to explain that such was my work as well, but it didn't prosper. He wanted to let me know that this all was very serious... the power to put something on the Internet can have grave consequences. I agreed; any reportage can have serious consequences. Then his questions: "Is this report authentic?" "Did Justice Weaver give you this and ask you to put it up at your website?" I had to explain that I believe to the best of my knowledge this is authentic. Justice Weaver did share this with me but she didn't ask me to put it up. I told her that was my intention. I did get in a question: "Don't you think this is newsworthy?" He indicated that he WAS looking into it. Next question: "Did you hear the tape?" I said I neither heard any tape nor saw any tape. I told him that I thought his most important job would be to seek corroboration from someone else at the conference. I thought he'd have better luck with that than I would.

Now, as for the other questions that I had, at the top of my list was this: Of all the stories he could have pursued from Justice Weaver's revelations, why pick up exclusively on that one...the use of bad language? Yes, it's egregious and unfortunate, but what Justice Young has said is nowhere near as serious as what he's done on the bench. (As an aside, in Justice Weaver's transcript, did you note how he changed his vote on the *Moxon v Moxon* to accommodate himself to then-Chief Justice Clifford W. Taylor? The result meant the difference between a Deny and a Remand [a kind of beneficent judicial do-over for the judge]. Interesting.)

I suspect that the answer is that it's a fairly easy story to report...much more simple, say, than a piece explaining Justice Young's take on the Common Law (he's agin' it). Either Justice Weaver was right that he'd said the "N" word or she was wrong. He admitted he said it. And now either she's right about when, where, and how he said it or she's wrong. Yes or no.

Most of the other stories are much more detailed...except for the one about Judge Mary Beth Kelly, who during her tenure as Chief Judge of The Third Circuit Court (Wayne County) earned herself a contempt citation that wouldn't go away, even after she appealed it to the Court of Appeals and the Supreme Court. Even Justice Young had to agree that she'd been playing outside the law.

But I didn't get the chance to ask that question, either.

I am sure Mr. White is doing his best. I trust that he will dig out this story and plenty of others relating to it. But his assertion that he is not a participant in this story is risible. As soon as you touch a story you become a participant.

[...]

Mr. White's reporting brought this story to hundreds of thousands of readers. It has a much larger impact because he decided to touch it. He will in some small or large way change the course of history. I'm very glad he did take this up and I hope he doesn't regret it, either. Yes, he's a participant, and we have no reason to think that he'll be anything other than as thorough, as objective, and as truthful as possible.[1402]

Really, I just wanted to know most of all what it was like to be lied to by a justice of the Supreme Court.

Ed White did write about the transcript story:

> Elizabeth Weaver provided a transcript of a court conference [....]
> It was intended to counter a black justice's explanation of how he had once used the N-word during private talks with other justices.
>
> But instead it raises questions about why—and how—a member of the state's highest court was recording her colleagues four years ago.
>
> "She probably committed a felony," said Justice Robert Young, Jr., referring to a state law that requires consent of all involved before recording phone conversations.
>
> Young, the justice who acknowledged using the N-word, said he believes Weaver recorded the court's discussion of cases on May 10, 2006, while participating by phone from northern Michigan where she lives.
>
> Weaver, who quit the court in August, said state law allows one party to a conversation to record it. She said Young was "trying to divert the public's attention" from his choice of words and the secrecy and "locker room" manner in which the court conducts public business.
>
> "It's a shame, it's a disgrace, and Young should himself be feeling shamed," she said.
>
> [...]
>
> Young reversed himself a bit Tuesday and said Weaver's version probably was right. He said he was quoting a disgraced former judge in Wayne Coun-

---

1402 David B. Schock, October 26, 2010—Ed White: "My story speaks for itself," My MI Court, 26 October 2010, http://www.mymicourt.com/?p=14.

ty who was considering a comeback in 2006, years after she was removed for denigrating minorities.

"I surely was not using it as a racial epithet. I was quoting the person who used it as a racial epithet," said Young, who is seeking re-election Nov. 2. "If I can be forgiven for remembering the emotion but not remembering the context after 4 1/2 years, I can live with it."

He said he's more troubled that Weaver recorded the Supreme Court's internal deliberations. Cliff Taylor, who was chief justice at the time, said he's shocked.

"This rogue judge was a nightmare on the court the whole time she served on it," Taylor said of Weaver. "And this is the capper. ... These discussions between judges have to be inviolately secret. Otherwise the system can't work."[1403]

I think it's unprofessional and unfair, when you're in the middle of a case, when we are doing court business, to tell a joke—and use the "N" word. And that's not acceptable, period, and it's certainly not acceptable at the Supreme Court when we're doing a case, anybody's case. You deserve better attention than that. And, furthermore, it was, in my opinion, a very strong racial remark. You don't use the "N" word even if you are African-American yourself. And it wasn't used in a way of protecting blacks or anything.

No, she'd not broken the law; she had well researched it before she released the transcript. And the charge that she had...?

Yeah. And that was all boloney, so then I produced the law that said I had every right to do that. And I didn't have to tell them [I was recording]. That's just the way it is. I was not in some secret club. My duty was always to the people, and that's the way I looked at it, that's the way I came into the court, and that's the way I left the court, like it or not.

And she was prepared to take the blowback. It came amidst the swirl of news stories and advertising campaigns. Early in 2010, the Democrats had little that would connect with voters. First, in April 2010, even before the court election season, they tried a reprisal of the "Sleeping judge ad" but this time with Young as the napper.

The Michigan Democratic Party's Web site has posted a contest,[1404] inviting participants to guess "How many times has Bob Young fallen asleep on the bench?" and the winner will get a Bob "Sleepy" Young t-shirt.

1403 Ed White, "Weaver says she recorded her high court colleagues; Young is troubled by recording of internal deliberations," *Detroit Legal News*, 28 October 2010, http://www.legalnews.com/detroit/752764/.
1404 "Bob Young Contest," Michigan Democratic State Central Committee, http://salsa.wiredforchange.com/o/1141/t/6083/questionnaire.jsp?questionnaire_KEY=354.

The site hauls out the statistic: "An insurance industry lawyer, Young has ruled with insurance companies and corporations 80 percent of the time," which would be fair game if it's true.

But another round of "sleeping judge" ads? Is this how we want to appeal to voters to select a Justice for our state's highest court?[1405]

It didn't fly, particularly given Young's reputation for frequent active questioning from the bench.

In their next excess, the Democrats fielded an ad that displayed a photo of a geeky Steve Urkel from the 1990's television show *Family Matters* morphing into Bob Young...

...while a voice says something like: "What is Steve Urkel as a grown-up? Bob Young," and then returns to the theme at the end by saying, "We don't need a clown on the bench."[1406]

Not surprisingly, late in the campaign the Democrats picked up on the Weaver assertions of Young's bad language, resulting in an ad that—described in a report from Justice at Stake Campaign, the Brennan Center for Justice, and the National Institute on Money in State Politics—"reached rock bottom."[1407]

The *Free Press* really didn't like the Democrats' ads and even though Dawson Bell had done a fact check in a story that verified Weaver's claim and Young's admission,[1408] the same day, editorial writer Stephen Henderson expressed his criticism. He noted the paper had not endorsed Young—opting instead for Mary Beth Kelly and Tom Davis. But the ads about Young were too much.

...Young's comments were, in the most honest reading of the transcript, an attempt at humor in parroting one of the remarks Ferrara made.

Should he have said it? Probably not. But the spin being put on his remarks by Weaver (who's a Republican, for the record) and some Democrats is pretty dishonest.

As I said before, I'm not a fan of Young's work. We didn't endorse him.

1405 Carol Lundberg, "Sleeping judge, the sequel," The Michigan Lawyer; A blog from *Michigan Lawyers Weekly*, 1 April 2010, http://michiganlawyerblog.wordpress.com/2010/04/01/sleeping-judge-the-sequel/.
1406 Stephen Henderson, "Democrats' racially tinged ads against Young beyond low," *Detroit Free Press*, 30 October 2010, A.8.
1407 Adam Skaggs, Maria da Silva, and Linda Casey, Charles Hall, ed., *The New politics of Judicial Elections 2009-10; How special interest "super spenders" threatened impartial justice and emboldened unprecedented legislative attacks on America's courts*, Brennan Center for Justice, Justice at Stake, and the National Institute on Money in State Politics, (Washington D.C., 2011), 12, http://newpoliticsreport.org/site/wp-content/uploads/2011/10/JAS-NewPolitics2010-Online-Text-Only.pdf.
1408 Dawson Bell, "Attack on Young; Fact check," *Detroit Free Press*, 30 October 2010, A.7.

But this kind of backwater racial politics is beneath even the lowest point of this vicious campaign.

Democrats all over the state should be embarrassed that this was done in their name.[1409]

With precious little time left before election day, the Republicans came back with robocalls featuring Michelle Engler, Young, and other voice talent. I received and heard the Engler call, but it was erased before I could record it from the phone answering machine. I know Michelle Engler had mentioned the Ku Klux Klan.[1410] When I first heard it, I thought that maybe she was meaning me; I had made a film about the Klan in Michigan,[1411] but it was hardly complimentary, and I have never been, nor wanted to be, a member. (As it turned out, in his lawyering days, former Democratic Party Chairman Mark Brewer had once represented a member of the Klan.) Here is text of one of the robocalls by a woman of some considerable ability:

Have you seen those outrageous ads about Bob Young? An organization led by a former member of the KKK is paying for racist ads attacking Bob Young, the only African American ON the Supreme Court. The *Free Press* calls it a bigoted campaign. This has got to stop. Do yourself a favor: grab a pen or a pencil and a piece of paper and write the name Bob Young and VOTE. Put it in your purse or your pocket and take it with you to the polls on Tuesday. Bob Young is OUR voice on the Supreme Court. Don't let the racists win. Please, vote for Bob Young on the non-partisan ballot on Tuesday. Thank you.[1412]

Young's voice work is less polished—he trips over "Baptists"—and it's a recording made over the phone, but his message is clear:

Hello, this is Supreme Court Justice Bob Young. As the only African American member of the Michigan Supreme Court I'm proud to have received the

---

1409 Stephen Henderson.
1410 Weaver also had received that call.

Michelle said that she knew that Justice Young was being falsely accused—but I don't think she used my name—and that he had not said such a thing. She was defending him. And then that was enough for me on Michelle Engler, whom I liked; I felt that she was one of the best things that ever happened to John Engler. But in retrospect now, if she had reduced herself to getting into something she knew nothing about—because how could she know what went on at that conference? She couldn't.

So the irony of that for me was that I knew—and had said—that Michelle Engler, interestingly enough, had been appointed to be one of the trustees of Freddie Mac. We had just been through and are still going through the mess of the failure of the trustees of Freddie Mac. And she had been a trustee for almost eight years, yet never publicly criticized the operations or performance of Freddie Mac. Then she quietly resigned about two weeks after things went bad—the big financial meltdown of September 2008.

(I had chronicled Michelle Engler's work there in a post, including her earning of $276,780 in 2008 as she was guiding the institution over—what some would call—the cliff. [David B. Schock, "November 2, 2010—The story is STILL going to come out," My MI Court, 6 November 2010, http://www.mymicourt.com/?p=20.
1411 David B. Schock, *The Klan In Michigan; Part One—The Klan of Reconstruction*, 2004, http://www.delayedjustice.com/?page_id=13.
1412 David B. Schock, "November 9, 2010—Still no script from Mrs. Engler, but how about this audio file from Justice Young himself?," My MI Court, 9 November 2010, http://www.mymicourt.com/?p=22.

endorsement of the Council of Baptist Ministers for my re-election. But I think it's a shame that every black candidate seems to face the same racial attacks you're hearing about me. The *Free Press* called it "back-water racial politics." None of these ads are true. I can't stop them from telling lies. But with your vote we can send them a message on Tuesday that enough is enough. [...][1413]

Weaver had no love for the Democrats' campaigns nor much respect for their leadership. And as much as it grieved her that they'd picked up her revelations and then had used them in an ad campaign, it seemed unavoidable.

We had discussed the likelihood of that happening. I said that it would have been better if her speech had come earlier; people would have had a chance to investigate, think, and talk about it. Instead it would be viewed as an opposition ploy, and Weaver was never in league with the Democratic Party. But it happened when it happened and as it happened.

It happened as it happened. Yes, if I had given that speech earlier, it might have been different. But I didn't. It was my highest sense of right at the time. We can learn from our mistakes.

Money and the Race for the Supreme Court

There was a lot of money being spread about in the 2010 race for the Supreme Court, more per seat than at any previous time in history: nearly $5.7 million for each of two seats (almost $11.4 million total). This from Michigan Campaign Finance Network:

> Michigan easily had the nation's costliest judicial elections in 2009-2010, fueled by a nasty TV ad blitzkrieg funded by special-interest groups, a new report by three nonpartisan legal reform groups discloses.

> [...] [M]ost of the special-interest spending stayed hidden from public view. The state Republican and Democratic parties channeled millions in secret money into election ads—evading accountability as they spent.

> Nationally, state high-court candidates and special-interest groups spent $38.4 million, and a growing portion of that money was spent by a small number of secretive special-interest groups. The 2010 high court elections were followed by a ferocious series of legislative attacks against the nation's court system.

> "Michigan has become a national symbol of special-interest pressure on our courts of law," said Bert Brandenburg, executive director of the Justice at Stake Campaign, a nonpartisan legal reform group.

1413 Ibid.

"The fact that Michigan led the nation in undisclosed spending in a state judicial campaign is a distinction of dishonor," said Rich Robinson, executive director of the Michigan Campaign Finance Network. "The Michigan legislature and our constitutional executives should be ashamed. Then they should get to work to require public disclosure of who is spending millions of dollars every election to influence our courts."[1414]

Oh, well that election was $11.4 million, and interestingly enough, Justice Davis had the most money contributed directly to him—over $900,000 [in candidate receipts]. And then the other candidates had receipts in various amounts down from that. Mary Beth Kelly didn't have really that much—maybe she had $400,000. She had all of this TV that went on about how just and fair she and Bob Young were, and she's not recorded as ever spending a dollar on TV ads. So who bought all her ads? ... Who-knows-what-PACs, where the money is unidentifiable? You know...People for Justice, or this or that as an example. What are they? And where did their money come from?

Michigan Campaign Finance Network did its best to answer that through its compilation of accounts:

> The 2010 Michigan Supreme Court campaign followed trends that have been in evidence since 2000: committees other than the candidate committees provided the majority of funds in the campaign, and a significant percentage of that spending was not disclosed in the state's campaign finance reporting system. Candidate committees were the source of a record low 23 percent of all spending in the campaign. Undisclosed spending reached a record-high 55 percent of all spending. Reported independent expenditures made up the balance.
>
> [...]
>
> Three-fourths of all spending in the campaign paid for television advertisements. Ironically, the top vote-getter in the campaign, Judge Kelly, was the only major party nominee who did not buy a broadcast television ad of her own. The Michigan Republican Party spent $3.4 million for Supreme Court ads touting Kelly and Young, only $650,000 of which was disclosed. On the other side, the Michigan Democratic Party spent $2,450,000 for unreported television ads attacking Kelly and Young.[1415]

Yes, Kelly was the top vote getter: 1,408,294. She had candidate receipts of $418,262, party independent expenditures (IEs) of $959,789, PAC IEs of $230,299, for total resources of $1,608,349. Party resources had accounted for $1,025,489 of that, 63.8 percent.[1416] Her cost per vote was $1.14.

1414 "Michigan high court races most expensive in nation in 2009-10," Michigan Campaign Finance Network, 27 October 2011, http://www.mcfn.org/press.php?prId=137.

1415 Rich Robinson and Barbara R. Moorhouse, *A citizen's guide to Michigan Campaign finance—2010*, Michigan Campaign Finance Network, (Lansing, Mich., 2001), 25, http://www.mcfn.org/pdfs/reports/MCFN2010_CitGuide.pdf.

1416 Ibid. A total of $218,450 of her candidate receipts came from committees, $199,812 from individuals.

Young came in second, with 1,310,986 votes. He had candidate receipts of $843,254, party IEs of $959,627, independent IEs of $230,237, for a total of $2,033,118 in resources. Of that total, party resources were $1,027,497, or 50.5 percent. Committee contributions accounted for $370,654 of his candidate receipts, individuals, $472,620.[1417] His cost per vote was $1.55.

Davis was a distant third with 908,642 votes. As Weaver asserted, he had the highest of the candidate receipts: $988,187. In addition, there were party IEs of $62,527, no independent IEs, for a total of $1,050,714 in resources. Of that, party resources accounted for $115,415, or 11.0 percent.[1418] His cost per vote was $1.16

Morris had 812,485 votes, not far behind Davis. She had candidate receipts of $353,387, party IEs of $43,507, no independent IEs, for a total of $396,894 in resources. The Democratic Party had supplied $51,848 of the total, 13.1 percent. Her cost per vote was almost 49 cents.[1419]

And Libertarian Bob Roddis had 262,645 votes. He reported not raising a penny.[1420]

But far more than the money that flowed to the candidates and their campaign coffers was the money spent on issue advertising...a total of $6.3 million, and that's just what Michigan Campaign Finance Network could track. A lot of money came from elsewhere and flowed around traditional measures of advertising income for television and radio stations' public files. Of candidate-focused issue ads—supporting Kelly and Young, or opposing Davis and Morris—the Michigan Republican Party put up $2.76 million and the Law Enforcement Alliance of America put up $930,000 for a total of $3.69 million. The Democratic Party put down $2.24 million to support Davis and Morris or to oppose Kelly and Young. The 21st Century Leadership Fund added $155,000, for a total of $2.6 million.[1421]

Rich Robinson had been sounding the warning, election by election, that things were getting out of hand:

> As with any election where there is undisclosed spending, voters were deprived of important knowledge of who was financially supporting whom.

The top ten contributors included: Michigan Republican State Committee, $61,606; Michigan Health & Hospital Assn./Health PAC $34K; Dickinson Wright PLLC $18,041; Automobile Club of Michigan PAC/ACPAC $15K; Michigan State Medical Society/MI Doctors PAC $15K; Frankenmuth PAC $10K; Michigan Chamber of Commerce PAC $10K; Michigan Farm Bureau PAC $10K; Miller Canfield $8,850, and seven couples at $6,800 each. [Ibid., 88.]
1417 Ibid., 25. His top ten contributors included: Michigan Republican State Committee $61,270; Michigan Health and Hospital Assn./Health PAC $34K; Michigan Assn. of Realtors/REALTORS PAC $34K; Michigan Farm Bureau PAC $33,700; Dickinson Wright PLLC $23,424; Michigan State Medical Society/MI Doctors PAC $20,504; Michigan Bankers Assn. PAC/MI BANK PAC $20K; Automobile Club of Michigan PAC/ACPAC $16,200; Frankenmuth PAC $15,881; Kienbaum, Opperwall Hardy & Pelton PLC $14,750; Miller Canfield $14,250. [Ibid., 88.]
1418 Ibid., 25.
1419 Ibid.
1420 Ibid.
1421 Ibid., 26.

However, the lack of accountability in Supreme Court campaigns is particularly troublesome. The U.S. Supreme Court ruled in *Caperton v Massey Coal Company* that a judge should not participate in a case involving a major campaign supporter, because the financial support may introduce an unacceptable probability of bias. That is, a judge should not rule in a case involving a party who had a substantial financial role in the judge's winning campaign because it deprives the financial supporter's legal opponent of his due process right to an impartial court hearing.

It should be assumed that parties who invest great sums in election campaigns are rational economic actors, and no party has a greater interest in the outcome of a Supreme Court campaign than a party with a high-stakes case in the appeals pipeline. Yet Michigan's conspicuously ineffective campaign disclosure regime deprives parties to litigation of the knowledge necessary to know when their due process rights may have been compromised, and when they rightfully could request a justice to disqualify himself. The fact that more than $20 million in the last six Michigan Supreme Court campaigns was unreported represents a toxic cloud shadowing the Court.

One other notable campaign finance development in the 2010 campaign was the $450,000 independent expenditure by the Michigan Association of Realtors corporate PAC for radio advertisements supporting Kelly and Young. The Realtors corporate PAC reported that $350,000 of its funds came from its "issues fund." This Russian doll construct allowed the Realtors to report spending but not contributors. They merely named the internal shell entity into which contributions were made.[1422]

Robinson is a man of restraint and few words; certainly he is not given to histrionics. He would rather, he has said, understate than overstate.

A little housekeeping here: those robocalls? The state Republican Party said they didn't come from them. The logical assumption is that they came from the Republican National Committee...someplace out of state. So, from where, then? Was the cost to produce and disseminate them ever reported?

...And Justice Young being outpolled by soon-to-be Justice Mary Beth Kelly as he had been by Elizabeth Weaver in 2002?

Justice Young just never comes in first in these elections.

1422 Ibid.

Chapter 27

After You've Gone
An Attempted Censure;
Maura Leaves and Brian Arrives;
The Trip to the AGC Courtesy of....

"Not pleased" would be one way to describe the frame of mind of the justices when it came to Weaver and her revelations before the 2010 election. "Furious" would be another. So furious, in fact, that they couldn't reason clearly. And their next move probably didn't do exactly what they hoped. Led by the Engler Three, the majority of the justices wanted to let Weaver know very clearly that she had displeased them mightily. At the very least, she was off their Christmas card list. So, they sent her a letter.

Dear Justice Weaver:

It is truly a sad day when this court is forced to censure a former colleague. Your action in recording and then in making public discussion that were part of the court's deliberative process, as well and internal court memoranda, compel us to do so.

None of your fellow justices was aware that you were tape-recording our private deliberation on cases. Had you requested our consent to record we would have refused it. We know of no instance in the past when a justice has secretly recorded court deliberations.

All members of the court but you had agreed to keep our deliberations on cases private. The only exception regards statements that reveal criminal or unethical activities. You, however, have maintained that you would use your best judgment as to what part, if any, of these private deliberations you would make public.

As you know, the reasons we deliberate in private on cases are several and include the same reasons juries deliberate in private. We wish to be able to speak freely, explore differing views, take straw votes and change our position on matters without concern for how sensitive matters might be construed in the media. Some matters we discuss would be injurious to innocent people if made public.

Since leaving the court you have made public material from court deliberations although it involves neither criminal nor ethical violations by a justice. Moreover, you have indicated an intent to continue to do so. Your stated goal—reform of the way justices are chosen—could surely be better accomplished without secret recordings and revealing private court deliberations.

We as justices owe a duty to the court and to the public to make clear that we do not condone your behavior as outlined in this letter. We also make clear, by issuing this letter, that we respect the court and the integrity of the decision-making process.[1423]

The letter was signed by Chief Justice Marilyn Kelly, and Justices Michael F. Cavanagh, Maura D. Corrigan, Robert P. Young, Jr., and Stephen J. Markman.

Alton Davis didn't sign. And Diane Hathaway dissented with this statement:

Because I respect the court and the integrity of the decision-making process, I do not sign this letter. In my opinion, issuing a formal censure, without any adjudicative proceeding, is inappropriate and disregards an individual's due process rights.[1424]

And she signed that instead. She stood up at the right time and with the right argument.

And despite their drive to keep internal deliberations very, very quiet, the justices released the letter to the press Nov. 22. It didn't matter that it suddenly might be a pending or impending matter if Weaver had reacted as she might have with a federal suit. Instead, after their giving it out to the press, she posted her analysis of the action:

Imagine that! I have been censured by the Michigan Supreme Court.

Now, what, exactly does that mean? The first two definitions in my dictionary relate it's a "1. strong or vehement expression of disapproval" and "2. an official reprimand, as by a legislative body of one of its members." Because the action to censure me was taken during the official administrative business of the court, and because it's delivered on court letterhead and ascribed to by five of the seven justices, I take this as an official action.

But this word "censure" carries more meaning that just that from my dictionary. It has a specific legal and constitutional meaning because it is used in our state's Constitution. Article VI, Section 30, Paragraph (2) provides:

1423 Marilyn Kelly, Michael F. Cavanagh, Maura D. Corrigan, Robert P. Young, Jr., and Stephen J. Markman, Letter of censure, My MI Court, 17 November 2010, http://www.mymicourt.com/?p=43.
1424 Diane Hathaway in ibid.

> On recommendation of the Judicial Tenure Commission, the Supreme Court may censure, suspend with or without salary, retire or remove a judge for conviction of a felony, physical or mental disability which prevents the performance of judicial duties, misconduct in office, persistent failure to perform his duties, habitual intemperance or conduct that is clearly prejudicial to the administration of justice. The Supreme Court shall make rules implementing this section and providing for confidentiality and privilege of proceedings.[1425]

In this action—as in so much else that it has done in recent years—our Supreme Court has been precipitous and acted outside the Michigan Constitution or the Code of Judicial Conduct. The important part of the above-quoted passage is "On recommendation of the Judicial Tenure Commission...."

You need to know that didn't happen. I received no notice of any proceedings against me or any recommendation of the Judicial Tenure Commission to the Supreme Court to censure or discipline me in any way.

What <u>did</u> happen is that on Wednesday, November 17, 2010, five (5) of the seven (7) justices of the Michigan Supreme Court violated the Michigan Constitution.

These five justices—Chief Justice Marilyn Kelly, and Justices Michael F. Cavanagh, Maura D. Corrigan, Robert P. Young, Jr., and Stephen J. Markman—signed a letter of censure and sent it to me. I found it on my doorstep Thursday. Further, they emailed the contents of their letter.

It's notable that Justices Diane M. Hathaway and Alton Thomas Davis did not sign the letter.

Further, Justice Hathaway added and signed the following statement:

> Because I respect the Court and the integrity of the decision-making process, I do not sign this letter. In my opinion, issuing a formal censure, without any adjudicative proceeding, is inappropriate and disregards an individual's due process rights.

Justice Hathaway can rest assured that I have violated no law, nor any of the Code of Judicial Conduct. In short, I have done nothing wrong. I have every right to do what I've done; I intend to do more.

And as much as I think openness at the court is appropriate, I did not disseminate the censure to the news media because I wanted to see just if and how this news would come out. So, how did it come to you? Through what

---

[1425] State Constitution of Michigan of 1963, Article VI, Section 30, http://www.legislature.mi.gov/(S(krlueum2i3l5ebfthudahzyr))/mileg.aspx?page=getobject&objectname=mcl-Article-VI-30.

channel, if not through me? Ah, yes, the court itself. This is a part of what I call error exposing itself.

As I see it, these five justices have made public their obviously unconstitutional and unjust attempts to censure my free speech, even as a retired justice. This is not the first time they've done so, and had they simply said they found my actions offensive or repugnant in letting you know about the character of Justice Robert Young and incoming Justice Mary Beth Kelly, and other matters at the court, I'd have had no issue or complaint; their opinions are their own. But when they use formal legal sanctions—as they have done here and as they have attempted in their illegal "gag order" of 2006—you have to recognize that something is seriously wrong, and it is not me.

As for yourselves, are you better off for knowing or would you prefer to remain in ignorance of the actions and the methodology of our Supreme Court? Are you better or worse informed to know that the likely new chief justice has used racial and sexual language during the course of his business at the court?

Speaking out to warn you has never been a personal campaign against these five justices, certainly not against Justice Young. I have long thought highly of his abilities and I still do; his deeds are another matter. My speech and writing is about the actions of this majority of justices and the cloak of unnecessary secrecy with which they have chosen to surround themselves as they undertake YOUR business. (And as you've seen, it's secret until they don't want it to be.)

I often have said that their ill-conceived acts are unworthy of them. I do so again in this case. It is another example of why the operations of the Michigan Supreme Court and the performance of some of its justices, its State Court Administrative Office, its Judicial Tenure Commission and Attorney Grievance Commission need investigation and reform.

For much of last 10 years of my almost 16 years as a justice of the Supreme Court, I worked from within with little success to reform the court for it to become less secret, more transparent and open, fair, just, orderly, and professional. My concern is that the court, as it now operates, is driven by special interests, partisan and personal agendas, and ideologies. This court is undeserving of the trust and confidence of the public.

You can tell that at least five justices of this court are more than passing nervous about other things I might make public. I have promised to open my files to those who are truly interested in understanding what's gone on at the state's high court. And those justices who see my work as worthy of censure must know that I have kept a lot of detailed records, something I was prompted to do when they first launched the campaign in 2003 to discredit me. It's possible that they may want to censure me again...and again. I hope they won't, but if they do they should pay attention to the Constitution. And they need to remember that the first and only time (as far as I know) they complained about me to the Judicial Tenure Commission (this past April) it all came to naught. They also might keep in mind that their actions are likely to be very closely examined at the federal level.

Throughout, I have tried to act in the best interests of the people of this state and always—ALWAYS—to tell the truth. Here's my continued pledge: as a retired justice I will work and speak out as long as there is potential for success in reforming Michigan's dual system of electing and appointing Supreme Court justices and for reform of the operations of the Supreme Court and its offices and commissions.

As for this latest attempt against me, this censure, I will continue to "Do right and fear not."[1426]

This time the news spread far and wide. Nathan Koppel, wondering in the *Wall Street Journal* Law Blog, put it this way:

What in the world is going on with the Michigan Supreme Court?

A high-court drama, the likes of which we have never seen, is now playing out in Wolverine country.

Former Justice Elizabeth Weaver, who retired this year after 16 years on the Michigan Supreme Court, evidently made secret recordings of internal court deliberations and has released transcripts of some of the meetings.

Yesterday, the court released a copy of a letter, signed by five current justices on the court, censuring Weaver.

[...]

We sense that we have not heard the last of this dispute.[1427]

That same day, the *Detroit Free Press* chastised Weaver in its editorial:

In her final six years on the court, Weaver was an increasingly independent voice who railed against both the Engler court's published jurisprudence and its administration of court business, which she regarded as excessively secretive.

1426 Elizabeth A. Weaver, letter in response to censure, My MI Court, 22 November 2010, http://www.mymicourt.com/?p=47.
1427 Nathan Koppel, "Former justice pulls back curtain on Michigan Supreme Court," *Wall Street Journal* Law Blog, 23 November 2010, http://blogs.wsj.com/law/2010/11/23/former-justice-pulls-back-curtain-on-michigan-supreme-court/.

We shared many of her concerns, especially her conviction that special in-terest contributions were undermining public confidence in the justices' independence. We believe, as she does, that the explosive growth of un-traceable campaign contributions compelled the need for reform of both the judicial selection process and the rules governing a justice's disqualification for conflicts of interest.

We were more skeptical of Weaver's assertion that most of the court's delib-erations should be public, and like her former colleagues, we were dismayed by her unilateral decision to release excerpts of case status conferences she had secretly recorded in an effort to embarrass Justice Robert Young, Jr., whose re-election Weaver opposed.

The leaked recordings betrayed the confidence of Weaver's colleagues with-out revealing any significant evidence of unethical behavior or even incivil-ity. Significantly, Monday's letter of censure was signed by both Chief Jus-tice Marilyn Kelly and Justice Michael Cavanagh, Democrats with whom the renegade Weaver frequently voted in her final years on the court.

If Weaver possesses records that document criminal or unethical behavior on the part of her former colleagues, she should bring them to the attention of the appropriate authorities. But the actions that earned her colleagues' censure appear to have been animated by more personal and puerile motives, and they disserve the reform agenda she purportedly hopes to advance.[1428]

Weaver had always denied that her criticism of the court had anything to do with criminal behavior. If she'd have observed that, she had promised that she'd have gone to the proper authorities. And, apparently there was nothing unethical to the *Freep* about a Supreme Court justice using the term "n____" and "slut" doing the business of the court. Perhaps because Young intended it in a humorous vein? And, despite the paper's horror that she'd make discussions of the court public, it was her constitutional right. It was an odd position for a newspaper that, had it learned of Young's behavior on its own initiative, likely would have had a field day with the language Young employed.[1429]

But the newspaper was not the audience Weaver was reaching for: it was the reading public.

1428 Editorial, "Secret recordings merit censure for ex-Justice Weaver," *Detroit Free Press*, 23 November 2010, A.10.

1429 The *cause célèbre* as of this writing was the political arrangement of State Representative Roy Schmidt of Grand Rapids and Republican House Speaker Jase Bolger. Much was being made of the text comments that were revealed though a FOIA request. [Paul Egan, "Texts give inside look at election fraud case," *Detroit Free Press*, 25 July 2012, Metro.] FOIA would have no authority with the Supreme Court, so without an inside source, it would be unlikely that the paper ever would have learned of Young's comments.

"After You've Gone..."

At the tail end of 2010, while she was still chief justice, Marilyn Kelly convened a task force to study the way justices were selected. The honorary chair was The Honorable Sandra Day O'Connor, senior associate justice of the U.S. Supreme Court. Joining Kelly as co-chair was James L. Ryan, senior circuit judge for the Sixth Circuit Court of Appeals. There were 24 other members. Very intentionally, Weaver was not one of them.

Voted off the court, Davis decided he'd retire and do something else. He'd previously said that fly-fishing was likely to consume a lot of his time if he wasn't elected.

> Davis said there was no personal rancor during his short five-month tenure on the Supreme Court and he has no regrets about taking the job.
>
> "It was very interesting work," Davis said. "There's not black-and-white there. Everything is a shade of gray with strong arguments to be made on both sides."
>
> Davis apparently had the opportunity to be reappointed to his old spot on the appeals court, but he opted to retire. He said it would have been foolish to return as a highly visible member of that court to issue opinions that would "just get swatted down" at the next level.
>
> "I have done this for 26 years and it's time to do something else," he said.
>
> Davis said he'll continue his work on a State Bar Association task force that is reviewing state court reform. The task force will issue a report in January to address changes to make state courts more accessible and more efficient.
>
> Davis said he would have appreciated a chance to rework the Supreme Court's efficiency.
>
> "Administratively, probably a lot could be done in that court to improve," he said. "I think they could conduct a lot more business in a lot less time with some administrative clarity."[1430]

And at the tail end of the year, before Rick Snyder took office, there was a substantive rumor that Justice Corrigan was going to leave the bench to take over the state's Department of Human Services (DHS). There were a lot of rumors about her possible replacement on the court: Court of Appeals Judges Jane Markey, Kirsten Frank Kelly,

---

[1430] Brian McGillivary, "Weaver reflects on state's top court; she served on the Michigan Supreme Court for 36 [sic] years," *Traverse City Record-Eagle*, 28 December 2010, http://record-eagle.com/local/x2036087094/Weaver-reflects-on-states-top-court. Weaver served as a judge for nearly 36 years of which almost 16 were at the Michigan Supreme Court.

and Rick Bandstra were early mentions. And Bandstra had announced his intention to step down from his bench.[1431]

And when the Supreme Court reorganized after the swearing in of Justice Mary Beth Kelly, Robert P. Young, Jr. was elected chief justice. He'd got his wish. While the vote tally was not released, you can bet it wasn't a unanimous selection. Had it been so, the public would have been so informed.[1432]

And January 14, 2011, Maura Corrigan was on her way to DHS to straighten out some serious problems, including revising the federal Child Welfare Settlement Agreement.[1433]

Of her departure, Young said:

> Justice Maura D. Corrigan [...] will stand out in the court's history for her "lasting achievements" as a jurist, administrator, and children's advocate, said Chief Justice Robert P. Young, Jr.
>
> "Her record is one that few have or will ever equal," Young said. "Maura Corrigan has met head-on some of this state's most difficult challenges, and she has succeeded brilliantly."
>
> [...]
>
> "Maura has been a wonderful colleague and friend," Young said. "I will miss her dearly on the court, but the children of Michigan will benefit from her passion to ensure that every child is well cared for. The children of this state could have no better friend or advocate."[1434]

And incoming was Brian K. Zahra, another Engler appointee to both the Wayne County Circuit Court in 1994 and the Court of Appeals in 1998.[1435] In his announcement, the new Governor especially lauded Zahra's intelligence:

1431 John Tunison, "Court of Appeals Judge Richard Bandstra of Grand Rapids to step down in January," *Grand Rapids Press,* 6 December 2010, http://www.mlive.com/news/grand-rapids/index.ssf/2010/12/court_of_appeals_judge_richard.html.

1432 Marcia McBrien, press release, "Robert P. Young, Jr., is state Supreme Court's new chief justice," Michigan Supreme Court, 5 January 2011. And when Young was again voted chief justice in 2013 the notice of his unanimous selection was made known. [Marcia McBrien, "Robert P. Young, Jr., elected to second term as chief justice," Michigan Supreme Court, 2 January 2013, http://www.courts.mi.gov/News-Events/press_releases/Documents/Robert%20P.%20Young,%20Jr.,%20elected%20to%20second%20term%20as%20chief%20justice.pdf.

1433 Tim Martin, "Corrigan says latest Michigan child welfare system report card sign of 'good progress,' but challenges lie ahead," *Grand Rapids Press,* 25 June 2012, http://www.mlive.com/politics/index.ssf/2012/06/child_welfare_michigan.html.

1434 Marcia McBrien, press release, "Justice Maura Corrigan ends Supreme Court tenure today; praised by Chief Justice Young for 'lasting achievements,'" Michigan Supreme Court, 14 January 2011, http://courts.michigan.gov/supremecourt/Press/MDC.pdf.

1435 Justice Brian K. Zahra, Michigan Supreme Court, http://courts.michigan.gov/courts/michigansupremecourt/justices/pages/justice-brian-k.-zahra.aspx.

"Judge Zahra's 16 years of judicial experience and his razor sharp intelligence will make him an outstanding addition to the court," Snyder said. "His integrity and consistent legal philosophy that judges are to interpret laws, not make them, gives me confidence that he will respect our system of checks and balances while upholding the rule of law."[1436]

When Governor Snyder appointed Zahra to the Supreme Court, I was certainly disappointed. But I doubt Snyder had even known of Zahra before he appointed him.

John Minnis of the *Detroit Legal News* reported the arrival and asked Justice Young his opinion.

> Robert P. Young, Jr., recently elected by the court to serve as chief justice, was pleased with Zahra's appointment.

> "This is an excellent choice, and I am delighted to add my personal welcome and congratulations to Justice Zahra," he said.

> Young said he has known Zahra almost since he began practicing law and cited Zahra's remarkable career as a lawyer and as a judge. He said Zahra is widely recognized as one of the state's top jurists and believed that the state high court has adopted more of Zahra's decisions than those of any other sitting lower court judge.

> "Justice Zahra will bring not only his considerable intellect but also his experience as a judge at all levels of our system," Young said. "As a jurist committed to following the rule of law, he is a worthy successor to my dear friend Justice Corrigan, who is departing to take on the challenge of protecting Michigan's abused and neglected children."[1437]

He is a Young protégé, and he didn't get to the Supreme Court without a good deal of special help from the Englerites.

As we noted in Chapter 4, Zahra was a two-time Engler appointment: first in 1994 to the Third Circuit Court (Wayne County) where he served until December of 1998, when Engler tapped him for the Court of Appeals.

But that doesn't tell much of the story. Zahra had been appointed to the Court of Appeals to fill the term of Maura Corrigan, who had been elected to the Supreme Court in November of 1998. He took office in January of 1999 and in 2000 ran unopposed in a low-key election; there were only 18 candidates for 14 seats on the Court of Appeals.[1438]

1436 Geralyn Lasher, "Snyder appoints Zahra to Supreme Court," State of Michigan, 10 January 2011, http://www.michigan.gov/snyder/0,4668,7-277-57577_57657-249164--,00.html.
1437 John Minnis, "Governor names Zahra to replace Corrigan; Supreme Court Chief Justice Young praises Zahra as 'excellent choice," *Detroit Legal News*, 11 January 2011, http://www.legalnews.com/detroit/831146.
1438 "'Low key' Court of Appeals race," *Michigan Lawyers Weekly*, 23 October 2000, http://milawyersweekly.com/news/2000/10/23/low-key-court-of-appeals-race/.

The 2006 election would be a different kind of election, but more about that in the next chapter.

It was clear he was an anointed favorite. Among other perks was the opportunity to play golf with the justices during judges' and justices' meetings on Mackinac Island. Weaver, who took up golfing late in life, found herself in a foursome with Zahra, Taylor, and Young.

Young and Taylor were occasional golfers—not particularly proficient; I don't think they played a lot—and I was then hardly any golfer at all, but Zahra was really good at it. I believe at one point, Zahra thought about going pro.

In addition to seeing him at conferences, Weaver came to know him though his work, which she saw on appeal.

He was ambitious and happy to be a part of the Engler farm team. He's one of theirs, and he will do what he's told.

Goodbye Carl

And in the order of things, Carl Gromek announced his intention to retire. His replacement was going to be Chad Schmucker, who had been first appointed a judge to the Jackson County Circuit Court by John Engler in 1991.[1439]

And when Gromek left, he went with honors.

> State Court Administrator Carl L. Gromek of Lansing, who is retiring this year, was honored today by the Michigan Supreme Court as "an exemplary public servant and consummate leader."
>
> In a resolution signed by the seven justices, the court noted that Gromek "has been entrusted with the highest management positions in the Michigan justice system, signifying the courts' great respect for him and his abilities."
>
> Chief Justice Robert P. Young, Jr., observed that "With Carl Gromek, it is not enough to say that he is a great administrator; he is a great leader. In the history of our state courts, no other person has filled so many management positions of the highest trust and responsibility."
>
> Young added, "Although he served the judicial branch for many years, Mr. Gromek never lost his private sector perspective, emphasizing fiscal responsibility, efficiency, and quality. Carl has never stopped pursuing the better way. He encouraged and pushed his colleagues to produce the best possi-

1439 Marcia McBrien, "Judge Chad C. Schmucker named State Court Administrator by Michigan Supreme Court; veteran jurist to oversee trial courts," Michigan Supreme Court, 10 March 2011.

ble work, but he never asked more of them than he demanded of himself. Thanks in part to his vision and advocacy, the future of our judicial branch is this: smaller, streamlined, better services, tax dollars saved."

Gromek was also recognized by Governor Rick Snyder. In a letter dated to-day, Snyder praised Gromek as a "great administrator and a highly respected person among your peers, community, and the state of Michigan ... You have truly impacted the administration of our justice system." The legislature also issued a special tribute to Gromek.[1440]

Off in Glen Arbor, Weaver had been revising her plan for the dual method of selection for Supreme Court Justices.[1441] Even though she had not been picked as a member of Kelly's task force, she made sure some members of the group had access to her reform proposals. She reasoned that she had been working on her plan for more than a decade and had given it her critical thought (informed by her experience). If it was helpful in the labors of the committee, so be it; she said she didn't care who got the credit, only that something got done.

As well, she had put her plan out to several of the state's newspapers, often with it appearing as an op-ed piece. She was calling and speaking with editors about the need for change and reform. And she was going about speaking to some of the groups that asked to hear her.

Off to the AGC

And then came the news March 15, 2011, that she was being investigated by the Attorney Grievance Commission (AGC). The matter was listed as "Re: Hon. Maura D. Corrigan as to Hon. Elizabeth Weaver, File No. 0665-11." The letter by AGC senior associate counsel Ruthann Stevens referenced a "recent" complaint against Weaver and attached a copy of the complaint that Corrigan, Markman, and Young had signed in reference to Weaver's conversation with Jon Muth after the conclusion of *In re Servaas*.[1442]

This was a mirror of the complaint the three had filed with the JTC. This one had been filed with the AGC on April 28, 2010. "Recent"? Eleven months had passed. Eleven! And why was Corrigan now the only complainant? What happened to the other two?

Weaver was not going to be shy about this; it was all going public. That opened the door for me to follow the story, so I did.

1440 Marcia McBrien, "Carl L. Gromek, State Court Administrator, honored by Supreme Court; Chief Justice Young: Gromek in "positions of highest trust" as leader of state judicial branch," Michigan Supreme Court, 6 April 2011.
1441 See Appendix A for Weaver's plan and its relevance with respect to the *Michigan Judicial Selection Task Force: Report and Recommendations, 2011*, [http://jstf.files.wordpress.com/2012/04/jstf_report.pdf.]
1442 Ruthann Stevens, letter to Elizabeth A. Weaver, 15 March 2011, http://www.justiceweaver.com/pdfs/letter40411sm.pdf.

First came a posting that began with the Stevens letter from the AGC, some background, and then Weaver's lengthy letter of April 4 in response, defending that she'd done nothing wrong. Further, she wrote the AGC had no authority in the matter; this was an impossible investigation because there was no way she could get an impartial hearing:

> For your further information I provide the following legal analysis. If it proceeds against me in this matter, the Attorney Grievance Commission's actions will be unconstitutional in violation of the Michigan and United States Constitutions and in violation of Michigan Court Rule MCR 9.116(B).
>
> In *Grievance Administrator v Fieger, supra,* then-Justices Taylor and Corrigan and current Justices Young and Markman asserted that I had leveled "irresponsible and false charges" against them and had undertaken to "falsely" impugn them. That is a statement that they have already concluded that I am dishonest. Then, in a public administrative session of the Supreme Court, now-Chief Justice Young stated in so many words that I am "dishonest" and "unethical." Then, in connection with *Brady v Attorney Grievance Commission,* 486 Mich 997 (2010), Justices Young, Markman and Corrigan sent to the AGC, a memorandum accusing me of assorted misconduct. Finally, those Justices filed requests for investigation, commonly called "grievances," with the JTC.
>
> It is plain from the just-recited history that two current Justices of the Supreme Court, Chief Justice Young and Justice Markman, have already determined that I cannot be believed and am guilty of the very misconduct alleged by Justice Corrigan. Were their separate opinion in *Fieger,* the materials they circulated in *Brady,* and their filing with the JTC of a grievance against me all that had happened, those two justices would, unquestionably, be disqualified from hearing this case should it progress to the Supreme Court. A majority of the court would, however, be available to hear the case. But, much more has happened, and what did happen means that the grievance against me by former Justice Corrigan cannot be processed any further without violating the Constitution of the United States.
>
> On November 17, 2010, five Justices of the Supreme Court, four of whom still sit on that court, publicly and in writing "censur[ed]" me for, among other things, the very conduct which is the subject of former Justice Corrigan's and Justices' Young's and Markman's grievance and your letter. Specifically, those justices castigated me for having made public material from the court's deliberations and for believing that I had authority to use my best judgment in deciding whether to do so. In other words, a majority of the court has already determined that not only am I guilty of doing the kinds of things former Justice Corrigan alleges, but that I have done what she and Justices Young and Markman allege.

The Supreme Court's "censure" of me establishes three facts: that the AGC cannot handle this matter any further; that the Attorney Discipline Board (ADB) cannot constitutionally adjudicate the matter, should it be presented to them; and, that the Supreme Court cannot review any of the ADB's decisions regarding me.

The letter of censure does not merely "pose [...] such a risk of actual bias or prejudgment" that proceeding any further with former Justice Corrigan's grievance "must be forbidden if the guaranty of due process is to be adequately implemented," *Caperton v C A Massey Coal Co, Inc.*, 556 US __; 129 S Ct 2252, 2263; 173 L Ed 2d 1208 (2009), quoting *Withrow v Larkin*, 421 US 35, 47; 95 S Ct 1456; 43 L Ed 2d 712 (1975); rather, that letter establishes unmistakable prejudgment by a majority of the court.

Because, plainly, the Supreme Court cannot hear this case, it would be unconstitutional to proceed with this matter. Any lawyer, a former Supreme Court justice included, against whom a request for investigation is filed with the AGC is entitled to review by the Supreme Court of the AGC's and the ADB's decisions. MCR 7.304(A), and 9.122(A). Such review is mandatory because the power of discipline belongs exclusively to that court. MCL 600.904. Discipline proceedings without the availability of Supreme Court review would violate that statute. Therefore, because no honest, meaningful review will ever be available to me in this case, proceeding with this grievance will violate Michigan law. Action by either the AGC or the ADB, without any possibility of review by the Supreme Court, would arrogate to those entities the control over the lawyers of this state, which the legislature has chosen to place in the Supreme Court, not in them.

In addition, *Caperton* **makes it clear that not only may the Supreme Court not be involved, given its prejudgment of** me, neither can the AGC or the ADB. That case reminded all that because "no man is allowed to be a judge in his own cause," no one can "choose [...] the judge in his own cause." Allowing either the AGC or the ADB to proceed would be the latter. The AGC "is the prosecution arm of the Supreme Court," MCR 9.108(A), while the ADB is "the adjudicative arm of the Supreme Court," MCR 9.110(A), and both are appointed by the Supreme Court. In other words, the Supreme Court has chosen all of the persons charged with deciding former Justice Corrigan's and Justices Young's and Markman's grievance. Under the circumstances of this case, that is constitutionally intolerable. For the AGC to do anything other than decline to entertain the grievance is forbidden by the core doctrines of separation of powers and due process.

Under other circumstances, the inability of the AGC and ADB to properly proceed could be remedied by MCR 9.131. Were only the AGC disqualified from proceeding, the court could itself review a request for investigation and appoint an independent attorney to investigate, file a complaint, and prosecute any complaint. MCR 9.131(A). Were the ADB disqualified, the chief justice could appoint a hearing panel and that panel's decision would proceed directly to that court. MCR 9.131(B). Neither the Supreme Court nor the chief justice may so act in this case, however. They are disqualified. Therefore, there is no way around the AGC's and ADB's respective disqualifications.

It also appears to be improper for the AGC to review the grievance because pertinent evidence may be testimony and a memorandum by one of its own employees, Mr. McGlinn, about a conversation he had had with Judge Servaas. The comments by Judge Servaas in his memorandum are hearsay and significantly inaccurate as to me. Were there no other problem, the situation could be handled by the procedures set out in MCR 9.131(A).

I also note that the JTC declined to take action on the complaint sent to it by former Justice Corrigan, and Justices Young and Markman. By letter dated September 27, 2010, it "dismissed" their request for investigation. MCR 9.116(B) dictates that the AGC "may not take action against a judge unless and until the Judicial Tenure Commission recommends a sanction." Obviously, the JTC did not recommend a sanction. It dismissed the grievance. The AGC has known this since September 2010, more than six (6) months ago. Therefore the AGC "may not take action" against me. The dictate of the subrule could not be clearer.[1443]

After Weaver's letter, at my website in following the story, I picked up with some queries, beginning with the question of competence at the AGC:

Concerning my assessment of incompetence, here are some questions for Ruthann Stevens at the AGC: Is this the complaint left over from almost a year ago? How often do complaints linger for eleven months before there is action? How did there come to be action now…just getting around to it? Or, did somebody in the office pick out this complaint to move on now? For what reason? Is this the way the AGC office normally handles a high-profile case? Was Maura D. Corrigan the sole complainant? Or, were the other two justices part of it? If so, why didn't the complaint say that? If not, where is the complaint from just Maura D. Corrigan.

Concerning the second possibility based on the actions of Maura D. Corrigan…actions that could be considered malicious, with evil intent, is this in her character? Is there any evidence that she might act in such a fashion?[1444]

1443 Elizabeth A. Weaver, letter to Ruthann Stevens, MyMIcourt.com, 4 April 2011, http://www.mymicourt.com/?p=101.
1444 David B. Schock, "April 5, 2011—What Dat? Incompetence of malice? Both?" My MI Court, 5 April 2011, http://www.mymicourt.com/?p=101.

By April 26, Ruthann Stevens was out of the picture, and in an unsigned letter, Weaver was informed that associate counsel Kimberly Uhuru was handling the case. It would hang fire a little while.

Because we'd opened Weaver's side of the investigation to public scrutiny, there were people wondering what had gone on. And some of them had opinions. Bill Ballenger from *Inside Michigan Politics*[1445] said:

> They should drop it and forget about it. But I don't know if they feel they can't because some future justice could engage in something like this. I don't see what good this is doing. [...] There is nothing coming the other way [from Justice Weaver] that I know of. She's not going after Corrigan. [Governor] Snyder ought to get to her [Justice Corrigan] and say 'Get off this.' I don't think it serves the justices well. [...] This is unseemly... their continuing to flail around in the cesspool.[1446]

At this point, it was still a "they" coming after Weaver, even though Corrigan was listed in the cover letter as the only complainant. Perhaps AGC Grievance Administrator Robert Agacinski could shed some light on the matter.

He dismissed the idea that perhaps Corrigan had relaunched this anew. No, it was an old request that the AGC was finally getting around to...nothing special there. And the reasons that ONLY Corrigan appeared as a complainant—even though both Markman's and Young's signatures were on the complaint—was a matter of housekeeping: in cases like this the AGC would call all the complainants to see if they still wanted to go forward. Perhaps two might say "no" and one might say "yes," and the complaint would go forward in the name of only one complainant. And there still might be three names on the original complaint.

So, perhaps Markman and Young said "no" but Corrigan said "yes." Weaver has said she suspects that Corrigan might simply have made a phone call around the time of her departure from the court and set the whole thing in motion. And, no, that's not the way the AGC is supposed to take complaints.[1447]

And there was shortly another change in the lead investigator. In a letter dated May 11, Weaver was notified the matter was being assigned to senior associate counsel Patrick K. McGlinn, the same fella who had worked the Servaas case.[1448] I wrote that things were getting stranger and stranger:

> Never mind for the moment that Justice Weaver has called Mr. McGlinn's third-party report [in the Servaas case] flat-out wrong, does this sound like

1445 *Inside Michigan Politics*, http://www.insidemichiganpolitics.com/Home.aspx.
1446 David B. Schock, "May 17, 2011—'Flailing around in the cesspool,'" My MI Court, 17 May 2011, http://www.mymicourt.com/?p=109.
1447 The proper method is outlined at the AGC website: "How to File a Request for Investigation," http://www.agcmi.com/pages/RequestInvestigation.html.
1448 AGC letter to Elizabeth Weaver, 11 May 2001, http://www.justiceweaver.com/pdfs/may10letter.pdf.

a good idea to have this staffer—who already is so deeply involved in the process—heading up the AGC investigation? Is this a bit like having the prosecutor also serving as the star witness in the case?

Sounded like time for another conversation [...] with AGC Grievance Administrator Robert L. Agacinski.

"The facts of the case would be determinative in the decision process as to how to proceed," he said. "If a staff member has a role in a case, it would depend. It's my judgment call. The staff members investigate; they don't provide evidence or testimony."

But didn't Mr. McGlinn already do that for the Supreme Court and before the JTC in the form of his memo?

Is there ultimately the appearance of a conflict of interest with Mr. McGlinn heading up the investigation for the AGC—whether or not [the conflict] exists in fact?

And with eleven other counsel members, why was this taken from Ms. Uhuru and assigned to Mr. McGlinn?

"It's really my call if there is some concern whether my staff have formed an opinion," said Mr. Agacinski. "It's really a function of whether the Grievance Commission is supervised properly. We haven't had issues in the eleven years I've been heading the office."[1449]

McGlinn followed with a letter to Weaver, formally specifying the one and only complainant:

You enquire why Director Corrigan is the only listed complainant. After Director Corrigan departed the court, she asked to be treated as a complainant.

If you believe the JTC disposition jurisdictionally preempts AGC consideration of this matter then please directly assert so.[1450] Should you assert that position, please provide a copy of the JTC disposition letter and be sure your assertion accounts for MCR 9.201(B)(3).[1451]

Finally, as you are aware, the Request for Investigation is not a determination of misconduct. This office is tasked with the duty and obligation to proceed with due diligence in investigative matters so that the Commission

---

1449 David B. Schock, "June 4, 2011—Now it's getting...strange," My MI Court, 4 June 2011, http://www.mymicourt.com/?p=113.
1450 She had.
1451 Michigan Court Rules, Chapter 9, Professional Disciplinary Proceedings, http://courts.mi.gov/Courts/MichiganSupremeCourt/CurrentCourtRules/1Chapter9ProfessionalDisciplinaryProceedings.pdf.

may properly determine how to conclude. That is what is taking place at this time.[1452]

The investigation may have been doing exactly what Corrigan had wished: taking a lot of time and energy. But Weaver responded to McGlinn with another lengthy letter supplying what she'd already sent and more. She reiterated that he could not proceed as witness and prosecutor, and there was no question in her mind that she got the law right in saying the AGC had no authority:

> When a grievance to the AGC replicates a grievance to the JTC about conduct related to a former judge's office or which was filed while a former judge was still in office, the AGC can proceed only if the JTC has recommended a sanction, although the AGC need not wait until the Supreme Court imposes discipline. If, however, a grievance is filed against a former judge after he or she leaves the bench and is not with respect to conduct related to the office, the AGC is allowed by MCR9.201(B)(3) to proceed without need of any input from the JTC.[1453]

And she included the dismissal of the complaint by the JTC.

And then she waited. On June 27th, she received a copy of the letter the AGC sent to Corrigan with this operative sentence: "The Attorney Grievance Commission determined that the evidence reviewed did not warrant further action by the commission."[1454]

In the same blog posting that contained the copy of the letter to Corrigan, this was my analysis:

> And, what about the motivation behind the complaint? That complaint had early on been dismissed by the JTC and it had no business being put before the AGC. A learned and intelligent Supreme Court justice should recognize that. Is this an effort to stir up trouble for Justice Weaver? (In one sense it caused more than enough trouble...it takes time and effort to answer baseless accusations.) Is this a payback? After all, both justices were off the court, there was nothing pending or impending before them. But there had been bad blood, at least bad blood on the part of Justice Corrigan: she had expressed her outrage on several occasions that Justice Weaver would dare to speak about decisions made at the high court after matters there had been concluded. [...]

1452 Patrick K. McGlinn, letter to Elizabeth A. Weaver, 20 May 2011, http://www.justiceweaver.com/pdfs/5202011sm.pdf.
1453 Elizabeth A. Weaver, letter to Patrick K. McGlinn, 6 June, 2011, My MI Court, http://www.mymicourt.com/?p=118.
1454 Patrick K. McGlinn, letter to Maura D. Corrigan, My MI Court, 27 June 2011, http://www.mymicourt.com/?p=121.

In the end, though, all the turmoil with the AGC redounds upon the origina-tor: Maura D. Corrigan. She looks less learned and intelligent, certainly less wise. She looks like she's seeking revenge.

All along I have been asking if this apparent desire for vengeance is in the nature of the character of Maura D. Corrigan. I don't know. But were I Gov-ernor Rick Snyder I would want to keep a close eye on an appointee who might have a penchant for settling scores. That can cause troubles when and where you least expect or want them.[1455]

Weaver was at last freed from the Attorney Grievance Commission to pursue her plans for court reform, but there had been a heavy price to be paid in defending herself from the bogus AGC complaint.

1455 Ibid.

Chapter 28

Is It Better Now?

The Englerites might have thought it a better court with Elizabeth Weaver gone. After all, there would be no more revelations of administrative matters, no more explanations after cases were concluded how and why decisions came down the way they did. So the newly reconstituted Engler Four could breathe easier. For the rest of us, though? That would depend on your point of view. There was no one there necessarily to alert the members of the public if and when bad things were being done at the Supreme Court. Still, news filtered to Weaver, and she saw that there was still ongoing unnecessary secrecy and deceit; things really hadn't changed all that much.

Like what? Three instances quickly come to mind.

The first-worst was the Waterstone affair.

Waterstone

This is yet another example of the ability and practice of the Supreme Court's discipline commissions—the JTC and the AGC—and its own administrative office (SCAO) to exercise power beyond their scope.

These arms of the Supreme Court have been allowed the incredible power, unchecked, unfettered, to be investigator, prosecutor, and judge. They bestow excessive leniency secretly or they persecute secretly, not always, but whenever they so choose. Confidentiality is stretched to mean unnecessary secrecy and to exclude just and fair process.

That is not their constitutional authority. The JTC may recommend but not decide in cases of judicial misconduct of a judge, censure, suspension, removal or retirement under rules made by the Supreme Court. The AGC is not even in the Constitution and exists and operates under the rules the Supreme Court creates for it. The SCAO—as created in the Constitution—is to perform duties assigned by the Supreme Court.

These arms of the court, the SCAO, JTC, and AGC are sometimes used to intimidate and/or extort as we've seen in Servaas, O'Sullivan, Gardner, Candy, and Bowling. Or they are sometimes used to hide judges' admitted criminal activity from the public and even the justices—as we've seen that in the case of Judges Gilbert and Root. It's here again in Waterstone.

The Waterstone case is yet another example that centers on the actions—or inactions—of the JTC in allowing a judge who condoned perjury to retire gracefully from the bench, even to the extent of allowing her to serve afterward as a visiting judge.

This lengthy and convoluted case started in 2005 while Weaver was still on the court, but it concluded after she left the bench. There are ins and outs, backs and forths...a lot to follow in what readers might have hoped would be an easy, last chapter. Well, you've made it this far. Take a breath and let's go....

Former Wayne County Circuit Judge Mary Waterstone[1456] had allowed testimony she knew was perjured in a major trial of cocaine traffickers. She made the decision in an effort she believed would keep alive a witness who was also a confidential informant. The decision forced her and others across the line.

It all started with a high-profile, high-value drug bust:

> [T]he suburban Inkster Police Department scored a major drug bust in 2005. Acting on a "reliable tip," officers reeled in 47 kilos of cocaine, the largest haul the Inkster authorities ever made.
>
> Swiftly taken down were Alexander Aceval, Ricardo "Richard" Pena, Chad Povish and Brian [sic.] Hill, and police estimated the value of the cocaine in the millions. The bust was highly celebrated by police and prosecutors, evidence that the war on drugs was working.[1457]

The arresting officers were Sergeant Scott Rechtzigel and Detective Robert McArthur. Povish had come to the Inkster Police as their tipster (in exchange for money, making him a confidential informant) and had, in fact, helped to set up the drug bust. And if that information came out, the officers cautioned the prosecutor (and later the judge) Povish would be a dead man. What followed led down a very slippery slope of allowing known perjured testimony to stand as unchallenged testimony in a trial.

Ed Wesoloski of *Michigan Lawyers Weekly* offered a gloss on the case up to April of 2010:

> What a mess.
>
> Back in 2005, when Mary Waterstone was still a Wayne County Circuit Court judge, the Wayne County prosecutor's office charged Alexander Aceval with narcotics trafficking and took the matter to trial.

1456 Waterstone was an Engler appointee to a district court bench in 1991. She was elected to the post in 1992, and was appointed by Engler to the circuit court in 1997, where she also was elected in 1998 (and reelected in 2000). Weaver says she was not, however, an Englerite.
1457 Clarence Walker, "A festival of lies: Perjury in a Michigan cocaine case," Stopthedrugwar.org, 13 June 2012, http://stopthedrugwar.org/chronicle/2012/jun/13/festival_lies_perjury_michigan_c.

Waterstone presided. Karen Plants handled the prosecution. The jury dead-locked. A new trial was scheduled for June 1, 2006.

But before his retrial, Aceval came forward with an amazing tale. At his first trial, he claimed, two cops took the stand and lied to protect a confidential informant's identity. Aceval alleged that the informant had lied as well. Okay, here's the really amazing part: Aceval said Plants knew about the perjury, had two *ex parte* hearings with Waterstone to tell her all about it, Waterstone sealed the hearing transcripts, didn't say a word to Aceval and *still let the case go to the jury.*

Aceval said all of this meant there should be no retrial, especially not with Waterstone presiding and Plants prosecuting.

Waterstone disqualified herself. The retrial proceeded as scheduled with a new judge, who unsealed the *ex parte* hearing transcripts. The transcripts revealed that the perjury was apparently tolerated in a woefully misguided, and ultimately unsuccessful attempt, to keep the informant's identity confidential.

The plot thickened with allegations that Aceval, before the retrial, convinced one of the prosecution's witnesses to do some lying of his own on Aceval's behalf.

The witness said that was indeed what happened and purged his testimony. The retrial was cut short when Aceval pleaded guilty to possession with intent to distribute more than 1,000 grams of cocaine.

Aceval repeated his allegations about Waterstone, Plants, the informant and cops in a federal-court suit filed on Nov. 30, 2006. Waterstone, naturally, was a named defendant. Because she was a judge at the time, the state Attorney General's office stepped up to defend her. On March 17, 2008, the federal court dismissed Aceval's case, which he had filed *pro per* while in prison, apparently because he didn't give the court his address.

Meanwhile, Wayne County Prosecutor Kym Worthy had a problem on her hands. Worthy decided that due to a clear conflict of interest, she could not initiate any criminal charges relating to the perjury. She asked the Michigan Prosecuting Attorney's Coordinating Council to assign a special prosecutor. The council was turned down by prosecutors from four different counties.

Attorney General Mike Cox stepped up to the plate and took the case.

While the AG's office was working up its investigation of Waterstone, the Court of Appeals was considering Aceval's appeal. No doubt about it, wrote Judge Kirsten Frank Kelly on Feb. 5, 2009:

defendant was denied due process because of the trial court's and the prosecutor's misconduct. However, here we stress that defendant was not convicted following his first trial; rather, the trial court declared a mistrial because of a hung jury. This was clearly the appropriate remedy. Although both the trial court's and the prosecutor's conduct was plainly reprehensible, the blameworthiness of either is not the critical factor, because the primary inquiry is the misconduct's effect on the trial. ...

In this case, the complained-of misconduct did not prejudice defendant because he received the remedy that was due him: a new trial.

For these reasons, defendant's constitutional due process claim must fail. [...]

Affirmed.[1458]

The AG's office issued felony charges against Waterstone the very next month. Waterstone responded that Cox's office defended her when Aceval sued in federal court and now wanted to prosecute her on basically the same facts. Waterstone argued that a conflict of interest prevented the AG from prosecuting her.

Up at the Michigan Supreme Court, Aceval was pressing his argument that his first trial had been too tainted to even permit a second trial, the one that ultimately resulted in his guilty plea. The MSC split 3-3 on taking the case, which meant the COA's affirmance of Aceval's conviction was left intact.[1459]

The 3-3 split resulted because Justice Maura Corrigan had agreed to be a character witness for Waterstone if her case ever comes to trial. [...]

Last month, the COA, in *People v Waterstone*, agreed with the former judge's argument that Cox's office had no business being in the case.

We conclude that the Attorney General violated the MRPC in undertaking the prosecution of defendant regarding misconduct in office in conjunction with the Aceval trial, where the Attorney General formerly defended her against Aceval's federal claims, *without first obtaining her consent.* [Wesoloski's emphasis, not the COA's.]

To remedy the conflict of interest, we direct that the Attorney General withdraw from the prosecution of this case.

1458 *People v Aceval*, Michigan Court of Appeals, 5 February 2009, http://coa.courts.mi.gov/documents/opinions/final/coa/20090205_c279017_75_22o-279017.pdf.
1459 Young, Weaver (who was still on the court at that point), and Hathaway voted against, Kelly, Markman and Cavanagh dissented.

As you might have expected, the AG sought leave to appeal.

Last week, the MSC ordered Waterstone and the AG's office to appear before the court and argue whether leave should be granted. Corrigan again
stated she wasn't participating because she might be called to testify for
Waterstone.

If the MSC ultimately rules that there is a conflict, it's back to square one.
The hunt for a prosecutor will begin anew, and, recall, they're not exactly
lining up at the gates for a crack at this one.

What a mess, and there's no end in sight.[1460]

There were really two paths that shared their origins and crossed and recrossed.
The first was the journey of Aceval through the courts. The second was that of Judge
Waterstone and her finally open admission that she had *ex parte* communications
with the prosecutor and then had allowed perjured testimony and had allowed
Aceval's prosecution with that testimony...and then her subsequent trip through
the legal system. (And she wasn't alone: in all, 13 members of the prosecution team
were defendants in the suit filed in federal court {and later dismissed} by Aceval's last
attorney, David Moffitt.[1461])

But Wesoloski was right: it was a mess, and it was going to get messier. In fact, it's
still a mess.

The matter for Waterstone zigged and zagged through the courts. When Wesoloski
left off—April 6, 2010—the Court of Appeals had disqualified the Attorney General's
office from taking on the matter in *Waterstone*. Then, on June 4, 2010, the Supreme
Court reversed the Court of Appeals opinion—the AG's office could prosecute—and
remanded the case to the circuit court.

In her concurring opinion, Weaver brought up the issue of Corrigan removing herself
from voting because she might be a witness. What was up with that?

I note that Justice Corrigan is not participating because as she states: "I am
not participating because I may be a witness in this case."

The Code of Judicial Conduct, Canon 2C states:

A judge should not allow family, social, or other relationships to influence judicial conduct or judgment. A judge should not use the prestige of
office to advance personal business interests or those of others. A judge

1460 Ed Wesoloski, "MSC to consider COA's conflict ruling in Waterstone case," The Michigan Lawyer;
A blog from *Michigan Lawyers Weekly*, 6 April 2010, http://michiganlawyerblog.wordpress.com/tag/mary-
waterstone/.
1461 Carol Lundburg, "A 'firm' conflict?" *Michigan Lawyers Weekly*, 17 May 2010, http://milawyersweekly.com/
news/2010/05/17/a-firm-conflict063/.

should not appear as a witness in a court proceeding unless subpoenaed.[1462]

On September 25, 2009, in *People v Aceval*, No. 138577, a related case to this
case, *People v Waterstone*, Justice Corrigan stated: "I am not participating because I may be a witness in a related case."

Regarding this statement, on September 28, 2009, *the Detroit News*[1463] reported: "Contacted at her home by *The News* on Sunday, Corrigan said, 'I was
asked to be a character witness, and I agreed.'"

Has Justice Corrigan agreed to be a "character witness" in this case as quoted in the *Detroit News*?

Has Justice Corrigan been subpoenaed in this case? If so, when?

What is Justice Corrigan's relationship, if any, to the accused defendant
Judge Waterstone?[1464]

*When she first claimed that she was likely to be a witness in a related trial, I had no idea what she
was referring to. I don't know if the others did or not. But when it finally came out, I knew that she
couldn't do it.*

In that same opinion, Justice Young came off the hook in his dissent trying to shut
down the matter. Waterstone, he said, had been "arguably" deprived of her rights
against self incrimination, he explained, citing the failure of the Attorney General's
office to let her know that she was the target of the ongoing investigation when she
responded in both an interview and a subsequent deposition:

> On November 25, 2008, the Attorney General's Special Agent, Michael
> Ondejko, met with the defendant at her home to deliver an investigative
> subpoena. During the 30-minute interview, Judge Waterstone spoke un-
> guardedly, once Agent Ondejko confirmed for her that the Attorney General
> was investigating the prosecutor that brought Aceval to trial, Karen Plants.
> A portion of the interview, which Agent Ondejko secretly recorded, pro-
> ceeded as follows:
>
> MR. ONDEJKO. I—I work for the Attorney General's Office now—
>
> MS. WATERSTONE. Right.

1462 Michigan Code of Judicial Conduct, Canon 2(C), http://coa.courts.mi.gov/rules/documents/8Michigan
CodeOfJudicialConduct.pdf.
1463 Doug Guthrie, "Supreme Court judge could be trial witness," *Detroit News*, September 28, 2009.
1464 *People v Mary M. Waterstone*, Michigan Supreme Court, 4 June 2010, http://coa.courts.mi.gov/documents/
sct/public/orders/20100604_s140775_55_140775_2010-06-04_or.pdf.

MR. ONDEJKO.—and I've been tasked with doin' an investigation into the perjury that occurred at the Pena/Aceval trial.

MS. WATERSTONE. Right.

MR. ONDEJKO. Well—and I've been through all the—the transcripts and talked to a lot of people. And I mean, just really doesn't seem to be any mystery. I mean, it—it pretty much is all black and white. But I guess—well, two things. There's a list of people that we're gonna do investigative subpoenas with; have 'em come in and—I don't know if you know John Dakmak?

MS. WATERSTONE. [inaudible]

MR. ONDEJKO. You remember? Okay. John is gonna be the assistant. He's now with the office.

MS. WATERSTONE. Yep.

MR. ONDEJKO. And he's gonna be the assistant in charge of that—those interviews. So we've got you on the list as well as about 20 others.

MS. WATERSTONE. As far as me.

MR. ONDEJKO. Yeah.

MS. WATERSTONE. This is in Karen Plants' investigation.

MR. ONDEJKO. Yes, yes. That's—

MS. WATERSTONE. I assumed that it—

MR. ONDEJKO. I—

MS. WATERSTONE. —that's what it was about.

MR. ONDEJKO. —should've mentioned that.

MS. WATERSTONE. That's okay. That was a—it was kind of an assumption, but I thought I should reclarify.

MR. ONDEJKO. Yeah. That's kinda, you know, that's what it centers around. And then the officers who, you know, perjured themselves.

After receiving this assurance that the Attorney General's investigation focused on the prosecutor, Judge Waterstone discussed the trial in detail.

Throughout the interview, Agent Ondejko did not inform her that she was a potential target of the investigation and did not advise her of her right to seek independent counsel or remain silent. And this interview occurred to Judge Waterstone's detriment notwithstanding the fact that the Attorney General's office had previously defended her in the federal litigation for the same conduct for which it is now prosecuting her. At the conclusion of the interview, Agent Ondejko served defendant with an investigative subpoena, ordering her to appear for a deposition on December 1, 2008.

The defendant appeared at her deposition without separate counsel. At the beginning of the deposition, Assistant Attorney General John Dakmak read the defendant her rights:

> MR. DAKMAK. You understand that you have the right not to incriminate yourself, give any act that could get you charged or potentially charged with a criminal act at any point. Do you understand that?
>
> MS. WATERSTONE. I do.
>
> MR. DAKMAK. And, of course, you have the right to consult with an attorney who could advise you on whether or not you should answer those questions. Do you understand?
>
> MS. WATERSTONE. I understand.
>
> MR. DAKMAK. ... Do you have any questions for me regarding your rights afforded to you under the Michigan [or] United States Constitution?
>
> MS. WATERSTONE. No. My understanding was this involved the investigation regarding Karen Plants; is that correct?
>
> MR. DAKMAK. Involving the investigation surrounding the trial of Alexander Aceval, Ricardo Pena, Wayne County Prosecutor's Office and the police department.
>
> MS. WATERSTONE. Okay. That's a little broader than I understood.
>
> MR. DAKMAK. Just so you know, we haven't narrowed it down to a defendant. We haven't charged anybody with a crime yet. We're investigating the acts, everything surrounding it. Do you understand?
>
> MS. WATERSTONE. I understand.
>
> MR. DAKMAK. Do you want to go forward and answer the questions we put forth to you today?

MS. WATERSTONE. Sure.

Noteworthy about this exchange is Mr. Dakmak's failure to disclose that Judge Waterstone was herself a potential target of the investigation. In light of the prior representation, I submit that it is at least arguable that the Attorney General had a duty to make a disclosure that Judge Waterstone was a potential target. Instead, Mr. Dakmak gave a very "lawyer-like" and non-committal answer that was designed to allay any concerns Judge Waterstone might have had about the deposition, thus providing his office cover to prosecute Judge Waterstone without truly informing Judge Waterstone what was occurring. The deposition lasted approximately an hour and a half, and Judge Waterstone discussed additional specific information regarding the Aceval and Pena trials.[1465]

A judge with Waterstone's experience wasn't stupid or naïve: she could figure what Dakmak was getting at. She had to know her conduct would be investigated. Even with his "vigorous dissent" Young was outvoted. (Hathaway had also voted with Young to grant.) The circuit court case could move forward.

On June 25, 2010, there was a request for reconsideration, which the court denied July 9.[1466] Again, Young and Hathaway would reconsider and grant leave. Corrigan—still—was sitting this one out because of her status as a "potential witness." At this point, the Supreme Court was officially out of the mix, and the matter was back at the lower court and then, again, at the Court of Appeals.

Weaver was long off the court when the matter was concluded. The *Free Press* reported the circuit court dismissed three of the four felony counts against Waterstone:

Originally, Waterstone faced four felonies, including neglect of official duties for holding secret meetings with Plants during the trial and allowing the perjury that hid Povish's role.

Last year, Wayne County Presiding Judge Timothy Kenny dismissed three of the counts, ruling the meetings were not a neglect of duty, but instead were deliberate acts taken out of concern for Povish's safety.

But Kenny ruled that Waterstone had to face trial for allowing the perjury to go to the jury—a five-year felony—because she had a duty to correct the lies heard in court. Kenny also said he would allow testimony explaining her actions.[1467]

1465 Robert P. Young writing in ibid., 4.

1466 *People v Mary M. Waterstone*, case history, Michigan Court of Appeals, http://coa.courts.mi.gov/resources/asp/viewdocket.asp?casenumber=140775&inqtype=sdoc&yr=0&SubmitBtn=Search.

1467 Joe Swickard, "Appeals Court dismissed last felony charge against ex-judge," *Detroit Free Press*, 12 April 2012, http://www.freep.com/article/20120412/NEWS01/204120452/Appeals-court-dismisses-last-felony-charge-against-ex-judge.

Waterstone's trial was on hold, pending an appeal. And on April 6, 2012, in a two-to-one-decision Court of Appeals Judges William Murphy and Christopher Murray delivered for her, dismissing the last count. Ed Wesoloski reported:

> The COA ruled that the Michigan Attorney General's office should have charged Waterstone under a misdemeanor statute for allegedly engaging in *ex parte* communications with the prosecutor and allowing perjured testimony at a drug trial.
>
> The felony statute, MCL 750.505, under which Waterstone was charged, punishes offenses that were indictable at common law, such as misconduct in office, unless there is a statute that specifically punishes the charged offense.
>
> The Attorney General's complaint against Waterstone charged her with "willfully neglecting" her judicial duties.
>
> MCL 750.478, the misdemeanor statute, specifically punishes public officials who have willfully neglected their duties.
>
> "Therefore, under the plain and unambiguous language in MCL 750.505, which is the statute relied on by the AG in regard to the four counts at issue, MCL 750.505 cannot be invoked as a basis to try and convict defendant," wrote COA Chief Judge William Murphy.
>
> The ruling means that Waterstone will not stand trial as currently charged.[1468]

Waterstone's reaction was relief:

> "I'm going to get a good night's sleep for the first time in three years," she said.
>
> [...]
>
> Waterstone's lawyers, Juan Mateo and Gerald Evelyn, said they welcomed the decision and hoped it ends the case.
>
> "It's a unique set of facts with this case, and for us, this is vindication for our position," Mateo said.
>
> "We're very pleased with the result, and we hope that this draws these matters to a close," Evelyn said.

1468 Edward Wesoloski, "Breaking news—COA: Felony misconduct charges against Waterstone dismissed, *Michigan Lawyers Weekly*, 6 April 2012, http://milawyersweekly.com/news/2012/04/06/breaking-news-coa-felony-misconduct-charges-against-waterstone-dismissed/.

> Even without an appeal, Waterstone could stand trial: [Judges] Murphy and Murray said there was nothing to bar Waterstone from facing a misdemeanor charge.

> Judge Michael Talbot was the dissenter on the panel, saying he would let the felony stand. The felony and misdemeanors have different elements and a jury could determine whether Waterstone's actions rose to a felony, Talbot said.[1469]

By just one vote at the Court of Appeals, Waterstone dodged the worst of the punishment she could have faced: five years in prison.

Prosecutor Karen Plants wasn't quite as fortunate. She served six months in jail and lost her license to practice law for two years.[1470] And, according to analyst and commentator Clarence Walker, the rest of the enforcement and prosecution team paid a high price:

> Officer Robert McArthur pleaded guilty to a misdemeanor charge of filing a false report and he, too, was ordered to serve 90 days in jail. Sergeant [Scott] Rechtizgel pleaded guilty to a similar charge but no jail time was ordered.[1471]

> A judge forced to retire in disgrace1472 and who barely escaped felony charges. An ambitious prosecutor forced to retire in disgrace, disbarred, and jailed. Two police officers forced out of their jobs and convicted of criminal charges. If those police officers and judicial officials had simply honored their oaths to uphold the law, such fates would not have befallen them.

> But that would have made it more difficult to win their case. And that desire to win at all costs trumped upholding the Constitution.[1473]

I know Mary Waterstone and I do like her. I remember she co-hosted a fundraiser for me at her house. I had thought she had been a good judge, but this allowing and concealing perjury was wrong, very wrong; she had made a terrible mistake in not saying "Wait a minute. We're going to adjourn this case." That was the mistake. She allowed herself to be put in a position where she didn't see a way forward. There is always something you can do, and it starts with the truth.

Weaver realized after the fact that the truth of the case against Waterstone would be found in the transcript of the interview by AG special agent Michael Ondejko and in her deposition before AG assistant attorneys John Dakmak and William Rollstin.

1469 Joe Swickard, "Appeals Court dismissed last felony charge against ex-judge," *Detroit Free Press*, 12 April 2012, http://www.freep.com/article/20120412/NEWS01/204120452/Appeals-court-dismisses-last-felony-charge-against-ex-judge.

1470 Joe Swickard, "Ex-top drug prosecutor disbarred," *Detroit Free Press*, 22 March 012. Metra A.4.

1471 They were the arresting officers in the case against Pena and Aceval.

1472 There is evidence she wasn't forced to retire; that will be subsequently offered.

1473 Clarence Walker, "A festival of lies: Perjury in a Michigan cocaine case," Stopthedrugwar.org, 13 June 2012, http://stopthedrugwar.org/chronicle/2012/jun/13/festival_lies_perjury_michigan_c.

Those were the same documents Young had referenced in his dissent. And those documents were in Weaver's files.

She had not personally consulted them at the time she voted with the majority to allow the case against Waterstone to go forward. After all, the issue before the court was simple: Did the AG's office have a right to prosecute Waterstone after defending her in her civil suit? The reading of the supplemental materials, the interview and deposition, could properly be and was left to her chief clerk who summarized it for Weaver, finding nothing to prohibit the AG's right to prosecute Waterstone.

There was no reason for me to read it then, but I did after I left the court. Waterstone continued to be an issue, and I went back to look at it. It was a revelation.

The Story Behind the Story

The interview and deposition would go a long way to explain what had occurred and why Young and Corrigan were deeply involved. In the interview and deposition, Mary Waterstone freely disclosed what occurred.

In the first place, Waterstone said that Prosecutor Karen Plants "was way over her head," in the matter.[1474] But, then, so was the judge, by her own admission. She was second-guessing herself. At one point or another, she said she should have called a bench conference as soon as she realized that perjured testimony had been delivered, she should have declared a mistrial—but then the defendant Aceval would have walked based on double jeopardy, and the confidential informant would have been revealed. She should have told Aceval's attorney at the time, Jim Feinberg, about the identity of the informant and the concealed communications, but she didn't fully trust Feinberg.[1475] This is how she put it: "I don't want to be the one who tells Jim Feinberg that Chad Povish is the guy. Because he'll be dead tomorrow."[1476]

She was confused about the right path to take.

> But I just frankly said, if I bring—to myself—I don't know what to do here. If I bring Jim Feinberg in and I tell him that there's been perjury, he's gonna go back and tell Aceval. I mean, he's makin' too much money [....] from a guy who just has brought in $27 million worth of cocaine, which made the courtroom reek.[1477]

> [...]

1474 Mary Waterstone in "Office of Attorney General interview with Mary Waterstone, Case Number AG2008-3016503A," 25 November 2008, unpublished, 13.
1475 Ibid., 14.
1476 Ibid., 28.
1477 In her deposition, she subsequently spoke of the odor accompanying the cocaine that was physically brought into the courtroom; it was strong and offensive, she said.

I said I just don't know what to do here. So the following Monday I was actually about to call Tim Kenny [Timothy M. Kenny, presiding judge of Wayne County's 28-judge criminal division[1478]], who's my—kind of my god-father—and say "Tim what would you do?" And Karen came down and said, "I'd like to meet with you. Mr."—what's the face—"Tim Baughman...." And you know, when Tim Baughman speaks, judges listen, defense attorneys listen, police officers listen. And she said, "Tim says the way to handle this is to have a sealed hearing."

So, I probably shoulda called Tim Kenny and asked him what he would do, but I just—I just thought, well, if Tim Baughman says that's the way to handle it....[1479]

The intent of the sealed hearing was that if Aceval were convicted, on appeal the use of perjured testimony would be revealed to a higher court. That court would then order a retrial. But Aceval wasn't convicted, and the matter didn't come out until after the "hung jury" verdict and the move to retry him.[1480]

Baughman's part in all this came up repeatedly in Waterstone's interview and deposition. During the deposition, Waterstone was being questioned why she didn't seek an additional legal opinion. She explained that she came up short:

Q: [...] [D]id you do any analysis or research yourself to find any case law throughout the United States that would support his position?

A: I did not. We were getting ready to go back to trial and I did not. I should have in retrospect. I don't have a—I didn't have a law clerk, I just—

Q: You didn't ask Ms. Plants to bring any supporting law with her and say, "Well, where does this idea come from? Show me the case. What does the Supreme Court say?" Anything like that?

A: No, I guess—no, I did not. I just took the word of the Oracle of Delphi, Mr. Baughman, and I was really mistaken and I'm sorry I did that, but I did.[1481]

You really see Judge Waterstone awakening. These AG attorneys are really probing, and they talk her through it, and she realizes it's a mess. She sees that she was being pushed into concealing perjury.

1478 Judge Timothy M. Kenny, http://judgetimothykenny.com/Bio.html.
1479 Mary Waterstone in "Office of Attorney General interview with Mary Waterstone, Case Number AG2008-3016503A," 16.
1480 The other defendant, Ricardo Pena, was found guilty in a first trial largely on the strength of his confession. In a second trial, he pled guilty to a reduced charge in exchange for his testimony against Aceval. [Curt Guyette, "Circle of Lies; Perjury and its consequences [in] a Wayne County court," *Detroit Metro Times*, 20 April 2011, http://metrotimes.com/news/circle-of-lies-1.1134801.] One of his attorneys was former judge Andrea Ferrara.
1481 Statement of Mary K. Waterstone *In re Perjury and Obstruction of Justice*, File No. 08-9094, AG# 2008-3016503, 1 December 2008, unpublished, 43.

She did it; she's not to be excused. She should have talked with Judge Kenny, and she likely would have had better counsel. She's realizing in this deposition that she's liable to get some jail time. Waterstone just believed in the "guru"—Baughman. She didn't realize the Wayne County prosecutors, Plants and Baughman through Plants, were apparently initiating and giving her ex parte advice against her judicial duty and her own interest. She was too close to the prosecution.

When Weaver's clerk read and summarized the file, she didn't reference Baughman.

She may not have understood just who he was and how important his direction was in this case.

So, who WAS Baughman, the guru and oracle? Timothy A. Baughman is the chief of research, training, and appeals with the Wayne County Prosecutor's office. He's held that job since 1986, but he's been with the office since 1975. According to the Wayne County website, he has some chops:

> He has appeared five times in the United States Supreme Court; in the first four cases he was successful, and the fifth was argued January 9, 2006, and is pending. He has also supervised the briefing and argument of four other cases in that court, as well as appearing over 60 times in the Michigan Supreme Court. He is the author of two books, and various articles on criminal law and criminal procedure. He served for eight years as an adjunct professor of law at Wayne State University Law School, teaching Criminal Procedure. He was appointed as Reporter by the Michigan Supreme Court for its Committee to Revise the Rules of Criminal Procedure. He lectures for the National College of District Attorneys, the Michigan Judicial Institute, the Michigan State Bar, the Prosecuting Attorneys Association of Michigan, and various state prosecutor's [sic.] offices around the country.[1482]

Baughman is very smart and had done a lot of good things in his career. But according to what Judge Waterstone says in her sworn deposition, Plants told her Baughman thought this thing up... he supposedly thought of this genius solution that would do everything but follow the law and would allow perjury to be concealed in a trial. At least Baughman's role in this should have been referred to the AGC and investigated.

And are the motivating factors that caused Corrigan to volunteer—apparently without being subpoenaed—to be a character witness for Waterstone (in violation of the Code of Judicial Conduct) and disqualify herself from the cases and for Young fighting against having the *Waterstone* case further explored explained in one simple phrase: Baughman was their friend, their man?

So, were Young and Corrigan trying to protect Baughman? And was the way to do that to make the *Waterstone* case go away?

1482 Timothy A. Baughman, Wayne County Prosecutor, http://www.waynecounty.com/wcpo_execof-fice_timbaughman.htm.

Are Young and Corrigan trying to cover up the ex parte *communication concerning concealing perjury that Waterstone's sworn deposition statement says went from Baughman to Plants to Waterstone? Should the JTC investigate Justices Corrigan and Young?*

There are deep ties among Corrigan, Young, and Baughman. For instance, Corrigan started her work as a Wayne County Assistant Prosecutor with Baughman. (She served until 1979.) Baughman spoke fondly of their time together during the dedication of the portrait of Justice Patricia Boyle in 2001:

> Chief Justice Corrigan and I began together working for Justice Boyle in the appellate department of the Wayne County Prosecutor's office. I like to tell people that this demonstrates that with some hard work and dedication at least one of us became something of a success in the profession and the other became a judge. There are many people here that I've worked [with] and appeared before whose professional and personal lives have led to close associations: Justice Boyle, Judge Ryan, Judge Borman, Judge Geraldine Ford, and many others, and, of course, the current court, many if not all of its members.[1483]

As well, Baughman's daughter, Lori Baughman Palmer, clerked for Corrigan at the Michigan Supreme Court following her 2001 graduation from Harvard Law and her undergraduate education at Albion College.[1484] And she now serves in the Wayne County Prosecutor's office. Her father is her boss.[1485]

Baughman has written many letters to Chief Justice Robert P. Young, Jr., as the head of the court, commenting on administrative orders and court reform,[1486] and he often appeared before the court at hearings.

But was it more than just business between Young and Baughman?

Of course they're friendly. Baughman is someone Young can count on to speak well of them. Don't you understand that sometimes those letters are requested or planned?

And by the time Corrigan and Young got into the act, Waterstone was long gone from the bench. Waterstone said in her deposition that she served out, retiring on Jan 1, 2007,[1487] a move she said she had planned since her election in 2000.[1488]

1483 Presentation of the portrait of the Honorable Patricia J. Boyle, Michigan Supreme Court Historical Society, 1 November 2001, http://www.micourthistory.org/special_sessions.php?get_id=13. That "current court" was dominated by the Engler Four: Taylor, Corrigan, Young, and Markman.
1484 Lori Baughman Palmer, Class of 1998, *Io Triumphe!*, Spring 2003, Volume 67, Number 4, 19.
1485 Carol Lundberg, "The family business; Father-daughter duo presents arguments to SCOTUS," *Michigan Lawyers Weekly*, 22 October 2010, http://milawyersweekly.com/news/2010/10/22/the-family-business/.
1486 There are examples that are revealed in an Internet search combining the names "Robert P. Young" and "Timothy Baughman."
1487 The court records indicate that Waterstone served through Dec. 31, 2006. It's a matter of one day. Is it of any significance?
1488 Statement of Mary K. Waterstone *In re Perjury and Obstruction of Justice*, File No. 08-9094, AG# 2008-3016503, 1 December 2008, unpublished, 57.

And wouldn't it seem likely that somewhere along the line, the Judicial Tenure Commission would be interested in all that transpired? Well, yes. Hesitantly, Judge Waterstone confirmed the fact in her deposition:

A: […] The answer is, yes, there was a grievance filed.[1489]

Q: Okay. And how was that resolved?

A: With a written reprimand and I was just reminded of not to allow perjury and that if it ever happened again when I was a visiting judge or finish[ed] my term—I was visiting judge then—it would be dealt with severely.

[…]

Q: There was no mention by the JTC, "You should leave now and then this goes away"?

A: No, no. As I said, I had planned it since 2000 and between this case and a murder case that I had at the very end, I said, "Boy, am I glad I'm leaving." I just had had enough because I never had…you know, I had been doing it 16 years. I never encountered anything like that.

Q: You had told us, I think, earlier that this case was a very unique situation for you?

A: Absolutely. I never understood why it wasn't done in federal court by federal prosecutors.[1490]

In the earlier interview with the AG's special Agent Ondejko, Waterstone put it this way: "I don't know why they didn't hand this over to the feds. It was way too big."[1491] Weaver had that figured out in about a minute.

There was a lot of money and credit involved in the $27 million drug bust. At some point, even Judge Waterstone says the police and prosecutor "had dreams of glory."[1492]

If Aceval went down, there was a lot of dough and honor that would accrue to the local police department.

So, Waterstone was retired and not driven from the office in disgrace. She had received a reprimand from the JTC, but—from her own testimony—still was able to serve as a visiting judge.

1489 The complaint was filed by Aceval himself, according to David L. Moffit, who was Aceval's last attorney. [David L. Moffitt, telephone interview with co-author Schock, 16 April 2013. For more documentation in the case consult his website: http://davidlmoffitt.com/media.html.]
1490 Statement of Mary K. Waterstone, 59.
1491 Mary Waterstone in "Office of Attorney General interview with Mary Waterstone, Case Number AG2008-3016503A," 18.
1492 Ibid., 20.

What I had heard was that she was able to take appointments as long as she let the court in which she would serve know what had occurred with respect to the perjury.

How could this be? Who would want this kind of a judge to sit?

This case is a whole book in itself, but it seems to me one part of the real story is missed here: the JTC handling of the matter early on, allowing Judge Waterstone to retire and still sit as an assigned judge without the Supreme Court or public knowing what was done.

It was only after the JTC investigation and slap on the wrist that the breadth and depth of Judge Waterstone's wrongdoing was revealed. If the matter had been left to the JTC, the public would never have known.

In his application for leave to appeal to the Michigan Supreme Court, Alexander Aceval's attorney, David Moffitt, had noted:

> ...[a] request for investigation [at the JTC] against involved former judge Mary Waterstone, [was] inexplicably dismissed without action 9-06.[1493]
> [...]

> The JTC ignored Judge Waterstone's conduct and let her retire, with no disclosure of its proceedings; the COA opinion says there is no remedy for such due process violations in Michigan and suggests we look, ironically, to the JTC.[1494]

Waterstone had retired not exactly with the honors and the cake, but not with the mud from the JTC, either. The investigation and the prosecution by the Attorney General's office was rightfully pursued. But even there, in the end, she got significant relief at the Court of Appeals.

Reading over Waterstone's interview and deposition in working on the book brought to light for Weaver what her colleagues on the bench are likely to have done:

Remember, this is the same time they—the remaining Engler three...Corrigan Young, and Markman—are trying to cook up ex parte communication charges on me with Jon Muth. They should have leveled ex parte communication charges against Judge Waterstone with the JTC, and they should have sent Tim Baughman to the AGC. But instead that's exactly what they did to me. They were very familiar with this. It hadn't really dawned on me that they could be covering up for Baughman. This could explain why Young was way off in his dissent. And it could explain why Maura was so off in her volunteering, in violation of the Judicial Conduct rule, to be a character witness for Waterstone. At the time, I was wondering why. If I had known of Baughman's involvement, then I could have brought out the need for investigation in this possible cover-up, and that may be what they feared most. So I believe they thought they needed to get to me first to distract me and only now do I think I know.

1493 David Moffitt, Application for leave to appeal, Michigan Supreme Court, 2 April 2009, 1, http://courts. michigan.gov/Courts/MichiganSupremeCourt/Clerks/Oral-Arguments/Briefs/11-10/138577/138577-AppellantApp.pdf. 1494 Ibid., 23.

Is It Better Now? The 2012 Election

The voters have spoken yet again. The 2012 election was the costliest ever for three Michigan Supreme Court seats.

There were three seats coming open during the 2012 election. Justice Stephen Markman had served his full eight, as had Marilyn Kelly. Kelly would not be able to run again because she was over 70. For the two eight-year terms, the Republicans had fielded Markman and Oakland County Circuit Court Judge Colleen O'Brien. The Democrats fielded Wayne County Circuit Court Judge Connie Kelly, and Bridget Mary McCormack, a University of Michigan law professor who served as associate dean for clinical affairs and co-director of the Michigan Innocence Clinic.[1495] Additionally, the Natural Law Party presented Doug Dern, a musician, factory worker, and attorney.[1496] The Libertarians offered attorneys Kerry Morgan and Robert Roddis.

The third justice up was Brian K. Zahra. Almost as soon as he was appointed in 2011 Zahra had to figure out how to run to retain his seat in the next election, a little more than a year away. When it rolled around he was facing a solid candidate, Shelia Johnson, a black woman judge (46th District Court, Southfield) who had been nominated by the Democrats. She posed a real threat. But there was another candidate, a most inexperienced young woman, University of Detroit Mercy adjunct law professor Mindy Barry, nominated by the U.S. Taxpayer Party. She had never run for office but the party that had put her forward had a slate of candidates for some of the state races. Still, there was something about her running that seemed disingenuous. .

Barry had served the minimum of five years as a member of the Michigan Bar—but barely—before she was eligible to run for the Supreme Court. The Democrats cried "foul."

> With election fraud and fake candidate shenanigans making plenty of news in Michigan, some Democrats believe they've identified a bogus candidacy for the Michigan Supreme Court.
>
> Grosse Pointe Park attorney Mindy Barry has filed to run for the high court as a Taxpayer Party candidate, but she's a former Republican House staffer who clerked for Michigan Supreme Court Chief Justice Robert Young, Jr., a GOP nominee.
>
> Democrats have nominated an all-female slate to try to unseat the two Republican nominees, Justices Stephen Markman and Brian Zahra, who face voters Nov. 6. Party Chairman Mark Brewer says the more candidates there

---

1495 Bridget Mary McCormack, faculty biography, Michigan Law, http://web.law.umich.edu/_faculty-biopage/facultybiopagenew.asp?ID=35.
1496 "Michigan Supreme Court candidates," *Detroit Free Press*, 24 October 2012, http://www.freep.com/article/20121025/NEWS15/310250205/Michigan-Supreme-Court-candidates.

are, the more it helps the GOP, and a female candidate is more likely to draw votes away from the Democratic nominees.

It looks like those trying to engineer a win for the Republican nominees "have taken a page from Speaker (Jase) Bolger's election fraud playbook and put a sham candidate into the race," Brewer said.

Barry, who sought a campaign finance reporting waiver by pledging she will spend less than $1,000 on her campaign, denied any such intent.

"I consider myself a Republican, but I am also a Taxpayer Party supporter," Barry said.

She said that when she clerked on the Supreme Court, she was aghast at how politicized it was.

Barry said she didn't think Markman was an offender, but she wouldn't discuss Zahra or Young.

Bolger was criticized in a county prosecutor's report for his involvement in a scheme to recruit a fake Democratic candidate to face Grand Rapids Rep. Roy Schmidt when Schmidt jumped from the Democrats to the Republicans in May.[1497]

Barry, meanwhile, answered the accusations and said her candidacy was valid. This was from her website:

The Michigan Democratic Party has accused me of somehow being a "fake" candidate designed to siphon away votes from the Democratic Party nominated all-female slate of candidates for the open Michigan Supreme Court Justice seats. Their accusations are unfounded and illogical. My candidacy provides a conservative alternative, as my background is clearly conservative.

The Democratic candidate in my race went so far as to say that I am not a "real" candidate because I am not "spending a lot of money" on my campaign. To this I ask, where does our democracy stand when a candidate has to "spend a lot of money" to be considered "real" by her competitors.

Obviously the Democratic Party is unhappy about alternative parties entering the political spectrum and I have caught their attention. They should campaign on their attributes, not worry about having to compete for the

1497 "Dems suspect fake GOP candidacy, *Detroit Free Press*, 12 August 2012, http://www.freep.com/article/20120812/COL05/308120118/Dems-suspect-fake-GOP-candidacy

votes of those who they feel will vote for someone simply because she is a female.[1498]

Could such a thing happen...that a fake candidate would enter the race to draw off votes? It's happened before, or at least contemporaneously. Consider the plight of the aforementioned House Speaker Jase Bolger and former state Senator Roy Schmidt (Grand Rapids), who switched party affiliation, turning from a Democrat into a Republican and then trying to raise a fake candidate—an acquaintance of his son's—to run against him.[1499]

And Mindy Barry DID draw enough votes from Judge Johnson to matter. In the unlikely event that every person who had voted for Barry (307,781) had instead voted for Johnson (1,470,000), Johnson would have won over Zahra (1,745,105).[1500]

We are creatures of habit. The first question concerning a possibly fake candidate was this: had it happened before?

Yes indeed, it had.

While Zahra had an easy time in retaining his Court of Appeals seat in 2000, 2006 was an entirely different set of circumstances. Suddenly there was competition. Both he and Kirsten Frank Kelly[1501] were up. And then Wayne County's Third Circuit Court Judge Diane Hathaway also entered the race.

The assessment was that Kirsten Frank Kelly had a lock on her seat, but that Hathaway, another woman with an Irish name AND a popular Democrat from the Detroit area, could beat Zahra. So it's possible they needed to run somebody to take votes away from Hathaway.

That would have involved the Englerites asking another individual to run as a fake candidate.

And another candidate with improbably meager experience <u>did</u> enter the 2006 COA race: Valerie White, Hillsdale County's chief assistant prosecutor. She described her candidacy as a way to meet new people:

> As for her chances of being elected, she says she sees her campaign as "basically an opportunity for me to just network and get my name out there in the event that something opens up in the future.

1498 "Fake Candidate?, Mindy Barry for Michigan Supreme Court, http://www.mindybarryformichigansupremecourt.com/-Fake_Candidate_.html.

1499 Paul Egan, "Investigation into conduct of Jase Bolger, Roy Schmidt draws mixed reactions," *Detroit Free Press*, 29 August 2012, http://www.freep.com/article/20120829/NEWS15/308290062/Investigation-into-conduct-of-Jase-Bolger-Roy-Schmidt-draws-mixed-reactions.

1500 Summary totals for partial term, Department of State, 4 Janurary 2013, http://miboecfr.nictusa.com/election/results/12GEN/13000002.html.

1501 She is no relation to former Attorney General Frank Kelley.

"I went into this very realistically (knowing) that this was an opportunity for me, coming from a small area, to get my name out without running against an incumbent judge or elected official here in our small county," says White.[1502]

Wasn't that interesting? I can guarantee you she had no chance of getting elected.

But she did have an opportunity to take votes away from Hathaway, and Weaver says Valerie White may have been just the go-to batter on the Englerites' farm team. The operative phrase is "may have been."

The ploy may have worked. In the election, Kirsten Frank Kelly easily outpolled everybody else to win re-election (340,429 votes; 35.5 percent). Zahra also won, but by a little less than 48-thousand votes (275,718; 28.8 percent). If the 113,877 votes (11.9 percent) that went to Valerie White had gone instead to Diane Hathaway (227,870 votes; 23.8 percent), Hathaway would have won over Zahra.[1503]

Interestingly, Zahra outspent everybody else in that Court of Appeals election: $335,267 as compared to Hathaway's $151,351, Kelly's $75,091, and White's $22,950.[1504]

Who could have known about her entering the race under false colors? It's likely that the head of the Republican Party might have known. At the time, that was Saul Anuzis.[1505] And Zahra would have known, and it's possible that his political mentor, Justice Robert P. Young, Jr. would have known. And of course White herself would have been in on it.

It's unlikely that the more experienced politicians would divulge such deceitful conduct, and unless White were talking about it, how would anyone ever know whether she was enticed to take a dive as an ersatz candidate or whether she took it in her own head to spend $22,950 just so she could meet people without disturbing those running for election in her own small community?

And where did that money come from? Well, $50 of it was her own. Other contributors made up a list of Republican high rollers. There is a reason to list them. The Michigan Chamber of Commerce topped White's supporters with $5K, followed by Michael Kojaian ($3,400), Alan Ackerman ($2K), Mike Jandernoa ($1,500), The Michigan Manufacturer's Assn. ($1K), Ron Weiser (later head of the Republican Party)($1K), Linda Hotchkiss (wife of Justice Robert P. Young, Jr.)($1K), Clifford Taylor, then Chief

1502 James Pritchard, Associated Press, "Odds against challengers in Michigan Court of Appeals races," *The Argus Press* (Owosso, Mich.), 23 October 2006, http://news.google.com/newspapers?nid=1988&dat=20061023 &id=hjUiAAAAIBAJ&sjid=M6oFAAAAIBAJ&pg=1900,3786472.

1503 Rich Robinson and Barbara Moorehouse, *2006 Citizen's guide to Michigan campaign finance*, Michigan Campaign Finance Network, (Lansing, Mich., 2007), 23, http://www.mcfn.org/pdfs/reports/07_MCFN_Cit_Guide.pdf.

1504 Ibid.

1505 Saulis "Saul" Anuzis was the head of the Michigan GOP from 2005-2009. [About, Saul Anuzis for RNC Chairman, http://www.anuzisforchair.com/inner.asp?z=2.]

Justice of the Supreme Court ($1K), Dennis Muchmore (a former vice president with the Michigan Chamber of Commerce and Governor Snyder's current chief of staff) ($750), Inheritance Automotive Group LLC ($500), Miller Canfield PAAC ($500), Richard McLellan ($500), and Peter Secchia ($500).   Throughout her campaign there was no other money raised. And all those campaign contributions were made at the start of her race, most in April, but the latest May 5. Beyond that White had in-kind contributions of $1,750 each from John Hemholdt and Joe Jones, both of Partner Strategic Communications Group in the Grand Rapids area. Finally, of all the money she raised, $19,275.21 went to either National Petition Management of Lathrup Village or Strategic Communications of Grand Rapids. Those are firms that go out to get enough signatures to put one on the ballot. And White needed signatures to get on the ballot; that's the only way—other than by appointment—to get on the Court of Appeals.

Those are some connected and powerful contributors, and many of them gave to Zahra as well, including the Chamber, Mike Kojaian. There was one little switchup in the couples' league: this time Robert P. Young, Jr. gave as did Lucille Taylor. Zahra, of course, had far more contributions and they were used for the more normal political activities associated with a campaign. And, he raised fund through the pre-election period.

But none of that was widely known or remembered in the 2012 election. Nor did it seem to matter much when Zahra retook the Supreme Court bench. (And when he ran for his seat in 2012, he did so with the support of Valerie White, who contributed $50 to both his campaign and that of Stephen Markman.)[1506]

White was herself running in the fall of 2012 for a probate judgeship in Hillsdale County. This time she was the primary financial supporter in her own race. What's more, none of her former high rollers turned out for her. She lost by fewer than 300 votes. Shortly after the election she found favor at the Supreme Court: on January 23, 2013, she was appointed to the Attorney Grievance Commission. Her term ends Oct. 1, 2015. She bears watching, as does Mindy Barry

And with a solid 4-3 majority and no swing vote, there was little dissent at the Supreme Court, at least little public dissent.

And Justice Zahra would be a vote for the Englerites. He could even vote against the Englerites if his vote was not needed and that's what he was told. That way he would seem to have some independence.

Markman also was returned in the 2012 election—although Bridget Mary McCormack took the top number of votes: 1,528,200.[1507] Markman came in second and retained his

1506 Contributor: Valerie White, Influence Explorer, http://data.influenceexplorer.com/contribution-s/#Y29udHJpYnV0b3JfZnQ9VmFsZXJpZSUyMFdoaXRlJmN5Y2xlPTIwMTImZ2VuZXJhbF90eXBlPXN0YW5kYXJk.
1507 Summary totals for two eight-year positions, Department of State, 4 January, http://miboecfr.nictusa.com/election/results/12GEN/13000000.html.

seat with 1,496,918 ballots. Connie Kelly was next (1,400,308), and then Colleen O'Brien (1,387,590), Kerry Morgan, (264,121), Doug Dern (219,128), and Bob Roddis (181,238).

And the cost for all the election activities set a new record, but one beyond calculation. Of the election, Peter Luke would write for the *Bridge* before February 2013, when the final on-the-record tally of $18.6 million was in:

> Rich Robinson of the Michigan Campaign Finance Network estimates that, at a minimum, 75 percent of the more than $15 [$18.6] million spent boosting the candidacies of Michigan Supreme Court candidates will remain hidden under the shroud of a 2004 secretary of state finding that continues to mistakenly characterize such spending as issue advocacy. That means the money poured into the political parties to finance TV, radio and mail need not be disclosed because federal courts have held that issue advocacy is a form of grass-roots lobbying.
>
> A lawyer who tried to lobby a justice would face disciplinary action. But a client with an appeal in the pipeline can write a million-dollar check to buy advertising in pursuit of a more understanding high court majority and the public would never know. Nor would they have cause to suspect that the money actually bought an outcome.
>
> Re-regulating independent advertising could wind up reducing the amounts of money now being spent. The forced disclosure of unseemly amounts of corporate, union and individual giving would make the appearance of corruption too embarrassing. Presumably.[1508]

That $18.6 million set the all-time record. And Robinson's Michigan Campaign Finance Network reported that most of the funding in the election was "dark money":

> Michigan's 2012 Supreme Court election campaign was the costliest and least transparent in state history, according to records compiled by the nonpartisan Michigan Campaign Finance Network (MCFN). Just $4.7 million out of the $18.6 million in spending documented by MCFN—25.4 percent—was reported through the State campaign finance disclosure system.
>
> The candidate committees of the six major-party nominees reported raising $3,442,367. The state political parties and a small number of political action committees (PACs) and SuperPACs reported making independent expenditures in the amount of $1,276,176. Overall spending reported to the Michigan Department of State totaled $4,718,543.

1508 Peter Luke, "Perhaps it's time to leave constitutional amendments to the legislature," *Bridge: News and Analysis from The Center for Michigan*, 20 November, http://bridgemi.com/2012/11/perhaps-it%E2%80%99s-time-to-leave-constitutional-amendments-to-the-legislature/.

Records compiled by MCFN from the public files of the state's television broadcasters and cable systems showed gross sales of $13.85 million for advertisements about the Supreme Court candidates that were not reported to the Department of State. Those advertisements were purchased by the Michigan Republican Party ($6.67 million), the Michigan Democratic State Central Committee ($6.17 million) and a DC-based nonprofit corporation called Judicial Crisis Network ($1.02 million).

A 2004 interpretation of the Michigan Campaign Finance Act published by the Department of State says that such advertisements are not campaign expenditures unless they contain words of "express advocacy," such as, "vote for," "vote against," "support" or "defeat." Since the advertisements are not treated as campaign expenditures, the contributions to the political parties and interest groups that pay for the advertisements are not disclosed either.

"This anachronistic interpretation of the Campaign Finance Act means that three-fourths of the money spent in this campaign was off the books," said Rich Robinson of the Michigan Campaign Finance Network. "The citizens of this state have no way to find out who was behind $14 million in dark money that was spent in the 2012 Supreme Court campaign."

There was additional spending in the campaign that MCFN has been unable to document with precision. For example, MCFN has collected 13 different direct mail pieces from the Michigan Republican Party about Supreme Court candidates. The party has reported that it made independent expenditures of $725,000 through Arena Communications for direct mail supporting unnamed candidates. It is not possible at this time to ascertain how much of the reported direct mail spending was related to the Supreme Court race.

Although the dark money in 2012 was a record, large volumes of unreported spending have occurred in every Michigan Supreme Court campaign since 2000. While spending by the candidate committees and reported independent expenditures has totaled $26.2 million since 2000, unreported spending for television "issue" advertising has totaled $34.7 million during that time. That yields an overall disclosure rate of just 42.7 percent.[1509]

Robinson, writing in a commentary that appeared first in the *Detroit Free Press*, repeated his warning:

We've been living with willful blindness instead of transparency and accountability in Supreme Court campaigns for more than a decade. The issue is not limiting speech. Those with the will and the way to spend $1 million in a campaign are free to do so. But they must be made to be accountable for it.[1510]

1509 "2012 Supreme Court race was state's most expensve, least transparent ever," Michigan Campaign Finance Network, 21 February 2013, http://www.mcfn.org/press.php?prId=173.
1510 Rich Robinson, "Guest Commentary: Who paid for those Michigan Supreme Court ads?" *Detroit*

Dark money? Lack of transparency?

Is It Better Now? Justice Young's Reforms

And beyond Judge Waterstone and the dark money of the recent election—and on a much smaller scope—were the actions of Chief Justice Young as he went about the land telling the public of the reforms he was making in downsizing the courts. One of the judges who encountered Young in his peregrinations put it this way in a communication to Weaver:

> Another example of the partisanship you were talking about is the 2011 Judicial Resource Recommendations: Michigan paid the National Center for State Courts $90,000 to update the method we use to calculate judicial workload. Four or five months ago, before anyone had seen the recommendations, the chief justice came to the presidents of each of the three associations [Michigan Probate Judges Association, Michigan Judges Association, and Michigan District Judges Association] and demanded that they support the recommendations, sight unseen, or any reductions would be immediate, not by attrition. When we did get the recommendations, we found that, instead of following the explicit recommendation of the NCSC about considering the actual number of quasi-judicial officers in jurisdictions targeted for reductions, they had attributed an average number for courts of that size, just as they had always done. In addition to that, the cut-off for a recommendation was moved from 1.0 plus or minus to .6 plus or minus, effectively doubling the number of reductions unnecessarily and as a matter of policy, not arithmetic. [....] Now, what we have is the chief justice going around with his chest puffed out about how we are all supporting the need for these reductions, when in fact he double-crossed us (and NCSC) and is now blackmailing us into silence with the threat of immediate reductions. Remember when Pogo said, "We have met the enemy, and he is us"?[1511]

Unless you are deeply in the know that math above will be opaque. The important part of it is this: the court opted out of following the NCSC recommendations it paid a lot for; and, by fiddling with the formula, twice as many judges were targeted for redundancy. Then, backed primarily by the State Court Administrator's Office, and joined by the Michigan Judicial Conference and Governor Rick Snyder, 45 trial and four Court of Appeals judgeships were set to dissolve into thin air.[1512]

Free Press, 9 November 2012, http://www.freep.com/article/20121109/OPINION05/311090016/Guest-commentary-Who-paid-for-those-Michigan-Supreme-Court-ads-. Robinson's essay also appeared as "Dark Money and Justice," Michigan Campaign Finance Network, 9 November 2012, http://www.mcfn.org/press.php?prId=171.

1511 Unidentified judge in e-mail to Elizabeth A. Weaver, unpublished.

1512 Judicial Resources Recommendation, State Court Administrative Office, August 2011, http://courts.michigan.gov/Administration/SCAO/Resources/Documents/Publications/Reports/Judicial-Resources/JRRSummary2011.pdf. [See also Ed Wesoloski, "Chief Justice Young to address House Judiciary Committee," The Michigan Lawyer; A blog from *Michigan Lawyers Weekly*, 18 October 2011, http://michiganlawyerblog.wordpress.com/tag/michigan-probate-judges-association/.]

And did it happen? Yes. More or less. On Feb. 14, 2012, the bill passed the House and was headed for the Governor's signature. Thirty-six judgeships were eliminated through attrition and another five through legislation.

> "This is the largest cut in judgeships ever accomplished in the United States—it is unprecedented," Young said.
>
> When complete, the cuts will save the state approximately $6 million per year. [...]
>
> Young noted that SCAO has recommended cutting judgeships for many years. "But past Legislatures weren't inclined to act," he said. "The Senate and the House have taken a much-needed step by cutting judgeships that are no longer justified by the workload. This right-sizing of our judiciary is the front edge of reforms we need to make for a more service-oriented and efficient court system."[1513]

No matter what he's told people, the fact of the matter was we were NOT overjudged. It's true that we had some judges in places where we didn't need them, but there were crying needs in other areas. The result is that many people will have to go much further and wait much longer for access to a court. This was not a wise consideration, but Justice Young wanted to make himself appear a leader of vision and resolve. But he achieved his political ends through deceit; in the end, it cannot prosper. We'll pay for it soon enough.

But Governor Synder in his 2013 State of the State address lauded the legislature for its role in the reductions, and then took the time to single out one individual:

> [W]e probably had the largest court reform, potentially in the United States, happen right here in Michigan, and it was in large part due to your work in the legislature. In particular, I want to thank Chief Justice Bob Young and the Supreme Court and the entire judiciary for their involvement in this process, which talked about performance measures for courts. It talked about court consolidation and it talked about concurrent jurisdiction. That fine work is going to continue and I want to compliment the court and all your fine work and your colleagues on moving ahead and bringing us leadership in the country on these topics. So, thank you.[1514]

And in the End...

1513 Marcia McBrien, "Judicial right-sizing bills pass House, head to Governor for signing; Chief Justice Robert P. Young, Jr. praises legislators for 'Doing the right thing for the courts and for the taxpayers,'" Michigan Supreme Court, 14 February 2012, http://courts.michigan.gov/News-Events/press_releases/Documents/PRFeb14-2012.pdf.

1514 Governor Rick Snyder, 2013 State of the State Address, *Journal of the House of Representatives, 97th Legislature, Regular session of 2013*, 16 January 2013, http://www.legislature.mi.gov/documents/2013-2014/Journal/house/pdf/2013-HJ-01-16-002.pdf.

With Chief Justice Young continuing on a court solidly influenced by John Engler, and with a new Engler majority, what had really changed?

"What was the good of it all?" I asked Weaver even though I had a good idea of the answer. I wanted to know if she thought her efforts were in vain.

No. Never in vain. It's true there's nothing fair and just about the way Justice Young conducted himself on the court. And it just got worse and worse. But still, I will tell you there were occasions when.... My heart always went out where Justice Young was concerned...and each one of them in their own ways. But especially Justice Young because he had the most potential, and to my way of thinking, he was the one who possibly could have gotten to the U.S. Supreme Court. But he didn't believe in "Do right and fear not." He believed you had to follow Engler, and you had to do things that you should not do. He just decided to follow—that's why he got to the Michigan Supreme Court. He was an appointee. He never was elected the first time. And maybe that didn't give him the confidence that he needed.

I don't dislike him. I know he thinks he REALLY dislikes me, hates me, or whatever it may be; I don't know. It appears that he really doesn't like me, I would say.

And that apparent dislike may have led him to do things he otherwise might not have done. And with Weaver revealing much of his bad behavior, the public knew about it.

I think Justice Young has disqualified himself from the U.S. Supreme Court. I would hope that there are people that are more mature and more honest, independent, and kind than Justice Young, because he's not proven that at the important times, that he will stand up for the truth. But he certainly appears stuck on the Michigan Supreme Court at the moment, for the next six years. He may not look at it that way, but he is. Even so, he has an open opportunity to be what he could be.

I think Justice Young just has to work through some of his problems, and they aren't my problems.

And the others who not only made her life at the Supreme Court so needlessly difficult, and who changed, diverted the course of justice in Michigan?

I believe everyone will work out their own salvation here or hereafter. I'm interested in trying to do it here
And the message is clear that the justices and the Supreme Court need reform inside out.

With the lax discipline concerning Judge Waterstone, we've pretty much had a thorough look at how the JTC—an agency of the Supreme Court—operates. In addition to Waterstone, consider the JTC performance in Gilbert, Gardner, Root, Servaas and, to a lesser extent, with Weaver.

Add to that the inappropriate actions of the AGC with lawyer Jim Ford and later with Weaver, and, most serious of all, the AGC's failure to act concerning JTC Director

Paul Fischer's actions directed at Judge Servaas. Then toss in the actions of the Court Administrator and his office with Judge O'Sullivan in Macomb County, Judge Servaas in Kent County.... Finally there are the unjust and ideologically or pragmatically motived actions of the justices to do what they've decided they wanted to do. It's clear this court system is in disorder, starting at the top.

Having been there and seen this from all sides, I am convinced that things are not growing better. We must get rid of opportunities for the justices and their commissions and offices to practice this kind of judicial deceit, tyranny, and unnecessary secrecy. They have held themselves beyond accountability.

Epilogue

The dark money and the budget-breaking investments of the last election would seem enough to draw attention to the ills at the Michigan Supreme Court. But there was more, even to the extent of more national notoriety; the election was hardly the last of it. In a scandal that rivals the ouster, conviction, and imprisonment of former Governor (1961-1962) and Supreme Court Justice (1971-1975) John Swainson for perjury before a federal grand jury in 1975,[1515] Justice Diane M. Hathaway found herself embroiled in a real estate transaction that involved a short sale on a home to avoid having to pay some $600,000. That occurred in 2011.

The story was revealed in May 2012 by WXYZ (Detroit) reporter Ross Jones.[1516]

Ross Jones and Channel 7 were right to pursue the story. Whether or not they were alerted to the story by Hathaway's political enemies is irrelevant. Their work was researched and thorough. They did the work as the Fourth Estate; the media and press are supposed to do it as enabled by constitutional freedom of the press. Too sadly, too often, too much of the press and media haven't and don't do it that way.

Other media picked up the story, but Jones stayed on top of it. Hathaway's attorney initially denied the allegations. But a federal probe revealed her wrongdoing. The result was Hathaway's Dec. 20, 2012 resignation (effective Jan. 21, 2013)—not made public until after the Judicial Tenure Commission charged her with six counts of fraud[1517] and called for her suspension,[1518] a move her attorney called "gratuitous."[1519] Hathaway went before U.S. District Judge John Corbett O'Meara, Jan. 29, 2013, in Ann Arbor.

Ed White was one of the reporters on hand to chronicle the event:

1515 For a new treatment of his fall from grace see Lawrence M. Glazer's *Wounded Warrior: The Rise and Fall of Michigan Gov. John Swainson*, Michigan State University Press, (East Lansing, Mich.) 2010.
1516 Ross Jones, "Did a Michigan Supreme Court Justice play a shell game to get out from her underwater home?," WXYZ TV, 9 May 2012, http://www.wxyz.com/dpp/news/local_news/investigations/did-michigan-supreme-court-justice-play-a-shell-game-to-get-out-from-underwater-home.
1517 Complaint, Formal Complaint No. 91, Judicial Tenure Commission, 7 January 2013, http://jtc.courts.mi.gov/downloads/FC91.Complaint.pdf.
1518 Petition for Interim Suspension, Formal Complaint No. 91, Judicial Tenure Commission, 7 January 2013, http://jtc.courts.mi.gov/downloads/FC91.PetitionforInterimSuspension.pdf.
1519 Melissa Anders, "Michigan Supreme Court Justice Diane Hathaway retires in wake of legal battle," mlive, 7 January 2013, http://www.mlive.com/politics/index.ssf/2013/01/judicial_tenure_commission_cal.html.

Diane Hathaway could face up to 18 months in prison under the terms of her deal with federal prosecutors. But her attorney, Steve Fishman, said after the hearing that he will ask a judge to sentence her to probation.

Hathaway, who resigned from the state's highest court last week, left the courthouse without commenting. U. S. District Judge John Corbett O'Meara allowed her to answer "yes" to a series of questions about her misdeeds that were read by Fishman.

Fishman told reporters that her crime was "dumb. It made no sense." He said he believes the bank, ING Direct, would have allowed the short sale even if Hathaway had disclosed everything.

"She feels terrible. She let down a lot of people," Fishman said.[1520]

This is a disaster. And Justice Hathaway, like some other past and present justices, has become a tragedy. During the almost two years we served together on the Supreme Court, she made many just decisions and took courageous stands. Diane became a dear friend.

While her fraud did not involve the business of the court, it certainly has an effect on and at the court, the judiciary, government, and society in general. It specifically determined her lack of fitness to continue to serve as a justice.

What she did was very seriously wrong. It was another instance of judicial deceit, dishonesty. Though perhaps not directly using the power and authority of the court to intentionally harm others or change the law for special interests or personal agendas, biases, and prejudices as in the case of the Englerites, her inexcusable fraud was dishonesty and deceit by a sitting justice—judicial deceit—for personal monetary gain.

And, yes, she did right to step down and plead guilty. But she waited too long to do it. When Channel 7's Ross Jones attempted to contact her and ran the story, she should have recognized then (if she didn't always know) her dishonest actions were fraud, and they disqualified her from serving as a justice. She should have taken immediate steps to remove herself from the court and accept accountability for her fraud.

At her May 28, 2013 sentencing, Justice Hathaway must accept the punishment that is handed to her without complaint or excuse. Then I hope that she will find the strength, motivation, and courage to use it in a positively transforming way.[1521]

It's interesting that one of the early voices calling for a revelation was that of Chief Justice Robert P. Young, Jr. He had spoken out as soon as the issue became public in May of 2012, urging Hathaway to "clear the air."[1522] Tammy Stables Battaglia and Paul

---

1520 Ed White, AP, "Ex-justice pleads guilty to bank fraud," *Grand Rapids Press*, 30 January 2013, A6,
1521 Hathaway was sentenced to serve a year and a day at the federal prison camp at Alderson, WV. With time off for good behavior, her sentence might run ten months. She surrendered both her law and real estate licenses earlier on.
1522 Dawson Bell and Joe Swickard, "Justice Young asks Hathaway to 'clear the air' on real estate deals," *Detroit Free Press*, 10 May 2012, http://www.freep.com/apps/pbcs.dll/article?AID=/20120510/NEWS06/120510029/Michigan-Supreme-Court-Chief-Justice-Robert-Young-Jr-.

Egan, reporting for the *Detroit Free Press*, asked Young for his reaction a few days before Hathaway made her plea:

> Michigan Supreme Court Chief Justice Robert Young, Jr. said Saturday that the charge and Hathaway's retirement "bring to a close an unhappy, uncharacteristic chapter in the life of this court."
>
> "When any elected official is charged with serious misconduct, the public's faith in its government institutions can suffer," Young said in the statement e-mailed to the Free Press. "This court, as an institution, will do what we have always strived to do: to uphold the highest ethical standards, render the best public service in promoting the rule of law for everyone, and do our utmost to deserve the trust the public has placed in us."[1523]

Even Chief Justice Young's comments—lip service, really—about restoring the integrity of the court lays the groundwork for an awakening by the people to demand and work for reform. When they contrast Justice Young's words with his actions, they'll know that something is seriously disordered and ongoing at the Supreme Court. The need is for reform and less secrecy—more transparency. If we don't reform the system, instances and occurrences of even good people doing bad things will continue.

Governor Snyder appointed 16th Circuit Court (Macomb County) Chief Judge David Viviano February 27, 2013, as Justice Hathaway's replacement. Viviano was 41 and had been on the bench for six years.[1524]

This appointment is that of another Englerite from the farm team. He was elected in Macomb on his father's name, a Macomb County political name. This is another example of the Governor having unlimited, unchecked power to appointed justices to the Supreme Court and accepting very limited and secret advice. Still, we hope for the best from Justice Viviano.

And so we draw this account to a close with some additional and final thoughts we gleaned during our interviews. They are not indented in the way we normally treat long quotes, but they are quotes nonetheless. Our speakers didn't necessarily intend these remarks as valedictory comments, so their placement here is an editorial choice.

Judge Steven Servaas: [1525]

Our court system is set up so if you have a legitimate dispute, from real small to super big—like life in prison, like losing your business, that kind of thing—you want to know that you'll get a fair shot.

1523 Tammy Stables Battaglia and Paul Egan, "Justice Diane Hathaway faces fraud charge in real estate sale," *Detroit Free Press*, 20 January 2013, http://www.freep.com/article/20130120/NEWS05/301200209/Justice-Diane-Hathaway-faces-fraud-charge-in-real-estate-sale.
1524 Press release, "Snyder appoints David Viviano to Michigan Supreme Court," State of Michigan, 27 February 2013, http://www.michigan.gov/snyder/0,4668,7-277-57577_57657-295946--rss,00.html.
1525 Steven R. Servaas, video interview with co-author Schock, 21 November 2011, rural Rockford.

But knowing human nature, you know we're smart enough to understand that sometimes that isn't true. So if a court makes a decision that you think is wrong or is not based on the law, you have another level of courts that is higher, where you can go, and they look at it.

And you're thinking that in this range of courts—two trial courts, two appellate courts in Michigan—that if you get up to the Supreme Court and you've got a question, and you don't think that you've gotten justice, that these people are going to, one, give you a fair shot, and, two, do the best they can to come out with a judgment that's based on the prior cases that have been decided, the equity in the case, and certainly not on anything that gives one party a head-start against the other, because what's the use? I mean, if that's the case that you've spent all this money, you've argued, and you get up to a court that's going to decide the case based on something besides the merits, then our system just doesn't work.

And the problem with the majority of the justices of the Michigan Supreme Court is, in my opinion, politically inspired by what they do. That affects all the courts, because what they hold on a certain question of law goes all the way down the chain to the Court of Appeals, to the Circuit Court, to the District Court. And what good is a judge that is not going to be fair? ...I mean fair, even if you disregard all the legal things they're supposed to do, when you go in there. I mean, he's no good at all in my opinion.

And corruption, you can corrupt somebody with money. It depends on what somebody wants what you can corrupt them with. And if they want political power, that corrupts them if they are not fair in deciding the case. And just in my opinion, based on what I've seen in my case, you know, I got all kinds of decisions that I don't think were based on the merits. [...]

I'd rather, I think, have a fair man deciding my case than a smart man who isn't fair. And I think that's probably what we have. The politics has kind of corrupted—not kind of—has corrupted the Supreme Court. That's the highest level of court in our state, and they're not held in much respect by the people that do polls, and, frankly, I don't think the lawyers in the state hold them in much respect. I certainly don't.

Jon Muth:[1526]

As I see it, we have the worst possible system today for selecting justices of the Supreme Court. And because of that system, where a justice really needs to be nominated by the party convention, it needs—to get on the ballot, a Republican has to be closely affiliated with the Religious Right and the Chamber of Commerce. That means to get on the ballot on the Democratic side, a candidate has to be closely affiliated with the Teachers' Union and the UAW.

So you're not finding anyone who has appealed to the moderate elements in either party. What you get is a Republican that's off to the right wing, because he or she has had to say

1526 Jon R. Muth, video interview with co-author Schock, 17 January 2012, Grand Rapids.

all the right things to get nominated, and on the Democratic side it's the same. And those people have a hard time finding a basis for a dialogue among themselves. And the cost of campaigns has made it such that you can't run unless you can convince powerful moneyed people on both sides that you're going to do them some real good if you get on the court.

Who cares enough to invest millions of dollars in a single judicial seat on the Michigan Supreme Court? Somebody who has something to gain by the direction or makeup of that court. And to think that after spending those millions of dollars and after candidates for the court having to appeal to certain political constituents to even get on the ballot, that that person, once elected, knowing that they're going to have stand for election again, is going to be of purely independent mind is Pollyannaish. It isn't gonna happen. It's not human nature. In fact, the system almost assures that the people it attracts to the office are going to be people with political agendas.

Judge Eugene Arthur "Bud" Moore: [1527]

I do think that something can be accomplished, and that's got to be a change in the way we've—at least in my view—the way we select our justices and who they are accountable to. They're not accountable to politicians; they're not accountable to the Governor; they're accountable to the people who are impacted by their decisions. And it isn't only their case-by-case decisions, it's the whole philosophy of whether there's trust, public trust. If the public doesn't believe a judge is truly nonpartisan, open-minded, not beholden to any group—be it business or labor, not prejudging, willing to listen to both sides, and follow the law, then there is no trust. Without trust, public confidence is lost and the system fails for all of us.

David Schock:

The ongoing and pervasive deceits at the Michigan Supreme Court may leave one incredulous. Once you recognize the lies, you wonder how in the world the majority carried it off so long and with such impunity.

I believe it comes to a matter of words. The Republican majority has repeatedly announced its dedication to conservative principles. But what kind of conservative would do what they've done? It really doesn't take much to reveal their position.

Dr. Russell Kirk,[1528] the author of *The Conservative Mind*, compiled what he called his Ten Conservative Principles.[1529] Kirk understood the temptations and dangers that confront the individual, especially one who is in and under authority. In particular, his

---

1527 Eugene "Bud" Moore, video interview with co-author Schock, 13 March 2012, Oakland County.
1528 He also was my doctoral mentor and advisor; for several years, I served as his amanuensis and assistant editor to *The University Bookman*.
1529 Russell Kirk, "A Conservatism of Thought and Imagination," 1993, http://www.kirkcenter.org/index.php/thought/.

Ninth Principle seems directed at a court that has arrogated to itself powers not in the Constitution:

> Politically speaking, power is the ability to do as one likes, regardless of the wills of one's fellows. A state in which an individual or a small group are able to dominate the wills of their fellows without check is a despotism, whether it is called monarchical or aristocratic or democratic. When every person claims to be a power unto himself, then society falls into anarchy. Anarchy never lasts long, being intolerable for everyone, and contrary to the ineluctable fact that some persons are more strong and more clever than their neighbors. To anarchy there succeeds tyranny or oligarchy, in which power is monopolized by a very few.
>
> The conservative endeavors to so limit and balance political power that anarchy or tyranny may not arise. In every age, nevertheless, men and women are tempted to overthrow the limitations upon power, for the sake of some fancied temporary advantage. It is characteristic of the radical that he thinks of power as a force for good—so long as the power falls into his hands. In the name of liberty, the French and Russian revolutionaries abolished the old restraints upon power; but power cannot be abolished; it always finds its way into someone's hands. That power which the revolutionaries had thought oppressive in the hands of the old regime became many times as tyrannical in the hands of the radical new masters of the state.
>
> Knowing human nature for a mixture of good and evil, the conservative does not put his trust in mere benevolence. Constitutional restrictions, political checks and balances, adequate enforcement of the laws, the old intricate web of restraints upon will and appetite—these the conservative approves as instruments of freedom and order. A just government maintains a healthy tension between the claims of authority and the claims of liberty.[1530]

Conservatives are judged by their actions, their articulated reasoning, their decisions, and not by platitudes. The adoption of conservatism by the members of the Engler-dominated court as a false cover—and all their other deceits—leads me to this conclusion: I have a right to a better Supreme Court.

Elizabeth Weaver:

We don't want to leave the impression that this is just a problem because of so-called conservative Republicans. While the so-called conservatives, the Republican Englerites, are the most recent offenders who perfected deceit, tyranny, and unnecessary secrecy at the Michigan Supreme Court, the so-called liberals, the Democrats, also had their less-perfected "go-at-it" for many years before. And unless there is genuine, thorough reform, both such groups (or new ones that may form) will continue

---

1530 Russell Kirk, *The Politics of Prudence*, Intercollegiate Studies Institute (Bryn Mawr, Penn.) 1993, 23-24. Also quoted at http://www.kirkcenter.org/index.php/detail/ten-conservative-principles/#nine.

the disgraceful see-saw battle for control of the Michigan Supreme Court. Special interest groups will manage to support and to control justices who, unrestrained and operating in unnecessary secrecy, will pursue their supporters' unjust agendas unless the justices' own personal ambitions, philosophical agendas, or biases and prejudices take priority to reach other unjust results.

What this is really about is spiritual wickedness in high places. "High places" means powerful places. And "spiritual wickedness" means extreme wrongdoing.

So, when in government, you have very smart people who have high positions of power, like Supreme Court justices, who are allowed to act in unnecessary secrecy, and who are willing to be deceitful— that means not telling the truth, withholding the truth, giving part of the truth, putting out inaccurate information, misleading information, or no information, and who are able to misuse and abuse that power—then what happens is that even good people can do very bad things. And that's what happened. It has happened in government and particularly what I witnessed at the Michigan Supreme Court and spent years from within, striving to correct and reform. Now it's up to the people to demand thorough reform and get it.

Appendix A
A Plan for Reform

The two main reasons for writing this book were to convey the need for reform in the way we select justices for the Michigan Supreme Court and to eliminate, by requiring more transparency, the unnecessary secrecy in which the justices individually and collectively perform their duties and operate and administer Michigan's judicial branch.

During her nearly 36 years on the bench, Justice Weaver has had a chance to look at how the various possibilities might play out, how other states pick their justices. And her opinion has evolved. Early on, she favored gubernatorial appointment. Once she understood the power that a Governor has to run the court with only four votes, she rethought her position. And she is a proponent of the diversity that arises in individuals that hail from the different parts of the state, so she favors election by districts. She also favors rotation in office, now something sorely lacking.

You cannot tell me with more than 42,000 lawyers in this state that ONLY seven people are now qualified for the job of Supreme Court justice. One of the problems is that the justices are there entirely too long when they serve term after term.

Among the varied opinions about how justices should be selected are those enumerated in the *Michigan Judicial Selection Task Force: Report and Recommendations.*[1531] In particular, the Task Force agreed that the dangers come from unchecked campaign spending, excessive partisanship, attack advertisements, a general lack of voter knowledge of candidates and the issues confronting the Supreme Court, the Governor's discretionary powers to fill mid-term vacancies, and a lack of judicial independence.[1532] But the report also suggested that we look at appointment (the report describes it as "merit selection") as the only way to people the Supreme Court.

That report, said Weaver, was a compendium of compromises; there was nothing to offend. But sometimes, strong opinions are necessary to lead.

1531 *Michigan Judicial Selection Task Force: Report and Recommendations, 2011,* [http://jstf.files.wordpress.com/2012/04/jstf_report.pdf.]
1532 Ibid., 4.

In her work on court reform, Weaver has come to the understanding that while some of the findings in the report warn of the dangers to an independent judiciary, it is what she describes as "unnecessary secrecy" that allows all the rest that's transpired. And there is nothing about that in the *Report and Recommendations*.

Here are portions of one of Weaver's recent speeches that lays out the danger:

> I believe we all want a Michigan Supreme Court in which we can have <u>trust and confidence</u>...a court peopled with truly independent, nonpartisan Supreme Court justices.

> Do we NOW have such a Supreme Court? From my almost 16 years Supreme Court experience, I say NO.

> Can we EVER have it? I believe, YES. (Or I wouldn't be here today.)

> But to have such a court, we need a Supreme Court of seven *independent justices* about whom we have *sufficient information* to hold each justice accountable for his/her individual and collective performance and administration of the people's judicial business.

> What is an *independent justice?*

> An *independent justice* is not agenda-driven and does not hold to and promote political party lines, or philosophies, or ideologies. An *independent justice* is dedicated to the rule of law, is impartial and courageous, exercises judicial restraint and self-discipline, applies common sense, and is wise, honest, fair and just, kind and charitable, orderly, civil and professional, open, not secretive, and non-partisan.

> How can we get such a Supreme Court in which we can have trust and confidence?

> First, we must find, develop, promote, and support to achieve solutions to two critical and chronic problems for and at the Michigan Supreme Court. They are:

> 1. The very obvious need to reform the system of selection of Supreme Court justices in order to make much more likely truly *independent justices* are elected and appointed.

> 2. The less obvious, but equally or even more important, need for transparency at the Supreme Court—transparency to eliminate the *unnecessary secrecy* under which the Supreme Court operates.

Unless *unnecessary secrecy* is eliminated, reform of the justice selection system will be futile. Selection reform alone will not solve the problems of and at the Michigan Supreme Court.

Our deeply flawed dual system of selection (the election and appointment of justices) that allows for political party nominations, exorbitant campaign spending with millions of dollars spent on often deceitful campaigns—untimely reported or not reported at all, the *unnecessary secrecy* and no transparency, and ignoring geographic diversity does not advance the cause and promotion of *independent justices*.

The flawed system produces power blocks of justices usually joining together with a majority of four (or more) votes to promote agendas of:

- Political parties and special interests
- Personal interests, philosophies and ideologies
- Biases and prejudices.

Further, at present all seven justices live in only four counties: Wayne, Macomb, Washtenaw, and Ingham—the "Detroit/Lansing Beltway." Those four counties make up only a little more than 33 percent of the state's population, leaving almost 67 percent of the people in the rest of the 83 counties with NO JUSTICES living in or close to their areas.[1533] And adding insult to injury, four of the seven justices have come from the same Detroit law firm.

As to exorbitant campaign spending, in the 2010 Supreme Court justices' campaigns at least $11.4 million was spent. Mind you, that was for only two seats. In the 2012 election—for three seats—at least $18.6 million was spent. [1534] Much of this is deceitful spending—untraceable, unidentifiable, and unaccountable.

Further, *unnecessary secrecy* allows for the misuse and abuse of the Supreme Court's huge powers of interpretation and discretion in decision-making and power of administrating (too often unjustly and unfairly) the operations of the Court itself and its offices (State Court Administrative Office [SCAO]), its commissions (Judicial Tenure Commission [JTC] and Attorney Grievance Commission [AGC]) and its boards.

1533 We identified that imbalance in a footnote in Chapter 25. It had dipped lower when Marilyn Kelly left the court and Bridget Mary McCormack took the bench in the wake of the 2012 election. But when Diane Hathaway resigned and Governor Snyder appointed Macomb's David Viviano on February 27, 2013, the percentage rose again so that now all the justices still come from four counties—Wayne, Macomb, Washtenaw, and Ingham—that represent only 33.26 percent of the state's population.

1534 And, according to Michigan Campaign Finance Network executive director Rich Robinson, that was a conservative tally, and it didn't necessarily mean that the outside investors were identifiable. ["2012 Supreme Court race was state's most expensve, least transparent ever," Michigan Campaign Finance Network, 21 February 2013, http://www.mcfn.org/press.php?prId=173.]

An example of this misuse and abuse of the Supreme Court power that resulted in the unfair and unjust treatment is the case of Kent County Judge Steven Servaas. ...A tyranny condoned by five Supreme Court justices when they refused to investigate or have investigated the egregious conduct of the JTC director in the Servaas and the *Brady v Attorney Grievance Commission* matters.

There are throughout this state including in the Lansing, Detroit, Traverse City areas and elsewhere in Michigan many other examples of the Michigan Supreme

Court's misuse and abuse of its power to administer the operations of the court system and of its power of interpretations and discretion in decisions.

Unnecessary secrecy is the crux of the problem. It allows the worst propensities in human nature—hatred, lust for power, revenge and deceit—to take root and grow. *Unnecessary secrecy* enables and facilitates people, even good people, to do bad things.

While some justices, sometimes even a majority of the court, have exhibited some of the worst propensities in human nature, Michigan Supreme Court justices, even when kind, collegial, charitable, orderly and professional, clearly should not "go along to get along" while doing the people's business.

Each justice must be free to fulfill his/her duty to the people—to inform them of what they need to know—no more, no less—as each justice deems necessary, about not only what the Supreme Court decides, but how, when, why, and where.

Canon 3A(6) of the Code of Judicial Conduct sets the proper standard for *temporary secrecy* for pending and impending proceedings. There should be no "gag order" as the majority of the Michigan justices asserted to attempt to keep any justice from speaking (communicating) to the public FOREVER about the decisions, performance, and operations of the Court.

The business of the Michigan Supreme Court does NOT deal with treason, sedition, national defense or international diplomacy where permanent secrecy is sometimes (often) necessary. The Court's work is basically dealing with people's lives—their property, businesses, families and freedom. There is no need for forever secrecy. Those who believe they must have "forever secrecy", a "gag order"—sometimes disguised as "deliberative privilege"—to do the Court's work are not ready or worthy of the privilege and responsibility to serve.

The Michigan Supreme Court should not be a secret club. Instead it should consist of seven truly independent justices who act in a transparent, open, accountable, independent manner. It should be the <u>SUPREME</u> example of conducting government business publicly, openly, fairly, orderly, professionally and justly.

It's a simple fact: An uninformed and misinformed public cannot make wise decisions on the suitability and performance of justices and the Supreme Court. As long as there is *unnecessary secrecy*, no transparency and no accountability can exist.

The proposed solutions for the needed reform of our dual system of selecting Supreme Court justices are seven specific proposals for reform, a seven-point plan that does *not eliminate* our dual system of electing and appointing Supreme Court justices, but *reforms* it. The proposed solution [listed below] grew out of common sense and my more-than 35 years' experience as a judge, justice and chief justice.

As you review and consider these solutions—the seven-point plan and other proposals (such as those from the spring 2012 report of the Task Force on Judicial Selection) ask yourself: are they rooted in basic American democratic principles for preventing, detecting and eliminating misuse and abuse of government power? That is, the democratic principles of:

- Rotation in office
- Check and balances
- Transparency—no *unnecessary secrecy*.

Do the proposed reforms contain and/or promote these principles?

Recognize and remember:

- The judiciary has the ultimate power—the power of interpretation. That's the power to have the last say on what something means and having it followed by the other branches and the people. That power of interpretation is combined with the power of administration of the courts, including making the court rules and appointments and combined with the power of contempt—to order jail (to take away personal freedom) and to order fines and costs (to take property).
- This power of the judiciary to interpret and have the last say and to administer the courts and make their rules is necessary for our system of government to function.
- Yet because it is so powerful, the judiciary is potentially the most dangerous branch if the power can easily be misused and abused by a power block of agenda-driven justices acting in a majority and in *unnecessary secrecy* through the unrestrained misuse and abuse of the judicial powers.

We need to guard against, prevent, and, if necessary, discover and correct the misuse and abuse of the Supreme Court's powers of interpretation and administration. We need reforms of the system for the selection of justices. And we need to eliminate *unnecessary secrecy* at the Supreme Court; it must be replaced with transparency in the justices' performance of their individual and collective powers or duties of interpretation and administration including constitutional affirmance of each justice's duty to the people, what the justice believes the people need to know—no more, no less. Justices who abuse and misuse their powers and who believe the court should be cloaked in secrecy are mistaken and not ready or fit to serve.

It is time to stop counting on our elected and appointed officials, special interests, the press, the rest of the media and "just anybody else" to lead in the preservation of our vital institutions like the judiciary and the Michigan Supreme Court.

It is time for everyone of us to take individual responsibility, to take the lead—to educate ourselves, our families, friends, neighbors, co-workers, local county, city, township, state officials, the press and the media, to recognize the problems and the need for reform at and transparency in the Michigan Supreme Court, and to join with others who have done the same, to propose and pursue to achievement the solutions through legislation and constitutional amendments in order to correct the problems and meet the needs.

It is time to Do Right and Fear Not. It's time to Demand and Get Reform.

And, finally, here is Justice Weaver's plan referenced above and elsewhere in this book for reforming the Michigan Supreme Court:

A Seven-Point Plan
for
Michigan Supreme Court Reform

Justice Elizabeth A. Weaver (Chief Justice 1999-2001; retired August 2010)

Here is my proposed solution, a seven-point plan for not eliminating our dual system of electing and appointing Supreme Court justices, but reforming it. Of note: the election of Supreme Courts justices is retained. There is no reason to assume that a system that allowed only appointments would be any less flawed and political than the current elections and appointments. Then too, why should we modify the Michigan Constitution in order to give us citizens less direct say in our government? There is nothing inherently wrong with elections; with accurate information, they allow the people to hold accountable their high officials. It's our justice selection process of party nominees and unregulated, untraceable, unaccountable, unidentifiable, deceitful spending, unchecked gubernatorial power to appoint justices for vacancies, lack of rotation in high office, and *unnecessary secrecy* that's doing us in.

Four of the proposals of the seven-point plan require legislative action and only three require constitutional amendment.

Concerning elections and appointments we should:

1. **Provide no political party nominations for elections. Supreme Court candidates would earn a spot on the ballot by petition—the same way trial and Court of Appeals judge candidates do.** [In 2010 former Senator Alan Cropsey introduced Senate Bills 1296-1300 to accomplish this, but no action was taken.] (To be achieved by legislation.)

2. **Achieve rotation in high office by limiting to only one term of a maximum of 14 years for any justice together with removing the upper 70 age limit as a qualification for running for the office of justice, and a justice never would be eligible for reelection or appointment.** In recent discussions much has been made of the idea of removing an upper age limit for the election of justices. Many would be well qualified to serve into their later years, but it could become a serious issue if there is no limit on their tenure at the Supreme Court. The 14-year limit will insure rotation in this office. (To be achieved by constitutional amendment.)

3. **Establish for the appointments process, a non-partisan advisory Qualifications Commission composed of 15 voting members and the chief justice as the non-voting chair. Five (5) attorney members to serve on the commission shall be submitted by the Board of Commissioners of the State Bar of Michigan and shall be appointed by the governor. Ten non-attorney members to serve on the commission shall be appointed by the governor.**

The process for appointment would require:

• The commission will meet and publicly provide in writing to the Governor two nonbinding recommendations within 60 days of a vacancy. Those written recommendations are to include why those two candidates are best qualified for a position on the Michigan Supreme Court.
• The Governor then can choose one of the two candidates recommended by the Qualifications Commission, or choose someone not recommended by the Qualifications Commission. If the Governor chooses someone not recommended by the Qualifications Commission, the Governor must give public, written reasons why her or his appointee is the best choice before or at the time of submitting an appointee's name to the Senate. The Governor

must submit the appointee's name to the Senate within 60 days of receipt of names from Qualifications Commission or lose the right to make an appointment. In such a case, the Senate must appoint one of the Qualifications Commission's recommended candidates.

• The state Senate must hold at least one public hearing on the Governor's appointee within 60 days of the Governor's appointment. The Senate has the right to confirm or reject the appointment by majority vote. If the Senate does not vote to confirm or reject the appointee within 60 days of the Governor's submission of the appointee, the Governor's appointment takes effect. If the Senate rejects the appointee by majority vote, the Senate must publish promptly its reasons in writing whereupon the Qualifications Commission will have 30 days to reconvene and begin the process anew. If the Qualifications Commission fails to timely reconvene, the vacancy shall be filled at the next general election for the remainder of the term.

• If both the Qualifications Commission and the Governor fail to timely and properly perform, the vacancy shall be filled at the next general election for the remainder of the term.

• The appointed or elected justice only serves for the remainder of the vacant term and shall not serve an additional term or partial term. (To be achieved by constitutional amendment.)

4. Require transparency and accountability in campaign finance reporting requirements. Allow no secret or unnamed contributors. This would involve real-time reporting (and within 48 hours for all elections). (To be achieved by legislation.)

5. Provide public funding. Use tax check-off money designated for gubernatorial campaigns for Supreme Court campaigns. (To be achieved by legislation.)

6. Provide election by district. The state should be divided into seven (7) Supreme Court election districts with one justice coming from each district. That will allow the geographic diversity in representation now so clearly absent. [In 2009 former Senator Michelle McManus introduced Senate Bill 745 to accomplish this; it had one hearing in committee in 2010 but no action was taken.] (To be achieved by legislation.)

7. Eliminate *unnecessary secrecy* and require transparency in the Supreme Court. Reaffirm every Michigan Supreme Court justice's duty to the people to inform them of what they need to know—no more, no less—as each justice deems necessary, about what the Supreme Court decides and how, why, when and where. Prohibit any attempt to keep any justice from communicating to the public forever about the decisions, performance and operations of the Court. Reaffirm as amendment to the Constitution the standard of only *temporary secrecy* for pending and impending proceedings in Canon 3A(6) of the Code of Judicial Conduct that provides: "A judge should abstain from public comment about a pending or impending proceeding in any court ..." (To be achieved by constitutional amendment.)

So, there it is: a proposed solution a seven-point plan growing out of my long experience as a judge and justice...and with a dose of common sense.

NOTE: To implement the Seven-Point Plan, a transition period will be necessary

A transition period will be necessary to reform and convert the present unchecked and unbalanced dual system of election and disorderly secret appointment of Supreme Court justices.

In the transition period the present election system of elections every two years of eight year terms for justices with incumbency designations would be converted to the reform system of one election without incumbency designations every two years of one justice for one of the seven election districts for one 14 year term (with no age limitation), with only one term of no more than 14 years for any justice, with no reelection or appointment of an elected justice, and with no reappointment or election for an appointed justice.

In addition, during the transition period the present disorderly secret appointment system of unchecked secret gubernatorial appointments of justices for vacancies would be converted to the transparent and open reformed check-and-balance system for vacancies filled by gubernatorial appointment with advisory committee recommendations and Senate confirmation for only the remainder of the vacant terms.

For example, assuming the necessary reform laws were adopted into law effective for the 2014 Supreme Court justices' election (by needed constitutional amendment vote of the people and/or the needed implementing legislation of the House and the Senate) the following transition rules would allow fairness to justices elected and/or appointed under the old system laws and holding office on or before November 1, 2014, the following one time exceptions:

• the terms for the elections during the transition period may be less but not more than 14 years;
• a serving elected or appointed justice would be able to run for election in his/her district one time as long as the justice's total number of years of service on the court if elected would be no more than 14 years.

The transition election terms, districts, and schedule would be as follows: The present Michael Cavanagh seat would be in District 1 with 14-year terms; Cavanagh with 32 years of service would not be able to run.

The present David Viviano seat would be in District 2 with a one-time, 12-year term and 14-year terms thereafter; Viviano with almost two years of service would be able to run.

The present Brian Zahra seat would be in District 3 with a one-time, 6-year term and 14-year terms thereafter; Zahra with almost four years of service would be able to run.

The present Mary Beth Kelly seat would be in District 4 with a one-time, four-year term and 14-year terms thereafter; Kelly would be able to run.

The present Robert P. Young, Jr. seat would be in District 5 with 14-year terms; Young, with more than 17 years of service would not be able to run again.

The present Bridget Mary McCormack seat would be in District 6 with a one-time, four-year term and 14-year terms thereafter; McCormack would be able to run.

The present Stephen J. Markman seat would be in District 7 with a one-time, 10-year term and 14-year terms thereafter; Markman, with more than 17 years of service would not be able to run.

Election Schedule

Election Year	Term	District#1	Dist#2	Dist#3	Dist#4	Dist#5	Dist#6	Dist#7
2014		14yr	12yr	6yr				
2016	No election for justices							
2018					4yr	14yr		
2020				14yr			4yr	10yr
2022					14yr			
2024							14yr	
2026			14yr					
2028		14yr						
2030								14yr

This should give those Michigan residents who are rightly concerned about the direction of justice in this state something to seriously consider.

Appendix B

Ten Principles for Living
Fundamental Tenets
of Responsible Behavior

By Justice Elizabeth A. Weaver

10. **Don't Attempt the Impossible.** But you decide what is possible. By all means listen to friends and relatives and even the experts, but ultimately decide for yourself what is right, what is possible or impossible to attempt.

9. **Do Your Best.** The reward is in the doing.

8. **Do Right and Fear Not.** It's simple to say but is not always easily accomplished. Followed, it will see you through life's temptations and challenges.

7. **Take Opportunities When Available.** They rarely come at what you conceive of as a perfect time.

6. **Avoid Unnecessary Disputes and Confrontations.** They cause friction, and friction wears things out.

5. **Don't Let the Turkeys Get You Down.**

4. **You Catch More Bees With Honey Than Vinegar But Sometimes You Need Vinegar To Clean The Windows.** Treat people as you would have them treat you.

3. **Realize That People Don't Always Do What's Right for the Right Reasons.** Just help yourself and them do what's right for whatever the reasons.

2. **Be Confident.** Don't Get Caught Up in Competition. Each of us has a reason for being. We need to have faith that we all have our own place in life—and that no one can do it for us or take it from us.

1. **Be a Goodfinder.** Be a person who seeks out the good in himself or herself and others.

While the business of the law and judiciary is serious, there still is room for fun and not taking one's self entirely too seriously. Former Chief Justice Elizabeth Weaver leads the 2007 Fourth of July Glen Arbor Kazoo Parade in what has become an annual tradition. (Photograph by Douglas Tesner, *Traverse City Record-Eagle.*)

Thanks

Elizabeth Weaver: To my mom and dad who gracefully expressed love, discipline, patience, meekness, and good deeds. Their influence determined the course of my life and made this book necessary.

David Schock: To my parents who taught me to abhor a lie and to love the truth.

In addition special thanks are owed to —

Transcriptionist Pegy Stanek, who was essential to this project.

Our editor, Amee Schmidt, of One Wet Shoe Media.

Kathleen King O'Brien and Mike Benedict for their careful reading, corrections, and thoughtful criticisms.

Our other readers who remain nameless here but who took the time to carefully read this long book and note their suggestions and reactions.

Rich Robinson, the executive director of the Michigan Campaign Finance Network, whose efforts to track deceitful spending in Supreme Court elections has been invaluable. His careful compilations have given Michigan citizens the analysis they need to make better decisions about the future of judicial selection. Without his organization, we'd be in the dark.

Social commentator and cartoonist Jef Mallett.
Karolee Hazelwood, office assistant, Grand Rapids History and Special Collections.
Patrick Jouppi, local history library assistant, Kalamazoo Public Library.
Attorney and reporter Jesse Green.
Attorney Mike Butler.
Pat Schellenbarger, former *Detroit News* and *Grand Rapids Press* reporter.
Attorney Andy Marks.
Attorney Rob Gaecke.
Ann Matteson, reference librarian, Detroit Public Library.
Ron Primeau.
David Bratt.
Cover designer Amanda Mary.

All the people who consented to be interviewed and a few who didn't.